Antiquities

EDITED BY

NICOLE LORAUX, GREGORY NAGY

AND

LAURA SLATKIN

TRANSLATED BY

ARTHUR GOLDHAMMER AND OTHERS
POSTWAR FRENCH THOUGHT, VOLUME III
RAMONA NADDAFF, SERIES EDITOR

THE NEW PRESS
NEW YORK

Pages viii–xii constitute an extension of this copyright page.

Published in the United States by The New Press, New York, 2001
Distributed by W. W. Norton & Company, Inc., New York

LIBRARY OF CONGRESS CATALOGING-IN-PUBLICATION DATA

Antiquities / edited by Nicole Loraux, Gregory Nagy, and Laura Slatkin ;
translated by Arthur Goldhammer and others.
    p.   cm — (The New Press postwar French thought series ; v. 3)
    Includes bibliographical references.
    ISBN 1-56584-376-2
    1. Civilization, Classical. 2. Classical literature — History and
criticism. 3. Classicists — France. I. Loraux, Nicole. II. Nagy,
Gregory. III. Slatkin, Laura M. IV. Series.

DE59 .A64 2000
938 — dc21   00–022323

The New Press was established in 1990 as a not-for-profit alternative to
the large, commercial publishing houses currently dominating the book
publishing industry. The New Press operates in the public interest rather
than for private gain, and is committed to publishing, in innovative ways,
works of educational, cultural, and community value that are often
deemed insufficiently profitable.

The New Press, 450 West 41st Street, 6th floor, New York, NY 10036

www.thenewpress.com

The New Press is pleased to acknowledge the Florence Gould
Foundation for its support of the Postwar French Thought Series.

Printed in the United States of America

9 8 7 6 5 4 3 2 1

Contents

PART II
CONVERGENCES OF SUBJECT

PART III
DIVERGENCES OF APPROACH OR SUBJECT

Series Preface

The aim of The New Press Postwar French Thought Series is to produce a multivolume anthology of seminal writings since 1945 that reflects the theoretical innovations and richness of French thought. Rather than reproduce excerpts of the canon of French authors, articles, and books already known to an English-speaking audience, the editors intend to generate, from the unique perspective of the Franco-American teams selecting texts, a new history of ideas proper to each discipline. Moreover, the collaboration of French and American editors has set in motion a productive dialectic which engaged them in the rethinking of their own disciplines. The resulting history will necessarily include texts and authors with whom specialists and non-specialists alike are familiar. But the context and problematics within which editors situate them will allow for the inclusion of other forgotten and unknown writings and thinkers whose dynamic influence has been ignored by previous critics.

RAMONA NADDAFF

Acknowledgments

This anthology reflects the collective efforts of an extended network of scholars united both by a commitment to the writings represented here and by a generous spirit of intellectual partnership; our debt to them is a pleasure to acknowledge. At various stages of the project we benefited from the literary and linguistic acumen of Sara Bershtel, Marie-Noëlle Bourguet, Jeannie Carlier, Kathleen Coleman, Antoine Compagnon, Marcel Detienne, Casey Dué, Mary Ebbott, Stella Georgoudi, Florent Heinz, Thomas Jenkins, Olga Levaniouk, Maureen McLane, Corinne Pache, Gloria Pinney, Pietro Pucci, Charles Segal, Regina Slatkin, and Froma Zeitlin; their judicious interventions greatly enriched this undertaking. Olga Levaniouk offered invaluable assistance from the outset, as did Fred Naiden, in the complex process of assembling our materials; Bruce King's scrutiny and discerning advice significantly improved the manuscript, as did the astute and careful attention provided by Jessica Blatt, Ted Byfield, Sarah Fan, Leda Scheintaub, and, especially, Tim Roberts. Arthur Goldhammer's translations, for this and the previous volumes in the Postwar French thought series, have established an unprecedented standard of eloquence. Ramona Naddaff and André Schiffrin, the guiding spirits of both this book and the larger inquiry of which it forms part, were models of thoughtful and patient counsel and encouragement throughout; both series and volume have been produced with the generous support of The Florence Gould Foundation. Finally, Amy E. Johnson and Patrice Loraux were our indispensable collaborators at every stage; this book would not have been possible without them.

This volume in the Postwar French Thought Series reflects as well a long-standing and devoted personal solidarity among its three editors. The American editors have chosen to diverge from their French confrère, however, in the matter of the book's dedication: from Greg and Laura to Nicole, with admiration, gratitude, and love.

NOTE ON FORMAT

The editors indicate omissions from the original texts by way of the sign: [. . .]. Such omissions, including the omissions of many notes, have necessitated the renumbering of the original footnotes or endnotes accompanying many of the original texts. In the endnotes of this book, references to articles or books that are not listed in the bibliography have been enclosed in brackets: for example, {Jaulin 1987} at page 81, note 2.

Permissions

Louis Gernet's "Dionysus," translated by John Hamilton and Blaise Nagy, pages 48–70 of *The Anthropology of Ancient Greece* (Baltimore and London: The Johns Hopkins University Press, 1981). Previously published as "Dionysos et la religion dionysiaque," pages 63–91 of *Anthropologie de la Grèce antique*, edited by Jean-Pierre Vernant (Paris: Maspero, 1968). Originally published in *Revue des études grecques,* vol. 66 (1953), pages 377–395. English translation copyright © 1981. Used by permission of The Johns Hopkins University Press.

Jean-Pierre Vernant and Pierre Vidal-Naquet's "The Masked Dionysos of Euripides' *Bacchae*," translated by Janet Lloyd, pages 381–42 of *Myth and Tragedy in Ancient Greece,* by Jean-Pierre Vernant and Pierre Vidal-Naquet. (New York: Zone Books, 1988). Originally published as "Le Dionysos masqué du *Bacchae* d'Euripide," pages 237–270 of *Mythe et tragédie en Grèce ancienne* (Paris: Maspero, 1972). Copyright © 1988 by Zone Books. Used by permission of Zone Books.

Stella Georgoudi's "The Twelve Gods of the Greeks: Variations on a Theme," translated by Corinne Pache. Originally published as "Les Douze Dieux des Grecs: variations sur un thème," pages 43–80 of *Mythes grecs au figuré de l'antiquité au baroque*, edited by Stella Georgoudi and Jean-Pierre Vernant (Paris: Editions Gallimard, 1995). © Editions Gallimard, 1995. Used by their permission.

Claude Mossé's "Heroes and Gods," translated by Arthur Goldhammer. Originally published as "Des héros et des dieux," pages 34–47 of *La Grèce archaïque d'Homère à Eschyle* (Paris: Editions du Seuil, 1984). © Editions du Seuil, 1984. Used by their permission.

Laurence Kahn's "Against the Rules: A Performative Sacrifice," translated by Florent Heintz. Originally published as "Contre les règles: un sacrifice efficace," pages 41–93 of *Hermès Passe ou les ambiguïtés de la communication* (Paris: Maspero, 1978). Copyright © 1978.

Claudine Leduc's "A Theology of the Sign in Greece: *The Homeric Hymn to Hermes [I]*, Commentary on lines 1–181," translated by Corinne Pache. Originally published as "Une théologie du signe en pays grec: L'hymne homérique à Hermès [I], Commentaire des vers 1–181," in *Revue de l'histoire des religions*, vol. 212 (1995), pages 6–49. © Presses Universitaires de France, 1995. Used by their permission.

Françoise Létoublon's "The Mirror and the Loop," translated by Arthur Goldhammer. Originally published as "Le miroir et la boucle" in *Poétique,* vol. 53 (1983), pages 19–36. © Editions du Seuil, 1983. Used by their permission.

Pierre Judet de La Combe's "Remarks on Aeschylus's Homer," in *Lexis,* vol. 13 (1995), pages 129–44. © 1995. Used by permission of Professor Vittorio Citti (Università di Trento, Italy).

Philippe Rousseau's "Rewriting Homer: Remarks on the Narrative of the Chariot Race in Sophocles' *Electra*" is seeing its first publication here.

Charles de Lamberterie's "Milman Parry and Antoine Meillet," translated by Arthur Goldhammer. Originally published as "Milman Parry et Antoine Meillet," pages 9–22 of *Hommage à Milman Parry. Le style formulaire de l'épopée et la théorie de l'oralité poétique,* edited by F. Létoublon (Amsterdam: Gieben, 1997). © 1997.

Emile Benveniste's "The Medical Doctrine of the Indo-Europeans," translated by Arthur Goldhammer. Originally published as "La doctrine médicale des Indo-Européens," in *Revue de*

NICOLE LORAUX,
GREGORY NAGY, AND LAURA SLATKIN

Introduction

This book is not about the status quo of French scholarship in Greco-Roman studies, that is, in "Classics." Rather, it concentrates on decisive trends of Classics research, especially in France during the second half of the twentieth century. The examples of scholarly writings collected in this book represent a distinctly French history of ideas in Classics. The impact of these writings extends from Classics to a wide range of research in the humanities and social sciences in general, especially in literary theory, philosophy, anthropology, sociology, history, and art history.[1]

The readings in this book, concerned as they are with Classics, raise fundamental questions about civilization. What are the origins of "Western" thought? That is, how do we trace the history of rational thought in the Western world? What, for that matter, does it mean to say "Western," and what is the ideological background for any distinction between "European" and "non-European"? The answers to such questions, both in breadth of generality and in depth of specificity, take shape here in a markedly French academic context.

The realia of Greek and Roman antiquity that abound in this Classics reader are interesting in their own right, but the interest for Classicists and non-Classicists alike is heightened by the spirit of investigation, in all its varieties, which animates this book. The questions raised by the myriad details of Classical antiquity that this book covers, ranging from such topics as the bureaucratic procedures of scribes working in the palace of Pylos at around 1200 [BCE] to the pioneering of democratic institutions in Athens at the end of the sixth century, engage French academic thinking in all its traditional and anti-traditional varieties.

---

[1] The single most authoritative source for ongoing bibliography on scholarship in Classics centers on a French enterprise: *L'Année philologique; bibliographie critique et analytique de l'antiquité gréco-latine* (Paris: Les Belles Lettres), starting with volume 1 in 1927 (some recent volumes: 62/63/64 for 1993/1994/1995). This series was founded by its first editor, Jules Marouzeau (1878–1964), who had earlier (1927–28) published *Dix années de bibliographie classique, 1914–1924*. The *Année* is now being electronically republished as *The Database of Classical Bibliography*, under the general editorship of Dee L. Clayman. The first electronic "volume," published in 1995, contains volumes 47–58 of the printed *Année*, covering the years 1976–87. Annual updates now cover volumes 59–60 (1988–89).

Amidst this vast array of scholarship, both in generalities and in details, what is at stake for contemporary French Classicists? The answer is stark in its simplicity: everything. The intellectual ambition of French Classics writ large is to define and even redefine the whole world by resituating all of it historically within its past as well as its present. After all, vast stretches of past history are to be traced primarily or even solely through the records and remains of Greco-Roman antiquity.

Many of today's leading figures in French Classical scholarship are paragons of modernity or even "postmodernity" in the eyes of some fellow Classicists in other academic cultures. Such impressions can mislead, however, if they are tied to the assumption that modern or "postmodern" perspectives in Classics are mere symptoms of an overall intellectual capitulation to ephemeral trends. It is clear that these same French Classicists consider themselves leaders, not followers, in modern and "postmodern" thinking. More important, they have been acknowledged as leading thinkers by such non-Classicist counterparts as Michel Foucault, Jacques Derrida, and Claude Lévi-Strauss. As we shall see, French Classicists are in the forefront of contemporary thinking on such vital topics as sexuality, *écriture*, and society itself.

Today's French Classicists have a great deal to say about "Western" thought. Unlike some of their Anglo-American counterparts, however, they tend to treat their subject more objectively as a living historical fact—not as some moribund fetish that needs to be propped up against the ever-fresh onslaughts of "theory" or even barbarism. This book is lacking in grim exhortations that call upon Classicists to man the ramparts of crumbling empires. It is pervaded, rather, by a far more easygoing atmosphere, one that fosters a general sense of intellectual optimism about "Western" thought. The French Classicists' freedom from cultural insecurity—as Classicists—is palpable.

There are reasons for such an attitude. The French Classicists' inherent optimism about themselves as active participants in a vital "Western" tradition, one that is ever self-renewing, stems in part from their philosophical training. Here we see a basic feature of their cultural *formation*: they know their philosophy, and they are not afraid to rethink everything, even the origins and the essence of philosophy itself.

It is this absence of intellectual insecurity that helps explain the French Classicists' alternative visions of "Western" thought, marked by an intellectual openness that seeks to establish an active engagement with other cultures. The range is humanistically all-encompassing: it extends from the monumental legacies of civilizations as disparate as those of China or India or the Near East all the way to the even more disparate but still commensurate values of the smallest-scale societies, such as those that still survive in remote regions like the Amazon Basin or Melanesia. In the long run, French Classicists view the term "Western" in terms of historical contingency, not manifest destiny.

All this is not to idealize French Classics. The cumulative history of the

French educational system brings with it some distinct disadvantages as well as advantages. A case in point is again their approach to "Western" thought: French Classicists may know their philosophy, but most of them learned it all in French, especially at the initial stages of their *formation* as students. Also, much of the philosophical learning in the earlier phases of a French student's education is mediated by hearing or reading the teacher, in place of direct exposure to primary reading. The absence of linguistic immersion in the texts of, say, the Enlightenment—when those texts happen to be in German or English rather than French—can easily lead to special kinds of cultural and intellectual blind spots. There are, to be sure, comparable blind spots in the education of Classicists trained in the Anglo-American or German or Italian or Spanish academic traditions. But the point is, miscommunications in Classical scholarship can be initiated from the French side just as easily as from other sides.

One focal point of potential misunderstandings is the ongoing academic struggle over establishing truth-values in humanistic disciplines. French conventions of argumentation are not always readily convertible in other academic cultures centering on the Classics, and there is a wide range in the blending of inductive and deductive reasoning even within the tradition of French Classical studies. Still, distinctively French patterns emerge in the style of answering Classical questions, even of asking them. The questions extend to the use and abuse of empiricism itself.

The sample writings in this reader are divided into three parts: (I) convergences of approach, (II) convergences of subject, and (III) divergences of approach or subject. Part I concentrates on relatively newer approaches leading to new perspectives that tend to redefine a given subject in the Classics (the writers include such influential figures as Jean-Pierre Vernant and Jean Bollack; also Pierre Vidal-Naquet, Marcel Detienne, and Nicole Loraux). Part II represents more traditional approaches, as in the case of text criticism (Jean Irigoin), history (Claude Nicolet), and epigraphy (Louis Robert). It also concerns the applications of relatively older methods to newer subjects (for example, Pierre Vidal-Naquet on hunting as initiation and François Hartog on the politics of defining what is alien, the "other"). The methods may be old, resistant to any radical redefinition, but the perspectives achieved are nonetheless new. Part III explores approaches and subjects that portend alternative directions. Some of these directions have been by and large ignored or undervalued in current research trends, while others represent distinct countertrends.

In the context of Part III, one figure who deserves special mention is Georges Dumézil.[2] Since this scholar's research in the humanities transcends

---

[2] A salient example is the complex argumentation that weaves its way through the 1,463 pages of Dumézil's masterpiece, *Mythe et épopée* I/II/III (Paris: Gallimard, 1968/ 1971/1973); there is a revised edition, featuring consecutive pagination, of the latest cor-

the world of Greco-Roman antiquity, and since his writings are particularly well known in English-language versions, no attempt has been made to present a sampling from the huge corpus of his published works, which are in any case too varied and detailed to accommodate the format of general essays. Still the potential impact of Dumézil's work on future Classical scholarship is signaled clearly and forcefully in the samples taken from the work of others in Part III, notably Émile Benveniste and Charles Malamoud.

The writers whose works are included in this collection, which can hardly be exhaustive, belong to two broad categories of Classicists: (1) those who are considered "mainstream" from an international (especially Anglo-American and German) point of view, such as Jean Irigoin, Michel Lejeune, and Louis Robert and (2) those who are associated with "schools" that have left a distinctive mark on the study of Classics. Part I of this book is dominated by the "schools of thought" category, while the "mainstream" category gravitates to Part II, though various "schools" make a strong showing there as well.

To be sure, many of the writers included in Part I might actively resist the idea that they belong to any particular school of thought. Even when scholars coalesce around a singularly preeminent intellectual presence, the group's self-definition can stay blurred. There are centrifugal as well as centripetal forces at work in the various "schools," and even in the "mainstream" of Classics research. Part III accommodates such centrifugal forces.

A prominent example of a distinctive school of thought is the "équipe" who have worked with Jean-Pierre Vernant at the Centre de Recherches Comparées sur les Sociétés Anciennes (later renamed as the Centre Louis Gernet) at 10 rue Monsieur le Prince, especially during the 1970s and 1980s.[3] Another

---

rected editions (1986/1986/1981), with a foreword by Joel Grisward (Paris: Gallimard, 1995). Although there is no single English-language version of this book, most of its parts have appeared in the form of smaller volumes bearing titles of their own. These books, as well as the other major works of Dumézil that have appeared in English, are tracked in C. Scott Littleton, *The New Comparative Mythology: An Anthropological Assessment of the Theories of Georges Dumézil*, 3rd ed. (Berkeley and Los Angeles: University of California Press, 1982). For a thorough survey of Dumézil's publications, see Hervé Coutau-Bégaire, *L'oeuvre de Georges Dumézil: Catalogue raisonné* (Paris: Économica, 1998). For an appreciation of the subtlety of Dumézil's methodology, with specific reference to the phenomena of polytheism, see Marcel Detienne, *Comparer l'incomparable* (Paris: Seuil, 2000), pp. 83–86. On the controversies surrounding the life of Dumézil, see Didier Eribon, *Faut-il brûler Dumézil?* (Paris: Flammarion, 1992). Dumézil himself reflects on these controversies in his *Le moine noir en gris dedans Varennes* (Paris: Gallimard, 1984) [*The Riddle of Nostradamus: A Critical Dialogue*, trans. Betsy Wing (Baltimore: The Johns Hopkins University Press, 1999)].

[3] For an overview, see Froma Zeitlin's introduction to Jean-Pierre Vernant, *Mortals and Immortals: Collected Essays*, ed. Zeitlin (Princeton, N.J.: Princeton University Press, 1991), pp. 23–24. She names as prominent "Vernantiens" in the "école de Paris": Pierre Vidal-

example is the group of Classicists associated with Jean Bollack at the University of Lille, building on the foundations of hermeneutics as formulated by Friedrich Schleiermacher, Karl Wilhelm Humboldt, August Boeckh, and Johannes Droysen.[4]

The very first two pieces of Part I, one written by Vernant and the other by Bollack, exemplify some of the most basic features that distinguish the new schools. They also reveal many of intellectual tensions (for example, Bollack offers some criticisms of the methods characteristic of the "school" of Vernant).[5] These distinctions and tensions are summarized in the final piece of Part I, derived from an introduction written by Marcel Detienne to the third edition of his groundbreaking book on archaic Greek poetics, *The Masters of Truth in Archaic Greece* (1996).[6] He examines the divergences between the "structuralists" who tend to be defined in terms of Vernant and the "hermeneutic school" associated with Bollack.[7] He also examines the convergences, focusing on the new generation of "hermeneutists" who apply the "sociology of culture" as pioneered by Pierre Bourdieu.[8] In general, he offers provocative retrospectives on "mainstream" French classicists ("the *littéraires*, as they are called on the Left Bank"[9]), on the "hermeneutists" associated with Bollack, and even on the "équipe" to which he himself does and does not belong; he raises questions, implicitly, even about the distinction between "équipe" and "Centre."[10]

Naquet (a co-founder of the Centre), Marcel Detienne, Nicole Loraux, Françoise Frontisi-Ducroux, François Lissarrague, Alain Schnapp, Claude Mossé, François Hartog. See also Ann Bergren and Froma Zeitlin, eds., *Texts and Contexts: American Classical Studies in Honor of J.-P. Vernant*, a special issue of *Arethusa* (15 [1982]). Note especially the piece by Charles Segal, "Afterword: Jean-Pierre Vernant and the Study of Ancient Greece," pp. 221–34.

[4] Closely linked to Bollack are Pierre Judet de La Combe, André Laks, and Philippe Rousseau, as well as Fabienne Blaise and Heinz Wismann. For a representative sample, see Fabienne Blaise, Pierre Judet de La Combe, and Philippe Rousseau, eds., *Le Métier du mythe: Lectures d'Hésiode* (Paris: Presses Universitaires du Septentrion, 1996). See also André Laks and Ada Neschke, eds., *La Naissance du paradigme herméneutique: Schleiermacher, Humboldt, Boeckh, Droysen* (Lille: Presses Universitaires de Lille, 1991).

[5] For an overview, see Giulia Sissa, "Philology, Anthropology, Comparison: The French Experience," *Classical Philology* 92 (1997): 167–71.

[6] 6. Marcel Detienne, *Les Maîtres de vérité en Grèce archaïque*, 3d ed. (Paris: Agora, 1993) [*The Masters of Truth in Archaic Greece* (New York: Zone Books, 1996)]. See in this volume, pp. 205–21.

[7] See Detienne, *Masters of Truth* (1996) in this volume, pp. 210–12.

[8] See Detienne, *Masters of Truth* (1996) in this volume, p. (209). See especially Pierre Bourdieu, *Esquisse d'une théorie de la pratique: Précédé de trois études d'ethnologie kabyle* (Geneva: Droz, 1972).

[9] See Detienne, *Masters of Truth* (1996) in this volume, p. 209.

[10] See Detienne, *Masters of Truth* (1996) in this volume, pp. 207–9. For avatars of the

It would be an exaggeration, however, to describe current trends of research emanating from the Centre as a falling out among members of the "équipe."[11] Throughout its history, the Centre has been a focus, a *foyer commun*, for centrifugal as well as centripetal impulses of Classics research, and even its self-definition is fluid rather than static. Witness its current designation, Centre Gernet, named after a Classicist whose research had exerted a singularly formative influence on the group, starting with Vernant himself. Pierre Vidal-Naquet gives this summary:

> In 1962, in *The Origins of Greek Thought*, Jean-Pierre Vernant established a framework that both Detienne and I share. . . To sum it up: "rational thought" arose within a specific political, economic, and social framework, namely, that of the city [*polis*], which itself only appeared through a decisive crisis of sovereignty, and within a special space unencumbered by the dominating presence of a Minoan or Mycenaean monarch modeled after Eastern "despots."[12]

This large-scale "framework" shared by Vernant, Vidal-Naquet, Detienne, and younger colleagues such as Nicole Loraux confronts the very essentials of European or "Western" civilization, centering on two basic topics: the transition from "myth" to "reason" (where myth too may or may not "contain" reason) and the formation of the *polis* or "city-state." For Vernant, Louis Gernet was the initiator of these two central topics, whence the current name of the Centre. Gernet's essay, "The Origins of Greek Philosophy" (Part I no. 3 in this book), is the impetus for one of Vernant's most influential essays, "The Spiritual Universe of the Polis" (Part I no. 1). The centrality of Gernet is reflected by the fact that three of his essays, including "Origins," have been included in the present collection.[13]

Centre, see Sissa, "Philology, Anthropology," 169, on the earlier work of Vernant in collaboration with scholars such as the Indologist Louis Dumont, the Sinologist Jacques Gernet, the Sumerologist René Labat, and the ethnologist Jean Guiart at the Centre d'Études et de Recherches Marxistes (CERM). In 1965, Fernand Braudel, as president of the École Pratique des Hautes Études en Sciences Sociales et Économiques, initiated the Centre de Recherches Comparées sur les Sociétés Anciennes.

[11] Such is the view of Arnaldo Momigliano, *Rivista storica italiana* 94 (1982): 784–87, reprinted in his *Ottavo contributo alla storia degli studi classici e del mondo antico* (Rome: Edizioni di storia e letteratura, 1987), pp. 381–84, with specific reference to Marcel Detienne's *L'Invention de la mythologie* (Paris: Gallimard, 1981) [*The Creation of Mythology*, trans. Margaret Cook (Chicago: University of Chicago Press, 1986)]. For a rejection of Momigliano's interpretation, see Detienne, *Masters of Truth* (1996) (p. 214 in this volume). For a review of Detienne's *Invention*, see Nagy, *Annales Économies Sociétés Civilisations* 37 (1982): 778–80.

[12] Pierre Vidal-Naquet, Preface to Detienne, *Masters of Truth* (1996), pp. 8–9.

[13] The 1981 English translations of Gernet's essays have been revised here, with corrections where needed (with the help of the original translators). In effect, then, the present

Vernant's self-effacing acknowledgment of an intellectual debt to Gernet should not detract from his own monumental accomplishments. Even the title of the original collection of Gernet's essays, as edited by Vernant and Detienne, reflects Vernant's large-scale research trajectory: *The Anthropology of Ancient Greece*.[14] This trajectory is defined not only by the "anthropology" of Louis Gernet but also by the "psychology" of Ignace Meyerson.[15] For Meyerson, "historical and comparative" psychology was the only truly Marxist psychology, as Detienne aptly describes it.[16] For Vernant, historical psychology and anthropology both become re-assimilated into a powerful new framework that transcends the earlier work of Gernet and Meyerson.[17]

The approaches of Gernet are more difficult to categorize. First of all, he was a Classicist who achieved an extraordinarily deep as well as broad understanding of ancient Greek society in general and of legal traditions in particular through a close reading of the texts (a hallmark is his work on Plato's *Laws*).[18] His editions of Athenian orators are classics in their own right.[19] For all practical purposes, Gernet's "anthropology" could just as easily be called sociology. To repeat: Vernant's own model of anthropology embraces the sociology of Gernet and the psychology of Meyerson, and it all comes together in his introduction to the aforementioned book of Gernet as edited by Vernant *and* Detienne, bearing the ex post facto title of *Anthropologie*.

There are glimpses of anthropological influences, less pronounced than that of Gernet, in a particularly influential collection of essays edited by Detienne and Vernant that bears the remarkable title *The Cuisine of Sacrifice among the Greeks*.[20] A thorough reading of *Cuisine* is an ideal point of entry for coming to

---

volume provides the reader with an authoritative abridged collection of Gernet's most important essays in Classics.

[14] The title of the 1981 English version, *The Anthropology of Ancient Greece*, reflects accurately the title of the French version edited by Vernant and Detienne: *Anthropologie de la Grèce antique* (Paris: Maspero, 1968). See also S. C. Humphreys, *Anthropology and the Greeks* (London: Routledge, 1978).

[15] Ignace Meyerson, *Écrits, 1920–83: Pour une psychologie historique* (Paris: Presses Universitaires de France, 1987).

[16] See Detienne, *Masters of Truth* (1996) in this volume, p. 217 n.6.

[17] For a salutary survey of pitfalls encountered by those who propose to "reconstruct" the intellectual trajectory of Vernant, see Detienne, *Masters of Truth* (1996) in this volume, p. 207.

[18] See especially Louis Gernet, *Droit et société dans la Grèce ancienne* (revision of 1955 ed.; Paris: Sirey, 1964).

[19] See for example Gernet, ed. and trans., *Antiphon, ca. 480–411 B.C.: Discours: Suivis des fragments d'Antiphon le sophiste* (Paris: Les Belles Lettres, 1954).

[20] Marcel Detienne and Jean-Pierre Vernant, *La Cuisine du sacrifice en pays grec* (Paris: Gallimard, 1979) [*The Cuisine of Sacrifice among the Greeks*, including essays by Jean-Louis Durand, Stella Georgoudi, François Hartog, and Jesper Svenbro (Chicago: University of Chicago Press, 1989)]. An important addendum: Guy Berthiaume, *Les rôles du mageiros:*

terms with most of the major agenda (both hidden and not so hidden) of current French intellectual life in the Classics.

The general methodology of *Cuisine* is based in part on the fundamental work of Emile Durkheim on the anthropology of sacrifice.[21] Far less attention, however, is paid to the equally seminal work of another leading anthropologist, Marcel Mauss,[22] whose emphasis on the *syntax* of sacrifice and of prayer has not yet received the attention that it deserves.[23] There is an added French twist in the title chosen by Vernant, Detienne, and their co-authors for this book about *sacrifice*. The cultural construct implied by the collocation of *cuisine* and *sacrifice* is a pointed challenge to the dead-serious Christian interpretation of sacrifice in the influential book of René Girard, *Violence and the Sacred*.[24] The implications, however, are far from merely playful. The descriptivist stance implied by the term "cuisine" offers a subtle counterpoint to the atavistic orientation of Walter Burkert's ambitious synthesis on Greek sacrifice, *Homo necans*, the perspectives of which tend to reach back all the way to the Palaeolithic era.[25]

There is a palpable distancing, in *Cuisine*, between the central event of shedding the blood of the sacrificial animal and the related events of cooking and

---

Étude sur la boucherie, la cuisine et le sacrifice dans la Grèce ancienne (Leiden: Brill, Mnemosyne Supplements 70 [1982]). A definitive book on Greek sacrifice in particular and religion in general remains Jean Rudhardt, *Notions fondamentales de la pensée religieuse et actes constitutifs du culte dans la Grèce classique*, 2d ed. (Paris: Picard, 1992). See also Jesper Svenbro, "La Découpe du poème: Notes sur les origines sacrificielles de la poétique grecque," *Poétique* 58 (1984): 215–32.

[21] Emile Durkheim, *Formes élémentaires de la pensée religieuse* (Paris: Alcan, 1910).

[22] Marcel Mauss, *Oeuvres*, 3 vols., posthumous edition by Victor Karady (Paris: Éditions de Minuit, 1968–69), vol. 1: *Les Fonctions sociales du sacré*, vol. 2: *Représentations collectives et diversité des civilisations*, vol. 3: *Cohésion sociale et divisions de la sociologie*.

[23] A notable exception is the work of an American scholar: Leonard Muellner, *The Meaning of Homeric EYXOMAI through Its Formulas* (Innsbruck: Innsbrucker Beiträge zur Sprachwissenschaft 13 [1976]), especially pp. 31–32. For important comparative contributions by Indologists, see Charles Malamoud, *Cuire le monde: Rite et pensée dans l'Inde ancienne* (Paris: Éditions la Découverte, 1989). See also Stephanie W. Jamison, *The Ravenous Hyenas and the Wounded Sun: Myth and Ritual in Ancient India* (Ithaca: Cornell University Press, 1991).

[24] René Girard, *La Violence et le sacré* (Paris: B. Grasset, 1972) [*Violence and the Sacred*, trans. Patrick Gregory (Baltimore: Johns Hopkins University Press, 1977)], with further elaborations in his *Des Choses cachées depuis la fondation du monde* (Paris: Grasset, 1978) [*Things Hidden since the Foundation of the World*, Book I trans. Michael Metteer, Books II–III trans. Stephen Bann (Stanford: Stanford University Press, 1987)].

[25] Walter Burkert, *Homo necans: Interpretationen altgriechischer Opferriten und Mythen* (Berlin: De Gruyter, 1972) [*Homo necans: The Anthropology of Ancient Greek Sacrificial Ritual and Myth*, trans. Peter Bing (Berkeley and Los Angeles: University of California Press, 1983)]. In the English translation, Burkert's topic has been reinterpreted as "anthropology."

distributing its meat for consumption by the sacrificing community. The shedding of the animal's blood in the central act of sacrificial killing, which belongs exclusively to the divine sphere, is complementary with the cooking and consumption of its meat, which extends to the human sphere. As Jean-Louis Durand observes in his incisive essay on sacrificial animals, the conventions of ancient Greek visual art consistently avoided showing the actual hemorrhage of the sacrificed animal at the precise moment when its throat is slashed.[26] Paradoxically, there seems to be no such "blackout" in representations of mythical human sacrifice. One vase painting, for example, shows the hemorrhage of Polyxena, daughter of Priam, at the precise moment when her throat is being slashed over a burning altar, with her blood spurting down toward the flames of the sacrificial fire.[27]

This observation is relevant to a central argument in Burkert's *Homo necans*. In his cross-cultural survey of the institution of sacrifice, specifically the sacrificial slaughter of animal victims, Burkert argues that sacrifice is a social mechanism for expiating guilt (in the broadest possible sense of this word). The fundamental guilt, in line with this formulation, concerns the capacity of one human to kill another human. The argument can be taken further: the institution of warfare, as reflected by Homeric descriptions of death in battle, is related to the institution of sacrifice.[28]

A premier example is the description of the three-stage death of Patroklos in *Iliad* 16, which reveals striking analogies to the description of the three-stage death of a sacrificial bull in *Odyssey* 3.418–63. In each case, the one who is first to strike stuns the victim from behind; the second to strike delivers the fatal blow; and the third administers the coup de grâce.[29]

Another example can be uncovered by tracing the etymological and contextual connections between the Greek verb *makhomai*, meaning "fight in battle," and the noun *makhaira*, designating the "sacrificial dagger," the prescribed implement used for dismembering the body of the sacrificial victim into the various cuts apportioned to various members of society.[30] In the myths concerning the death of the hero Pyrrhos, son of Achilles, we see a formalization of

---

[26] Jean-Louis Durand, "Greek Animals: Toward a Topology of Edible Bodies," in *Cuisine of Sacrifice*, pp. 87–118, especially p. 91.

[27] London amphora 97.7.272; this is figure 7 in the English-language version of Durand's piece (not "figure 8," as indicated on p. 91) and figure 3 in the French version.

[28] Gregory Nagy, *Pindar's Homer: The Lyric Possession of an Epic Past* (Baltimore: Johns Hopkins University Press, 1990). See especially the observations on p. 143 n. 40, which form the nucleus of the remarks in the next five paragraphs of the present discussion.

[29] Steven Lowenstam, *The Death of Patroklos: A Study in Typology* (Königstein: Verlag Anton Hain, Beiträge zur klassischen Philologie 133 [1981]), p. 165.

[30] Richard P. Martin, *Healing, Sacrifice and Battle: Amêchania and Related Concepts in Early Greek Poetry* (Innsbruck: Innsbrucker Beiträge zur Sprachwissenschaft 41 [1983]).

this connection: the impetuous young warrior, falling into a brawl with the priests of Apollo on the occasion of a sacrifice held in the god's sacred precinct at Delphi, is overwhelmed, slaughtered, and carved up like a sacrificial victim by the sacrificing attendants, each wielding a *makhaira* (Pindar, *Paean* 6 and *Nemean* 7).[31]

Beyond the general argument that the institution of warfare is related to the institution of sacrifice, a more specific point can be made: the descriptions of the deaths of warriors in Homeric poetry serve as a compensation for the absence of ritual detail in descriptions of the slaughter of animal victims. Homeric poetry, as a medium that seems to have reached its synthetic pan-Hellenic status by virtue of avoiding the parochial concerns of specific locales, specific regions, tends to avoid realistic descriptions of ritual, including ritual sacrifice.[32] This is to be expected, given that ritual sacrifice, as for that matter any ritual, tends to be a strictly localized phenomenon in ancient Greece.[33] What sacrificial scenes we do find in Homer are highly stylized, devoid of the kind of details that characterize real sacrifices as documented in the epigraphical evidence.[34]

In real sacrifice, the ritual dismemberment of the sacrificial victim corresponds to the ideological articulation of the body politic: this is an essential point that pervades the 1979 book *Cuisine of Sacrifice*.[35] Moreover, the disarticulation of the body in sacrifice presupposes the rearticulation of the body in myths of immortalization.[36] Given, then, that Homeric poetry avoids delving into the details of disarticulation as it applies to animals, in that it avoids the realia of sacrificial practice, we may expect a parallel avoidance of the topic of immortalization for the hero. By contrast, the local practices of hero-cult, contemporaneous with the evolution of Homeric poetry as we know it, are based on religious notions of heroic immortalization.[37]

---

[31] Gregory Nagy, *The Best of the Achaeans: Concepts of the Hero in Archaic Greek Poetry* (Baltimore: Johns Hopkins University Press, 1979; rev. ed., 1999), pp. 118–41. See also the French translation by Jeannie Carlier and Nicole Loraux, *Le Meilleur des Achéens: La Fabrique du héros dans la poésie grecque archaïque* (Paris: Seuil, 1994), with an introduction by Nicole Loraux (pp. 9–17; note especially p. 16 for her comments on *sacrifice*).

[32] Nagy, *Best of the Achaeans*, pp. 118–41.

[33] Nagy, *Best of the Achaeans*, pp. 132–34, 217.

[34] For which see Friedrich Puttkammer, *Quomodo Graeci victimarum carnes distribuerint* (Königsberg: Kuemmel, 1912).

[35] See especially Marcel Detienne and Jesper Svenbro, "The Feast of the Wolves, or the Impossible City," in *Cuisine*, pp. 148–63. Besides the writings collected by Vernant and Detienne in their 1979 book, see Jesper Svenbro, "À Mégara Hyblaea: Le Corps géomètre," *Annales économies sociétés civilisations* 37 (1982): 953–64. See also Nicole Loraux, "La Cité comme cuisine et comme partage," *Annales économies sociétés civilisations* 36 (1981): 614–22.

[36] Nagy, *Best of the Achaeans*, pp. 208–9.

[37] Nagy, *Best of the Achaeans*, pp. 151–210. On the dichotomy of heroes as viewed in

While personal immortalization is a theme too localized in orientation for Homeric poetry, the hero's death in battle, in all its staggering varieties, is an acceptable topic for the universalized perspectives of epic. Homeric poetry compensates for its avoidance of details concerning the sacrifices of animals by dwelling on details concerning the martial deaths of heroes.[38] In this way, the epic poetry of the ancient Greeks, in describing the deaths of heroes, can serve as a compensation for sacrifice.[39]

Finally, the polytropic title *Cuisine* evokes yet another vital aspect of the anthropological "framework" shared by Vernant and his colleagues. It comes under the general heading of "structuralism"—a term overused, often in oversimplified ways, by some Anglo-American Classicists. The key "structuralist" model for Vernant and his earliest research partners, notably for Detienne and Vidal-Naquet, has been Claude Lévi-Strauss. There are two books by Lévi-Strauss that have been particularly influential for this group: *Structural Anthropology* and *The Raw and the Cooked*.[40] The agenda of the second book, which explores cultural dichotomies of the natural and the artificial, of nature and culture, in terms of metaphorical oppositions involving "raw" and "cooked" categories, is indirectly reflected in the title of *Cuisine*.

Reductive usage in the application of the term "structuralism" goes back to the 1960s, when Classicists were first exposed to the idea of "structuralist" approaches to antiquity in general and to myth in particular. The work of Lévi-Strauss, as we have seen, is widely recognized as the main moving force in the shaping of "structuralist" approaches to myth. Still, many English-speaking teachers and students of the Classics continue to rely not on Lévi-Strauss but on Geoffrey Kirk for guidance on these approaches.[41] Kirk, who is a Classicist

---

poetry (both Homeric and Hesiodic) and heroes as viewed in cult, see the incisive observations of Jean-Pierre Vernant, *Mythe et pensée chez les Grecs: Études de psychologie historique*, 2d rev. ed. (Paris: Éditions la Découverte, 1985), pp. 86–106, especially pp. 100–106. The English-language version, *Myth and Thought among the Greeks* (London: Routledge and Kegan Paul, 1983), is based on the 1st edition (Paris: Maspero, 1965), and needs to be updated.

[38] See again Nagy, *Pindar's Homer*, p. 143.

[39] In a related tradition, the epic poetry of the Indic peoples, we see the ultimate logical extension of such a line of thinking: in the *Mahābhārata*, a warrior's death in battle is sacrifice itself. See Alf Hiltebeitel, *The Ritual of Battle: Krishna in the Mahābhārata* (Ithaca, N.Y.: Cornell University Press, 1976; repr. ed., 1990, Albany: State University of New York Press).

[40] Claude Lévi-Strauss, *Anthropologie structurale* (Paris: Plon, 1958) [*Structural Anthropology*, trans. Claire Jacobson and Brooke Grundfest Schoepf (New York: Basic Books, 1963)] and *Le Cru et le cuit* (Paris: Plon, 1964) [*The Raw and the Cooked*, trans. John and Doreen Weightman (New York: Harper and Row, 1969)]. For a critique of his methods, see Renate Schlesier, "Lévi-Strauss' Mythology and the Myth," *Telos* 77 (1988): 143–57.

[41] G. S. Kirk, *Myth: Its Meaning and Functions in Ancient and Other Cultures* (Berkeley

and not an anthropologist, distances himself from the methods of Lévi-Strauss, with consequences that have been described as follows by Gregory Nagy:[42]

> What results is that readers are scared away from consulting directly the anthropological perspectives of Lévi-Strauss himself. I suggest that not enough credit is being given to the methods of Lévi-Strauss in analyzing the myths of small-scale societies like the Bororo of central Brazil, even if we may agree with [Edmund R.] Leach that not enough attention is being paid to the contexts of performance.[43] The works of Lévi-Strauss, I maintain, remain models of "structuralist" techniques in revealing the richness and complexity of human thought in the institutions of so-called "primitive" societies. For many who read Kirk, however, the myths of small-scale societies like the Bororo will seem more like a foil for showing the distinctness and in many instances the purported superiority of the myths of the ancient Greeks. Such an attitude is criticized by Marcel Detienne in an essay bearing the ironic title, "The Greeks are not like the others" [*Les Grecs ne sont pas comme les autres*].[44]

Despite his self-distancing, Kirk's interest in the work of Lévi-Strauss is tantamount to a "revolt from classicism" in the opinion of some English-speaking Classicists: one of them singles out Kirk as an example of "scholars who have begun to take seriously the bizarre myths of primitive peoples," making these myths "seem deeper and truer than the human scale and coherent logic of the myths of Homer."[45] Other Classicists, however, have succeeded in developing comparative methods of applying the systematic study of myth to the actual poetics of Greek literature, on the level of form as well as content.[46]

---

and Los Angeles: University of California Press, 1970) and *The Nature of Greek Myths* (Harmondsworth: Penguin, 1974).

[42] Gregory Nagy, *Homeric Questions* (Austin: University of Texas Press, 1996), p. 118.

[43] E. R. Leach, critical introduction to *Myth*, by M. I. Steblin-Kamenskij (Ann Arbor: University of Michigan Press, 1982), pp. 1–20.

[44] Marcel Detienne, the first chapter of *Dionysos mis à mort* (Paris: Gallimard, 1977), pp. 17–47 [*Dionysos Slain*, trans. Mireille Muellner and Leonard Muellner (Baltimore: Johns Hopkins University Press, 1979)]. See especially the remarks at pp. 12–13 (the English version) concerning Kirk. At one point in his 1970 book on myth (p. 179), Kirk says about the ancient Greek heroes: "The Greeks are *a special case*. In the mythology of most other peoples, heroes . . . are either inconspicuous or absent" (emphasis added).

[45] Jasper Griffin, *Homer on Life and Death* (Oxford: Clarendon Press, 1980), p. 173.

[46] Richard P. Martin, *The Language of Heroes: Speech and Performance in the Iliad* (Ithaca: Cornell University Press, 1989; rev. ed., 1992); Laura Slatkin, *The Power of Thetis: Allusion and Interpretation in the Iliad* (Berkeley and Los Angeles: University of California Press, 1991); and Leonard Muellner, *The Anger of Achilles: Mēnis in Early Greek Epic* (Ithaca: Cornell University Press, 1996). See also Laura Slatkin, "Les Amis mortels," *L'Ecrit du temps* 19 (1988): 119–32, and the remarks of Loraux (pp. 12–14 as in n. 30 above).

It is questionable, in any case, to link Kirk with "structuralists." He is in fact the antagonist of "structuralists" in a notorious debate about the methods of structuralism. This debate, facetiously known as the "lettuce wars," centers on the symbolism of lettuce in the myths and rituals associated with the love-hero Adonis.[47] The methodological problem can be summed up this way: when a structuralist argues that "A" stands for "X" in context "L," a critic may object, "But look, here is a counterexample in context 'M' where 'A' stands for the opposite of 'X'!" Such counterargumentation misses a basic principle of semiotics: a given sign means what it means only in relation to other signs within the same system of signs, but its meaning is arbitrary when it is viewed outside of that given system. If indeed lettuce "means" sterility in Greek myths about Adonis, as Marcel Detienne argues, then it is pointless for Kirk to cite as a counterexample various cases where lettuce happens to "mean" fertility, as in Egyptian myths.[48]

Whether or not the word "structuralist" is the most apt designation for these new Classicists of France, one thing is for sure: they have created their own intellectual momentum, and they are leaders, rather than followers, in applying the methods of structuralism.[49] Besides Vernant, Detienne, Vidal-Naquet, and Loraux, many other names stand out. What follows is a list of distinguished contributions, arranged along general lines of methodology:[50]

---

[47] G. S. Kirk, "The Spicy Side of Structuralism," *Times Literary Supplement*, 18 Aug. 1978, pp. 22–23, reviewing Marcel Detienne, *Les Jardins d'Adonis: La Mythologie des aromates en Grèce* (Paris: Gallimard, 1977). Kirk's review is included in this volume.

[48] See Detienne in the afterword to the 1985 reissue of *Les Jardins d'Adonis*, trans. Froma Zeitlin as "Afterword: Revisiting the Gardens of Adonis" (Princeton: Princeton University Press, 1994), pp. 133–45, of *The Gardens of Adonis: Spices in Greek Mythology*, trans. Janet Lloyd (Hassocks, Sussex: Harvester, 1977).

[49] For the foundations of structuralism, see Ferdinand de Saussure, *Cours de linguistique générale*, ed. Charles Bally and Albert Sechehaye, with the collaboration of Albert Riedlinger (Paris: Payot, 1916), critical reedition by Tullio de Mauro (Paris: Payot, 1972). Saussure makes a key distinction between *synchronic* and *diachronic* levels of linguistic analysis. For Saussure, synchrony and diachrony designate respectively a current state of a language and a phase in its evolution ("De même *synchronie* et *diachronie* désigneront respectivement un état de langage et une phase d'évolution" [p. 117]). For methodological precision, Nagy, *Homeric Questions*, p. 4, suggests that these terms be applied consistently "from the standpoint of an outsider who is thinking about a given system, not from the standpoint of an insider who is thinking within that system." Further, *diachronic* and *synchronic* are not the equivalent of *historical* and *current* respectively: "Diachrony refers to the potential for evolution *in a structure*. History is not restricted to phenomena that are structurally predictable" (Nagy, p. 21 n. 18). Compare Pierre-Yves Jacopin, "Anthropological Dialectics: Yukuna Ritual as Defensive Strategy," *Schweizerische Amerikanisten-Gesellschaft*, Bulletin 52 (1988): 35–46, especially 35–36: "Both synchrony and diachrony are abstractions extrapolated from a model of reality."

[50] The sublistings are in alphabetical order.

History—François Hartog,[51] Nicole Loraux,[52] Pauline Schmitt Pantel,[53]
   Pierre Vidal-Naquet[54]
Social Anthropology and Semiotics—Claude Calame,[55] Jesper Svenbro[56]
Philosophy—Barbara Cassin,[57] Patrice Loraux[58]
Psychoanalysis—Laurence Kahn[59]
Religion—Philippe Borgeaud[60]
Iconography and Art History—Stella Georgoudi,[61] Françoise Frontisi-
   Ducroux,[62] François Lissarrague,[63] Alain Schnapp[64]

---

[51] François Hartog, *Le Miroir d'Hérodote: Essai sur la representation de l'autre* (Paris: Gallimard, 1980) [*The Mirror of Herodotus: The Representation of the Other in the Writing of History*, trans. Janet Lloyd (Berkeley and Los Angeles: University of California Press, 1988)].

[52] Nicole Loraux, *L'Invention d'Athènes: Histoire de l'oraison funèbre dans la "cité classique,"* 2d ed. (Paris: Payot, 1993) [*The Invention of Athens: The Funeral Oration in the Classical City*, trans. Alan Sheridan (Cambridge, Mass.: Harvard University Press, 1986)].

[53] Pauline Schmitt Pantel, *La Cité au banquet: Histoire des repas publics dans les cités grecques* (Rome: Ecole française de Rome, 1992).

[54] Pierre Vidal-Naquet, *Le Chasseur noir: Formes de pensée et formes de société dans le monde grec* (Paris: Maspero, 1981) [*The Black Hunter: Forms of Thought and Forms of Society in the Greek World*, trans. Andrew Szegedy-Maszák, foreword by Bernard Knox (Baltimore: Johns Hopkins University Press, 1986)].

[55] Claude Calame, *Le Récit en Grèce ancienne: Énonciations et représentations de poètes*, preface by Jean-Claude Coquet (Paris: Meridiens/Klincksieck, 1986) [*The Craft of Poetic Speech in Ancient Greece*, trans. Janice Orion (Ithaca: Cornell University Press, 1995)]. See also his *Choruses of Young Women in Ancient Greece: Their Morphology, Religious Role, and Social Function*, trans. Derek Collins and Janice Orion (Lanham, Md.: Rowman and Littlefield, 1997). This book is in effect the second edition of volume 1 of Calame's *Les Choeurs de jeunes filles en Grèce archaïque* (Rome: Edizioni dell'Ateneo & Bizzarri, 1977).

[56] Jesper Svenbro, *Phrasikleia: Anthropologie de la lecture en Grèce ancienne* (Paris: Éditions la Découverte, 1988) [*Phrasikleia: An Anthropology of Reading in Ancient Greece*, trans. Janet Lloyd (Ithaca: Cornell University Press, 1993)].

[57] Barbara Cassin, *L'Effet sophistique* (Paris: Gallimard, 1995).

[58] Patrice Loraux, *Le Tempo de la pensée* (Paris: Editions du Seuil, 1993).

[59] Laurence Kahn, *La Petite maison de l'âme* (Paris: Gallimard, 1993).

[60] Philippe Borgeaud, *Recherches sur le dieu Pan* (Rome: Institut suisse de Rome, 1979) [*The Cult of Pan in Ancient Greece*, trans. Kathleen Atlass and James Redfield (Chicago: University of Chicago Press, 1988)].

[61] Stella Georgoudi, *Des Chevaux et des boeufs dans le monde grec: Realités et représentations animalières à partir des livres XVI et XVII des Géoponiques*, preface by Marcel Detienne (Paris: Daedalus, 1990).

[62] Françoise Frontisi-Ducroux, *Du Masque au visage: Aspects de l'identité en Grèce ancienne* (Paris: Flammarion, 1995).

[63] François Lissarrague, *L'Autre guerrier: Archers, peltastes, cavaliers dans l'imagerie attique* (Paris: Editions la Découverte, 1990).

[64] Alain Schnapp, *Le Chasseur et la cité: Chasse et érotique dans la Grèce ancienne* (Paris: Albin Michel, 1997).

The "iconographers" in this list merit special attention because of their extraordinary publication record. Their medium of publishing lends itself to a particularly strong showing in English-speaking circles. The premier example is a book jointly written by several of them:

> Claude Bérard, Christiane Bron, Jean-Louis Durand, Françoise Frontisi-Ducroux, François Lissarrague, Alain Schnapp, and Jean-Pierre Vernant, *La Cité des images: Religion et société en Grèce antique* (Lausanne and Paris: Fernand Nathan, 1984) [*A City of Images: Iconography and Society in Ancient Greece*, trans. Deborah Lyons (Princeton: Princeton University Press, 1989)].

In the present volume, only a glimpse of the "iconographers' " wide range of interests can be covered, as represented by the writings of Françoise Frontisi-Ducroux and Stella Georgoudi in Part II. There is much more to be seen and read, however, in *City of Images*, which can serve as a complement to *Antiquities*.

Two other American collections complement our *Antiquities*:

> John J. Winkler and Froma Zeitlin, eds., *Nothing to Do with Dionysos? Athenian Drama in Its Social Context* (Princeton: Princeton University Press, 1990)[65] and David M. Halperin, John J. Winkler, and Froma Zeitlin, eds., *Before Sexuality. The Construction of Erotic Experience in the Ancient Greek World* (Princeton: Princeton University Press, 1990).[66]

This introduction began—and now ends—with a citation from the works of Jean-Pierre Vernant as the last entry in the last footnote. Vernant in many ways epitomizes the importance of French research in the Classics over the second half of the twentieth century. His contributions to the study of Classical antiquity, like the studies of French scholars in general, have been prodigious. There are in fact so many dimensions to this era of French Classical scholarship

---

[65] See especially the following contributions:
Nicole Loraux, "Kreousa the Autochthon: A Study of Euripides' *Ion*," pp. 168–206;
François Lissarrague, "Why Satyrs are Good to Represent," pp. 228–36;
Jesper Svenbro, "The Interior Voice: On the Invention of Silent Reading," pp. 366–84.
[66] Nicole Loraux, "Herakles: The Super-male and the Feminine," pp. 21–52;
François Lissarrague, "The Sexual Life of Satyrs," pp. 53–81;
Maurice Olender, "Aspects of Baubo: Ancient Texts and Contexts," pp. 83–113;
Françoise Frontisi-Ducroux and François Lissarrague, "From Ambiguity to Ambivalence: A Dionysiac Excursion through the 'Anakreontic' Vases," pp. 211–56;
Giulia Sissa, "Maidenhood without Maidenhead: The Female Body in Ancient Greece," pp. 339–46;
Jean-Pierre Vernant, "One . . . Two . . . Three: Erôs," pp. 465–78.

that our main worry is that so much had to be compressed into so little space. Still, this treasury of French Classical scholarship gives an idea of the range of work accomplished, and of its staggeringly wide cross-cultural applicability. It is a lasting legacy of intellectual precision and brilliance.

PART I
Convergences of Approach

JEAN-PIERRE VERNANT

The Spiritual Universe of the *Polis*

1962

In this chapter of his influential first book, Vernant specifies the pre-conditions for the emergence of the city-state, an innovation that is here recognized not principally as a social and economic transformation, but as "a decisive event in the history of Greek thought." Vernant's discussion shares concerns with Gernet's "Origins of Greek Philosophy" (in this volume), which provides a model for recognizing pre-philosophical antecedents and also introduces an account of the secularization—and therefore democratization—of wisdom and the authority it confers. Private, secret, and unalienable wisdom (the privilege of the king and of priestly or aristocratic families) gave way to an accessible, transferable, and genuinely public wisdom that could be established by means of discourse and dispute and disseminated in writing, set forth es to meson— "into the middle" of communal space. The prestige of public speech and the new visibility of power in action found their crucial complement, finally, in a new basis for affinity that subsumed family, tribal, and local ties in a larger concept of "alikeness" that allowed civic identification to flourish. (For a complementary investigation of the politics and ideology of isonomiē, "equality under the law," that builds on Vernant's discussion, see the selection by Lévêque and Vidal-Naquet, Cleisthenes the Athenian [in this volume]). Not the least intriguing aspect of Vernant's analysis is his ascription of this key development to the changing technology of war; hence it is Sparta's military preoccupation that first gave rise to institutions embodying equality among citizens, even as, by default, Sparta left "to others the honor of fully expressing the new conception of order, in which the city became a balanced and harmonious cosmos under the rule of law."

T he advent of the *polis* constitutes a decisive event in the history of Greek thought. Certainly, on the intellectual as well as the institutional level, the *polis* went through a number of stages and a variety of

From *The Origins of Greek Thought*, trans. Janet Lloyd (Ithaca, NY: Cornell University Press, 1982), pp. 47–69 ["L'univers spirituel de la 'Polis'," in *Les origines de la pensée grecque* (Paris: Presses Universitaires de France, 1962), pp. 40–61].

forms, and only in due time did all of its consequences become known. From the very outset, however, which we can place between the eighth and seventh centuries, it marked a departure, a genuine innovation. With the *polis*, social life and human relations took on a new form, and the Greeks were fully aware of its originality.[1]

The system of the *polis* implied, first of all, the extraordinary preeminence of speech over all other instruments of power. Speech became the political tool par excellence, the key to all authority in the state, the means of commanding and dominating others. This power of speech—which the Greeks made into a divinity, *Peithō*, the force of persuasion—brings to mind the efficacy of words and formulas in certain religious rituals, or the value attributed to the "pronouncements" of the king when he rendered final *themis*, "judgment." Actually, however, we are dealing with quite a different matter. Speech was no longer the ritual word, the precise formula, but open debate, discussion, argument. It presupposed a public to which it was addressed, as to a judge whose ruling could not be appealed, who decided with hands upraised between the two parties who came before him. It was this purely human choice that measured the persuasive force of the two forms of address, ensuring the victory of one speaker over his adversary.

All questions of general concern that the sovereign had to settle, and which marked out the domain of *arkhē*, "sovereignty," were now submitted to the art of oratory and had to be resolved at the conclusion of a debate. They therefore had to be formulated as a discourse, poured into the mold of antithetical demonstrations and opposing arguments. There was thus a close connection, a reciprocal tie, between politics and *logos*. The art of politics became essentially the management of language; and *logos* from the beginning took on an awareness of itself, of its rules and its effectiveness, through its political function. Historically, rhetoric and sophistry, by analyzing forms of discourse as a means of winning the contest in the assembly and the tribunal, opened the way for Aristotle's inquiries, which in turn defined the rules of proof along with the technique of persuasion and thus laid down a logic of the verifiably true, a matter of theoretical understanding, as opposed to the logic of the apparent or probable, which presided over the hazardous debates on practical questions.

A second feature of the *polis* was the full exposure given to the most important aspects of social life. We can even say that the *polis* existed only to the extent that a *public* domain had emerged, in each of the two differing but interdependent meanings of the term: an area of common interest, as opposed to private concerns, and open practices openly arrived at, as opposed to secret procedures. This insistence on openness led to the progressive appropriation by the group of the conduct, knowledge, and procedures that originally were the exclusive prerogatives of the *basileus*, or the *genē* that held *arkhē* and their exposure to public view. On the intellectual level, this double impulse toward democratization and disclosure had decisive consequences. Greek culture took form by opening to an ever-widening circle—and finally to the entire *dēmos*, "community"—access to the spiritual world reserved initially for an aristocracy of priests and warriors. (Homeric epic is an early example of the process: from court poetry, sung first in the halls of the palace, it was freed, expanded, and transformed into a poetry for popular festivals.) But this broadening involved a radical transformation. Knowledge, values, and mental techniques, in becoming elements of a common culture, were themselves brought to public view and submitted to criticism and controversy. They were no longer preserved in family traditions as private tokens of power, and their exposure to public scrutiny fostered exegeses, varying interpretations, controversies, and impassioned debates. Now discussion, debate, polemic became the rules of the intellectual as well as the political game. The community's inexorable control was exercised over the creations of the mind no less than over the operation of the state. The law of the *polis*, as distinguished from the absolute power of the monarch, required that both be equally subject to a "rendering of accounts," *euthunai*. They could no longer be imposed by the authority of personal or religious prestige; they had to demonstrate their validity by processes of a dialectical sort.

Speech became the instrument of the city's political life; on the strictly intellectual level, writing became the medium of a common culture and permitted the complete dissemination of knowledge previously restricted or forbidden. Borrowed from the Phoenicians and modified to permit more precise transcription of Greek sounds, writing was able to fulfill this function of communication because it had become almost as widely known and used among citizens as the spoken language. The oldest known inscriptions in the Greek alphabet show that from the eighth century onward it was no longer a matter of specialized knowledge, reserved for scribes, but a technique in general use, freely diffused among the public.[2] Along with recitation from memory of texts by Homer and Hesiod—which remained traditional—writing constituted the basic element of Greek *paideia*, "education."

Thus we can understand the significance of a demand that arose with the birth of the city: the writing down of the laws. Setting them down not only ensured their permanence and stability but it also removed them from the private authority of the *basileus*, whose function was to "speak" the law. Thus they became public property, general rules that could be applied equally to all. In Hesiod's world, before the rise of the city, *dikē*, "justice," still operated on two levels, as though divided between heaven and earth. Here below, at the level of the small Boeotian farmer, *dikē* was a determination of fact subject to the whim of the kings, "devourers of gifts." In heaven it was a sovereign divinity, remote and inaccessible. But as a result of the public exposure provided by the written word, *dikē*—without ceasing to be regarded as an ideal value—could be incarnated on a strictly human level. It could emerge as the law, a principle at once common to all and superior to all, a rational standard that was subject to

discussion and modification by decree but which nevertheless expressed an order that was understood to be sacred.

Individuals who decided to make their knowledge public by means of writing did so either in the form of books, such as those that Anaximander and
Pherecydes are said to have been the first to write, or those that Heraclitus
deposited in the temple of Artemis at Ephesus, or in the form of *parapēgmata*,
monumental inscriptions on stone similar to those on which the city engraved
the names of its magistrates or its priests (private citizens recorded astronomical observations or chronological tables based on them). Their ambition was
not to make a display of their own discoveries or opinions; in setting forth such
a message *es to meson*, "into the middle," they wished to make it the common
property of the city, a standard that would, like the law, be applicable to all.[3]
Thus disclosed, their wisdom would take on a new consistency and objectivity;
it would become the truth. We are no longer dealing with a religious secret,
reserved for some elect few who had been favored by divine grace. Certainly
the truth of the sage, like the religious secret, revealed what was fundamental,
unveiled a higher reality that far transcended the mass of humanity; but in
being committed to writing, it was wrenched from the closed circle of the cults
and displayed in broad daylight before the gaze of the whole city. Those who
wrote thus recognized that their message was within the reach of all by right,
and agreed to submit it, like political debate, to the judgment of all, in the hope
that in the end all would acknowledge and accept it.

This transformation of secret wisdom into a body of public truths has a
parallel in another area of social experience. The early priesthoods, which belonged to certain *genē* of their own and claimed special intimacy with a divine
power, were appropriated by the *polis* for its own uses, once it had become
established, and turned into official city cults. The protection that the deity had
formerly reserved for his favorites would henceforth be extended to the entire
community. But to speak of a city cult is to speak of a public cult. All the old
sacra, badges of investiture, religious symbols, emblems, *xoana* (wooden images), jealously preserved as talismans of power in the privacy of palaces or the
crannies of priestly houses, now moved to the temple, an open and public place.
Within that impersonal space, which faced outward and which now projected
the decoration of its sculptured friezes toward the outside, the old idols were in
turn transformed. Along with their hidden character, they lost their quality as
efficacious symbols and became simply "images," with no ritual function other
than to be seen, no religious meaning other than their appearance. Of the large
cult statue lodged in the temple to represent the god, one could say that all its
esse, "being," now consisted of *percipi*, "perception." The *sacra*, formerly
charged with a dangerous power and withheld from public view, became a
spectacle in full view of the city, a "lesson on the gods," just as the secret
chronicles and occult formulas shed their mystery and their religious force to
become the "truths" debated by the sages in full view of the city.

Still, it was by no means without difficulty or resistance that social life was thus brought into full public view. The process of disclosure occurred by stages; in every area it met with obstacles that limited its progress. Even in the high classical period, secret governmental practices preserved a form of power that worked in mysterious ways and by supernatural means. The Spartan regime offers the best examples of these hidden procedures, but the use of hidden sanctuaries as tools of government, private oracles reserved exclusively for certain officials, and undisclosed handbooks of divination kept by certain leaders is equally well attested elsewhere. In addition, many cities entrusted their survival to the possession of secret relics: the remains of the hero, whose tomb could be revealed to no one, on pain of destroying the state, save to those officials who alone were qualified to receive such dangerous information when they took office. The political value attributed to these secret talismans was not simply a survival of the past; it answered definite social needs. Did not the city's safety necessarily set in motion forces that eluded the calculations of human reason, elements that could not be appraised in debate or foreseen at the close of deliberation? This intervention of a supernatural power whose role was ultimately decisive—Herodotus' Fate, Thucydides' *Tukhē*, "Chance"—must be taken into account and given its place in the political system. Public worship of the Olympian gods could answer to that function only in part. That worship had to do with a divine world that was too general and too remote; it defined a sacred order that was exactly the opposite of the secular sphere where the city's administration was located, as the *hieros* (sacred) was opposed to the *hosios* (secular). The desacralization of an entire plane of political life had as its counterpart an official religion that kept human affairs at arm's length and was no longer directly involved in the vicissitudes of *arkhē*. Yet however clear-sighted the political leaders and however wise the citizens, the assembly's decisions bore on a future that remained fundamentally opaque and the intelligence could not altogether grasp. So it became essential to ensure as much control over that future as possible by other means—means that called into effect no human abilities, but rather the power of ritual. The political "rationalism" that presided over the city's institutions was certainly in sharp contrast to the old religious procedures of government, but still it never went so far as to abolish them.[4]

In the religious sphere, moreover, associations based on secrecy developed at the fringes of the city and alongside the public cult. Sects, brotherhoods, and mysteries were closed groups, with hierarchies of ranks and degrees, modeled on the initiation societies. Their function was to single out, through a series of ordeals, an elect minority who would enjoy privileges not available to the mass of people. But in contrast to the initiations to which the young warriors, the *kouroi*, had once been subjected, which conferred power upon them, the new secret groups were confined to a purely religious sphere. In the framework of the city, initiation could now bring only a "spiritual" transformation, with no political connotations. The elect, the *epoptai*, were the unsullied, the saints. Akin to the divine, they were indeed dedicated to a special destiny, but they would meet it in the hereafter. The preferment they would gain belonged to another world.

The mysteries offered to all those who wished to undergo initiation, with no restriction of birth or rank, the promise of a blissful immortality that had once been an exclusively royal privilege; they disclosed to the wider circle of the initiated the religious secrets that had been the sole property of such priestly families as the *Kērukes* and the *Eumolpidai*. But despite this democratization of religious privilege, the mysteries were never revealed to the public. On the contrary, what defined them as mysteries was their claim to attain to a truth that was inaccessible by any normal route and which was not to be "exposed" in any way, to gain a revelation so exceptional that it gave access to a religious life unknown to the state religion and reserved for the initiated a destiny that had nothing in common with the ordinary condition of citizens. Thus secrecy, in contrast to the public character of the official cult, acquired a special religious significance: it defined a religion of personal salvation whose goal was to transform the individual independently of the social order, to bring about in him, as it were, a new birth that would pluck him from the mass of people and permit him to reach a different plane of life.

But in that same area, the inquiries of the earliest sages were proceeding to overtake the preoccupations of the religious groups until they sometimes merged with them. Their teachings, like the revelations of the mysteries, claimed to transform the individual from within, to lift him to a higher state, to make of him a unique being, almost a god—a *theios anēr*, "godlike man." When the city fell victim to disorder and pollution and turned to such a sage to ask the way out of its difficulties, it did so precisely because he seemed a being apart and exceptional, a holy man isolated and removed to the fringes of the community by his whole manner of life. Conversely, when a sage addressed himself to the city, in speech or in writing, it was always to transmit a truth that came from above, and which even after its disclosure did not cease to belong to another world, one alien to ordinary life. The early wisdom thus took form as a sort of contradiction that arose from its paradoxical nature: it divulged to the public a knowledge that it proclaimed at the same time to be unavailable to the majority. Was not its purpose to unveil the unseen, to make visible the world of *adēla*, "unknown things," that hid behind appearances? Wisdom revealed a truth so marvelous that it could be won only at a cost of painful effort—so marvelous that it remained, like the vision of the *epoptai*, hidden from the eyes of the common people. To be sure, the secret had to be formulated in words— but the mass of people could not grasp its meaning. Wisdom brought the mystery out into the public square; it examined it and studied it, and still it did not altogether cease to be a mystery. For the traditional initiation rites that guarded

access to the forbidden revelations, *sophia* or *philosophia* substituted other ordeals: a rule of life, a road of *askēsis*, "training," a path of inquiry that—along
with the methods of discussion and argumentation, or the new mental tools
such as mathematics—preserved the ancient divinatory practices and spiritual
exercises aimed at concentration, ecstasy, and the separation of the spirit from
the body.

From its birth, then, philosophy was to find itself in an ambiguous position.
In its inspiration and its development it was related to both the initiations into
the mysteries and the disputations of the *agora*; it wavered between the sense of
secrecy peculiar to the cults and the public argument that characterized political activity. Depending on the place, the time, and the trend, it might, like the
Pythagorean sect in sixth-century Magna Graecia (southern Italy), be organized in a closed brotherhood that refused to entrust a purely esoteric doctrine
to writing; or it might, like the Sophistic movement, become completely integrated with public life, presented as a preparation for the exercise of power in
the city and offered freely to any citizen by means of lessons paid for in cash.
Greek philosophy perhaps never completely extricated itself from the ambiguity of its origins. The philosopher would continually waver between two attitudes, hesitate between the conflicting temptations. At times he would claim
that he alone was qualified to direct the state; arrogantly taking the place of
god–king, he would take it upon himself, in the name of "knowledge" that
elevated him above ordinary men, to reform all social life and rule the city as
sovereign authority. At other times he would withdraw from the world to im-
merse himself in a purely private wisdom; gathering about him a few disciples,
he would set out with them to establish his own city within a city. Turning his
back on public life, he would seek salvation in learning and contemplation.

To the two aspects I have indicated—the magic spell of the spoken word
and the increasingly public conduct of affairs—another feature was added to
mark the spiritual universe of the *polis*. Those who made up the city, however
different in origin, rank, and function, appeared somehow to be "like" each
other. This likeness laid the foundation for the unity of the *polis*, since for the
Greeks only those who were alike could be mutually united by *philia*, joined in
the same community. In the framework of the city, the tie that bound one man
to another thus became a reciprocal relationship, replacing the hierarchical relations of submission and dominance. All those who shared in the state were
defined as *homoioi*, men who were alike, and later more abstractly as *isoi*, or
equals. Despite everything that might set them at odds with one another in the
day-to-day business of social life, on the political level the citizens conceived of
themselves as interchangeable units within a system whose law was the balance
of power and whose norm was equality. In the sixth century this image of the
human world was precisely expressed in the concept of *isonomia*—that is, the
equal participation of all citizens in the exercise of power. But before it had

acquired this fully democratic meaning, and before it had inspired such institutional reforms as those of Cleisthenes, the ideal of *isonomia* was able to convey or to extend communal aspirations that went back to the very origins of the *polis*. There is some evidence that the terms *isonomia* and *isokratia* served in aristocratic circles to define an oligarchical regime that contrasted with the absolute power of one man (the *monarkhia* or *tyrannis*). In this regime, *arkhē* was reserved for a small number to the exclusion of the majority but was divided equally among all members of that elite group.[5] That the requirement of *isonomia* was able to acquire such strength by the end of the sixth century, that it could justify the popular demand for ready access by the *dēmos* to all civic offices, may no doubt be explained by the fact that it was rooted in a very old egalitarian tradition, and even responded to certain psychological attitudes of the aristocracy of the *hippeis*. It was in fact this mounted military nobility that first established a correspondence between martial qualifications and the right to participate in public affairs—a correspondence that was never again questioned. In the *polis* the status of the soldier coincided with that of the citizen: anyone who had a place in the city's military structure had by the same token a place in its political organization. But after the middle of the seventh century, modification in equipment and a revolution in combat technology transformed the figure of the warrior, completely altering his social status and his psychological makeup.[6]

The appearance of the hoplite, a heavily armed line soldier, and his use in close formation on the principle of the phalanx, struck a decisive blow to the military prerogatives of the *hippeis*, "horsemen." All those who could bear the costs of their hoplite equipment—that is, the small free landowners who made up the *dēmos*, such as the *zeugitai* in Athens—were assigned to the same level as those who owned horses. But here, too, the democratization of the military function—formerly an aristocratic privilege—entailed a complete reshaping of the warrior ethic. The Homeric hero, the stalwart charioteer, might still live on in the figure of the *hippeus*; he no longer had much in common with this citizen-soldier, the hoplite. What counted for the *hippeus* was the individual exploit, splendid performance in single combat. In battle, a mosaic of face-to-face duels between *promakhoi*, "champions," military worth was asserted in the form of an *aristeia*, a wholly personal superiority. The warrior found the boldness that enabled him to perform such brilliant feats of arms in a sort of exaltation or warlike frenzy, *lussa*, into which he was thrown, as though beside himself, by *menos*, the ardor inspired by a god. But the hoplite no longer engaged in individual combat; if he felt the temptation to engage in a purely individual act of valor, he was obliged to resist it. He was the man of elbow-to-elbow warfare, of shoulder-to-shoulder struggle. He was trained to hold ranks, to march in formation, to throw himself directly against the enemy, to take care not to leave his position at the height of battle. Martial virtue, then, no longer had anything to do with *thumos*, but consisted in *sōphrosunē*—a complete mastery of self, a constant striving to submit oneself to a common discipline, the coolness necessary to restrain those instinctive pressures that would risk upsetting the discipline of the formation as a whole. The phalanx made of the hoplite, as the city made of the citizen, an interchangeable unit, one element like all the others, and one whose *aristeia*, or individual worth, must never again be demonstrated except within the framework imposed by coordinated maneuvers, group cohesion, mass action—the new instruments of victory. Even in war, *eris*—the desire to overcome an adversary, to affirm one's superiority over another—must give way to *philia*, the spirit of community; the power of the individual must yield to the law of the group. When Herodotus mentions—as he does after each account of a battle—names of the cities and the individuals who proved bravest at Plataea, he gives the palm among the Spartans to Aristodemus, one of the three hundred Lacedaemonians who had defended Thermopylae, and who alone had returned safe and sound; anxious to clear himself of the opprobrium the Spartans attached to his survival, he sought and found death at Plataea in the performance of noble exploits. But it was not to him that the Spartans awarded the funeral honors that were bestowed only on the very best, as the prize of bravery; they denied him the *aristeia* because, fighting in fury like a man deranged by *lussa*, he had broken rank.[7]

This account strikingly illustrates a psychological attitude that is evident not only in the realm of warfare but on all levels of social life, an attitude that marked a decisive turning point in the history of the *polis*. There came a time when the city rejected the traditional modes of aristocratic behavior, which tended to exalt the prestige of individuals and of *genē*, reinforce their power, and raise them above the mass. Thus it condemned as excess, as *hubris*—in the same category as martial frenzy and the pursuit of purely personal glory in combat—the display of wealth, costly garments, magnificent funerals, excessive displays of grief in mourning, behavior that was too flamboyant in women or too confident and bold in aristocratic youths.

All these practices were now rejected because, by accentuating social inequalities and the sense of distance between individuals, they aroused envy, produced discord within the group, threatened its equilibrium and cohesion, and divided the city against itself. What was now extolled was an austere ideal of reserve and restraint, a severe, almost ascetic way of life that obscured differences of manner and rank between citizens in order to bring them closer together, to unite them like the members of one big family.

In Sparta the military seems almost certainly to have played the decisive role in the advent of the new mentality. The Sparta of the seventh century was not yet the state whose originality would call forth in the other Greeks an admiration mixed with shock. At that time it was caught up in the general movement that was carrying the aristocracies of the various cities toward extravagance, causing them to wish for a more refined existence and to seek out profitable undertakings. The break came between the seventh and sixth centuries. Sparta turned in upon itself and became frozen in those institutions that dedicated it wholly to war. It not only repudiated the display of wealth, but closed itself off to all foreign contacts—no commerce, no craft activity. The use of precious metals was prohibited, and so was the use of gold and silver currency. Remaining outside the main intellectual currents, Sparta now neglected the arts and letters for which it had once been famous. Greek philosophy and thought therefore appear to owe it nothing.

But one can only say "appear." The social and political changes that the new techniques of warfare brought to Sparta, which turned it into a city of hoplites, expressed at the institutional level the same demand for a balanced human world, regulated by law, which the sages were formulating on a strictly conceptual level elsewhere, in cities that were experiencing mutinies and domestic upheavals for want of a solution like the Spartans'. Scholars have rightly insisted on the archaism of those institutions to which Sparta adhered so obstinately: age groups, martial initiation rites, secret societies. But we must also stress other features that placed Sparta ahead of its time: the egalitarian spirit of a reform that abolished the ancient opposition between *laos* and *dēmos* in order to establish a corps of citizen-soldiers, defined as *homoioi*, each of whom in the beginning had a portion of land, a *klēros*, exactly equal of that of every other. To this form of *isonomia*, "equal shares" (perhaps later there was a second distribution of land), must be added the communal aspect of social life that imposed the same austere regimen on everyone, which in its abhorrence of luxury codified even the way a private house was to be built, and which instituted the *sussitia*, communal meals for which each man furnished monthly his allotted portion of barley, wine, cheese, and figs. It must finally be noted that Sparta's regime, with its double royalty, the *apella*, "assembly," the ephors, and the *gerousia*, "council of elders," achieved an "equilibrium" among social elements that represented opposing duties, virtues, and values. On that reciprocal equilibrium was based the unity of the state, with each element kept by the others within limits it might not overstep. Plutarch thus assigned to the *gerousia* the function of a counterweight that maintained a continual balance between the popular *apella* and the royal authority, aligning itself now on the side of the kings to keep democracy in check, now on the side of the people to check the power of any one person.[8] In the same way, the institution of the ephors represented a martial element in the social body, "junior" and belonging to the people, in contrast to the aristocratic *gerousia*, whose "senior" traits of levelheadedness and wisdom were needed to counterbalance the martial daring and vigor of the *kouroi*.

In the Spartan state, society no longer formed a pyramid with the king at its apex, as in the Mycenaean kingdoms. All those who had submitted to military training and the series of tests and initiations it entailed, and thus had a *klēros* and took part in the *sussitia*, had been raised to the same level. That level was what defined the city.[9] The social order thus no longer appeared to depend on the sovereign; it was no longer bound to the inventive power of an exceptional individual, to his activity as an organizer. On the contrary, it was the social order that held the power of all individuals in check, setting limits on the urge to enlarge one's scope. The social order came first with respect to power. *Arkhē* in reality belonged exclusively to the law. Any individual or faction that tried to secure a monopoly on *arkhē* threatened the *homonoia*, "unanimity," of the social body by such an attack on the balance of all other forces, and thereby put the city's very existence at risk.

But if the new Sparta thus acknowledged the supremacy of law and order, its purpose in doing so was to prepare for war; the reshaping of the state was above all a response to military preoccupations. The *homoioi* were more thoroughly drilled in the practice of battle than in the disputations of the *agora*. Thus in Sparta speech could never become the political tool it was elsewhere, or take shape as discussion, argumentation, rebuttal. In place of *Peithō*, the force of persuasion, as an instrument of the law, the Lacedaemonians extolled the power of *Phobos*, that fear which made all citizens bow in obedience. They boasted of relishing only brevity in speeches, and of preferring sententious and pithy turns of phrase to the subtleties of debate. For them speech was still *rhētrai*, those quasi-oracular laws to which they submitted without discussion and which they refused to expose to public scrutiny by writing them down. However advanced Sparta may have been, it left to others the honor of fully expressing the new conception of order, in which the city became a balanced and harmonious cosmos under the rule of law. It was not the Lacedaemonians that could define and explicate, in all their consequences, the moral and political ideas that they were among the first to embody in their institutions.

TRANSLATED BY JANET LLOYD

NOTES

[1] See V. Ehrenberg, "When Did the Polis Rise?" *Journal of Hellenic Studies* 57 (1937): 147–59 and idem, "Origins of Democracy," *Historia* 1 (1950): 519–48.

[2] E. J. Forsdyke, *Greece before Homer: Ancient Chronology and Mythology* (London, 1956), p. 18ff. See also remarks of Préaux 1959.

[3] See Diogenes Laertius 1.43; letter from Thales to Pherecydes.

[4] The role of divination in the political life of the Greeks comes to mind. In general, it may be noted that every civic office still had a sacred character. But it was the same with politics as with the judiciary. In the legal framework the religious practices that originally had value in themselves became a prologue to the hearing of each case. Similarly, the rites to which civic officers still submitted on taking office, such as sacrifice and oath taking, constituted the formal structure and no longer the internal strength of political life. In this sense, there was indeed secularization.

[5] Ehrenberg, "Origins of Democracy," recalls that the song of Harmodios and Aristogeiton honors the *eupatridai* for having made the Athenians *isonomoi*; see also Thucydides 5.62.

[6] See A. Andrewes, *The Greek Tyrants* (London, 1956), ch. 3; F. E. Adcock, *The Greek and Macedonian Art of War* (Berkeley, 1957). On dating the appearance of the hoplite, see P. Courbin, "Une Tombe géométrique d'Argos," *Bulletin de correspondance hellénique* 81 (1957): 322–84.

[7] Herodotus 9.71.

[8] Plutarch *Life of Lykourgos* 5.11. Aristotle *Politics* 1265b35.

[9] Of course, alongside the citizens and in contrast to them, the city included all those who in varying degrees were denied the privileges of full citizenship: in Sparta, the *hupomeiones*, *perioikoi*, helots, and slaves. Equality stands out against a background of inequality.

JEAN BOLLACK

Reflections on Philological Practice

1977

This apologia pro vita sua *needs little introduction. Bollack is a grand master of Classical hermeneutics (see the Introduction), and here he undertakes a definitive statement that sets forth both his methodology and its applications to the Classics.*

To edit a page of Aeschylus or Plato, to pick apart its sentences or verses, in a word, to understand, is to discover that the composition that emerges not only from a long and consistent tradition but also from the work of the modern science that is the heir to that tradition differs to a considerable extent from the text preserved in some cases only in discontinuous fashion in the footnotes and critical apparatus while living as well in the upper portion of the page, in the lines printed for normal reading. To interpret that continuous text is often to rewrite it in accordance with a different grammar. This splitting of the text calls for explanation. It cannot be the result of error, since analysis invariably derives from, and is justified by, specific conditions, nor can it be the result of a taste for contradiction. Indeed, it calls for reflection on the boundaries of hermeticism and the very possibility of communication.

Several books on classical authors, which were also critical editions of their texts, have led me to reflect on the reasons for some of the difficulties peculiar to the practice of philology. Anyone who establishes and translates canonical texts must inevitably confront, in the text itself, not only the protean interpreter shackled by authority but also academic manners.

Most readers have no idea that they are reading Marulle in Lucretius, Usener in Epicurus, or Diels in Heraclitus. Interpretation is vulnerable. It cannot stand up against conjecture. If texts were corrected, there must have been all sorts of good reasons, reasons still valid today, because the same prejudices are still around and because the tradition has the virtue of existing and the force of the fait accompli.

From "Réflexions sur la pratique philologique," *Social Science Information* 16 (1977): 375–85.

In two studies, one of Pindar, *Olympian* 2.83–88, and *Pythian* 2.52–73 (paper read to German philologists at the Mommsen-Gesellschaft, Bochum, 25 May 1972 [. . .]), the other on Homer (introduction to a seminar on the adventures of Odysseus at the École Normale Supérieure on 27 January 1973),[1] I considered two noteworthy cases:

> in the first, the lyrical self, the subject of the poem under examination, had over the course of history, and already in the hands of the scholiasts, turned into a biographical person and an anecdote;
>
> in the second, epic description had condensed into a world of mythical or geographical realities (the Planctae added to Charybdis and Scylla) that owed their existence solely to the finesse and artifice of Homeric discourse.

In both cases, the fabrication of interpretable subject matter grew out of arbitrarily focusing on certain isolated elements of the narrative. In the case of Pindar (*Olympian* 2), moreover, the assertion of intrinsic hermeticism was ignored. Examples of similarly distorted descriptions in the works of the most widely read authors are presumably legion.

These free and "creative" readings are, for all their flights of fancy, impoverished in comparison with the effort that would be required to establish the neglected dimension of the work in a systematic manner. Instead of analyzing the literal sense as a sign, it is explained as an accident, interpreted as a discordance or incoherence. When the problematic terms are integrated, however, it becomes clear that the logic of the text is definitely not that on account of which those terms were mistaken for discordant. Of course a sentence can conceal error as well as truth, and the demiurge that it possesses might even be capable of tracing the wakes of phantom sailors upon the seas. The Ancients used to say that there was a Heraclitus for fools (Diogenes Laertius) and no doubt a Homer as well. Some interpretations are satisfied with separating out what the genesis of the work melded together or with recomposing what it divided.

It would be easy, and unjust, to scoff at the effort invested in the cumbersome apparatus of philological demonstration. Immediate access to the text is urgently required. Yet it is impossible to base interpretation on the naked text without taking account of the history of interpretations. Not that the centuries have provided increasingly accurate approximations to the truth. Nor is there any reason to believe a priori that there should be profit in mixing the variety of existing ingredients in new ways. But apart from the fact that the selected text cannot be justified without recognizing and refuting the reasons for which it was altered in the first place, the text itself exists only to the extent that one interpretation wins out over others (the hermeneutic circle also applies to discoveries having to do with the text's duration). No reading can take shape in a vacuum devoid of other readings. The correct interpretation becomes clear only when confronted with all the possibilities.

Quite apart from this heuristic justification, no reading is convincing that does not justify itself by refuting other readings. Merely by virtue of its difference, it would seem more esoteric than the text it purported to explain. To convince, admittedly, it is not enough to criticize. In a culture that has always been based on the explication of texts, most readings exist only so that the institution, wherever it happens to be found, can function, and as a form of practice. The sheer quantity and mass of publications then constitutes an insurmountable obstacle, and that obstacle does not become smaller simply because its actual interest is less.

Like technique in general, philological technique tends to become autonomous with respect to its object. Texts become part of the literary cultural heritage, which is a recognized asset, a form of capital. The division of labor, which is problematic in a field that does not adapt readily to the distinction between technicians and users, is nevertheless legitimated by the sheer number of potential users. Many technicians, including some of the most productive, are pleased to say that they are completely in the dark when it comes not only to the "ultimate signified" but to meaning in general, whatever it might be, yet they go on blindly processing raw material for delivery in suitable form to the technicians of meaning. This divorce marks as suspect all histories of philosophy and most chapters in the history of science. Without foundation, suspended in midair above an ill-defined subject matter, constructions bear down on interpretations, that is, on texts.

In Empedocles there is an elaborate but entirely forgotten theory according to which the sun that we see is the reflection onto the vault above of light from the earth. Not only does this theory explain certain surviving sentence fragments, it is also richer than a mere opinion on a point of science would be because it makes us see the positions of all the bodies in the universe as those positions relate to it.[2] Similarly, the system of blue eyes and black eyes is in itself the complete, coded expression of a theory of vision.[3] Now, these two facts, discovered in a voluminous doxographic summary, are all but irremediably absent from histories of astronomy and optics because their place in a specific constellation did not allow them to be readily incorporated into a linear history of scientific progress, and progress is necessarily the guiding idea of nearly all specialized histories.

No doubt the division of labor is inevitable in practice, but it is unacceptable in theory and is perpetuated only by self-interest.[4] If this reliance on partial competence is to be eliminated, the history of philology can no longer be a history of humanists and scholars[5] or even a history of the perfection of techniques; it must proceed against the current by seeking to situate interpretations with respect to the historical conditions that determine them—not that such a procedure can take us to the meaning that lies in the difference between the object that properly belongs to the science of discourse and the object that one pursues in interminable doxography. In this way, at least, philology, that mirror of incomprehension, can become a precious instrument for the study of society. In the future, one might be able to show that what the history of philology and interpretations reveals is also valid for current cultural systems. Even today, translations are steeped in national traditions.

II

At the end of the nineteenth century, the *philologisch-historische Methode* found itself in radical contradiction with its object. Reflection on the constitution of knowledge, the subject of traditional hermeneutics, had been reduced to its most rudimentary form, to the point where it became a mere footnote to "formal" philology, patterned on what was known as *Realphilologie.*[6] The discipline, whose mission was now mainly to polish and correct, refused to despair over this thankless task, taking pride instead in the act of censorship: "It is the role of formal philology to follow the expression of thought, which is sometimes defective, and, up to a point, to correct the creative work" (Gercke). As psychologist and therapist, the analyst of written expression appears when the hermeneutic task is complete.

In order for a fundamental science like exegesis to have failed in this way, to the point of restricting itself, of censuring itself in the act of censuring, so as to devote itself exclusively to the hothouse culture of correction and excision, philology must have been undermined by an internal contradiction. Paradoxically, censorship defended values that were not its own. Setting itself up as a science and therefore, in order to be accredited as science, viewing all objects as equivalent, it ultimately came to treat authors in a mercenary fashion, leaving their reputations in the hands of a vague and discredited aesthetic. It hid its lack of judgment behind a vast scientific apparatus. Material problems were regarded as more serious than intellectual ones. In his *Introduction to Greek Tragedy*, Wilamowitz wrote that "if Euripides' poems were not corrupt, Hermann would not publish them."[7]

Philological censorship is in power wherever it is charged with a pedagogical mission, but it uses weapons having nothing to do with pedagogy to increase rapidly the quantity of its material. A breakneck pace of production was not the least of the vices encouraged by the *philologisch-historische Methode*. By its reckoning, Classical antiquity had no further raison d'être, even if philology scrupulously performs its mission, which was to serve Classical antiquity.

The contradiction revealed itself whenever a critic showed that he was capable of producing discourse of two different types, depending on whether he was representing science within the university or extolling the values that guaranteed his institutional position.[8] It was also apparent in the war between official science and the circles that reacted against it by celebrating the religion of aestheticism. In the Homeric question, for example, the controversy between analysts and unitarians was almost entirely defined by this necessary tension between dignitaries and marginal figures. The former were invested with the authority of the university, the latter justified by faith. It proved impossible to get beyond the contradiction by calmly examining the issues in order to provide unitarianism with a scientific foundation, as it were.

In the nineteenth century, the honing of such tools as compilation and classification of manuscripts, textual history, and paleography offered incomprehension the support of material accident.

After a certain date, for example, lacunae and interpolation flourished: at some point between 1850 and 1860, the editions of Bernays, Lachmann, Munro, and Brieger shattered Lucretius by introducing more lacunae than had ever been accepted previously, to the point where one of these editors expressed amazement at the richness of his harvest. In the case of Epicurus, I have shown the imaginary extent of the corruption in *La Lettre d'Epicure*.[9] Further work on Epicurus can be found in *La Pensée du plaisir*, and it will be summarized in the edition of *La Lettre à Pythoclès*. One can take all the interpolations in an Aeschylean tragedy, as Pierre Judet de La Combe and I have done in the case of the *Agamemnon*, and show that all stem from difficulties of understanding, some of them traditional, which for one reason or another could not be resolved in any other way.[10] The fact that people are now ready to condemn such excesses does not change the basic situation, because they do not recognize the connection with the practice of resolving problems of meaning by invoking accidents. In order to bring the vanished "meaning" back to life, it has to be incorporated into some sort of explanatory system.

Although the appeal to systems of representation and psychological and mental structures provided interpretations and, above all, interpretative grids, these had little to do with the understanding of individual works. True, the inventors of these interpretative devices were looking for a complete, illuminating hermeneutic meaning, but they borrowed their lighting directly from social reality (generational conflict, *polis* and *genos*, and so on), which turned everything into a pure abstraction that was all too quickly magnified to the scale of an entire culture or period. Plays and poems became mere examples to be hammered home repeatedly, ipso facto. But the evidence of such examples is suspect. Because the essayists of the various structuralist schools had no interest in the unique meaning of each work, they did not really make use of the traditional tools of textual criticism and therefore failed to criticize the inherited meanings of texts.

To be sure, individuality of expression has been recognized as a distinct historical form since the time of Wilamowitz, a form that has been studied not only in terms of systems of representation but also in conjunction with types of instruction and rhetorical habits.

Under the influence of ethnology and anthropology, formalists abandoned all reference to the humanist norm in favor of specific forms of expression. The alienation of the author's point of view appeared once more. Apart from the fact that in the case of authors like Pindar (see Bundy)[11] and Lucretius (see Schrijvers)[12] one could ask whether the textbook explained the author or the author the textbook, this second-degree normalization imposed a schematic assimilation that precluded in-depth exploration of the esoteric dimension or "allegorical" level of the work. Compared with psychologically oriented criticism, all that was sacrificed was a certain type of simplification, such as that derived from biographical knowledge, for instance.

III

The constitution of a horizon of representations is no doubt indispensable but cannot be achieved in this way. Historians, convinced in advance of the otherness of the subject matter and the possibility of historical objectification and less likely to naturalize the foreigner than to assume his existence, project current prejudices onto the past, if only by indiscriminately applying models taken from many sources. Nothing is more historically determinable than the introduction of explanatory schemes considered a priori to be historically applicable.

In a course taught regularly at the University of Berlin from 1809 to 1865,[13] August Boeckh defined philology as a historical science, which he treated as a universal discipline, alternating with philosophy as Castor alternated with Pollux. But his idea of philology also included a historical dimension, which for him was characteristic of all knowledge. Although remote, the object for him involved the interpreter directly, hence the interpreter was led to judge what he knew ("alien ideas are not yet ideas for me"). The universal philologist (his concept), capable of knowing everything because all objects of history are known through him, introduced distance only in judgment, which was no longer historical when it appropriated the foreign. Boeckh exhorted the philologist to free himself from his condition and rise above the integrated object in order to view it in its atemporal objectivity. For him it was a matter of knowing what he knew, which was already known by someone else. The judgment brought to bear on the critical act resulted in an appropriation, so that the doubled object was no longer the object known by the alien author but belonged to the knowing subject. Historical distance was abolished not only by the concept of universal history but also by the approval or invalidation of the act of judgment.

The hermeneutics of Boeckh, who was also one of the founders of historical science, thus reconciled the need for investigation and criticism, on the one hand, with the need to maintain privileged values of concern to us, on the other hand. It was similar in many ways to the hermeneutics codified by Ast (1808),[14] which, in the tradition of Schelling's philosophy of identity, held that it was impossible to purge objects of their historical contingency in order to grasp the movements of the one spirit. By contrast, other eighteenth-century German theorists and idealist philosophers had, like Hölderlin, in view of the paradigmatic nature of antiquity, come to accept its absolute otherness, in virtue of which modernity was able to recognize itself.

Ast's theory, which asserts the possibility of identification, made no less a problem of distance, whereas later philologists, giving up on appropriation, also gave up on knowing the distant object and in the end assimilated it.

IV

Determined by his own position in history and society, the interpreter, as artisan of his own subject matter, stands at a distance from his object—in the case of works of antiquity, a distance so great that the difference in time offers little support. The distance cannot be measured; it is absolute. Indeed, if we can only understand the unknown, we must learn to turn that very tension to our advantage.

Furthermore, the same distance exists between Heraclitus and his contemporaries, or between Epicurus and his: remoteness in time is coupled with difference within synchrony.

In order to objectify, one has to be willing to turn things studied into fixed markers, lives into facts, theatrical works into opaque events, thoughts into bodies. But what one grasps can only be, in the instantaneous act of grasping it, a movement in search of itself, an inflection in a phrase. What one is after is not the known, common meaning but the unknown, the unsaid that reveals itself in combination with the literal text. That is the specific object of philology, an object that it shares with no other science.

Since philology, especially in its positivist, documentalist phase, sought the literal meaning, it gave up on allegory, on the *sensus spiritualis* which it took to be gratuitous and superfluous, with the result that it also missed the *sensus litteralis* to which it had thought it prudent to confine itself. This is because the relation between the two is not arbitrary, as philologists believed. Allegory is not simply the transfer of sense from one register of thought to another, as when the Stoics interpret Homer or the Church Fathers interpret the Old Testament. The "allegory" that transforms frozen discourse by "speaking differently" (*allēgorein*) is part of expression. A sentence cannot be reduced to what it says. There is also another sentence that can be read in the work of another author or in a different part of the same work, so that any sentence can contradict any other.

The example of Heraclitus is particularly striking, because with the discovery of the principle of implicit correction I was able, in *Héraclite ou la séparation*,[15] to show that nearly all the adages, as brief as they are, deny some assertion and even deny the negation of some assertion. In many cases, the two prior stages are not attested, yet they can be extrapolated.

In the work of other authors, allegorical practice refers not to formulas implicit in a literary culture but to other parts of the work, thus constituting a kind of "thick expression." This stratification has nothing to do with the notion of levels of meaning, which implies differentiated levels of consciousness. The virtual meaning revealed by these complex compositional settings must not be confused with the return of a repressed feeling. Rather, the practice is related to a mode of writing that we know from the biographical lore of Servius: Virgil every day dictated a large number of verses to a slave. Later he winnowed those verses down to just one. In this case, the "allegory" consists of all the eliminated verses, which reappear elsewhere in some other form.

Here, no doubt, we are using the single term *allegory* to describe a phenomenon that has a variety of applications, and when further work has been done it may be possible to classify these various uses in relation to ancient theories of *obscuritas*. There exists both a closed form, in which the elements of the text must be related to one another in order to decipher it, and an open form, in which autonomous structures overlap. The first corresponds to the philosophy of Being, the second to atomism. One is obscure at first and becomes clearer as one reads, the other seems clear but becomes more complicated as one reflects on it. Yet the richer the deeper meanings that one extracts, the more subjective they seem. Philology should be able to offer criteria for distinguishing fantasy from science and for judging the appropriateness of interpretations which, because they are astonishing, seem personal.

The literal sense is decisive. Once a text is settled, this literal meaning is not an "interpretation" of the interpreter. The philologist is bound by the interpretation that is the text. This literal meaning is not a definite thing that can be moved about like a pawn and related to other meanings in some sort of formal game for the simple reason that the author has already played the game. The "allegory" has produced the grammatical construction. The arrangement of words is what it is because it is determined by other arrangements entailed by the author's decision.

The point, then, is not that the sentence bound by these internal constraints refers to a single signified. *Because the project includes and contains polysemy,* it is inconceivable that this polysemy should escape. All the variants of interpretative desire that cannot be located on the axis that is the project, which is historically situable though only by interpretation, are beyond the strict limits of philology and hermeneutics. The work is inexhaustible, but only in its own terms, respecting its autonomy. Aristotle was quite capable of deriving answers from Empedocles' poem that Empedocles never gave. But he was right to add immediately: "If one had said this to him, he would not have said no."[16] This avowal sets limits to polyvalence. No doubt it is difficult to draw a line between those elements of which the author makes full use and those which simply work for him, but that is what must be done. The teleology of the project encompasses both.

Thus ambiguity must not be posited as a principle of composition, and authors who have done so, whether for Heraclitus or for the tragic poets, miss the significance revealed by the procedure they are studying, which assumes a thetic act before adding in the author's own countersense.

Readings that supplant the work and transform it, canceling out its peculiarities through a process of assimilation or using it as a point of departure, are new projects on the part of the commentator. The stages of this aftereffect (*Wirkungsgeschichte*) interest the interpreter of the primary work only to the extent that they cloud its comprehension.

Le propre / difference is another criterion. Among all the improbable meanings, one stands out (*probatur*), but it is even more unexpected than the others. The limit, the criterion here, is presumably the whole, provided that this arrangement is absolutely differentiated by its peculiarity. Although a parallel passage can never confirm an interpretation, repetition in different contexts cannot be pointless.

Peter Szondi says this in his analysis of a poem by Paul Celan: "Even if— and this in itself is doubtful—one could claim that one or more . . . expressions in the two places are identical and that the supposedly certain interpretation of one of the passages seems to clarify the meaning of the same word in the line one is trying to understand, that line becomes clear without being understood because it is what it is only in this particular use, which at first resisted comprehension."[17]

If agreement with other homologous parts provides the means to decide, it is only on condition of knowing at every moment that the agreement is composed of distinct and imperceptible properties, which in turn settle the matter. Coherence is established in a circular fashion, and there may be no end to the circle.

Ultimately, the result is determined by experiment. Since one of the conditions of the experiment is to reproduce the movement of the work in a literal reading, all possible directions can be explored. The only thing that can end the experiment is the hermeneutic efficacy of each of those directions. Correct explanation is more fruitful than error.

TRANSLATED BY ARTHUR GOLDHAMMER

NOTES

[1] See Bollack 1975 and 1976.

[2] See Bollack, *Empédocle* II, fr. 332–39, and the commentary in *Empédocle* III, pp. 263–77 (Paris, 1969).

[3] *Empédocle* II, fr. 420, § 8 and 437–38, and the commentary in *Empédocle* III, pp. 335–68ff.

[4] On the division of the field of philology, see the preface to *La Pensée du plaisir:* "Pourquoi Epicure?" (Paris, 1975), pp. ix–xliii, esp. pp. xxiv–xxix.

[5] On the history of humanists, see J. E. Sandys, *A History of Classical Scholarship* (Cambridge, 1908); A. Gudemann, *Grundriss der Geschichte der klassischen Philologie* (Leipzig and Berlin, 1907); and R. Pfeiffer, *History of Classical Scholarship*, vol. 2: *From 1300 to 1850* (Oxford, 1976).

[6] A. Gercke, *Einleitung in die Altertumswissenschaft* (Leipzig and Berlin, 1910), p. 35 (ch. "Methodik").

[7] "Einleitung in die griechische Tragödie," p. 239, in U. von Wilamowitz-Moellendorff, *Euripides Herakles*, vol. 1 (Berlin, 1889).

[8] Bollack 1975, 12–13.

[9] Bollack, Bollack, and Wismann 1971.

[10] Bollack and Judet de La Combe 1981.

[11] E. L. Bundy, *Studia pindarica* (Berkeley and Los Angeles, 1962).

[12] P. H. Schrijvers, *Horror ac divina voluptas: Etudes sur la poétique et la poésie de Lucrèce* (Amsterdam, 1970).

[13] A. Boeckh, *Enzyklopädie und Methodologie der philologischen Wissenschaften*, ed. E. Bratuscheck (Leipzig, 1886).

[14] F. Ast, *Grundlinien der Grammatik, Hermeneutik und Kritik* (Landshut, 1808). On Ast, see P. Szondi's contribution to J. Bollack and H. Stierlin, eds., *Einführung in die literarische Hermeneutik* (Frankfurt, 1975), pp. 135–54.

[15] Bollack and Wismann, 1972.

[16] Aristotle *Metaphysics* A 10, 993 a23.

[17] P. Szondi, "Lecture de Strette," *Critique* 288 (1971): 387ff.

LOUIS GERNET

The Origins of Greek Philosophy

1945

In this remarkable distillation, Gernet places his initial emphasis on "origins": "I am interested in the philosopher as a human type [and] the idea the philosopher has of himself." Moving from pre-Socratic Parmenides and Empedocles to the Plato of the Phaedo, *Gernet confirms the presence of an Orphic-Pythagorean strain of mysticism even in the foundations of the rationalist value system that characterized the intellect as arbiter of truth, simultaneously orienting the "Western" development of philosophy and of science. By linking the philosopher's journey of inquiry to the themes of initiation, revelation, and the authoritative power of "privileged knowledge," Gernet not only establishes the religious, indeed prehistoric, antecedents of the philosopher's prestige, but also underscores a prime tenet of his own scholarly investigations: the historian's conviction that cultural creations — even those as arresting and influential as Hellenism, the "Greek miracle" — yield to our understanding "only when we start seeing the new as nothing more than alterations of the old."*

The question about the origins of Greek philosophy is only part of a larger question concerning the origin and development of Hellenism itself as one of the major factors enriching our own civilization. Even so, the problem of Greek philosophy's origin is the beginning of what we call philosophy as such, or to put it another way, it is the basis of the intellectual activity whereby man, through reason and reflection, attempts to define the meaning of the world and his place in it . . .

What are the conditions in which such a bias in favor of intellectual comprehension could assert itself? We speak of reason and rational truth; these and

From *The Anthropology of Greece*, trans. John Hamilton and Blaise Nagy (Baltimore and London: The Johns Hopkins University Press, 1981), pp. 352–64 ["Les origines de la philosophie grecque," *L'Anthropologie de la Grèce antique,* ed. J.-P. Vernant (Paris: François Maspero, 1986), pp. 415–31; first published in *Bulletin de l'enseignement public du Maroc* 183 (1945): 1–12].

similar terms characterize Hellenism as it is most often represented. But it is origins that concern us here; and origins, since they are antecedents, are not of the same order as the phenomena that follow them. Previously, scholars did not look for antecedents, and they hardly even speculated on the matter. For a long time, the idea that Hellenism in general was created *ex nihilo* was implicit, and it was only startling discoveries that forced us to admit that classical Greece had a very long past . . . In my own account, *ne sutor ultra crepidam*, I will deal only with one aspect of the "origins" question: I am interested in the nature of the philosopher as a human type, the behavior of some of the first representatives of this type, the idea that the philosopher has of himself, and what others on occasion made of him.

From the end of the seventh century [BCE] to the middle of the fifth—the period of the pre-Socratics—philosophy, in the modern sense of the word, already existed in many respects, but it manifested itself in forms and expression that are often rather confusing for us. Yet it is precisely these forms and expressions that from our perspective can be the most instructive.

As a point of departure, I will take the extant prologue of Parmenides' philosophical poem . . . The poet tells how he is brought by a chariot to the gates where the paths of Night and Day diverge: their keys are in the possession of the goddess *Dikē* (Justice). His guides are the Daughters of the Sun, and the road he traverses is that of the goddess who alone directs the man of understanding. The gates open and the goddess, after receiving him in friendship, shows him the paths of knowledge: the one leading to Truth and the other leading to the illusory opinions of mortals. (Parmenides deals with these in a special section of his systematic presentation.)

Even a quick glance at such an unusual narrative (the letter of which we have respected) reveals a masterful conception; the perception of philosophical truth is represented in the form of a revelation and is the end product of a mystical journey . . . The problem is to discover the real emotional and practical force of Parmenides' poetic images. In order to answer such a question, it is first necessary to ask if his images have any precedents.

That there are precedents is beyond doubt. We are already familiar with one, namely, the entire body of apocalyptic literature that we know existed in the archaic period. In it, especially within the circles one would call "Orphic," the theme of a "descent to the underworld" appears, a theme that is somewhat analogous to that of Parmenides' prologue. Of more immediate interest is another motif, namely, the "journey to heaven," a very ancient theme that, perhaps under the secondary influence of Eastern thought, has had as long a life as the other. To ask which of the two influenced Parmenides is perhaps useless, for we may be dealing with a synthesis of images . . .

The mystical tradition that shapes these images for the purposes of a doctrine of salvation can deviate in the direction of a philosophy without ceasing to be mystical. In the prologue of Parmenides, one image is used for two purposes: the image of the "way." It appears elsewhere, where it is no less haunting, and it has to have had a corresponding reality in the Mystery religions . . . For the individual elect, who is assured that he has the truth, revelation, associated as it is with the image of the "way of inquiry," is becoming knowledge that is already, strictly speaking, philosophical. Such is the case with Parmenides.

We are led to hypothesize, then, that there may have been some transformations from past mystical thought to philosophy, understood in its strict sense. An attempt can be made to identify some of these transformations.

Parmenides profits from a certain advantage. For him the philosopher is someone entirely set apart and especially chosen. Intimately connected with such a view is the idea of a revelation that precedes what we would term a theory of knowledge. Implicit in a theory of knowledge is what has traditionally been referred to as a psychology, in the metaphysical or, more exactly, mystical sense. All of this can be recognized as the datum of a nascent philosophy—indeed, of an entire philosophical tradition—and there is reason to search for its original significance.

The theme of the philosopher as a unique or even superior person is one that Plato enjoys developing in several ways, especially in the *Phaedo*, in which he connects it with asceticism. The superiority is a reality, or rather a firm belief of those involved, and is confirmed by a society's acceptance or hostility . . . A very early locus communis of Pythagorean literature recalls the hierarchy, acknowledged by the sect's members, that was established according to degrees of advancement (a phenomenon that obviously corresponds to the different degrees of initiation in the mystery religions). According to Varro, at the head of this hierarchy is the one who is called *beatus*, in the sense that he is *doctus*, *perfectus* and *sapiens*. *Sapiens*, a term inspired by religious scruple, is really a euphemism for "philosopher." *Perfectus* is certainly a translation of the Greek word that signifies the highest level of achievement and *initiation*. *Doctus* refers to the science that may already be partly one of the numbers. But it is a "science" of a very special kind, for it is communicated, in secrecy and through an initiation into a mysterious truth, only to the sect's inner group. The term *beatus*, although it seems jejune, is nevertheless interesting. Its Greek equivalent, *eudaimōn*, will have a long history in Greek philosophy: the ethics of the Greeks are "eudaemonistic," since they involve a quest for the summum bonum which itself involves the happiness of the individual . . .

Our interest in Pythagoreanism stems from a desire to examine a tradition of mystical sects to which philosophy owes not only a vocabulary and some of its metaphors but also, from the beginning, a direction of thought. Since we attach special importance to the idea of a "grace of state," it is worth noting that in the archaic age this tradition has been taken up by isolated figures who have taken it upon themselves to be missionaries. Very little is known about them, and this only from legend. They seem to have been profoundly engaged in a similar form of religious thought; but in certain respects they are also the authentic predecessors of the philosopher. For if the philosopher, as is usually the case, desires to create a "school"—that is, to establish the equivalent of a confraternity—it is by his singular deeds of boldness that he qualifies as a founder. Here we are speaking of men like Abaris, Aristeas, Epimenides, Hermotimus—and others, to whom one might add Pherecydes, who is already a philosopher of sorts. These men primarily practiced purification and divination; but theological and cosmological teachings were also attributed to them. Moreover, even in the legends, they have some connection with Pythagoras.

What is the nature of this prerogative they proclaim and authorize for themselves? It has two elements but is still one: these men are in special and direct contact with divinity, and this contact is manifested by the miraculous revelation they are granted.

The first element fits in perfectly with the thinking of mystical sects; or, even better, it is at their core. Minimally, it involves "becoming similar to a divinity" through a special asceticism and certain rites. But there is a much higher goal: for the truly elect, the "road of life" is a means of divinization . . . In Platonism, when applied to a philosopher, expressions such as *theios anēr* retain some of their original force.

Another expression from Platonism highlights the nature of a prerogative that is at once the consequence and the guarantee of eminent dignity: *theia moira*, "divine portion." It designates a kind of divine election of the philosopher. In particular, it connotes the aptitude one has for philosophical understanding, the talent that makes such knowledge possible. When Plato wants to make the concept of this knowledge present and vivid, he has recourse to comparisons from the mysteries. Truth is perceived in a kind of *epopteia*—that is, in a vision analogous to the one reserved for those initiated in the higher mysteries. This concept is not an isolated example but plays an integral role in Platonism. It inspires some of the famous allegories or myths in the *Symposium* and *Phaedrus*; and in Aristotle's earliest philosophy, where the idea is inherited, one discovers the outline of a theory that approaches an intuition of initiation and *enthousiasmos* . . .

That a philosophical transition had already taken place in Parmenides has already been noted. But in his case the myth of revelation is not simply poetic. It is essentially the myth of the soul's journey. In what might be described as its materialistic form, the myth has some obvious antecedents in the legendary material about ecstatic visionaries. While he was asleep, Epimenides' soul left his body and was lifted into the sky. It was also said to have the power of leaving his body at its pleasure in order to meet and confer with the gods. And the souls of other inspired figures also wander. In addition, Epimenides claimed to have lived several lives. But in this milieu, this idea no longer seems original. The idea that souls make journeys is expanded and given some definition in the concept of their transmigrations. Here again an idea is seen that appears to us to be an arbitrary and isolated fantasy. But it played a large role in all religious speculation and in the elaboration of one of philosophy's principal ideas. In an age preceding and propaedeutic to philosophy the doctrine known as metempsychosis can be identified as the major and, without doubt, historically necessary basis upon which the idea of the soul, as distinct and independent of the body, developed. Admittedly, before the Pythagoreans and similar groups, this "mystical" notion was not a radically new idea; but in their hands it became a decisive turning point. This calls for a few words of explanation . . .

It is after his journey to the underworld that Pythagoras reveals to those assembled at Croton the chain of his earthly careers. Existence in the underworld is a necessary link in the chain of a soul's destiny. This idea is almost constant and basic to the different varieties of Greek mysticism. It happens that an express concept of psychological continuity combines with this theme, but it is a form of continuity which does not happen automatically; it is granted only to the elect and is the result of their labor. This doctrine appears in a sect to which Pindar alludes. The Isle of the Blessed is the paradise reserved for those having the energy to guard their souls from evil after having made three sojourns in one world and the other. In order to preserve this continuity, a set of procedures exists. Purification is especially significant in the whole scheme of mystical associations, and its history culminates in Plato's *Phaedo*: there, though expressly preserved by him in a defused and intellectualized way, it is philosophically transformed (as has also been the case with the correlative idea of *anamnēsis*). Indeed, all this is part of the same discipline, a discipline where positive practices are the obligatory complement, or the obverse, of negative ones. We are interested only in the discipline's connections with the idea of the soul's salvation, a concept whereby the soul, through purificatory trials and ecstatic adventures, not only preserves itself but in a way achieves its own victory . . . The idea of the soul, which Platonism eventually assimilated, had formerly been associated with something similar to a shamanistic discipline.

In the notion of the vocation of philosopher, and in all the thinking that underpins it, we recognize a heritage and catch a glimpse of derivatives that point to a very long history. Is it possible to shed some light on this history, and thereby better understand a certain kind of philosopher?

Among the pre-Socratics it is Empedocles who seems to provoke the most interest . . . It is his person, or, to be more exact, the kind of person he was and the ambitions he professed, that holds our attention.

He introduces himself at the beginning of his poem *The Purifications*. (Empedocles is even more of a poet than his elder Parmenides.) Since he is no longer a mortal, he goes among his "friends" as a god. As soon as he enters the towns, people press in around him and pay him homage. Some ask him for oracles; others seek cures for their illnesses. He promises to teach his disciples remedies against old age, the art of stopping the winds, and the power of bringing rain in time of drought or dispelling it in time of floods. He will even grant his disciples the power to "bring back a dead man from the underworld" . . .

Curiously, when these traits are taken together, they produce a figure that is familiar to us from ethnology. One of the major subjects of the *Golden Bough* is kingship. The king is responsible for the material prosperity of his group because he has power over the elements; because magical power resides in him; and finally, because he is in his own persona god himself . . . After seeing in the philosopher a successor to the kind of inspired person who reveals not only characteristics of the ecstatic seer but also the ambitions of a prophet and healer, we now recognize in him a more ancient, yet striking, reminiscence: the relic of the "king-magician," one whose unique character and authority derive from his ability to control nature, from his infused science of divination, and from his miraculous feats of prehistoric "medicine" . . .

Why is it that these images and beliefs, belonging to extremely distant ages, were able to cross over so many centuries? Such a question involves a problem that is not really our concern to treat extensively: social prehistory. Nevertheless, something should be said about it in an attempt to understand the strange avatar of the "primitive king," which in the person of Empedocles arouses our curiosity.

At the dawn of Hellenism we still catch a glimpse of religious associations that have been inherited by the *genē* of the nobility; and these *genē* last into the historical period . . . In the archaic period, their life is not in the *polis* but in the mystery religions, in the confraternities, and with those who might be called the magicians of Greece. In this period a number of innovations occur which are more or less interdependent. And it might be observed that the most remote tradition is renewed rather than broken. The vocations of those who have been inspired had to have some relation with the religious power embodied in certain heroes by the guilds of the Healers, Singers and Dancers, Pacifiers or Winds, Men of the Vine of Fig Tree. That is to say, this religious power was embodied in some king from a distant past. Between a myth of "kingship" and the myth of these heroes there is an analogy that one might term functional. It turns out that their legend is only partially attested; what it indicates is the survival of a medicine man. It is a paradox of history that the collective memory is crystallized in an actual person: and it is the philosopher of the fifth century [BCE] who resurrects for us the model of the type in its fullest . . .

In any case, we understand better certain aspects of philosophy in ancient Greece. Apropos of the philosopher himself, we have taken up the question of the *theios anēr* and its connections with the old idea of the "inspired man" and with the concept of the initiate in higher degrees of "secret societies." And here there is a strange coincidence, for the same expression is used by Xenophon at the end of his *Oeconomicus* in an unexpected context. He applies it no longer to an aptitude for knowledge but rather to the aptitude to exercise authority. Found in such a rich context, this usage of *theios anēr* implies a very precise kind of thinking that Xenophon was incapable of inventing. Such a notion is similar to that of the inspired philosopher and continues the idea of initiation (even the word is there), one involving a kind of power granted by divine election. Plato, after all, does not allow us to forget that *theia moira*, itself the divine privilege that gives a man access to true knowledge, also consecrates him for authentic kingship. No doubt, such considerations are valuable only in the ideal order . . .

Even if we know little of the political theory of the first philosophers, we know that in general they had one. And on occasion they were regarded as lawmakers. According to them, a political philosophy is the crowning point, the "achievement" in the Greek view, of all philosophy. This imperious tradition can be explained by recourse to the origins of philosophy.

In fact, the claim inherited by the philosopher from a prehistoric past is not really codified in the actual *polis*. Beforehand it was disavowed by the *polis*. The very conditions that made the philosophical movement possible could not support the quasi-religious assent that domination by sages would have demanded. One can see this almost symbolically in the history (or legends) of the Pythagorean communities and their failed attempts at governing . . . It is as if one activity, no longer capable of functioning in the political order, is diverted to a priestly class that no longer commits treason because it no longer has the temptation to do so.

It must be said that we have noted antecedents rather than a transition . . . There are other facets of the subject . . . Must these aspects remain unintelligible to us? The formula "Greek miracle" is a convenient one, but it is only a formula. What is labeled a miracle is really a creation. And perhaps in human history creations are contingent and gratuitous in nature. But they have their antecedents and preconditions. We have seen, in some of the traditions, that they could have had their own prime matter. We will begin to learn about these creations only when we start seeing the "new" as nothing more than alterations of the "old."

TRANSLATED BY JOHN HAMILTON AND BLAISE NAGY

PIERRE LÉVÊQUE AND PIERRE VIDAL-NAQUET

Cleisthenes the Athenian

1964

This selection offers a semantic inquiry into the word "democracy," which did not yet exist at the time of the reforms of Cleisthenes as described by Herodotus, in conjunction with the term "isonomia." An important examination of the texts of Herodotus, through which the authors discover that "isonomia," a political term, is closely associated with the incipient notion of "democracy" at the end of the sixth century BCE.

"Isonomy and Democracy"

Was it democracy that the great Alcmeonid established? Herodotus had no doubt of it. After describing the marriage of Megacles and Agarista, the daughter of Cleisthenes of Sicyon, he simply states: "From this marriage came Cleisthenes, who reorganized the Athenian tribes [*phulai*] and instituted the democratic regime in Athens" (Herodotus 6.131);[1] Aristotle is no less categorical in his brief description of the reforms: "When the people held power, Cleisthenes was their guide and leader" (*Constitution of Athens* 21.1). "The people had confidence in Cleisthenes" (21.1). His conclusion is particularly sharp: "In the wake of these changes, the constitution became more democratic [*dēmotikōtera polu*] than it was under Solon" (21.1).

In fact, the question is not a simple one, and few matters have been as clouded by, on the one hand, the extremely rapid evolution of political institutions and vocabulary in the fifth century and, on the other hand, the polemics of the end of the century and the subsequent period. The very text of Herodotus that we just quoted will help us to grasp and enumerate the difficulties. When the Alcmeonid Megacles married Agarista "according to the Athenian law" (Herodotus 6.130), he was the representative of a wealthy and important

From "Isonomie et démocratie," in *Clisthène l'Athénien: Essai sur la représentation de l'espace et du temps dans la pensée politique grecque de la fin du VIe siècle à la mort de Platon* (Paris: Les Belles Lettres, 1964), pp. 25–32.

Athenian family that can safely be described as having harbored oligarchic ambitions. The marriage itself was, as "marriages of tyrants"[2] generally are, rather unusual, not because it violated, as did other, similar marriages, a religious taboo but because Cleisthenes' choice of a bride was preceded by an astonishing competition that went on for a year while he tested the qualities of the various aspirants (Herodotus 6.128). The marriage also provided Herodotus with the opportunity to discuss the fate of Cleisthenes' family: "He took his name from his maternal grandfather, the Sicyonian. With him Megacles had a son, Hippocrates. Hippocrates was the father of another Megacles and another Agarista, named for Agarista, the daughter of Cleisthenes. She married Xanthippos, son of Ariphron. While pregnant, she had a vision in a dream in which she saw herself giving birth to a lion, and a few days later she bore Xanthippos a son, Pericles" (6.131).

For Herodotus, there is clearly a continuous line connecting Cleisthenes of Sicyon, Cleisthenes the Athenian, and Pericles. History seems to disappear in favor of repetition within a lineage of identical actions and political attitudes. If Cleisthenes the Athenian "imitated" his ancestor from Sicyon,[3] might Pericles not be adhering closely to the family tradition of the Alcmeonids, who were among the historian's primary sources? But there is ambiguity in this idea. The Sicyonian was a tyrant, but as such he was obliged to seek the support of the *dēmos* against the nobility. Pericles, who oversaw the final phase of Athens' evolution into a democracy, nevertheless, according to a famous remark of Thucydides, imposed government by a single person. How did Cleisthenes the Athenian define himself in this tradition, in which tyrannical authority was coupled with democratic options? Should he be seen not as the founder of democracy but as one of those "princes," or *fürstliche Herren*, who, according to H. Berve, still dominated Greek cities in the late sixth century and deliberately set themselves above the *nomos*, which summed up the teachings of civic life?[4] Appealing as this interpretation is, we are inclined to reject it entirely. What we can say with assurance, moreover, is that it was not an interpretation shared by Herodotus, who, as we have seen, regarded Cleisthenes as the founder of democracy (*dēmokratiē*).

But did this notion and the word that designated it exist more than half a century before Herodotus wrote? A semantic investigation is in order before we return to the case of Cleisthenes proper.

In a brilliant essay,[5] Victor Ehrenberg tried to show that in *The Suppliants* Aeschylus used if not the word democracy itself then at least a periphrasis involving its two constituent elements: [. . . *dēmou kratousa* (*kheir*) . . .].[6] We can no longer follow him, however, when he ascribes this tragedy to the period immediately preceding Marathon. In fact, the 1952 publication of a papyrus fragment (*Pap. Oxy.* XX 2256, fr. 3) of the didascalia for the *Danaids* of Aeschylus forces one to assign the production of the tetralogy a date not prior to 468 (the date of the first production of a play by Sophocles) and perhaps even under the archonship of Archimedes in 464. At the end of the sixth century and the beginning of the fifth, if the democratic idea existed, it was not expressed by the word *dēmokratia* or any related expression.[7]

In the famous dialogue of the three Persian chieftains on different political constitutions, in which Herodotus compares the virtues of monarchy, oligarchy, and popular government (Herodotus 3.80–82), Otanes of course argued in favor of democracy. He summed up his case as follows:

> The rule of the people . . . has the finest of all names to describe it—isonomy [*isonomia*]; and, secondly, the people in power do none of the things that monarchs do. Under a government of the people a magistrate is appointed by lot and is held responsible for his conduct in office, and all questions are put up for open debate [. . . *es to koinon*]. For these reasons I propose that we do away with the monarchy and raise the people to power; for everything resides in number [. . . *to pollon*].[8]

If, in this celebrated passage, isonomy is thus formally identified with democracy, it is clear that the former notion is prior to the latter and must be treated separately.[9] In fact, Herodotus' text alerts us to this: it is striking to find Megabyzus, who favors oligarchy, criticizing both democracy and monarchy, and Darius, the future monarch, attacking both oligarchy and democracy, while Otanes directs his criticism solely at monarchy, to which he ascribes all the classic features of tyranny. It is as if Otanes were speaking as a representative of a time before oligarchy and democracy were clearly distinguished and isonomy simply meant opposition to tyranny.[10] A brief study of the use of the word *isonomia* and the related words *isēgoria* and *isokratia* confirms this initial impression. It is striking that Herodotus used these words only in describing things that occurred in the late sixth and very early fifth century:

1. After the fall of Polycrates of Samos (circa 518), the tyrant's successor, Maiandros, had this to say: "I did not approve the conduct of Polycrates, nor should I that of any other man who sought to reign as a despot over his equals [*despozōn andrōn homoiōn*]. Therefore, now that Polycrates has met his end, I intend to place power in the center [. . . *es to meson*] and proclaim isonomy for you" (3.142).[11]

2. In 506, commenting on Cleomenes' ill-fated attempt to seize power in Athens and the Athenians' victory over the Chalcidians, Herodotus wrote: "This shows that equality [*isēgoriē*] prevails not only in isolated instances but generally. When governed by tyrants, the Athenians had no better fortune in war than any of their neighbors, but once the yoke was flung off, they proved the finest fighters in the world" (5.78).

3. At the very end of the century, the Corinthian Socles, representing a moderate oligarchy, was astonished at the mere thought of the Lacedaemonians "abolishing egalitarian regimes" (*isokratiai*) and "restoring despotism in the cities" (5.92a).

4. Finally, around 500, on the eve of the Ionian revolt, Aristagoras "abdicated from tyranny and established equal rights in Miletus (*isonomiē*) in order to induce the Milesians to support his rebellion," and, adopting an institution that appeared in Athens shortly after Cleisthenes' reform, appointed generals in each city (5.37-38).

In fact, in the vocabulary of fifth-century historians, the word *isonomos* and its derivatives seem to have been closely connected with the regimes that grew up in opposition to tyranny in the late sixth century and which Sokles of Corinth did not distinguish in any way from the Lacedaemonian regime. So, when the Thebans sought to explain their earlier attitude to the Plataeans, they said: "our city was at that time neither an isonomous [*isonomos*] oligarchy [*oligarkhia*] nor a democracy [*dēmokratia*]" and misleadingly described their former regime as a tyranny (Thucydides 3.62).[12]

Before Herodotus, only two texts used the noun *isonomia* or the adjective *isonomos* from which it derived. Ehrenberg traces the famous *skolion* of the Tyrannicides,[13] familiar to both democrats and aristocrats in Athens,[14] back to the period immediately after the Murder of Hipparchus, circa 514–510: "Harmodius and Aristogeiton . . . when they killed the tyrant, made Athens isonomous [*isonomoi*]."[15]

Isonomous Athens was thus Athens freed from rule by tyrants. Finally, a fragment of Alcmeon of Croton, an author familiar to the Pythagoreans who apparently lived in the late sixth or early fifth century, defined health as an isonomy of forces (*dunameis*) such as cold and heat, sour and sweet, and so on, whereas illness was portrayed as a monarchy of these same forces.[16] For this philosophical physician, isonomy was thus an internal law regulating the functioning of an organism, which he explained in terms of an analogy with the body politic.

The notion of isonomy thus seems to date from a period in which "oligarchs" were not yet completely distinct from "democrats," namely, the end of the sixth century, which was in so many respects a turning point.

In the foregoing, we have left untranslated the word *isonomia*, which does not so much define as adumbrate a regime in which those who participate in public life do so as equals, a word whose sense the modern notion of "equality before the law" fails to capture.[17] As J.-P. Vernant puts it, "the ideal of *isonomia* may reflect or extend communal aspirations that go back . . . to the origins of the *polis*,"[18] and in fact it began to take root in the aristocratic city when the phalanx of hoplites, in which each soldier is as important as any other, replaced the Homeric fighter. But even a superficial study of Greek political vocabulary suffices to show that it also introduced some fundamentally new ideas. Isonomy is a purely *political* notion, distinct in this respect from *isomoiria*, that is, from the division of the land demanded by peasants in the time of Solon, which Solon refused to grant.[19] Solon was an arbiter who, when the city was shaken by the call for justice, responded with this judgment: "I drafted the laws in the same way for the good and the wicked, established a straight judgment [*dikē*] for every man."[20] [. . .] According to the ideal of *isonomia*, the body politic, no matter how limited, contains neither "good" nor "base"; everyone is equal. This may involve, as Ehrenberg says, an "equality of peers,"[21] but in any case some sort of equality is intended. Since the time of Solon, the debate had shifted from the economic to the political sphere. To establish isonomy was, to borrow Herodotus' phrase, to place *arkhē*, "authority," *es to meson*, "into the center." Historically, the ideal of isonomy corresponds to the moment when more than one Greek city, perhaps following a trail marked out quite early on by the Spartans in the time of the Lycurgan reform, attempted to solve its problems not by calling upon an arbiter, a foreign lawgiver, or a tyrant[22] but through the operation of its own institutions, its own *nomos*.[23]

It remains to be seen to what extent Cleisthenes' reform and history fit this overall view, and to what extent the personal destiny of the Alcmeonid, heir to a long aristocratic family tradition, can be related to the major political transformation that occurred in the late sixth century.

TRANSLATED BY ARTHUR GOLDHAMMER

NOTES

[1] English translation by A. de Sélincourt (New York, 1955), p. 435, as revised by A. R. Burn.

[2] L. Gernet, "Mariage de tyrans," 1954, pp. 44–53.

[3] Cf. Herodotus 5.67. It was natural for Herodotus to make the Sicyonian the model for the Athenian because mythical traditions frequently associated the grandson with his *maternal* grandfather, to whom he was entrusted for upbringing. [. . .] The temptation was all the greater because Cleisthenes bore the name not of his paternal grandfather, as was common in Athens, but of his maternal grandfather, which was less common.

[4] H. Berve, "Fürstliche Herren zur Zeit der Perserkriege," *Die Antike* II (1936), pp. 1-28. [. . .]

[5] "Origins of Democracy," *Historia* 1 (1950), pp. 515–18 (on Aeschylus, see pp. 517–23).

[6] *Suppliants* 603–4.

[7] For us, Herodotus remains the first attestation of this word in its Ionian form. To be sure, he was certainly not the man who coined the word. [. . .]

[8] Sélincourt translation, p. 238, as revised by A. R. Burn.

[9] On the notion of isonomy and its relation to the prior notion of *eunomia* and the subsequent notion of democracy, see esp. Ehrenberg, "Origins of Democracy," pp. 515 ff. [. . .]

[10] We know that for Herodotus the dialogue among the Persian chieftains was a historical fact, and that he was critical of contemporaries who did not believe it had actually taken place (6.42).

[11] Sélincourt translation, p. 262, as revised by A. R. Burn. On this text, see Vernant 1962, 123.

[12] Here we leave aside any consideration of the meaning of the words *isonomia* and *isonomos* in the political language of the fourth century.

[13] "Das Harmodios Lied," in *Festschrift A. Lesky: Wiener Studien* 69 (1956), pp. 57–69.

[14] Cf. Aristophanes *Acharnians* 980; *Wasps* 1223; *Lysistrata* 632, and corresponding scholia.

[15] Diehl, vol. 2, p. 181, 10–12.

[16] Aetius 5.30.1.

[17] In Sophocles' *Oedipus Rex* (579), Creon, speaking of Jocasta, says to Oedipus: "You therefore reign over this country with rights equal [*ison*] to hers."

[18] Vernant 1962, pp. 52–53.

[19] Fr. 23, 8–10 (Diehl), in *Constitution of Athens* 12.3.

[20] Fr. 24, 18–20, in *Constitution of Athens* 12.4. On Solon's political thought, see [. . .] J.-P. Vernant, 1962, pp. 77–79.

[21] 1950, 531.

[22] "Each person was to return home and concern himself with his personal affairs; he [the tyrant] would take charge of all public [*koina*] affairs": Aristotle *Constitution of Athens* 15.5. These words, ascribed to Pisistratus, are the best definition of tyranny.

[23] Were there democracies in Greece before this time? The problem remains open. [. . .]

NICOLE LORAUX

Greek Civil War and the Anthropological Representation of the World Turned Upside-down

1995

As the title suggests, this article examines ancient Greek discourse on civil war as the occasion for a chaotic, inverted, and perverse human behavior—behavior that would seem to require a primarily anthropological analysis when it descends from the merely inhumane or inhuman to the non-human, for example in the practice of literal or metaphorical cannibalism. Loraux's meticulous examination of the semantic fields of certain key terms used by the historiographers—among them the Greek words for civil strife, throat-slitting, and bestial cruelty (with associations of raw-flesh eating)—is complemented by her investigation of the same terms as deployed by such archaic poets as Hesiod and Theognis. Loraux argues that civil strife—stasis, a crucial word in her corpus—must be seen not as a threat to, but rather as constitutive of, the political; representations of stasis that focus on bestiality and animality—on strife as an anomaly—serve, she argues, to obscure its political centrality. Turning to Thucydides for a crucial distinction between the actions characteristic of civilized men and those of a degraded and regressed human nature, Loraux poses and suspends the question of how to read Man: "anthrōpos or anēr? A theological-anthropological reading or a purely political one?" Loraux thus follows the Greeks and insists on a double, critical reading of strife, as simultaneously political and anthropological, a function of man as both "anthrōpos and anēr." Interdisciplinary in its sources (which range from the Iliad *and Herodotus to Le Roy Ladurie and the French newspaper* Libération*) and its perspectives, this essay's conclusions challenge, in effect, the disciplinary categories and boundaries available to describe the phenomenon under study, both for the original historiographer and for the scholar of today.*

From "La guerre civile grecque et la représentation anthropologique du monde à l'envers," *Revue de l'histoire des religions* 212 (1995): 299–326.

Mozambique. At least six refugees were devoured by lions after returning to their abandoned homes in Naico (North). The wild animals had invaded villages deserted since the civil war. Naico had
been a dead city for the five years that war raged between Renamo
and the Mozambique Liberation Front (Frelimo, now in power).

—*Libération*, 23 September 1993

"Truly, the sky will sink beneath the earth, and the earth will hover
above the sky; men [*anthrōpoi*] will make their home in the sea, and
fishes[1] will reside where men [*anthrōpoi*] once lived, because you
Lacedaemonians, having laid waste to the egalitarian regimes [*isokratias*], are
making ready to restore tyranny in the cities, tyranny that is the most unjust
and bloodiest [*adikōteron, miaiphonōteron*] thing that there is among men [*kat'
anthrōpous*]."[2]

It is in connection with the subject of tyranny that the Corinthian Sokles
resorts—effectively, moreover—to the rhetoric of the world turned upside-
down (in Herodotus 5.92). But the discourse on tyranny shares enough com-
monplaces with the figure of *stasis* (the Greek word for sedition or dissension)
that one can include this statement in the very full dossier of Greek representations of civil war. Nevertheless, I will turn to Polybius as the point of departure
for my reflections on *stasis* as chaos, where I understand the latter term in its
ordinary sense rather than as "a gaping opening," which is what it means in, for
example, Greek cosmogonic poetry.

A SAVAGE "*STASIS*" IN ARCADIA

In Book 4 of the *Histories*, Polybius describes the *stasis* that left the small Arcadian city of Kynaitha spattered with blood. In this city, we are told, there were
constant major disputes [*akatapaustais kai megalais . . . stasesi*], throat-
slittings [*sphagas*], reciprocal proscriptions, pillaging, and redistribution of
land. To this point the description of the civil war in Kynaitha is little different
from the all but canonical description of *stasis*. Polybius does not stop there,
however. He tells us that the exiles asked to be allowed back into the city. No
sooner was their request for restoration of full rights of citizenship granted
than they began plotting against their fellow citizens: "Even as they swore
oaths of loyalty over the sacrificial victims [*ta sphagia*], they were already plotting impious acts [*asebeias*] against the gods and against those who had placed
their trust in them" (17.11). Polybius then tells how the plotters opened the city
to the Aetolians, who massacred many of their fellow citizens, and reports the
unanimous judgment of Greek opinion, namely, that for all their misfortunes,
the Kynaitheans "were seen to have endured the most just of fates" [*pantōn*

anthrōpōn dikaiotata, 19.13]. He offers his own diagnosis: in order to explain how the "savagery" [*agriotēs*] and "cruelty" [*ōmotēs*] of the citizens of Kynaitha could be so at odds with the "humanity" [*philanthrōpia*] characteristic of the Arcadians (20.2), he remarks on the Kynaitheans' grave neglect of education (in the proper sense of *mousikē*), which led to their "savagery" [*agriotēs*, 21.11]. Ultimately, if we believe Polybius, they had "reached a stage of bestiality so complete that one saw no greater or more constant impieties [*asebēmata*] in any other Greek city" (21.6). To be sure, there is nothing surprising about the fact that rhetorical inflation may accompany the account of a *stasis*, especially when it is presented as paradigmatic. In what follows, however, we will focus in particular on the text's sustained use of the language of savagery in connection with a civil war.

It is of course appropriate to begin the examination of the use of such language by looking at Polybius's own frame of reference: his thought is apt to be couched in terms of "humanity" versus savagery or bestiality.[3] But as the Arcadian historian himself suggests in his digression on music, where he elaborates something like a theory of climate (20.4–7, 21, 5), we must above all take account of the peculiar nature of Arcadia: "humanity" itself originated there, yet it is a place abounding in signs of ever-threatening savagery compensated by opposing signs of civilization's responses to that threat.[4] According to Philippe Borgeaud, this "peculiar cultural status," by virtue of which "the Arcadian is . . . on the threshold" because "in Arcadia humanity has not yet totally divorced itself from its savage or nomadic origins,"[5] is exactly what the events in Kynaitha demonstrate: there, in the Hellenistic period, the barbarization (*ensauvagement*) so feared by the inhabitants of Stymphalos took place; a similar barbarization, in the form of a return to cannibalism, had threatened the citizens of Phigalia in the fifth century.[6]

Because Polybius's text "realizes," *but in figurative language*, the immemorial threat that had hung over the Arcadians, must we read into the verb *apethēriōthēsan* the idea of *allēlophagia*, "eating one another," where the historian spoke only of "bestiality," with no further details? The question is serious: at stake is not only the method of reading texts—do we or do we not need to pay close attention to the various linguistic registers of which a narrative is constituted?—but also our whole general reflection on the phenomenon of *stasis*. Must we conclude that all *stasis*, whether in Arcadia or not, was by definition a form of savagery? Such an interpretation is hinted at by Françoise Frontisi when, on the basis of the example of Kynaitha, she asserts that "*stasis*, the kind of civil war in which man *ceases to be a disciplined citizen and descends to the level of the wild animal devouring its own kind in a form of allēlophagia*, is seen as the most monstrous form of regression."[7]

Confronted with such an analysis, I ask myself whether *stasis* in and of itself was in fact one form, be it "the most monstrous," of an idea of the city centered on the possibility of a "return to savagery"? In that case, civil war would fall entirely within the limits of Greek anthropological discourse, of which it would be merely one figure. It would then be appropriate to situate *stasis* in the cultural realm of civilization rather than in the political realm, where citizens are not so much "disciplined" (as the humanity of the *anthrōpoi* is in opposition to the animal kingdom) as *politicized*, as virile men [*andres*] are supposed to be. Furthermore, the answer to this question has implications for the status to be assigned to anthropological discourse in a text by a Greek historian: is this discourse actually present as such in the accounts of *stasis*, or is it merely used in a more or less ad hoc way and in a metaphorical manner?

These questions are all the more crucial to my way of thinking because I have for some time now been trying to show, often with, but at times against, the apparently most widely shared representations, that *stasis* was an integral part of the Greek idea of the political, even if the Greeks themselves regularly tried to deny its political dimension by treating civil war as a calamity, meteorological[8] or epidemic[9] but in any event heaven-sent and therefore at odds with the normal functioning of the city, which in this perspective could only be peaceful.

It is therefore important for me to determine the actual role that the representation of *stasis* as savagery occupied in Greek discourse, beginning with the historians. This calls for taking a fresh look at Polybius's text. I shall focus on two ways of designating—or should I say two metaphors for?—*stasis* as extraordinary murder: the use of the noun *sphagē*, the word for sacrificial slitting of the throat (4.17.3; 4.21.8), and the verb *katasphazō*, which describes the completion of the act of throat-slitting (4.18.4 and 7), and the themes of savagery [*agriotēs*] and cruelty/crudity [*ōmotēs*], associated with the bestiality of the behavior of the Kynaitheans. It is worth pausing to analyze the use of these two linguistic resources.

"*SPHAGĒ*," CIVIL WAR, AND SACRIFICE

Let us begin, therefore, with *sphagē*, a recurrent term for denoting massacres of fellow citizens from Xenophon to Diodorus of Sicily and beyond. For the historians I cite here, this was clearly the ultimate horror—and one should mention in passing that this implies that, even in the context of sacrifice, the act of throat-slitting, though part of an accepted festive practice,[10] was problematic, because the word *sphagē* in other contexts became the primary metaphor for seditious murder.

In Xenophon's *Hellenica*, for example, "throat-slitters" are seditious killers in Elis (3.2, 28) and Corinth (4.5.5, 5.1.34). Although the act itself, understood in terms of duration and repetitive monstrousness (Polybius 4.57.9), was usually characterized by the verb *sphazō* (*Hellenica* 4.4.3) or, more commonly, its composites *apo-* (*Hellenica* 5.4.12, 7.4.26; Diodorus 12.57) and *kata-sphazō*, the recurrent use of *sphagē* subsumed the totality of seditious murders under the generality of throat-slitting in Elis, Corinth, and Corcyra (*Hellenica* 3.2.29, 4.4.2; Diodorus 13.48.2). This "extreme proximity of sacrifice and murder" has been noticed before and subjected to pertinent analysis in order to show how the use of sacrificial metaphors reveals the very meaning of the sacrifice itself.

Here, however, we are more interested in seditious murder than in sacrifice, and while we must try to interpret the sacrificial dimension introduced by the language of *sphagē*, our primary concern is with the meaning of civil war.

In substituting *sphagē* for *phonos*, did the Greek historians mean to suggest that for each camp the adversary was "reduced to animal status"? A simple logic would require this to be the case, but in this instance the imaginative operation seems to have been more complex.

Indeed, in the absence of any animal metaphor, explicit[11] or implicit, in these accounts of civil war, there is reason to doubt that this was the case: unlike certain episodes of the modern era, well known to historians,[12] dissension in Greek cities was rarely interpreted in terms of animalization. So that, in an obviously paradoxical way—given that we are dealing with a rite whose victim was actually, with few exceptions,[13] always an animal—it has to be said that, in terms of sacrifice, the scenes on which the Greek imagination dwelt most insistently assigned the victim role to a human rather than an animal.[14]

Let us therefore focus on what the use of the name of the sacrificial act to designate murder would suggest in and of itself: that seditious individuals, blinded by hatred to the point where they slit the throats of other men, quite simply "forget" that the only way for humans to communicate with the gods is through animal offerings. It is the diversion of this act from the sacrificial space within which it is normally contained into the space of civil strife in the *agora* that reveals the fundamental impiety [*asebeia*] of civil war, which for all the historians is the essential characteristic of *stasis*.

The recurrence of episodes of seditious *sphagē* during sacrifice is indeed remarkable: at such times the vocabulary of throat-slitting, caught between its metaphorical use and its more realistic meaning, plays on itself. We may read an instance of this between the lines of Polybius's account, according to which the Kynaithean rebels supposedly conceived their dark design "even as they were swearing an oath over the victims [*sphagia*],"[15] and a few chapters later it becomes explicit with the description of massacres [*sphagas*, Polybius 4.22.3, 34.3] in Lacedaemonia, where seditious youths seized the occasion of an armed procession to slit the throats [*apesphaxan*] of the ephors conducting a prescribed sacrificial rite [*thuousi*, 35.3].[16]

Since tradition credits Polybius with having written a "tragic" history, it is natural to look next to tragedy, which took a particular pleasure in playing on the sinister overtones of the sacrificial vocabulary: in Euripides' *Electra*, for example, Orestes kills Aigisthos in the middle of a sacrifice,[17] while the orchestration of murder's sacrificial overtones is what gives meaning to the *Oresteia* from *Agamemnon* to the *Eumenides*.

Yet Polybius was not the only writer of historical prose to describe such scenes: for example, Xenophon, who never fails to mention a regular sacrifice, is also capable, when a massacre occurs in a sacred place, as in Corinth, of restoring to the word *sphazō* all the violence implicit in the impiousness of the seditious act [*hoi anosiōtatoi . . . esphatton kai pros tois hierois*]. Indeed, such descriptions hark back beyond tragedy to Hesiod, who was not only the Greeks' official "theologian" but also, for that very reason, their authorized spokesman in matters of anthropology. When Polybius, commenting on events in Lacedaemonia, observes that

> the temple offered security to all who took refuge in it, even those condemned to death. But in the cruelty [*dia tēn ōmotēta*] of their audacity, they became so contemptuous of this that they slit the throats [*katasphagēnai*] of all the ephors around the very altar and table of the goddess (4.35.4) [18]

how can we avoid thinking of Hesiod's list of crimes, which opens with a description of the mistreated suppliant (*Works and Days* 327), or of the apocalyptic announcement of an epoch worse than the age of iron, when hosts will no longer respect guests and companions no longer respect each other (*Works and Days* 183)? These themes occur repeatedly in Greek tradition [19] but primarily in accounts of *stasis*, where the darkest stain attaches to the massacrers of suppliants, from the Alcmeonidae, who killed the kin of Kylon on the Acropolis, where they had taken refuge next to the statue of Athena (Herodotus 5.71), to the "rich men" of Megara, who, according to Herodotus (4.91), were never able to calm the wrath of Demeter Thesmophoros because, in their zeal to make prisoners of their enemies, they had not hesitated to cut off the hands of a man clinging to the entrance of the goddess' temple, in which he had sought refuge.

In Hesiod, as is well known, the origin of the human condition lies in the foundation of sacrifice. If impious parody of sacrifice on the very site of its canonical exercise is surely a sacrilege that disrupts the communication that sacrifice normally establishes between gods and men, those who engage in sedition are guilty in addition of regression to a less-than-human condition.

There are, however, other historical texts that tend to contradict the figurative use of the verb *sphazō* in the context of murder or suggest an association not of civil war with sacrifice but rather one of *stasis* with *polemos*. [20] To be sure, the latter association is just as disturbing to the mind, but its implications are quite different, because instead of the theme of humanity, whose mere evocation generally suffices to indicate the existence of a transgression, we have the notion of an equal struggle among *andres*.

There is a text of Xenophon that condenses these two frames of reference and establishes virtual relations between them. The astonishing richness of this text has not always been recognized, especially because the conspiracy it describes was nipped in the bud, so that one has to deduce from the preparations for conflict how the battle might have unfolded. I am speaking of Book 3 of the

Hellenica and the Kinadon conspiracy that came close to changing the face of Sparta in 397.

LACEDAEMONIAN INTERLUDE

As is inevitable with Xenophon, the preamble is sacrificial. Shortly after becoming king, Agesilaus ordered one of the prescribed civic sacrifices, at which time a soothsayer saw in the victims' entrails the signs of a dreadful conspiracy. A second and third sacrifice only confirmed the magnitude of the danger facing the small group of citizens, who were seemingly surrounded by enemies. No sooner had a fourth and final sacrifice warded off the threat, with considerable difficulty, than an informer came forward and revealed the plot, which involved a vast number of noncitizens, and its leader, whose obvious qualities had not been enough to win him full Spartan citizenship (3.3.4). The informant told how, when Kinadon was questioned about the arms that such a mass could muster, he had distinguished between those who, like himself, were members of the military contingent and therefore had arms at their disposal (and for whom the conflict was a kind of *polemos*) and the horde of others. As for the masses of workers,

> he led them to the ironmonger's and showed them many knives, swords, skewers, axes, hatchets, and sickles. "These, too, are weapons," he said, "for all the men [*anthrōpoi*] who work the earth, the forest, and the quarries. As for the other trades, they generally have tools, which are sufficient arms, especially against men who carry none." (*Hellenica* 3.3.7)

Kinadon's presentation of these makeshift weapons is troubling. He clearly divides them into two categories: before considering *tools* [*organa*], which are to be the weapons of artisans and are not enumerated but dealt with in a comprehensive statement, Kinadon lists objects that appear to have no generic denomination but only individual names. It is as if the knife [*makhaira*], the sword [*xiphos*], the skewer [*obeliskos*], the hatchet and ax [*pelekus, axinē*], and the sickle [*drepanon*] were not categorized as tools. This is indeed the case: an attentive reader will recognize that this list is really an enumeration of instruments of sacrifice.[21] This point has not generally been noticed, perhaps because nothing explicit is stated in the text. In contrast to the staging of sacrifice, in which the sacrificial knife is treated not as a weapon but only as an instrument,[22] the Lacedaemonian conspirators restored the *makhaira* to its status as a weapon. But the knife, and even more the hatchet and sickle (which normally denoted agriculture exclusively[23]), are problematic "weapons," to say the least, when the combatants brandishing them are not barbarians but Greeks: in some cases, in fact, it is a matter of desperate combat, in which citizen-soldiers like the last square of Spartan *Homoioi* at Thermopylae abandon the hoplite's disciplined methods of combat, while in other cases, as here, these are weapons used by noncitizens.

In this respect as well, Sparta was probably an exception among Greek cities, because when noncitizens rebelled, they were able to express authentically political demands.[24] This, by the way, meant that their uprising was like a *stasis*, in contrast to slave rebellions elsewhere in the Greek world.[25] Nevertheless, when it came to noncitizens of Lacedaemonia, Kinadon traced something like a boundary line between conspirators who were regular soldiers (and who thus exemplified the quasi-legitimate proximity of *stasiōtēs* and *stratiōtēs*, seditious rebels and soldiers),[26] and those who used sacrificial instruments as weapons and who therefore would certainly have deserved to be called "throat-slitters" if their rebellion had come to pass and been recorded in a historical narrative. As we have seen, however, neither group of potential rebels actually achieved their aim.

We are not quite finished with them, however. For even if they did not complete their rebellion, all without exception were credited, unlike the *Homoioi*, with a wish that, had it been realized, would have taken them to the bottom of the scale of transgressions even more surely than a misplaced sacrificial practice. This was a wish for cannibalism, or, more precisely, to eat raw meat, as Kinadon put it, if we are to believe the informer's account. Indeed, after claiming that the "whole mass of Helots, *Neodamōdes* [newly enfranchised], *Hypomeiones* [subordinate citizens], and *Perioikoi* are of one mind" with the conspirators, he added: "Whenever these people spoke of the Spartiates [that is, of the citizens of Sparta], not one of them could conceal the pleasure he would take in eating them, even raw [*kai ōmōn*]" (*Hellenica* 3.3.6).

Thus the adjective *ōmos*, in its most sinister and concrete sense, suddenly crops up in this astonishing text. What are we to make of this eating of raw flesh? It would be too easy simply to dismiss it as an idiom peculiar to Xenophon by adducing another instance in the historian's work[27] or as an almost proverbial expression, because we know that topoi that use this sort of formula must be taken very seriously. Nor will it profit us simply to add this statement to the chapter on *sphagē* by asserting that "in a liminal situation, *sphagē* calls into question the boundary between civilized order . . . and a realm of chaos ruled by pure violence, much as wild animals without laws or justice . . . devour one another."[28] For it is not clear that a veiled allusion to *sphagē*, like the one we think we have identified in a list of weapons that are also sacrificial instruments, belongs to the same linguistic register as an openly avowed wish to eat raw flesh.

This, to be sure, is a question of manner, but in this instance the manner is important, especially since in the accounts of civil wars it is in fact a reciprocal *throat-slitting* in which the rebels engage, even where the sense is said to be figurative. What is it about eating raw flesh? In what manner—metaphorical or literal—is it evoked in this history of a *stasis*? The time has come to look beyond the text of Xenophon that has occupied our attention thus far.

Cannibalism as Fantasy

If we are to clarify Kinadon's formula, we must look hard, because eating raw flesh (which we take here, as in Xenophon, to be akin to cannibalism) is not a recurrent explicit feature of ordinary narratives of *stasis*.

True, in Theognis one finds the expression of a wish to "drink the black blood" of the enemies who have dispossessed him of his property (347–49). But since the poet in this is identifying himself with a "hideous dog"—and possibly even with an Erinys[29]—the literary dimension of such a statement is obvious. In any case it bears emphasizing that, as in Xenophon's text, this is only a *wish*, which also relates this text to the expression of similar wishes in the *Iliad*: Achilles, for example, gives in to his wrath sufficiently to wish that he might eat Hector's flesh after cutting his body to pieces (*Iliad* 22.346–50),[30] while Hecuba expresses a symmetrical wish to sink her teeth into Achilles' liver (24.212–13), and Zeus credits Hera (4.34) with "devouring Priam, his sons, and the other Trojans raw" (*ōmon*). Yet nothing in these passages from the *Iliad* indicates that the "wish" thus formulated is anything other than an intense expression of a very powerful hatred. And when the same Theognis expresses his fear "lest the *hubris* that destroyed the raw-eating [*ōmophagous*] Centaurs also destroy the city" of Megara (541–42), it would be reading too much into the text to deduce, on the basis of a literary comparison, a monstrous civic consumption of raw flesh from the mythical and traditional behavior of hybrid creatures.

If we are to believe another passage in Theognis, the "savages" are already in the city in the form of new citizens who only yesterday were peasants clad in animal skins and ignorant of the city's justice and laws (*nomous*) and who graze (*enemonto*) like deer outside the walls (54–57). But this text tells us far more about the gap between *nomos* and *nemesthai*, the traditional image of peasant savagery,[31] or the sentiments of an aristocrat confronted with an inversion of the hierarchy,[32] than about any traditional practice of eating one's own kind— particularly since the intruders inside the walls of the city are not real lions from Mozambique but harmless metaphorical deer.

What else can we place under the heading of eating raw flesh in a time of *stasis*? Surely nothing that refers to the recurrence of the theme of cannibalism during the Wars of Religion in France, even though "fantasy" in general took precedence over reality, as it did in Romans during the carnival of 1580.[33] Because the accusation of cannibalism was then rooted in the Protestant critique of holy communion, images of transgression derived their legitimacy from religious polemic. It is best to refrain from projecting this kind of pattern onto Greek thought, which was reluctant to imagine *allēlophagia* in the city even in order to denounce *stasis*. We know that only the cynics dared to rehabilitate the eating of raw flesh.[34]

If we refuse, as I believe we must, to attach other than a general and figurative meaning to the bestiality of the Kynaitheans in Polybius's text, we can, for

want of anything better, cite the *allēlophagia* coupled with "incestuous cannibalism"[35] with which the Pythia threatened the Phigalians (*s' allēlophagon thē-
sei takha kai teknodaitēn*) if they did not promptly calm Demeter's wrath
(Pausanias 8.42.4–7). But if this text can in all rigor be associated with Polybius's
text because, like Kynaitha, the Arcadian city of Phigalia exemplified the constant danger of regression that all of Arcadia faced, [36] it is nevertheless true that
there is no question of *stasis*, only impiety.[37] Once again, moreover, it is only a
threat that is involved here, and a threat that was obviously never carried out.

Hence we make no claim that there was a regular connection between civil
war and man-eating. If we are looking for a substantial connection, it makes
more sense to look at texts concerning the relation between tyranny and eating
raw flesh: Kypselos is described as a "strong lion and eater of raw flesh"[38] in the
Pythia's oracle to the Corinthians (Herodotus 5.92),[39] and in Plato's *Republic*,
the tyrant and protector of the people becomes a wolf and, after tasting the
"blood of his kind" [*emphuliou haimatos*], "savors with impious mouth and
tongue the blood of his kinsmen" [*phonou xuggenous*, 8.565d–66a].

We are still dealing only with metaphors. If we really want "actual," con-
summated raw-flesh eating, we have to look to barbarian countries and tribes
that were either cannibalistic by nature or could become so, as did the soldiers
of Cambyses astray in the desert, according to Herodotus (3.25). But since this
story involved an unjust expedition sent by a mad king against those liminal
men, the Ethiopians, who would deny that such a story was partly fictional?
Indeed, the essence of Herodotus's story has nothing to do with realism: it lies
rather in the careful description of the slow degradation of the starving army's
diet and in the fact that the word *cannibalism* occurs only in indirect discourse,
in the account of the report to Cambyses of the "horrible act," which is then
designated rather formulaically as *allēlophagia*, a way of alluding to the well-
known that resembles the quoting of a proverbial phrase.

An even more interesting passage can be found in Book 1 of Polybius's *Histories*, in the celebrated account of the Carthaginian mercenaries' revolt, which
ends in cannibalism. But this remarkable text needs to be carefully analyzed:
although Polybius does not hesitate to apply the term *stasis* to a "savage" uprising in a barbarian country and the word *apothērioō* dots his narrative,[40] there is
no *stasis* by the time the monstrous act occurs and there has been none for some
time; more than that, "bestiality," whose largely abstract character *apothērioō*
had previously denoted, has now reached a new phase, that of incarnation or
realization, surpassing the limits beyond which the human animal ceases to be
human.[41] At this point the *allēlophagia* occurs—and very quickly, at the end of
the narrative. The historian comes back to it twice: after describing the famine
that "made it necessary for them to devour one another" (84.9), he mentions
only (enemy) prisoners and slaves as victims of cannibalism (85.1), as if, even in
monstrousness, a certain minimal norm was still observed by the mercenaries.

They surrender before devouring one another. Though bestial, a man is still a man. In other words, even in a condition beyond *stasis*, one does not eat *one's own kind*.

A fortiori, it follows that to the Greek mind, the horrors of *stasis* were without overt affinity with cannibalism, even in extremis. Taken all in all, those horrors were still *human*. Reasoning by analogy, one might argue that in the recurrent proximity of *limos* (famine) with *loimos* (plague, the traditional metaphor for civil war),[42] the imagination provides for the possibility of such a figure. But it is only a prospective possibility on the horizon of discourse, in no case an obligatory figure. Note, moreover, that in the passage from Hesiod that is surely the earliest occurrence of the pair *limos/loimos*, the calamities that beset the unjust city do not take the form of civil war: it is certainly not *stasis* that occurs there, nor is it *eris*, the incarnation of multifarious Strife, as real as it is redoubtable, nor even *neikos*, the Hesiodic name for conflict; rather, according to Hesiod's theology (and Greek theology generally), death and sterility are the punishments for impiety and excess.

In that case, would it be too bold to claim, through an only slightly paradoxical application of Hesiod, that civil war, by respecting the order that defines human *dikē* in contrast to the *allēlophagia* intrinsic to animals (*Works and Days* 276–80), still comprises its share of "justice"?

The question is a delicate one, for although it is true that Heraclitus asserted, in lapidary form, an equivalence between conflict and justice,[43] few political thinkers have dared to draw that unflinching conclusion. So rather than dwell any longer on archaic poetry and the thought of philosophers, we shall switch, prudently, to another angle of attack, one that is certainly less "fundamental" but also less dangerously provocative and more appropriate to the corpus with which we have been dealing up to now.

Let us therefore turn once again to historiographic discourse. It is high time that we looked at one historian whose very name I have thus far avoided mentioning: the paradigmatic historian, Thucydides.

"STASIS," OR "ANDRES" AS VICTIMS OF HUMAN NATURE

To be sure, Thucydides is no stranger to the "ferocious" representation of *stasis*. As if to comment on the idea of an irresistible impulse to transgress the limits of horror—illustrated by a father murdering a son or by the massacre of suppliants in the temple of Dionysus—his discussion of the phenomenon begins with the adjective *ōmos*, which characterizes the very essence of civil war.[44] But that is all: Thucydides says no more, and, knowing the degree to which his writing generally resists any allegorical interpretation,[45] we would do well to refrain from reading the figurative but abstract reference to ferocity as in any sense an allusion to cannibalism.

Whether one describes this as a bias in favor of "secularization" or, as I would prefer to put it, "politicization," the fact remains: Thucydides is by no means fond of describing transgressions in detail, and although *stasis* as described in his text has all the usual characteristics, starting with impiety and the murder of suppliants (3.81.2–3 and 5),[46] the historian never wavers from the sobriety that is the hallmark of his style: thus, in the discussion of civil war, the analysis of faction ends in the rather euphemistic statement that "pious conduct [*eusebeiai*] was not customary in either camp" (3.82.8), and he does not apply the term *sphagē* to any massacre at the altar.

No doubt someone will object that the single, unique occurrence of this word in Thucydides' work is in a seditious context: the oligarchs of Corcyra, trapped in a building surrounded by their enemies, commit suicide with the very arrows their enemies have used to try to kill them (4.48.3). A closer look reveals, however, that just as the appellation *loimōdēs nosos* (plaguelike malady) is aimed at severing the plague from all the mythic-religious connotations attached to *loimos*, the use of the word *sphagē* tends to rule out any sacrificial reading, even metaphorical. Indeed, besides the fact that any reference, even implicit, to a sacrificial background for suicide is in itself unthinkable,[47] there are no grounds for treating the building in which the oligarchs are trapped, and which Thucydides is careful to describe only in terms of its imposing dimensions, as a temple. Hence we are forced to recognize that the use of the word *sphagē* restricts its meaning to the strictly anatomical sense of "throat."[48]

Before leaving the subject of impiety, a comparison may help to clinch my point. Consider the use of the same type of perjury in the context of *stasis* by both Polybius and Thucydides. In one, the Kynaithean exiles no sooner return home than they begin plotting against the democrats who invited them back; in the other, in Book 4 of *The Peloponnesian War*, the Megarean exiles are restored to office and behave in a similar way by forcing the people to sentence their enemies to death and by establishing "a regime oligarchical to the utmost degree" (Thucydides 4.74.2–3). But whereas Thucydides is content to point out that the exiles initially swore all the oaths they were asked to and leaves it to the reader to judge the gravity of their perjury, Polybius insists that oath and treason are simultaneous (recall that even as the exiles are swearing by the *sphagia*, they are already contemplating their crime) and applies the most emphatic possible term to their behavior: these seditious conspirators are plotting "acts of impiety" [*asebeias*: Polybius 4.17.11]. Thus the conclusion, which is moral in Polybius (despite their misfortunes, the Kynaitheans are deemed to have suffered the justest of fates [*dikaiotata*], 4.19.13), is factual in Thucydides, who is confident that a mere statement of the facts will be more powerful than an expression of outrage: "Of all the regimes newly founded by a faction," the historian writes soberly, "this one owed its existence to the fewest men and lasted the longest time" (4.74.4).

Yet as remarkable as these literary and philosophical choices may be, what seems to me most essential in Thucydides for our purposes is the way in which he focuses on a tension that is overt in *stasis* and that we have already detected in various places, a tension between two figures of sedition: the citizen as *anēr* and man as *anthrōpos*. In this respect, Thucydides' historiography is ideal for anyone who wishes to test the conventional figures of anthropological discourse with respect to Greek civil war.

Ever since Theognis described the "insurrections and murders of virile men" [*staseis te kai phonoi andrōn*], civil war had been associated with *andres*, or citizens, the active force within the Greek city. After setting civil war in motion, they become its subjects, but being obedient to its destructive force, they are at the same time its "objects."[49] In Thucydides, this reversibility, characteristic of murder as well as the battlefield,[50] becomes singularly complicated.

Civil war attacks *andres* as such, that is, as virile men, inextricably citizens and soldiers. But it does not simply wipe them out by delivering them, at the hands of adversaries who are their fellow citizens, to *androktasiai*, a form of martial "slaughter" that according to Hesiod's *Theogony* is, along with Battles [*Makhai*], Murders [*Phonoi*], and Quarrels [*Neikea*], a child of Struggle [*Eris*], itself principal daughter of dark Night (228–29). For Thucydides, civil war obliges its victims to suffer a meritless death: by driving them to suicide, especially by hanging (3.81.3, 4.48.3), it forces them to behave, admittedly under duress, in ways that in the Greek mind carried feminine connotations.[51] That this was no accident but a structural necessity is shown by the space devoted in the discussion of *stasis* in Book 3 to the vicissitudes of the virile definition of man: in fact, courage, understood as an inherent virtue of the *anēr* (*andreia*), is foremost among the values affected by the general inversion of the meaning of words that comes about as a result of civil war.[52]

When Thucydides attempts to name the cause of this destructive inversion, it turns out that, after *stasis* and its catastrophic effects, blame is to be laid at the door of human nature [*phusis anthrōpōn*] itself.[53] Hence we see how the historian could both allow Greek anthropological discourse to influence his text, if only in the minimal form of the adjective *ōmos*, and try to keep it at a distance. For since the plague had reduced the very citizens of Athens whose courage was lauded in the funeral oration to their all too human nature, human nature was for the *anēr* at once the source and area of their regression.[54] This is true throughout *The Peloponnesian War*.

This position is certainly original when compared with the Hesiodic tradition, which spoke not of human nature but of the human *condition*, or, rather, the human *order*, governed by the "law" [*nomos*] that Zeus prescribed for men, whose name is *dikē*. Since the human order is defined as a norm, the major risk is that man may regress to something less than human. For Thucydides, by contrast, because the *anēr* was all valor, civil war degraded him by reducing him to his nature as *anthrōpos*.

Anthrōpos or *anēr?* A theological-anthropological reading or a purely political one? The question is complicated, because it involves a tension internal to the Greek man and gives rise to a variety of possible interpretations. It may even happen that a figure whose dominant connotation, to judge by its recurrence among the city's thinkers, is undeniably political (for example, the metaphor of the city as ship in the turbulence of civil war) traces its remote origins back to the Hesiodic discourse on the human condition. It is clear, however, that the dilemma runs through all of Greek thought, where it receives a variety of responses, not always unequivocal. To confine our attention to the work of Xenophon, note, for example, that in the Kinadon conspiracy the historian distinguishes between *andres* and *anthrōpoi*, with the leader himself designated as *anēr* (*Hellenica* 3.3.11), while his makeshift army consists of *anthrōpoi* (3.3.7). But Xenophon can also unambiguously blame the *stasis* on the *anthrōpoi* alone, as he does in discussing the affairs of Phleious, where he distinguishes between the small group of seditious "men"[55] who betray their city and the *andres* who are its citizens (*Hellenica* 5.3.16).

Anthrōpoi or *andres*, *anthrōpoi* and *andres*: we will not attempt to choose between the two models, any more than the Greeks did. Since we are dealing with a phenomenon peculiar to the city, we tend to prefer the political version of civil war, particularly since the anthropological representations have been shown to be fragmentary (abstract bestiality but not cannibalism), frequently allusive, interpolated into the heart of another discourse, and always scattered through texts of which they never constitute the sole register.

Thus to reduce *stasis* to savagery alone is to risk obliterating its significance for the Greeks by covering up the disturbing connections between civil war and *polemos* (which, paradoxically, transform it into something like an order) and *dikē*, especially when, because transcendent Justice is embodied in the city in positive judicial procedures, or *dikai* (which we may translate as trials), we can associate, as Plato emphatically does, *dikai kai staseis*, trials and dissensions, or, as Aristotle does, treat the judge [*dikastēs*] as a "divider in two" [*dikhastēs*].[56]

These are disturbing connections, to be sure, but we must do justice to this straddling of boundaries that the Greeks were bold enough to imagine despite their preference for clear-cut distinctions. Otherwise, we risk depoliticizing the city through a "mental dodge": by manipulating the horror that rivets the texts, thought prevents itself from thinking.[57]

I am prepared to offer the following hypothesis: *stasis* was like any other civil war from early modern history right up to the present day. It gave concrete political form to horror,[58] but that alone does not entitle us to identify with chaos something that interferes with our powerful desire for order.

TRANSLATED BY ARTHUR GOLDHAMMER

Notes

[1] *Nomos*: pasture, residence, abode (Chantraine 1968). If *nomos* is to be understood here as "abode," there is no reason why the overdetermined sense "pasture" may not also be present in the world turned upside-down: men have become animals, indeed, animals out of place in their new environment. Finally, even if, in the context of Sokles' speech, *isonomia* is replaced by *isokratia*, the implicit reference to the word *nomos* cannot be ruled out.

[2] Beginning with the use of the term *miaiphonos*, an epithet applied to Ares in the *Iliad* and to the seditious in Xenophon (*Hellenica* 4.4.6), but one might also mention the way in which, in Theognis, the pregnant city engenders a strong man, a "restorer" of *hubris* (43–44), as well as *stasis* (51–52: *ek tōn gar staseis te kai emphuloi phonoi andrōn/mounarkhoi te*), or even the violent leader of a crude *stasis* (1081–82). Note, moreover, that while the Platonic tyrant drinks the blood of his ancestors (*Republic* 7.565e), *stasis* sheds *haima emphulion* (Pausanias 2.20.2).

[3] Confining our attention just to Book 4, see, on humanity: 14.7 (*anthrōpinōs*), 23. 1 (*ta dikaia kai philanthrōpa*), 54. 5 (*philanthrōpōs*); see also the use of the verb "to civilize" in the passage under study (21.4: *exēmeroun*; 21.11: *hēmerōsin*). Savagery: 77.4 (*turannon agrion*); bestiality: 3.1 (the *thēriōdēs bios* of the Aetolians).

[4] In the immediate vicinity of Kynaitha, at Lousoi (Polybius 18.9–11), Artemis was celebrated as *Hēmerasia*, because she supervised Melampous's purification of the daughters of Proïtos (Pausanias 8.18.8); in Kynaitha itself, the only two cults mentioned by Pausanias are a festival of Dionysus and the spring *Alussos*, which cures one of *lussa*, "madness" (8.19.2–3).

[5] Borgeaud 1979, 37, 39, followed by Vernant 1990a, 144.

[6] Ibid., 33–38.

[7] Frontisi-Ducroux 1981, 48 (emphasis added).

[8] See Pindar *Paean* 9.

[9] See for example Frontisi-Ducroux 1981, 48 and n. 59.

[10] Vernant 1990, 173.

[11] Such as that which placed the 1870 massacre of Hautefaye under the sign of "the animal metaphor" (Corbin 1990, 98) and the "lexicon of hogs" (ibid., 100–111).

[12] On animalization as an obvious theme of the Carnival of Romans, see Le Roy Ladurie 1979, passim, and especially 240 (the "bestiary" of the Carnival).

[13] On the question of human sacrifice, see Henrichs 1981.

[14] Tragedy, of course, played on this, always in a perfectly ambiguous way: here the victims were not *andres* but young girls, who were more readily animalized—for the imaginary cannot entirely neglect the real—as heifers and fillies; see Loraux 1985, 62–68.

[15] The Mantineans would later indicate their horror at the impious Kynaithean *sphagē* by purifying their city in the prescribed manner, carrying victims (*sphagia*) around their territory in procession after a visit from Kynaithean envoys (Polybius 4.21.8).

[16] By extracting the verb (*apo-, kata-*) *sphazō* from its sacrificial context and placing it in the context of civil war, the text suggests the murderous nature of the act, whereas *thuō* denotes the sacrificial norm by omitting the slitting of the throat.

[17] Scene analyzed by J.-L. Durand, "Bêtes grecques," in Detienne–Vernant 1979, 146–48.

[18] On *bōmos* and *trapeza* see Durand 1986, 116–23.

[19] For example, Theognis 143–44; on the "iron age" in Megara, see Nagy 1985.

[20] See Loraux 1984, 203–4, and especially 1993a, 107–18.

[21] This is obvious in the case of *makhaira*: see Detienne–Vernant 1979, 234; *xiphos*: ibid., 184; *obeliskos*: ibid., 148, 154–55, 180, 185; *pelekus*: ibid., 178, 258 (note that this is Por-

phyry's term for Sopatros' hatchet (see Durand 1986, 44ff.); *drepanon*: ibid., 204–5. For ax (*axinē*), I have not yet found any sacrificial use, but Homer and Herodotus treat it as a weapon (for the latter, at 7.64, it is a Sacian weapon). Compare the double meaning, both ritual and aggressive, of the rakes, brooms, and threshing flails brandished by the dancers of Saint-Blaise in Romans in 1580 (see Le Roy Ladurie, 1979, 201–2).

[22] Detienne-Svenbro, in Detienne–Vernant 1979, 234.

[23] Durand 1986, 49, interprets the presence of a hatchet in the Sopatros story as a source of confusion, because in the mythical source the hatchet introduced "an agricultural type of activity into the sacrificial zone." But the connection between sacrifice and agriculture is complicated in the Kinadon story, in which the sacrifice is implicit while the tools for working the earth are explicitly appropriated for the purpose of seditious violence.

[24] Vidal-Naquet 1981, 219, 225.

[25] {See Paradiso 1995.}

[26] See Loraux 1993, 118.

[27] *Anabasis* 4.8.14 (Xenophon's speech to his troops): "those people," *kai ōmous dei kataphagein*.

[28] Quotation from Vernant 1990a, 177.

[29] See Nagy 1985, 71–74 and 75 (for comparison with Odysseus).

[30] The very formulation of this wish, with Achilles desiring that *his anger* unleash itself to the point of driving him to cannibalism, as if his *ego* could not accept responsibility for such an act even fictively, indicates the force of the taboo. What is more, Achilles (like Hecuba, who, in her despair, expresses herself in the first person (24.212) knows full well that in reality "it is the dogs and the birds who will feast" on Hector's corpse.

[31] See Frontisi-Ducroux 1981, 36, and, for the connection between animal skins and savagery in the dress of helots, A. Paradiso, *Corps spartiate*, forthcoming in N. Loraux and Y. Thomas, eds., *Le Corps du citoyen* (but dressing in animal skins often connotes a situation in which the world is turned upside down: see Le Roy Ladurie 1979, 215–16). No doubt Gregory Nagy (1985, 44 n.) is right to observe that line 24 of Theognis (*oute dikēn oute nomous*) evokes the Cyclops of the *Odyssey* (9.215), but the allusion is both too discreet and too limited to the question of justice for it to be possible to bring in the Cyclops' eating of raw flesh, which Nagy does not do.

[32] Ibid.: "The *kakoi* turn the community inside out (Theognis 56–57), upside down (Theognis 679)."

[33] Le Roy Ladurie 1979, 215–16, 233.

[34] See Detienne 1977.

[35] The expression is that of F. Lestringant 1982.

[36] See Borgeaud, cited in n. 5.

[37] The relation between *stasis* and impiety is not reversible: while all *stasis* is impious, impiety does not necessarily imply civil war.

[38] Like Dionysos *Omēstēs*: see Alcaeus, fr. 129 Campbell, v. 9.

[39] In Sokles' speech, with which this study began: for Herodotus, tyranny is even more of a symbol of the world turned upside-down than *stasis* is.

[40] See I.67.6, 70.1, 79.8 (in strong opposition to Geskon's *philanthrōpia*, 81.9). Compare this with the single occurrence in the story about Kynaitha.

[41] In 67.6, animalization is the ultimate end, representing a stage beyond normal human wickedness. In 80.10, the bodies of Geskon's executed partisans seem to have been devoured "as if by beasts" (*hōsper hupo thēriōn*): with this comparison, a line has been crossed; in 81.9, bestiality seems to be one possible state of human nature, an excess of which takes men beyond their nature. But it is also true that already, in 81.7, Polybius the Stoic observed that "no animal exhibits a ferocity (*ōmoteron*) more complete than

man." All this unfolds against a background of constant opposition between bestiality and *philanthrōpia*.

[42] Hesiod *Works and Days* 240–45 (the city of unjust men); Thucydides 2.44.3 (the plague). *Limos*, like *loimos*, was often conceived as the punishment for sacrilege (see Hesiod, *loc. cit*, and, e.g., Herodotus 6.139).

[43] Diels-Kranz fr. B 80.

[44] Thucydides 3.82.1: *Houtōs ōmē <hē> stasis proukhōrōse*. Note, moreover, that all the occurrences of *stasis* are condensed in Book 3: 3.36.4 (to characterize a political decision that goes beyond the limits of the political), 3.84.1 (*stasis*), 3.94.5 (the Eurytanes, savage Aetolians, with incomprehensible language [*kai ōmophagoi*]).

[45] On the phenomenon of demetaphorization, especially in the passage on the plague, see "Un Absent de l'histoire? Le Corps dans l'historiographie thucydidéenne," forthcoming, in N. Loraux and Y. Thomas, eds., *Le Corps du citoyen*.

[46] In 3.81.3, the statement that the suppliants kill one another "in the sanctuary itself" suffices to suggest the magnitude of the transgression. Note the difference from Polybius's text quoted above and in n. 30.

[47] Except in Euripidean tragedy, which confuses the orders at will (the suicide of Menoikeus in the *Phoenician Women* or of the daughters of Erechtheus in *Erechtheus*).

[48] The method of suicide involves the throat, whether by hanging or plunging an arrow into the throat.

[49] Theognis 51 [. . .]. Recall that in the catalogue of children of the Night, Eris gives birth *androktasias te neikea te* (*Theogony* 228–29).

[50] On this reversibility, of which the exemplary incarnation is the figure of Ares, see N. Loraux 1986b, 335–54 and 1987, 101–24.

[51] See Loraux 1989.

[52] On this general inversion of signs, see Loraux 1986; on the inversion of all things associated with *andreia*, see Loraux 1989, 287–89.

[53] Thucydides 3.82. 2: *heōs an hē autē phusis anthrpōpōn ēi*. See also 3.84.2 (*anthrōpeia phusis*).

[54] By contrast, since the nature of women simply sets a limit below which they must not sink (2.45.2), *stasis* allowed them to outdo themselves in an exceptional way: see Loraux 1989, 289–91.

[55] Using other categories and other oppositions, we might well translate this as "individuals."

[56] Loraux 1995.

[57] I borrow this formulation from Marie-Danièle Demélas.

[58] This is not to say that horror in politics has nothing to do with humanity, as the celebrated chorus in *Antigone* proves in the case of the Greeks.

NICOLE LORAUX

Epilogue:
Once Again, the Woman, the Virgin,
Female Athenians

1981

The Children of Athena *explores the relationship between Athenian ideas about citizenship and myths about the origins of the city and its offspring, tracing an Athenian topography within which the role of women is radically circumscribed—in practice as well as in the imagination; beyond the city limits, it locates Athenian democracy's particular exclusion of women from civic activity within a pervasive traditional discourse about women as an intrinsically "separate race." Here, as in* The Experiences of Tiresias *[see selection II.4], Loraux's work brings to the structural study of myths a precise historical framework, as well as perspectives from psychoanalysis, to yield a historical anthropology that (as exemplified also in the work of Pierre Vidal-Naquet) bypasses the assumed antinomy between historicism and structural analysis. Here, as elsewhere [see Loraux 1997], Loraux is interested in the tensions and fissures that the ideology of civic harmony seeks to reintegrate. A second edition of* The Children of Athena, *nine years after the first, provided the occasion for Loraux's reflections here on the controversies stirred by her argument that, despite Athens' claims to inclusiveness, "female Athenians* (Athéniennes) *do not exist"—and her forceful exposition of a "politics of ideas about men and women."*

The announcement of a new edition of *The Children of Athena* immediately provoked my desire—or perhaps revealed my need—to write a few more pages, eleven years after the completion of this book, and nine years after its publication. Desire or necessity—I could not say. But I

From *The Children of Athena: Athenian Ideas About Citizenship and the Division Between the Sexes*, trans. Caroline Levine (Princeton: Princeton University Press, 1993), pp. 237–51 [Afterword to the second edition of *Les enfants d'Athéna: Idées athéniennes sur la citoyenneté et la division des sexes* (Paris: François Maspero, 1981).]

write these few pages after the fact to thank Olivier Bétourné for including this book in the collection of "Points" editions. And to make a point myself by taking stock of the current situation.

This undertaking involves mentioning a few names, expressing some regrets, and examining the forceful arguments of several critical responses. Most of all, it entails admitting in 1990 that I am essentially still in agreement with the book that I published in 1981. It is not that *The Children of Athena* is anything like the "last word" on the subject of autochthony as it is linked to Athenian representations of citizenship and images of the division between the sexes. Other books can no doubt be written on this subject—indeed, they have been, and will be again—but this is the only one I could have written, and so I have done.

It is not that one could not find gaps or, as I both know and suspect, some inaccuracies of detail here or there. I take full responsibility for these lapses and errors, yet I will not take them up here since readers have already absorbed the book in its original form. But it looks as if Erichthonios and Pandora have become favorite topics for Hellenists over the last ten years—we can ascribe this phenomenon to the spirit of age, if we wish—and I seize the opportunity to write this epilogue so that I can enter briefly into the heart of these debates, which, in 1981, I never suspected would be in the making, or so richly sustained.

First of all, I should mention the works that were written without reference to this book, but which, to my great satisfaction, have shared many of its conclusions. I will not attempt to provide an exhaustive list, but here are just a few examples: an article on the birth of Erichthonios, in which both the "mother" and father of the autochthonous Athenian are assured of their proper roles; a study on the Parthenos statue of Pheidias as an incarnation of the city; and—though not addressing the same questions as this book—a monograph on Greek images of fertile dew.[1]

Under the second rubric, I should cite the contributions made by certain readers of the book. Once again, I am choosing very selectively and no doubt unfairly. First, then, the "users": one insists on "the virgin and politics"; another turns the analysis of autochthonous filiation around to serve some very personal reflections about "circular filiation"; and a third, according to the routine game of association, condenses Anna Freud and Athena into "Annathena."[2] But it is only right, as a matter of ethics, to pause for a while over additions and criticisms: one is the kindly and generous critique of Claude Lévi-Strauss, which reformulates a question I had posed in inadequate terms (following Hume, it is true, but unaware of the fact) on the subject of Athenian prohibitions against incest;[3] and two articulate critics who rely on a different interpretation of Athenian autochthony: Pierre Brulé reconstructs the myth with spirit and conviction in a book on "the religion of the girls" of Athens, and Marcel Detienne, in his typically keen and lively way, responds, point for point, to all those propositions that he, for his part, considers too militant for his taste.[4] I will return to this later.

Then there are the inevitable adjustments and corrections that historians of ancient Greece know they are doomed to make whenever recent archaeological discoveries invalidate canonical interpretations that are merely borrowed from a long tradition, since we lack the ability to make effective use of those instruments which might challenge the prestige of scientific authority. The grotto of Aglauros, for instance, is no longer north of the Acropolis, as we had been told, but east of it, at the foot of the ramparts of the sacred enclosure.[5] I acknowledge this all the more willingly because the correction changes nothing in my project, but only affects the map of the Acropolis I used, which I found in someone else's work, and have therefore simply left as is,[6] entrusting my readers with the responsibility of mentally moving the contested grotto.

Finally, I could modify a book centered on the question of the gender of politics by joining more recent, thoughtful studies to a more classically political perspective, citing the instances and uses of the myth of autochthony in the relations Athens maintained with the world outside—in the sphere of ideas. We would certainly have a better understanding, then, of how representations of a "pure" lineage should be distinguished from modern racist ideologies. And we would commit ourselves to the opposition that often recurs in official rhetoric, between the autochthons—who have always been there, right from the beginning—and the citizens of "other cities," who are forever immobilized in their status as "newcomers," eternal metics on their own civic earth.[7] And we could wonder about the inherent aporia built into an ideal whose formulation can only be a negative one.[8] But that would be a different book, and one that would not necessarily be relevant. It is therefore time to enter right into the heart of the subject. Which brings me back, as I predicted, to express a few regrets before turning to examine the most strongly articulated critiques.

The regrets, then. Or, rather, to give just a selection: a hesitation and a single regret.

When interpreting the gesture of the divine child toward Athena, was I too hasty in believing that I could interject a reference to the rites of the Amphidromia? Pierre Brulé thinks so, and has said so very plainly.[9] I admit that I found these observations disturbing—those which concerned the Amphidromia, at least, if not the interpretation of the gesture made by Erichthonios, which I have always seen as directed toward a paternal figure. Yet perhaps we should both reflect on Annalisa Paradiso's interpretation of the rite, which comes at the end of a careful reexamination of the evidence pertaining to the Amphidromia. Her study takes the feminine role into account along with that of the male: "Once *delivered again by Hestia* and *recognized by his father*," she observes, "the newborn at last enters into his paternal *oikos*."[10] And since this is certainly Hestia's domain, it is worth asking whether the goddess is as exclusively "familial" as we hear over and over again. It seems as though there now is a trend toward a redefinition of Hestia and the *hestia* in distinctly political terms.[11] In short, I am wary of trying to settle the question, and gladly leave the ritual of the Amphidromia to those more competent than I in matters of rites of integration. After all, a little doubt is never a bad idea.

As for my regret—its name is Plato. In spite of a long-standing desire to study what Plato makes of Athenian autochthony in his work, I have never confronted the question in all its detail, neither in this book nor in any other study. Whether through pure chance or through reverence, I do not know. If I had to rewrite that particular page from *The Children of Athena*, I would no longer be satisfied with the mere assertion that the Platonic version of collective autochthony "is an isolated if not a polemical one with respect to the dominant tradition," since, contrary to this tradition, Plato resolutely places the emphasis on the mother. Others have noticed this quasi-anomaly in the *Menexenos* and elsewhere; I myself have returned to this less orthodox aspect of the Socratic (or Aspasian) *epitaphios*.[12] But if in the past, in the wake of my *Invention of Athens*, it seemed both legitimate and necessary to organize the group of *epitaphioi* into a coherent corpus, characterized—with some exceptions—by its orthodoxy, I would now be glad to clarify my choice of the *Menexenos* in the light of the rather unusual reevaluation that all of Plato's work tends to make, when confronting the maternal figure, in what is obviously a deliberate move.

But once again, now is not the time for regrets, and I come to those essential questions which have been amply debated over the last ten years.

The honor of opening this list of questions goes to the paradigmatic feminine, since there has been a considerable number of studies on this subject.

Let us therefore begin with Pandora. Or to put it better, since I have confined myself to the text of the *Theogony*, let us begin with the woman introduced by Zeus into the world of men. Insisting on her status as an artifact, I saw her as a kind of denial of the supposed omnipotence of the agrarian metaphor, in which woman is a field to be plowed. It is certainly an institutional metaphor in the Athenian ceremony of marriage, but historians of Greek religion tend to turn it a little too hastily into an inevitable representation. In opposing this standard reading, I insisted—I persist on insisting—on the quality of *thauma*, which distinguishes the woman: a marvelous object, pure imitation, a copy of herself.

Reading Hesiod again, Pierre Lévêque was just as intent on rediscovering a mother-goddess in Pandora as I was in trying to distance her from this figure, and he "connected" this image of "terrifying femininity," this incarnation of the curse that is feminine sexuality, to the primordial cohort of Great Mothers—especially when they turn terrible.[13]

The horizon of fertility is not far off. It has been reinstated, with all of its prerogatives, by Pierre Judet de La Combe, who confirms Pandora's status as the mother of humanity.[14] His project is, of course, entirely different from mine, since I wanted to read Hesiod's text for itself alone and not from the insufficiently hermeneutical perspective of its "reception."[15] Hence, situating "Pandora" (though it would be better not to use this name when the issue is the textual economy of the *Theogony*, in all its specific details)[16] in the continual process of generation, which makes up the history of the gods, requires that we see her as a "rupture" that defined the particular status of men when faced with the gods. With her creation, men become mortal in the very movement of the text, as the transition from *anthrōpoi* (586) to *thnētoi anthrōpoi* (588) confirms. This is an important point, and I can do no more than give wholehearted support to this fine analysis of the text, which focuses on narrative development. But since the woman introduces the ultimate division between humankind and the gods, I confess that I do not grasp why these lines should apply more to the question of men and gods than to that of woman and her status, as if there were no necessary link between them. Moreover, along with the shift noted by Judet de La Combe, I will persist in emphasizing what it is (also present and just as crucial in this passage) that brings human men (*anthrōpoi*) to become virile men (*andres*), and, when faced with the category of women, to discover they are merely one half of humanity.

But Jean Rudhardt had already urged readers of Hesiod to accept a devastating revision. "Pandora"—and of course the woman from the *Theogony* cannot escape this name—is not the first woman.[17] To temper the abruptness of this formulation and to put it more precisely, she is not the first feminine being: she is simply the first truly human woman, committed to life in civilized society. This disclosure is in order and deserves to be examined more closely.

Until Rudhardt, and the force of the evidence he marshaled for his conclusions, no one had gone so far as to formulate the idea that the feminine, in the *Theogony*, extends well beyond the woman fashioned by Hephaistos; therein lies an important observation. It is perfectly true that the distribution of masculine and feminine roles in the world of men is very different from the situation among the gods, and, to define the feminine in Hesiodic terms, we ought to "consider all the feminine beings whom [the poet] describes, from monsters to goddesses."[18] But as far as mortal women are concerned, the affair is much more complicated: if "mortal creatures" had been in existence since the first generations of the *Theogony*—such as Medusa, an example cited by Rudhardt—there is nothing to indicate that they were, in fact, "women"; on the contrary, in Hesiod's text, everything points to an absolutely indecipherable status when it comes to the opposition between men and gods.[19] As for the "worthy mothers" in the *Works and Days*, who acquire an existence by the side of the men of the silver race, they are only needed for the sake of the narrative: there must be mothers to watch over these overgrown children, and nothing gives us license to introduce these maternal figures from the *Works and Days* into the mythical chronology of the *Theogony* in order to construct a single and distinctive linear time, a line that reaches beyond the difference in the narrative strategies that distinguishes the two texts.

The woman in the *Theogony* is certainly not the first feminine being in the poem. Yet since she is a *thauma* destined for humankind, we must see her as that unique product, that rupture of a former existence that the first woman represents for men. And the proof is even more secure, since nothing in the text claims that the goddesses served as a model for Hephaistos in these circumstances, as in the case for Pandora in the *Works and Days*. Thus, I will not hesitate to repeat myself on this point: the only model for this woman, which is paradoxically also her essence, is indeed the *parthenos*.[20]

Parthenos: a "sexually available" being among mortals, to borrow an expression from Ann Bergren;[21] and a virgin among the goddesses. A virgin like Athena, who is the single figure that gives the present book its unity.

Let us take another step, one already taken elsewhere in the course of the book. Let us dare to maintain that what constitutes a *parthenos*, both in the human world and among the gods, is her virginity. Throughout this book, against all received definitions of *parthenos*—all sociologically based in their characterization of her as a "marriageable girl"—I wanted to restore meaning to this term, both as the chapters of the book unfolded and in its index. The logic of the texts and the logic of the Greek imaginary invited me to do so, without, however, prompting me to focus explicitly on the Greek definition of virginity. This task has now been accomplished, thanks to Giulia Sissa's research in her work *The Virginal Body*.[22]

Parthenia is thus not only a negative status, and "its relevance is not limited to one period of a woman's life"—here, Sissa's argument seems conclusive to me. In order to give meaning to the word, we must understand how it is related to "a specific attitude in matters of sexuality." It is not that this virginity without a hymen is something that can be detected on the bodies of young girls, since only the child of the virgin, the *parthenios*, can verify the fact that a girl was indeed seduced by a god. As for the sequel, the vaginal lips of the *parthenos* close up again on her lost *parthenia*, and only trials of virginity can bring her secret to light.[23]

So much for the human girl and the deceitful virgin-woman of the *Theogony*. But, as for the goddesses, virginity can only be absolute—that is, its loss is truly "irreparable." The virgin Athena, whatever she might be, and whatever might be said about her, is not the "mother" of Erichthonios, unless we make use of an infinite set of quotation marks. At most, as Pierre Brulé correctly observes, she is his "false mother."[24] However, after having copied this phrase, I will follow a vastly different route from Pierre Brulé.

In spite of the bold constructions that Brulé superimposes on the myth of Erichthonios, I continue to consider only the "ideas" of classical Athens relevant to my project—that is, the story of the divine child's birth, as told by texts and vases of the fifth century. Far from being a mere accessory, Athena plays an essential part as the object of Hephaistos's desire and as the *trophos* (nurse) who receives the child from Earth the mother; like a father, she guarantees his *paideia* so that the autochthonous child can become a real citizen of Athens, or even better, so that he can be the paradigmatic citizen that he is, right down to the peculiar conditions of his birth.

Since the aim of my book is an analysis of the thought processes that take place *hic et nunc* around the myth of autochthony in classical Athens, the search for the origin of the story is not my concern. It is possible—although I confess that I am not wholly convinced—that in a very distant, prehistoric past, the "mother" of Erichthonios was not Athena,[25] or even Gē, but the "ancient mother" Agraulos, who, in the course of history, was gradually deprived of her generative power as a goddess-mother without a masculine partner. In other words, Ge, and then Athena and Hephaistos (in a word, the entire story, which is what disturbs me), have only been introduced as a later reworking of the myth. At the beginning, then, there would have been nothing to imagine or to dream about concerning an event as unthinkable as it is unrepresentable, since solitary births are never recounted. But anyone who wants to capture a sense of the myth *within* the city will not be so interested in the origin of the myth—so dear to Brulé—and will be more concerned with the myth itself, since the story constructs an origin for Athenians to use in their daily lives of the present.

I do not mean that there is not a great deal to be derived from the system of the "religion of young girls," which Pierre Brulé, in his zeal for reconstruction, patiently and passionately exposes, in all its complex workings, especially the "repulsion" displayed on the Acropolis toward "adult feminine sexuality."[26] But the most remarkable thing is that the entrenchment of the myth in the present and the search for origins meet, in perfect accord, around the purely masculine interpretation of Athenian autochthony in the classical city—to such an extent that I take credit for all that is said in Brulé's book about the "ambiguity of the role of the woman in the Athenian matrimonial system": "She transmits; she *is* not. But the quality of blood cannot be perfected without her. She transmits autochthony, but does not possess it in her person."[27] Let us transpose this situation into the theater of Dionysos, where it will be subject to the techniques of condensation that belong to the tragic genre. Kreousa is the woman—or the girl—from Athens, who will ultimately transmit autochthony, after all the problems have been dramatized, right up to the moment of her transition to the intention to commit murder.[28]

Kreousa interests me in the *Ion* just for this reason: she is a reflection, in tragedy, on what autochthony makes of the women of Athens. This choice doubtless led me to pass over other important aspects of this play in silence, such as the Dionysiac dimension, with the echo effects that join Ion to Dionysos, who, like him, is twice-born, and like him, is both a stranger and a native of his land. But once more it is against the background of autochthony that I return to the *Ion*—that is, to Kreousa as *parthenos* and as mother, as *epiklēros* (heiress) and as the paradoxical bearer of autochthonous lineage.

From this perspective, I attach great importance to a study by Arlene Saxon-house[29] written without any actual contact with "Autochthonous Kreousa." The conjunction between us (and there has indeed been one) is all the more valuable to me because of the differences that dictate the specific characteristics of our two sets of questions. Her piece moves from one Athenian lie to another, from Plato's "beautiful lie"—which, as we know, is an autochthonous affair—to the lie that remains at the end of the *Ion*, which leaves Xouthos out of the picture, but also leaves out the collectivity of the Athenians, which is a far more serious matter. Thus, the essay examines the difficulties inherent in the concept of autochthony and its treatment in tragedy—the genre that, after the fact, examines the way the myth functioned. Since Saxonhouse's aim is to present the city, this contractual creation, as if it were a natural entity from the beginning, the myth of autochthony is seen as an operator of exclusion: the original exclusion of "others." And here ideas about autochthony come to contradict and limit that other Athenian representation of Athens, as a city "open" to foreigners. It is a denial of conflict, excluded from the story of origins as it must be excluded from the contemporary life of the city;[30] and it is also a denial of women, who, from the outset, are excluded from the founding of Athens as well as from the procreation of the first Athenian. It is peculiar to the tragic genre to make the myth work on itself, and in the *Ion* there is a kind of critical "revision"[31] of the principles of autochthony. Revealing what I, for my part, had called the "dark face" of autochthony leads to a direct look at the violence of the story of origins and at the exclusion that is obscured beneath the praise of pure Athenian stock. But since the exclusion of women contains within it the seeds of all the other issues, it is the problem of woman that tragedy tackles first of all, with all the effectiveness peculiar to fiction. In Saxonhouse's reading, woman, in the person of Kreousa, is reintroduced into the period of origins at the close of the play. I would even say that she is integrated into the time of the necessary continuation of Athens. And through the relation that is constantly questioned between mother and son, maternity is finally recognized as a central part of the Athenian system of citizenship.

Comforted by this interpretation, whose coherence brings essential elements to my own reading, as it is defined in this book, and supported in my hypothesis that there is much to be understood from the *Ion* on the question of the gender of politics, I hold more than ever to the analyses I developed under the rubric "Autochthonous Kreousa." Indeed, under this heading, we must sense both an oxymoron (since, in the logic of the civic myth, women are not, and should not be, autochthonous) and an invitation to reexamine the orthodoxy of citizenship, paradoxically refocused in the figure of the "female Athenian."

One "female Athenian"? Perhaps. But more than one female Athenian? Let us open up the subject once again.

Female Athenians, as I have claimed, do not exist. In this phrase, I was condensing a linguistic fact (the documented absence of the term *Athēnaia*), a story

about the women's loss of the title of female Athenians (which strongly resembles an *aition*), and the avoidance of heterosexual reproduction in the myth
of the birth of Erichthonios. The first point has been contested, as a way of
unsettling—and why not?—the entire structure. *Athēnaia* certainly does exist,
they say, in an inscription concerning the priestess of Athena Nike, who was
chosen from "among the female Athenians," as Marcel Detienne affirms.[32] But
if we want to produce an *Athēnaia*, it would be better not to look for her in the
restoration of an epigrapher: indeed, the text, which has holes in the worst
possible places, stops right here at the crucial moment—the ending, masculine
or feminine, is missing. Obviously, if we wished, *ex Athēnaiōn hapa* could be
completed in the feminine (*ex Athēnaiōn hapa[sōn]*), but we could also legitimately presume that the priestess was chosen *ex Athēnaiōn hapa[nton]*—from
among the Athenians. All the *Athenians*: if the *identity* of a woman necessarily
passes through that of a man—father, or husband—then the men, not surprisingly, are those givers of identity, who, by definition, will furnish any Athenian
woman they like with her institutional framework.[33] But also, she would be
chosen from *all* the Athenians—which means that the priestess would have
been chosen democratically, out of the entire Athenian collective, with no preference accorded to a particular *genos*. In short, the example is not so devastating
as it was supposed to be. Thus, I am betting that we must wait for another,
better-documented *Athēnaia* to come along, if I am to revise my somewhat facile formulation.

In fact, the real question lies elsewhere for Marcel Detienne. It is the very
idea of a purely masculine autochthony that he challenges, in favor of a feminine autochthony.[34] A generalized autochthony, then, as much feminine as
masculine, but above all, the "autochthony of female Athenians"—as if, when
we follow the texts that regularly decline autochthony in the masculine, we
have already embarked on the (inadvisable) route of denouncing a city of
males. The privileged representative of this happy autochthony in the feminine, which would eliminate conflicts in all reflections of the city, is Euripides'
Praxithea, the wife of the autochthonous king Erechtheus and the "heroine" of
the tragedy that bears her husband's name (since the tragedy is indeed called
Erechtheus and not *Praxithea*).[35] Through Praxithea, Detienne claims, "respect
should be paid to the female Athenians, to the strength of the women of Athens, who are autochthons with no complexes about it."[36] That is all well and
good. My project is certainly not to return to the whole series of controversies
about Praxithea. I would simply point out that when it is a matter of a tragic
character and not of an ordinary "female Athenian," it is hazardous to attribute
a psychology to her, whether she has a "complex" or not—what is good for
Oedipus is good for Praxithea, and if one insists on calling up the "complexes"
of female Athenians, why not point straight at Praxithea, for whom a daughter
is just a poor substitute for the male children who could defend the country,
and who sacrifices her daughter only because she has no sons to send off to

war?[37] I will add, to avoid any quarrel over words, that it would certainly be appropriate to agree about the meaning of the word *autochthōn* from the beginning. If we take the word to mean the offspring of the "earth itself" is the term still pertinent and applicable for Praxithea, who is the daughter of a river? Let us hope, then, that a kind of discriminating typology of primordial creatures might be established, in which the autochthonous child would have its place and the daughter of the river hers. But let us leave the issue here, since what is at stake goes far beyond autochthony.

Did writing *The Children of Athena* simply mean yielding to the spirit of polemic, which, "here and elsewhere, means denouncing the injustice done for millennia to the condition of women"? If describing amounts to denouncing, I will certainly have to admit to it (although I am not sure that the most active female practitioners of women's history would be satisfied with such an equivalence). But what kind of book could it be, if it had no other project than simply to *comprehend* the mechanisms that guide a certain set of thought processes? Indeed, I am not absolutely positive that these thought processes, in their largest and most general sense, are Greek alone. Will the "war of the sexes" be discussed, or will it be "taking a position on the gender of mythology"? The reader will have guessed that this book is aimed not at mythology but at politics (a politics of ideas about men and women). Can we admit, then, that in a society that reserves politics for men—such as the privilege of representing the paradigm of humanity, to cite the major example—it is the feminine, whether we like it or not, that discriminates,[38] because the task of gathering the imprint of all the hesitations, problems, and patterns of compromise always reverts to the feminine, as to the *khōra* in Plato's *Timaeus*. Which is how we get to Praxithea, and to Kreousa, who are specifically called "autochthonous" here.

It is the task of the readers, if they so wish, to choose between the gender of politics and feminine autochthony. But in doing so, let them be aware, at least, that there is no statement about Athens, even when cloaked in the terms of scientific neutrality, that does not nourish very contemporary passions. I was naive if I thought I could escape from them. But then, I never really believed I could.

The debate—indeed, all the debates called up in these few pages—remains open, even if, for clarity's sake, I have been eager to tell which of the sides was mine. May this controversy remain always open and may its arguments be always further refined.

And let us continue to discuss, at length, the question of the sexual identity of the "true" children of Athena.

TRANSLATED BY CAROLINE LEVINE

NOTES

[1] Miralles 1982 {May 1984} and Boedeker 1984, whose fifth chapter, entitled "Dew and Athenian Autochthony," accepts the essential conclusions proposed by *The Children of Athena*; the perspective as a whole, however, presents a kind of analysis I would never have imagined (which is why I include this study here).

[2] {Jaulin 1987} Daraki 1985, 142–52, and Trilling 1983.

[3] Lévi-Strauss 1983. I would like to come back to this question in my book *La Famille d'Oedipe*, which will be published by Editions de Seuil.

[4] Brulé 1987, 13–175; Detienne, in Sissa and Detienne 1989, 231–54 and 288–92.

[5] {Dontas 1983} has proved this point.

[6] See 150 and 197: the maps are borrowed from {Travlos 1971}.

[7] See Loraux 1990b, especially 119–29. Parker (1988, 195) makes the excellent point that "Athenians en masse were invited to despise other states (Dorians above all), just as an aristocrat might despise a metic. Athenians were, so to speak, the only authentic citizens of Greece, all other groups were mere immigrants." Thus, by setting up an opposition between autochthons and citizens in name, Praxithea in Euripides' *Erechtheus* aims less at metics, as Detienne 1989a, 240, suggests, than at citizens of other cities.

[8] Loraux 1990b, 129–33. Another aporia is that of an autochthonous *oikein*, since as Casevitz 1985 has shown, *oikein* means a residence plain and simple, and not some natural relationship to the soil one may occupy.

[9] Brulé 1987, 58–59, and 61–65 on *Les Enfants d'Athéna*.

[10] {Paradiso 1988} 212 (my italics).

[11] Hestia: see Detienne 1989a, 85–98. {The hestia: Leduc 1987.}

[12] See Saxonhouse 1985, who insists on the denigration of the feminine in the autochthonous tradition (258), emphasizes the absence of the male god Hephaistos in the *Menexenos* (259), and ascribes this omission to Aspasia, who is called the "mother" of the discourse. Return to the *Menexenos*: see {Loraux 1990c, 30}.

[13] Lévêque 1988.

[14] Judet de La Combe (with the collaboration of Rolet), "'Pandore' dans la *Theogonie*," working document for the Hesiod colloquium, Lille, October 1989.

[15] I would respond to Judet de La Combe that the idea of reception depends not only on the historicity of the periods in which it is read but also on that of the text itself, which always lends itself, in one form or another, to a plurality of readings. The "race of women" is certainly Hesiodic.

[16] Or else I run the risk of incurring the same criticism that the author himself addresses to J.-P. Vernant for having seen two "versions of the myth" where there are in fact two texts.

[17] Rudhardt 1986.

[18] Ibid., 239. For a project of this kind, see {Loraux 1991}.

[19] The only pertinent opposition is in line 278, between Medusa *thnētē* and her *athanatoi* sisters. The monsters can die, but they are not humans.

[20] Judet de La Combe's grammatical arguments are not enough to convince me that we should understand lines 513–14 as "He received the virgin of Zeus as woman." In that case, we would still have to take account of the very powerful effect—of distance and proximity at the same time—caused by the carrying over of *parthenon* to the beginning of the next line (*gunaika/parthenon*).

[21] Bergren 1989, 19 (as well as 10 and 20).

[22] {Sissa 1987, 100–109; quotation, 101}.

[23] Ibid., 127 and 137–39.

[24] Brulé 1987, 56.

[25] Ibid., 123 and 139, analyzes Athena's "many-sided" nature as reflecting all the phases of femininity: *pais, parthenos, mētēr*, young, adult, and old. Why then as a last resort does he describe her as "rather mannish" on the vases (139), a half-concession that has no impact on the analysis he makes in the rest of the chapter?

[26] Brulé 1987, 139.

[27] Ibid., 395. Marcel Detienne refers to this last phrase, which he views as a "timid conclusion": Sissa and Detienne 1989, 290 n. 64.

[28] Kreousa does not kill Ion, but she is in effect a murderer, if, as {Zeitlin 1989, 184 n. 27} observes, "the ambiguity in Greek between the indicative statement (of action fulfilled) and the conative of attempted action blurs the boundary between 'killing' and 'trying to kill.'"

[29] Saxonhouse 1985.

[30] {Saxonhouse 1986, 264.} By contrast with the Theban version of autochthony, the Athenian version aims for a peaceable type; see Isoc. *Panath.* 120–25, and my recent commentary on this passage: Loraux 1987, 27.

[31] {Saxonhouse (1986, 272)} uses this word: it means a revision or recreation of autochthony, just as in Euripides' *Erechtheus*, Praxithea's act of realignment is meant as a refoundation.

[32] *IG*, I2 24, cited by Detienne in Sissa and Detienne 1989, 240.

[33] Mossé 1983, who also observes that "the priestess, just like the other magistrates, is chosen from among all the female Athenians," insists that religion was an "integrating factor for the women in the community" (152). But it is still not certain that even on these grounds they were anything but "the legitimate wives of Athenian citizens" (153).

[34] "Feminine autochthony is not unthinkable," notes Daraki 1985, 152.

[35] Even if the "real hero is named Praxithea rather than Erechtheus": Detienne in Sissa and Detienne 1989, 239, just as Ion, whether we like it or not, is the eponym for the tragedy, and not Kreousa. We should no doubt distinguish between the "heroine" (Antigone is one, in a tragedy that is not called *Kreon*) and the female character who serves to focus certain problems of the play.

[36] Detienne in Sissa and Detienne 1989, 245.

[37] Austin frag. 5, 22–26 (*anti thēleiōn stakhus / arsēn*).

[38] See Loraux 1990a, 7–26.

PIERRE VIDAL-NAQUET

The Black Hunter Revisited[1]

1986

In Memory of Moses and Mary Finley

This article is an all-purpose retrospective on the pathfinding work of Vidal-Naquet concerning the theme of the "black hunter" in a wide variety of ancient Greek myths. In its historical contexts, this mythological theme reflects clearly the ritual patterns of initiation from pre-adult male age-classes. Combining rigorous historical methodology with the perspectives of social anthropology, Vidal-Naquet demonstrates the central relevance of myths about the "black hunter" to the very structure of ancient Greek societies. In the end, he also validates the comparative methodology of Georges Dumézil, who adapted the heuristic techniques of comparative linguistics in reconstructing the "ideologies" of societies (see also the Introduction, note 2).

Like many of its brothers in ambiguity, the "Black Hunter" has a double birthday. Like the First international, it is a French child educated in England. As "Le Chasseur Noir," this paper was first given in Paris, on 6 February 1967, at the Association pour l'Encouragement des Études Grecques, and, a year later (15 February 1968), in Cambridge at the Philological Society. I owe it to the truth to say that in Paris the audience remained mute. In Cambridge, on the contrary, there was a lively discussion, not only among the classicists but also with no less an anthropologist than Edmund Leach, now Sir Edmund. A few months later the paper was first published in Cambridge, on the initiative of the late Denys Page, in a translation by Janet Lloyd and with a dedication to the late Moses Finley, and a little later in Paris.[2] One may easily note here a structural opposition in the form of a chiasmus: in Cambridge, in the university where eminent classicists—Jane Harrison, Francis MacDonald Cornford—were also anthropologists, it was in a purely

From *Proceedings of the Cambridge Philological Society* 212 (1988): 126–44.

philological publication, the *Proceedings*, that the paper was published. In Paris, where the anthropological tradition of classical studies remained, with Louis Gernet and Henri Jeanmaire, and, more recently, with Jean-Pierre Vernant, outside the university proper, it was in the *Annales* that the paper was published.

Marx used to say that man raises problems only when he is able to solve them. I do not pretend to have *solved* any problem, but I am sure that the appearance of a problem is not haphazard. Some years before, I had read a useful little book by Angelo Brelich[3] on the connection between war, religion, and the initiation of young men, which is one of the topics of the "Black Hunter." When it was published I sent my paper to Brelich in Rome, and he answered that he had just given to the printer what became his major book, *Paides e parthenoi*.[4] However, if there was some originality in the "Black Hunter," it was not the subject of the initiation of young men. The pioneer study of the topic had been Henri Jeanmaire's *Couroi et courètes* in 1939, and considerably earlier, his 1913 paper on the Spartan *krupteia*.[5] Nor was it original—indeed it was fairly common—to compare the Attic *ephēbeia* and the Spartan *krupteia*. Rather, the "Black Hunter" was, if not the first attempt to use structural analysis in the classical field,[6] the first endeavor, as far as I know, by a Greek historian, to use specifically, if critically, Lévi-Straussian concepts to understand some features of ancient Greek society.

I said "by a Greek historian"—regarding Moses Finley as a "reality principle"[7]—and I spoke of ancient Greek society; the two are linked together. The problem for me was not the study of Greek myths as such, as it was and partly still is for M. Detienne in Paris, E. Pellizer in Trieste, or J. Fontenrose in California; my problem was the study of the relation between some mythical data and a historical or, rather, a political society.

What was the central intuition of the paper? It was related not to Athens but to Sparta, and was an answer to a question raised by Jeanmaire in 1913. What was the military role of the *krupteia*, this strange institution of Sparta? Did these very select young men, the *kruptoi*, who ran in the mountains during wintertime and killed helots with cunning, undergo a military preparation? Jeanmaire protested: "The whole of Spartan military history cries out against the idea of turning the Spartiate hoplite into a tracker in the bush, clambering over rocks and walls."[8] My answer was that we should read this contract as a table of social opposition. The *kruptos* was to the hoplite what the mountain was to the plain, the *gumnos* youth to the man in armor, the winter to the summer, the cunning killer of helots to the face-to-face fighter of the phalanx, the night to the day, and, of course, the raw to the cooked.

From Sparta, I jumped to Athens, and tried to explain the original myth of the *Apatouria*, the festival of the Phratries, when the young ephebes were admitted into the society of men and citizens. It was the story of Melanthos, the black champion of Athens, using *apatē*, guile, to vanquish Theban King Xanthos, the Fair One. Why was such a strange and "black" story used as a model for the ephebes? The contrast with their famous oath, an oath where they promised to behave like hoplites, was as striking as the opposition between the Spartan *kruptos* and the hoplite. At the Cambridge meeting, Edmund Leach generalized my remarks, observing that in many societies, when one had to undergo a *rite de passage*, the contrast between *before* and *after* was violently underlined, for instance boys dressing up as girls just before their admission into manhood. My third point, after Sparta and Athens, was of course hunting. At that time, Greek hunting was very poorly studied.[9] I had, however, some direct evidence proving, for instance, that a Macedonian noble was not permitted to recline on a couch at a banquet, as grown men did, until he had killed a boar *without the aid of nets*.[10] I found in the *Laws* of Plato[11] and in some other documents the idea of opposing a hoplite-type of hunting, practiced for instance in Sparta, and a pre-hoplite or ephebic type of hunting, using guile, nets, and night. As for the Black Hunter himself, he is a figure who does not exist in Greek literature or documentation, although I have found him at least once in recent literature with no reference to my essay, learning that on occasion he used a boomerang. The Black Hunter, for better or worse, is a creation of mine—it was, however, a title in the French wolf-hunting system—and when I had to choose an image for the jacket of the book bearing this title, I found (on the suggestion of Nicole Loraux) a Black Hunter not in Greek art but in a picture by Uccello in the Ashmolean Museum in Oxford.

Of course my Black Hunter did not lack Greek models. One was the already mentioned Melanthos, the hero of the *Apatouria* tale, the example proposed to the Athenian ephebes, who used to wear a black cloak on some solemn occasions, the fighter who was victorious over Xanthos in the black country (*melainai*), and who was patronized by Dionysos Melanaigis.[12] But Melanthos is not a hunter. A second model is the not less mythical figure of Melanion, whose story is partly sung by the chorus of old men in Aristophanes' *Lysistrata*:[13]

> Let me tell you a little story
> I heard when I was a boy
> How
> There once was a youth [*neaniskos*] called Melanion, who was so appalled at
> the prospect of women he flew to the mountains rather than marry.
> And he hunted hares
> And he set his snares
> With his dog there,
> And never came back for anyone!

But of course, I did not forget that Melanion, the husband of Atalanta, was also the hero of the hunt of the boar of Calydon, a heroic and collective hunt if ever there was one.

I took the Black Hunter as a symbol of the ephebe who misses the *rite de passage*. I took him also as a symbol of a transitory status, and this has been widely misinterpreted—to my astonishment. The reason why the ephebe swears to behave like a hoplite seems to me only too obvious: for the young man *apatē*, guile, is the present, the straightforwardness of the hoplite, the future.

That was "Black Hunter" in 1968. Has he remained unchanged until today? Yes and no. To use a French rhetorical figure, the "Black Hunter" is like Johnny's knife. You may change the blade and change the shaft, it is always Johnny's knife. When I republished the paper in various languages, I of course corrected some inaccuracies, pointed out by reviewers or critics, and added some new evidence, but tried essentially to enlarge the field of the study, by working on neighboring topics: *ephēbeia* and tragedy in Sophocles' *Philoctetes* and in the *Oresteia*,[14] *ephēbeia* as a case study of the relation between history and anthropology,[15] and very recently, Alexander, the royal hunt and the ephebic hunt.[16] When the time came to make a book of my various studies, I could not find a better title than *The Black Hunter*.

Indeed the "Black Hunter" has generated much discussion and controversy. Some scholars have at least accepted my main arguments and, among them, the scholar with the best knowledge of the fourth-century ephebic inscriptions.[17] Sometimes also they have been dismissed, politely by J. K. Anderson, violently by V. di Benedetto who speaks of mystification.[18] Some scholars, of course, were able to add further evidence.[19]

When I now read the original paper, I certainly feel less ashamed at some inaccuracies—there may remain some even in the most recent publication— than at a general tendency to take the various sources at face value, whatever they were, scholia, lyric poetry, mythography, as if all of them could give the same kind of evidence for social history. For instance I even wrote: "Everyone knows, as is confirmed by vase illustrations, that until the time of Herodes Atticus' bounty the Athenian ephebes wore a black chlamys."[20] This was rightly censured by P. G. Maxwell-Stuart,[21] and this shows that in those days, I had the naive, or at least unsophisticated, conception—perhaps shared by Maxwell-Stuart himself—that vase painting could give this kind of realistic evidence. Thanks to the work of some of my younger colleagues in Paris, such as Alain Schnapp and François Lissarrague,[22] I now know that the question was a red herring. I should indeed have known that in archaic and classical times in Athens, the duel, not the phalanx, is the normal form of fighting portrayed *on the vases*, but something obviously very different happened on the battlefield.

If the major weakness of the original paper was in the treatment of the evidence, my first task in revisiting it is to give some examples of how the sources should be treated. I will begin with Homer. Strangely enough, Homer was practically absent from my paper. I did, indeed, mention Dolon, the cunning wolf, and Melanthios, the treacherous goatherd, but not Odysseus and the famous hunt with the sons of Autolycus in *Odyssey* 19, a clearly initiatory episode, which is rightly quoted at the very beginning of J. K. Anderson's recent book. The question I, as a disciple of Moses Finley, who once revisited the *World of Odysseus*,[23] would raise about Homer is a central one, and not only for Homer. How far are we speaking of an institution in an *existing* society, and how far are we speaking of an epic figure or tale? I think I am able to give, in relation to the Black Hunter, an example of both. But, of course, an institution is much less visible than an epic figure. The more familiar the institution is to the audience, the less it will be nominated. We have to infer it from the poem.

It is Benedetto Bravo who made the point I will now develop.[24] When the aged Nestor in *Iliad* 11 (670–762) recalls the time when he was in his *hēbē* (*hōs hēbōoimi*, 670), he describes the quarrel his people had with the Eleians over cattle-rustling. The result was a *razzia* of cattle, but this *razzia* was also a war, a *polemos* (684). Nestor killed his enemy, "and Neleus was glad in his heart that so much had come my way, who was young to go to the fighting."[25] So does Nestor begin his war experience. But, a little later in the same book, the people of Pylos have to participate in a new war, a war with all the *laos*, a war using horses. Neleus refuses to let Nestor participate, he hides his horses, *ou gar pō ti m'ephē idmen polemēia erga* (719), "he thought I was not yet skilled in the work of warfare." Nestor did indeed fight, but secretly and on foot. How are we to explain this discrepancy? It has been suggested that the whole passage is late, and even "grotesquely out of place,"[26] which even if true would not much affect the problem. Is Nestor, this "garrulous old man,"[27] senile? Has he forgotten in verse 719 what he had said in verse 684? This is certainly a kind of "psychological" explanation which should now be set aside. Bravo's suggestion is that we have here *two* kinds of wars, one in which young people, *neoi*, are allowed to fight a war that ends with a return to Pylos by night, and one for adults wearing breastplates (cf. 709, 718), which begins explicitly with dawn (723, 735). The whole of the sequence has no meaning at all, if we do not admit that the opposition between the adult and the ephebe functioned perfectly in "Homeric times." Between the first and the second battle, the ephebe becomes an adult. Nestor is now on the other side of the *hēbē*. This, I suppose, was a normal practice of the world of Odysseus.

But we can also identify in the poems a figure much nearer to the Black Hunter as ideal type, I mean the younger son of Priam and brother of Hector, the "husband" of Helen, Paris-Alexandros, whose double name is a remarkable feature. Paris has been rightly described as *"un héros inachevé,"*[28] an incomplete hero. What was a succession in the *life* of Nestor coexists in the *appearance* of Paris. He is a warrior who kills three people in the *Iliad*, less than Hector but more than Sarpedon. At his first appearance, Paris' costume and equipment are a surprise.[29] He is actually double, archer and normal fighter, male and female, carrying a bow but also two spears, "strange equipment for one also carrying a bow, but . . . also unusual for a spearman."[30] Strange equipment also is his leopard skin, comparable to Dolon's wolf-skin "for night work" in Book 10. Hector insults him: he has "carried away a fair woman, whose lord's kin were spearmen and fighters" (3.48–49), but man and warrior he is not, having only *ta dōr' Aphroditēs* (44), "the favors of Aphrodite," and the deficiencies of an ephebe. When Paris wounds Diomedes in Book 11, the same insults are repeated by the Achaean hero: "you archer, foul fighter lovely in your locks, eyer of young girls. If you were to make trial of me in strong combat with weapons (*sun teukhesi*), your bow would do you no good at all, nor your close-showering arrows" (11.385–87). The bow in the poems has a double meaning. It is an instrument of sovereignty, of Lord Apollo, of Lady Artemis, of Odysseus in his palace. It is also on the side of hunters, which is not in the *Iliad* a heroic activity,[31] associated with Pandaros,[32] on the side of traitors, with Pandaros again, of bastards (Teucer), of inferior peoples (the Locrians of the second Ajax). It is the typical weapon of the Black Hunter. It is sometimes suggested that Paris' strange equipment could be the sign, if not of "a cultural difference," "at least of a different way of looking at things."[33] Its meaning has nothing to do with any foreign culture, it is perfectly clear inside Greek culture, and I could repeat more or less what I said in commenting on the equipment of another ephebe, Jason in Pindar's Fourth *Pythian*.

And, of course, outside the *Iliad*, we have the whole legend of Paris-Alexandros, the dream of Hekabe, the education in the wild, the pastoral life, the first marriage with Oenone, another figure of the wild, the victory at the race, a classic ephebic trial . . . How far did Homer know of all these legends? At least to some extent. He does not describe the judgment, but alludes to it, speaking of the "courtyard," *messaulon* (24.29), where the Trojan prince and shepherd received and insulted the goddesses. Paris passes in Homer from an excess of savagery to an excess of civilization, making love, to give one example, in the middle of the day (3.441–46), which is certainly opposed to standard Homeric morality, although two deities, Zeus and Hera, can make use of the same liberty (14.292–351). Nobody, however, can treat the Homeric biography of Paris as a direct social document like one of "Chieftain X." Like every piece of art, the relation between the portrait of Paris and real society is the relation between dream and reality, according to Freud in *Traumdeutung*. Homer freely uses condensation (*Verdichtungsarbeit*), displacement (*Verschiebungsarbeit*), figuration (*Darstellung*). I would say that the youth of Nestor belongs to social history, the eternal youth of Paris does not. I could also comment at length on the same opposition in classical times, for instance between Jason of Pindar and the Plataean warriors who left besieged Plataea as *monokrēpides*, that is, using the equipment of young men going through a *rite de passage*.[34]

I wish here to interrupt my historical analysis for a moment, precisely to speak of what constitutes, in my opinion, an historical analysis in these matters. For we have to face two extreme and, I believe, radically false attitudes.

The recent book by J. K. Anderson on *Hunting in the Ancient World* begins by stating that it "is concerned with hunting for sport among the ancient Greeks and Romans, especially the practical details described in the texts and illustrated by archaeological evidence." Anderson immediately adds that "several related matters of greater importance are here only touched upon or altogether neglected," and, among them, "the hunt as a source of literary images."[35] Certainly one could object that the definition of sport in antiquity is perhaps not as obvious as it seems. However, my main question is: Is it possible totally to separate hunting as a practice and hunting as "a source for literary images"? Studying "Hunting and Sacrifice in Aeschylus' *Oresteia*,"[36] I have tried to show that these images had a meaning which was not purely "literary." And how are we to distinguish the images as sources for literary analysis from the pictures—I mean the vase paintings and the sculptures abundantly commented on in Anderson's book—as sources for documentary evidence? And how does he comment on them? When he has to discuss boar hunting as a technique and as a "sporting business as dangerous [in classical times] as it had been in the Age of Heroes"—a formula totally void of meaning, for there was no heroic age, except *in the mentality* of Homer and post-Homeric poets and educators—Anderson quotes at length a section of Xenophon's *Cynegetica* (10.1–8, 10–18) and adds simply: "This admirable description requires little in the way of either interpretation or comment."[37] What is admirable indeed is the idea that a text of Xenophon is transparent and requires no comment, as if Xenophon's handbook was not a chapter in the history of Greek *paideia*, comparable, for instance, with Plato, as if it could have been written in the fifth century and not after the crisis of the Peloponnesian War, with the new reflections on *tekhnē*, characteristic of the Sophists, with the new vision of the Past, which provokes Xenophon to propose new ideals in the name of ancient education. But, actually, J. K. Anderson does comment on Xenophon on boar hunting; he comments on this text simply in quoting[38] extensively a description of the François Vase (circa 560 [BCE]) by Sir John Beazley, as if both Beazley and the picture of the Calydonian hunt were equally transparent, as if the technical remarks of Xenophon could be paralleled with the story of Meleager and Atalanta, and as if Beazley himself did not precisely refer to things which have nothing to do with the *technique* of boar hunting, but are related to the topic studied in the "Black Hunter," the problem of age groups, for instance: "Peleus is beardless: this adventure is thought of as taking place when he was quite young, before his marriage."[39] Certainly Anderson knows that one cannot simply add Beazley to Xenophon, but he writes as if he did not.

May I add simply that the history of technique and practice is certainly not the history of values, of ideology or self-affirmation. But how can we understand, for instance, why during the Peloponnesian War *apatē* appears in Pericles' mouth and Thucydides' narration as the great specialty of Sparta and of its Peloponnesian allies, if we ignore the old Spartan pretension to be paragons of the hoplite ideal?[40]

But if the bad habits I am criticizing, with Anderson's book as a symbolic target, exist, the opposite defect also exists only too widely, and most especially in France. The equivalence sometimes proclaimed, under the influence of linguistics and specifically of Roland Barthes, between a fact of language and a fact of society leads to absurd conclusions. If this equivalence existed, why should we distinguish the world of Odysseus from the world of Quintus of Smyrna or of Tzetzes? I am myself a historian of *l'imaginaire*, as is said, and I admit in theory that the Imaginary is a part of reality, but I must immediately add that some parts of reality, are, to modify slightly Orwell's famous formula, "more real than others." I heartily agree with Simon Goldhill that there was in Athens a "city of words,"[41] and my colleagues and friends in Paris and Lausanne have published *La Cité des images*,[42] but if the city of images was to be separated from the city of politics it would, as N. Loraux has opportunely reminded us,[43] lose its principle of intelligibility. Let me give an example of what is, in my opinion, a good use of these methods. François Hartog[44] has shown with insight that the Scythians in Herodotus 4 were understood as cunning ephebes, and even hunting, nomadic ephebes. So in Herodotus, the Greek *ephēbeia*, an institution that we discovered in the Homeric world, becomes a semantic category or, in Lévi-Straussian terms, a symbolic operator.[45] Hartog reminds us also of the famous equivalence in Photius's *Lexicon*[46] between the Scythians and the ephebes among the Eleians. This is confirmed by Attic vases where there is some equivalence and possible commutability between Scythian archers, hunters, and ephebes in opposition to hoplites.[47] Paris-Alexandros in myth is, on the vases, one of these Scythian archers.[48] But if the *ephēbeia* becomes a semantic category it is, of course, as F. Hartog and other scholars know, because it has been and is still felt as a Greek institution.

This institution I have left as it is perceived in the Homeric text. Was it a common Greek institution? This is a reasonable supposition, but we have, of course, no possibility of proof. It seems however, very likely that as the various types of city-states evolved they gave rise to very different forms and meanings for this institution. In Athens the *ephēbeia* of the city, for young men aged from 18 to 20, became distinct from the *ephēbeia* of the phratry, where the age group was 16 to 18.[49] In the famous Chapter 42 of Aristotle's *Constitution of Athens*, *ephēbeia* is described as an aspect of citizenship and, indeed, the chapter is devoted to citizenship. At this time, I mean after Epicrates' *nomos peri tōn ephēbōn*, the law on *ephēbeia* supported by Lycurgus circa 335/4,[50] *ephēbeia* is a military duty of two years, mainly in the fortresses on the periphery of Athens, with practically nothing recalling a *rite de passage*, except the fact that "during these two years of garrison duty, the ephebes wore a chlamys and cannot be involved in a lawsuit either as plaintiff or as defendant, so that they will have no excuse for absenting themselves. The only exceptions are cases concerned with an inheritance or with an heiress; or when a man has to take up a hereditary priesthood in his family" (*Constitution of Athens* 42.5). We may read in this rule the "trace" of a rite of seclusion, but in the time of Lycurgus and Aristotle this was not so. Indeed, as I myself have emphasized,[51] the admission of a young man into the deme of his father, that is, into citizenship, precedes military service: recognition of citizenship precedes the "probationary period" and is definitely not its consequence. But this of course is the end of a long evolution. We know that the *ephēbeia* existed long before Lycurgus;[52] we know also, thanks to Philippe Gauthier, that in the time of Xenophon's *Way and Means* (ca. 355), *ephēbeia* did not concern *all* young citizens.[53] Finally we know that Aeschines was an *ephēbos* during his youth,[54] circa 371/70. This being said, we have no direct evidence on the Athenian *ephēbeia* in the time, let us say, of Pericles.

To solve this problem we have to use a very different method, making comparisons *inside* the Greek world, and not only between Athens, Sparta, and Crete, as I did, more or less, in 1968. Some scholars probably still imagine that, after the "hoplite reform," the phalanx suddenly succeeded directly the so-called Homeric duel. I have tried to show elsewhere that the Homeric duel is, historically speaking, a fiction,[55] and certainly the anonymous phalanx is another fiction. The truth is that most cities used to train elite military groups, of 300 or 1,000 soldiers, sometimes with archaic names, like the *hippeis* in Sparta, and the chariot drivers (*hēniokhoi*) and *parabatai* (soldiers standing beside the drivers) in Thebes.[56] These groups existed in Sparta as in Athens, in Crete as in Argos, in Megara as in Elis, and in Syracuse. The very existence of these groups is not unaffected by history. Xenophon describes the 300 *hippeis* as young people recruited by three *hippagetai*,[57] but in the battle of Thermopylae Leonidas had with him 300 soldiers who were not chosen from among the *hippeis* alone. They included also some citizens with children (*epilexamenos andras te tōn katesteōton triēkosiōn kai toisi etuwkhanon paidaes eontes*).[58] In Athens, the "300 elite soldiers" (*hoi triēkosioi logades*)[59] function like an institution at the battle of Plataea (479 [BCE]). Did this institution survive the evolution of the radical democracy? We still find a group of 300 *logades* during the siege of Syracuse.[60] Was it the "traditional" group, if I may use that expression, or a group recruited on the spot?[61] My personal choice is for the second hypothesis, because these people are associated with other chosen soldiers who are lightly armed (*psiloi*),[62] something that would not have been conceivable at the beginning of the century.

Is there a link between the ephebes, or the equivalent of the ephebes, and these elite groups? This seems at least probable in some cities of Crete: according to a famous text of Ephorus,[63] when the *erōmenos* who had been abducted by his lover to live in the country, hunting and racing, comes back to the center of the city, he becomes a member of the group of the *kleinoi*, the illustrious. I think we may reasonably accept the demonstration by Jeanmaire that in Sparta the very elitist group of the *kruptoi*, when they became full adults, took the name of *hippeis*.[64] We know that the Argive group of the 1,000 *logades* who were, according to Thucydides, educated by the city, *dēmosiai*, as professionals in warfare were recruited among the *neōteroi* "who were at the same time the most vigorous in body and the most wealthy," a detail which did not prevent the city, according to Diodorus, from "freeing them also from every other service to the state and supplying them with sustenance at public expense." Diodorus' final formula is: "These people therefore, by reason of the expenses incurred for them and their continuous training, quickly formed a body of athletes trained to deeds of war."[65] Neither in Argos nor in Elis nor in Megara[66] do we see anything like the Spartan *kruptoi*.

In Thebes, if we are to accept what Plutarch says of the Sacred Band[67] as composed of *erastai* and *erōmenoi*, we must also admit that the ephebes — however they were called at Thebes — were associated with members of the older generation inside the three hundred, but we know also that here, too, the institution was transformed at least twice in the fourth century, first by Gorgidas and then by Pelopidas or Epaminondas.[68] In other places the separation between ephebes and *logades*, selected soldiers, disappears. There is a notice in Hesychius[69] to the effect that "three hundred" was simply another name for the ephebes. This was undoubtedly the rule in Cyrene. In that city since the end of the fourth century the official documents distinguished those who have and those who have not *hēba*.[70] There existed a group of *triakatioi* who are simply the first age group in the army. Their officers, the *triakatiarkhai*, sometimes associated with the officers of the *peltastai*, take in imperial times the name of *ephēbarkhoi*. Like the Athenian ephebes they are on the other side of the archaic *ephēbeia* but do not seem to form the totality of an age group. Even the name of "three hundred" is a fiction, a legacy of the tradition.[71]

So, with Athens, Sparta, Thebes, the Peloponnesian cities and Cyrene we have quite different lines of evolution. The Athenian ephebe is only a very distant relative of the Spartan *kruptos*. To tell the truth, the only young people one could compare to the Spartan *hippeis* or *kruptoi* in classical Athens are not boys but girls, I mean the little "bears" of the Brauronia about whom we have some information in a few famous lines of the *Lysistrata* (638–47) and, not without many problems, through the excavation in Brauron.[72] The transformation in Athens of the age group system was otherwise radical, and Aristotle's interpretation is a correct reflection of the present, not the past. Between the Spartan *kruptos* and the Athenian ephebe there is the same distance as between the *boulē* and the *gerousia*, between the *ekklēsia* and the *apella*.

There is another Greek or, better, Athenian institution I have to consider and this is theater. Insofar as the tragic poet sees ancient myth with the eyes of the fifth-century citizen, the encounter between the "Black Hunter" and tragedy was unavoidable. For ancient myths are full of stories about *rites de passage*, about heroes living their childhood in the wild and, once grown to manhood, coming to claim their patrimony. Many of these heroes found their way into tragedy: Orestes, Jason, Paris-Alexandros whom I have already mentioned, are examples among others.[73] Oedipus himself can be described as a misguided ephebe. In a footnote to the original "Black Hunter,"[74] I announced that I was going to analyze Sophocles' *Philoctetes*, and most specially the figure of Neoptolemos, in the light of my hypothesis. This promise at least I fulfilled,[75] but what was interesting, finally, in the *Philoctetes* was not so much Neoptolemos himself as the couple formed by the exile, Philoctetes, the old wounded man living in the wild with the sole help of his bow, and the young champion, Neoptolemos, the ephebe accomplishing by guile his first exploit that qualified him for manhood, both becoming soldiers for the city-state under the walls of Troy. I still think the example was a good one. Certainly others would have been as good, perhaps even better. I am thinking of the *Ion* of Euripides in which we see a young boy fighting birds at the beginning of the drama and becoming at the end a citizen of Athens and the eponymous ancestor of the Ionians.[76] Even better, the *Bacchae*. Pentheus is a hoplite king who first tries to use hoplitic methods to expel the new god Dionysos. In a famous scene, he disguises himself as a woman, regressing to the status of ephebe, and goes to the mountain as a scout to spy on the women, a true Black Hunter if anyone was, but is himself hunted and killed.

My paper on the *Philoctetes* has been subject to various attacks by Vincenzo di Benedetto and, with greater courtesy, by R. P. Winnington-Ingram.[77] About these critics and about my hypothesis I will make three points, one specific and two more general. Winnington-Ingram admits that "an audience of Athens might have seen him [Neoptolemos] in the light of their ephebate," but he has what he considers a decisive objection. Neoptolemos, he writes, "does not in fact operate within the wild environment." So V-N's theory "falls to the ground," and, with some majesty, my critic adds: "It is a neat pattern which might have formed the basis of a play but it does not correspond to the reality of this one." This is a nice example of a complete misunderstanding. One can deny that Neoptolemos is an *ephēbos* in the technical meaning of the word, but how can we deny that he operates in the *eskhatiai* (144), in an island that is *ouk oikoumenē*, "not inhabited" (221), a detail that is invented by Sophocles? My second point will be to underline a remarkable coincidence. As has been observed by Maria Grazia Ciani,[78] in 1969—so with no influence from my paper—Robert Silverberg published a science-fiction novel, *The Man in the Maze*.[79] The place of the action is a planet called Lemnos, and, undoubtedly it is a tale inspired by Sophocles' tragedy. It is the story of an exploit accomplished with a guide, under the control of an old politician, in which a young man becomes qualified for adulthood. So, at least, I have not been alone in interpreting as I did the tragedy of Sophocles.

My third point is perhaps more surprising. Neither my critics, which is natural, nor myself, which is less normal, paid any attention to the myth of Neoptolemos. I should have noticed years ago that the name of the hero means "he who is, by himself, a new war,"[80] a perfectly appropriate name for an ephebe, a new warrior, that he has a double name—Neoptolemos-Pyrrhos, exactly like Paris-Alexandros, and that he is the inventor, or at least, one of the inventors of the *pyrrhikhē*,[81] according to a tradition already alluded to by Euripides,[82] an invention he made when for the first time, apparently, he killed in a war; his victims were Eurypylos, and Telephos.[83] The *pyrrhikhē* is a warlike dance performed by *enoploi paides*, which is easily interpreted—with as many proofs as one may wish—as expressing the transition between boyhood and adulthood. That was how Plato took it,[84] and so too do modern commentators;[85] the *pyrrhikhē* could be described as the equivalent, in dance, of the oath of the ephebes. As for Neoptolemos, he seems to be, like Paris-Alexandros or Dorian Gray, something like a permanent youth.[86]

These notes are enough, I suppose, to make acceptable the idea of a link between at least some tragedies and the *ephēbeia*. Is it possible to go further, to be more radical? In an extremely interesting paper, published in 1970,[87] J. P. Morel has commented on the famous Livian excursus in Book 7 of the Roman History on the origins of Roman theater. He points out that in Roman archaic times, the *iuuentus* was an organized body and played a role at least in the text of Livy. But the *iuuentus* did not create tragedy. What J. P. Morel, after Livy, suggests, is that the *iuuentus* helped to create *atellana* and a kind of parodic theater, including a form of *satura*. For this there are parallels in many societies. In a very recent paper J. J. Winkler thinks he can go much further, and characteristically entitled his text—a new look at the old subject of the origins of tragedy—"The Ephebes' Song: *Tragōidia* and *Polis*."[88] Although there are in this paper many extremely interesting remarks, I do not think I can accept the general thesis developed in it, and as it presents itself as an offspring of the "Black Hunter," I feel compelled to raise at least some doubts as to its total legitimacy.[89]

J. J. Winkler tries to make two major points. He explains the word *tragōidos* not as "billy-goat singer," which is undoubtedly obscure and has received no convincing explanation, but by the term *tragizein*, used by Aristotle[90] to mean "the breaking or changing in voice, that adolescent boys experience." *Tragōidoi* began as a slightly jocular designation, not because their voices were breaking (that was long past and anyway no one whose voice is breaking can sing well) but because they were identified with those undergoing social puberty.[91] So the tragic chorus would be a socially bleating chorus, hence the symbolic use of a word linked with the billy-goat, the *tragos*. This unfortunately seems to me unfalsifiable in Popperian terms and self-contradictory.

Moreover the question is: Have we any evidence, as J. J. Winkler thinks he has, *proving* that the tragic chorus was composed of ephebes? On this crucial point no text can be quoted. The major document on which Winkler relies is the Pronomos vase, a quite exceptional piece of the late fifth century,[92] which is generally held to commemorate the representation of a Satyric drama,[93] as exceptional, I dare say, for the representation of theater on *Attic* vases as the

Chigi *olpē* is exceptional for the representation of forms of fighting on Corinthian ware.[94] "The painter," writes Richard Seaford,[95] "seems to have a specific drama in mind, for most of the satyrs are labelled with ordinary Athenian names." Actors and satyrs on this vase have masks in their hands. All the masks are bearded, but the satyrs—by contrast to the actors—are unbearded, and J. J. Winkler asserts that "they are iconographically speaking ephebes."[96] This may be true, and surely there is an interesting contrast between the chorus and the role it performs. But even if we accept, as is generally done, that in the fifth century tragic poets had a single chorus for the tragedies as well as for the satyric drama, this document is both too exceptional and too late to allow generalization. Besides, one can argue that there is definitely some likeness between satyrs and ephebes: on the Attic vases, one can be exchanged for the other. Both are *metaxu*, between savagery and culture, as they are between childhood and maturity. As R. Seaford points out,[97] the liberation of the satyrs from captivity and servitude is one of the most common themes of the plays, and this may be related to an initiatory procedure. Unfortunately I see nothing of this kind in the figures who are the chorus in the tragedies.

It is now time to bring this paper to an end. I shall not, however, conclude without mentioning another problem that was explicitly discussed at the very end of the original "Black Hunter." In the opposition between the archaic ephebe, or *kruptos*, and the hoplite, two patterns of war are implied, night and day, guile and face-to-face, individual and collective, disorder and order—it being admitted, of course, that the "disorder" is here a constructed one, an organized disorder. We should not, for instance, take for *historical* the opposition we see between the *lussa* of the Homeric hero and the *sophrosunē* of the citizen at war. The Homeric war has also its order and the citizens their disorder. Here comparison may help. There are many types of comparison and one is free to use sociological and ethnological methods, but I am thinking of the specific mode of comparative studies created by Georges Dumézil in his Indo-European studies.

As early as 1940 in the first edition of *Mitra-Varuna*, Dumézil discovered the bipartition of the first of his three functions, the function of sovereignty. Mitra is order, Varuna disorder, violence, and the same is true in the early "history" of Rome, of Numa and Romulus. The question I raise is: Is there not also such a bipartition in the second function, the war function? In some of Dumézil's major works we can find many hints of the hypothesis in relation to the Indian world as well as to Scandinavia,[98] but there is no systematic treatment of Rome.[99] Quite recently, Olga M. Davidson discovered exactly the same two models of war in the Iranian *Books of Kings* of Ferdowsi,[100] the Iranians being, of course, on the side of order and their enemies, the Turanians, on the side of disorder. If this hypothesis, I mean the idea of a bipartition of the second function, has any value and future, whether in the Greek world or elsewhere, it will be worked out by someone who has a competence that I lack. This seems a suitable conclusion.

NOTES

[1] This is a revised version of the Corbett Lecture, delivered at Cambridge on 2 May 1986. During this visit to Cambridge I saw Moses and Mary Finley for the last time. My warmest thanks go to the Faculty Board of Classics for this invitation and to Iris Hunter and my friend Geoffrey Lloyd for checking my English. [Publication of this paper was assisted by a grant from The Corbett Fund.]

[2] "The Black Hunter and the Origin of the Athenian Ephebeia," *Proceedings of the Cambridge Philological Society* n.s. 14 (1968): 49–64; "Le Chasseur noir et l'origine de l'éphébie athénienne," *Annales E.S.C.* 23 (1968): 947–64.

[3] *Guerre, agoni e culti nella Grecia arcaica* (Bonn, 1961).

[4] Rome, 1969.

[5] H. Jeanmaire, "La Cryptie lacédémonienne," *Revue des études grecques* 26 (1913): 121–50; *Couroi et courètes* (Lille, 1939).

[6] One could quote J.-P. Vernant's work on Hestia and Hermes; cf. now his *Mythe et pensée chez les grecs* (1985), pp. 155–201.

[7] Cf. *Le Chasseur noir* (2d ed., 1983), p. 19 (*The Black Hunter* [1986], p. xxiv).

[8] Cf. Jeanmaire, 142 n. 5; Cartledge, "Hoplites and Heroes: Sparta's Contribution to the Technique of Ancient Warfare," *JHS* 97 (1977): 11–27 (*Sparta* [Darmstadt, 1986], pp. 387–425, 470); N. Loraux 1977, 105–20.

[9] The major work was O. Manns, *Über die Jagd bei den Griechen* (Progr. Kassel, 1888), pp. 7–38; (1889), pp. 3–20; (1890), pp. 3–21. We have now J. K. Anderson, *Hunting in the Ancient World* (Berkeley, 1985), and we shall soon have Alain Schnapp's doctoral dissertation. For a very brief presentation cf. A. Sherratt, "The Chase, from Subsistence to Sport," *The Ashmolean* 10 (Summer 1986): 4–7.

[10] Athenaeus 18a.

[11] *Laws* 7.822d–4a.

[12] For the sources, cf. "Black Hunter," pp. 51–54.

[13] Vv. 781–96 (Dickinson's translation).

[14] Cf. my essays in J.-P. Vernant and P. Vidal-Naquet, *Myth and Tragedy in Ancient Greece* (1981).

[15] Cf. [. . .] *The Black Hunter.*

[16] Cf. "Flavius Arrien entre deux mondes," in *Arrien, histoire d'Alexandre le grand* (1984), pp. 355–65.

[17] O. W. Reinmuth, *The Ephebic Inscriptions of the Fourth Century B.C.* (Leiden, 1971), p. 126.

[18] Anderson, *Hunting in the Ancient World*, p. 159 n. 3; V. di Benedetto, "Il *Filottete* e l'efebia secondo Pierre Vidal-Naquet," *Belfagor* 33 (1978): 191–207 (repr. in *Filologia e marxismo: Contra le mistificazioni* [Naples, 1981]).

[19] Cf., e.g., P. Schmitt, "Athéna Apatouria et la ceinture: Les Aspects féminins des Apatouries à Athènes," *Annales E.S.C.* 32 (1977): 1059–73; I shall refer later to important evidence given by B. Bravo and P. Gauthier.

[20] "Black Hunter and the Origin," p. 54.

[21] Cf. P. G. Maxwell-Stuart, "Remarks on the Black Cloaks of the Ephebes," *Proceedings of the Cambridge Philological Society* n.s. 16 (1970): 113–16.

[22] Cf., e.g., J.-P. Vernant, Cl. Bérard and others, *La Cité des images* (1984).

[23] Cf. *The World of Odysseus* (2d ed., 1977), pp. 142–58.

[24] B. Bravo, "Sulân: Représailles et justice privée contre les étrangers dans les cités grecques," *Annali della scuola normale di Pisa, classe di lettere e filosofia* 10.3 (1980): 675–987, esp. 954–57.

[25] *Iliad* 11.683–84; here and elsewhere I quote Lattimore's translation.

[26] W. Leaf, *The Iliad* (New York, 1900), pp. 465–66.

[27] Ibid., p. 466.

[28] This is the title of the unpublished dissertation of my former pupil Ariadni Gartziou-Tatti (Ecole des Hautes Études des Sciences Sociales, Paris, 1985).

[29] G. S. Kirk on *Iliad* 3.17–20; Kirk does little to explain this surprise. Paris' cuirass is borrowed from Lycaon (the wolf-man), cf. 3.333.

[30] Ibid.

[31] Cf. Annie Schnapp-Gourbeillon 1981, 135–48.

[32] Son of another Lycaon.

[33] C. R. Beye, *The Iliad, the Odyssey, and the Epic Tradition* (Garden City, N.Y., 1968), p. 49.

[34] Pind. *Pythians* 4.96, Thucyd. 3.22; cf. *Le Chasseur noir*, pp. 101–102, 116, 154–5; *Black Hunter*, 69–70, 72–108.

[35] Anderson, *Hunting in the Ancient World*, p. xi.

[36] Title of one my three studies in *Myth and Tragedy*.

[37] Anderson, *Hunting in the Ancient World*, p. 53.

[38] Ibid., pp. 53–54.

[39] J. D. Beazley, *The Development of Attic Black-figure* (Berkeley, 1951), p. 32, quoted by Anderson, *Hunting in the Ancient World*, p. 53.

[40] Cf. note 8 above, and the comments of E. Heza, *Eos* 62 (1974), p. 44, and of S. Saïd and M. Tredé, *C&M* 36 (1985), pp. 65–85. The main Thucydidean references are 2.39, 3.30.2, 5.8; on ambush and surprise in general cf. W. K. Pritchett, *The Greek State at War*, vol. 2 (Berkeley, 1974), pp. 156–89, and vol. 3 (1979), p. 330.

[41] *Reading Greek Tragedy* (1986), pp. 57–78.

[42] Cf. note 22, above.

[43] "Repolitiser la cité," *L'Homme* 97/8 (1986): 239–55.

[44] 1980, 59–79.

[45] For a good use of this tool in the ancient field cf. P. Borgeaud, "L'Animal comme opérateur symbolique" in *L'Animal, l'homme, le Dieu dans le Proche-Orient ancien* (Cahiers du C.E.P.O.A., 1986), pp. 13–19.

[46] s.v. συνέφηβος.

[47] F. Lissarrague, *Archers, peltastes et cavaliers. Aspects de l'iconographie attique du guerrier* (diss., École des Hautes Études de Sciences Sociales, Paris, 1983).

[48] On the "Scythians" see also F. S. Brown and Wm. Blake Tyrrell, "'Εκτιλώσαντο: A reading of Herodotus's Amazons," *CJ* 80 (1985): 297–302.

[49] I mentioned this point in "Black Hunter and the Origin," pp. 50–51, relying heavily on {Labarbe 1953}.

[50] Lycurgus, fr. 25, edited by Sauppe.

[51] "Recipes for Greek Adolescence."

[52] Cf. Reinmuth, *Ephebic Inscriptions*, pp. 123–38.

[53] 1976, 190–95.

[54] *On the Embassy*, p. 167.

[55] Cf. the preface to P. Mazon's translation of the *Iliad* (1975), pp. 22–26.

[56] Diod. Sic. 12.70; in general cf. M. Detienne, "La phalange: Problèmes, et controverses," in J.-P. Vernant, ed., 1968, 119–42; G. Hoffmann, "Les Choisis: Un Ordre dans la cité grecque?" *Droit et culture* 9/10 (1985): 15–26 (with the essential references).

[57] *On the Constitution of the Spartans* 4.3.

[58] Herodotus 7.205; cf. Loraux, "La Belle Mort," p. 117.

[59] Herodotus 9.21.

[60] Thucydides 6.100.1 (a reference I owe to A. Andrewes).

[61] In Syracuse the Athenians had to fight a group of 600 (not 300) *logades*. Half of them died, which is the traditional function of these elite soldiers (Thucydides 6.96.3, 97.4).

[62] *Kai tōn psilōn tinas eklektous hōplismenous* (6.100.1).

[63] *FGrHist* 70 F 149 (in Strabo 10.483), a text commented upon by, among others, D. Briquel, "Initiations grecques et idéologie indo-européenne," *Annales E.S.C.* 37 (1982): 454–69, and Jeanmaire, *Couroi et courètes*, pp. 450–55.

[64] Ibid., pp. 540-52; Cf. Xen. *On the Constitution of the Spartans* 4.3. The *hippeis* were recruited from among the *hēbōntes*.

[65] Thucydides 5.67.2, Diodorus Siculus 12.75 (Oldfather's translation except for the detail). This group of 1000 *logades* has obviously succeeded in Argos to the archaic group of 300 whom Herodotus describes fighting their Spartan counterpart (1.82; cf. Pausanias 2.38.4–5).

[66] For Elis, Thucydides 2.25.3; for Megara, 5.60.3.

[67] *Pelopidas* 14.18–19.

[68] Other than Plutarch, the main sources are Diodorus Siculus 12.70, Polyaenus 2.51, Athenaeus 13.602a (from Hieronymus the Peripatetic).

[69] *Triakatoi hoi ephēboi kai to sustēma autōn.*

[70] For this distinction cf. *Supplementum Epigraphicum Graecum* ix.72, 34–40.

[71] The bulk of the evidence is given by Luni, *Quaderni di archeologia della Libia* 8 (1976), pp. 223–84, esp. 236–55. For the officers cf. *Supplementum Epigraphicum Graecum* ix.7 (Schwyzer 234), 14 and 51, ix.9.51, ix.742 (the *triakatarkhai* take the name of *cphēbarkhoi*); Eustathius on *Iliad* 8.518 mentions the fact that in Cyrene the ephebes were called the three hundred. I owe my knowledge of these documents to Catherine Dobias-Lalou, whose doctoral dissertation will contain a thorough analysis of this evidence.

[72] Cf. *Le Chasseur noir*, pp. 197–99, *Black Hunter*, pp. 145–47 and, most recently, R. Osborne, *Dēmos, The Discovery of Classical Attika* (1985), pp. 154–72.

[73] Cf. J. J. Winkler, "The Ephebe's Song: *Tragōida* and *Polis*," *Representations* 11 (1985): 27–62, esp. 32–35.

[74] Page 63 n.3.

[75] "Le Philoctète de Sophocle et l'ephébie," *Annales E.S.C.* 26 (1971): 623–38 (*Myth and Tragedy*, pp. 175–99).

[76] This is a suggestion of Yangos Adreadis, who has promised to develop it.

[77] Cf. Di Benedetto, "Il Filottete," pp. 115–36; R. P. Winnington-Ingram, "Sophoclea," *Bulletin of the Institute of Classical Studies* 16 (1979): 1–12, esp. 10–11. I shall make a detailed reply to these two papers (among others) in a forthcoming essay.

[78] "Filottete delle galassie," *Sigma* 7 (1981): 15–25.

[79] This book was translated into both Italian and French, and it is the French version with which I am familiar.

[80] I am here indebted to M. Casevitz.

[81] Cf. Scholiast to Pindar *Pythians* 2.127, Hesychius s.v. *purrikha, purrikhas, purrikhizein,* Diomedes *Ars grammatica* 3 (in *Grammatici Latini* 1.475), Lucian *On Dancing* 9.

[82] *Andromache* 1135; cf. J. Pouilloux in J. Pouilloux et G. Roux, *Enigmes à Delphes* (1963), p. 117.

[83] On Eurypylos cf. Pausanias 3.26.9, Hyginus *Tales* 112, Strabo 13.584.

[84] *Laws* 7.796b-c; cf. also Athenaeus 14.631c, *Aristoxenos de phēsin hōn hōi palaioi gumnazomenoi prōton an tēi gumnopaidikēi eis purrikhēn ekhōroun pro tou eisienai eis to theatron.*

[85] On the *pyrrhikhē* cf. J. C. Poursat, *Bulletin de Correspondence Hellenique* 92 (1968): 550–615, and particularly P. Scarpi, *Dialoghi di archeologia* n.s. 1 (1979): 78–97.

[86] He was still a νεανίας at the time of his death at *Andromache* 1104.

[87] J. P. Morel, *Revue des études latines* 47 (1969): 208–52; cf. also the other papers by J. P. Morel quoted in *The Black Hunter*, pp. 347–48.

[88] Cf. note 73 above.

[89] I must, however, admit that I am proud to be the originator of such a valiant enterprise.

[90] *HA* 7.581a21–7, *GA* 5.787b32–8a.

[91] Winkler (n. 82), 47–8.

[92] *ARV*² 1336, frequently reproduced, e.g. A. Pickard-Cambridge, *The dramatic festivals of Athens* (Oxford, 1968), fig. 49, R. Seaford, *Euripides: Cyclops* (Oxford, 1984), fig. 3.

[93] David Lewis informs me that he believes it to be the description of a dithyrambic chorus.

[94] This will be demonstrated in a forthcoming paper by F. Lissarrague.

[95] In his valuable edition of the *Cyclops* (n. 92), 3.

[96] Winkler (n. 73), 39.

[97] *Cyclops* (n. 92), 33–6.

[98] Cf., e.g., *Mythe et epopée* (Paris, 1968), 63–5, *Heur et malheur du guerrier* (Paris, 1985), 140, 161–8.

[99] Strangely enough, in *Mitra-Varuna* (Paris, 1948²), 48–54 Dumézil draws a parallel between *Luperci* and *Flamines* as between *iuniores* and *seniores*. He takes it for granted that the *Luperci* belong to the first function, while quoting Valerius Maximus 2.2 who defines them as *equestris ordinis iuuentus* (49). I wonder if this should not be reassessed. I thank John Scheid for documentation on these topics.

[100] O. M. Davidson, "The Crown-Bestower in the Iranian book of Kings," *Papers in honour of Professor Mary Boyce* (1985), pp. 61–148, esp. 81–7.

LOUIS GERNET

Political Symbolism: The Public Hearth

1951

*In "Political Symbolism: The Public Hearth," Gernet begins by identify-
ing the hallowed but publicly accessible Hearth (Hestia) of the Greek polis
with such other social spaces or sites as the hero's tomb and the
omphalos—both potent focal points that predate the city as "symbols that
have to do with the unity of the group." Existing simultaneously with the
private hearths of families and the reciprocal public hearth of every other
polis, the* Hestia *has economic as well as religious associations. Its perpetual fire functions in numerous festivals and rites connoting public authority, civic identification, and an emphasis on communal prosperity, as
embodied in shared identification, and an emphasis on communal prosperity, as embodied in shared access (literal, or by representatives) to common
meals. "We are presented with multiple themes; the preeminent quality of
such symbolism is its polyvalence," notes Gernet. Nevertheless, by subtle
argument, he concludes that the "aura or myth" surrounding the Hearth is
less a survival than a deliberate feature of its construction: "For the foundation of the Hearth remains the sole relic precisely because it was the symbol of a sudden change. . . . By supposition a religious symbol, the
Hearth is something quite different from a literary metaphor, but it is on
the way to becoming one. In a period of crisis, it had the privilege of conveying what lay at the heart of the city." Gernet's analysis here is a model of
how "to study the 'signified' in terms of the 'signifier' in order to make
contact with some historical values that other modes of thought no longer
preserve."*

There is no need here to insist on the importance the examination of
symbols has for our understanding of human society, symbols that
have to do with the unity of the group. To study the "signified" in

From *The Anthropology of Ancient Greece*, trans. John Hamilton and Blaise Nagy (Baltimore and London: The Johns Hopkins University Press, 1981), pp. 322–37 ["Sur le symbolisme politique: le Foyer Commun," in *Anthropologie de la Grèce antique,* ed. J.-P.
Vernant (Paris: François Maspero, pp. 382–403); first published in *Cahiers internationaux de
sociologie* 11 (1951): 22–43].

terms of the "signifier" is to study a social mode of thought that is at times actually richer, since it is not expressed in the usual sort of language; but it is, in its own way, no less organized. On encountering it, we discover that it is the means of making contact with some historical values that other modes of thought no longer preserve.

In ancient Greece we find a number of these symbols, which by definition belong to the category of space; they are centers. The tomb of a hero can be a center. Since the hero's world has a special connection with the city, it can appear alone or in the company of other symbols. In fact, the rock of the agora also is a center; it seems to have a long history, and its functions, while quite diverse, have a marked legal dimension. It is used for proclamations of public authority, inaugural oaths of high magistrates, publication of legal acts such as adoptions, ancient forms of punishment such as exposure of the condemned at the pillory, and so on. Here we discover the reflex of an object's special *power*—for example, the agora rock (which nevertheless remains a rock of investiture). Here we also find the feeling of collectivity that consecrates or ratifies this power, as well as the spatial representation of the group, reflected, for example, in the treatment of an adulteress at Aeolian Cyme; as a form of shameful exposure, she is first seated on the rock, then led through the town on the back of an ass, just as the *pharmakoi* are forced to go through the town in their role as scapegoats.

Another symbol that long precedes the city—it survives in the historical period only in a religious tradition in which it becomes specialized and loses much of its force—is the *omphalos*, a bulge in the earth or a conical rock that is more or less a cult object. Its mythical implications are still striking; it is related to the *numen* of the earth itself. The *omphalos* is also the center of the earth, the place where, in Delphi, its most celebrated locale, two eagles met after flying from the two ends of the earth . . . The *omphalos* is also connected with a form of mantic activity that we know was formerly practiced for legal purposes: Themis, the Delphic variant of *Gē* (the keeper of the oracle), has a special connection with the *omphalos* "for judgments that are certain"; and Themis is the name of the primitive "justice" that appears to have been administered by the "kings" of the king-magician type. This is a very ancient way of thinking; but at times it till survives behind a much more modern mode of thought . . .

But the symbol we will now examine characterizes the city best; it can pass for being as ancient as the city, and it lies at the heart of the political institution. We are referring to the public Hearth. By hypothesis, it has connections with a social creation that contributed to ancient man's beginnings; it is, however, a creation that is not so remote that it is completely beyond the reach of the historian; and it is a creation whose meanings can be illuminated by a kind of projection, which is both institutional and, in the larger sense, mythical.

Aristotle tells us of the truly central importance of this Hearth (*Hestia*).

He describes it as a religious function that depends on the government, the function "that especially concerns communal sacrifices: that is, all those that the law ascribes not to the priests but to the magistrates, who get their dignity from the communal Hearth, and who are at times called *arkhontes*, at other times kings, and at still other times *prutaneis*" (*Politics* 1322b.26ff).

The word that is translated as "dignity" (*timē*) has come to apply, inter alia, to the public function; it means fundamentally an honor, a prerogative or privilege, an attribute that is religious in nature or that refers to things religious. It comes down to admitting that in the concept formulated by Aristotle—an observer who was rather disinterested in the origins of beliefs—the *timē* of the magistrate is his religious qualifications, or even the magistracy itself; the two are apparently closely connected. We might even ask if our text does not preserve a relic of a ritual that consecrated or empowered the magistrate through a direct bond or contact with the Hearth. In any case we can see a preestablished association between the *Hestia* and the organs of public authority; there was even something like a personal relationship, which could have some historical significance in terms of the origins of the city . . .

To describe better this idea of the Hearth, let us recall that it is not exclusive; it is open to the outside world. In a sense, the Hearths of various cities presuppose one another. The hospitality they provide strangers is one of their most characteristic features. For example, the invitations that are extended to certain religious ambassadors are invitations "to the public Hearth of the city"; they are accompanied by gifts of protocol that attest to the traditional demand for generosity and the need for some kind of "communion at a distance." . . . In addition, the pervasive quality and quasi-national use of the symbol are confirmed by a noteworthy extension of it. At certain specified times (whether exceptional or periodic), the "renewal" of the cities' fires takes place for the benefit of a prestigious sanctuary that figures as a pan-Hellenic symbol: after being defiled by the presence of barbarians in the Second Persian War, the Hearths at Delphi were restored, and each year thereafter an Athenian procession went to fetch a new fire from the Hearth of Delphi.

But correlatively, the Hearth of the city is no less an expression of the city's personal existence. There is a deity, Hestia, who belongs to it and who alone possesses it as her domain. If the social era in which Hestia appears did not, as a rule, favor mythical personification, one finds here a special exception: Naucratis, a Greek colony founded on Egyptian soil, celebrated yearly the birth of its own *Hestia Prutanis*.

These preliminary remarks will do. What remains now is for us to define the meanings that are implicit in the Hearth and—through the behavior of those affected—the articulations of a social mode of thought.

Let us first place this kind of thought in its context within a historical (or prehistorical) perspective.

In principle the Hearth is a family matter. And it is "the immediate family" that is involved; at least so it seems from our evidence, which cannot go back very far. One might even ask (keeping in mind archaic ceremonies such as the Amphidromia, in which the newborn child is paraded around the Hearth) if the limited vitality of the household *numen* does not owe something (by way of reflection) to that Hestia who is, above all, the projection of the public Hearth. It is true that only afterward, and on the model of individual Hearths, could the notion of the city Hearth be established. All the same, it is not a quasi-epitome or composite image of the others. There is more to the city Hearth than to the individual ones.

In fact, this creation could well presume a social memory; still, the past that it recalls and transforms measures up to it in proportion. The public Hearth emanates from the king's Hearth. This prehistoric reality is attested by archaeology (but only for the Mycenaean period), and the preeminent value of the king's Hearth still survives here and there in poetry. But what is also attested is the continuity that links the king's Hearth to the public one. The disposition of certain archaic temples, where in exceptional cases a city Hearth is installed and preserved, reproduces the plan of the *megaron*, the king's residence, the place of a cult attached to the person of the leader, and a place of which the *hestia* was a central feature. There exists here a past whose meaning has been faithfully preserved by legendary tradition. Witness Erikhthonios of the Athenian acropolis and his association with the goddess's Hearth (*sun-hestios*). This is a past from which Aeschylus does not feel so far removed; in a scene of supplication in which the connection between the two has dramatic value, he indicates successively a confusion and an antithesis between the royal Hearth and the Hearth of the city.

There is a mythology of the royal *hestia*. At times it flourishes even in lyric images; and certain elements persist sporadically in legend. It is at his Hearth that Agamemnon, in Clytemnestra's prophetic dream, plants his royal scepter; it sprouted foliage that shaded all the land of Mycenae. In its association with the twofold image of royal power (the scepter and the Hearth), the ancient theme of the blossoming staff here takes on unique significance: it refers to the coming of the son, who is avenger and successor. Life and perpetuity—above all, the Hearth (indeed, the fire of the Hearth) ought to be symbol of these. In some Italian legends with Greek backgrounds, the future king is born from the Hearth itself. In Greece, "the external soul" of Meleager resides in the firebrand on the Hearth which the Parcae designated for the hero at the time of his birth. This is a relic of royal rituals, as the legend of Eleusis itself suggests; and we find the mythical infant in a specific relationship with the Hearth. Such a notion is often injected with a specific meaning for the benefit of legendary kingship. It is very striking that on the basis of these traditional images a ritual designation, one connected with the public Hearth, seems to have been borrowed in the historical period: the "child of the Hearth" represents the city to the Eleusinian divinities. His title signifies literally "he who comes from the Hearth" or "he who emanates from the Hearth" (*aph' hestias*).

In this conception of the public Hearth, which might at first be regarded as theoretical and somewhat artificial, the vigor of a very ancient image has not yet completely died out. Heritages of this kind persist with some stubbornness. The *Hestia* sometimes rejoins the very prehistoric symbol of the *omphalos*. In the same way that the Roman *mundus*, generally distinguished as it is from the altar of Vesta in the story of the origins of the city, nonetheless supplied for Vesta her first geographical site (according to one tradition), so also the *omphalos* of Delphi was accepted as the seat of Hestia (an event preserved in religious language). Thus we see that the royal mythology of the Hearth is itself sustained on a perennial basis, one where the idea of the earth and its dark powers remains ever present. And this idea is maintained in the city itself. If it is not the usual thing for a Hearth to be a hero's tomb, there is at least one example showing that it can be. There is, in addition, the proximity of chthonian divinities and their mysterious rites within the agora.

The Hearth of the city is surrounded by an aura of myth; this was apparently necessary in order for a new reality to be understood. The newness, more than anything else, is perceivable; and in comparison with the past, one can already see changes in the way the symbolism functions.

In the most ancient representation, it is the signification of the fire which appears to be primary—the fire and its continuous life in the heart of the human world. Its intended meaning is certainly not lost. The rites of the Hearth's renewal continue to make this meaning tangible; and the image of the Hearth in which the central fire is constantly renewed is naturally associated with the perpetuation of the group over generations. This element appears in the prayers of deprecation or benediction which guarantee such perpetuity. But it seems that the force of this suggestion has worn away.

In reality we are presenting here a history that is not simple. In the beginning the cities may have reclaimed the perpetual fire in a quasi-archaic way; when the first buildings were erected as homes for the gods (and one suspects that his moment was laden with institutional and psychological significance), the plan we have already noted for certain archaic temples (which eventually developed into public Hearths) could have been so general that as a result, poetic tradition quite creditably gives to Hestia (as the power of fire) the privilege of having her place in every temple. But in the public Hearth as such, the concrete and ancestral idea of this power does not allow itself to be blurred. In the historical period there is even a tendency for its importance to reappear; perpetual fires exist which are distinct from the public Hearth. And it is interesting that the kind of thought associated with this phenomenon is a form of archaizing piety, which reveals a rather self-conscious memory of past ages. The "lamp" of the Erechtheum in Athens is a perpetual flame in a residence of mythical royalty. In Argos, a flame "of Phoroneus" is kept burning—Phoroneus, a "First Man," an inventor of fire. In Boeotia, at the sanctuary of a "confederate" Athena, the myth associated with a cult amounts to a quasi-historical narrative: long ago Iodama the priestess had been *petrified*; the fire on her altar was renewed every day, and the formula "Iodama lives and asks for fire" was intoned. This tale contains an image that is a survival of the past, and it is acknowledged as such: maintaining the fire—in general, and perhaps in the royal house—is the office of a female priesthood. The religion of Vesta is evidence of this in Rome, as is the cult of perpetual fires in Greece, some of which might be termed rather specialized and hardly more than local survivals. But the service of the city *Hestia* requires male personnel, which makes it, by definition, even more "political."

For what is stressed in this cultural reality is politics, in all its depth and resonances. This idea of the public Hearth is perceptible, but it is so intentionally. There is no other symbol like it, and in no comparable designation do we find a more domineering and impersonal form of government. In contrast, it is instructive to note a reaction in a milieu that is otherwise quite artificial, a reaction that may be a kind of *ricorso*: Augustus transformed the state cult of the Vestals into the cult of the imperial household.

In essence, what the symbol of the public Hearth expresses is the belief that the polis can have its own identity and presence; the symbol's richness is found above all in its manifestations, which are "implicit." It is best to begin our consideration of this symbol in the area of religion—all the more so because this area possesses its own distinctive mode of thought.

Let us return to Aristotle. His text, which in a way has served as our epigraph, leads us to examine thoroughly the religious meanings of the public Hearth. As we have seen, Aristotle distinguishes between two kinds in the cult. The first is limited to a sacerdotal ministry that is more or less separate and usually hereditary, since it represents the ancient monopolies of *gentes* (the Eumolpids and other sacral *genē* of Eleusis could provide extreme examples). The history and theory of the city within the *Politics* often take note of this. There is here a domain that is recognized by the city, an assignment defined by "law," by *nomos*; and *nomos* is imperative rule derived from a collectivity that represents (etymologically) the principle of distribution. Here we are dealing entirely with social and religious history . . . Opposed to this principle within the regime of the city is the principle of organization—that is, law that commands and subordinates. But there is more, a second kind of significance in the cult, one that has as its sign and instrument the public Hearth. Aristotle's terse and abstract language provides important testimony. Doubtless, the religion of the city can be regarded from one point of view as a synthesis or federation of cults that are older than the city itself (local, patrimonial, and others.) But city religion also has its own significance; it claims a kind of individuality. The "public sacrifices" that have as their center (at least in the ideal sense) the "public Hearth" affirm a collective existence, which in itself is an eminently religious matter. Was the symbolism of lighting the fires of other altars at the central Hearth a general practice? Aristotle's expression could imply it. It is attested several times; and that is enough for it to be the source of a readily identifiable mode of thought . . .

An Athenian festival that is characterized by striking archaisms (though it is doubtless not one of the oldest festivals) is organically connected with the Prytany: it is the festival of Dipoleia, whose central act was, it seems, the sacrifice of an ox on the Acropolis. This is the origin of the term *Bouphonia* (literally, "murder of the ox"). As far as its alleged origins are concerned, we find several mythical versions, all of which are ingenious; but they still convey the psychology of a religious action, which the myths make explicit. The earliest sacrifice was sacrilegious: when an ox approached the altar of Zeus *Polieus* (Zeus "of the city" and Zeus "of the acropolis") and ate the offerings of cereal reserved for the god, the angry priest struck it down with an ax. Upset over his impiety, he fled. A famine resulted and the Delphic oracle was consulted; it offered pardon for the past and legislation for the future: thenceforth the sacrifice would have to take place each year and in the same way. In fact, the events in the rite are almost exactly like those in the legend. Conforming to the last part of the story, the rite was concluded in the Prytany, where a make-believe judgment took place (and where, moreover, animals and objects causing death to men continued to undergo judgment well into the classical period). Responsibility was imputed to the ax (or to the sacrificial knife), which was then thrown outside the borders of the town. What is the "semantic force" of these details?

Every sacrifice involves sacrilege: this hypothesis is evident from the fact that the victim is an object of special respect and protection. The victim is an ox, an animal used for labor; and an ancient but still living tradition commands genuine religious reverence. In addition, the theme of the heinous sacrifice with the same victim (but one that is finally accepted) is illustrated in legends that have found their way into the Herakles cycle and that serve to justify certain aberrant rites . . . In any case, the victim, which is revived in order to be harnessed to a plough (yet another symbol of final pacification), naturally brings the earth's blessings. But the victim's immolation, which is supposed to assure these blessings, at first produces a troubling and disquieting feeling in which the city, through symbols of an agrarian religion, is personally involved. The city assumes this formidable act vis-à-vis the divine world as represented in the person of the god, who by name is in direct contact with the city. In the myth, the first man to perform sacrifice consents to take on his office only if the *responsibility* for the ritual murder is shared by all. This, in effect, is what happens: the guilt is shared. Understandably, it is the conclusion that gives sense to the entire scenario. The last act takes place at the public Hearth; the religious drama is resolved in a legal one where innocence is finally proclaimed as certain, and a consecration is guaranteed which exists from this point on. Finally, the victim's flesh provides food for a communal meal . . .

We can see yet another aspect of this moral security that as such had to be acquired. In the representation of the public Hearth, the symbolism of nourishment plays a large role. The Hearth, in general, is naturally associated with food; in the institution of the city, this meaningful aspect is put into rather high relief. We find it in the Roman cult of Vesta, a cult that may well have come from a Hellenic tradition. A fragment of Cratinus makes us think of some of its practices: there is some question in the fragment of the baking of barley grains on the very Hearth of Athena (that is, the question deals with a technique of feeding whose archaism survives in Italic ritual, but which is also attested in Greek legend). In addition, we know that the anxiety about food is translated into a lively expression in Hestia's domain. Plutarch tells us of an annual ceremony that is celebrated even in his day in his native city, Chaeronea. It is the Expulsion of Hunger, celebrated by each *pater familias* at his own expense and in his own home; but the chief magistrate celebrates it at the public Hearth. A slave is struck with the branches of an *agnus castus* (used elsewhere in "apotropaic" rituals); he is then pushed through a gate while these words are intoned: "Outside famine; inside, health and wealth." The concept of a *daimōn* to be expelled is found in Athens under the same name: next to the Prytany, a sacred terrain is set aside for *Boulimos* (Famine).

Above all, or at least often, the Prytany brings to mind the meals served in its halls. But through a number of practices, wherein a vital and concrete "representation" is diffused, we can trace a mentality that has many different purposes but is possessed of an autonomy that is—despite everything that could be confused with it—worth emphasizing. *Hestia* is synonymous with eating publicly. A whole group of terms is connected with the idea, but the central image never disappears. We know what it means to welcome someone to the Hearth: whether it involves a permanent or hereditary right, and whether it concerns an occasional invitation or the obligatory participation of magistrates, the etymology can be seen in related terms. In the derivations, the central idea remains intact . . .

Let us return, then, to the fundamental idea of the city *Hestia*. Obviously it does not monopolize the symbolism it contains. In ancient Greece, as elsewhere and more so, the common meal appears as an institution at every stage and in fact on every level; but it appears with some social, even historical, meanings that are quite diverse and that, in a way, build gradually on one another . . .

By hypothesis, the public Hearth involves only certain beneficiaries. In the privilege accorded them, there is manifest both the unity of the city and the totality of citizens participating (at the Hearth) through representatives. The symbol could first have been one of belonging, and a sign of being integrated into a collective body; one can see this as a possibility even in Athens, where only returning envoys are usually welcomed at the Hearth. For the fourth century B.C.E., this is above all a mark of honor; but in fact the reception is not a reward, since one does not even know what the envoys did (and on one occasion there was a dispute on precisely this point). The envoys are received at the public Hearth, just as individuals also returning from abroad would be received at their family Hearth, by means of certain rites of desacralization and reintegration. The only thing is that in the city, collectivity as a special power appears to be the dominant idea. We mention a very suggestive myth of the welcoming of heroes under the guise of a legendary *agapē* only in passing, because it is not localized at the public Hearth (in the tale of Orestes, during the Athenian Anthesteria it is set in a nearby building, which is the site for the reunion of the *thesmothetai*). But it goes without saying that participation is a right for representatives of public authority; still, it is more essentially an obligation.

As far as the beneficiaries are concerned—that is, those who receive some recompense or other concession (it seems that at times there was a kind of rotation in the assignment of this right)—the symbolism operates with that "moderation" which is itself the mark of the city. We have the regulations governing the Hearth from Naucratis (where one ate rather well on festival days, but in general the fare was rather meager in the Prytany). It is both problematic and instructive, but we have something even better from Athens. The moralizing Plutarch must have been correct when he interpreted a law of Solon in classical terms: to refuse the common meal implies "contempt" for the city, and to profit from the public meal more often than is right amounts to "greediness" (*pleonexia*).

In this deliberately managed symbol, the idea attached to the public Hearth remains communal: what is expressed directly, from the fact that there is a city Hearth as well as individual family ones, is a form of concrete solidarity that makes the well-being of all the well-being of each; it is the very constitutive nature of the city. This nature reveals itself strikingly and fully in theory, in actual events, and even in forms of behavior. At the core there is always the notion of public property: everyone should have access to it, and everyone on occasion exercises his claim to it or participates in it. The system of festivals, the distributions, and indeed the attraction of a windfall to share in—many elements convey this tenacious notion. It is in conjunction with it, and in the sphere of economics, that we must first deal with the institution of the Hearth.

Curiously, in opposition to this kind of thinking there is yet another kind, one that has to do with state organization and, under the state's aegis, with economic individualism. Are they in opposition or complementarity? The fact is that the two antithetical notions have equal links with Hestia and represent two extremes between which societies have always found it difficult to strike a balance. And the Greek city, a rather complex reality, attests to precisely the alternative to both of these extremes.

Sometimes there is nothing more instructive than a manual of the interpretation of dreams. One specialist in this area tells us that when Hestia appears in a dream, she signifies the city council and the treasury that contains public revenues. We could perhaps say that a state is born in the ancient city when a state treasury develops. Hestia is directly involved with this basic element. In Cos . . . Hestia's epithet is *Tamia*. It is, to be sure, an ancient word, with significations of "feudal" and religious royalty; but within the structure of the state, it has supplied the somewhat premature designation of "treasurer." With regard to this *Hestia Tamia*, the Cos ritual contains something suggestive: as soon as the victim is selected, it is led into the agora; the owner then announces that he has made a gift of the animal to his fellow citizens, and that they in turn must pay the price to Hestia. Thus we see that in an essentially monetary economy the value of cattle can be put up at compound interest by a Hestia who in the city's service is still independent of the total body of citizens. This increase in value is owed to the generosity of a donor; one immediately recognizes here a *leitourgia*. The "liturgies," or tasks freely assumed by an individual, especially at festivals (one of these *leitourgiai*, the organization of a banquet, is called *hestiasis*), represent an adaptation within the structure of the city and a kind of "nationalization" of the "gift ethic," a practice that predates the city but that is in a way put to use for the city's own purposes. The city is not an abstract entity, and one of its major components is affirmed in its religious life.

In the case of the Greeks, and in the course of this very compromise, the city's structure appears to correspond to that of a "discreet" economy dominated by the principle of *suum cuique*. This same principle sometimes supplies the Greeks' early moral philosophers with a definition of justice. Some features of a religious vocabulary dealing with the Hearth are interesting in this regard. One of the divinities associated with Hestia at her sanctuary in Naucratis is Apollo *Kōmaios* (Apollo "of the villages," whose epithet is a form that predates the city; the name sometimes remains tied to topographical subdivisions of the city). Perhaps it is not by chance that we find at Ainos, a colony in Thrace, an Apollo with the same (or practically the same) name who presides over the sale of *real* estate. There is some historical insight to be gained from the name of a divinity in Arcadian Tegea: here, groups of altars are built around a public Hearth on a site dedicated to Zeus *Klarios*. The career of the word *klaros* is well known: at first it referred to a kind of "fief": but in the classical period it came to mean true individual property—that is, a patrimony. In any case, one thing is certain (and the archaism preserved through tradition is striking): the first act of the Athenian archon, whose relationship with the Prytany was personal—he resided there from the earliest times—was to proclaim that "each person will remain, until the very end of the archon's magistracy, owner and master of the property he owned before the archon's entry into office."

In studying the Indo-European roots of representations of myth dealing with the functioning of society, Georges Dumézil has pointed out the opposition and alternation between "totalitarian" and "distributive" economies. In clearly defined forms he shows that at the dawn of history the symbolism of *Hestia* permits us to recognize the antithesis between two analogous concepts; and within the organism of the city (fragile and restless, as are all human creations), *Hestia* shows us the ideal of a synthesis of these concepts.

We are presented with multiple themes; the preeminent quality of such symbolism is its polyvalence. Moreover, behind the psychological material, whose testimony from an already-classical Greece appears to be in a state of almost complete deterioration, one can still find elements of continuity: how, for example, the symbols of nourishment can, with the context of festivals, be associated with sentiments of religious community. One can also see how these symbols convey an idea of the eternal, of social unity, and indeed of discipline or order. One would like to recapture all of this.

To do so is to put it within a context. Mauss observed that if in the study of man and society, we only take into account "collective representations," "the collective psychology" will suffice as a special chapter on psychology only; but there is another dimension—that is, society itself, and consequently its history. In the symbolism of the public Hearth it is already of great interest that economic solidarity especially asserts itself, and it does so as something fundamental. What is more, the different directions in which the symbolism leads allows us to identify a specific stratum: the social age that the foundation of Hearths points to is one in which an individualist economy, the type more or less rejected by the organizations we have identified in the background (peasant communities, "male societies," beneficent kingships, and so on), is integrated into a new form of unity. And this stage is not part of an "abstract chronology." We are fortunate to hit upon something like a historical fact that the convergence of literary, linguistic, and institutional dates places around 800 [BCE] For the foundation of the Hearth is first the symbol of the creation of the city. Vague as this creation was in the archaic period, it still reveals a "point of maturation."

This is a moment of history of which the public Hearth remains the sole relic precisely because it was the symbol of a sudden change. Because of this, in the classical period there will be a certain ambiguity in the nature of the Hearth. Although it will preserve some of its religious features, it will do so within a network of thought that no longer belongs to its origins. The echoes we detect in the festivals that have an organic relationship to the Hearth: that *Stimmung* which is really stifled within a tradition of *mos maiorum*—these must correspond historically to historical crises. In the founding of the city, we sense a religious eruption; and we sense it too in the semidarkness of legends, in the acts of certain innovators, and in certain associations . . .

But perhaps from the beginning, this novelty of the *Hestia* owes its mark of a practical mentality to its more or less spontaneous nature. It is a fact that the symbolism of the Hearth—from all evidence, so weak in mythological development—seems in history to have disengaged itself from ancient contexts. This in contrast to the forms of thought verified in the very symbols from which that of the Hearth emerges. Despite their persistent proximity, chthonian connections no longer appear in the symbolism of the Hearth. The Hearth's symbolism excludes the element of mystery and rule based on a religious secret; but survivals of these elements are not entirely lost in a tangential but otherwise innocuous tradition. The symbolism of the Hearth is synonymous with publicity; the very representation of the social space that is bound up with its symbolism is itself something new. Men arrange as they will the mathematical disposition of land; it can be almost anything. Where the center is an arbitrary—indeed a theoretical—matter. Even in legend, a Hearth can be removed at will. No doubt colonies remained faithful to the piety that had them take their fire from the *mētropoleis*; but colonization, above all a manifestation of civic vitality, conditions men to disregard prescribed places. Let us also say that the ancient meanings, which are not really so ancient, have been obliterated . . .

Let us go back to where we began. The *Hestia* touched a political reality that from the earliest days the Greeks characterized as rational, almost preordained. Its true destiny was to initiate a mode of thought which no longer used it except as a deliberate symbol. This means that it was no longer needed for the functioning of institutions in which Hestia's earliest qualities were manifest . . . In Athens the name of a tribunal, the name of a formality preceding a court case, and certain aspects of Plato's laws attest to the memory of a substantial link between jurisdiction and the Hearth—but in effect, only the memory of such.

By supposition a religious symbol, the Hearth is something quite different from a literary metaphor, but it is on the way to becoming one. In a period of crisis, it had the privilege of conveying what lay at the origin of the city. But the turning point it signaled put Greece on its own course: the major innovations of Hellenism asserted themselves very rapidly. We have outlined some of them here.

TRANSLATED BY JOHN HAMILTON AND BLAISE NAGY

JEAN-PIERRE VERNANT

Hestia–Hermes:
The Religious Expression of Space
and Movement in Ancient Greece

1963

Building on Gernet's study of the public hearth, Vernant dwells on the Hestia half of the polarity "Hestia–Hermes." While his starting point in this 1963 essay is the attested affinity between Hestia and Hermes in the twelve-god Olympian pantheon (cf. Georgoudi in this volume), Vernant follows Gernet's lead in moving quickly outward to a variety of evidence elaborating the social context these deities reflect and the institutions and actions they sponsor: "Whether concerned with facts affecting marriage, lines of descent, the heritage of the family klēros, *the domestic status of husbands and wives, the social and psychological contrasts between men and women, their activities within the house and outside, the double aspect of wealth and of land improvement . . . it seems that the spatial values associated with a center [sic: Hestia], immobile and withdrawn, had their regular counterpoint in the opposite values of an open space, unstable, a place of distance, contacts, and change [Hermes]." In addition to emphasizing social realities, including those of sexual dichotomy, this study resonates with many others in this volume in its concern with reciprocal concepts, here embodied in the two Olympians. "Furthermore, this very complementarity which is an attribute of the two deities implies that there is a contradiction or internal tension in each of them that gives their characters as gods a basic ambiguity"—an ambiguity that has mesmerized modern scholarship, with Hermes second only to Dionysus as its focus (cf. Kahn, Leduc in this volume).*

This translation omits most of Vernant's analysis of the tragedians' versions of the Electra story, as well as details of the institution of the epiklēros *and the ritual of the* amphidromia.

From J.-P. Vernant, *Myth and Thought Among the Greeks*, trans. H. Piat (London, Boston, Melbourne, and Henley: Routledge & Kegan Paul, 1983), pp. 127–76 ["Hestia-Hermès: Sur l'expression religieuse de l'espace et du mouvement chez les Grecs," in *Mythe et pensée chez les Grecs: Études de psychologie historique* (Paris: François Maspero, 1965), pp. 97–145.

On the base of the great statue of Zeus at Olympia, Phidias carved the twelve gods. Between the Sun (Helios) and the Moon (Selene), the twelve deities, in pairs, were disposed in the orderly arrangement of a god and goddess in each couple, while in the center of the frieze, in addition, appeared Aphrodite and Eros[1]—the two deities (feminine and masculine) who preside over unions. In this series of eight divine couples there is one pair that poses a problem: Hermes and Hestia. Why are they matched? Neither their genealogies nor their legends can explain this association. They are not husband and wife like Zeus–Hera, Poseidon–Amphitrite, Hephaestus–Charis; nor brother and sister like Apollo–Artemis and Helios–Selene; nor mother and son like Aphrodite–Eros; nor even protector and protégé like Athena–Heracles.

What is the link that, in Phidias' mind, unites a god and goddess who appear to be without connection? It can hardly be ascribed to the sculptor's personal fancy. The artist of classical times was bound to conform to certain models when creating any sacred work of art: his creativity could be expressed only within the forms laid down by tradition. Hestia—the name of a goddess but also the noun designating the hearth—was less suited to anthropomorphic representation than the other Greek gods and goddesses. She is seldom depicted and when she is it is often, as sculpted by Phidias, in the shape of Hermes' partner.[2] In the plastic arts, as a rule, therefore, the Hermes–Hestia association is invested with real religious significance. It is there to express a definite structure in the Greek pantheon.

Meagerly represented in the arts, Hestia is even more poorly served in the mythical tales: a remark concerning her birth in Hesiod and in Pindar, an allusion to her virginal status in the *Hymn to Aphrodite*. We would know practically nothing about her that could explain her relations with Hermes were it not for a few lines in a *Homeric Hymn to Hestia* that have come down to us. In this text the two deities are associated in the closest possible way. The hymn opens with six lines invoking Hestia, followed immediately with six lines of invocation to Hermes, whose protection is sought "in agreement with the worshipful goddess who is dear [*philē*] to him"; and it closes with two lines addressed to the god and goddess jointly. On two occasions the poet stresses the feeling of friendship which Hermes and Hestia nurture for each other. This mutual *philia* explains why Phidias could place them, together with the other couples, under the patronage of Aphrodite and Eros. Nevertheless this reciprocal affection is based neither on blood ties nor on ties of marriage nor on personal interdependence. It is the result of an affinity of function, for the two powers are present in the same places and carry out their complementary activities side by side. Neither relations nor spouses nor lovers nor vassals—one could say that Hermes and Hestia are "neighbors." Each is related to the terrestrial sphere, the habitat of a settled people. The "hymn" sings that the two gods "in friendship together dwell in the glorious houses of men who live on the earth's surface [*epikhthonioi*]."[3]

That Hestia should reside in the house goes without saying: in the middle of the quadrangular *megaron* the rounded Mycenaean hearth marks the center of the human dwelling. According to the *Hymn to Aphrodite*: "Zeus the father gave her [Hestia] a high honor instead of marriage and she has her place in the midst of the house [*mesōi oikōi*]."[4] But Hestia represents not only the center of the domestic sphere. Sealed in the ground, the circular hearth denotes the navel that ties the house to the earth. It is the symbol and pledge of fixity, immutability, and permanence. In the *Phaedrus* Plato evokes the cosmic procession of the twelve gods.[5] Ten deities proceed in the wake of Zeus who leads them across the heavens. Only Hestia remains at home and never leaves her abode. For the poets and philosophers, Hestia, the node and starting point of the orientation and arrangement of human space, could be identified with the earth, immobile at the center of the cosmos. According to Euripides, "the Sages call the Earth-Mother Hestia because she remains motionless at the center of the Ether."[6]

Hermes too, though in a different way, is associated with man's habitat, and, more generally, with the terrestrial sphere. In contrast to the distant gods who dwell in an outer region, Hermes is a familiar god who frequents this world. Living among mortals on terms of intimacy, he introduces the divine presence into the very heart of the world of mankind. As Zeus says to him in the *Iliad*: "Hermes, seeing thou lovest above all other to companion a man (*hetairissai*). . . ."[7] And Aristophanes salutes him, of all the gods, as the most "friendly to man."[8] But if he thus manifests himself on earth, if, with Hestia, he inhabits the dwellings of mortals, Hermes does so in the form of the messenger (Hermes *angelos*—it is by this name that he is specifically invoked in the *Hymn to Hestia*), as a traveler from afar and one who is already preparing to depart. Nothing about him is settled, stable, permanent, restricted, or definite. He represents, in space and in the human world, movement and flow, mutation and transition, contact between foreign elements. In the house, his place is at the door, protecting the threshold, repelling thieves because he is himself the thief (Hermes *lēistēr*, the robber, *pulēdokos*, the watcher at the gates, *nuktos opōpētēr*, the watcher by night),[9] for whom no lock, no barricade, no frontier exists. He is the wall-piercer who is pictured in the *Hymn to Hermes* as "gliding edgeways through the keyhole of the hall like the autumn breeze, even as mist."[10] Present at the front doors of houses (Hermes *pulaios, thuraios, strophaios*), he also stands at the gateways of towns, on state boundaries, at crossroads (Hermes *trikephalos, tetrakephalos*),[11] as a landmark along paths and tracks (Hermes *hodios, enodios*), and on tombs—those gateways to the underworld (Hermes *khthonios, nukhios*). In all places where men, departing from their private dwellings, gather together and enter into contact for the purpose of exchange (whether for the exchange of ideas or for trade), as in the *agora*, or for competition as in the stadium, Hermes is present (Hermes *agoraios*, Hermes *agōnios*). He is the witness to agreements, truces, and oaths between opponents; he is the herald, messenger, and ambassador abroad (Hermes *angelos, diaktoros, kērukeios*). A wandering god, the patron of the roads both on and leading to the earth, he is the travelers' guide in this life, and, in the other, escorts souls to Hades—and sometimes brings them back (Hermes *pompaios, kataibatēs, Psukhopompos*). He leads the dance of the *Charites*, brings in the four seasons in their turn, attends the change from waking to sleep and sleep to waking, from life to death, from one world to another. He is the link, the mediator between mortals and the gods, both those of the world above and those of the underworld. The Albani villa bust of him[12] bears the inscription: *coeli terraeque meator*; and Electra addresses him in these words: "Herald (*kērux*) supreme between the world above and the world below, Oh nether Hermes, come to my aid and summon me the spirits beneath the earth to attend my prayers."[13] But though he may mingle with humanity, Hermes remains both elusive and ubiquitous. He makes an abrupt appearance where least expected, only to disappear again immediately. When there was a sudden pause in the conversation and silence reigned, the Greeks used to say: "Hermes is passing."[14] He wears the helmet of Hades, which grants the wearer invisibility, and winged sandals that abolish distance. He carries a magic wand that transforms all he touches. He is the unpredictable, the unexpected meeting. In Greek a godsend is *to hermaion*.

Through this profusion of epithets, this variety of attributes, Hermes appears as an extraordinarily complex figure. He has been thought so baffling that it has been suggested that in the beginning there must have been several different Hermes gods which later merged into one.[15] The various characteristics that are combined in the general makeup of the god seem, however, to fall into order more easily if he is considered in light of his relations with Hestia. If they form a couple in the religious belief of the Greeks, it is because the two deities belong to the same plane, their action applies to the same field of reality, and their functions are interrelated. Now, as regards Hestia, no doubt is possible: her significance is obvious, her role is strictly defined. Because her fate is to reign, forever immobile, at the center of the domestic sphere, Hestia implies, as her complement and her contrast, the swift-footed god who rules the realm of the traveler. To Hestia belongs the world of the interior, the enclosed, the stable, the retreat of the human group within itself; to Hermes, the outside world, opportunity, movement, interchange with others. It could be said that, by virtue of their polarity, the Hermes–Hestia couple represents the tension that is so marked in the archaic conception of space: space requires a center, a nodal point, with a special value, from which all directions, all different qualitatively, may be channeled and defined; yet at the same time space appears as the medium of movement implying the possibility of transition and passage from any point to another.

Obviously, by interpreting the Hermes–Hestia relationship in terms of these concepts, we distort them. The Greeks who worshipped these deities never saw them as symbols of space and movement. The construction/ structuring of a pantheon was ruled by a logic that is not in accordance with our criteria. Religious thought obeys its own rules of classification. It defines and classifies phenomena by distinguishing between different types of agent, by comparing and contrasting various kinds of activity. In this system space and movement are not yet interpreted in the form of abstract ideas. They remain implicit in that they are incorporated in more material and more dynamic aspects of reality. If Hestia is apparently capable of "centering" space while Hermes can "mobilize" it, that is because as divine powers they are the patrons of a series of activities undoubtedly dealing with the organization of earth and space, and even constituting, in terms of praxis, the framework within which, for the ancient Greek, the experience of space took place—but which nevertheless covers a very much wider field than that implied when we talk of space and movement.

The relationship of the Greek Hestia to the Roman Vesta has given rise to many a controversy.[16] In Greece there was no persona or function comparable to the Vestal virgins. It is, however, difficult not to believe that, in the beginning, the tending and care of the Mycenaean hearth, and in particular the royal hearth, was a sacred office performed by women and that this duty fell on the daughter of the house before her marriage.[17] Louis Deroy has even argued that the word *parthenos* (virgin) is a functional designation denoting she who tends the fire.[18] Whether that is true or not, if fire as such (the sacrificial fire as much as that of the forge or the cooking fire) is related to Hephaestus, a male god, the round altar of the domestic hearth is, on the contrary, associated with a female deity and a virginal one. The usual explanation in terms of the purity of fire is not satisfactory. For one thing, Hestia is not fire but the altar-hearth; and for another, Hephaestus, who is precisely the incarnation of this power of fire, is anything but "pure."[19] In order to interpret these facts, therefore, it would be better to go back to the *Homeric Hymn to Aphrodite* and the short passage concerning Hestia, which is moreover sufficiently explicit.[20] The hymn exalts Aphrodite's supremacy: nothing can withstand her, neither beasts nor men nor gods. But the goddess's prerogative is not the brutal domination, the physical coercion appropriate to the warrior deities. Her weapons, even more successful, are those of tenderness and charm. No creature, in the heavens, on earth, or in the sea, can escape the magic powers of the forces she mobilizes in her service: *Peithō*, persuasion, *Apatē*, alluring charm, *Philotēs*, the bonds of love. In all the universe there are only three goddesses to withstand her magic arts: Athena, Artemis, and Hestia. Unshakeable in their determination to remain virgins, they oppose Cytherea with hearts so staunch and with such high resolution that neither the wiles of *Peithō* nor the fascinations of *Apatē* succeed in changing their sentiments or altering their status. This fixity of purpose, this obstinacy in refusing to change, is particularly emphasized in the hymn with regard to Hestia. Wooed by Poseidon and Apollo, who both desire her, Hestia firmly (*stereōs*) rejects their suit, and to make this refusal irrevocable she takes the grand oath of the gods—"that which can never be retracted"—and vows to remain an eternal virgin. There can be no doubt that Hestia's function as goddess of the hearth is related to the permanency of her virginal status: the text specifies that Zeus gives her the right to take up her residence at the center of the house *in compensation for* the nuptials she has renounced forever (*anti gamoio*). For Hestia, the wedded state would be the negation of the values that she represents at the heart of the house (house, *oikos*, signifying both the dwelling place and the human group inhabiting it): values of fixity, permanence, seclusion. Does not marriage, after all, imply a twofold transformation of the young girl—of herself as a person and of her social status? On the one hand it is a form of initiation by which she accedes to a new status, to a different world of human and religious realities,[21] and on the other it uproots her from the domestic milieu to which she belonged. Once she is established at her husband's hearth she becomes part of another house.[22] More generally speaking, the union of the sexes is a contract and, of all contracts, the one that involves the two greatest natural opposites—the male and the female. In this connection, one of the essentials aspects of Greek *kharis* should be emphasized: *kharis* is the divine power that is manifest in all aspects of gift-giving and reciprocity (the round of generous liberality, the cordial exchange of gifts), which, in spite of all divisions, spins a web of reciprocal obligations,[23] and one of the oldest of all of the functions of *kharis* is the giving of herself by a woman to a man.[24] Thus it is not surprising that Hermes, who is closely linked with the *kharites* (Hermes *kharidōtēs*) should also play a part in the union of the sexes and should appear side-by-side with Aphrodite as the true patron of *Peithō*, of the persuasive arts capable of shaking the most fixed resolves, of changing the most confirmed opinions.[25]

But the analysis can go deeper. In Greek the domestic sphere, the enclosed space that is roofed over (protected), has a feminine connotation; the exterior, the open air, a masculine one. The woman's domain is the house. That is her place and as a rule she should not leave it.[26] In contrast, in the *oikos*, the man represents the centrifugal element. It is for him to leave the reassuring enclosure of the home, to confront the fatigues and dangers of the outside world, to embrace the unknown; for him to establish contacts with the outside, to enter into negotiations with strangers. Whether engaged in work, war, trade, social contacts, or public life, be he in the country or in the *agora*, on sea or on land, man's activities carry him into the great outside. Xenophon is merely expressing the common belief when, after contrasting mankind with the beasts as needing a roof over their heads instead of living in the open, he adds that the gods have endowed men and women with opposite characters. Body and soul, man is made for the *erga hupaithria, ta exō erga*, the open-air life and outside activities; the woman for the indoor life, *ta endon*. And so "to the woman it is more honorable to stay indoors than to go out into the fields, but to the man it is unseemly to stay indoors rather than to attend to the work outside."[27]

There is, nevertheless, one instance when this orientation of the man toward the exterior and the woman toward the interior is reversed. In marriage, in contrast to all other social activities, it is the woman who is the mobile social element, whose movement creates the link among different family groups, whereas the man remains tied to his own hearth and home. The ambiguity of the female status lies thus in the fact that the daughter of the house (more closely linked to the domestic sphere by virtue of her femininity than is a son) can nevertheless not fulfill herself as a woman in marriage without renouncing the hearth of which she is in charge. The contradiction is reconciled in the sphere of religious representation by the image of a deity who personifies those aspects of feminine nature that are permanent, while remaining, through her virginal status, a stranger to the element of mobility. This "permanence" of Hestia's is not only of a spatial kind. As she bestows on the house the center that sets it in space, so Hestia ensures to the domestic group its continued existence in time. It is through Hestia that the family line is perpetuated and remains constant, as though in each new generation the legitimate offspring of the household were born directly from "the hearth." Through the goddess of the hearth, the function of fertility, dissociated from sexual relations (which, in an exogamous system, postulate relations between different families), can appear as an indefinite prolonging of the paternal line through the daughter, without a "foreign" woman being necessary for procreation.

This dream of a purely paternal heredity never ceased to haunt the Greek imagination. It is openly expressed in the tragedy *Eumenides* when Apollo proclaims that maternal blood can never run in the veins of the son, seeing that "the mother of what is called her child is not its begetter; the begetter is the man, he who plants the seed, whereas she doth preserve the sprout as a stranger would tend a stranger."[28] It is this dream that doctors and philosophers disguise as scientific theory when they uphold, as Aristotle did, for instance, that in procreation the female emits no seed, that her role is entirely passive, that the active regenerating function is exclusively male.[29] It is the same dream that is discernible in the royal myths in which the newborn child is compared to an ember from the paternal hearth. The stories of Meleager, of Demophoon,[30] recall the Latin legends—mostly Greek in origin—in which the king's son is born from a brand or spark leaping from the fire into the lap of the virgin tending the hearth.[31] The ritual appellation of the hearth-child (which, in the historic age, designated the city's representative to the deities of Eleusis) has very much the meaning and significance accorded it by Gernet when he specifically emphasized the close relationship which in Greece links the hearth and the child: the *pais aph' hestias* represents, in its true sense, the child "issue of the hearth."[32] And, as we shall see, it is in this context that the ritual of the *amphidromia* should be understood, whereby the newborn child, seven days after birth, is attached to its father's hearth.

Hestia thus incarnates, pushed to its limits, the tendency of the *oikos* toward self-isolation, withdrawal, as though the ideal for the family should be complete self-sufficiency economically,[33] strict endogamy in marriage. This ideal does not confirm with Greek reality. But it is nevertheless present in family institutions and the forms they take to ensure their continued existence—it is one of the axes round which the domestic life of ancient Greece was organized.

[. . .]

In a masculine society such as that of Greece the woman is normally regarded from the man's point of view. And from this standpoint she fulfills, through marriage, two major social functions between which there is a divergence if not complete polarity. In its oldest form (and among the nobility to whose circles epic poetry introduces us), marriage is a formalized transaction between family groups and the woman is one element of the exchange. Her role is to seal the alliance between opposing groups. Like a ransom, she may be the means of bringing a vendetta to an end.[34] Among the gifts exchanged as a normal accompaniment to the marriage which set the seal on the new agreement there is one of particular value because it is explicitly given in exchange for the woman, and is in fact the price paid for her. This is the *hedna*, a very valuable commodity of a very definite type: prize animals from the flocks and herds, especially male cattle, of great prestige value, and for which exaggerated claims of size and number are made. By this marriage practice of purchase, the woman becomes one of the commodities of the exchange. Being mobile in the same way as other commodities, she is simply the medium for gifts, exchanges, and abduction.[35] In contrast, the man who welcomes the spouse to his house (it is *sunoikein*, cohabitating with the husband, which defines the state of marriage for the wife) represents the landed property of the *oikos*, the *patrōia*, generally inalienable, which through the rise and fall of succeeding generations maintains the bonds between the family line and its native soil. This idea of a symbiosis, or, even better, of a communion between a plot of earth and the human group that cultivates it, exists not only in religious thought (witness the myths of autochthony: men asserting they are the "sons of the soil" they inhabit) and in the rites of sacred ploughing (which we shall have occasion to consider later on). It is also evident, with remarkable persistency, in the city institutions. As the term *oikos* has both a familial and a territorial meaning, it is easy to understand the undercurrents that, in a fully mercantile economy, hamper transactions of purchase and sale in the case of family landed property (*klēros*). Equally comprehensible is the refusal to grant strangers the right to own land belonging to "the city" because this is the privilege and right of the "native" citizen.

Marriage, however, does not consist solely in this form of commerce between families. It also allows men of a particular lineage to found a family and
so ensure the continued survival of their house. From this further standpoint
the Greeks viewed marriage as a form of ploughing the soil (*arotos*), the
woman symbolizing the furrow (*aroura*), and the man the ploughman (*arotēr*).
This imagery, almost obligatory for the tragic poets,[36] but employed also by the
prose writers,[37] is something much more than a mere literary device. It is in
line with the declaration of the plighting of troths in the stereotypical style
made familiar by the comedies. The father, or in his absence the *kurios* who is
authorized to arrange the daughter's marriage, pronounces as the pledge of
betrothal (*enguē*): "I bestow this girl in order that ploughing should bring forth
legitimate children."[38] Plutarch, referring to the existence in Athens of three
ceremonies of sacred ploughing (*hieroi, arotoi*), remarks: "But most sacred of all
sowings is the marital sowing and ploughing [*gamēlios*] for the procreation of
children."[39]

The woman, who at one moment figures as an element of commerce,
equivalent as movable property to the wealth of flocks, is now identified, in her
procreative function, with a field. Paradoxically, however, she personifies not
her native soil but that of her husband. This must be, for otherwise the sons,
issue of the ploughed furrow, would not have the religious qualifications to
take over the paternal property and work the land productively. Through
Clytemnestra, but also in opposition to Clytemnestra, the "stranger," it is the
land of Mycenae which fosters the germination and growth of the tree that
casts its shadow over all the land of the house of the Atrides, marking its
boundaries in the process. This shadow (*skia*) projected by the royal scion, born
of the hearth, rooted at the center of the domain, possesses beneficent properties. It protects the land of Mycenae. It transforms it into a domestic enclosure,
a place of security where each feels at home, protected from want, in a climate
of family friendship.[40] Handed down from father to son, the *sacra*, privilege of
royal houses or of certain noble *genē*, ensure simultaneously the defense of the
land against dangers from outside, internal peace with justice, and the fertility
of the soil and flocks. Should a prince be unworthy or illegitimate, the land, the
flocks, and the women will be barren, and war and dissension will be rife. But
if the rightful king acts according to the rules and upholds justice, then his
people will flourish in boundless prosperity: "The earth bears them victual in
plenty, and the oak bears acorns upon the top and bees in the midst; his woolly
sheep are laden with fleeces; his women bear children like their father."[41] It
seems legitimate to believe that the practice of sacred ploughing, which was
still the custom right up to historical times, and which, in the city, was carried
out by such priestly families as the Bouzygai, was an extension of ancient royal
rites designed not only to introduce and regulate the agricultural calendar but
also to promote, through the act of tilling, the marriage of the king to his land,

as in earlier times Jason was joined to Demeter on thrice-ploughed fallow land.[42]

The need for the husband to summon a "strange wife to his home," there to personify the family land where his children will grow seems less paradoxical if a further aspect of Hestia is considered. In the words of the Homeric hymn: "For without you [Hestia], mortals hold no banquet where one does not duly pour sweet wine in offering to Hestia both first and last."[43] It is therefore Hestia's prerogative (*timē*) to preside over repasts which, beginning and closing with an invocation to the goddess, form a cycle enclosed within time as the *oikos* forms an enclosed circle in space. Having been cooked on the altar of the domestic hearth, the food engenders a religious fellowship among the table companions. It creates a kind of common identity among them. From Aristotle we know the epithet used by Epimenides of Crete for members of the *oikos*. He called them *homokapoi*,[44] that is, those who eat at the same table, or, according to another reading, those who inhale the same smoke, *homokapnoi*. By virtue of the hearth the table companions become "brothers" as if of the same blood. Thus the expression "to sacrifice to Hestia" has the same meaning as our proverb that charity begins at home. We are told that when the ancients sacrificed to Hestia no portion of the offering was given to anyone. The household shared their collective repast in privacy and no stranger was allowed to participate.[45] Under the sign of the goddess the family circle shuts itself in, the domestic group strengthens its ties and asserts its unity in consuming food forbidden to the stranger.

But there is a counterpart to this. The verb *hestian*—in both of its generally accepted meanings: receiving in the home and accepting at the table—is usually applied to the guest who is being feasted in the house. The hearth, the meal, the food, also have the property of opening the domestic circle to those who are not members of the family, of enrolling them in the family community. The suppliant, hounded from his home and wandering abroad, crouches at the hearth when he seeks to enter a new group in order to recover the social and religious roots he has lost.[46] And the stranger must be led to the hearth, received, and feasted there, for there can be neither contact nor exchange with those who have not first been integrated within the domestic space. Pindar wrote that at the ever-spread tables of sanctuaries where Hestia was the patron goddess, the justice of Zeus *Xenios* was respected.[47] Relations with strangers, *xenoi*, are thus the province of Hestia as much when receiving a guest in the home as when returning to one's own house after a journey or an embassy abroad. In both cases contact with the hearth assumes the value of deconsecration and reintegration within the family space. The center symbolized by Hestia defines, therefore, not only a closed and isolated world: it presupposes, as a corollary, other analogous centers. By exchanging goods, movement of people (women, heralds, ambassadors, guests, and table companions), a network of "alliances" is built up among domestic groups. Thus, without being part of the family line of descent, an outside element can become, in more or less permanent fashion, joined to and integrated within a household other than its own. This is the way in which the "stranger" wife enters her husband's *oikos* through the ritual of the *katakhusmata* and becomes part of his home. And for as long as she dwells in her husband's house, she can by virtue of her procreative powers assume that attribute of permanency, continuity, and attachment to the soil which is personified by Hestia.[48]

[. . .]

It has been seen how the child that Agamemnon implanted in his hearth at the center of the kingdom overshadowed, as it grew, all the land of Mycenae, or, in other words, extended to the farthermost limits of the territory the protective shadow that makes the house a covered shelter, an intimate realm where women can feel at home.[49] In contrast to the open air, dazzling with sun and light during the day and filled with dread in the dark of night, the hearth space, shaded and feminine, implies, in the semidarkness of the fireplace, security, tranquillity, and even a certain easy softness incompatible with a state of virility. [. . .] If, as in Plato's own formula, the woman "imitates" the earth by receiving the seed that the male implants in her, the house, like earth and woman, receives and keeps in its heart the wealth the man has brought to it. The enclosure of the dwelling place is intended not only to shelter the family group. Domestic goods are also kept there where they can be gathered together, stored, and preserved. It is thus not surprising to see the goddess, who symbolizes the interior, the center, and fixity, directly associated with this function of the dwelling place, which inclines the life of the *oikos* in two directions. First, and in contrast to the circulation of riches under Hermes' patronage (exchange, profits, and expenditure), there is a trend toward accumulation (a tendency that in ancient times took the form of collecting food supplies in jars in the storeroom and accumulating precious objects such as *agalmata* locked up in the coffers of the *thalamos*; when a monetary economy was established this became capitalization). Second—and in contrast with the communal forms of social life—there is the tendency toward appropriation. Within the framework of a distributive economy,[50] each house appears to be bound up with a plot of ground. Each household is separate and differentiated and wants to have full control of the *kleros* on which it subsists and which distinguishes it from other domestic groups.

Under the title of Hestia *Tamia*, the hearth goddess assumes this joint role of the concentration of wealth and the delimitation of the family patrimonies. In the palaces of the Homeric kings, the *tamia* was the thrifty housekeeper who organized the household work and watched over the provisions.[51] In city times the word *tamias* was used to describe the treasurer administering the state funds or the sacred treasures, the property of the gods. There are two confirmations of Hestia as the patron of the gathering in of the riches even in a later period. The first is in Artemidorus, who states that when Hestia or images of her are seen in a dream by one who is a citizen, this symbolizes "the public revenue funds."[52] The second, connected with a ritual of Cos alluded to in a third-century inscription, includes a significant detail. It concerns a sacrifice to Zeus *Polieus* with whom Hestia is closely associated in the feast. Among the cattle presented by the groups of different tribes the animal to be sacrificed is selected after a long procedure probably similar to that employed at Athens at the *dipolies*. The victim, having thus been selected, is led to the *agora*. Its price, valued in terms of money, is publicly declared by the herald (*kērux*). Its owner then declares that his fellow citizens should pay this amount, not to Zeus, but to Hestia. As Gernet remarks, the value of the bullock in a monetary economy is "capitalized" by Hestia, who is guardian and guarantor of the wealth of the city.[53]

On the other hand, we should also stress Hestia's relationship with what this same writer calls a discretionary economy, dominated by the *suum cuique*. At Tegea the communal hearth of the Arcadians was associated with a Zeus *Klerios*, the apportioner (cf. *klēros*, "portion," "patrimony")—an epithet that recalls the first allocation of Arcadian land divided by drawing lots between the three sons of Arcas.[54] In Athens, the first act of the archon (the magistrate who, we are told by Aristotle,[55] derives his office from the communal hearth, and who, from the earliest days, always resided in the prytaneum),[56] once he is installed, is to have proclaimed by the herald that "all men shall hold, until the end of his office, those possessions and powers that they held before his entry into office."[57]

Such testimony is concerned with the communal hearth, the Hestia of the city, which became the center of the state and symbol of the unity of the citizens. The better to appreciate it, we should place it in its historical perspective and relate it to what can be ascertained of a more ancient past, before the city-state, when Hestia was not yet the communal hearth but the family altar, and symbolized most specifically the superior virtues of the royal house.[58]

But there are two aspects to the wealth of the king—one could even say two opposite poles. On the one hand there are goods that can be collected and stored in the palace: food supplies, of course, but various types of *agalmata*, cloth; precious metals; *sacra* invested with power, used as symbols of authority; coats of arms; instruments of investiture. Penelope, in Odysseus' palace, goes down with her women into the depths of the *thalamos* where the master has locked up his treasures[59] of cloth placed in coffers, bronze, gold, and wrought iron, and lastly the bow that Odysseus alone can bend, which appears later in the poem as the instrument of his vengeance, the symbol and restorer of the lawful sovereignty. The word *keimēlia* is applied to all these objects emphasizing that they are goods which are immobilized, intended to stay in place (cf. the verb *keimai*, "to be laid," "immobile").[60] The other aspect of royal wealth is represented by flocks and herds.[61] On the level of economic values these form a contrast to the treasure, as does the interior to the exterior, the static to the mobile, the domestic enclosure to the open space of the *agros*. In contrast to the world of town, house, and even cultivated fields, what Greeks call *agros* is actually the pastoral sphere, land for pasture, open country to which the animals are led or where wild animals are hunted—the wild and distant country filled with herds.[62] When Xenophon contrasts men with beasts it is precisely because men need a roof over their heads, while herds live *en hupaithrōi*.[63] Moreover the word denoting grazing stock, *probaton*, is vivid enough: in its true meaning it signifies that which moves, that which goes forward. The phrase *keimēlion kai probasis* (which, through the antinomy of *keimai*, "to be lying down," and *probainō*, "to go forward," expresses the twofold aspect of wealth taken as a whole),[64] emphasizes clearly the contrast between riches that "lie" in the house and those that "run" in the country. Across the sweep of the *agros* the herdsman Hermes[65] (Hermes *Agrotēr*, Hermes *Nomios*) drives the flocks, controlling them with his magic staff. As god of the shepherds[66] he has power over them, just as Hestia, the domestic goddess, is patron of the goods within the house.[67] In the closing words of the Homeric *Hymn to Hermes*, Zeus commands "that Hermes should be lord (*anax*) over the cows in the fields, the horse and mules, the lions, the boars and dogs, and over the sheep that the wide earth nourishes and over every four-legged animal (*pasi d'epi probatois*)."

But it is not only in their wandering that the herds exemplify the aspect of movement in wealth. They also constitute the first form of riches, which, instead of remaining constant, has the capacity to increase or diminish. First, because with the complicity of Hermes, the cattle thief, neighbors' lands can be raided and the booty added to one's own herds. And also because if Hermes *epimēlios*, Hermes *polumēlos*[68] (of abundant herds) favors you, the stock will multiply and your riches will beget riches. Ownership and the preservation of goods are the domain of Hestia. But the movement of riches which can either increase or decrease, and acquisition and loss, depend, as does exchange, on the god, who, like Hecate (so Hesiod tells us) knows how to "increase [*axein*] the livestock in their sheds—the herds of cattle, the flocks of goats, the long columns of sheep heavy with wool: he makes the few the many and the many the few."[69] Later on, in a fully mercantile economy the Greeks had no difficulty in recognizing the ancient god of the shepherds beneath the features of their god of trade. In the movement of money, which, through the action of interest, is self-increasing, they could still discern the increase of livestock multiplying at regular intervals. They used the same word, *tokos*, for interest on capital and for the newly born animals brought forth at the turn of the year.[70]

[. . .]

The feast of the *amphidromia* focused on the hearth implies, in terms of the space with which it is concerned, that same polarity expressed for the Greeks, in the arrangement of their pantheon, by the Hermes–Hestia couple. And we have, therefore, to extend our investigation to further rituals concerning the hearth-goddess, in order to discover what form of spatial representation they may involve.

Two examples, in this respect, seem particularly illuminating. Knowledge of the first comes from a text of Plutarch, who is a firsthand witness, as it were, about a ritual in Chaeronia, the birthplace of the author.[71] The rite of expulsion of hunger (*boulimou exelasis*) in the Boeotian city took place on two levels: each individual conducted the rites for his own family within the home, and at the same time the *archōn* followed the ritual on behalf of the group, at the communal hearth of the city. The ceremony was identical in the two cases. A slave was beaten with a willow rod (*rhabdos*)[72] and pushed outside across the threshold, while the exclamation: "Hunger out, Riches and Health within"[73] was pronounced. The rite is based on the opposition between an enclosed and fixed interior where the wealth is kept (Hestia), and the exterior to which the injurious forces of hunger are expelled with the very staff of Hermes.

In Athens the same opposition characterizes the organization of the space where the *Prutaneion*, the seat of Hestia Koine, is situated. In its immediate vicinity was a piece of land dedicated to *Boulimos*, Hunger.[74] This was evidently a field that was always left to lie fallow, which, lying in the heart of the humanized space of the city, represented the wild land that man must not lay hands on for this would be a sacrilege for which the punishment was famine.[75] In relation to the *Prutaneion*, the *Boulimos*, field is, therefore, the counterpart of the *Bouzugion*, the field at the very foot of the Acropolis which was annually subjected to a ritual ploughing by the *Bouzugēs*[76] in the name of the city. One further point should be made: while conducting the ploughing ceremony which periodically renewed the union between the original Athenian peoples and their native soil and deconsecrated the Attic earth for them to use and cultivate freely, the *Bouzugēs* uttered curses that fell on the newly turned soil and ensured its productivity. The priest anathematized on the one hand "Those who refuse to share water and fire" (referring to the space of hospitality—Hestia), and, on the other, "Those who do not point the way for wanderers [*planōmenois*]" (referring to the space of the traveler—Hermes).[77]

The second example is from the Achaean city of Phares, near Patrai.[78] It concerns a divinitory ritual of a rather special kind which associates Hestia and Hermes very closely. A stone statue of Hermes, bearded and foursquare, stands in the middle of a vast *agora*, surrounded by a peribolus. Oracles are uttered by the god who is called *agoraios*. Facing this statue of Hermes is a hearth (Hestia). It includes, besides the altar, a number of bronze lamps bound with lead. The procedure for the delivery of oracles was as follows. At dusk, the person consulting the oracle enters the *agora*. First he goes to the hearth where he burns incense, fills the lamps with oil, and lights them. Then he puts on the altar of Hestia a coin of the country, no doubt sacred, and termed a "bronze." Then only does he turn to Hermes and whisper in the god's ear the question he wants answered. Having done this, he puts his hands over his ears and walks off to get out of the *agora*. As soon as he has left the peribolus and got outside (*es to ektos*), he removes his hands from his ears, and the first voice he hears, as he goes on his way, will provide him with the god's answer.

In this instance the *agora* is a circumscribed place around a specific center, under the twofold patronage of Hermes *agoraios* and Hestia. It is in front of Hestia, in the center, that the person coming from outside to consult the oracle first stops. By contact with the hearth in the actions of incense burning and lamp lighting all round the goddess, the stranger is infused with the religious qualities necessary to be able to consult the local oracle. And he pays his consultation fee to Hestia because it is she, in the divine couple, who represents the force of permanency and storage. In contrast, the way in which the oracle is consulted emphasizes the volatile aspect of Hermes. The god's answer is revealed first through the very movement of the questioner who must start walking before he can learn it; second, at the moment he leaves the enclosed space of the *agora*, when he enters exterior spaces; third, in catching the sound of a voice—an elusive, faint, imperceptible *phōnē*, the voice of the firstcomer who happens to cross his path; last, in the distance imposed between the question asked in the center of the *agora* (in the same way as the consultation fee is paid in the center, there to remain forever) and the answer supplied by the outside, in a space other than that in which his statue is erected.

This study took as its point of departure the presence in the Greek pantheon of a particular and well attested structure: the Hestia–Hermes couple. From analyses of texts which stress the bonds uniting the god and goddess has emerged the relationship each has with specific and contrary aspects of space. This has led us to abandon the domain of purely religious representation and to direct our study no longer exclusively to the ideas of the Greeks regarding their gods but toward the social systems of which these ideas seem a part. The various institutions discussed refer specifically, in the very way they function, to the hearth and the religious values it represents. This body of institutional practices, gravitating around the hearth established as a fixed center, expresses one aspect of the archaic experience of space in ancient Greece. To the extent that these practices constitute a well-regulated and orderly system of conduct they imply a mental organization of space.

Whether concerned with facts affecting marriage, family relationships, lines of descent, the heritage of the family *klēros*, the domestic status of husbands and wives, the social and psychological contrasts between men and women, their activities within the house and outside, the double aspect of wealth and of land improvement—our aim has always been to throw light on the structures of thought pertaining to space, as testified in the interplay of symbolic representations and structures of behavior. It seems that the spatial values associated with

a center, immobile and withdrawn, had their regular counterpart in the opposite values of an open space, unstable, a place of distance, contacts, and change.

Nevertheless, the analysis has been one-sided. We have consistently approached it from the point of view of Hestia and the center. So Hermes has
been seen only as Hestia's complement, the god appearing as the antithesis of
the goddess. In order, therefore, to complete the study of the relationship of
these two deities, the approach should be changed and the investigation carried
out from the converse point of view, this time from the standpoint of Hermes,
through the study of the groups of images evoked by the god in the Greek
conscience and the activities and institutions of which he is the patron. But
before abandoning the subject of Hestia it should also be pointed out that the
polarity that is so marked a characteristic of all the goddess's relations with
Hermes is such a basic feature of archaic thought that it appears as an integral
attribute of the hearth goddess, as though part of Hestia already belonged to
Hermes.

In order to fulfill her function as the power conferring on domestic space its
center, its permanence, and its confines, Hestia, as has been said, must root the
human dwelling place in the ground. This is the significance of the Mycenaean
hearth, that *fixed* altar-hearth. This in fact gives a chthonic aspect to the "epich-
thonic" goddess dwelling on the earth's surface. Through her the house and
the household enter into contact with the underworld. In a fragment of the
Phaethon,[79] Euripides identifies Hestia with Demeter's daughter, Kore, who,
sometimes reigning at Hades' side and sometimes living in the world of men, is
responsible for establishing communication and passage between the two
worlds separated by an insurmountable barrier.

Furthermore, in the Mycenaean *megaron* the circular hearth welded to the
ground is in the center of a rectangular space bounded by four columns. These
reach to the roof of the house where they enclose an open lantern through
which smoke escapes. When incense is burned, or meat is cooked on the
hearth, or when, during a meal, the portion of food dedicated to the gods is
consumed by the flames of the fire lit on her domestic hearth, Hestia sends the
family offerings up to the dwelling place of the Olympian gods. Contact between earth and the heavens is established through her in the same way as she
acts as a passageway to the infernal regions.

The center, of which Hestia is the patron, represents for the domestic group
that spot of earth which enables terrestrial space to be stabilized, demarcated,
and determined. But it also, conjointly, represents the passageway par excellence, the channel of communication between normally separate and isolated
cosmic levels. For members of the *oikos* the hearth, the center of the house, also
marks the path of exchange with the gods beneath and the gods above, the axis
through which all parts of the universe are joined together. Another image
evoked by the hearth is that of the mast of a ship firmly fixed in the deck and
raised straight up toward the sky.

Should we believe, like Louis Deroy, that there is an early link between the hearth and the mast or colonnade, postulated by the lexicographical analogy, which, even in Homer's language, changed the old word *hestiē*, "hearth," into *histiē*, which means a colonnade, the confusion of the two terms being explained by the fact that the Mycenaean hearth was surrounded by wooden pillars, *histoi*, supporting the roof-lantern (*melathron*)?[80] Hesychius, we know, comments that *hista* = the altar of the hearth (*eskhara*) and the mast of a ship; and again that *histia* = the woman who weaves, because *histos* also denotes, apart from column and mast, a loom (always upright among the Greeks) that seems firmly fixed in the ground while reaching upwards.

It should be noted, in any case, that in Plato, who is so faithful to the teachings of the sacred writings and the suggestions of the ancient myths, the figure of Hestia, alone of all the gods to remain immobile at home,[81] is merged, in the final myth of the *Republic*,[82] with the great goddess Anagke, the Spinner, enthroned at the center of the universe. On her knees Anagke holds the spindle whose movement controls the rotation of all the celestial spheres. It is itself fixed to the great shaft of light in the center of which Anagke is seated, and which, rising straight as a mast or a column, stretches from top to bottom right through the sky and the earth, uniting the entire cosmos in the same way as the various parts of a boat are linked together from prow to poop.

Immobile, but mistress of the movements around her, central in the same way as a main shaft traversing a machine throughout and holding its component parts together: this is the image of Hestia that Plato appears to have inherited from the oldest of the Greek religious traditions. That is why when he claims, in the linguistic game of the *Cratylus*,[83] to reveal the secrets of the divine names, Plato, the academy philosopher, suggests a double etymology for the word Hestia. Of his two contrary explanations Plato certainly gives his preference to one rather than the other. But it is very significant that he should present them, in spite of their antinomy, as two equally possible interpretations of the same divine name. For some Hestia corresponds with *ousia*, which in Greek is sometimes also called *essia*, that is, the immutable and permanent essence. But for others essence is termed *ōsia* because, like Heraclitus, they think that all that exists is mobile and that nothing remains static. According to these latter everything is caused by and based on the impetus of movement (*to ōthoun*), which they term *ōsia*.

Hestia as the principle of permanence, Hestia as the principle of impetus and movement—in this twofold and contradictory interpretation of the name of the hearth goddess we recognize the very foundations of the relationship which opposes and unites, in a single contrasted couple joined in unbreakable "friendship," the goddess who immobilizes space around a fixed center and the god who renders it completely and everlastingly mobile.

TRANSLATED BY H. PIAT

NOTES

[1] Pausanias 5.11.8

[2] On the Sosibios vase, Hermes follows Hestia [cf. P. Raingeard, *Hermès psychagogue: essai sur les origines du culte d'Hermès* (Paris, 1934), p. 500]; bicephalic columns with masculine and feminine heads of Hermes and Hestia [. . .]; on Hermes habitually associated with Hestia as a couple among the twelve gods [. . .].

[3] *Homeric Hymn to Hestia* 1.11ff.; cf. also lines 1–2: "in high dwellings of all who walk on earth (*khamai*)." In his *Interpretation of Dreams*, Artemidorus classes Hestia and Hermes among the epichthonian deities in contrast to the celestial and subterranean gods.

[4] *Homeric Hymn to Aphrodite* 29–30.

[5] *Phaedrus* 247a.

[6] Euripides fr. 983N2; cf. Macrobius 1.23: "If Hestia remains alone in the house of the gods, it means that the earth remains motionless at the center of the universe." Cf. also the saying of Philolaos: "That One who remains in the middle of the sphere is named Hestia" (Diels and Kranz, *Die Fragmente der Vorsokratiker*, 7th ed. (Berlin, 1956), vol. 1, p. 410 line 12. Note also the expression in the Homeric *Hymn*, line 3: "Hestia's status in the home is immutable (*heirēn aidion*)."

[7] Homer *Iliad* 24.334–335.

[8] Aristophanes *Peace* 392.

[9] *Homeric Hymn to Hermes* 14–15.

[10] Ibid., 146–147.

[11] The triple or quadruple representation of the face of the god was precisely what enabled him to control simultaneously all directions in space.

[12] L. R. Farnell, *The Cults of the Greek States* (Oxford, 1896), vol. 5, p. 62 n. 2.

[13] Aeschylus *Libation Bearers* 124ff.

[14] Plutarch *On Garrulousness* 502F.

[15] Cf. also J. Orgogozo's interesting study "L'Hermès des Achéens," *Revue de l'histoire des religions* 136 (1949): 10–30. [. . .]

[16] See references in L. Deroy's "Le Culte du foyer dans le Grèce mycénienne," *Revue de l'histoire des religions* 137 (1950): 32 n. 1.

[17] Cf. Louis Gernet, "Sur le Symbolisme politique en Grèce ancienne: Le Foyer commun," *Cahiers internationaux de sociologie* in this volume at pp. 100–11 as "Political Symbolism: The Public Hearth." In his *Life of Numa*, 9–11, Plutarch remarks that the tradition was maintained in Greece of a female priesthood to tend the sacred fires. The responsibility fell not upon virgins, as in Rome, but on women abstaining from all sexual relations. During the city period, the ministry of the communal hearth became essentially a political function and was for this reason reserved for men. It should be noted that, already in Homer, the cult of Hestia was relegated to the background.

[18] Deroy, "Le Culte," 26–43.

[19] On the "generating" fire, see Plutarch *Life of Camillus* 20.4; *Social Matters* 7.4.3.

[20] *Homeric Hymn to Aphrodite* 20–30.

[21] Concerning the rites that, on the eve of marriage, mark the renunciation of the previous state, cf. Euripides *Iphigenia in Tauris* 372–375, and the remarks of L. Séchan, "La légende d'Hippolyte dans l'antiquité," *Revue des études grecques* (1911): 115ff. On the rite of hair shearing, for marriage as for mourning a relative, cf. *Palatine Anthology* 6.276, 277, 280, 281. In Sparta the young bride's head was shaved all over: see Plutarch *Life of Lycurgus* 15.5.

[22] On the *katakhusmata*, the rites concerning the integration of the wife in the household of her husband, cf. E. Samter, *Familienfeste der Griechen und Romer* (Berlin, 1901), p. 159. The bride was led to the hearth, perhaps even seated beside it (in the crouching attitude

of the suppliant), and her head was covered with sweetmeats, *tragēmata*, particularly dried fruit, dates, nuts, figs. The same ritual was followed with a new slave on his first entering the house to which he was to belong. In that case it was the mistress of the house (*despoina*) who officiated as the representative of the hearth.

[23] On *Kharis*, presiding over free exchange and gift giving, cf. Aristotle *Nicomachean Ethics* 1133a.2. [. . .]

[24] Plutarch *On Love* 751d.

[25] Hermes, associated with Aphrodite in her role as *Peithō*: inscription of Mytilene to Aphrodite *Peithō*, and, among others, Hermes, *Inscriptiones Graecae* 12.2.73; Plutarch *Precepts for Marriage* 138c. Associated with Aphrodite in her role as the "schemer" (*Makhanitis*), Pausanias 8.31.6; when she is *Psithuros* of the "seductive murmurings," cf. Harpocration s.v. *Psithuristēs*: the Athenians worshipped Hermes under the name in association with Aphrodite and Eros. On Hermes *Peisinous* at Cnidos, cf. Farnell, *Cults of the Greek States* (Oxford, 1896–1909), p. 70 n. 43.

[26] "A virtuous woman should stay at home; only light women appear on the streets": Menander fr. 546, Edmonds.

[27] Xenophon *Oeconomicus* 7.30; cf. Hierocles in *Stobaeus* 4.1, 502H: "Man's job is in the fields, in the *agora*, the affairs of the city; women's work is spinning wool, baking bread, keeping house." In the *Against Neaera* 122, Demosthenes, defining the married state (*to sunoikein*), gives special emphasis to the domestic vocation of the spouse as the guardian of her husband's hearth in contrast to the functions of courtesans and concubines: "Mistresses we keep for the sake of pleasure, concubines for the daily care of our persons, but wives to bear us legitimate children and to be faithful guardians of our households [*tōn endon phulaka pistēn*]."

[28] Aeschylus *Eumenides* 658–661; cf. also Euripides *Orestes* 552–555 and *Hippolytus* 616ff.

[29] Aristotle *Generation of Animals* 1.20, 729a. "A theory of this type, deprived of all contact with the object is pure myth," remarks Marie Delcourt in *Oreste et Alcméon: Etude sur la projection légendaire du matricide en Grèce* (Paris, 1959), p. 85.

[30] On Meleager, cf. Apollodorus 1.8.2; Aeschylus *Libation Bearers* 607ff. The brand (*dalos*) in the hearth is a kind of "double" or the outsoul of Meleager. The child will die when the brand, placed in a casket (*larnax*) by his mother, is consumed by fire. This was decided by the *moirai* seven days after his birth—a date that corresponds, as we shall see, with the celebration of the *amphidromia*, the rites that integrate the newborn child into the home of its father. On Demophoon, cf. Homeric *Hymn to Demeter* 239ff. The goddess, nurse to the royal baby, hides it in the fire like a brand (*dalos*).

[31] Legends of Caeculus and Servius Tullus. The comparison is made by Gernet, *Sur le Symbolisme*, p. 27.

[32] Gernet, ibid.

[33] Cf. A. Aymard, "L'Idée de travail dans le Grèce archaique," *Journal de Psychologie* (1948): 29–50.

[34] On the woman offered in wedlock as *poinē* of the vendetta, cf. Glotz *Solidarité de la famille dans le droit criminel en Grèce* (Paris, 1904), p. 130.

[35] The ritual bears witness to the persistency of this aspect of abduction in marriage; Plutarch *Life of Lycurgus* 15.5; *Roman Questions* 271d 29.

[36] Aeschylus *Seven against Thebes* 754; Sophocles *Oedipus Rex* 1257; *Antigone* 569; Euripides *Orestes* 553; *Medea* 1281; *Ion* 1095. [. . .]

[37] Plato *Cratylus* 406b; *Laws* 839a.

[38] Menander *A Close-Cropped Girl* 435–436, fr. 720, Edmonds: *tautēn gnēsiōn paidōn ep' arotōi soi didōmi*. Cf. Benveniste, 1936, 51–58.

[39] Plutarch *Precepts on Marriage* 144b.

[40] Sophocles *Electra* 421–423; Aeschylus *Agamemnon* 966.

[41] Hesiod *Works and Days* 232ff.

[42] Hesiod *Theogony* 969–971.

[43] *Homeric Hymn to Hestia* 1.5ff.; cf. Cicero *De natura deorum*: *in ea dea, omnis et precatio et sacrificatio extrema est.* Cornutus c. 28: Hestia is at once *prōtē* and *eskhatē*; she is the beginning and the end.

[44] Aristotle *Politics* 1252b 15.

[45] Zenobius 4.44; Diogenianus 2.40.

[46] As did Odysseus in the palace of Alcinous: *Odyssey* 7.153–154.

[47] *Nemean Odes* 11.1ff.

[48] On the *katakhusmata* rites, see note 22, above. The bonds between the man and his wife are the same as those which unite two antagonistic groups who have become guests and allies after an exchange of oaths has substituted a peace agreement between them for a state of war. It is the same word, *philotēs*, which denotes intimate relations between spouses and the contract that establishes a fictitious relationship between recent antagonists with a view to binding them by reciprocal obligations. Cf. Glotz, *Solidarité*, p. 22. In the love story of Aphrodite and Ares there is no doubt some phrase-spinning, but basically what we see here are institutional realities with all the behavior patterns and psychological attitudes that they govern. On the ties uniting the wife to the home of her husband, cf. Euripides *Alcestis* 162ff. Before dying, Alcestis invokes Hestia, the domestic goddess of the conjugal hearth. She addresses her as *despoina*, "mistress," and entrusts her children to her.

[49] Sophocles *Electra* 416ff. This text should be compared with the *Agamemnon* of Aeschylus, 965ff. In both cases the man is the root (*rhiza*) implanted in the earth, which, developing into a tree protecting the house, confers on the hearth (*hestia*) its "shadowed" character. Aeschylus makes Clytemnestra say, when she is pretending to welcome Agamemnon joyously on his return: "For if the root still lives, leafage comes again to the house and spreads its over-reaching shade against the scorching dog-star; so, now that thou hast come to hearth and home, thou showest that warmth hath come in wintertime; aye, and when Zeus maketh wine from the bitter grape, then forthwith there is coolness (*psukhos*)."

[50] On the contrast between totalitarian and distributive economies, cf. G. Dumézil, *Mitra-Varuna* (New York, 1988), p. 155ff.

[51] A full study has yet to be made of the figure and functions of the Homeric *tamia*, and her relations with Hestia. One or two points should be stressed: in Odysseus' palace Eurycleia is the attendant, the nurse, and the one who tends the fires. In his youth Laertes had obtained her, in exchange for twenty bullocks, from her father, Ops (the Eye), son of Pisenor. The heralds in Ithaca were recruited from this family (*Odyssey* 2.38). In the palace Laertes had honored Eurycleia on equal footing with his wife but had refrained from any intimate relations with her (*Odyssey* 1.431). She had suckled Odysseus, whom she calls her child. It is on her suggestion that Autolykos, the boy's maternal grandfather, is asked to choose a name for the newborn child (*Odyssey* 19.403). Her role is to watch unceasingly over all the goods of the house. Her vigilance, care, and foresight are much praised. She is an accomplished *phulax*. These are the qualities that Xenophon insists should belong to the *tamia* (*Oeconomicus* 9.11). She should have no weaknesses, whether for food, drink, sleep, or men; she must have a perfect memory. But the true *tamia*, the best *phulax* of the wife, should be the wife herself (9.14–15).

[52] Artemidorus 2.37; cf. Gernet, *Sur le Symbolisme*, p. 38.

[53] On the Cos ritual, cf. Gernet, *Sur le Symbolisme*, p. 33 [p. 109 in this volume].

[54] Pausanias 8.53.9.

[55] *Politics* 1322b ff.

[56] Aristotle *Constitution of Athens* 3.5.

[57] Ibid., 56.2.

[58] On the historical relations between the royal Mycenaean hearth and the city communal hearth, cf. Farnell, *Cults of the Greek States* (Oxford, 1896–1909), p. 350ff.

[59] *Odyssey* 21.8ff.

[60] Note the expression, *keimēlia* (*Iliad* 6.47 and *Odyssey* 11.9). In the first book of the *Odyssey* Telemachus offers his guest a gift, saying: "Thou mayest go to thy ship glad in spirit and bearing a gift costly and very beautiful, which shall be to thee a *keimēlion*, even such a gift as dear friends give to friends." Again, in the twenty-third book of the *Iliad* (618), Achilles gives to Nestor a cup: "Take this now, old sire, and let it be a *keimēlion* for thee, a memorial of Patroclus's burying"; cf. also Plato *Laws* 913a.

[61] The presence among the herds of Atreus of a lamb with a gold or purple fleece is the sign that Pelops's son is born to be king. Occasionally Hermes is presented as having himself engendered the golden lamb, the symbol of royal investiture (Euripides *Orestes* 995). In any case it is he who intervenes to reestablish the legitimate sovereignty when Thyestes, in his contest with Atreus, fraudulently presents the royal beast that belongs to his brother's flocks. The relations of Hermes with the ram, the symbol of royalty, are the same as those which associate him with the *skēptron*, the mobile symbol of sovereignty that the god of exchange transmits from Zeus to the house of the Atridai, in the same way as he brings them the golden ram. In Orgogozo's study (see n. 15), there are some interesting remarks on Hermes's place in the myths of the golden fleece and his associations with the function of royalty.

[62] On the significance of the *agros*, cf. P. Chantraine 1956, 34–35.

[63] Xenophon *Oeconomicus* 7.19.

[64] On the significance of *probaton* and the opposition *keimēlia–probasis*, E. Benveniste 1949. The double aspect of wealth could also be expressed in a formula such as Hesiod's (*Works and Days* 308): "Through work men grow rich in flocks and substance, *polumēloi t' aphneioi te.*" *Aphneios* is in fact related to a different type of riches from herds. It is wealth that is stored in houses or cities. In the *Odyssey* 1.392, the term refers to a house; in the *Iliad* 2.570, to a town—Corinth. On Corinth *aphneios* cf. Thucydides 1.13.5. See also *Odyssey* 1.165, where the contrast is emphasized between "light-footed" men (*elaphroteroi podas*) and men weighed down with possessions of the kind of riches constituted by gold and precious cloths (*aphneioteroi*).

[65] Hermes *agrotēr*, cf. Euripides *Electra* 463; Hermes *nomios*, cf. Aristophanes *Thesmophorriaznsae* 977.

[66] Cf. Simonides of Amorgos, fr. 18 Diehl: Hermes, patron of shepherds. We are reminded of the importance, in the religious plastic arts, of the figure of Hermes Criophorus bearing a ram on his shoulders.

[67] Cf. Scholia to Aristophanes *Ploutos* 395.

[68] Hermes *epimēlios*, cf. Pausanias 9.34.3; Hermes *polumēlos*, cf. *Iliad* 14.490.

[69] Hesiod *Theogony* 444ff.

[70] Cf. Aristotle *Politics* 1258b.

[71] Plutarch *Social Matters* 693F.

[72] It is hardly necessary to recall that the *rhabdos* is an attribute of Hermes which confers on this god the patronage of certain "expulsion" rituals, especially those that Eustathius (*Odyssey* 22.481) calls *pompaia* (cf. Hermes *pompos*, Aeschylus *Eumenides* 91; Sophocles *Ajax* 832): When the *pompaia* are celebrated and the sullied are expelled to the crossroads, a *pompos* is held in the hands, which is said to be nothing else but the *kērukeion*, the wand of Hermes; from this *pompos* and the word *dios* comes the word *to diopompein*, sacred expulsion.

[73] "*Exō boulimon, esō de plouton kai hugieian!*"

[74] *Anecdota Graeca*, Bekker, 1.278.4; G. Verrall and J. Harrison, *Mythology and Monuments of Ancient Athens* (London, 1890), p. 168.

[75] On the relations between this type of sacrilege and "devouring hunger," cf. the story of Erysichthon, Callimachus *Hymn to Demeter* 30ff.

[76] Plutarch *Precepts on Marriage* 144a–b.

[77] *Paroemiographi graeci*, edited by Gaisford, p. 25; *bouzugēs*, cf. Farnell, *op. cit.*, pp. 3, 315 n. 7. On the domestic symbolism of fire and water, cf. Plutarch *Roman Questions* 1: in Rome, the new bride has to "touch fire and water." It was doubtless a rite of integration in her husband's home as were the *katakhusmata* in Greece.

[78] Pausanias 7.22.1ff.

[79] Euripides fr. 781, 55 N². Porphyrius, in Eusebius *Praeparatio evangelica* 3.11, also associates Hestia with the subterranean deities.

[80] Deroy "Le Culte," 32 and 43.

[81] Plato *Phaedrus* 247a.

[82] *Republic* 616ff.; cf. P.-M. Schuhl, "Le Joug du bien, les liens de la nécessité et la fonction d'Hestia," in *Mélanges Charles Picard* (Paris, 1949), vol. 2, p. 965ff.

[83] Plato *Cratylus* 401c–e.

JEANNIE CARLIER

Voyage in Greek Amazonia

1979

*In contrast to the anthropologists' literal explorations, Jeannie Carlier's so-
journ among the Amazons is frankly an intellectual adventure, in which
narrative confluences are navigated and steppes of testimony traversed. Her
goal is a more nuanced understanding—not of a reconstructed Amazon
society that may or may not have existed in history—but of the Greek polis, whose norms (and nightmares) the mythic traditions of Amazonia vividly exemplify by means, as Carlier argues, of the "dynamics of inversion."*

> Stories about the Amazons have had a peculiar fate. In other cases,
> myth and history have their own clearly distinct domains.
>
> —Strabo 11.5.3

To disentangle history from myth, to separate the plausible from the
implausible, to discover the original historical kernel beneath the mystification, to pinpoint the sociohistorical origin of the legend—these
are things by which scholars fascinated by the Greek narratives concerning
these women without men and slayers of males are repeatedly tempted.[1] I have
no desire to discourage them. Like many others, however, my own view is that
the only interesting way to visit the land of the Amazons is to reconnoiter the
imagination—the Greek imagination, to be sure. If, moreover, the stories of
the Amazons require a referent in the real, we will find it in the Greek city
itself. It is there that we find the noninverted world in terms of which we shall
attempt to interpret the various inverted worlds described in the several versions of the Amazonian myth.

To the Greeks, the Amazons were triply other. They were women, with
all that that implied for a Greek about animality and undisciplined violence.
They were anti-male, *antianeirai*, and, as was pointed out quite early on,[2] this

From "Voyage en Amazonie Grecque," *Acta Antiqua Academiae Scientiarum Hungaricae*
27 (1979): 381–405.

definition played on the double meaning of *anti*, implying that they were both the equals and the enemies of males. And finally, they were barbarians. The various versions of the myth are merely variations on the degree of otherness in these three respects (dangerous femininity, inversion of sexual roles, barbarism). For one can be more or less different, and given a single norm one can construct a variety of inverted figures through partial and variable inversions. Compared with other bodies of work in which the Greeks dealt with otherness, the Amazonian legends are ideal for exploring the procedures of the imagination. The very profusion of versions and variety of contradictions that wreak havoc with historicist approaches provide both the raw material for and the justification of this type of interpretation.

To begin with, I want to recall briefly what the Greek norm was in at least one respect, namely, the distribution of sex roles, and to ask how the Greeks saw the Amazons. The condition of women was summed up in a celebrated remark of Demosthenes: "Courtesans we have for pleasure, concubines for daily care of our persons, and wives to provide us with legitimate offspring and to keep faithful watch over the household."[3] The realm of women was thus strictly divided into three sharply differentiated roles: male pleasure, housekeeping, and production of sons who resembled their fathers, or, in other words, the continuation of the male line. As mothers of citizens (though not citizens themselves), silent in politics, excluded of course from warfare and hunting, and marginalized even in religion, Greek women had no destiny other than to serve men and the city of men. The greatest merit a woman could achieve was not to be talked about by men, whether for good or for ill.[4]

But the Amazons were talked about, at length. Known since the time of Homer as redoubtable warriors, they performed exploits, set out on expeditions, rode horses, hunted, and behaved like men. They lived apart from males or else subjugated them and used them as docile slaves. Masculine behavior, segregation, and domination of males are the characteristic features of those whom the Greeks called Amazons in all versions of the myth. The Amazonian world had fringes, however. Sarmatian women, who lived like warriors but did not exclude or dominate males, lived on its frontiers, as we shall see. In many respects they resembled Amazons, but the Greeks hesitated to call them by that name: true Amazons had no husbands.

BEFORE AND ELSEWHERE

Most Greek myths were situated in the remote past, in the heroic age prior to or contemporary with the Trojan War. They constituted an "archaeology" in the Greek sense: the Gorgons had vanished, the Trojan War was over, the Chimera was defeated. What was novel about the Amazons was that the Greeks were not entirely certain that they had completely vanished. It was possible that they still existed a thousand years after Troy on the fringes of the known world, one people among others and different only by being somewhat more exotic. The Amazons thus occupied a distinctive place in myth, belonging on the one hand to "archaeology" and on the other to ethnography. The various versions of the myth reveal something like a hesitation to choose between two temptations of the imaginary: in order for the victory of the hero (Heracles or Theseus) to have been complete, the Amazons had to have been totally exterminated. But if no Amazons remained after Heracles' expedition or Theseus' and the Athenians' victory in Attica, then there could be no lovely tales of Penthesilea battling Achilles at Troy or Alexander's encounter with the queen of the Amazons and no absorbing descriptions of the strange customs of contemporary Amazons. Greater verisimilitude could be achieved by pretending that these stories pertained to a tribe that inhabited a remote but accessible land, for anyone who wished to see for himself could then do so simply by embarking on a lengthy journey.

Some versions of the myth therefore presented the Amazons as still extant, while others relegated them to the realm of "archaeology." Still others confused the issue by subterfuge. It is easy to understand why Lysias, in a funeral oration rehearsing the great exploits of his Athenian ancestors, would have chosen to exterminate the last Amazon for the greater glory of Athens:

> To them alone it happened that they were able neither to draw lessons from their mistakes in order to exercise better judgement in the future, nor to return home and report their defeat and the valor of our ancestors. For they perished here, on our very soil, paying a just penalty for their folly. They immortalized the memory of our city's valor, but their own country they plunged into obscurity through the catastrophe that befell them here. Because these women unjustly coveted the land of others, they justly lost their own.[5]

Speaking in a different context where patriotism was not of the essence, Diodorus was more subtle and devious. To be sure, a state governed by women was contrary to nature, and the Amazons were just as monstrous as the fantastic creatures of which Heracles rid humanity; they must disappear:

> the race of Amazons was entirely destroyed by Heracles . . . for, in his desire to be the benefactor of the entire human race, he deemed it aberrant to overlook the fact that one of the nations was being governed by women (*gunaikokratoumena*).[6]

Here, Diodorus was speaking of the Libyan Amazons, the oldest of all. The better-known Amazons of the Thermodon were also exterminated by Heracles,[7] but that did not prevent Diodorus from recounting their expedition to Attica,[8] Penthesilea's combat at Troy,[9] or Alexander's encounter with the queen of the Amazons.[10] We must assume that the extermination was not total.

Leaving a small "residue" of Amazons was a rather blatant but indispensable ruse if the story was to continue to be useful.

Authors who extended the existence of the Amazons into the historical period frequently sought to link "archaeology" to ethnography. There was more than one way to do this. In Herodotus, for example, the transition from archaeology to ethnography proceeds from radical Amazonism to a quasi-normal contemporary situation. The Amazons of old became the Sarmatian women of Herodotus' day, women who waged war but also took husbands. Pompeius Trogus took the opposite approach: following a "historical" event in the distant past, ordinary women became out-and-out Amazons, and so they remained until the time of Alexander or even Caesar.

Partaking of both "archaeology" and ethnography, the Amazonian legends can therefore be read either as stories of origins, that is, of the "other" who came "before," or as stories of "barbarians," that is, of the "other" who lives "elsewhere."

Yet although Amazonian texts are in several respects similar to descriptions of barbarians, they differ in other respects. In texts about barbarians, readers are confronted with a reality different from that of the Greek world (and with an interpretation of that reality). In order to make the other (the Scythian, Egyptian, Persian, or what have you) intelligible to the Greek audience, writers had to employ an interpretative framework familiar to their readers. Greek ethnographers accordingly made abundant use of techniques of inversion. In the case of the Amazons, since there was no reality, it was no longer a matter of interpretation but rather one of producing a purely imaginary account. The writer was thus freer but at the same time more strictly conditioned by canonical reference to the Greek norm.

To Believe or Not to Believe

Did the Greeks believe in their stories about the Amazons? No opinion poll will ever answer the question. We can, however, measure the extent to which the authors of Amazonian narratives believed what they said and expected to be believed and how they went about making their stories credible.

When fourth-century Attic orators praised Athens and its warriors, they never failed to include among the great exploits of their ancestors the Athenian triumph over the Amazons in the time of Theseus.[11] The attack on Attica by these barbarian women was seen as a prefiguration of the expedition by Medean and Persian barbarians, in no way less historical.[12] Even allowing for the stilted quality of patriotic speechifying, it is clear that Theseus' exploit would not have been invoked so consistently had it not been accepted by most listeners as historical. In any case, assuming that we cannot know but only infer what the audience really believed, we can say that it was a law of the genre of patriotic speeches to speak *as if* no doubt about the reality of the Athenian victory were possible.

Some ancient historians simply present the Amazons as a historical or even contemporary reality without citing any sources and without any of the verbal devices used to imply doubts such as *phasi,* "they say," *legetai,* "it is said." And if there was no shred of doubt on the part of the narrator, neither was there any incredulity to combat on the part of the reader. Quintus Curtius[13] and Diodorus[14] recount the story of Alexander's interview with the queen of the Amazons, while Pompeius Trogus and his compilers[15] trace the history of the Amazons from their remote but historical origins to the time of Julius Caesar. Similarly, Plutarch never questions the raid on Attica: "That they came by crossing the frozen Cimmerian Bosporus, as Hellanicus recounts, is hard to believe. But that they camped virtually in the city is a fact attested by place names and by the graves of those who perished."[16] He compared versions and pointed out an inconsistent tradition: "clearly a fable, a pure fiction."[17] This was a way of saying that there was nothing fabulous about his own account.

In his remarks on the "archaeological" Amazons, Diodorus takes an ambiguous and for that reason interesting position. Speaking of the Amazons of Libya, he warns us that his tales are going to seem "extraordinary and strange."[18] This is because most people believe that only the Amazons of the Thermodon in Asia Minor existed. "The truth is different, for the Amazons of Libya are far older and accomplished some notable exploits."[19] Indeed, it is because they are older that memory of them has vanished. The better-known Amazons of the Thermodon inherited the glory of the Libyans. Diodorus, however, is prepared to attribute to the Libyan Amazons what he has found "in the work of many ancient poets and historians as well as a certain number of more recent historians."[20] He hopes to convince by citing numerous witnesses. His wish to be believed is obvious, as is his sense that it would be easy not to believe. Strangely, however, his account is punctuated with expressions such as "tradition has it that" (*phasi, muthologeitai*), whereby the narrator declines responsibility and hides behind what other people say. When, moreover, he recounts the exploits of the Amazons of the Thermodon, whose existence he says is acknowledged by "most people," he precedes his remarks with a striking double caveat: "Since we have mentioned the Amazons, we do not think it out of place to discuss them, even if what we say, because of how extraordinary it is, may look like a myth."[21] Here, again, the discussion is introduced by *phasi* and ends with an exhortation to belief: "afterwards, the race, humiliated, lost all its strength, so that in recent times, even though some people speak of their prowess, *it is generally believed that the ancient tales [arkhaiologiai] of the Amazons are made-up fables.*"[22] In other words, Diodorus takes note of the incredulity, explains it, contests it, but also shares it to a certain extent since he precedes his narratives with locutions such as "it is said." It is as if he wished to persuade us not that the Amazons actually existed and accomplished the exploits that he recounts but that there exist traditions about them which he is faithfully reporting.

Since the Amazons have not gone out of existence, there are people who have encountered them while traveling in their country or because the Amazons themselves have traveled. "Theophanes [of Mytilene], who went on an expedition with Pompey and traveled to the land of the Albanians, says that the Geles and Leges, Scythian tribes, live between the Amazons and the Albanians. . . . Other authors, most notably Metrodorus of Scepsis and Hypsicrates [of Amisos], to whom these places are also not foreign, state that they live in the vicinity of the Gargarians."[23] Plutarch tells us that during the same campaign of Pompey "Amazon shields and boots" were found on a battlefield after the battle.[24] More than that: "Among the hostages and prisoners of war were many women, whose wounds were no less severe than those of the men. And they seemed to be Amazons, either because the Amazons are some tribe who live nearby and were called upon as allies or because the barbarians in this place generally call all women warriors Amazons."[25] And of course the accounts of Alexander's meeting with the queen of the Amazons were based on the testimony of supposed eyewitnesses.

Eyewitness testimony is open to challenge, however. Arrian uses the story of this encounter to demolish the myth of the Amazons. His argument is as follows: 1) The best historians do not mention this interview. 2) If the story is true, the Amazons must be false: they were probably just women trained to ride horses and equipped as Amazons. As Appian did with respect to Pompey's prisoners, Arrian here implies that the term Amazon has been stretched: is any mounted female warrior an Amazon, and can one therefore ascribe to any such warrior the traditional characteristic traits? 3) If the story were true, the Amazons must have been around in Arrian's time, in which case Xenophon would have encountered them in Asia Minor in the course of his *Anabasis*. Here, the testimony of a traveler who saw nothing is taken as counterevidence. 4) Arrian doubts in any case that the Amazons ever existed.[26]

The most explicit and detailed doubts were expressed by Strabo. After reporting, in the most skeptical of terms, what Metrodorus and Hypsicrates said about Amazons living close to Gargarians, Strabo rejects all the traditions concerning the Amazons in a text that considers both the extent to which such stories, whether about the "archaeological" Amazons or the contemporary ones, should be believed and the extent to which they are in fact believed without justification:

> When it comes to the Amazons, however, the same fantastic stories are told now as in the ancient times. Who indeed would believe that an army, city, or people of women could ever be put together without men? And not only be

put together but proceed to invade the territory of its neighbors? And not only subjugate its immediate neighbors and advance as far as what is today Ionia, but launch a military expedition across the sea as far as Attica? For this is the same as saying that the men in former times were women and the women men. And yet people say the same things about them even now, and the situation is all the more peculiar in that people are more willing to believe the ancient tales than the present ones.[27]

[. . .]

In authors of stories about the Amazons as well as readers whose opinions we can sample only indirectly, we thus find a range of beliefs as to their veracity: historical truths, glories of Athens' past, travelers' accounts presented as truthful, simple reports, stories recounted for pleasure, myths dismissed as having been invented out of whole cloth yet recounted by the very authors who denounced them. What is certain is that stories about the Amazons circulated throughout antiquity for a millennium: they were evidently a pleasure to recount and to hear as well as to think about.[28]

[. . .]

To conclude this survey, we must go back to the text of Demosthenes that defined the place of women in Greek society. The key terms of this definition, it will be recalled, were pleasure, household, and reproduction. If we look at all the Amazonian traditions, what we find, despite their discrepancies and their hesitancy to choose between a model in which man stands opposed to woman and a model in which Greek stands opposed to barbarian, is nothing less than a society in which the female is male and vice versa. The males of Amazonia are deprived of political power and speech, forbidden to know their own sons, confined to household chores and child care, and compelled to make love eagerly and procreate abundantly for the sole benefit of the opposite sex; their condition is thus a remarkably accurate reflection of the condition of women in Greece. Amazonia was indeed the Greek world turned upside-down.

Before Cecrops invented the city, the Athenians by their own account lived in a society not unlike the Amazonian: marriage did not exist, promiscuity was general, and fathers did not know their own sons. Women participated in government: they voted. Outnumbering men by one vote, they elected instead of Poseidon the goddess Athena as protectress of the city. In the wake of this event, they were excluded from power once and for all. Marriage was then instituted as a way of producing legitimate sons by imposing strict controls on female sexuality. What deep reasons impelled the Greeks for a millennium to invent anti-cities in which women held or shared power and controlled the reproductive process? To be sure, every society defines itself by contrast to others. Telling stories about the "other"—the Amazon, the barbarian, the people of prehistory—is one way of recognizing and defining oneself. But in these

Greek stories of women in power and women in arms, there is something else as well. As fully domesticated as the Greek woman, courtesan, concubine, or spouse may have been and as firm a grip as men may have had on power, they were never fully certain of their power. Greek male anxieties about the omnipresent and never fully domesticated threat of female violence and excess reveal themselves in a number of ways: in stories about women taking arms and shedding blood, sharing power and controlling reproduction, and rejecting marriage like Atalanta; in the belief that women were more apt than men to live and reproduce without the aid of the opposite sex; and, more concretely, in the refusal to allow women to wield the sacrificial knife, even in the sacrifices of the Thesmophoria that were specifically reserved for them.[29] No doubt the function of the Greeks' stories about Amazons was to point up the monstrousness of a society in which male values were stood on their head. More than once, the stories stress the perversity, cruelty, and barbarity of such a society. It is as if by telling these stories, men—for the stories in question were indeed told, or at any rate written down, by men—hoped to warn both themselves and their docile companions about the dangers of any attempt to rebel against the male order. As if to stand that order on its head in fiction was a way of ensuring its perpetuation.

The Greeks are not the only people to have believed in the Amazons. Although most serious Hellenists consider them to have been creatures of legend, some feminists in recent years have attached importance to the idea that they actually existed.[30] During a lecture at a French university on the condition of women in antiquity, female students proclaimed: "We had our kingdom, the Amazons ruled." And one committed feminist declared that any woman who cast doubt on the actual existence of the Amazons deserved the death penalty. In the United States the word "Amazon" is applied to a woman who lives alone or with another woman but shares a man's bed for a time for the sole purpose of having a child that she intends to bring up alone. Amazonia has been reborn as the founding myth of a new kind of female power, of a way of life independent of men and a rejection of traditional sex roles. If, however, I am correctly interpreting the Greek stories, the price of this co-optation has been a total reversal of meaning. The Greeks were expressing their anxieties, their rejection of a monstrous society, but this is now taken as a model, a source of confidence and hope: since real women were once able to act as veritable males, why can't real women do so again today? No doubt the model is not totally satisfying to those with truly open minds, since it does not eliminate oppression but only changes its sign. And of course no feminist dreams of establishing a society utterly without males or in which all males are reduced to servitude: Amazonism is at most an ancient reference, and the myth requires substantial revision before it can serve as a model. With such revisions, however, a two-thousand-year-old male discourse has been taken up by today's women. A living myth, it has once again become capable of carrying an ideological charge, but the opposite of that which the Greeks bestowed on it.

TRANSLATED BY ARTHUR GOLDHAMMER

NOTES

[1] The literature, both before and after Bachofen, is abundant. For a recent bibliography, see Samuel 1975.

[2] *Etymologicum magnum* 3.35.7; Eustathius, *Commentary on the Iliad* 6.186 [. . .].

[3] *Against Neaira* 122.

[4] Pericles in his funeral oration, Thucydides 2.45.2.

[5] Lysias *Funeral Oration* 6. See also Isocrates *Panegyric* 4.70.

[6] Diodorus Siculus 3.55.3.

[7] Ibid., 4.16.4 and 2.46.4.

[8] Ibid., 4.28.

[9] Ibid., 2.46.5.

[10] Ibid., 17.77.1–3.

[11] "All Athenian orators who eulogize soldiers killed in battle make special mention of the Athenian exploit against the Amazons" (Arrian *Anabasis of Alexander* 7.13.6).

[12] The paintings of the Stoa Poikilē in Athens depicted the battle of Marathon *and* Theseus' battle with the Amazons.

[13] 6.5. 24–32.

[14] Diodorus 17.77.1–3.

[15] Pompeius Trogus, fr. 36 b Seel = Justin 2.4 [. . .].

[16] *Life of Theseus* 27. 2.

[17] Ibid., 28.1

[18] Ibid., 3.52.2.

[19] Ibid., 3.52. 1.

[20] Ibid., 3.52. 3.

[21] Ibid., 2.46. 3.

[22] Ibid., 2.46.6.

[23] Strabo, who reports these travelers' opinions (11.5.1), is himself radically skeptical.

[24] *Life of Pompey* 35. 5.

[25] Appian *The Mithridatic Wars* 103.

[26] Arrian *Anabasis of Alexander* 7.13.2–6.

[27] Strabo 11.5.3. The last sentence is ambiguous and could also mean: "more willing to believe the ancient tales than reports about contemporary Amazons."

[28] And pleasant to represent visually as well: there are countless representations of Amazons in ceramic, and Amazonomachiae are found on monuments as important as the Parthenon, the Athenian treasury at Delphi, the Theseion of Athens, and the shield of the Athena Parthenos by Phidias.

[29] See Detienne 1979, 183–214.

[30] See F. d'Eaubonne's preface to Samuel 1975.

FRANÇOIS HARTOG

Frontiers and Otherness

1980

As his title suggests, Hartog's study of Herodotus shares goals with Jeannie Carlier, for whom the Amazons defined, by implication, the Greek citizens who imagined them as embodied opposites. In this essay, part of his examination of Darius's expedition against the Scythians, Hartog focuses on the spatial analogy of the frontier, offering two examples: the ring composition comprising the "characteristically Scythian" behavior of Anacharsis and Scyles, and the account of Salmoxis, a religious figure of the Getae whose identity is hard to pin down. (The Salmoxis analysis is omitted from this translation.) These complementary stories, both of which turn on transgression (or willed oblivion) of geographical and cultural frontiers, also raise the question of what frontiers are recognized by the gods—and what role the mythographic narrator plays in demarcating "otherness."

The question of otherness raises that of frontiers. Where does the break dividing the same from the other occur? The Scythians are nomads and, spatially, Scythia is an "other" space to the extent that it is an inaccessible place. As Darius learns to his cost, throwing a bridge across the Ister dos not suffice for truly entering Scythia. He exhausts himself in this mockery of a hunt and emerges from it defeated, without ever even setting eyes upon his adversaries. However, this "otherness"—that is to say, the apparent absence of any fixed frontier—cannot be dissociated from the narrative of the war itself. It can only be understood in the context of the protagonists in this narrative. In one sense, the Ister certainly is a frontier (the Scythians do not seek to cross it, and when Darius crosses back over it in his retreat, he is saved). In another sense, though, it is not, for it does not provide "access" to the Scythians, whose aporia remains unaffected by it. Thus, even from a purely spatial point of view, the frontier may be understood in a number of ways.

From *The Mirror of Herodotus: The Representation of the Other in the Writing of History*, trans. Janet Lloyd (Berkeley: University of California Press, 1988), pp. 61–84 ["Les frontières et l'autre," in *Le Miroir d'Hérodote: Essai sur la représentation de l'autre* (Paris: Gallimard, 1980), pp. 81–127].

Two other episodes in the Scythian *logos* make it possible to pose the question of the frontier, this time not in a geographical but in a cultural sense: first, the misadventure of Anacharsis and Scyles, both Scythians of high nobility; second, the story of Salmoxis, a figure of uncertain identity. The two texts offer two opposing approaches to the frontier theme. Anacharsis and Scyles in effect "forget" the frontier between the Greeks and the Scythians and suffer the consequences. In the Salmoxis episode, on the other hand, the Black Sea Greeks attempt, by every conceivable means, to make it impossible to "forget" the distance that separates them from the Getae.

The question of a cultural frontier leads to the organization of divine space: is the world of the gods affected by geographical and human frontiers? Also, these two texts afford us a glimpse of the narrator in operation. In the story of Anacharsis and Scyles he makes the addressee think that he is seeing the Greeks through the eyes of the Scythians; in the story of Salmoxis, in contrast, he shows the Scythians as seen by the Black Sea Greeks. These two stories thus relate respectively to either side of that imaginary line traced by the frontier: in the first, the Greeks are seen through the eyes of "others"; in the second, "others" are seen through the eyes of the Greeks.

ANACHARSIS AND SCYLES: CIRCUMSCRIBING A TRANSGRESSION

The stories of Anacharsis and Scyles should be read together, and in relation to one another (Herodotus 4.76–80). The destinies of Anacharsis and Scyles were "analogous" (*paraplēsia*). That similarity is the justification for considering them together even if they are chronologically separated, Scyles having "lived long after Anacharsis." Herodotus presents them as two examples illustrating a rule of Scythian behavior, and his narrative, which begins by setting out the rule governing such behavior, ends by calling it to mind: "As regards foreign usages, the Scythians [as others] are remarkably loath to practice those of any other country, particularly those of Greece" (Herodotus 4.76). That is the lesson the addressee is specifically invited to learn from the two episodes.

Taking as my starting point this manifest organization of the text, I should like to suggest a hypothesis concerning the logic of this *logos*: are not the different codes that operate in these two stories to some extent homologous?

First, who are the protagonists in these two stories? In the story of Anacharsis, the cast, in order of appearance, consists of Anacharsis, the Cyzicenes (who are engaged in celebrating a festival), a Scythian (who denounces Anacharsis's behavior to the king), and, finally, King Saulius, who, Herodotus tells us, is in reality Anacharsis's own brother (it is he who kills Anacharsis). To this list we should add a divine personage: the Mother of the Gods. We may already at this point note that, like Dionysus in the other episode, the Mother of the Gods is simply the mute object of a cult: the narrative does not tell us whether or not these deities appreciate the cult of their new devotees.

Next, the story of Scyles: it involves Scyles, the Borysthenites (who worship Dionysus Bacchus), one particular Borysthenite (who reports the whole affair to the Scythians), the principal Scythians, "who saw him among the revellers . . . and told [*esēmainon*]" the other Scythians about it, and, finally, Octamasades, Scyles' brother, whom the Scythians adopt as their leader; he it is who later puts Scyles to death.

Second, who are Anacharsis and Scyles? Herodotus is at pains to trace the genealogy of Anacharsis and produces a witness to bear him out: Tymnes, one who was in the confidence of the late King Ariapeithes (Herodotus 4.76). Anacharsis is the paternal uncle of Idanthyrsus; Idanthyrsus's father is Saulius, so Anacharsis and Saulius are brothers.[1] The important point is that Anacharsis belongs to the Scythian royal family. His biography is given in a most summary fashion: "Anacharsis, having seen much of the world [*gēn pollēn*] in his travels and given many proofs of his wisdom [*sophiēn pollēn*] was coming back to the Scythian country [*ēthea*]."[2] It was also said of Solon that he had seen much of the world (*gēn pollēn*) and had shown much *sophiē* (Herodotus 1.130). In Herodotus, Anacharsis is not included among the Sages and is not related directly to Solon, but both were men for whom travel and *sophiē* were linked.

Scyles is not just a member of the royal family but is the king himself. He is, however, a bastard, one of his father's many illegitimate children. He is nevertheless different from his brothers, in that his mother was Greek; she is not native-born (*epikhōriēs*) but came from Istria (Herodotus 4.78), and she "taught him to speak and read Greek" (ibid.). Scyles is thus a double personage, half Scythian, half Greek; he is *diglōssos*. When his father is assassinated, the kingdom passes to him, as does his father's wife. But Herodotus does not tell us how he came by the throne or how he qualified for the title despite the fact that his father had at least one legitimate son, Oricus (ibid.); nor did he, earlier, explain why Anacharsis did *not* obtain the throne, which instead passed to his brother.

A comparison between these two "biographies" enables us to make an observation about the logic of the narrative: the travels of Anacharsis and the bilingualism of Scyles occupy parallel structural positions in the two narratives and also serve the same function in their development. To travel and to be bilingual come down to the same thing: both are dangerous, for they lead to forgetting frontier and thus to transgression.[3]

How do Anacharsis and Scyles move from one place to another? What spaces do they cross? In the cases of Scyles, the schema is quite simple: he moves to and fro between the *ēthea* of the Scythians (the word denotes an animal's lair, one's habitual domicile) and the town of the Borysthenites, namely, Olbia. He leaves the Scythian space, a space more animal than human, where he feels ill at ease (he detests the Scythian lifestyle) and sets off for the town, but the narrative specifies that he leaves his train on the outskirts (*toi proasteioi*, Herodotus 4.78) in that intermediary zone outside the domain of the *ēthea* but not yet in that of the *astu*. It is as if it were impossible for the Scythians to progress any further, for *they* are not bilingual.

[. . .]

But "as it had to be that evil should befall him" (Herodotus 4.79), the story now becomes a narrative of his last journey of all. He gets back to the Scythian *ēthea* but the Scythians, having seen what they were not supposed to see, rise up against him, whereupon he flees to Thrace. Because of what he has done, the Scythian space is now forbidden to him. The Scythians assemble on the banks of the Ister, ready for battle, and the Thracians do likewise, massing on the opposite bank. The Ister, then, clearly represents a frontier between the Scythians and the Thracians. The two kings make a deal: "Return my brother to me and I will return yours." As soon as Scyles has crossed back over the Ister, he is executed. The text even specifies "on the spot," on that side of the river (Herodotus 4.80). He can set foot in the Scythian space only to be met with death. These are the stages of Scyles' last voyage.

Anacharsis leaves the Scythian space altogether. After a long absence, he travels back to the *ēthea* of the Scythians (Herodotus 4.76). When he puts in to Cyzicus, the Milesian colony, he is still in Greek space; then he lands in Scythia and immediately plunges into the wooded region known as the Hylaia. A Scythian sees him and informs the king, who, upon seeing the scene, immediately kills Anacharsis. In this second case, the spatial schema is very simple: Anacharsis passes from a Greek space into the Scythian space. Yet I think that two questions are posed: (1) Is the Hylaia a completely Scythian space or is it a particular, even marginal, part of that space? (2) What is the position of the town of Cyzicus in relation to the "Greek space"? Is it a particular part of that space? These are questions that cannot be answered simply by examining the journeys from a geographical point of view. The only possible way to tackle them is to take account of the semantic content and the cultural codes.

Let us consider the action of the two stories: the narrative concerning Anacharsis is much more starkly told than the other. Having seen the Cyzicenes celebrating the Mother of the Gods, Anacharsis vows that if he ever reaches home he will devote a similar ceremony to her. On his return, he immediately fulfills his vow, as piety demands. Yet Saulius kills him with an arrow.

The story of Scyles is more elaborate, but three principal points can be noted. Each time Scyles returns to the town, his first action is to shed the Scythian "robe" (*stolē*) and adopt Greek clothing (*esthēs*); more generally, he adopts the Greek style of life (*diaitē Hellēnikē*) in every respect. The second point concerns his relations with women: he receives the kingship and also his father's wife, Opoia, but he also marries another woman, whom he installs in the house he has had built in Olbia. There is a problem here: Opoia is described as *astē* (Herodotus 4.78), which the translators and commentators render as "native"; in other words, according to them she is Scythian. The second wife is called *epikhōriē*, that is to say, "local," but the translators and commentators explain that she was born in the town and so is Greek. So Scyles appears simply to have acted as his father did before him. That is to say, the translators are here reversing the usual meaning of these words and that, at their limit, their meanings are interchangeable: *epikhōriē* means "native" but also "of the town," and *astē* means "of the town" but also "native." All the same, perhaps we should recall the beginning of Chapter 78, which states that Scyles was born from a woman of Istria and definitely not from a native (*oudamōs epikhōriē*), the opposition between the town and the country in this case being indicated by precisely the use of *epikhōriē*.

Might it not be that Scyles' actions are more complex than is assumed? He marries Opoia, a woman from the town but who lives in Scythian space; then, in Olbia, he marries a woman who is *epikhōriē*, a native, but he has her live in the Greek space or, rather, within the enclosure of her vast residence, whose precise position is uncertain; it is not known whether it fully belongs to the spatial fabric of the city. The principle behind his actions might thus be confusion—to muddle up both people and spaces.

Finally, consider the religious domain: he practices the Greek religion and wishes to become an initiate (*telesthēnai*) of Dionysus Bacchus. As in the case of Anacharsis, Scyles' piety occasions his death, for what is piety to the Greeks is the height of impiety to the Scythians.

From a logical point of view, then, the two accounts establish an equivalence between traveling and being bilingual. From that point on, the number and complexity of the sequences may vary but they all speak of confusion and its attendant dangers, above all in the religious domain; only death can put a stop to such disorder. We must now examine the two stories again, this time imbuing the various sequences with their full semantic content and tracing out the cultural codes that provide their context and are at the same time conveyed by them.

What is the Hylaia? In Greek the word means "wooded" but also "wild"; as is to be expected, the forest belongs to the border spaces and thus to wildness. But what is the situation in Scythia? According to Herodotus, the Hylaia is situated along the shore of the sea, bordered by the Borysthenites to the west and the territory of the "farming Scythians" to the north (Herodotus 4.9, 18, 54, 55, 76). Its distinctive feature is that, in contrast to the rest of the country, it is covered with trees and, furthermore, trees of every kind. And it has another peculiarity: it was in the Hylaia that Heracles encountered the Mixoparthenos with whom he was then united; according to the Black Sea Greeks, the Scythian people were the issue of that union. These observations provide justification for assigning the Hylaia a rather special place within the Scythian space; they do not, however, tell us enough to determine the meaning of its peculiarity with any precision. [. . .] All the same, Saulius's arrow there found its mark and killed Anacharsis.

Just as, once its doors are closed, Olbia offers Scyles shelter to do things that the Scythians must not behold, similarly the Hylaia, into which Anacharsis plunges (*katadus*) (Herodotus 4.76), provides him with a hidden place where he can celebrate a cult the Scythians refuse to recognize. But as well as the protection this dense forest offers, has it not another aspect that makes it a suitable place for a celebration in honor of the Mother of the Gods? It is the only wooded region in the country; and the cult of the Mother is associated with trees and plants. Tradition has it that the Argonauts founded the cult of the Mother, at Cyzicus. To atone for the murder of the hero Cyzicus, the Argonauts, on Mount Didymus "under the shelter of some tall oaks, the highest trees that grow," established a sanctuary of the goddess, and Argus himself carved from a vine root the *xoanon* revered ever since that time. It thus seems that within the Scythian space the Hylaia was the most suitable place for a "transplantation" of the cult of the Mother of the Gods.

In the story of Scyles the spatial pattern is simple: Olbia lies to one side, Scythia to the other. But why, in Anacharsis's case, is there first Cyzicus and then the Hylaia? Why both? Would it not be perfectly plausible for a Scythian to surprise Anacharsis in Cyzicus, engaged with the Cyzicenes (like Scyles with the Borysthenites) in celebrating a *pannukhis*, and subsequently to have him assassinated as he lands in Scythia? This is not necessarily a foolish question. Nevertheless, it seems to have been impossible for the narrative to adopt that story line: the distance separating Cyzicus from Scythia is too great, too much sea lies between them. At Cyzicus, Anacharsis "vowed . . . to this same Mother of Gods that, if he returned to his own country safe and sound, he would sacrifice [*thusein*] to her . . . and establish a nightly ritual of worship [*pannukhis*]" (Herodotus 4.76). Such prayers would have been perfectly reasonable, since Cybele was also a "lady of the sea."[4] She was called upon in time of storm,[5] sailors made her *ex voto* offerings,[6] and "on the headlands" of the Mysian coastline her temples stood "like lighthouses of salvation."

From a spatial point of view we may thus regard the Hylaia as the double of Cyzicus in Scythian territory, the difference being that here Anacharsis no longer has the right to worship the Mother; his piety becomes impiety. The comparison between Cyzicus and the Hylaia thus reinforces the latter spot's exceptional character, noted above: it is Scythian territory but it is also something else. Olbia, however, does lie outside the Scythian space, and the town walls symbolize that extraterritoriality. These walls block the view and conceal what is going on inside them, but they are not altogether beyond the Scythian territory: spying Scythian eyes can always look in from atop the walls. Through the metaphor of looking, the narrative conveys the spatial ambiguity of the Hylaia and Olbia: even when you are screened by the forest or the fortifications, a look, whether a chance one or one with intent to harm, may at any time discover you.

One more relationship should be considered: having posed the question of the respective positions of Cyzicus and the Hylaia, and of Olbia in relation to the space of Scythia, we must examine that of the relation of Cyzicus and Olbia to the space of Greece. It is a question that, in truth, it is not possible to answer for the moment; but both were colonial towns. For Herodotus, Olbia is an "emporium" inhabited by "Greeks" (4.2); more specifically, the Borysthenites "say that they are Milesians" (Herodotus 4.78). In other words, Borysthenites is a colony of Miletus and between the two cities exists an agreement of reciprocal political rights. Cyzicus is also a colony of Miletus, and a similar agreement probably existed between these two cities. As to the question of whether the Cyzicenes and the Borysthenites were considered marginal peoples within the space of Greece, not on a geographical level, of course, but from the point of view of the shared knowledge of the Greeks, there is so far no evidence on which to base a reply.

What is the position of the Mother of the Gods and of Dionysus, on the one hand, in relation to the space of Scythia and, on the other, in relation to the space of Greece? That is the next question. It boils down to asking what it was that Anacharsis and Scyles did wrong. How did they contravene the Scythian cultural codes (as conveyed to us through Herodotus's narrative, of course)? In relation to the space of Greece that means, why did they choose the Mother and Dionysus in preference to, for example, Apollo or Hera? So the question to which these few chapters of the *Histories* point is that of the place occupied by the Mother and Dionysus within the Greek pantheon. Why are these two deities chosen by two non-Greeks and why are they regarded by the Scythians as the symbols of Greekness?

[. . .]

It can be shown that both Anacharsis and Scyles contravene the Scythian cultural codes. The list of deities in the Scythian pantheon includes neither Dionysus nor the Mother of the Gods. They have no place there, even under other names (Herodotus 4.59). We may be sure that were that not the case, Herodotus would have been at pains to give the translation. Furthermore, a basic rule of the Scythian religion is to make no use of statues, altars, or temples except those dedicated to Ares (ibid.). Now, how does Anacharsis celebrate his ritual in honor of the Mother? He sounds a tambourine but also wears around his neck the *agalmata* of the goddess. As for Scyles, as soon as he has entered Olbia he offers up sacrifices "in accordance with the customs of the Greeks," visiting temples and sacrificing upon altars.

In the case of Scyles, there is also the problem of initiation. It appears that so long as he contented himself with visiting Olbia and living there in the Greek fashion, the Scythians tolerated his transgression, which hardly amounted to more than his bilingualism. When he departed from Olbia and dressed once again in the Scythian costume to return to the *ēthea* of the Scythians, that was the end of it: there was no confusion, no "overlapping" of the *nomoi* of one space onto the other. But initiation seems to have upset this clear division. Why? Precisely because initiation makes a lasting, irreversible change of status; it is meaningful only in the context of a separation established between a "before" and an "after." So even if Scyles readopts the Scythian costume as usual at the end of his visit, he remains an initiate of Dionysus Bacchus for all that. The Scythians cannot tolerate that: it is an "overlapping" and thus must be punished.

On the "Greek side," the solemnity of this initiation is indicated, in the narrative, by the intervention of the gods. To put it more clearly: the text appears to purvey two opposed points of view at the same time. On the one hand, this initiation is simply "the occasion, the pretext" (Herodotus 4.79) for punishing Scyles, for whom "it had to be that evil should befall him" in any case; on the other, it is something solemn, since immediately before it the god sends an "extremely impressive omen [*phasma megiston*]." However, this opposition is resolved to the extent that the two expressions do not operate on the same level: the first is an interruption arranged by the narrator, made by the anonymous voice of destiny and tragedy; the second is an assertion, within the narrative, of the importance of the initiation.

In Olbia, Scyles has had himself built a "great and costly" house surrounded by a wall of "sphinxes and griffins wrought in white marble" (ibid.). There is something inappropriate and exaggerated about this mansion: it is more barbarian than Greek. The griffins, which appear to guard it, are creatures from the edges of the world. According to some, they are "the guardians of the gold" that live between the Arimaspians and the Hyperboreans (Herodotus 3.116, 4.13, 27, 29). By erecting this enclosure, Scyles establishes his own difference within the city. And what is the omen that "the god," that is to say Zeus, is about to send? It is a thunderbolt that will strike the enclosure and reduce it to ashes (Herodotus 4.79). What is Zeus trying to tell Scyles at the very moment when he is about to become initiated? Just as the thunderbolt, by destroying this wall, does away with the separation between the two spaces, so the initiation, for which he is preparing himself, in a sense abolishes the distance between Greek space and Scythian space; and this transgression of one space upon another is a serious matter. But, needless to say, Scyles is incapable of fathoming the meaning of the omen and so goes ahead with the ceremony, which is to lead to his death.

Herodotus is at pains to describe the circumstances of the death in some detail. We have noticed the importance he attached in his narrative to establishing and recording the fact that Anacharsis was killed by his own brother, Saulius. The introduction of these two brothers is easily explained. They are the closest relatives to Anacharsis and Scyles respectively, and they are also their doubles. But these are the doubles that represent the good side. In contrast to their brothers, they remained totally faithful to the Scythian *nomoi*, and it is consequently they who are the most appalled by the transgression. They are without doubt the best qualified to punish and eliminate the guilty ones, to whom the Scythian soil is henceforth forbidden ground.[7] Not content simply to execute them, the Scythians annihilate their very memory; they are wiped out, have never so much as existed, "and now the Scythians, if they are asked about Anacharsis, say they have no knowledge of him" (Herodotus 4.76).

Anacharsis and Scyles choose to honor two deities on whose account they meet their deaths: the Mother of the Gods, and Dionysus. Why this particular choice? Why those deities rather than others? To the objection that the question is a pointless one since that was the choice the narrative made, I would suggest that it is worth attempting to understand what the Mother of the Gods and Dionysus represent in the *Histories* and in the fifth century; to put it in a more precise and unpretentious way, let me suggest that the Mother of the Gods and Dionysus appear in the very place where a number of cultural codes intersect, and Herodotus's narrative may enable us to formulate a number of hypotheses on the topography of that place.

Cyzicus and Olbia are situated on the very edges of Greek space. Might we postulate a homology here and suggest that the same might be said of the Mother of the Gods and Dionysus?

The Mother is referred to as such only here, in this chapter of the *Histories*: even if we are told nothing more about her position, she is thus certainly linked with Cyzicus.[8] [. . .] Kybele is one of only three gods for whom Herodotus suggests no equivalent "in the Greek language": in Herodotus's "dictionary" no translation is supplied for the name Kybele. In short, her only point of anchorage within the space of Greece is Cyzicus, and the only Greeks who devote a cult to her are the Cyzicenes.

Dionysus is much more widely known and figures in numerous pantheons. [. . .] Honored in distant lands and revered in mainland Greece as well, he seems to be present everywhere.

To discover how his influence spread, who—according to Herodotus— received it from whom, we must pose the question of the god's origin. As always when it comes to origin, we must heed a number of voices: here, those of the Greeks, the Egyptians, and the narrator.

Dionysus (like Heracles and Pan) is considered by the Greeks as one of the most recent of the gods (*neōtatoi*, Herodotus 2.145); he is said to have been born the daughter of Cadmus. Furthermore, as the Greek story has it, "now [*nun*], no sooner was Dionysus born than Zeus sewed him up in his thigh and carried him away to Nysa, in Ethiopia beyond Egypt" (2.145–46). For the Egyptians, on the other hand, Dionysus belongs to the third generation of the gods.

[. . .]

The narrator, for his part, is totally opposed to the Greek version. In the first place, on the strength of the "inquiries" he has made, he believes that virtually all of the Ounomata of the gods came to Greece from Egypt: *punthanomenos houtō heuriskō eon* (2.50). Dionysus was introduced as follows (2.49): "I believe that Melampus learnt the worship of Dionysus chiefly from Cadmus of Tyre and those who came with Cadmus from Phoenicia to the land now called Boeotia. . . . It was Melampus who taught the Greeks the name of Dionysus and the way of sacrificing to him, and the phallic procession [*to ounoma kai tēn thusiēn kai tēn pompēn tou phallou*]."

The Greek story consequently becomes untenable. Herodotus makes that very clear by pointing to the chronology: between Dionysus, the son of Semele, and "myself," one thousand years at the outside have elapsed, whereas according to the Egyptian calculation, fifteen thousand years separated Dionysus and Amasis (Herodotus 2.145). Now, the Egyptians are quite "certain" (*atrekeōs*) of their date "seeing that they had always reckoned the years and chronicled them in writing."

One conclusion to be drawn is that the Greeks are mistaken, for they have confused the time when they learned of this god and the time of his birth. Another is that the Greeks came to know of Dionysus (and likewise Pan and Hermes) "later" (*husteron*) than the other gods (Herodotus 2.146). Finally, no doubt Dionysus did have a foreign origin but, for Herodotus, that is true of most of the Greek gods.

On the evidence of the *Histories* alone, these then are the places where the Mother of the Gods and Dionysus are recognized, and that is who they are. If the Mother of the Gods does seem a truly marginal figure, the procession of Dionysus, in contrast, is (apparently) known everywhere, throughout the non-Greek space as well as the Greek one. But the interesting question that the text now raises is the manner in which Dionysus and the Mother of the Gods operated as criteria of Greekness not only for the Scythians and Greeks but also for the actual addressees of this discourse, Herodotus's audience. When the narrator shows, in Book 2, that Dionysus is of Egyptian origin, he at one point uses an important *a contrario* argument: "I will not admit that it is a chance agreement between the Egyptian ritual of Dionysus and the Greek; for were that so, the Greek ritual would be of a Greek nature [*homotropa*] and not but lately introduced" (Herodotus 2.49).

In other words, one proof of the foreignness of Dionysus, in the narrator's view, is the fact (which he is content simply to state, without explaining or glossing it) that practices followed in the cult addressed to him are not *homotropa* with those of the Greeks: his cult is thus a reminder of his non-Greekness. That is the first proposition to be found in the *Histories*.

There is another, perhaps less explicit but equally interesting. It occurs in the passage on the Geloni (4.108). [. . .] The construction of a *polis*, the establishment of sanctuaries, and the celebration of festivals in honor of Dionysus are thus all associated as so many actions which are no longer surprising once the reader is told that the Geloni had Greeks for ancestors. In this particular case, to look no further, Dionysus functions as a criterion for Greekness. Is there a contradiction between these two propositions? There is not, because they do not operate on the same level or refer to the same time: in one case it is a question of origins, in the other of the (narrator's) present time. Thus, even if the expression "to honor Dionysus with Bacchic festivals" was not initially in keeping with Greek practices, with the passing of time it may well have become a way of indicating Greekness.

At all events, Dionysus is a familiar figure along the shores of the Black Sea. That is frequently attested, but the fact remains that the testimony of Herodotus is the most ancient. Pippidi tells us, for example, that at Callatis there were not only *Xenika Dionysia*—that is to say, the ritual banquets organized in honor of Dionysus[9]—but also a public cult (*thiasoi*), a sanctuary consecrated to the god, and a month of Dionysus.[10] In short, his was an extremely active presence (well attested during the Hellenistic period), and that goes not just for Callatis but for the entire length and breadth of Scythia Minor.[11]

[. . .] Some scholars have wondered whether the *thiasoi* were reserved for women,[12] but men certainly participated at Olbia, since when the Scythians catch sight of Scyles he is taking part in the *thiasos*. As to whether the status of the *thiasos* was official, we may note that in Olbia everything took place quite publicly in the streets if the town.

This prompts one further remark. In support of the thesis that the place of Dionysus was considered to be outside the city itself, mention has often been made of the fact that even when the god has been adopted, he does not enter the town. When the places in which mysteries take place are mentioned, it is always a matter of a wild place in the *agros*; remember, too, that the people of Smyrna celebrate his festival "outside the walls [*exō teikheos*]" (Herodotus 1.150); and consider, finally, the name by which he is sometimes known, *propoleos*, "in front of the town." However, to return to Olbia, it must be admitted that here the initiation and procession take place inside the town; Scyles has seen to it that the gates are closed. When the Scythians, positioned up on the tower, behold the procession, Scyles is described, in a word, as "acting as a Bacchant," which means that the *pompē* demands that the initiates sing and dance in honor of the god.

As for the Mother of the Gods, who addresses a cult to her? Herodotus is content here too to do no more than mention the "Cyzicenes," a term that covers men as well as women. For Hasluck, on the contrary, it is clear that the Greeks considered her cult to be "barbarian" and that her religion "was probably for the natives. . . . The Mother was always a foreigner to the Cyzicenes, though a foreigner that must be conciliated." Now, as proof that this cult was regarded as barbarian by Greeks, Hasluck cites the example of Anacharsis in the text of Herodotus; yet Anacharsis is assassinated by the Scythians precisely for having introduced a cult imported from Cyzicus! As to his second claim, the insertion of that "probably" no doubt dispenses him from substantiating it. Who else, then? According to a tradition that is difficult to date and that is echoed in particular by the scholium to Aristophanes and by Iamblichus, the zealots of the Mother were recruited above all from among women and effeminate males. Note also the legend recorded by the *Suda* and Photius on the origin of her introduction in Athens. [. . .] At the end of the fifth century the Mother had her own building on the agora, so it seems that the question of her "foreignness" was no simple matter;[13] sometimes rejected, sometimes a marginal figure, sometimes admitted to the very center of the city, she occupied a whole range of positions.

To close this excursus with an example of an extreme test, let us cite Clement of Alexandria:

> Blessings be upon the Scythian king. . . . When a countryman of his own was imitating among the Scythians the rite of the Mother of the Gods, as practiced at Cyzicus, by beating a drum and clanging a cymbal and by having images of the goddess suspended from his neck after the manner of a priest of Cybele, this king slew him with an arrow, on the grounds that the man, having been deprived of his own virility in Greece [*anandron gegenēmenon*], was now communicating the effeminate disease [*thēleias nosou*] to his fellow citizens. (*Protreptica* 24.1)

Anacharsis became a zealot of the Mother, a veritable Metragyrtes. Moreover, there is no doubt in the mind of Clement of Alexandria that practicing the cult of Kybele is a criterion of Greekness—in other words, a failing. Anacharsis is in truth killed not for having introduced foreign *nomoi* but for having become "effeminate" or, rather, for having lost his virility among the Greeks and for seeking to teach this "effeminate disease": so Kybele is Greek, and the Greeks are women!

The Scythians, for their part, totally reject the Mother and Dionysus, applying the rule set out by Herodotus. When Saulius sees Anacharsis, he promptly slays him, without a word, as if any explanation or justification were quite unnecessary: the crime is patently clear, the punishment immediate. In the case of Scyles the scenario is slightly different: Dionysus is not only foreign but induces madness—two excellent "reasons" for the Scythians to reject him. This raises the question of the relationship between Dionysus and *mania*. In the *Bacchae*, Pentheus is driven out of his mind by Dionysus, who leads him to Citheron disguised as a woman,[14] for the very reason that he persists in refusing to recognize him and wants "to break his neck." This is one type of *mania*, but there is another, that which afflicts Agave and her companions who are wandering over the slopes of the mountain, for they too have "outraged" Dionysus, "denying that he was truly god" (*Bacchae* 912). [. . .] Blinding, loss of reason, and *mania* are all punishments for refusing the god recognition. Once this logic of *mania* is established, it is easy to understand why Pentheus, when discovered perched in his tree, dies for having seen "forbidden sights" and having pursued "what one should flee" (*Bacchae* 1297).

In the case of Scyles, however, the situation is in many respects reversed. Here it is the Scythian leaders who lie in wait (*lathrē*) at the top of a tower. They are the ones who see what they should not see, yet it is they who deal the death-blow; it is they who totally reject the god, yet they too who speak of *mania* and accuse others of madness. And when the Borysthenite seeks them out, he pre-tends to speak their language as an expression of his scorn for them: he repeats the words that Herodotus ascribes to the Scythians in explanation of their con-duct,[15] and even goes so far as to refer to Dionysus as a *daimōn*.

The Scythians' failure to understand Dionysus might—and herein, per-haps, lies the cunning of the narrator—be a way of suggesting that the one who is mad is not the one we think it to be; that, in the last analysis, the real madmen are perhaps those who are the first to denounce madness in others. But this incomprehension on the part of the Scythians is also a ruse in another sense. What the Scythians interpret as *mania* in the performance of the *thiasos* may well give every appearance of *mania*, but the point is that it *is* only an appearance; in other words, *mania* is as different for *bakkheuein* as those who accept him. However, the Scythians are incapable of seeing beyond the appear-ances, so their discourse does not know what it is saying.

At this point we find ourselves back with the theme of the discourse of the ethnologist, which *does* tell the truth. It is the discourse of the one who knows, because he knows the circumstances and the results. The Scythians, for their part, do not differentiate between, for example, feathers and snow,[16] and call what they should call snow feathers, just because snowflakes "resemble" feath-ers; similarly, they cannot distinguish between being afflicted with *mania* and being a Bacchant, because the two appear to be one and the same thing.

Such, then, were the lives and deaths of Anacharsis and Scyles, and all be-cause they forgot the existence of frontiers. [. . .]

FRONTIERS AND OTHERNESS

Anacharsis and Scyles both met their deaths as the result of transgressing a frontier. The one, in the Hylaia, celebrated the mysteries of the Mother, alone; the other, inside the walls of Olbia, became an initiate of Dionysus Bacchus. This "forgetfulness" of the Scythian *nomoi* must be punished, by virtue of the rule the narrator has stated: the Scythians refuse to adopt foreign *nomoi*. In short, the narrative of their misfortunes is just one more illustration of the great general law that "custom rules the world."

The story of Anacharsis and Scyles, just as much as that of Salmoxis, hinges on the interplay between the near and the far. Dionysus, who is recognized within the walls of Olbia, is not at all understood outside them, and Bacchana-lian "revels" are interpreted by the Scythians as "being mad." The spatial prox-imity is transformed into a cultural distancing. [. . .]

But, in an implicit fashion, the near and the far also operate on another level. From the point of view of Herodotus's addressee, what does the choice of the Mother of the Gods and Dionysus tell us? Both are certainly important deities of Cyzicus and Olbia, which are situated on the margins of the Greek world. But, as we have seen, it is much too simplistic to assume a direct homology between a representation of geographical space, on the one hand, and a representation of divine space, on the other; to suggest that the geographical marginality is matched by a similar marginality where the gods are concerned, that the Mother and Dionysus stand, in relation to the rest of the Greek pantheon, in the same position as Cyzicus and Olbia in relation to the rest of the Greek world. To do so would be to overlook their capacity to move from those margins into the interior and to be present in several places at once.

All the same, so that their radical rejection (on the part of the Scythians) may be as meaningful as possible to Herodotus's addressee, perhaps these two powers, the Mother and Dionysus, should be seen as both Greek and, at the same time, as close to the Scythians. The fact is that they must be perceived to be Greek by the addressee if the behavior of the Scythians is to make sense and in order to illustrate the general rule put forward by the narrative. But they must also be recognized to be close to the Scythians not only geographically but culturally, if their rejection is to astonish and take on its full meaning. These are deities that it ought to be possible for them to accommodate easily (by reason of their origin, the rituals they entail, their "barbaric" aspect); yet these are the very deities that they utterly reject (as Greek). In this way, the explicit moral of the story is further reinforced: truth lies on this side of the frontier, error beyond it.

In the narrative of the misfortunes of Scyles, the narrator does not directly intervene to counterpoint the opinions he ascribes to the Scythians. It is left up to the reader to appreciate the extent to which they confuse *mania* and *bakkheuein*. The Salmoxis episode presents a richer structure and is therefore even more interesting. The discourse of the Black Sea Greeks seems to be truthful discourse that is sure of itself, that records the true facts of the case (Salmoxis is a charlatan), that knows more about the Getae than they do themselves.[17] But it is then overlaid by a direct intervention from the narrator which, in effect, ruins the reassuring and reductive explanation given by the Black Sea Greeks and reopens the question of the identity of this figure. Salmoxis may be a man or a *daimōn*, he may have been the former and now be the latter, or he may be something else again; in the last analysis, the mark of his "otherness" is this open-endedness. I believe that is the sense of Herodotus's final *khairetō*, that third-person imperative, "farewell," or "that is enough of that." The *khairetō* is also saying, "it is for you to decide."

TRANSLATED BY JANET LLOYD

NOTES

[1] This is the first way that Herodotus tackles the genealogy of Anacharsis. Then, as if to substantiate it from a different angle, he approaches the question again: Anacharsis is the son of Gnurus. All that remains to be done is show that Saulius is also a son of Gnurus, but Herodotus does not do so at this point.

[2] For Herodotus the geographer, the earth is a continuous space and Anacharsis has traveled through much of it. His fault is, precisely, to have forgotten that some frontiers cannot be crossed.

[3] Confirmation of this equivalence is to be found in the tradition relating to Anacharsis. Diogenes Laertius (1.101) gives him a Greek mother and makes him bilingual, as if this element borrowed from the biography of Scyles could also "be attached" to him and as if it were necessary to reinforce his "traveling," which, on its own, did not suffice to set him apart.

[4] H. Graillot, *Le Culte de Cybèle* (Paris, 1912), p. 290.

[5] Diodorus 3.55.8: Myrna the Amazon invokes her. Apollonius Rhodius 1.1098–99.

[6] *Bulletin de Correspondance Hellénique* 23 (1899): 591.

[7] Ambushed by his brother, Anacharsis is shot with a bow and arrow, like a hunted animal, whereas Scyles is beheaded. Note that the punishment suffered by Scyles is that inflicted on perjurers (4.60), since perjury is a threat to the royal hearth.

[8] On Kybele and Cyzicus, cf. W. Hasluck, *Cyzicus* (Cambridge, 1910). It is worth noting that Herodotus does not speak of a cult, an "initiation," or orgies in this connection. He mentions a festival (*ortē*), a sacrifice (*thusein*), and a nocturnal watch (*pannuchhis*); the word *pannuchhis* is also to be found elsewhere meaning a vigil in honor of the Mother, in particular in Euripides' *Helen* 1365.

[9] D. Pippidi, *I Greci nello Basso Danubio* (Milan, 1971), p. 127: "For the Greeks of Dobrugia, who had carried him with them aboard their ships, Dionysus was a national god, worshipped as a secular tradition, with titles that reappear in Megara and Asia Minor."

[10] D. Pippidi, "Xenika Dionysia à Callatis," *Acta antiqua academiae scientiarum Hungaricae* 16 (1968): 191–95.

[11] Cf. also G. Hirst, "The Cults of Olbia," *Journal of Hellenic Studies* 23 (1903): 24–53.

[12] On the obscurity of these early theories, cf. Festugière 1972, 14–16. The *Thiasatai* of the *Frogs* include both men and women.

[13] On the Mother of the Gods, see Will 1960, 95–111, for whom the Great Mother arrived in mainland Greece from Ionia as early as the sixth century. Pindar mentions her and is interested in her cult: Pythian 3.77, fragments 48 and 63, edited by Boeckh. Cf. also DuPont-Sommer and Robert 1964.

[14] Euripides *Bacchae* 912–14; Jeanmaire 1951, 105–106.

[15] Herodotus 4.79: "They say that it is not reasonable to set up a god who leads men on to madness." So this is clearly an intervention on the part of the narrator.

[16] Herodotus 4.31. Cf. Dumézil 1978, 339–51.

[17] The fact that it is possible to regard Salmoxism as an avatar of Pythagoreanism rebounds upon Pythagoreanism: it is a mirror effect. From the point of view of the general knowledge of the Greeks, comparison between the two is bound to be at least admissible, even if it is made by the distant citizens of Olbia and even if Salmoxis was Pythagoras's slave.

CATHERINE DARBO-PESCHANSKI

The "I" of the Inquirer:
The Function of Critical Discourse

1987

Catherine Darbo-Peschanski's study foregrounds the nature and principles of Herodotean inquiry rather than its subject; she delineates an epistemology that privileges the multiplicity of voices and opinions through which a logos *is constructed, rather than the authority of the narrator to establish a preemptive truth. The "critical knowledge" of the inquiring "I," the first-person narrator, regularly yields to the "immediate knowledge" of his informants. Thus where the "I" of the historian asserts itself, in Book 2 of the* Histories, *we must look for explanations; Darbo-Peschanski finds them in Herodotus's situating of himself in relation to his predecessors.*

Whoever skims through the imposing mass of the *Histories* is bound to make the following observation: the inquirer affords himself only very little opportunity to speak in his own name, especially if one thinks of the ominous way he vigorously takes possession of his text in the preamble. He shows restraint not only because he lets other voices resound next to his—we will come back to this—but also because most of the time he manifests himself only briefly, in the course of a digression or in a short statement. Longer passages, namely those which go beyond mere traces or fleeting allusions, are worth noticing for their scarcity. Let us examine some definite facts and figures.

In Book 1, the first-person singular appears about sixty times, in fifty cases only within brief statements which our author uses either to announce a coming section or to allude to a past one: for instance, when he vows to tell later why Cyrus overthrew Astyages, his maternal grandfather and king of Media (1.75); or when he goes back, in one sentence only, to what he just said about the Milesians (1.69). Always in a dozen words, he sometimes gives his own

From "Le 'je' de l'enquêteur: La place du discours critique," in *Le discours du particulier: Essai sur l'enquête hérodotienne* (Paris: Editions du Seuil, 1987), pp. 107–12.

personal impression, makes a conjecture, confesses his inability to solve a problem, alludes to his search for information, agrees or disagrees with a particular version of the facts he is interested in, refuses to impart what he knows, or else notes what is left in his own days of such-and-such monuments or dedications. These interventions are quite dry and lack the support of any kind of argumentation: whether arbitrary or perfunctory, they take up very little space (two words, one line at the most) within the enormous mass of other *logoi* which, on the other hand, are copiously expanded upon.

There remains a dozen other passages in which first-person speech is given more importance, mostly because, next to interventions similar to those just mentioned, the author either makes statements of intent about the way he proceeds, or agrees to argue. We should note, however, that these passages rarely exceed twenty lines in our modern editions. The inquirer, for instance, claims that a gold vessel dedicated at Delphi was a gift from Croesus: he knows the name of the man from Delphi who, in order to ingratiate himself to the Spartans, engraved the precious object with an inscription making them appear as its generous donors (1.51). Elsewhere as well, he explains the reason why Ionia had twelve cities, a much more speculative approach by which he attempts to verify a fact rather than to show how he has become convinced of its existence (1.145).

The analysis of Book 1 we have just conducted is equally valid for Books 3 to 4 and establishes the author's reserve as one of the *Histories'* main features.

Book 2, however, represents an important exception to this rule. If we try to determine how frequently the author speaks in the first person in Book 2, we are bound to observe that the phenomenon described above undergoes a complete reversal. Thus, out of Book 2's 182 paragraphs, about 115 (63 percent) contain statements made in the first person; in 70 out of these 115 passages (38 percent of the total), the author speaks at some length, and can even be the only speaker (2.22, 24, 116, 117, and so on). This leaves 45 paragraphs (25 percent of the whole) containing only brief asides. We see Herodotus transcribe the questions he asked, explain why he undertook a particular investigation, discuss various versions of the facts which his informers gave him, compare these versions in order to analyze them critically, and finally, give the results of his own experience constantly. In the first thirty-four chapters he thinks aloud, which for him is entirely exceptional.

What is more, the entire book is riddled with transition paragraphs in which Herodotus both recapitulates the sources he has used up to that point, and announces the ones he is going to use from then on (2.28–29; 99; 147). The fact that he so clearly delineates the origins and stages of his text shows how he encompasses the entire course of the book in one dominating glance, which is not without consequence for his audience and for the role he grants his informers.

While he simply lets the former speak everywhere else in his *Histories*, in Book 2 he only lends them the right to speak. He establishes himself as the owner of his text and does not hesitate to use this right to step into the narratives offered to him, to evaluate them, to supplement them, and especially to guide them; for, more than anywhere else, he shows how he personally *selects* the themes he is about to address—he is always ready to ask new questions and to initiate new debates.

How are we to explain this reversal? It has been suggested that Book 2 provides evidence for how Herodotus evolved from geography, which would cover the beginning of his work (Books 1 to 4) to history, which would prevail at the end (Books 5 to 9). Hecateus' *Periēgēsis* would have served as a model for geographical passages, and the only reason why Book 2 presents some structural originality is because Herodotus must have revised his entire work and modified it according to his most recent methodology. This theory, which reduces the originality of Book 2 to an originality of method derived from the *Histories'* genesis, raises several unavoidable objections. First of all, there is no proof that Book 2 was ever composed separately from and prior to the rest of the work. Second, why should one rely on the Egyptian *logoi* to qualify Book 2 as a geographical work, and then make the observation that the markers lending it a specifically geographical quality were thoroughly scrambled when the work underwent the unifying revision which gave it its final form? Such a position comes close to being a *petitio principii*. Finally, a comparison of Book 2 with Book 4 raises a third objection. These two books, which, supposedly, were geographical and Hecatean at first, and then were reworked, are nonetheless very different. It is true that, in Book 4, Herodotus presents major territories (Scythia, Lybia), just as he presents Egypt in Book 2; granted, he deals in Book 4 with questions of origins, natural environment, local customs, and the past. However, this presentation is far more cursory than that of Egypt. We are entitled to think, therefore, that Book 2's originality depends primarily on its contents, namely Egypt; only from this point on (that is, only secondarily), because Herodotus was influenced by a strong Ionian tradition which consisted in commenting and speculating on this particular region of the globe (a tradition, of course, to which Hecateus belongs), did he adopt a way of writing and relating to his text which he did not feel the need to use elsewhere to such a large extent. But this approach is not unusual enough in the *Histories* that it should not be subsumed, like many others, under the general notion of inquiry which Herodotus puts in the singular (1.1); similarly, it should never be given the anachronistic title of *geographical method*.

Herodotus is indeed fascinated with Egypt. In his eyes, this region is still able to enjoy a kind of Golden Age, all thanks to the beneficial influence of the Nile; and even if these wonderful times will eventually come to an end (2.13–14) when the Nile finally amasses so much alluvial deposit that it is no longer able to flood the plain, Egyptian people—or at least those settled downstream of Memphis—keep enjoying them. Benevolent Nature saves man if not the entirety at least most of his agricultural work: "As things are at present these people get their harvests with less labor than anyone else in the world, the rest of the Egyptians included; they have no need to work with plough or hoe, or to use any of the ordinary methods of cultivating their land; they merely wait for the river of its own accord to flood their fields; then, when the water has receded, each farmer sows his plot, turns pigs into it to tread in the seed, and then waits for the harvest. Pigs are used also for threshing, after which the grain is put into store" (2.13, trans. Burn).

Egypt was also a pioneer in many areas. Its inhabitants were "the first of all men" to invent the year and its twelve divisions through astronomical observation; they were the first to use the names of all twelve gods (2.4); the first to make it a law not to engage in sexual intercourse with women in sanctuaries and to purify themselves after each sexual act if they wished to enter these sanctuaries (2.64). Elsewhere, they are presented as the inventors of divination and are said to possess the largest amount of prophecies in the whole world thanks to a good archival system. Finally, they are singled out as having first formulated the doctrine of the immortality of the soul (2.123).

Furthermore, says the inquirer, after ending his study of the natural environment in general and the Nile in particular, Egypt carries the day on account of all the marvels it contains (2.35): "About Egypt I shall have a great deal more to relate because of the number of remarkable things which the country contains, and because more monuments that beggar description are to be found there than anywhere else in the world. That is reason enough for my dwelling on it at greater length" (trans. Burn). Egyptian wonders include the pyramids, the inhabitants' diet and how it gives them health and longevity, as well as how much they know about the past (2.77).

Finally, Greece itself, including Solon in some of his laws (2.177), took Egypt as a model. In this respect, Herodotus's statement is as provocative as Critias's later story in which Egyptian priests call Solon, the Athenian wise man, together with all the Greeks, children with a short memory. Even Greece bows to Herodotus's Egypt.

But it would be a mistake to think that the inquirer himself is solely responsible for this fascination and to argue, as some commentators do, that he is obviously biased toward Egypt in Book 2. Or else, one has to concede that he shares this bias with many Ionians. For even though Athens did not come into contact with Egypt before 489, the Ionians entered the country as early as Psammetichus's reign, a fact to which the *Histories* themselves bear witness: "To the Ionians and Carians who helped him to gain the throne Psammetichus granted two pieces of land, opposite one another on each side of the Nile, which came to be known as the Camps" (2.154, trans. Burn). This is why, ever since then and up until the reign of Amasis, Ionian and Carian mercenaries have become involved in Egypt's important historical events (3.1). Subsequently, the peace of Callias caused Ionians and Egyptians to share a common destiny. Finally, both people were heavily involved in trade relations: Greek colonies had sprouted all along the Nile, sometimes on the occasion of military expeditions such as the one led by Cambyses: "During the campaign of Cambyses in Egypt, a great many Greeks visited that country for one reason or another: some, as was to be expected, for trade, some to serve in the army, others, no doubt, out of mere curiosity, to see what they could see." Egypt, therefore, played an important role, both culturally and economically, for the Ionians, so much so, in fact, that going on a trip down the Nile appears as a requisite for inquisitive traders and intellectuals alike. Herodotus seems to have followed a tradition that was still alive in his own times.

In fact, ever since a landmark study by Camille Sourdille, the reality of Herodotus's own personal trip to Egypt is no longer questioned. Sourdille even managed to demonstrate that it had been but a short visit: from the end of July to the beginning of December of the same year. Exactly in which year it took place has provoked much controversy; but commentators agree on a date between 460 and 447 at the latest. There remains to be determined what the inquirer saw with his own eyes, what he was able to understand, and to whom he was able to ask questions. Generally, the brevity of his trip, the language barrier, and the various interests expressed by his informers suggest that the author of the *Histories* was able to gain only a superficial view of Egypt: this is why scholars tend to emphasize the importance of written sources and oral tradition in his work.

It seems, then, that by evoking Egypt at such length and with such partiality, Herodotus makes his own personal contribution to a particular kind of *topos* which Thales, Xenophanes, Pythagoras and Hecateus all contributed to shaping. Because he is dealing with an already much-discussed topic, he is forced to leave a strong individual mark on his material by means of vigorous and open polemicizing: the theme has become so mundane that whoever wants to address it anew needs to clearly state his views. The inquirer is particularly eager to show that the north of Egypt was only recently formed as part of the Nile's alluvial deposits, while Anaximander held the opinion that the world was originally covered with water. He also gives *his own* explanation for the flooding of the Nile (2.19–27), a problem that Thales had already tackled. Finally, by describing the history and geography of Egypt, Herodotus clearly emulates Hecateus.

If the inquirer, in Book 2 more than anywhere else in the *Histories*, displays such a substantial amount of speculation and lets the mechanisms of his research appear so clearly, it is because, dealing with a theme so recurrent in his own culture, he can only make space for himself by taking into consideration what his predecessors and contemporaries have said and the issues they have raised. The Greeks, and the Ionians in particular, were fully prepared to comprehend the subtle interplay of similarities and differences which the inquirer uses to define his own place within a tradition whose former masters, when they are known, are not always mentioned by name.

Once this is established, and however numerous the inquirer's personal interventions may be within Book 2, one should note that passages where he speaks in his own name, and which are developed enough to allow for analysis, occupy only 13 percent of the entire *Histories*. What remains to be done now is to investigate this reserve and to study how Herodotus organizes in his work a whole concert of voices other than his own.

TRANSLATED BY FLORENT HEINTZ

FRANÇOISE FRONTISI-DUCROUX

Living Statues

1975

In this part of Frontisi-Ducroux's study of artisanship, the author takes a combination of literary evidence and physical objects as her point of depar-ture, comparing ancient catalogues (by Pausanias and others) of sculpture attributed to the legendary Daedalus with the archaeology of Greek statu-ary through the seventh and sixth centuries [BCE]. The course of her analy-sis, which draws on the history of Greek religious ritual and on comparative mythology, separates a "rational" stratum of tradition—ascribing Daed-alus' prestige to his technical innovations in wooden representations of the gods—from a far broader archaic conception that linked the works of Daedalus to the automata of Hephaistos, worked in metal but internally animated. The "open eyes" and "separated legs" of Daedalus-sculpted gods are shown to gain their power from something quite different from aes-thetic illusion; rather, they symbolize the enigma of divinity, with its elusive mobility and charged charisma.

In Athens, Daedalus was seen primarily as a sculptor: the Greeks placed him at the origins of their art. According to Apollodorus,[1] in a tradition followed by Hyginus,[2] he was the inventor of *agalmata*, or statues repre-senting the gods. Diodorus simply credited him with decisive progress in ar-chaic statuary, but the legend according to which he was the ancestor of the Athenian sculptors was apparently widely disseminated. We find an allusion to it in a remark by Socrates, who, as the son of a sculptor, claimed Daedalus as an ancestor.[3] Ancient historians of art were apt to associate him with the first known artists. Thus Endoios, Daedalus' faithful disciple, was reputed to have accompanied his exiled master to Crete. The early-sixth-century Cretan sculp-tors Dipoinos and Scyllis were said to be pupils and perhaps even sons of Daed-alus, supposedly his children by a woman from Gortyn.[4] According to Polemon, Simmias of Athens, the author of an old Dionysus in stone, was his

From "Statues vivantes," in *Dédale: mythologie de l'artisan en Grèce ancienne* (Paris: François Maspero, 1975), pp. 95–117.

brother.[5] Clearchus, to whom Pausanias attributed the oldest bronze statue, was said to be a pupil either of Dipoinos and Scyllis or of Daedalus himself.[6] And when no direct filiation could be established, Pausanias still attributed the skill of the Cretan artists to Daedalus, for the greater glory of Athens.[7] Other contemporary sculptors were judged against Daedalus and found wanting, including the Aeginetan Smilis and one of his successors, Onatas.[8] Finally, Daedalus was also the eponymous hero of the *Daidalidai*, the deme to which Socrates belonged.

Under the circumstances, it was only natural for any number of temples to boast of possessing a work by Daedalus. Pausanias compiled a list of those he regarded as authentic: a Herakles in Thebes, the Trophonios of Lebadea, a Britomart at Olos in Crete, an Athena at Knossos, and an Aphrodite at Delos dedicated to Apollo by Theseus. Two works were destroyed: the Argives' offering at the Heraion, and the *agalma* brought from Omphake to Gela in Sicily.[9] Mention is made elsewhere of two *xoana* of Herakles, one, naked, in Corinth, the other between Messenia and Arcadia.[10] To these statues Pausanias added the *khoros* of Ariadne at Knossos, a white marble statue that was mentioned by Homer; its nature is still a matter of controversy.[11] Although Daedalus was a citizen of Athens, the city possessed only one work by its premier sculptor, a folding chair in the Erechtheion.

In addition to the evidence offered by Pausanias, we also have that of Apollodorus, who mentions an image of Herakles at Pisa in Elis, and of Stephanus of Byzantium, who mentions an Artemis *Monogissēnē* in stone in Caria and two statues representing Daedalus and Icarus in the Electris Islands. Finally, Skylax mentions an altar of Poseidon in Libya that contains two sculptures or bas-reliefs.

With this somewhat tedious chore of listing works out of the way, it is worth noting that nearly all the statues of Daedalus are *xoana*. The technical term *xoanon* (derived from the verb *xeō*, to scrape or polish) originally denoted an image carved in wood, but it could also be applied to statues covered with metal.[12] In listing the works of Daedalus, Pausanias uses the words *xoanon* and *agalma* interchangeably. The latter term had no technical significance. Its meaning was much more extensive: it covered anything that could be a cause of joy,[13] including finery, ornament, and offerings. More specifically, it referred to statues erected in honor of a god but not necessarily images of that god. Nevertheless, all of Daedalus' statues represent gods, and all the ones mentioned by Pausanias are wooden *xoana*. Pausanias is always careful to mention the metal and precious gems with which ancient idols were covered. The workmanship must have been fairly primitive, or so we infer from details concerning the statue of Aphrodite at Delos: it was a small *xoanon* of which the right hand had been destroyed and stood not on feet but on a square base.[14] Indeed, the ancients were disconcerted by the "simplicity" of these works, to

judge by the rather embarrassed reaction of Pausanias, who was quite a con-
noisseur of ancient artifacts: "Everything Daedalus did is of rather strange appearance, yet there is something remarkable and inspired about these
works."[15] And to judge also by the less respectful sarcasms of Socrates: "If
Daedalus were alive today and produced the works to which he owes his renown, he would seem ridiculous in the eyes of our sculptors."[16]

These astonished reactions were due to the contrast between the appearance
of the works ascribed to Daedalus and the leading role traditionally assigned to
him. When he was not credited with having invented the statue, his talent was
praised as being responsible for all the important progress in archaic art: according to Diodorus, this included such sculptural features as open eyes, legs
spread apart, and arms detached from the body and outstretched.[17]

Before Daedalus, statues therefore had closed eyes, legs joined, and arms
attached to bodies, and some were without hands, feet, and eyes altogether.
Some were nothing more than a plank or beam, similar to the herms that still
existed in the classical period.

This tradition actually reflected the evolution of statuary that archaeologists
have uncovered. The art of sculpture progressed from the pre-Hellenic idol,
whose body was a cylindrical or tetragonal piece of wood, to the so-called "dedalic" statue. This rather imprecise term was borrowed from ancient historians
of art, themselves in disagreement as to its meaning.[18] According to Jenkins'
classification,[19] the term "dedalic" applies to the entire seventh century and
suggests a schematic, rigid modeling in two dimensions adhering strictly to the
law of frontality. The statuette known as the *Lady of Auxerre*, which dates from
the middle of the seventh century, is a good example of this style. But what
Diodorus describes is even more remote from the old, crudely fashioned
wooden *xoana* that so astonished Pausanias. The details he gives—legs separated, arms outstretched—suggest the dedalic statue of the seventh century,
the beginnings of the archaic style as we know it from stone statuary: for example, the Cleobis in the museum of Delphi, represented in a walking posture.

Thus there are two levels of contradiction: the progress that ancient tradition ascribed to Daedalus suggests the archaic statuary of the sixth century.
The term "dedalic," which itself comes from antiquity, refers to the more rigid
modeling of the previous century. Furthermore, the "reality" reported by Pausanias concerns an even earlier stage. One of Daedalus' works, the *xoanon* of
Aphrodite at Delos, with "a square base instead of feet," was therefore footless,
just like the works of his mythical predecessors.[20]

The epithets "without hands" and "without feet" that define the works of
the most ancient sculptors can therefore refer either to the most primitive type
of idol, the stone pillar or wooden block, and thus to a pure, aniconic symbol of
a divine presence, or to a *xoanon* carved in wood, with the merest indication of
arms and legs firmly attached to the body. But they may also refer to another

reality. This tradition of primitive statues without hands and feet may, according to a suggestion of Waldemar Déonna,[21] be based on an erroneous interpretation of mutilated statues, damaged by time or by man: statues with hands cut
off or missing pieces of stone or wood.

As for epithets alluding to the blindness of statues,[22] they can be explained in
the same way—by total omission of the eye or by technical clumsiness in representing the open eye ("archaic exophthalmia"), giving an impression of
blindness, or even by erosion or fading of the paint that represented the eyes.[23]
With technical progress, more deeply set eyes with more distinct eyelids and
painted pupils made statues seem to possess the power of sight, while at the
same time the separation of the limbs from the body gave an impression of
movement.

As represented in ancient tradition, however, Daedalus' statues were far
more than a reflection of a real evolution. These works had characteristics that
eluded any aesthetic reality. They were perceived as being so lifelike that they
seemed to see and to move.[24] They were like living beings. For Diodorus and
other rationalist authors,[25] the statues were simply images, a view that reflected
precisely the progress for which Daedalus was responsible. All the evidence
insists on the perfection of the illusion that these images produced. Apollodorus reports that Herakles, deceived by a *xoanon* that Daedalus had made of
him, struck his own statue, believing in the dark that he was confronting an
enemy.[26]

This lifelike quality clearly went beyond the realm of imitation, however. A
whole tradition, recounted by Plato in the *Meno*, emphasized the miraculous
mobility of Daedalus' works. Did they not have to be bound to prevent them
from fleeing?[27] Not only could they run,[28] but they also possessed the powers
of sight and even speech.[29] Since the immobility of statues was proverbial, the
agitation of these works was all the more paradoxical. Their movements had
none of the stiff rigidity of automata but seemed, like the contraptions of Hephaistos, to be governed by an inherent intelligence. This inspired Aristotle: "If
every instrument could, on command, perform its work as the statues of Daedalus and tripods of Hephaistos are said to do."[30]

In fact, these statues were invested with a magical form of life, even if Philip
the Comic did attempt to give an amusing explanation of their powers. According to him, Daedalus had animated his wooden statue of Aphrodite by
pouring mercury into it.[31] Athena possessed the secret of this magic life, and
she had vouchsafed it to the Rhodians, whose "roads were lined with figures
resembling living things on the move."[32]

Daedalus' statues thus belong to a series of works of which Athena and
Hephaistos were the authors. There were of course tripods that transported
themselves (*automatoi*) to the assembly of the gods, and golden "servants" that
helped the crippled god to move: "They were made of gold, but they looked
like real maidens. In their hearts dwelt a kind of reason; they also possessed

voices and strength. By the grace of the immortals, they were able to do work."
Hephaistos was also the creator of the gold and silver dogs who guarded the
palace of Alcinous, as well as of an even more astonishing work, Talos, the
man of bronze, who was assigned by Minos to keep watch over Crete, about
which he made regular rounds.[33] He was also responsible for Pandora, who
was formed from earth with the help of Athena, who, according to Plato's
Protagoras, also assisted Prometheus in the creation of man. This variety of
works calls to mind the work of the potter and thus makes us think of terra-
cotta statues. But modeling in clay is also an indispensable step in the fabrication of statues from molten bronze,[34] and a vase from the Berlin Museum
shows Athena making a clay mold of a horse.[35] Thus for two gods to fashion a
living being out of clay was an activity not unrelated to their other creations.

Pandora, covered with *daidala*, can thus be categorized as a living *daidalon*.
Similarly, the golden servants were the creation of a divine artisan, a master of
daidala. The tripod automata were equipped with *daidalea* handles. And as for
Talos, we shall see later on just how "dedalic" this fantastic creature was. The
statues of Daedalus, the quintessential *daidala*, are thus right at home in this
series of magical works, and the mysterious life of the latter is reason enough to
account for the legendary mobility of the former.

The animation of Daedalus' statues must also be related, however, to several
other categories of mythical and ritual evidence. When this has been done, we
will be able to map the *xoanon*'s field of representation (all of Daedalus' statues
were *xoana*).

Plato's remark in the *Meno* about the need to bind Daedalus' statues is
matched by certain ritual practices whose meaning was no longer apparent in
the classical period. Consider, first of all, the existence of various bound statues,
which are mentioned by Pausanias: at Phigalia in Arcadia, the *xoanon* of Eury-
nome, a mermaid goddess whose temple was opened only once a year, was
bound in chains of gold. In Sparta, the old statue of Enyalios was fettered,
while the cedar image of Aphrodite Morpho was chained and veiled. At Or-
chomenos, the bronze statue of Actaeon was bound to a rock by an iron chain.
And finally, in Phocis, Pausanias saw an ancient image of Demeter wrapped in
bandages. But were these also bonds?

In addition to these examples of bound statues, there is evidence of the periodic binding of statues of the gods. The best known example was recorded by
Athenaeus.[36] In Samos, during the festival of the Tonaia, an effigy of Hera, a
xoanon, was taken by the priestess and hidden in a wicker case by the river.
When it was recovered, the bonds of wicker were removed, and the statue was
purified and replaced in the temple.

It seems legitimate to associate this practice with the epithet attached to the
little *xoanon* of Artemis Orthia in Sparta: "*lugodesma*." The statue, a small,
lightweight *xoanon*, was supposedly discovered in a thicket encased in bonds of
agnus castus, which held it upright.

Conversely, in Rome, a statue of Saturn had its legs bound permanently by a woolen thread that was untied for the Saturnalia.

For these facts Pausanias offers two types of explanation. In the case of Enyalios, the bonds are a symbol whose meaning is the same as the absence of wings on the Athenians' Nike Aptera: the purpose of the fetters is to keep the god with the Athenians.[37] In the case of Actaeon, the purpose was to immobilize and neutralize a troublesome and pernicious phantom by chaining its effigy.

Neglecting certain differences of detail, the goal in both cases is to fix a mysterious power (phantom or god), initially by giving it a material incarnation in wood or metal. Actaeon's *eikōn* and Enyalios's *xoanon* can thus be seen as signs of an immaterial, elusive, and invisible reality, which they localize and materialize without affecting the supernatural efficacy of the power in question. In addition, a further material sign is required to hold this mobile and fugitive power fixed in one place.

The existence of bound statues is only one example of the mobility of the *xoanon*, however, though to be sure an example that reveals that mobility with particular clarity. It is also apparent in most of the ritual practices and legends associated with divine images of this type. Indeed, mobility is part of the concept of such images: small, light, and easily transportable, the *xoanon* was different from earlier representations or, rather, incarnations of the divine presence—beams, pillars, sacred trees, *betyles* or herms, all things rooted in the soil that fixed and localized divine power.[38] With the *xoanon*, the sign that manifests the god's presence was no longer linked to a specific place; it could be, and was, moved about. The festivals in which the icon figured involved a series of practices that emphasized its mobility. It was first hidden, then shown. It was washed, adorned, carried about, and transported from one sacred site to another before finally being brought back to its temple. The cult of Athena in Athens involved all these activities: the Palladion was taken once a year to Phaleron and immersed in the sea. During the Panathenaia, it was given a new *peplos*, woven by the Ergastinon. In the Plynteria the idol was undressed and veiled.[39] In Argos, ceremonies in honor of the goddess apparently included an episode in which a priest fled into the mountains with the *xoanon*, which was also transported to the temple of Inachos to be washed. In Athens, the *xoanon* of Dionysus was taken on a chariot from the Limnaion to the Boukoleion on the second day of the Anthesteria, apparently to be united with the wife of the archon-king. Such practices establish a contrast between the *xoanon* and the massive, immobile cult statue of stone housed in a temple for all the city to see; the latter succeeded the *xoanon* but did not replace it altogether, since *xoana* continued to play a central role in certain ceremonies.

Finally, mobility was an important theme in the legends that revolved around the *xoanon*. The divine idol came from afar, sometimes from the world of the gods, often from a foreign country, sometimes brought by human agents, like the Lugodesma, which came from Tauris with Orestes, or the Aphrodite of Delos, which Theseus and Ariadne took with them in flight, other times by themselves, mysteriously. It was an object of desire that people stole and fought over—the icon itself and the divine power that it embodied. The story of the Palladium is exemplary in this respect: dropped from Olympus into Troy, this *xoanon* made the city invulnerable until Odysseus and Diomedes made off with it. It was then claimed by Argos, Sparta, Athens, and Rome, each eager to possess the ancient idol of the goddess. This was because possession carried a religious privilege along with it, a privilege that was a sign of special power accorded by the goddess to the individual or group that possessed the icon. The image of the god was thus a token of royal investiture in the same way as other talismans that played a similar role in analogous myths: Agamemnon's sword, which was honored as much as a divine idol in Chaeronea, Diomedes' shield in Argos, ring, cup, tripod, and necklace.

The functional parallelism, attested by myth, between the *xoanon* and other types of *sacra*, or precious objects invested with religious significance and political power, places this sort of divine image (which Daedalus was credited with inventing) among the *agalmata* defined and analyzed by Louis Gernet. We saw earlier that this category subsumed nearly all the *daidala*. Daedalus' statues therefore had every reason to flee. Their mobility signaled either the imperceptible presence of a god or their function as a ritual object or instrument that mimicked divine action in its various manifestations or else symbolized a political power that claimed divine investiture but could, like any talisman, escape its possessor. Or, finally, the mobile icon could also be a precious object, which, apart from any religious or political value it might have, was also a symbol of wealth and economic power, a circulating currency, a token of value, a movable good.

All four aspects of the *agalma*'s meaning—economic, social, political, and religious—contributed to the magical mobility of the *xoanon*. Originally, the *xoanon* was merely one segment of this larger category, the word *agalma* meaning a feeling of joy or exultation as well as the precious object or opportunity to make an offering that was its cause. But the semantic evolution of the term, which came to denote that exemplary offering, the divine image,[40] made it almost synonymous with *xoanon*. Even in this case, however, the notion of *agalma* remained independent of the material of the divine image and its technique: engraved metal, relief, sculpture in the round, painting, or woven fabric. From the point of view of technique, therefore, the *xoanon* can be seen as a category of *agalma*.

Analysis of one of the primary characteristics of Daedalus' statues, mobility, thus reveals the wealth of meaning in this mythical motif. Behind the image of the animate *xoanon* that takes flight if not tied down, it is possible to detect echoes of the technical and aesthetic revolution that occurred in Greek sculpture in the seventh and sixth centuries: the conquest of expression and movement. But it would be wrong to ignore the equally significant reflections of a series of highly complex representations whose economic, social, political, and religious overtones define the semantic field of *agalma*, the category that encompassed the divine, the *xoanon*, and the *daidalon*, sometimes distinct, sometimes not.

Were these representational schemes, most likely quite old, revived in the sixth century, as Waldemar Déonna has suggested,[41] by the contrast between the stiff, constricted old images and the impression of liberation and life spurred by the sight of *kouroi* and *korai*?[42] This is more than likely, and it would explain the paradox of a tradition that attributes to the works of Daedalus the technical characteristics of sixth-century cult statues and the mythical properties of the *xoanon*, or divine effigy, of the previous period. A certain contradiction was expressed in the contrast between two views of the divine figure, incarnated by two types of plastic sign and reflecting two different conceptions of the divine. One, essentially symbolic, manifested a mysterious and active power, while the other was much more an image, a representation of the god and spectacle for the eye: here, the divine was expressed through its form, reproducing that of the human figure, which in the case of the *xoanon* was merely indicated in the most rudimentary way. The second conception succeeded the first in time but did not entirely supplant it. *Xoana* were still being fabricated and consecrated in the classical period, and the gods they represented apparently continued to figure in any number of ritual practices that supplemented the public cult of the city.

Thus far we have neglected the other innovations attributed to Daedalus, focusing exclusively on the impression of mobility in his works, no doubt because of the interest Plato and his contemporaries took in the problems of representing movement by plastic means. The lifelike impression of Daedalus' statues was also ascribed to their gaze, however, and the traditional claim that he had "opened the eyes of statues" could be analyzed in a similar way.

I have already mentioned Déonna's explanation for the epithet *aommatous* (eyeless) that was applied to works prior to Daedalus': failure to grasp older plastic conventions, lack of skill on the part of older sculptors in representing the eyes (in contrast to the more confident technique of later works), or, finally, an impression of blindness caused by the fading of the paint used to represent the pupil of the eye.

Déonna loses no time, however, in pointing out that this explanation is inadequate. In the two articles cited above, he discusses evidence from both myth and ritual that sheds considerable light on Daedalus' talent for bringing statues to life.

Indeed, myths from many different civilizations (Amerindian, Australian, and Oriental) feature the theme of the demiurge who brings statues to life by giving them eyes and a mouth. All forms of figurative representation of the human or divine face are involved: there is the story, for example, of the Chinese painter who did not dare to paint eyes on his human subjects lest they get up and run away.

These myths can be related to certain rituals for the consecration of statues. In Tonkin, for instance, a statue was consecrated by drawing a line with black paint between its two eyes. In the case of ancient Egypt, moreover, we know about the ritual from the tomb of Tutankhamen, which contained a text listing the various procedures for bringing statues to life and the formulas that were uttered in conjunction with them: "I open your mouth, I open your eyes, I open your legs." Similar formulas and techniques are also attested in the case of Babylonia.

To be sure, this evidence is not directly applicable to the Greek world, but certain beliefs concerning the evil effects of the gaze of divine images allow us to hypothesize that a background of similar representations existed. Might not a fear of this kind explain the stone *kolossoi* of Selinos, which have hair and ears but no eyes or mouth? Or the mysterious female figures of Cyrene, with smooth faces totally devoid of features or, later, partially veiled? The role of the *kolossos* was to provide a substitute for the absent cadaver,[43] to fix the impalpable presence of the dead person or invisible divine power. Although the latter was mobile and transportable and the former half-buried at a fixed location, in both cases the gaze was apparently an important representational feature in these two different types of plastic sign. In the *kolossos* "with empty eyes," blindness seems to have been a quality equivalent to the immobility of stone, expressing death itself. For the *xoanon*, imbued with supernatural life, belief in the efficacy of the gaze was expressed in two ways: the veil that covered the face of Aphrodite Morpho may have protected the faithful from the effects of the divine gaze as much as from the sight of the divine image. Either could be harmful. Contemplating the image of a god could cause blindness, while to be gazed upon by a god could cause madness. This double danger—of either looking upon the face of a god or falling under a god's gaze—actually reflects a principle of reciprocity that appears to be a constant feature of the concept and expression of vision in Greek. The term *ōps* denotes both the eye and sight—the organ and the faculty—as well as the face, visage, or aspect—the object of vision.[44] The same reversibility characterizes the adjective *tuphlos*, which describes not only the blind person but also that which is hidden, obscure, invisible. The two equivalent notions, *to see* and *to be seen*, stand opposed to the antithetical couple consisting of the terms *blind* and *invisible*. The first pair of words belongs to the realm of light, the second to the realm of darkness or fog that envelops the kingdom of the dead, the realm of Hades, the invisible one— *A-idēs*—whose magical helmet possesses the virtue of invisibility. To die is to disappear from the world of the visible, but it is also to be frozen, transformed into stone, as indicated by the symbolism of the head of Gorgo, who turns to stone living creatures who make their way into the kingdom of the dead, or the eye of Medusa, whom Perseus must defeat without looking at her, with his eyes closed, while he himself has been made invisible by the helmet of Hades.

This opposition between the visible and the invisible is also present in the representational range of *xoanon*, where it appears in the form of an alternation: the divine image is often hidden, veiled, or enclosed. Only priests are allowed to see it. Access to the temple is forbidden. Periodically, the temple is opened, and the *xoanon* is unveiled and shown to the faithful. The practice of first hiding and then showing the *xoanon* is central to the rituals in which it figures, as important as the behavioral contrast we analyzed earlier: that of first immobilizing the divine idol, if need be by tying it down, then setting it loose and manipulating it or carrying it about—in a word, animating it. Indeed, are these two types of behavior not synonymous? Are they not analogous expressions of the same reality, the revelation by a visible sign of the active presence of a god, the manifestation, through movement, of its supernatural efficacy? In other words, as we might speculate from the well-attested equivalence between the blind or invisible and the petrified, mobility and sight both connote life. And the two legendary features that distinguished the statues of Daedalus— unbound limbs and open eyes—were synonymous metaphors, redundant expressions of a single signified: sculptural representations of the mystery of divinity. But these characteristics were closely associated with a particular form of figuration, namely, the *xoanon*, and the representation of divinity that it embodied. The statue was yet another sign, which revealed a power conceived of as an active force present in the world. Later, in the era of the large cult statue,[45] image would replace symbol, and the idol would become the form, spectacle, and representation of an ideal essence standing outside the world.[46]

[. . .]

This analysis of Daedalus' statues does not actually coincide with any narrative sequence. We began with various facts about Daedalus' works, especially their reputation for mobility and lifelike qualities. These facts had little to do with the thread of the narrative, of which they formed nothing more than a traditional element.

Analysis revealed that this theme had several layers. There were, first of all, the very ancient mythical and ritual traditions that defined the representational range of *xoanon*, which, like *daidalon*, was partially incorporated in the broader system of the word *agalma*, a complex notion that combined values that we consider distinct: economic, social, aesthetic, and religious.

Upon this archaic substrate later authors built a more "rational" structure in their attempts to historicize the personage Daedalus by situating him in

relation to the evolution of Greek statuary. The price of this "historical reconstruction" was a series of contradictions and distortions of the original data, to
which new plastic and aesthetic significations were added by assigning Daedalus a key role in the representation of movement. But the primary effect of all
this was to conceal the legendary artisan's original association with metalwork-
ing while emphasizing his role as a sculptor in wood, thought to be the only
possible precursor of the later Greek sculptors.

TRANSLATED BY ARTHUR GOLDHAMMER

NOTES

[1] Apollodorus 3.15.8.

[2] Hyginus *Fabulae* 274.

[3] Plato *Alcibiades* 121a; *Euthyphro* 11b.

[4] Pausanias 2.15.1.

[5] Polemon *FGrH* 3.136 fr. 73.

[6] Pausanias 3.19.7.

[7] Ibid., 8.53.8.

[8] Ibid., 3.17.6; 5.25.12.

[9] Pausanias 9.40.3; 9.11.4, and 9.39.8.

[10] Ibid., 2.4.5; 8.35.2.

[11] *Iliad* 18.550; Pausanias 1.27.1.

[12] C. Picard, *Manuel d'archéologie grecque* (Paris, 1935), vol. 1, pp. 86–87.

[13] *pan eph' hōi tis agalletai* (Hesychius).

[14] Pausanias 9.40.4.

[15] Pausanias 2.4.5.

[16] Plato *Hippias major* 282a.

[17] Diodorus Siculus 4.76.

[18] See, for example, Cassius Dio 1.97; Pausanias 7.55; 5.25, 13; Philostratus *Life of Apollonius* 6.3. According to B. Schweizer, who is following K. Reinhardt, Democritus was the first to consider Daedalus as a historical sculptor and to interpret the magical life of his statues as reflecting the progress of statuary in the seventh and sixth centuries (see Hanna Philipp, *Tektonōn Daidala* [Berlin, 1968], pp. 51, 63). The author believes that this connection was made before the fifth century.

[19] R. J. M. Jenkins, *Dedalica* [. . .] (Cambridge, 1936).

[20] See n. 14.

[21] W. Déonna, "L'Image incomplète ou mutilée," *Revue des études anciennes* 32 (1930): 321.

[22] *aommatous—summemukotas tous ophthalmous—tois men ommasi memukota.*

[23] Déonna, "L'Image," and "Les Yeux absents ou clos des statues de la Grèce primitive," *Revue des études grecques* 48 (1935).

[24] Diodorus 4.76.

[25] Palaephatus *On the Incredible* 22.

[26] Apollodorus 2.63. Perfect imitation of reality was also characteristic of Daedalus' other works, such as Pasiphae's cow, the honeycomb of the temple of Aphrodite Erycina, etc. (Diodorus 4.77).

[27] Plato *Meno* 97d. The same allusion to the disconcerting mobility of these statues can also be found in the *Euthyphro* 11c–d.

[28] Dio Chrysostom *Orations* 37.9.

[29] Euripides *Hecuba* 838.

[30] Aristotle *Politics* 1.2.5.

[31] Quoted by Aristotle *De anima* 1.3.

[32] Pindar *Olympian* 7.52. The Rhodian tradition was linked to the Telchines, magician-artisans who were the first artisans of metal and the first to sculpt statues of the gods.

[33] Apollodorus 1.140; Apollonius Rhodius *Argonautica* 2.1051.

[34] This point is developed in a subsequent chapter of the book from which this selection is excerpted.

[35] *Corpus vasorum antiquorum* (Berlin, 1990–), 3 pl. 145, F. 2415.

[36] Athenaeus 526, 1,672 (cf. Pausanias 4.4.4).

[37] Pausanias 3.15.7.

[38] The analysis that follows is based on an unpublished study by J.-P. Vernant, "De la Figure des dieux."

[39] L. Farnell, *The Cults of the Greek States* (Oxford, 1896–1909), pp. 305, 1,262.

[40] The notion of *agalma* was then quite close to that of *anathēma*.

[41] Déonna, "L'Image."

[42] And reactivated in the time of Plato (which explains the allusions in the *Meno*, *Euthyphro*, and *Timaeus* 19b–c) by the exploration of expression and movement by contemporary sculptors, Lysippus in particular (Schuhl, *Platon et l'Art de son temps* [Paris, 1952], p. 94ff.).

[43] Vernant 1965, 251–64.

[44] This ambiguity of active and passive is also found in other languages: cf. French *vue*.

[45] Archaeological discoveries in Keos have revealed the existence of large cult statues in the fifteenth century B.C.E. We must assume that the technique was lost throughout the Greek Middle Ages. On the birth or rebirth of the large statue, see Picard *op. cit.* Chs. 6 and 7.

[46] Hence Plato's fundamental hostility to art, which belongs to the illusory domain of appearances, and the concessions that he sometimes makes to the works of art, to the extent that the work preserves a reflection of the idea and allows one to make a representation of it.

GEOFFREY KIRK

The Spicy Side of Structuralism

1978

Marcel Detienne's research on the symbolism of lettuce in the myths and rituals of the ancient world in The Gardens of Adonis *can serve as a keynote for articulating, in all its rich complexities, the "French structuralist" approach to Classics. It has become an intellectual flashpoint for highlighting different academic styles of argumentation in different "Classics" cultures. The differences seem particularly pronounced in the case of Gallic and Anglo-American styles. Geoffrey Kirk's "lettuce war" with Detienne is a telling example.*

T*he Gardens of Adonis* is an English version—well translated, but marred by serious misprints—of a book that made quite a stir when it appeared in France some six years ago. Marcel Detienne uses the Adonis myth as starting and finishing point for an attractive excursion through the various implications of aromatics and spices in ancient Greek thought and experience. What made the stir was not, of course, just this, but rather that a substantially structuralist analysis of Adonis seemed to result in a completely different assessment from that advanced by Frazer in *Adonis, Attis, Osiris* of 1906 and subsequently incorporated in *The Golden Bough*. It has therefore been accepted by many—including Jean-Pierre Vernant, who contributes an ample and interesting introduction, and Lévi-Strauss himself, who wrote a glowing review of the original version in *L'Homme*—that we have here a unique demonstration that a Lévi-Straussian analysis could be rigorously directed not only (as Paul Ricoeur once suggested) to the myths of tribal societies, but also, as should be the case according to structuralist theory, to those of more developed Western cultures. Others, including Pierre Vidal-Naquet, had found that the methods of *Mythologiques* could illuminate occasional aspects of Greek myths—creatures like the Centaurs and Cyclops, for instance. But no full-scale structuralist analysis had been successfully applied to the Greek material, nor had it been thought possible to do so. It was therefore a relief to committed

From *The Times Literary Supplement*, 18 August 1978.

structuralists when Detienne did just that, and came up with a new and positive result. Or did he?

The birth of Adonis from Myrrha, "myrrh-tree," leads the author directly to a consideration of Greek tales about the origin of myrrh and other aromatics. Herodotus tells us that they all came from Arabia, the land of spices, and regales us with fantastic stories of the way they are gathered. Even the learned Theophrastus could later believe that cinnamon and cassia (both in fact from the Far East) were of South Arabian origin, like frankincense and myrrh; and even these last two were confused by the elder Pliny. They were exotic substances, and science was not at home with them. [. . .]

Detienne, at any rate, is led rapidly by Herodotus to the famous Lévi-Straussian polarity of Above and Below, significant, of course, for the relations of gods and mortals, and not least so for people who cast aromatic spices into the flames of sacrifice to be carried with the rich fat-laden smoke into the upper air. Among other marvels Herodotus told how cinnamon-twigs are made up by great birds into nests high up on inaccessible cliffs; whereas cassia grows in a lake, protected by fierce batlike creatures. Theophrastus varies the latter tale: it is cinnamon, not cassia, it grows in deep glens, not a lake, and is protected by snakes, not bats. But this shows all the more clearly, according to Detienne, that what is really at issue, what is structurally essential and significant, is the opposition of Above (cliffs!) and Below (deep glens!). Other polarities, too, are discovered, with great and typical ingenuity; all is welded into a nexus of oppositions and mediations, and the pages are dotted with those structuralist diagrams that conceal so much and say so little. But the nexus remains an exceedingly loose one, and moreover it turns out to have very little point—that is, explicative or reflective value when applied as a code to different levels of experience—even by common structuralist standards.

This learned interweaving of heterogeneous beliefs and mythical motifs concerned with aromatics is significantly different from Lévi-Strauss's painstaking analysis of an arguably unique and unusually complex corpus of myths from Amazonia, in which he was enabled [. . .] to compare manifold local and to some extent temporal variants of a traditional theme or tale and discern—rather than simply conjecture— those elements which are structurally indispensable and those which can be varied more or less at will. In order for myth-elements to be significant, at anything beyond the narrative level, their relations with each other have to be shown to be specifically determined in some sense, which means not to be simply banal or axiomatic. For example, the appearance of dualities, pairs, polarities or opposites does not of itself entail that a mediation is being sought. [. . .]

One trouble about Detienne's deployment, in his first and most fundamental chapter, of Greek ideas about the origins of spices is they seem to depend so clearly on a few simple assumptions; mainly that spices owe their smell to hot and dry conditions, that they come from a hot, distant and exotic land, that they are gathered and distributed in exotic and mysterious ways. They are hard to get, expensive, and play a serious role in such important activities as religion, sex, and cooking; it is hardly surprising, then, that they should come within the scope of marvellous tales and ingenuity-motifs, which (like most folktale-motifs) are not entirely cut off from real life. Such categories of high and low, or wet and dry, as can be detected in these tales are more plausibly interpreted as obviously concomitants of *inaccessibility* than as typically structuralist polarities to reflect a cosmological or a social code.

Once again there is a profound difference between Lévi-Strauss's salutary doctrine of scrutinizing the implications for a myth-making society of every plant, creature, institution or artifact that may appear in a myth, however incidentally—of assessing their cultural and ecological value as accurately as one can—and the practice, exemplified quite often by Detienne, of amassing details about details until something turns up that can be plausibly regarded as the opposite of something else—as though that necessarily mattered.

Thus I doubt whether Herodotus's cinnamon-gatherers, who use hunks of meat to attract the giant birds (who then fly up with the lumps, which being too big for the nests send the precious twigs tumbling down the cliffs to the gatherers below), are significantly opposed to his cassia-gatherers, who wrap themselves in skins in order to brave the giant bats, by the opposition, conscious or otherwise, of Inside (meat!) to Outside (skins!). That kind of claim is little more than a tic of modern analysis; and I dare say that in the present case there is no more to the matter than that meat is an obvious bait for vulturelike birds, and skins a natural protection against aggressive flying creatures.

The argument takes on new life when it returns to Adonis himself. Detienne sees this Greek version of an Eastern demigod as a symbol of excessive and abnormal sexuality developed to set against, and thereby to confirm, regular marital relations directed to the production of legitimate children. There is some truth in his view of the myth and cult of Adonis (although the implications are wider than that); but not so much because of any association with aromatics, which increase sexual allure both within and outside marriage, or even with lettuces, which were grown as part of his ritual and were also associated with his death, as because the festival of the Adonia was celebrated by women of easy virtue and their lovers, whereas the regular female festival of fertility, the Thesmophoria, was entirely confined to women, and primarily respectable ones at that. [. . .]

In fact, the emphasis was not so simple, as might have been seen by the investigation of another paradox: precisely that of the apparent respectability of the ritual actions in Adonis's festival, in contrast with the dubious nature of its clientèle. The mounting of ladders to the rooftops, the exposing there of the "Gardens of Adonis"—swiftly growing seeds of wheat, barley, fennel, and lettuce, planted in broken crocks—and the tending of them till they withered in the sun, scarcely constitute a *risqué* or a titillating business [. . .]. On the other hand, the ladies of the Thesmophoria devoted much of their ritual fervor to the muttering of dirty words and the handling of model genitalia, even apart from the more solidly agrarian performance of mixing seed-corn with decayed lumps of pig's flesh dredged up by specially designated matrons from underground chambers. Clearly, the public festival could afford to follow the crude and ancient rituals without fear, the newer and more private cults could not; but there is more to it than that.

There is a risk that Detienne, if he has illuminated certain aspects of the Adonis cult, has more seriously obfuscated others, not so much by his omission of many implications of the women's festivals as by his evident desire to replace Frazer's "disappearing god" with something entirely different, a structuralist paradigm in fact. For Adonis *is* a fertility god, after all, and one who symbolizes the disappearance and reappearance of the crops, as well no doubt as much else. That is strongly suggested, to begin with, by his Near Eastern prototypes—prototypes by which poor simple-minded Frazer was rightly impressed, but which Detienne dismisses [. . .]. For it seems hard to deny that the structuralist preoccupation with synchrony is often accompanied by an undue carelessness with respect to the diachronic: in short, over basic historical methodology where evidence about the past is germane. Thus Detienne, in arguing against the need to pay attention to Adonis's Near Eastern origins, claims that "Neither . . . the Syrian Tammuz, nor—*a fortiori*—the Sumerian Dumuzi, are clearly enough drawn in the oriental tradition" to throw light on the Greek Adonis.

But that "*a fortiori*" gives the game away, for what Detienne must mean is that we inevitably know less and less about the past the further it stretches away from us: the evidence for Dumuzi is generally earlier than that for Tammuz, therefore it must be less full and reliable. That is, of course, a very serious methodological mistake, and the truth is, in the present case, the very opposite: for we know little enough about Tammuz but a considerable amount about his non-Semitic ancestor, Dumuzi. If Detienne had turned his learning eastward he would have remarked much that is highly relevant to the proper understanding of the Greek Adonis.

For no one denies that Adonis was somehow introduced into Greece from the Near East: his name is derived from the Semitic *adon-ai*, "lord," used in particular to address Tammuz, the Akkadian and Syrian form of Sumerian Dumuzi. Dumuzi was a complex figure, but by the end of the third millennium B.C. he had certainly become a god of fertility associated with sheep, with grain and with the date-cluster. He was originally the mortal lover of Inanna, goddess of love and "queen of heaven," just as Adonis was the beautiful boy-lover of Aphrodite [. . .]. More recently it has become clear that Dumuzi's place in the "House of Dust" is taken for half of each year by his sister Geshti-nanna (just like Castor and Polydeuces in the later Greek myth), allowing him to come to life again with the new season's reemergence of fertility. Nothing suggests that Tammuz was not believed to do much the same. If Adonis, the Greek Tammuz, ritual mourning and all, did not have such connotations, where is the evidence for it? Nowhere at all, except in a shaky intellectual construction whereby Adonis can *only* exist as a counterpart to Demeter in matters of human sexual relations. Moreover there is important evidence, of which Detienne seems unaware, to indicate that Adonis retained, in the very details of his mythical biography that Detienne finds most significant, the colouring and associations of the ancient Sumerian demigod.

Lettuces, strangely enough, are a case in point. Adonis's associations with aromatic plants are disappointingly restricted to his mother's name and transformation, and to the seductive role of unguents in the parallel tale of one Phaon of Lesbos, where we come closest (but not close enough) to finding the manifold variation that is an essential element of structuralist mythinterpretation. It is undeniably interesting that Phaon shares with Adonis the detail of attempting to hide among lettuce plants before his death, or having his corpse placed among them afterward. The relevance of this odd detail, according to Detienne, is that lettuce is a sign of sterility; not only was it one of the plants that grew and decayed so prematurely in the ritual "Gardens," it was also, as both comic and medical writers of the fourth century B.C. onward testify, a food that when taken in excess induces impotence. The association with lettuces of both Adonis and Phaon (who through the use of his magic unguent became irresistible to women), either at or just before death, emphasizes the impotence and infertility that result from a premature and excessive use of sexuality.

I admire the ingenuity of this suggestion and the care with which it is developed, but I question whether it is necessarily or even probably correct. There are two main difficulties, the first of them being that lettuce, although in excess it may have produced the soporific state to which Benjamin Bunny is an important witness (our French author cannot be blamed for being innocent of this), and even downright incapacity, remained a favorite food of the Greeks, as both Theophrastus and the culinary authority Athenaeus (to whom the comic testimonies are due) clearly imply. [. . .] The other difficulty is that the Near Eastern mythical tradition which Detienne so steadfastly ignores suggests a very different symbolic value for lettuces. According to Kramer they were a favorite plant among the Sumerians, and I have noticed that fragments of the lovesongs imagined as sung by Inanna to her young lover, none other than Dumuzi himself, demonstrate that they were also a favorite symbol, not of sterility and decay, but of sexual attractiveness and desirability!

[. . .] The Mesopotamian evidence suggests that any association between lettuces and Dumuzi's descendant Adonis may depend on the desirable and erotic connotations of the plant and not at all, as Detienne maintains, on connotations of infertility. There are other possibilities, too; the mention of myrrh is intriguing, and Adonis's attempts to hide among lettuce plants to escape the conventional wild boar that was attacking him may likewise depend, in some indirect way, on a detail of the tale of Dumuzi's death [. . .].

On the whole Detienne's interpretation of the myth and ritual of Adonis is neither proved nor probable. The demigod's Asiatic connections and background simply cannot be disregarded; indeed, they appear to motivate some of the most conspicuous, because least standard, details of the Greek accounts. That Tammuz and Dumuzi were among other things fertility figures is undeniable, and there is no good reason for seeing Adonis as implying a reversal, rather than a reflection of that role. Structuralist theory urges us to disregard historical influences and the more obvious kind of cross-cultural comparison in assessing an assumed pattern of synchronous interests and structures; but structuralist theory is probably too doctrinaire in this respect, or at least too abstract in its formulation to be practically useful.

Other foreign cults absorbed by the Greeks—of Cybele, Bendis or Isis— did not undergo drastic reversals of values or of the character of the deity in its broad lines. Why, in default of specific evidence to the contrary, should Adonis have been different? On the other hand, Frazer's picture of the disappearing fertility god is certainly too simple and too uncritical in glossing over some complicating details in the Greek versions.

Detienne is right to emphasize that, and to make the point that all these fertility rituals, the Thesmophoria included, had developed by the Classical period strong implications for social relationships which went beyond mere questions of fertility, whether vegetable, animal or human. His book, although it fails as a serious structuralist document, is suggestive enough in its way, and is a useful compendium of ancient information on aromatics and spices; not the least of its virtues is that it often displays an antiquarian charm and elegance that remind one of Norman Douglas or—dare one say it?—Frazer himself.

A Letter on Kirk's Review of *The Gardens of Adonis*

Kirk's review inspired this letter from a reader of The Times Literary Supplement, *published 15 September 1978 under the heading, "Lettuces."*

Sir,—I should like to support G. S. Kirk's excellent review of Marcel Detienne's Adonis (August 18) by pointing out that there was yet another ancient fertility god with aphrodisiac lettuces: the Egyptian Min, who was depicted standing ithyphallic among his lettuce leaves.

JACK LINDSAY

Castle Hedingham, Essex

A Reply to Kirk et al.

In The Times Literary Supplement *of 22 September 1978, the Cambridge anthropologist Edmund Leach replied to the preceding letter's evidence for Frazerian thinking in the purlieus of Essex, and also to Kirk.*

Sir,—Jack Lindsay, like G. S. Kirk, simply does not understand Detienne's argument. For contemporary social anthropologists the category "fertility god" is as empty of meaning as its coeval "totemism." That "Egyptian Min was depicted standing ithyphallic among his lettuce plantations" is no more a refutation of Detienne's association of lettuces with a wet and chilly antisexuality than is the fact that Śiva is frequently depicted in yogic meditation sitting ithyphallic among the snows of the Himalayas.

EDMUND LEACH

The provost's lodge, King's College, Cambridge

MARCEL DETIENNE

Afterword:
Revisiting the Gardens of Adonis

1994

*"More than ever," writes Detienne in this afterword to his original 1972
book on the gardens of Adonis, "comparative studies must be differential."
In other words, the process of comparing the institutions of different cultures should result in a clearer appreciation of each culture as an individual
system in its own right, not in blurred generalizations about supposedly
universal meanings. If the symbolism of lettuce means one thing in the
myths and rituals of ancient Greece, it does not follow that we should expect the same meaning in the analogous myths and rituals of, say, ancient
Egypt. If lettuce means one thing for the Egyptian god Min, it could still be
quite the opposite for Adonis. In Detienne's lively account, the Egyptian
lettuce was "flung" at him by a critic, whose attack was then answered by
none other than the noted Brtitish anthropologist Sir Edmund Leach; in
effect, Leach vindicated Detienne, "hurling" the lettuce back at the critic.
It seems doubtful that Leach's remark, printed here at p. 182, will be the
last word in the "lettuce war" that started with Kirk's review. After all, as
Detienne himself remarks in this overarching essay, "structuralist analysis is
a heuristic enterprise." Still, Detienne may have succeeded in putting an
end to the assumption that the symbolism of any given myth is universal.
"Like every interpretation," as Detienne notes, "the structuralist analysis of
myths entails constraints and imposes limits."*

I s there any news to report about the beautiful lover brutally separated from
Aphrodite by an enraged or jealous boar? What new information, reaching us from the East or elsewhere, have we learned about the young demigod, who dies amid the fruits of the earth before returning to life perhaps, or,

From *The Gardens of Adonis: Spices in Greek Mythology*, trans. Janet Lloyd (Atlantic
Highlands, NJ: Humanities Press, 1977), pp. 133–45 [afterword to the 2nd ed. (Princeton:
Princeton University Press, 1994)].

if not immediately, then the next year for sure? For lurking just behind the gardens, the women of Athens, the cries, the laments, there is the East, both the near and the far.

Etymology calls: Adonis-*Adon* means Lord just as Baal means Master. The Phoenicians are there, the Syro-Palestinian world too, and Canaanite traditions as well. Then there is Sumer, Dumuzi before Tammuz. The sleuths go back in time. The Phoenician fellow could have been sighted at Sumer well before berthing in Mediterranean ports—Byblos, the Piraeus, Alexandria. Yes, indeed, everything begins at Sumer, including the erotic values of "lettuce" (*hassu*, derived from Sumerian HI-IS), but the mists there are thick. Orientalists with trained eyes point to the Syro-Phoenician horizon where superhuman figures are celebrated in rituals with funerary connotations.[1] These critics check off for our benefit those forebears who somewhere between Ugarit and Tyre always achieved divine status. These are the god-kings of remote cities, kings who were dead[2] or slumbering before being roused in a ceremony we know nothing about, but is one plausible enough at any rate, given that Melqart, Master of Tyre, awakens at the behest of his official "resuscitator,"[3] and this time well attested, as our philologists say, nodding their heads sagely. Perhaps at Ugarit there is even a garden filled with royal ancestors in the king's palace,[4] but it seems so very far away from the little roof gardens, the festive ladders, and the daughters of Athens mourning for the lover of Aphrodite. Must we then listen to the wailings of the Moabites in an oracle issued by Isaiah that calls up the withering of plants, the land returning to desert, and the bloodied waters of Dimon?[5]

And what of the great cosmic myth, they ask me. What of the seasonal rhythms of the earth, vegetation alternating between exuberant life and terrifying death? Indeed, we know at least two different versions of this myth, barely separated by eighteen centuries. And so? One, the most complete, was written by Sir James Frazer in several hundred pages of *The Golden Bough*, while the second, consisting only of a few lines, is explicitly presented as a story told by a very local exegete at the end of the second century [CE.] This version is noted by Origen, the Christian philosopher of Alexandria, in connection with the text of Ezekiel.[6] "The god whom the Greeks call Adonis is called Tammuz, as they say, among the Jews and among the Syrians. . . . It seems that certain sacred ceremonies take place each year. First he is bewailed as though he had ceased to live, and secondly there is rejoicing on his behalf as if he were resurrected from the dead. Those who pride themselves on interpreting the myths of the Greeks and what is called *mythic theology* say that Adonis is the symbol of the fruits of the earth that are mourned when they are sown but whose growth is a cause of joy for those who cultivate them."[7]

Kinship with Tammuz, resurrection from among the dead, seasonal rhythms regulating the cycle of cultivated plants: the exegeses of some "theologians of myth" attach to Adonis those principal features that were to make such a strong impression on Frazer the mythologist. And others (such as the Abbé Loisy), drawn in turn to interpretation under the influence of Frazerian tales that were put into circulation in the modernist period, discover there the model of Christ resurrected in the lover of Aphrodite-Astarte. This is a reading that Father K. Prümm violently refutes in a *Supplement* to the *Dictionnaire de la Bible*.[8] Although by the 1960s the quarrel between pagan mysteries and Christian mystery already seemed anachronistic, the spokesman of Christian orthodoxy speaks ironically of the pitiful "triumph of death" granted to a little hero of vegetation, who cannot, however, be wrested away from the cyclical course of nature.

One day perhaps we will know more about Tammuz, Dumuzi, and the Semitic variants of a mythology that associates sexual activity with agricultural practice. We already have at our disposal a sufficient number of versions to glimpse the transformations of a young lord into the position of a mediator between two worlds, or two mistresses, or between poles otherwise specified.[9] But it happens that all these variants are written in Greek and told by Greeks, even in the area of Byblos, homeland of the Phoenician hero. And if structural analysis has value in a domain that is truly its own, it is to put the emphasis on an inventory of differences between the Adonia of Byblos, Alexandria, and Athens. Not to postulate, as some Orientalist readers have done on their own,[10] that there is some essential core to the figure of Adonis, embedded in his first epiphany at Sumer, even if we do not find it preserved in the pure form of a ritual,[11] one that over the expanse of millennia could reveal the truth about the nature of a god or a demigod.

Return then to the Adonia, but this time the Adonia of other cities, which our initial study, published in 1972, had omitted, so as to respect in the first instance the constraints imposed by the single ethnographic context of an Athens that included both the roof gardens of this festival and the Thesmophoria of Demeter. Return at the same time to the tales of both Alexandria and Byblos, and to the often explicit body of myths that tell us about certain features and patterns of the festival, but that do not imply at every moment the evocation of such rhetorical figures as the "god of renewal," "vegetation spirit," or "eternal return."

Of the three principal versions of the festival of the Adonia—Athenian, Alexandrian, and the one from Byblos—the first,[12] which is also the most ancient, places the Phoenician hero, it is true, in a context of the agrarian type, whose ritual emblem is spelled out in the ceremonial of the little gardens. Yet everything indicates that the Adonis of the Athenians cannot be a god of vegetation, but is even the exact opposite. The little gardens entrusted to fragile pots of clay or transferred into modest baskets grow in eight days under the heat of the summer sun. The Adonia are celebrated in the days of the Dog Star, the full noontime of the solar year. No sooner do the young shoots turn green than they quickly wither, desiccated by the burning rays of the sun. In fact, these hasty plantings are, as it were, brought close to the sun: borne by women who carry them up on ladders,[13] they are placed on the roofs, midway between earth and heaven. As imitations of cultivation, the gardens of Adonis are at the other extreme from the cultures of Demeter, of worked land, of fields in which fruit-bearing seeds slowly ripen in the rhythm of the seasons, where men raise and harvest cereal foods—wheat and barley—that are made into bread for mortals and are the staff of life for the living.

The horticulture of Adonis, where the verdant borders on the withered, is entirely envisaged by the Greeks as the negation of cereal culture and the order of Demeter. From Plato to Simplicius an entire tradition condemns the Adonian gardens for being cultures without crops and essentially sterile. They are images of everything that is delicate, superficial, lacking maturity, and without roots: gardens of stone, cold, impenetrable like the mask of death. Is this view just the deviant reading of some "puritan and misogynist" philosophers[14] who understood nothing about the stories of a Phoenician young man surrounded by women?

This negation in the Athenian Adonia of a true cultivation of plants is supported all the more by the fact that the Greek mythological tradition insists on the seductive aspect of Adonis together with his relation to spices and perfumes. Born of Myrrha, who was transformed into myrrh following incest with her father, the child Adonis, invested with an irresistible seductiveness, arouses the desire of both Persephone and Aphrodite. Seducer of divinities from opposing realms, Adonis, as far as the Greeks are concerned, is neither a husband nor even a virile being. Heracles is of the same opinion. Adonis is nothing but a lover and an effeminate, whose worshippers, adds Plutarch, are recruited among women or among androgynes. The young boy with the abundant seed, precocious lover of beautiful mistresses, signifies an inverted figure of marriage and of fertile sexual union. His surplus sexual power is only the reverse side pointing to a lack of maturity, associating premature sexual union with fruitless seeding. Destined to fall into a garden of stone, the seed of Adonis can never take root as in the case of good and legitimate seed. The seducer's itinerary follows the trajectory of his gardens: deprived of progeny, condemned to perish in the flower of his age, Adonis passes suddenly from spices to lettuce—from the myrrh tree that confers on him the power of seduction to the vegetal plant of a cold and damp nature that receives him as he lies dying after his failure in the hunt, and thus fixes him in the site of impotence, for which lettuce is a well-known emblem in one sector of Greek tradition.

Seduction is indeed the theme around which the festival of the Athenian Adonia is played in its two phases. The first seems to speak of the sterility of seeds cast finally into spring waters or the sea, while the other, with its "gathering of aromatics," seems to hail the pleasure of perfumes and the promises of seduction. The two phases, so discretely inscribed in the constraining time of a ritual, appear, so to speak, like two concurrent ways of defining Adonis: from the city's point of view, by the failure and inversion of the serious and solemn order of Demeter; and from within, for the worshippers and their lovers celebrating the virtues of extramarital pleasure although still in the intimacy of private dwellings, separated from the invasive regimentation of the politico-religious world. This is perhaps why those who write the history of Athens recall the women's pseudo-funerary laments around figurines and little gardens only in the context of the departure of the Sicilian expedition, that military adventure that was to result in a tragic end for the Athenian city.[15] In the Adonia of Athens, nothing indicates any return invitation. No whiff of an allusion to an Adonis coming back to life, or even, more discreetly, as still alive. Matters are not the same at Byblos.

Byblos is the homeland of the Phoenician figure masked under its Hellenized name.[16] But the oldest representation we know doubly disguises this fact through a tale that comes from Cyprus but is told by Greeks. The Cypriot Adonis is called Gauas,[17] and the Muses plot his ruin. The boar kills him, Aphrodite weeps. Here Adonis' story concerns the misfortunes of a hunter, treated as an antihero, but whose place in the ritual or festivals seems eclipsed almost entirely by the Lady of Byblos, a grand bisexual Aphrodite, with her numerous sanctuaries and her mysteries in which the initiates receive a phallus and bit of salt, symbols of the birth of a goddess come from the sea and the foam. And before the Hellenistic period? Absent from the royal inscriptions of Byblos between 1000 and 800 [BCE], Adonis of Gibla only emerges from the shadows with Lucian's ethnographic inquiry into the Syrian goddess, in the second century CE. Here, unlike other cultic places, it is the territory of Byblos in its entirety that is inhabited by Adonis and by the festival in his honor. Two sanctuaries of Aphrodite demarcate the kingdom of Byblos: one on the Acropolis, the other in the mountains, in Aphaca, where the river Adonis arises, the Nahr Ibrahim, whose waters are dyed with blood each year in commemoration of the mortal wound inflicted on Adonis by the boar in that very same country.[18] The ceremony mobilizes the entire land, men and women alike. A public, one might even say national, festival punctuated by two arresting moments: a great mourning with lamentations and a sacrifice of a funerary type, "as befits a corpse"; then, a procession to escort a living Adonis "into the open air."[19] The distinctively Phoenician features are all the more difficult to detect since the exegetes of Byblos in Lucian's time tended to give greater importance to the Egyptian Osiris, regarding their own Adonis as merely the other's local supernumerary.[20] True, Egypt's presence is found in Byblos from the third millennium on, but this time the relation is of an exegetical type that Plutarch, the author of the *Treatise on Isis and Osiris*, does not anywhere mention, while in the "Alexandrian" version Isis's quest takes an otherwise uncharted detour by Byblos.[21] Turned into Osiris, Adonis gets lost again right in the heart of his own home ground. He disappears, swallowed up by another power, who annexes him all the more securely, since although Osiris has the rank of a cosmic god, this same divinity also rules over the dead and over life in the other world.[22]

In the festival at Byblos, there is not a word about gardens or other agrarian practices. On the contrary, Lucian notes an unusual form of sexual behavior. During the period of lamentation, the women, who refuse to let their hair be shorn, must prostitute themselves for an entire day, but only with strangers, and donate what they are paid for this transaction to the sanctuary of Aphrodite. Forcible prostitution that punishes a crime and penalizes the guilty parties.[23] A funereal prostitution that seems at the opposite pole of the erotic exchanges found in the Adonia at Athens. The traditions of Cyprus insist on maintaining this distance in relating how the daughters of Kinyras, king of Paphos and father of Adonis, were condemned to prostitute themselves with strangers before being sent into exile or transformed into rough stone by the decree of Aphrodite, whose power they had denied.[24] Here again, prostitution is a punishment that, in its extreme form, seems to lead to a metamorphosis into stone.[25]

It is from the metropolis of the Ptolemies that Byblos in the second century CE gets the starting signal for the Adonia. Sometimes it is the portent of a "head" of papyrus brought by sea to the port or Byblos. Lucian confirms having seen it during his stay there. Sometimes it is a letter written by the women of Alexandria for the benefit of their sisters of Byblos: a message placed in a sealed jar and thrown into the sea to announce that Adonis has been found.[26] And each year, in the same period, the devotees of Aphrodite cease their lamentations when they learn that their mistress is no longer separated from her Adonis. Is the very ancient Byblos an offshoot of the young Alexandria where the festival of Adonis begins in joy and pleasure?

In the Alexandria of the Ptolemies, the Adonia take the form of a spectacle: a representation, with a chorus and actors.[27] When Aphrodite weeps for the death of Adonis, the chorus groans and laments; when she ascends from the underworld and says she has found the one she was seeking, all rejoice with her and begin to dance. A spectacle conducted in sanctuaries.[28] According to Cyril of Alexandria, but in the fifth century [CE], the representation ends in the happiness of a reunion. According to the narrative of Theocritus in the third century [BCE], however, the festival-spectacle held in the palace of the queen Arsinoe, wife of Ptolemy Philadelphus, begins with songs that relate the union of the two lovers seated under a bower of dill and before whom are deposited the fruits that the trees bear, delicate gardens in silver baskets, golden alabasters filled with Syrian perfume, and finally, all sorts of cakes in the form of creatures that fly or walk.[29] But the ceremony's second phase, which begins the next day, opens with a funereal procession: the women as a group transport the figurine of Adonis outside the city, where the waves foam on the shore. Hair dishevelled and throats bared, they strike up a lugubrious song. It is a procession that reverses the *pompē* at Byblos when the living Adonis is taken out in the open air. But Theocritus' poem ends with the mention of the demigod Adonis, the only one among the heroes of ancient Greece (Agamemnon, Hector, the Pelopids, the Pelasgians, and Lapiths) who alternates between upper and lower worlds.[30] "Next year," it is said at Alexandria, but only while the statuette of Adonis is being cast into the sea together perhaps with the little gardens and the fruits.

At an interval of several centuries (almost eight) in the same Alexandria, the double erotic life of Adonis could be acted in either the joyful or funereal mode. In this little theatrical ritual with its alternation of mourning and gladness of rejoicings and lamentations, the women, as at Athens, occupy a premier role, but in a city more vast, more open, and radically cosmopolitan, where neither seduction nor horticulture seems to have the same meaning. The gardens placed in the midst of fruits and cakes have become the emblem of lovers fulfilled, and the same reclining Adonis can just as well be a guest at a banquet of pleasure as a recumbent figure presented for lamentation.

Lacking all reference to Adonis or to a far-off Tammuz, the hasty little gardens are available for many scenarios: possible "experimenting" with the harvests of the year, as some Egyptians did in the tenth century [CE], according to Birouni;[31] offerings on the tomb of Christ in the course of Holy Week in northern Greece today; or in modern, if not Brahmanic, India, the "offering of shoots" (pots of seedlings left to sprout in darkness), which can take place in domestic rites as in temple festivals, symbolizing in the sacrificial domain the destroyed world of the victim Goddess or the seed of a new day of the world under the sign of the fertile Goddess.

More than ever, comparative study must be differential: the goddess of Hinduism, Earth, kingdom, queen and wife of the sacrificer-king cannot be the equivalent of either the son of Myrrha on Athenian roofs or the consort of the Lady of Byblos in a Phoenician country. With such changing patterns, multiple historico-ethnographical contexts, and strata of meanings that are rich in different ways, structuralist analysis cannot be reductive, and nonvariant elements are not some hasty and premature generalizations. For example, the Hopi Indians practice an agrarian rite, called Powamu, that is designed to promote the germination and growth of food plants. Claude Lévi-Strauss insisted not long ago on its similarities to the gardens of Adonis: the same "forced growth, out of season, gardens in miniature placed in pots."[32] But this resemblance gives us the right to draw up a closely matched list of oppositions between the two artificial plantings: the season (February instead of July); the place (subterranean sanctuaries instead of roofs of houses); heat (hothouse fires in midwinter instead of the fires of Sirius); and so on. This series of oppositions still awaits being put to the test, of both ethnographical context and mythic patterns displayed by the Hopi Indians or other Indian mythologies called to mind by such unusual practices.

If the analysis is combinational, it is not necessarily interminable. Like every interpretation, the structuralist analysis of myths entails constraints and imposes limits. True, instead of collecting worldwide the largest number of miniature gardens, it chooses to privilege abstract schemas, with the help of which it undertakes to reconstruct an organized semantic field and to articulate the elements that form part of the same pattern. Structuralist analysis is a heuristic enterprise: lettuce associated with the death of Adonis points toward the story of Phaon hidden by Aphrodite in a lettuce patch, or again toward a solitary Hera, dreaming of giving birth alone and adroitly munching on a juicy heart of lettuce before giving birth to Youth, Flower of the pubis, Hēbē.[33] In the Adonis pattern, according to native exegetes, lettuce is explicitly myrrh in reverse. On the other hand, in Hera's entourage a seminal lettuce makes an appearance outside a garden. It is a kind of plant, whose nature suggests we make an inventory of the various humors to define the relations between lactation, menstruation, production of seed, the body (feminine and masculine), and the mechanics of vital fluids. Only then should we introduce lettuce from Sumer (of the third millennium) and from Babylon situated somewhere between a nipple (masculine, close to Marduk) and a head of hair (of the wife, subject of a love song).[34] Or, in the absence of any certain relation with Tammuz or his lookalike, should we just put all this on hold? If the second solution seems the best one, it is not always obvious to these critics.

Let us take the hunter Adonis confronted with the destiny of Atalanta, the huntress transformed into a wild beast through hatred as much of marriage as of Aphrodite. This Adonis undergoes a metamorphosis into a flower, recorded in Book 10 of Ovid's collection of myths.[35] The blood of Adonis gives birth to the anemone: a flower defined in the Ovidian tale by a series of traits, some of which are explicit, fully spelled out, while others are implicit but to different degrees. For the explicit side, the anemone gets three points: (1) it has the same color as the blood from which it springs; (2) it resembles the color of the pomegranate that conceals its seeds under a supple skin; (3) it is poorly fixed; too light, it falls, detached, ineffectual; it cannot be enjoyed for long; it is ephemeral. If I interpret these features by putting them back into the system of oppositions I earlier reconstructed in this volume, I could say, in the first instance, that they all emphasize the negative aspect of Adonis' metamorphosis. The anemone is red like the flower of the pomegranate, but the similarity is only expressed to indicate an absence in the blood-flower of any promise of fruits. There is a lack, a deprivation of the fecundity concealed beneath the skin of the fruit of the pomegranate, which we know was offered to the new bride on her wedding day. The anemone of Adonis is situated at the opposite pole from the one of ripe fruits: without roots, it is fragile, a breeze wafts it away. It confirms the proverbial sterility of the "gardens of stone" that are the outcome of the Adonia.

In addition to these clear facts that frame this explanation, there is the implicit fact of the pattern "anemone," that is, a symbolic value among those shared traditions in Greece about plants and botanical species: the anemone is a flower without an odor, more precisely, a rose without a scent. Why mention this characteristic "without an odor"? I am afraid we must. In fact, in Ovid's tale, when Aphrodite brings about the metamorphosis of her beloved, she does so in open and even aggressive competition with the transformation of Mintha into perfumed mint. Aphrodite intends to pull off the same feat that Persephone also accomplished. The implicit feature "without odor" is therefore invoked by a detail of Ovid's version, a detail that would remain unexplained and seem merely gratuitous if we were not informed about the equivalence between the anemone and the scentless rose, and therefore about the ultimate state of Adonis, doomed to a scentless destiny.

The lack of perfume confirms and repeats the failure of a seducer who, in Ovid's own version, was born from the myrrh tree into which the figure of his mother, Myrrha, had vanished. And Aphrodite's lover, having become an anemone, comes to occupy the least-favored place on the scale of lovers turned into plants: the tree of incense for Leucothoe, the perfumed herb for Mintha, and for Adonis, the flower that is only a scentless rose.

Without feeling compelled to endorse the principle of an interpretation of this kind, one can still acknowledge the not inconsiderable advantage of enriching rather than impoverishing myths, provided, however, that the inquiry is not falsified by any a priori scheme. In the sequence just used as an example, the appearance of the anemone at the end of an unfortunate hunt comes to reinforce and redouble in the botanical code the itinerary that leads from myrrh to lettuce. Let us add that even in the mythic tradition there is a version, adopted by the Alexandrian poet Nicander, that combines lettuce and anemone in the same order: one serves as a ludicrous refuge from the violence of the boar, while the other is born from the mortal wound of its victim.

At this point, the analysis could come to a stop, the interpretation could consider itself satisfied and could keep quiet from now on, unless perhaps to savor the pleasure of finally having come home, by returning to the version from which it first started out. The intrusion of the implicit aspects of the myth could go no further than this and could leave the field open to the analysis of forms, semiotic practices, and everything that concerns the ways in which the story is told. But would we not then be abandoning mythology at the expense of a myth that is arbitrarily separated from the whole to which it belongs? Let us take up again the symbolic pattern of the anemone in Greek culture. In the shared knowledge, where popular hearsay merges into encyclopedic erudition, doctors and botanists recall that among the plant's virtues is the fact that it encourages the production of milk and favors the flow of the menses. The anemone's role in menstruation and lactation would then shift the flower born from the blood of Adonis in the direction of feminine fertility and would, as a result, have to connect it to the world of Demeter—that is, to a power with which until now Adonis would seem to have nothing but essentially negative relations. True, Ovid's version denies any value of fecundity and fertility to the anemone of Adonis, but that very denial does not fold the version of the myth back upon itself. Rather it stimulates us to use it, combine it with other myths, even those that show up in the simple evocation of the dual value of the anemone. It is easy, in fact, to show that in botanical lore menstruation and lactation are directly affected by a series of plants such as the *agnus castus* ("chaste tree"), lettuce, and mint, along with the anemone, and that a pattern takes shape through the relations among these four vegetal species. These relations operate in stories about the figure of Hera when she engenders her daughter Youth (Hēbē) from a lettuce she consumed, creating a pattern grafted onto a split between two planes: the first pertaining to the fertility of the feminine body, pointing toward the production of legitimate children, and the second, directed toward amorous pleasure, ratified by one and/or the other sex.

The details of the demonstration matter little. The question is only of ascertaining whether the critic, who takes mythology as an object of knowledge, is not constrained by that very fact to appeal to the greatest amount of implicit information. The inquiry would be interminable; no doubt, if at the outset we did not restrict the field of investigation to the contours of a society—that is, if we did not decide to keep at the start to only those traditions, beliefs, stories, and symbolism that Greek culture as a whole put into play.[36] But this in its totality. Crossing through texts, leaping over chronologies, pushing aside the gatekeepers of History (although it may mean sneaking back through the window here or there), the analyst of myths must recover those networks of relations, sets of patterns, and kinds of knowledge shared by proverbs, table manners, travel stories, botanical descriptions, medical discourses, and treatises on animals in the form of bestiaries. For its subject—mythology—is not so much the body of stories captured by writing from the fifth century [BCE] on—this "library" with a knowledge about myths—as it is the mythology-frame,[37] the system of thought that includes the whole set of the basic tales of Greek society, the symbolic horizon on which myths and their alternate versions are transformed into one another and thereby attain a kind of autonomy. At least this is how it appears to the analyst's eye.

A mythology then as a system of symbolic representations that would always exceed the narrative genre of a mythic story. A mythology to be constructed by interpretation, through relations of transformation of myths or groups of myths among themselves, but always by mobilizing the beliefs, values, forms of knowledge, and the common sense of symbols in which the myth(s) lie hidden in gestures, ceremonies, and rituals, small or great. And perhaps the analysis, getting back to work once again, will be able to identify certain structures that are bearers of cultural memory. For instance, in the Greek case, botanical and zoological taxonomies with an animal and vegetal symbolism that crosses through the entire span of a culture's life from one end to the other, and, by the strength of its patterns, that clusters around a few recurrent animals or certain dominant plants, seems to organize at a deep level the production and transformation of mythic discourse.

TRANSLATED BY FROMA ZEITLIN

NOTES

[1] Above all, the works of {Ribichini 1979, 1981a, 1981b}.

[2] Perfumed or interred in myrrh instead of the honey of Spartans: {Grottanelli 1984}.

[3] Bonnet 1988 (especially 174–79). For the "Awakening": Bonnet 1988, 33–40.

[4] Bonnet 1988, 420–25.

[5] Bonnet 1987. Also in the book of Isaiah, {Delcor 1978}. Critique in {Ribichini 1981a, 94–98}.

[6] *Selecta in Ezech.*, VIII, 12 in *Patrologie grecque*, 13, c. 798–800 Migne.

[7] Plutarch's warning is aimed at similar "theologians of myth": *De Iside* 65, 377B: "the numerous as well as tiresome people, whether they be such as to take pleasure in associating theological problems with the seasonal changes in the surrounding atmosphere, or with the growth of the crops and seedtimes and ploughing; and also those who say that Osiris is being buried at the time when the grain is sown and covered in the earth and that he comes to life and reappears when plants begin to sprout" (trans. F. C. Babbitt).

[8] "Mystères" in the *Dictionnaire de la Bible*, Suppl. vi, 1960, c. 115–19. In 1943 the same scholar had strongly upheld the monotheism of the Greeks, those pure Aryans. This is the notion that A. J. Festugière had immediately repudiated in *Revue des études grecques* 57 (1944): 252–56, criticizing Father Prümm.

[9] On models of the mediator: Lévi-Strauss 1979, 175.

[10] Recently, for example, Soyez 1977, 90 (concerning 73–74) or {Soyez 1978, 1192}.

[11] This is the contention of the unitary reading proposed by Will 1975.

[12] By chance, of course. We must summarize the specific features to facilitate the process of differential comparison.

[13] Again on the subject of the ladders: a relief from the Agora: C. M. Edwards, "Aphrodite on a Ladder," *Hesperia* 53 (1984): 59ff.; a vase from Altamurra associating a scene of the Adonia (a ladder, a woman holding the little "gardens") and an Aphrodite on a goat, thus the Epitragia. . . . Cf. the connection between music and climbing, Soyez 1984.

[14] Will 1975, 94.

[15] Cf. Plutarch *Nicias* 13.10–11; *Alcibiades* 18.5. The Adonia in high summer: J. Servais, "La date des Adonies d'Athènes et l'expédition de Sicile," in *Adonis*, ed. Ribichini (Rome, 1984), pp. 89–93.

[16] A convenient discussion in Sznycer 1981.

[17] Lycophron *Alexandra* 828–33, and *Scholia to Lycophron* 831, ed. Scheer, 265.25–26, etc. Cf. Soyez 1977.

[18] Soyez 1978. Indirect relation with the Dog Star. [. . .]

[19] {Roux 1967.}

[20] Lucian *De dea Syria* 7.

[21] *De Iside* 15.357a.

[22] Plutarch the mythologist is right. We must not confuse everything. And ever since Gardiner's observations in 1915 concerning Frazer's Osiris, the Egyptologists have demon-

strated the complexity of Osiris, his story and his festivals. Cf. E. Chassinat, *Le Mystère d'Osiris au mois de Khoïak 1–11* (Cairo, 1966–68).

23 Before and after Eusebius, this issue has always been of considerable interest for the Christian family. Facts in W. Kornfeld, *s.v.* "Prostitution sacrée," *Dictionnaire de la Bible, Supplément*, fasc. 47, 1972, c. 1356–74; Y. Hattar, *La triade d'Héliopolis-Baalbeck: Son Culte, sa diffusion à travers les textes littéraires, les documents iconographiques et épigraphiques*, vol. 2 (Leiden, 1977), pp. 425–62.

24 Ps.-Apollodorus *Bibliotheca* 3.14.3; Ovid *Metamorphoses* 10.220.42. Group of myths analyzed by J. Rudhardt, "Quelques notes sur les cultes chypriotes: En Particulier sur celui d'Aphrodite," in *Chypre des origines au Moyen Age* (Geneva), pp. 109–54.

25 Lucian *De dea Syria* 7.

26 Cyril of Alexandria *Commentaires à Isaïe*, II.3 in *Patrologie grecque* 70, c.441 Migne.

27 Cf. A. S. F. Gow, "The Adoniazousai of Theocritus," *Journal of Hellenic Studies* 58 (1938): 180–204.

28 Cyril of Alexandria, ibid.

29 Theocritus 15.111–18.

30 Theocritus 15.136–44.

31 Indications of the same type in Paladius, in the *Geoponica*, and taken very seriously by Baudy 1986, who gives an economico-religious reading of the gardens, which he pursues down to the very last details of interpretation.

32 Lévi-Strauss 1972, 100.

33 Detienne 1989, 31.

34 I follow closely the information given me in June 1975 by J. Bottéro, who substantially qualifies Kramer's interpretations used by G. S. Kirk (1978). True, there is also a seminal lettuce in Egypt between Horus and Seth, to say nothing of the erection of the god Min after swallowing a *lactuca sativa*. A question, certainly, to be pursued for Egyptian myths. This is the lettuce flung at my head by J. Lindsay to trip me up (*Times Literary Supplement*, 15 Sept. 1978, 1026), but it was immediately hurled back with vigor at its author by E. Leach (*Times Literary Supplement*, 22 Sept. 1978) [both in this volume at pp. 176–82].

35 A specific analysis with appropriate references pertaining to its use in Detienne 1980, 114–17; 128–31.

36 Jacob 1987.

37 Detienne 1989, 185–86.

PAUL VEYNE

Social Diversity of Beliefs and Mental Balkanization

1983

Paul Veyne's Did the Greeks Believe in their Myths? *deliberately challenges the assumptions underlying much historiographic and anthropological perspective on ancient Greece. The generalization of the title is strategic, designed not only to provoke and unsettle but also to encourage a contemporary analogy (more readily, perhaps, than* Did the Tlingit—*or* Aymara, *or* Mixtecs—Believe in their Myths?*); and indeed, the volume claims that both credulous and critical attitudes existed, not only in different classes within a society but within individual writers, depending on the goals of their thought at a particular moment, and verges on the relativism of Bacon's jesting Pilate. As the chapter below demonstrates, however, Veyne is prepared to detail the rationalizations employed to assert or reject the authority of sources, to stipulate the category of heroes (rather than gods) as a skeptic's "litmus test," and to explore the political conditions favoring the "capacity to simultaneously believe in incompatible truths" that he dubs "the Balkanization of the symbolic field."*

T he Greeks distinguished between two domains: gods and heroes. For they did not understand myth or the mythmaking function in a general way but evaluated myths according to content. Criticism of the heroic generations consisted in transforming heroes into simple men and giving them a past that matched that of what were called the human generations, that is, history since the Trojan War. The first step of this criticism was to remove the visible intervention of the gods from history. Not that the very existence of these gods was doubted in the least. But in our day the gods most often remain invisible to men. This was already the case even before the Trojan

From *Did the Greeks Believe in their Myths?*, trans. Paula Wissing (Chicago and London: University of Chicago Press, 1988), pp. 41–52 ["Diversité sociale et balkanisation des cerveaux," in *Les Grecs ont-ils cru à leurs mythes?: Essai sur l'imagination constituante* (Paris: Editions du Seuil, 1983), pp. 52–69].

War, and the whole of the Homeric supernatural is nothing but invention and credulity. Criticism of religious beliefs indeed existed, but it was very different. Some thinkers purely and simply denied either the existence of a particular god or, perhaps, the existence of any of the gods in which the people believed. On the other hand, the immense majority of philosophers, as well as educated people, did not so much criticize the gods as seek an idea worthy of divine majesty. Religious criticism consisted in saving the idea of the gods by purifying it of all superstition, and the criticism of heroic myths saved the heroes by making them as probable and lifelike as simple men.

The two critical attitudes operated independently, and the most pious minds would have been the first to remove from the so-called heroic epoch the childish interventions, miracles, and battles of the gods that Homer presents in the *Iliad*. No one thought of stamping out Infamy[1] and transforming the criticism of heroes into a war machine or guerilla attack of allusions against religion. This is the paradox: there were people who did not believe in the existence of the gods, but never did anyone doubt the existence of the heroes. And with reason: the heroes were only men, to whom credulity had lent supernatural traits, and how could anyone doubt that human beings now exist and have always existed? Not everyone, on the other hand, was disposed to believe in the reality of the gods, for no one could see them with his own eyes. As a result, during the period that we are going to study, which extends for almost a millennium, from the fifth century [BCE] to the fourth century [CE], absolutely no one, Christians included, ever expressed the slightest doubt concerning the historicity of Aeneas, Romulus, Theseus, Heracles, Achilles, or even Dionysus; rather, everyone assumed this historicity. Later on we will shed some light on the presuppositions governing this long-standing belief. First we will describe which Greeks believed in what throughout these nine centuries.

A mass of folkloric superstitions, which sometimes also were found in what was already called mythology, existed among the populace. Among the educated classes this mythology found entire acceptance, as much as it did in Pindar's day; the general public believed in the reality of Centaurs and accepted the legend of Heracles or Dionysus with an uncritical spirit. [. . .] Lastly, the learned formulated historical criticism of the myths with the success with which we are already familiar. The sociologically odd result is this: the ingenuousness of the people and the criticism of the learned did not go to war for the triumph of Reason, nor was the former culturally devalued. It followed that each individual, if he belonged to the ranks of the learned, internalized something of a peaceful coexistence in the field of relations of symbolic force, which resulted in half-beliefs, hesitations, and contradictions, on the one hand, and, on the other, the possibility of juggling different levels of meaning. It was from the latter, in particular, that an "ideological"—or, rather, rhetorical—use of mythology emerged.

[. . .]

It cannot be doubted that the Greeks believed in their mythology for as long as their nurses or mothers told them such tales. [. . .]

But which myths did nurses tell children? They certainly spoke to them of the gods, for piety and superstition required it. They frightened them with bogeymen and Lamias; they told them sentimental stories about Ariadne or Psyche for their own amusement, and they wept. But did they teach the children the great mythic cycles: those of Thebes, Oedipus, the Argonauts? Did not the little boy, and the little girl as well,[2] have to wait until they were under the grammarian's authority to learn the great legends?

[. . .]

The people had their legends, in which certain myths were mentioned. There were also heroes, such as Heracles, whose name and nature—if not the details of his adventures—everyone knew. Other purely classical legends were known through songs. In any case, oral literature and iconography made the existence and fictional modality of a mythological world familiar to all, even if not all the details were familiar. Only those who had attended school knew the fine points. But, in a slightly different way, has this not always been the case? Do we really believe that classical Athens was a great civic collectivity where all minds acted in concert, where the theater ratified the union among hearts, and where the average citizen could pass any test about Jocasta or the return of the Heraclidae?

The essence of a myth is not that everyone knows it but that it is supposed to be known and is worthy of being known by all. Furthermore, it was not generally known. A revealing phrase occurs in the *Poetics* (9.8).[3] One is not obliged, says Aristotle, to restrict oneself to hallowed myths if one writes tragedy: "It would be absurd, in fact, to do so, as even the known stories are known to only a few, though they are a delight nonetheless to all." In a general way the Athenian public were aware of the existence of the mythical world in which tragedies took place, but they did not know the details of the stories. Nor did they need to know the fine points of the Oedipus legend in order to follow *Antigone* or *The Phoenician Women*. The tragic poet took care to reveal everything to his audience, just as if he had invented his plot. But the poet did not place himself above his public, since myth was not supposed to be known. He did not know any more about it than they did. He was not writing learned literature.

All of this changes in the Hellenistic period. Literature is intended to be learned. Not that this is the first time that literature has been reserved for an elite (Pindar or Aeschylus were not exactly popular writers), but it demands a cultural effort from its audience that excludes the amateurs. Myths then give way to what we still call mythology, which will survive until the eighteenth century. The people continued to have their tales and superstitions, but mythology, now a matter for the learned, moved beyond their reach. It took on the prestige of the elite knowledge that marks its possessor as belonging to a certain class.[4]

During the Hellenistic period, when literature became a specific activity that authors and readers cultivated for its own sake, mythology became a discipline that soon would be studied in school. This does not mean that mythology dies—quite the contrary, in fact. It remains one of the great elements of culture and never ceases to be a stumbling block for the literate. Callimachus gathered rare variants of the great legends and local myths, not out of frivolity (nothing is less frivolous than Alexandrianism), but patriotic piety. It has even been supposed that he and his disciples traveled the Greek world with the deliberate intention of collecting such legends. Four centuries later, Pausanias traveled throughout Greece and combed the libraries with the same passion. Once it had become a matter for books, mythology would continue to grow, but what was published was garbed in the taste of the day. [. . .] Myth is put into manuals, thereby undergoing a codification that will simplify it and cast the great cycles as official versions and strand the variants in oblivion. [. . .] The serious side of the matter still remained: What was one to think of this mass of tales? Here there are two schools, which we wrongly conflate in the too-modern term the "rational treatment of myth." On the one hand were the believers, such as Diodorus, but also Euhemerus; on the other were the learned.

Indeed, there existed a believing but educated public that demanded a new type of supernatural, which must no longer be situated, beyond matters of truth and falsehood, in an ageless past. It was to be "scientific" or, rather, historical. For it was no longer possible to believe in the supernatural in the old way. The reason for this shift is not, I believe, to be found in the Sophistic *Aufklärung* but in the success of the historical genre. To be accepted, myth must henceforth pass for history, and this mystification then takes on the deceptive appearance of a rationalization. This transmutation produces the falsely contradictory aspect of Timaeus, one of the great purveyors of the genre. He wrote a history "full of dreams, prodigies, incredible tales, and, to put it shortly, craven superstition and womanish love of the marvellous."[5] The same Timaeus gives myths a rational interpretation.

Many historians, writes Diodorus, have "avoided as a difficulty the history of fabulous times" (1.3). He is intent on filling this gap himself. [. . .] No great importance was accorded the myths found in the works of the historians, even if they did not admit to writing myths; for, as Strabo says, we know that they had no other intent than to entertain and astonish by means of an invented supernatural (Strabo 1.2.35). However, the marvelous of the Hellenistic period has a rational cast, so that the moderns are mistakenly tempted to see in it a battle for truth and enlightenment.

In fact, there were readers for whom the need for truth obtained and others for whom it was not a factor. A passage from Diodorus acquaints us with the case. It is difficult, says this historian, to narrate the history of mythical time, if only because of the imprecision of the chronology. Such inexactness makes it impossible for many readers to take mythical history seriously (Diodorus 4.1.1).

Furthermore, the events of this distant time are too far away and too unlikely to be readily believed (Diodorus 4.8). What can be done? The exploits of Heracles are as glorious as they are superhuman. [. . .] These readers who apply the false principle of current things to Heracles are also mistaken in wanting things to happen on the stage as they do in real life. And this is to show a lack of respect for the heroes:

> When the histories of myths are concerned, a man should by no means scrutinize the truth with so sharp an eye. In the theaters, for instance, though we are persuaded there have existed no Centaurs who are composed of two different kinds of bodies nor any Geryones with three bodies, yet we look with favor upon such products of the myths as these, and by our applause we enhance the honor of the god. And strange it would be indeed that Heracles, while yet among mortal men, should by his own labors have brought under cultivation the inhabited world, and that human beings should nevertheless forget the benefactions which he rendered them generally and slander the commendation he receives for the noblest deeds.

The test is revealing in its adroit ingenuousness. We can sense here the uneasy coexistence of two programs of truth, one of which is critical, the other respectful. [. . .] Diodorus, who plays to his audience, here becomes a one-man band. He manages to see things with the eyes of those in one camp, to give right-thinking people the impression that he reconciles the critics' viewpoints for them, and, finally, to place himself on the side of the orthodox. He seems to show bad faith because he expresses the respectful belief of the first in the critical language of the second. This at least proves that the believers were always numerous. In their modernized versions, Heracles and Bacchus were no longer divine figures but gods who were men or divine men, to whom humanity owed civilization. [. . .]

Just as in the archaic period, the human past was seen to be preceded by a wondrous period that formed another world, real in itself and unreal in relation to our own. [. . .]

In this civilization, nothing was seen beyond a nearby temporal horizon: [. . .] the Homeric period and the heroic generations constituted antiquity in the eyes of this ancient civilization. [. . .] Already Herodotus was opposing the heroic to the human generations. Much later, when Cicero wants to be charmed by a philosophical dream of immortality and gives it the character of an idyll in the Elysian fields, he takes pleasure in thinking that in these meadows, where learned discourse abounds, his soul will converse with that of the wise Ulysses or the sagacious Sisyphus. [. . .]

The learned, we see, are not easily deceived; but by the first paradox they doubt the gods much more easily than they do the heroes. For example, Cicero: in politics or ethics he is perceptibly the equal of Victor Cousin, and he is quite capable of believing in what agrees with his interests. On the other hand, he has a religiously cold temperament, and in this area is incapable of professing something that he does not believe. Any reader of his treatise on the gods will agree that he does not believe in the latter very much and that he does not even try to make a different impression for the sake of political expediency. He lets it appear that in his day, as in our own, individuals were divided on matters of religion. Did Castor and Pollux really appear to a certain Vatienus on a road outside Rome? The question was discussed among the devout of the old school and the skeptics. [. . .] Now the same Cicero, who believes neither in the appearance of Castor and his brother nor, undoubtedly, in their very existence, and who does not hide it, fully admits the historicity of Aeneas and Romulus. Furthermore, no one was to question this historicity until the nineteenth century.

Here is a second paradox: almost everything that is told about these characters is only an empty tale, but the total of these zeroes makes a positive sum. Theseus indeed existed. Cicero, from the first page of his *Laws*, pleasantly jests about Romulus' supposed apparition after his death and about good king Numa's conversations with his nymph Egeria. In his *Republic* he does not believe that Romulus was the son of a god who had impregnated a Vestal Virgin, either: a venerable tale, but a tale nonetheless. Nor does he believe in the apotheosis of the founder of Rome; the posthumous divinization of Romulus is but a legend fit for naive times. Nevertheless, Romulus is a historically authentic person, and, according to Cicero, what is strange about his divinization is precisely that it had been invented in the middle of the historic age, for it takes place after the seventh Olympiad. In the matters of Romulus and Numa, Cicero questions everything except their very existence. To be precise, a third paradox appears here. Sometimes the learned seem very skeptical about myth as a whole and consign it to oblivion with a few well-chosen words. At others, they seem once again to have become completely credulous. This restoration of belief happens each time that, confronted with a given episode, they wish to be serious and responsible thinkers. Is this bad faith or half-belief? Neither. Instead, they are wavering between two criteria of truth, one of which requires the rejection of the marvelous, the other the persuasion that it is impossible to create a gratuitous life.

[. . .] Since the archaic period the value of the word "myth" has shifted. For example, when an author no longer frames his tale as his own but puts it in indirect discourse, "A myth says that . . . ," he is no longer claiming to make a bit of information, floating in the air, well known to all. He is withdrawing from the game and letting each one think what he pleases. "Myth" has become a slightly pejorative term, describing a suspect tradition. [. . .]

Ephorus will refrain from stating his approval, but he and his peers will also refrain from offering any condemnation. And here begins the second movement we mentioned: the return to credulity by means of methodical criticism.

A true background lies behind every legend. Consequently, when the historians move from the totality, which is suspect, to the detail and to individual myths, they once again become cautious. They question myths as a group, but not a one of them denies the historicity forming the basis of any legend. The moment it is no longer a question of expressing his overall doubt but offering a verdict on a specific point and pledging his word as a serious scholar, the historian begins to believe again. He clings to the task of sorting and safeguarding the true kernel.

We have to be careful here. When Cicero in his *Republic* and Titus Livy in his preface admit that the events "before Rome was born or thought of" are known only "in the form of old tales with more the charm of poetry than of a sound historical record," they are not offering a glimpse of modern historical criticism or foreshadowing Beaufort, Niebuhr, and Dumézil. They are not condemning the general uncertainty about the four centuries following the city's foundation and the absence of any contemporaneous documents. They are complaining that the documents related to an even older period are not certain. For these documents exist. They are traditions, but they are suspect, not because they date from a long time after the fact but because credulity has entered into the matter. What Livy and Cicero refuse to support is the divine birth of Romulus or the miracle of Aeneas' ships transformed into nymphs.

Knowledge of legendary times, then, emerges from a mode of knowledge that is completely habitual to us but that made the ancients uncomfortable when it was applied to history: criticism, conjectural knowledge, and scientific hypothesis. Speculation, *eikasia*, replaces confidence in tradition. It will be based on the notion that the past resembles the present. This had been the foundation on which Thucydides, seeking to do more than tradition, had already built his brilliant but perfectly false and gratuitous reconstruction of the first days of Greece.

Since this principle makes it equally possible to purify myth of its portion of the marvelous, it becomes possible to believe in all legends, which is what the greatest minds of this very great period did. [. . .]

Earlier the object of naive credulity, hesitant skepticism, and daring speculations, myth is now treated with a thousand precautions. But these precautions are very calculated. When filling out the contours of some legend, the writers of the Hellenistic and Roman periods seem to hesitate. They often refuse to speak in their own name. "People say . . . ," they write, or "according to myth." But in the next sentence they will be very definite concerning another point of the same legend. These shifts between daring and reserve owe nothing to chance. They follow three rules: state no opinion on the marvelous and the supernatural, admit a historical basis, and take exception to the details. One example will suffice. Narrating Pompey's flight toward Brindisi and Durazzo after Caesar had crossed the Rubicon, Appian speaks of the origins of the town of Durazzo, the ancient Dyrrachium, on the Ionian Sea. The town owes its name to Dyrrachus, the son of a princess "and," people say, "of Neptune." This Dyrrachus, states Appian, "had Heracles as an ally" in a war that he waged against his brothers, the princes, and this is why the hero is honored as a god by the people of the regions. These natives "say that during the battle Heracles mistakenly killed Ion, his ally Dyrrachus' own son, and that he threw the body into the sea so that this sea would take the name of the unfortunate one." Appian believes in Heracles and the war, rejects Neptune's paternity, and gives the locals credit for an anecdote.

Among the learned, critical credulity, as it were, alternated with a global skepticism and rubbed shoulders with the unreflecting credulity of the less educated. These three attitudes tolerated one another, and popular credulity was not culturally devalued. This peaceful coexistence of contradictory beliefs had a sociologically peculiar result. Each individual internalized the contradiction and thought things about myth that, in the eyes of a logician at least, were irreconcilable. The individual himself did not suffer from these contradictions; quite the contrary. Each one served a different end.

Take for example a philosophical mind of the first order, the physician Galen.[6] Did he, or did he not, believe in the reality of centaurs? It depends.

When he is speaking as a scholar and laying out his personal theories, he speaks of the centaurs in terms that imply that for himself and his most select readers these marvelous beings had barely any present reality. Medicine, he says, teaches reasonable knowledge, or "theorems," and the first condition of a good theorem is that it be perceivable by the senses. "For, if the theorem is unrealizable, in the manner of the following statement, *The centaur's bile relieves apoplexy*, it is useless because it escapes our apperception." There are no centaurs, or at least no one has ever seen one.

[. . .] If no one in Galen's time had ever taken the legend of centaurs literally, why would the philosophers have needed to speak seriously of these things and reduce them to mere likelihood? If no one had believed them, why would Galen himself have had to deliberately distinguish between those who did and did not believe in them? Moreover, Galen, in his great book on the finality of the parts of the organism, fights for a long time the idea that mixed natures, such as centaurs, could exist. He could not have done this without ridicule if centaurs did not have their believers.

But when the same Galen no longer seeks to impose his ideas but to win new disciples, he seems to pass to the side of the believers. Summarizing his whole view of medicine in one hundred pages and determined to give the most lofty idea of this science, he offers an account of its high origin: the Greeks, he says, attribute the discovery of the different arts to the sons of the gods or their familiars. Apollo taught medicine to his son Asclepius. Before him, men had only a limited experience with some remedies, herbals, "and, in Greece lay therein, for example, all the knowledge of the centaur Chiron and the heroes of whom he was the teacher."

This historical role accorded to a centaur is assuredly only pompous, conventional language. It is certainly what antiquity called rhetoric, and rhetoric was the art of winning more than the art of being right. In order to win—that is, to convince—it was doubtless necessary to start with what people thought rather than to rub the jury the wrong way by telling them that they were mistaken on everything and must change their worldview to acquit the accused. [. . .] This is not to say that rhetoric is not without philosophical dignity. I mean quite the contrary: that philosophy and truth both operate on the basis of interests. It is not true that, when they have a motive, intellectuals must be lying and that they are disinterested when they tell the truth. Galen had every reason to tell the truth about centaurs and deny their existence when his interest lay in the victory of his personal ideas among his disciples rather than in the recruiting of new ones. Exploring minds have different aims and tactics, depending on the circumstances. We are all in the same situation, even if we, and our disciples with us, take our jealousies to be righteous indignation and make a lofty idea of our scientific and ethical disinterest. [. . .]

But since this politics of ideas is often unconscious, it is internalized. It is difficult, for example, not to begin to believe a little in the foreign dogmas against which one has formed an offensive or defensive confederacy. For we line up our beliefs in accordance with our words, so that we end up no longer knowing what we truly think. When he was relying on popular belief in centaurs, Galen, for want of cynicism, must have been caught up in a whirl of noble and indulgent verbiage and no longer knew too well what he thought of it all. In such a moment are born these modalities of wavering belief, this capacity to simultaneously believe in incompatible truths, which is the mark of times of intellectual confusion. The Balkanization of the symbolic field is reflected in each mind. This confusion corresponds to a sectarian politics of alliance. Regarding myth, the Greeks lived for a thousand years in this state. The moment an individual wishes to convince and be recognized, he must respect different ideas, if they are forces, and must partake of them a little. Now we know that the learned respected popular ideas on myth and that they themselves were split between two principles: the rejection of the marvelous and the conviction that legends had a true basis. Hence their complicated state of mind.

Aristotle and Polybius, so defiant when they are confronting myth, did not believe in the historicity of Theseus or Aeolus, king of the wind, out of conformity or political calculation. Nor did they seek to challenge myths, but only to rectify them. Why rectify them? Because nothing that does not presently exist is worthy of belief. But then, why not challenge it all? Because the Greeks never admitted that the mythmaking process could lie to everyone about everything. The ancient problematic of myth . . . is bounded by two dogmas that were unconscious, for they were self-evident. It was impossible to lie gratuitously, or lie about everything to everyone, for knowledge is only a mirror; and the mirror blends with what it reflects, so that the medium is not distinguished from the message.

TRANSLATED BY PAULA WISSING

NOTES

[1] The French reads "nul ne songeait à écraser l'Infâme . . ." The reference is to Voltaire's famous slogan *Écrasez l'infâme!*, "Crush the wretched thing!"—the "wretched thing" being religion, which he viewed as a source of superstition, ignorance, intolerance, and fanaticism.—TRANS.

[2] For little girls followed the teachings of the grammarian but stopped before reaching the rule of the rhetorician; I add that classes were "co-educational": little girls and boys sat side by side listening to the grammarian. This detail, which seems little known, is found in Martial 8.3.15 and 9.68.2, and in Soranus, *On the Maladies of Women*, Ch. 92 (p. 209, edited by Dietz); cf. Friedländer, *Sittengeschichte Roms* (Leipzig, 1919), vol. 1, p. 409. Mythology was learned in school.

[3] Aristotle *Poetics* 9.8. W. Jaeger, *Paideia* (Paris, 1964), vol. 1, p. 326.

[4] This is the idea Trimalchio has about it (Petronius 39.3–4, 48.7, 52.1–2).

[5] Polybius 12.24.5.

[6] We will cite, in order: Galen *On the Best System, To Thrasybulus* 3 (*Opera*, vol. 1, p. 110, edited by Kühn); *On the Opinions of Hippocrates and Plato* (5.357 Kühn; for the expression "reduce legend to verisimilitude," see Plato *Phaedrus* 229e, which Galen transcribes almost verbatim); *On the Use of the Parts of the Body* 3.1 (3.169 Kühn; 1.123 Helmreich); *An Introduction, or the Doctor* (14.675 Kühn). Note that here Galen mentions Asclepius in a rhetorical vein, but at the same time he had made a private devotion to him (vol. 19.19 Kühn), the sincerity of which the example of his contemporary and equal in devotion, Aelius Aristides, forbids one to suspect. This did not prevent the same Galen from having a demythologized idea of the gods; like many of the learned, he thought that Greek polytheism was the popular deformation of the true knowledge of the gods, who are nothing other, literally, than stars, which are considered as so many living beings, in the ordinary meaning of the word, but endowed with faculties that are more perfect than those of men. For the surprising pages that this anatomist wrote on the perfection of these divine bodies, see *On the Use of the Parts of the Body* 17.1 (vol. 4, pp. 358–60 Kühn).

MARCEL DETIENNE

Return to the Mouth of Truth

1996

*This important essay was designed by Marcel Detienne to serve as an intro-
duction to the American edition of his influential book,* The Masters of
Truth in Archaic Greece. *Its importance, however, goes even beyond the
central topic of the book, which can be formulated as a basic question: what
are the historical facts that link poetry with the ever-changing cultural constructs of universal truth in ancient Greek civilization? Detienne's introduction goes on to broaden this question: how is the actual study of Greek
civilization linked with the search for truth in contemporary scholarship?
Pointedly, Detienne reaches beyond the world of French Classics scholars:
here he is speaking not only as Directeur d'Études and holder of the Chaire
des Religions de la Grèce of the École Pratique des Hautes Études, Fifth
Section (Sciences Religieuses), Paris, but also as the simultaneous holder of
the Basil L. Gildersleeve Professorship of Classics at the Johns Hopkins
University in Baltimore, the historical birthplace of graduate-level teach-
ing and research in Classical Philology in the United States (see Ward W.
Briggs, Jr, and Herbert W. Benario, eds.,* Basil Lanneau Gildersleeve: An
American Classicist *[American Journal of Philology Monographs in
Classical Philology, volume 1; Baltimore: The Johns Hopkins University
Press, 1986]). In this essay, Detienne's professorial voice addressed simultaneously the French and the Anglo-American worlds of classical scholarship. "La bouche de la vérité" has developed an American accent.
Reviewing thirty years of his own thinking, Detienne sets out here to "reexamine the assumptions and procedures" and to "consider a number of methodological problems." His essay provides a fitting coda for readers of Part I
of* Antiquities. *It marks an opportunity for reflection and retrospection.*

In archaic Greece, since the time sculptures first depicted walking figures,
paths suddenly opened on to the "Meadow of Truth" where the Plain of
Alētheia came into view. Even more secret tracks led to the Fountain of

From *The Masters of Truth in Archaic Greece,* trans. Janet Lloyd (New York: Zone
Books, 1996), pp. 15–33 [preface to the American edition of *Les Maîtres de vérité dans la
Grèce archaïque* (Paris: François Maspero, 1967)].

Oblivion or the icy waters of Memory. One day in Crete, the herb gatherer
Epimenides fell into a sleep so deep, without beginning or end, that he had all
the time in the world to speak in person with Truth. In the sixth century [BCE],
Truth, *Alētheia*, figured as one of the intimate companions of the goddess who
greeted Parmenides and guided him to "the unshakable heart of the perfect
circle of Truth."

For inquirers of the archaic and of beginnings, Truth provides a fascinating
archaeology, ranging from Hesiod's Muses to the daughters of the Sun, the
guide of the man who knows. Two or three earlier forays into the notion of the
"demonic" and the adaptation of Homeric and Hesiodic themes in the
philosophico-religious circles of Pythagoreanism had already convinced me it
was productive to follow the paths leading from religious to philosophical
thought.[1] I had begun to examine the subject in a brief article published in 1960
and completed my inquiry in 1965 in my Ph.D. dissertation at the Université
de Liège.[2] Its starting point was a simple observation: in archaic Greece, three
figures—the diviner, the bard, and the king of justice—share the privilege of
dispensing truth purely by virtue of their characteristic qualities. The poet, the
seer, and the king also share a similar type of speech. Through the religious
power of Memory, *Mnēmosunē*, both poet and diviner have direct access to the
Beyond; they can see what is invisible and declare "what has been, what is, and
what will be." With this inspired knowledge, the poet uses his sung speech to
celebrate human exploits and actions, which thus become glorious and illuminated, endowed with vital force and the fullness of being. Similarly, the king's
speech, relying on test by ordeal, possesses an oracular power. It brings justice
into being and establishes the order of law without recourse to either proof or
investigation.

At the heart of this kind of speech as it issues from these three figures is
Alētheia, a power belonging to the group of religious entities who are either
associated with or opposed to her. *Alētheia*, who is close to Justice, *Dikē*, forms a
pair with sung speech, *Mousa*, as well as with Light and with Praise. On the
other hand, *Alētheia* is opposed to Oblivion, *Lēthē*, who is the accomplice of
Silence, Blame, and Obscurity. In the midst of their mythico-religious configuration, *Alētheia* pronounces a performative truth. She is the power of efficacy
and creates being. As Michel Foucault would later put it, true discourse is "discourse pronounced by men who spoke as a right, according to ritual."[3] *Alētheia*
and *Lēthē* are not exclusive or contradictory in this way of thinking; they constitute two extremes of a single religious power. The negativity of silence and
oblivion constitutes the inseparable shadow of Memory and *Alētheia*. In the
name of this same power, the Muses, the daughters of Memory, possess not only
the ability "to say many false things that seem like true sayings" but also the
knowledge to "speak the truth."[4]

What place do the Sophist and the philosopher have in the lineage of the
"Masters of Truth"? How does their speech differ from the efficacious speech

of the diviner, the poet, and the king of justice, speech that conveys reality? How does the transition occur between one type of thought where ambiguity is a central feature of both its mode of expression and its logic to another kind of thought where argumentation, the principle of noncontradiction, and dialogue, with its distinctions between the sense and the reference of propositions, apparently announce the advent of a new intellectual regime?

It seemed to me that an understanding of the sociohistorical context might contribute to this genealogy of the idea of truth. During my research on the Pythagoreans, I gleaned signs of a process which set in motion the gradual secularization of speech. The most important sign was to be found in the military assembly since it conferred the equal right to speech on all members of the warrior class, those whose very position allowed them to discuss communal affairs. The hoplite reform, introduced in the city around 650 [BCE], not only imposed a new type of weaponry and behavior in battle but also encouraged the emergence of "equal and similar" soldier-citizens. At this point, dialogue—secular speech that acts on others, that persuades and refers to the affairs of the group—began to gain ground while the efficacious speech conveying truth gradually became obsolete. Through its new function, which was fundamentally political and related to the *agora*, *logos*—speech and language—became autonomous. Two major trends now developed in thought about language. On the one hand, *logos* was seen as an instrument of social relations: How did it act upon others? In this vein, rhetoric and sophistry began to develop the grammatical and stylistic analysis of techniques of persuasion. Meanwhile, the other path, explored by philosophy, led to reflections on *logos* as a means of knowing reality: Is speech all of reality? If so, what about the reality expressed by numbers, the reality discovered by mathematicians and geometricians?

I then began to study the rise and fall of *Alētheia*, particularly the way *Alētheia*, once devalued in sophistic thought, found itself linked in the discourse of Parmenides and early metaphysics with the immutable Being that is always self-identical and strictly governed by the principle of noncontradiction.

Thirty years later, with the publication of this careful translation by Janet Lloyd, whom I thank most warmly, I have the occasion to reexamine the assumptions and procedures of this early work as well as to consider a number of methodological problems. In 1958, at the Ecole Française de Rome in the Piazza Farnese, where my analysis of the "demonic" led me to consider various forms of mediation, Louis Gernet sent me his essay "Les Origines de la philosophie."[5] For many years already I had been reading the work of this Greek scholar who, in the 1980s, in the shrine on rue Monsieur-le-Prince, was to become the object of some veneration by the devotees of the Centre de Recherches Comparées sur les Sociétés Anciennes and its left-wing historiographer, Riccardo Di Donato, who, with Marxist zeal, traveled from Pisa to organize the liturgy of its "founding heroes."[6] In that brief essay—which was very difficult to find until Jean-Pierre Vernant and I republished it in 1968, with other essays, in *The Anthropology of Ancient Greece*—Louis Gernet pointed out the importance of identifying how "mythical concepts, religious practice, and societal forms . . . were involved in philosophy's beginnings."[7] Gernet paid close attention to the figure of the philosopher, his way of behaving as if he had been "chosen," his view of his position and knowledge in the world and in the city. In the same year, 1958, in the Piazza Farnese, as I came to realize the fascination Greece exerted on ethnology, Claude Lévi-Strauss's *Structural Anthropology* revealed to me new ways of analyzing and theorizing "mythical thought," which Greek scholars hardly dared mention, even among themselves.[8] Underlying my inquiry into the religious configuration of truth was Ernst Cassirer's and Antione Meillet's hypothesis that language guides ideas, vocabulary is more a conceptual system than a lexicon, and linguistic phenomena relate to institutions, that is, to influential schemata present in techniques, social relations, and the contexts of communicative exchange.

Speech and its use in the early city was my subject then, and my inquiry today continues along the same two general lines. The first concerns the practices of the assembly, which developed out of hundreds of experiments involving models of a political space. Closely linked to this is the nature of the environment in which the many reflections on speech, its effects, techniques, and relations with the world and with other people occurred. I am currently analyzing ways of using speech and modes of behavior in the assembly from a comparativist perspective, considering Ethiopian communities, Cossack societies, and the commune movement in Italy.[9]

The second line of study follows in the wake of *Themis*, examining schemata of creation and foundation ranging from oracular pronouncements, through the procedures for opening and closing assemblies, to the domain of decisions engraved on stones set up in the unfixed space of nascent cities.[10] Michel Foucault, in his 1970 inaugural lecture at the Collège de France, discovered in archaic Greece the province governing our own "will to knowledge" or, more precisely, our "will to truth."[11] To me he seemed to be referring to the landscape of truth sketched in my own inquiry. Once we jettison the poorly defined earlier identification of "power and knowledge," the desire to speak the truth seems, in retrospect, to have been very marked among the masters of truth in early Greece. Such a will or desire is expressed both by the Hesiodic Muses and by the Bee-Women of the young Apollo.[12] Similarly, in the political domain, a desire for practical effectiveness is always explicit: it is found across the board, from the ritual formula of the herald who opened the assembly with the question "Who wishes/desires to speak for the city?" to the formula repeated in thousands of decisions legibly carved in stone and carefully positioned where they could be read by "whoever had the will/desire to do so."[13] The philosophers wasted no time in attempting to monopolize this desire for truth. But the city was spared such a monopoly, thanks to its use of speech and the practices of the assembly—although this development was, at the same time, altogether in line with the will and desire of those who were obsessively establishing the forms for the government of men by men.

Such an inquiry into not only the semantic field of *Alētheia* but also the protohistory of philosophy and the changes in the archaic world was bound to evoke reactions, silent or vociferous, from the three academic disciplines in a position to judge the validity of the enterprise: philology and history, of course, but also anthropology, if it could overcome its complexes vis-à-vis those other two and their international prestige—in Europe, at least. One might have expected the historians to pay some attention to an essay on the "hoplite reform," but the potential of categories of thought constituted no part of any history program, modern or ancient.[14] Moses I. Finley was wary of anything outside the socioeconomic sphere, even politics in the strict sense of the term. Pierre Vidal-Naquet, working at that time with Pierre Lévêque on Cleisthenes and the intellectual transformations accompanying his great political reforms, was the sole exception; I am now even more appreciative of his work than I already was at the time. But what about the philologists, the *littéraires*, as they are called on the Left Bank?

Observers of the intellectual scene have long recognized that the tribe of historians is divided into "nationalists" (about three-quarters of the group) and the rest, of whom there are remarkably few in a "nation" such as present-day France.[15] The tribe of philologists—to which, as an archaeologist of the Truth, I am bound to return—has always fallen into two distinct species: the philologist who thinks and the one who dispenses with thinking. The latter, it must be said, is invariably the more prolific, regardless of climate or circumstances. However, the hermeneutic school of Lille, Germanic and philosophical in its inspiration, undoubtedly belongs to the first species.[16] Won over by a sociology of culture *à la française*, that is, by the works of Pierre Bourdieu, some members of this group have even manifested an interest in anthropological approaches that may illuminate certain important aspects of Greek culture. Examples of such areas including writing, considered a cognitive practice, and its effects on the modalities of certain types of knowledge; also earlier work in "mythology" or "mythical thought" as it relates to the practices of such an explicitly polytheist culture from the time of Homeric epic to almost the end of antiquity.[17] A recent international colloquium on Hesiod, admirably organized by interpreters from the hermeneutic school, combined philosophy and anthropology with philology, that most eminent of all disciplines.[18] Since F. M. Cornford, Hesiod, author of the *Theogony*, has indeed been recognized as a precursor to philosophical discourse, but the inclusion of anthropology was not as predictable. This was especially so since, in the sociocultural context of this colloquium, what was labeled "anthropology" seemed to range from essays produced under the sign of a so-called historical psychology that was sometimes comparative as well; the works of historians of the *Annales* school, with their inventories of mentalities; and inquiries into the structures of myths, ranging from Georges Dumézil's studies to the ambitious work of Lévi-Strauss.[19] The "structural" analyses of the major narratives of Greece were obviously bound to irritate the more or less strict hermeneutists. Nevertheless, an important question had thankfully been raised: Do Hesiod and the truth of the Muses really fall into the province of a "science of literary works" as represented by the hermeneutists?

Heinz Wismann has addressed this question in his comments on studies of Hesiod.[20] Is it legitimate to apply to the author of the *Theogony* the modern hermeneutic principle on which the coherence of the work's meaning resides, in the last analysis, on the autonomous decision of a single individual?[21] The constraints of this principle involve accepting the work in its autonomy, the coherence of its meaning, a unitary project, an author at work, and a peerless interpreter responding to the appeal of a peerless author. Comparison is never even envisaged—which discourages from the outset any reference to anthropology, since anthropology was born comparativist. Out of loyalty to its own principles, elaborated between a reading of Plato and a reading of the New Testament at the end of the nineteenth century, philological exegesis cannot accommodate an analysis of historico-ethnographic context.[22] Institutional practices such as ordeals by water, prophecy via incubation, and Orphico-Dionysiac funerary rituals are barred from the magic hermeneutic circle, as are all the representations of memory and oblivion that throng the cultural field in which Hesiod belongs. On the grounds that they are "external" to the text— Hesiod's text—those "data" are considered to have no bearing on the literal meaning that alone gives access to the "sole meaning" of the work. "Structuralist school essayists"—as Jean Bollack has called them—are thus completely dismissed, along with their claims to understanding a Greek culture which is reduced to a certain number of great literary or philosophico-literary texts.[23]

A great deal is certainly at stake here, as is demonstrated by the state of contemporary "Classical studies" in the United States and its unceasing focus on "great texts" and their exegesis. In truth, Classical studies devotes itself to maintaining certain privileged values, without the slightest concern for analyzing cultural systems as a way of understanding the mechanisms of human thought across different cultures. Yet for "structural essayists," as for members of the French school of hermeneutics, the subject of Hesiod's poem is clearly speech—not only its status and authority but also its representation by the poet and the Muses. We all recognize that from Homer to Hesiod the relationship between the bard and the daughters of Memory undergoes a transformation and becomes more complex. In the *Iliad*, the Muses are all-knowing, and, thanks to them, the poet can see perfectly into both the bards' and the daughters' camps. As the servant of the Muses, the bard can recount what happened when the Trojan horse entered the city of Apollo and Hector. Instructed by the

Muses, he sings now for Odysseus, now for others, of what unfolded before his blind gaze, as though he himself were present in the days of the Trojan War.[24] But Hesiod of Ascra speaks in the first person as well as the third. An author who is both poet and prophet is present and is chosen by the Muses, who now assume new modalities of speech. Wismann is right to emphasize this point: "They say that they know how to say false things [*pseudea*, which I would translate as "deceptive" things] that seem to be real, but at the same time know how to make true things understood."[25]

Here the Muses are understood to be reflecting on the subject of narrative and its structures. The order of discourse, *logos*, thus has a double register: one of fine fiction, which is certainly by no means rejected, the other of "true understanding." According to Wismann, the latter means "seizing upon the structures of the narrative" or "the narrative of the true structures," and so on.[26] *Alētheia* thus designates the register of the intelligible, that of true understanding of the work produced by Hesiod and his post-Homeric Muses. Both levels are in the province of the daughters of Memory, as is shown by comparing the representation of the three Bee-Women in the *Homeric Hymn to Hermes*. These Bee-Women instruct Apollo himself—in divination, no less— according to a double register: "From their home, they fly now here, now there, feeding on honeycomb and bringing all things to pass. And when they are inspired [*thuiōsin*, "they leap," like Thyiades possessed by Dionysus] through eating yellow honey, they are willing [*ethelein*] to speak the Truth [*Alētheia*]. But if they be deprived of the god's sweet food, they speak falsely [*pseudesthai*] in the distress that assails them."[27] Here a comparison with the knowledge of a diviner is fundamental; fortunately for hermeneutics, it can be justified by the definition found in one of the "great texts":[28] the *Iliad* declares that Calchas is able to speak of the present, the future, and the past.[29] In both cases, there are thus two registers: with the Bee-Women for Apollo the diviner, and with the Muses, for Hesiod, there is both poet and prophet. The difference between them lies in the honey, the means of ecstasy. Hesiod's Muses, more down to earth despite being Olympians, feel no need for ecstasy, not even in the customary form of nectar and ambrosia. The "desire/will" of the Bee-Women, similar to that of Hesiod's Muses, diminishes the mechanical nature of the food of truth and thereby reduces the distance between the two groups.

While hermeneutics may successfully explore the double register of Hesiodic speech, it refuses to understand memory and oblivion in their ethnographic and religious contexts, as I myself have done in this book.[30] A hermeneutist must interpret literally, at the level of the words: *lēthē* must mean "a kind of awareness," the counterpart to *alētheia*, "things of which we are no longer unaware"—and this, we are told, means we have "true comprehension of them."[31] *Mnēmosunē*, or Memory, a divine power married to Zeus as were first *Mētis*, then *Themis*, and finally Hera, dissolves into a platitude, a most ridiculous outcome. She becomes simply "good memory," because "we must remember what has already been said about perceiving *Alētheia*."[32] Yet the signs provided by Hesiod are certainly clear enough: on Mount Helicon, the Muses appear close to the altar of Zeus;[33] they "breathed a voice into" the poet (*empneuein*), as does Apollo when he gives the elect the knowledge of the present, past, and future.[34] In the *Theogony*, *Lēthē*, far from being simply "a kind of unawareness," is just as much a divine power as are the Words of Deception, the *Pseudeis Logoi*, who are listed among the Children of the Night, along with Sleep and Death.[35] No thoughtful study of speech in Hesiod's poems could neglect the most immediate Hesiodic context, the work itself. Similarly, ignoring the Old Man of the Sea, who is listed among the Children of the Deep (*Pontus*), leads one to ignore another essential passage in the *Theogony* and to fail to ponder "the truth" implied by the king of justice, his prophetic knowledge, and his other powers.[36] What kind of *explication de texte* begins by sweeping under the rug whole chunks of the work, without the least explanation?

Interestingly enough, it is the American Hellenists at Harvard University, such as Gregory Nagy and Charles P. Segal, who have paid the most attention to the mythico-religious aspects of memory and oblivion and their relation to blame and praise, no doubt because they recognized the paramount importance of wider horizons of knowledge and were disinclined to consider a cultural system simply as a more or less rich collection of separate and autonomous works.[37] In spite of all the philologists' skepticism, the most important recent discoveries have established the ancient and complex nature of the works and practices of philosophico-religious circles. The first discovery was that of the oldest Greek book, the Derveni Papyrus of ca. 380 [BCE], a scroll from the library of Orpheus containing rich philosophical commentaries on the Orphic poems.[38] Next came new gold tablets, from Hipponion in Magna Graecia and Pelinna in Thessaly, which establish both the "Bacchic" nature of the initiation reserved for the bearers of these engraved lamellae and the sacred path along which they were carried, at the end of which the dead man or woman accedes to life in all its plenitude.[39] A kind of Bacchic and Orphic ritual from the end of the fourth century [BCE] in turn testifies to the importance of writing in philosophico-religious circles fascinated by the interplay between memory, oblivion, and truth.[40] Finally, on the shores of the Black Sea at Olbia, a colony of Miletus, excavators from what was then the Soviet Union discovered bone tablets bearing graffiti from 500 [BCE]. Beneath the three terms *Life-Death-Life* and alongside the words *Orphic* and *Dionysus* was *Truth* (*Alētheia*). On another slender tablet, parallel to the pair *Peace-War* stood the words *Truth-Deception* (*Alētheia-Pseudos*). Finally, on a third tablet, beneath a shortened version of the name Dionysus was inscribed *Soul* (*Psychē*), which was associated with *Alētheia*.[41]

The philosophico-religious circles of the late sixth century were thus deeply involved with the subject of Truth, the very Truth which, rightly or wrongly,

Martin Heidegger regarded as the essential element of Greek philosophy and which was at the heart of philosophical discussion during the "overthrow of metaphysics" between the time of the Greeks and "our own time."[42] Few scholars of antiquity or educated readers are aware of how carefully Heideggerians and "deconstructionists" have built a veritable wall to separate themselves from the explorations of Greek scholars. The Hellenists are perhaps at fault in not realizing that the only real innovator in Greek thought is Heidegger; still, these scholars continue to publish and publicize documents, texts if not whole works, from the diverse world of archaic Greece. The barrier seems insuperable. Even lucid critics of successive interpretations of Heidegger's view on Truth seem to accept at face value his notion of the "unconcealed" or the "deconcealed," making no attempt to deconstruct it or set it alongside those archaic representations of *Alētheia*. André Doz, one of the boldest of those critics, as uninformed as the most obdurate of them about the discoveries at Olbia and Derveni, has written, "We ought to take a closer look at the word *alēthēs*."[43] On the other hand, many Greek scholars probably do not know that, for Heidegger and his disciples, the history of philosophy and hence the establishment of the meaning of *Alētheia* are part of the very history of being.[44] Clearly, this does not make it any easier to initiate a debate on the modalities of concealment, oblivion, and memory in Greek thought and culture.

From the perspective I have adopted from the start, no etymology can be singled out as infallible (thank God). At least from Parmenides on, Greek philosophers recognized that to think it was necessary to debate and argue. When an etymology seems bad or fantastic no appeal to higher grounds can confer authority on it. In the context of the same inquiry, it is important to remember that it is partly because of the etymology of the word *polis* that the field of politics is left out of the analysis offered by Heidegger and his followers, intent as they are on the "overthrow of metaphysics." During a seminar, Heidegger once said (and he later wrote) that the word *polis* comes from *polein*, an ancient form of the word meaning "to be." Such an etymology is entirely arbitrary; there is simply no convincing, verifiable "true meaning" for *polis*. Even so, there was no reason for such an elementary piece of information to inhibit thought on the *polis* from developing: if the city, or *polis*, is based on the verb "to be," that in itself demonstrates that the *polis* must be the site of a total unveiling of Being.[45] Thus, the city cannot have anything in common with "politics" in the trivial sense of *to politikon*. So, goodbye politics.[46] The "philosophico-religious" aspect was not even mentioned in connection with either the mundane world or the world of the Beyond.

It is worth pausing to reflect on this matter since, for a nondebate, the fallout continues.[47] To my knowledge, not a single disciple of Heidegger has ever questioned this feeble etymology. A few later insisted that, for Heidegger, politics is not a category or a field like ethics or ontology. Politics, with its foundation rituals, gods, and autonomy articulated through so many practices, does not exist. It vanishes into thin air, leaving no trace, useless and unknown. In fact, on closer examination, ever since Heidegger's *Being and Time*, politics in the common sense of the word has been heaped with scorn. It constitutes an obstacle in the process of *Dasein*, the process of what is existent, which is determined by its concern for self and which can assume possession of itself only by turning away from the mundane social elements of life and from the city and its pointlessly loquacious public places. In this connection, only one philosopher, Dominique Janicaud, braver and more lucid than the rest, has sought to understand how Heidegger's thought laid itself open "to what happened to him."[48] I refer, of course, to the recent past, 1933: the philosopher of *Dasein* supported Adolf Hitler's national socialism, maintained a hermetic silence on the genocide of the Jews, and afterward failed to produce any philosophical critique of his "incidental" support of the Nazi party. It may not have had much to do with the so very Greek concept of truth, but it may not be totally unconnected with the equal scorn heaped on what Heidegger calls "Anthropology." For his disciples and devotees, the term incorporates the inquiries historians of archaic Greece have conducted both on the philosophico-religious circles and on forms of thought discovered through methods that lead neither to familiar places nor to the heart of "great works."

Finally, two additional matters are worth raising here. The first concerns the "mythical thought" that, I maintain, possessed a true consistency yet also was "overthrown." The second deals with the "social and mental" conditions that made possible the deep changes I explore through the history of the concept of Truth.

In a grudging review of a work in which I considered the presuppositions of the essentially Greek category of "myth," Arnaldo Momigliano noted my disaffection toward studies of the transition from mythical to rational thought in Greece, an issue he considered well established by then.[49] Momigliano, usually a much more perceptive observer, believed that this disaffection indicated a break with the analyses Vernant had been working on ever since his *The Origins of Greek Thought*. But Momigliano was mistaken, as we all are at times. He had completely misunderstood the intentions of my book, *The Creation of Mythology*.[50] The aim of this book was to reflect on and provoke thought about the category of "myth" and its place in Lévi-Strauss's analytic methods—methods I myself had experimented with (the first to do so in a Greek context, I believe), in 1972 in *The Gardens of Adonis*.[51] Momigliano did not realize that I had been so successful in convincing Vernant of the need to rethink the category of narratives known as "myth" that Vernant himself had explained in the popular periodical *Sciences et avenir*, with my *The Creation of Mythology* solely in mind, that "today Greek mythology is changing its meaning."[52] Unlike Momigliano, Vernant was not upset by this at all. In fact, at this point it even seemed to suit him.[53]

However, the question here concerns the "mythical thought" that was so important in the inquiry I began in 1960. At that time it was mediated through Louis Gernet, who from time to time referred to the ideas of Hermann Usener, yet spoke of them with all the conviction of a disciple of Emile Durkheim and possibly of Ernst Cassirer; Cassirer had devoted a whole volume of his 1924 *Philosophy of Symbolic Forms* to "Mythical Thought."[54] Following in Gernet's footsteps, Vernant set up a new "framework": "mythical thought"—"positivist, abstract thought," or, put another way, the transition "from myth to reason."[55] Lévi-Strauss, for his part, had not yet said enough on the subject. *The Raw and the Cooked*, the first volume of his *Mythologiques*, appeared in 1964, and it was not until I was prompted by the comparison between "alimentary codes" and Pythagorean sacrificial practices to try new methods of analyzing Greek myths that I saw how new meaning could be given to "mythical thought."[56]

Insofar as thought of a global nature incorporates a number of different types of experience, mythical thought or ancient religious thought made it possible to elaborate the most convincing configuration of poet, seer, and king around a single model of speech with shared gestures, practices, and institutions. Now, as then, an analysis of the trajectory of *Alētheia* from Hesiod to Parmenides provides a unique opportunity to observe the changes in the mechanisms of the intellect at work in the beginnings of philosophical thought. I am now planning to develop those religious and mythical representations of speech in the direction of *Themis*, positioned between the oracle, Apollo, and the assemblies.[57] I have no intention of writing the history of a "psychological function" such as memory; this is in no way the aim of an inquiry devoted to detecting traces of *Alētheia* in the many places where the tribe of philosophers do not venture.[58] Nor do I intend to seek what might intuitively seem to be "the" logic behind "mythical thought," for any such notion would be quite artificial. Rather than make the inquiry hang on a contrast between *a* principle of ambiguity and *the* principle of contradiction, I prefer now to emphasize the diversity of the configurations that include *Alētheia* and the comparison that should be made between the orientations of the various frameworks encountered during this first reconnoiter. Perhaps it is no longer enough to know that Truth also has a history and that, once Parmenides had depicted the Goddess as revealing the Way of Truth to him, Truth had to be proved, argued, and put to the test of refutation.[59]

From the time of my earlier inquiry into Truth and its double registers to my comparison between different ways of beginning—the central theme of "Transcrire les mythologies"—I chose to concentrate on instances of rupture and radical change.[60] My reasons for doing so were twofold. The first reason, explicit and factual, is that the Greek data are full of abortive beginnings and sudden impulses, which the Greeks are vibrantly aware of through the very force of reflection animating these new kinds of knowledge. The second reason has become clearer in the course of my comparative studies: conditions that involve profound change and abrupt breaks with the past make it easier to select apt comparisons between cultural systems. In the case of the *Masters of Truth*, the comparison remained internal: between two types of men, two successive configurations, two models of speech. Between Hesiod and Parmenides, the determining factors seem to have been the passage of time and the change of context. I wanted to analyze the social and mental conditions of the transformation of truth between Epimenides and Parmenides. Simply noting that there was a discontinuity seemed unacceptable, particularly since the contrast between two models of speech, the "magico-religious" and the "dialogue-speech," became explicitly obvious in the earliest days of Greek culture and the Greek city. What I then called the "process of secularization" was first manifested in a social framework whose practices and representations, so important in the formation of the city, were found described by the time of Homer's poems, particularly in the *Iliad*. Now more than ever, the assembly practices and the representations of space that made for egalitarianism in warrior circles, which are described in epic, seem to me to be essential for an understanding of the increasing importance of the *agora* in the first Greek cities of the eighth century as well as for the development of the model of *isonomia* in the "political" world of the seventh and sixth centuries.

In the variegated landscape of the journeys from "mythical thought" to the "positivist and abstract thought" that found support in the mind of the city, a certain furrow was visible from the start. With this rift came a different kind of speech, a different framework, a different kind of thought, marked by temporal divisions (the eighth century for Homer; the mid-seventh century for the qualitative leap represented by the "hoplite reform"; between the two, the first circular *agora* laid out on the ground by the founders of the Magna Graecia cities from about 730 on). These matters are worth following up and keeping under observation, however difficult, even today. With the advantage of hindsight, I will avoid referring in the future to "undeniable relations" between a major phenomenon such as "the secularization of thought" and changes as rich and complex as "the emergence of new social relations and unprecedented political structures." Given the scarcity of evidence in archaic Greece, it was tempting to make too much of the coherence between widely differing aspects of the culture and to connect them boldly with a network of interrelations between a different kind of social and mental phenomena, which in many cases it was barely possible to glimpse.

In a careful and intelligent analysis of *The Masters of Truth*, Maurice Caveing has pointed out the large gap between a kind of egalitarian and secular scene and the formulation of, or at least insistence on, a principle of noncontradiction in the field of Parmenides' *Alētheia*.[61] Certainly, I was somewhat cavalier in pronouncing on what many earlier scholars had solemnly defined as "a great social fact."[62] Its importance could not be doubted, and to simply sum it up as I did must have sounded quite incongruous. The juridical and political exercise of these two theses or two parties certainly deserves a study that takes account of their respective forms and procedures. However, it does seem more justifiable to stress the role that the technique of mathematical demonstration may have played in sixth-century Greece, together with the insistence on non-contradiction within this new kind of knowledge, as Caveing did in 1968. The debate on "common matters" (*ta koina*) within a space of equality is not necessarily directly related to the debate between intellectuals on the rules of reasoning, the forms of demonstration, and the criteria of conceptual analysis.[63] Indeed, the recent comparativist studies of Geoffrey Lloyd have revealed the complexity of this laboratory of new rational thought with all its various types of knowledge, its competitive frameworks of rivalry, its different types of proof, and its ways of distinguishing between discourse that is true and discourse that is not.[64] Still, in any project involving an increasingly refined comparison between modes of reasoning and ways of formulating or establishing the truth, there is even today a place for *The Masters of Truth*.

TRANSLATED BY JANET LLOYD

NOTES

[1] In chronological order: "Homère, Hésiode et Pythagore: Poésie et philosophie dans le pythagorisme ancien" (1962); "De la Pensée religieuse à la pensée philosophique: La Notion de *Daimōn* dans le pythagorisme ancien" (1963); "Crise agraire et attitude religieuse chez Hésiode" (1963).

[2] "La Notion mythique d'*Alētheia*" (1960).

[3] Foucault 1972, 218.

[4] Hesiod *Theogony* 27–28, trans. R. Lattimore (Ann Arbor, 1959).

[5] L. Gernet, "Les Origines de la philosophie," in this vol. at pp. 41–47.

[6] These "founding heroes" were I. Meyerson, with his "historical and comparative" psychology (the only truly Marxist psychology, as he and his most loyal disciples claimed), L. Gernet, and J.-P. Vernant (possibly somewhat despite Gernet). I will consider elsewhere the "service" performed at that time by R. Di Donato and its reception.

[7] M. Detienne, L. Gernet, J.-P. Vernant, eds., *The Anthropology of Ancient Greece*, p. 353.

[8] See in particular ch. 11, "The Structural Study of Myth."

[9] This work is currently in progress as part of the program of the research group, "Histoire et Anthropologie: approches comparatives" at Ecole Pratique des Hautes Études/Centre National de la Recherche Scientifique, Université de Paris, and Johns Hopkins University.

[10] For an analysis of the current state of studies on this subject, see *Annuaire de l'École Pratique des Hautes Etudes* 99 (1990–91): 243–46.

[11] Foucault 1972, 218–20.

[12] Hesiod *Theogony* 27–28 (*ethelein*); Homeric Hymn to Hermes 558–63 (*ethelein*).

[13] The formula used by the herald is found in Euripides *The Suppliant Women* 438–39 (*thelein*), trans. F. W. Jones (Chicago: University of Chicago Press, 1958); concerning the formula inscribed on stones designed to be legible and visible (*boulesthai*), see Detienne 1992 [1988], 41.

[14] Detienne, "La Phalange: Problèmes et controverses" (1958).

[15] See the historian of France in the role of "priest of the nation," as he appears in P. Nora's part-historical, part-narcissistic work, *Les Lieux de mémoire*, 7 vols. (Paris: Gallimard, 1984–92). See, in particular, *Débat* 78 (1994), in which a comparison with other European nations prompts Nora to suggest that France possesses a historical predisposition to memory. In France, a nation given to commemoration, any comparative approach that would first insist on a critical analysis of the "categories" involved is derailed. The most pertinent remarks about this "very French" enterprise have come from outside, either from the United States or from a sociological perspective: J.-P. Willaime, "'Lieux de Mémoire' et imaginaire national," *Archives des sciences sociales des religions* 66.1 (1988); S. Englund, "De l'Usage du mot 'nation' par les historiens et réciproquement," *Le Monde diplomatique* (March 1988), 28–29.

[16] Among other programmatic and polemical writings, I would single out J. Bollack, "Réflexions sur la pratique philologique" [in this vol. as "Reflections on Philological Practice," pp. 31–40].

[17] I have in mind P. Judet de La Combe, who welcomed the collective work *Les Savoirs de l'écriture en Grèce ancienne*, which I edited. I am even more grateful to him because, at about the same time—between 1984 and 1988—I presented my ideas on "The Gods of Writing" at the Townsend Lectures (February–April 1987) at Cornell University, to an audience convinced, apparently on the basis of strong arguments, that the only "god of writing" was Jacques Derrida, a fact that rendered null and void the ideas of Palamedes, the Egyptian accounts of Thoth, and the Orphics' pronouncements on letters, the *grammata*. In a book I intend to write one day, I will also try to understand why the stories of "Mr. Palamedes" seemed so ridiculous to an audience that had been treated to revelations from the High Priest of Writing. I have presented an initial sketch of the mythical and intellectual representations of inventive writing in two chapters of *L'Ecriture d'Orphée*, pp. 101–30.

[18] "Rencontre internationale Hésiode: Philologie, Anthropologie, Philosophie" (October 12–14, 1989), published as *Le Métier du Mythe*, ed. Blaise et al. (1996).

[19] This range is detectable in Bollack, "Réflexions," pp. 379–80, which refers to the explanations of "essayists of the structuralist schools" that appeal to "the system of representation and mental and psychological structures." He criticizes them for not being interested in the "unique meaning" of a work and for throwing light on works "by means of borrowing directly from social reality." A vague reference to "the influence of ethnology and anthropology" rules out any reflection on procedures for analyzing the narratives of "mythology" within the field of a *Greek* ethnographical context (cf. Detienne, afterword, "Revisiting the Gardens of Adonis," [in this vol, pp. 183–94]).

[20] Three mimeographed texts mark the development of H. Wismann's approach: Bollack's seminar (1976); document for the Hesiod colloquium (1989); "Propositions pour une lecture d'Hésiode" (1993). I henceforth refer to them by their years.

[21] {Wismann 1993, 3.}

[22] Laks and Neschke 1991.

[23] Ibid., 379.

[24] Ford 1992 draws attention to the complexity of epic poetics.

[25] {Wismann 1989, 5.}

[26] {Wismann 1976, 5,} used the expression "immediate transparency of the meaning." He also defined *Alētheia* as "the level of true comprehension" (1989, 6) or as "the symbolism of the structure" (1989, 7), "the structures that the narrative's self-consciousness makes it possible to grasp" (structural muses?). In the 1993 version, p. 7, the only thing remaining is the work (*Theogony*), deploying "true meanings that philosophy will continue to work upon in order to derive its systems from it."

[27] *Homeric Hymn to Hermes* 558–63, trans. H. G. Evelyn-White (Cambridge, Mass.: Loeb Classical Library, 1914).

[28] A philologist can be recognized from afar by his stretched-out neck, slightly twisted as a result of his looking back, upstream, toward the works of the past or earlier authors; with the past before him, he walks backward.

[29] *Iliad* 1.70.

[30] Between 1976 and 1993, the horizon of thought involving "Truth-Memory-Oblivion" that emerged from my 1965 studies received no attention, whereas flat, basic philology (e.g., H. J. Mette and T. Krischer) was deemed worthy of discussion. Such tactics are not unconnected with the strategy of "the philologist's profession."

[31] {Wismann 1989, 6.} In 1993, 6, he was content simply to allude "to the regulating principle of memory," *Mnemosunē*, which is thus taken simply as the antonym of *Lēthē*, from which *Alētheia* is derived with a privative *a*. In his "Autorité et auteur dans la *Théogonie hésiodique*" (published in Blaise et al. 1996; see n. 18 above; pp. 41–52), Nagy produced a critique of the interpretation suggested by T. Cole, "Archaic Truth," *Quaderni urbinati di cultura classica* 13 (1983). While emphasizing again the essential relations between "memory" and "truth" in poetic thought Nagy (p. 35), tries to show that Hesiod's expression *alēthea gērusasthai* is meant to refer to a whole corpus of pan-Hellenic myths felt to be radically different from the local versions that are invariably at odds with one another.

[32] {Wismann 1989, 10.}

[33] Hesiod *Theogony* 4, 31, followed at 32 by "the power"—for Hesiod, inspired by them— "to sing the story of things of the future, and things past," i.e., in the same fashion as the diviner, with mantic speech (at 31 *thespis* is found alongside *aoidē*), trans. R. Lattimore (Ann Arbor, 1959).

[34] These powers include the power of the Muses, the power of speech. As early as 1965, Greek scholars such as Nagy and Segal recognized that, as powers of sung speech, the Muses, whose remarkable names constitute a theology of articulated song, represent an essential aspect of self-conscious reflection on speech and language. Hermeneutics—at least in the case of Wismann 1989, 8—seems to discover this unaffected by any evidence other than that found in the literal meaning.

[35] Hesiod *Theogony* 211–32; *Thanatos* and *Hypnos* at 212; *Mōmos*, blame, at 215; *Apatē*, deception, at 224; *pseudeis logoi*, words of deception, at 229. As I have pointed out, Hermes reigns over *pseudea* as well as *haimulioi logoi*, which directly affects both Pandora and the fact that speech is shared by men and the gods.

[36] Hesiod *Theogony* 233–36.

[37] See Nagy 1979, 1990. [See also Segal 1998—eds.]

[38] The Derveni Papyrus was discovered in 1962, announced by S. G. Kapsomenos in 1964, and "edited" by M. L. West (*Zeitschrift für Papyrologie und Epigraphik* 47 [1982]) in anticipation of the delayed publication by the discoverers themselves.

[39] G. Pugliese-Carratelli, *La Parola del passato* 29 (1974); K. Tsantsonoglou and G. M. Parassoglou, "Two Gold Lamellae from Thessaly," *Hellenika* 38 (1987): 23–25.

[40] See F. Graf, "Textes orphiques et rituel bacchique: à propos des lamelles de Pélinna," in Borgeaud 1991. On the specificity of the choice of writing and books in the Orphic movement, see Detienne 1989, 101–32.

[41] M. L. West, "The Orphics of Olbia," *Zeitschrift für Papyrologie und Epigraphik* 45 (1982): 17–30.

[42] A good guide to the paths taken by *Alētheia*, as seen by Heidegger, is M. Zarader, *Heidegger et les paroles de l'origine*, 2d ed. (Paris: Vrin, 1990), pp. 49–82.

[43] See A. Doz, "Heidegger, Aristote et le thème de la vérité," *Revue de philosophie ancienne* 1 (1990), in particular p. 96.

[44] See ibid., 76.

[45] See M. Heidegger, *Introduction to Metaphysics*, trans. R. Manheim (New Haven: Yale University Press, 1959); see also Heidegger, *Gesamtausgabe*, vol. 53 (1984), p. 100; cf. pp.

98–99. Heidegger's interpreters tell us that it is not just a matter of the way a word is put together or linguistic motivations. Heidegger attempted to illuminate what the Greeks themselves did not understand; e.g., "concealment totally rules the essence of being"; *Alētheia* is an "enigma," where the veiling and unveiling of Being meet. An unveiling of veiling? Why not? Clarifying and flushing out? But all this is a matter for Heidegger and his *own* poetic and philosophic reflection on being. The Greeks are simply used as hostages. However, if one believes that Heidegger tries to clarify "the basis for what they said and thought," as Zarader, p. 82, does, this interpretation, like all others, ought to come to terms with objections, recognize its mistakes, and discuss arguments coming from other horizons. There can be no masters of truth where there is no demonstration in the "geometric" manner.

[46] Heidegger goes even further, claiming that neither Plato nor Aristotle thought out the essence of the *polis* (*Gesamtausgabe* 53 [1984], p. 99). Who is correct? His followers are on the run and still running.

[47] An open discussion supported by textual evidence may be found in D. Janicaud, *L'Ombre de cette pensée: Heidegger et la question politique* (Grenoble, 1990). I have reviewed it in both France and Italy; see M. Detienne, "Pour une anthropologie avec les Grecs," in A. Bonnard, ed., *Civilisation grecque*, vol. 1, 2d ed. (Brussels: Editions Complese, 1991). All these publications have been greeted with impenetrable silence. I am returning to this and will continue to do so in connection with the project sketched out in "Pour une anthropologie."

[48] I refer to Janicaud, *L'Ombre de cette pensée.*

[49] A. Momigliano, *Rivista storica italiana* 94 (1982): 184–87.

[50] Detienne 1986. Momigliano was not alone in misunderstanding this.

[51] See Detienne 1994.

[52] "La Mythologie grecque change de sens," an interview with Jean-Pierre Vernant by Henri de Saint Blanquat, *Sciences et avenir* (January 1982), 105–10.

[53] This had not been exactly the case when, in 1974–75, at the ex-Sixth Section, I embarked on a historiographical and critical analysis of ancient and contemporary representations of "myth" and "mythology."

[54] Gernet 1981, 96, 102, 104, 150; E. Cassirer, *Philosophy of Symbolic Forms*, vol. 2: *Mythological Thought* (New Haven: Yale University Press, 1953).

[55] See Vernant 1983, in particular the chapter "From Myth to Reason."

[56] The comparison emerged from Lévi-Strauss's 1970 seminar and was published as "La Cuisine de Pythagore," *Archives de sociologie des religions* 29 (1970). I used these methods for more than three years (École Pratique des Hautes Etudes, sixth section, 1969–72) in connection with bees, honey, Orion, and Orpheus, although I have not yet published any of this work except "Orphée au miel," 1974. I have sketched this "new meaning" in the afterword to *The Gardens of Adonis*, in this vol., pp. 183–94 and "Mito" (in *Enciclopedia delle scienze sociali* [Rome, 1995]).

[57] See the seminars on *Themis* summarized in the *Annuaire de l'Ecole Pratique des Hautes Études: Sciences religieuses* 49 (1990–91).

[58] On the "psychological function," see I. Meyerson, *Journal de psychologie normale et pathologique* 66 (1969): 376–77.

[59] For two approaches to Parmenides, fr. 7.5–6, see D. Furley, "Truth as What Survives the *Elenchos*: An Idea of Parmenides," in P. Huby and G. Neal, eds., *The Criterion of Truth* (Liverpool, 1989), pp. 1–13; N. L. Cordero 1990, 207–14.

[60] See Detienne 1994, in particular "Ouverture" and "Manières grecques de commencer."

[61] M. Caveing, "La Laïcisation de la parole et l'exigence rationnelle," *Raison présente* (January 1969): 85–98.

[62] I am thinking here of pp. 100–101 in ibid., at the end of the chapter "Le Procès de laïcisation."

[63] In my inquiry into writing and its new intellectual subjects, I stressed this point: even if writing down laws shaped the public space and the field of politics, it was the intellectuals—philosophers, doctors, and geometrical astronomers—who used writing to invent unprecedented subjects that opened up the intellect to new paths of exploration; see Detienne, "L'Écriture et ses nouveaux objets intellectuels en Grèce," in Detienne 1994. I return briefly to this point in "Ouverture," in Detienne 1994.

[64] {Lloyd 1990,} is an original and rich comparison of different models of reasoning, taking as its starting point an important inquiry into types of proof, verification, and argumentation between rival types of knowledge.

PART II
Convergences of Subject

MICHEL LEJEUNE

Dāmos in Mycenaean Society

1965

A model of rigorous empiricism, Lejeune's analysis of the bureaucratic lan-
guage of the "Linear B" tablets of the second millennium [BCE] (mostly
from the palaces of Knossos = KN and Pylos = PY) yields important new
socio-historical perspectives on the meaning of the Greek word dāmos *as*
the ancestor of "Western" concepts of democracy. For background on the
"Linear B" script as a reflection of "Mycenaean" society, see Palmer 1980,
27–56.

1. The Mycenaean tablets attest the word *dāmos*:

a) In composite anthroponyms such as, perhaps, *[da]-mo-ke-re-we-i* (dative, PY Fn 324) = *Dāmoklewei*, and surely *e-ke-da-mo* = *Ekhedāmos* (nomin., PY Cn 285; dative, KN Uf 1522), *e-u-da-mo* = *Eudāmos* (KN B 799, X 57; TH Z 853), *e-u-ru-da-mo* = *Eurudāmos* (KN X 166);

b) in the nominative (representing an activity of the *dāmos*) as subject of *do-se* = *dōsei* (PY Un 718; cf. § 7), and of *pa-si* = *phāsi* (PY En 704; cf. § 8);

c) in the dative after the preposition *paro* (equivalent construction, in Myce-naean, to Attic-Ionic *para* + genitive, to indicate origin) in the formula (cf. § 6) "so-and-so holds (*e-ke* = *ekhei*) such and such an allocation of land from the *dāmos*" (*pa-ro da-mo*), a formula that is encountered ten times in the Pylian cadastres in series Ea (52, etc.; scribe 43), twenty-eight times in series Eb (347, etc.; scribe 41), thirty-six times in series Ep (212, etc.; scribe 1), and two times in Eq 59 (scribe 43);

d) in the genitive in -*ō* at Knossos: twice in an inventory of draft oxen (C 59.2, 3), which, for the localities *da-22-to* and *tu-ri-so* respectively, records (ideogram: BULL) six *da-mo we-ka-ta* = *dāmō wergatai* once in another inven-tory (C 911: small animals allocated to subaltern or servile personnel), in which of the recipients, *qa-di-ja* (line 6), is designated by two characteristics, *po-ku-te-ro* (obscure term) and *da-mo do-e-ro* = *dāmō doelos* (see § 5 b);

e) probably also at Knossos (if the first character, of which only faint traces remain, is indeed *da*-) in the genitive in -*oio*, in the scant fragment B 7038:

da]-mo-jo MAN[, in which we find variety 103 of the ideogram MAN, reserved specifically for subaltern or servile personnel: apparently, mention of the same kind as *da-mo do-e-ro* (above, d);

f) in the form *da-mo*, in an indeterminable case owing to lack of context, in the scant fragments PY Fn 1427 and KN E 845;

g) as basis of the adjective *dāmios* in the formula (which appears once, PY Ea 803, scribe 43) "so-and-so holds his allocation (in kind, term *o-na-to = onāton* understood) of the *dāmos*," *e-ke da-mi-jo = ekhei dāmion*, very likely equivalent (§ 6 and note 23) to *e-ke pa-ro da-mo* (above, c);

h) as basis of the composite adjective (first term *opi* = Att. Ion. *epi*) *o-pi-da-mi-jo*, employed substantively to denote men (husbandmen in this case) who work the land of the *dāmos* and for the benefit of the *dāmos* (§ 5 b): hog farmers (PY Cn 608.2), cattle farmers (who number 60 for the locality pi–82: PY An 830.12);

i) as the first term of a composite *da-mo-ko-ro* (PY Ta 711, On 300; KN L 642, X 7922), which will be discussed later (§§ 10–12).

2. The notion of *dāmos* can be clarified by what we know or can guess about the Mycenaean social system (§§ 4–5) and (§§ 3–4) by discussion of texts in which the word appears (§§ 5–13). But the fact that our sources are account records means that our information is incomplete and often unclear about institutions that transcended everyday material realities. Furthermore, the information varies widely from site to site: to date there is nothing about Mycenae or Thebes, and the information about Pylos is far more detailed than that about Knossos. As a working hypothesis (given the fact that the rare Knossian data do not contradict the Pylian data), we may assume that the propositions that follow are valid for all Mycenaean kingdoms circa 1200.

At the lowest level, production in Mycenaean society seems to have relied on slavery. The existence of slaves (*do-e-ro, do-e-ra*) is attested by the sources, as well as by their character as entities for sale[1] and by hereditary transmission of the servile condition.[2]

The idea that the "free" population was itself divided into three classes corresponding to the three "functions" that Georges Dumézil saw as defining the hierarchy of primitive Indo-European society has been put forward as a working hypothesis by L. R. Palmer, myself, and others.[3] It does not conflict with our data but is not substantially corroborated by them either, for the data are fragmentary and more suggestive than explicit on crucial matters. Still, the hypothesis remains plausible.

Classified under the head of the "first function," that of political and religious sovereignty conjoined, is the complicated administrative and cult apparatus that we can glimpse through our texts, together with a host of civil and religious functionaries (whose precise responsibilities generally escape us). But this is not enough to prove the existence of a class as such. It is also true that the word *wanax* applies in the texts both to the Pylian chief of state and to certain gods. But does this suffice to justify the assertion that the two sources of sovereignty are twinned? To be sure, in Homer, both Agamemnon and Apollo are *anax*, but we are apt to think that this is the result of a purely verbal tradition, referring to an earlier state of civilization in which states were governed, if not by divine kings, at least by priest-kings. But what proof is there that already in the Mycenaean stage the ambiguity of the term *wanax* was not something other than a linguistic heritage from an outmoded stage of social development? In any case, the singular and eminent character of "sovereignty" in the state was indicated by the derivative of the adjective *wa-na-ka-te-ro* ending in *-teros*. It implies the existence of two distinct domains, one containing everything that comes under the head of the *wanax*, the other containing everything else.

The Mycenaean state certainly included an advanced military organization with a warrior aristocracy that waged war in chariots.[4] This is perhaps as close as we come to a genuine "class." In each Pylian realm there was also a personage[5] whose title was *ra-wa-ke-ta* = *lāwagetās*, and various bits of evidence suggest that he was the second most important person in the state after the *wanax*.[6] We will assume that this personage was the representative of the "second," or warrior, function. Thus far, however, it is only by analyzing the word, and attributing to *lāwos* the meaning that the term still has in Homer, that we deduce the warrior nature of the *ra-wa-ke-ta*, for this personage appears in our account books only by way of his "civil house" and its associated lands.

We come now to the "third function." To what extent did nonslave peasants and artisans constitute a "class"? To what degree was it organized? To what level of the administrative structure (village or township, district, or province) did such an organization belong? At the state level, was there a personage or personages who symbolized the *dāmos* as well as the *wanax* and the *lāwagetās*? These are the questions that we would like the texts concerning the *da-mo* to answer, but in fact, as we shall see, the evidence is incomplete. [. . .]

4. The existence of compound anthroponyms with *dāmos* as a first or second term (§ 1 a), parallel to compound anthroponyms with *lāwos* as a first or second term (*ra-wo-do-ko* = *Lāwodokos*, etc.; *a-ke-ra-wo* = *Agelāwos*, *a-pi-ra-wo* = *Amphilāwos*, etc.) seems to prove that, as far back as the Mycenaean age, the general notion of a civil class (*dāmos*) existed in parallel with that of a military class (*lāwos*), and shows that the two notions could equally well be represented in the "noble" register of anthroponymy ("noble" by tradition, even if, for example, the *Ekhedāmos* of PY Cn 285 and the *Agelāwos* of PY Cn 599, were in fact small livestock breeders).

Yet while it is plausible that *lāwos* was only a class denomination (which explains why **ra-wo* in isolation does not appear in our texts, since the military class manifested itself concretely in various units such as the *o-ka* [. . .]), we may ask whether, apart from proper names (where it evokes a general notion), the word *da-mo*, used in isolation, did not always denote a particular unit, a socially and geographically defined segment of the civilian population; or, in other words, whether there was any concrete existence of anything other than *dāmoi* in the plural.

The *lāwos* was no doubt an abstraction. But it had a head, the *lāwagetās*, and there are no grounds for challenging the uniqueness of the *ra-wa-ke-ta* in either Pylos or Knossos.

While all the Pylian *ra-wa-ke-si-jo*, or people belonging to the "house" of the *lāwagetās*, are mentioned[7] by only one[8] of our cadastres (Ea+Eq 59: scribe 43), it is nevertheless true that the *wa-na-ka-te-ro*, the people of the "house" of the *wanax*, are mentioned only[9] in cadastre Eo/En of *pa-ki-ja-ni-ja* (scribe 41 for the first version, 1 for the second). No doubt the *temenē*[10] of the two great personages were located in different regions, along with their "houses," that is, the personnel attached to the *temenē*. Nevertheless, one should not infer from this that there was any division of territorial authority between *wanax* and *lāwagetās* or a plurality of *lāwagetai*.

For Knossos[11] one text appears to create difficulties, the catalog of men. As 1516, whose first rubric, *ko-no-si-ja ra-wa-<ke>-si-ja*, if read as "estate of the *lāwagetās* of Knossos," might suggest that there were several *lāwagetai* in Crete. In fact, the words should be read as "estate of *lāwagetās* at Knossos. The text lists the personnel of several "houses." It begins with Knossos, the location of the *temenē* of the Cretan *lāwagetās*. It continues with [. . .] *to*, the location of the estate of the *basileus*[12] *a-nu-to*; and then with *se-to-i-ja*, the site of the estate of the *basileus su-ke-re*. It must have continued on one or more additional tablets, which have not been recovered.

If the *lāos* constituted a class, that class had, in each Mycenaean kingdom, one supreme representative in the person of the *lāwagetās*. We must now examine the data pertaining to the *dāmos* and the "third function" in the light of this information about the "second function."

5. In our texts, the *da-mo* appears as a local administrative entity with an agricultural function:

a) It owned land, a portion of which was parceled out to individual beneficiaries who enjoyed rights to what the land produced (§ 6) while another portion certainly remained the undivided property of the community.

b) This undivided portion was probably exploited collectively. It is plausible to imagine the "slaves of the *dāmos*" (§ 1 d, e) and the "beasts of burden of the *dāmos*" (§ 1 d) being used on it, as both were collective property. Cow and hog breeders *o-pi-da-mi-jo* (§ 1 h) raised the communal livestock.

c) The *dāmos* produced crops and livestock that enabled it to sustain communal personnel and obtain necessary commodities through barter. This production also allowed it to meet its tax obligations to the Palace and its religious obligations (cf. § 7) to the temples. No doubt the communal income came partly in the form of dues in kind paid by those to whom communal lands were distributed and partly from collective exploitation of the undivided communal land.

d) The *dāmos* appears to have been managed by a council of farmers, probably under the supervision or control of a functionary representing the Palace (§ 8).

6. Our Pylian cadastres distinguish between parcels (*ko-to-na* = *ktoiniai*, § 9) of two sorts, the so-called *ki-ti-me-na* (= *ktimenai*) and the *ke-ke-me-na* (= **kekesmenai?*). The pair of great cadastres Eo/En and Eb/Ep from *pa-ki-ja-ni-ja* separately consider the *ki-ti-me-na* lands (Eo/En) and the *ke-ke-me-na* lands (Eb/Ep). The *dāmos* is concerned only with the latter. Just as scribe 41 established both preparatory documents Eo and Eb, and scribe 1 took responsibility for both final drafts En and Ep, so, too, did scribe 43 establish both preparatory documents (Ea+Ec 481+Eq 59) for two other cadastres, one of *ki-ti-me-na* parcels,[13] the other of *ke-ke-me-na* parcels,[14] concerning a region other than *pa-ki-ja-ni-ja*. The final draft of these two cadastres either was not done or has not been recovered. Although the mention of the *da-mo*[15] and that of the *ke-ke-me-na* character of the lands concerned are not explicitly conjoined, we may assume that either mention in Ea is enough to indicate a legal situation analogous to that in cadastre Eb/Ep, to which the following observations will be limited.

The activity of the *dāmos* was to take certain parcels of its *ke-ke-me-na* lands and assign the usufruct[16] of that land to certain individuals. The beneficiary was then said[17] to hold (*e-ke* = *ekhei*) the parcel in question in usufruct (*o-na-to* = *onāton*) by allocation[18] from the *dāmos* (*pa-ro da-mo* = *paro dāmōi*). Allocations of this type were not normally transferable to third parties.[19]

In fact, out of an Ep total of *ke-ke-me-na* land that can be evaluated at more than 8,000 liters of seed, those allocated as *e-to-ni-jo*[20] represented more than 1,000 liters; those allocated as *ka-ma*[21] represented nearly 5,000 liters; those allocated as *o-na-to pa-ro da-mo*, with which we are especially concerned here, represented roughly 2,000 liters The beneficiaries of the latter were (cf. § 9) called *ko-to-ne-ta* = *ktoinetai*; they numbered roughly fifty.

The *ko-to-neta* included (for roughly one-third of the *o-na-ta pa-ro da-mo*, hence roughly one-twelfth of the *ke-ke-me-na* land) a privileged subcategory, the *ko-to-no-o-ko* = *ktoinookhoi*,[22] a group of twelve members (*a-da-ma-o*, III; *a-i-qe-u*, XII; *a-tu-ko*, IV; *a3-ti-jo-qo*, I; *ke-ra-u-jo*, IX; *ko-tu-ro2*, XI; *ku-so*, VIII; *pa-ra-ko*, X; *pi-ke-re-u*, VI; *ra-ku-ro*, VII; *ta-ta-ro*, V; *wa-na-ta-jo*, II). They are listed at the top of the cadastre (Ep 301.2–14), owing to their personal importance (we shall see in § 8 that they may have been a sort of "board of directors" for the *dāmos*) rather than the physical extent of their allocations *pa-ro da-mo*.[23] These, though not purely symbolic, were generally not very impressive. I am inclined to view them as token allocations to board members, most of whom were in other respects well endowed (see below). It is plausible to assume, moreover, that the first man named, *a3-i-jo-qo*, who also has the largest allocation (174 liters), was the head man of the group.

Furthermore, nearly all of our *ko-to-no-o-ko* had other land holdings. Two of them were also *ka-ma-e-we* (holding *ke-ke-me-na* land): *ko-tu-ro2* (Ep 617.13 = Eb 839) and *pa-ra-ko* (Ep 617.11 = Eo 173), and there may also have been a third, if the restoration *[pi-ke]-re-u* in Ep 617.6 = Eb 177 is correct. Six were also *te-re-ta* (holding *ki-ti-me-na* land): *a-da-ma-o* (En 659.8 = Eo 351), *a-i-qe-u* (En 659.12 = Eo 471), *a3-ti-jo-qo* (En 74.11 = Eo 247), *pi-ke-re-u* (En 74.20 = Eo 160), *ra-ku-ro* (En 659.15 = Eo 281), *wa-na-ta-jo* (En 609.3 = Eo 211); and two others had just become so:[24] *pa-ra-ko* (Eo 224.3) and *ta-ta-ro* (Eo 224.7). Each of these prominent individuals thus held not only the *o-na-to* of the *ko-to-no-o-ko* but often other allocations two to four times larger.[25]

To sum up, then, the *pa-ki-ja-ni-ja* cadastres show that a quarter of the *ke-ke-me-na* land was divided among roughly fifty *ko-to-ne-ta* as *o-na-to pa-ro da-mo*. These fifty or so *ko-to-ne-ta* included the twelve *ko-to-no-o-ko* (§ 8) along with other beneficiaries, most of whom had ties to the cult (*i-je-re-u*, *i-je-re-ja*, *ki-ri-te-wi-ja*, thirty or so *te-o-jo do-e-ro* or *do-er-a*, etc.). The remaining three-quarters were divided among two types of parcel, the *e-to-ni-jo* and the *ka-ma*.

What we do not know is what procedures were used to make these assign-ments,[26] for what period of time they were made, or what payments in kind were exchanged for them. Furthermore, it is extremely likely that the term *ke-ke-me-na* did not apply to all the land of the *dāmos* but only to that which was distributed in this form (which, it may be worth mentioning in passing, supports etymological interpretations of *ke-ke-me-na* based on the idea of par-celing out: root of κεάζω). Indeed, we must assume that in addition to the land that was distributed as *o-na-to pa-ro da-mo*, *ka-ma*, or *e-to-ni-jo*, an important reserve of undivided land remained (§ 5). But this land does not appear in the cadastre (which was an official record of land distribution).

Of course one might object that, before anything else is mentioned, includ-ing the *ko-to-no-o-ko*, inventory Ep begins (Ep 301.1 = Eb 818) with a line giv-ing the size (132 liters) of what is called *ke-ke-me-na ko-to-na a-no-no*, and *a-no-no* (*an-ōnos*) appears to have the form of a privative corresponding to *anā-tos*. But this cannot be the undivided land of the *dāmos* for two reasons. First, it is unlikely that the communal property of *pa-ki-ja-ni-ja* that remained under collective ownership accounted for only 1.5 percent of the total land. Second, we find (in other cadastres[27]) individual assignments from these *a-no-no* lands. It would appear, therefore, that what was *a-no-no* was the small amount of the land of the *dāmos* intended for distribution (*ke-ke-me-na*) and temporarily un-assigned but available for subsequent distribution. Our cadastres had no need to account for the lands of the *dāmos* that were to remain collective property, hence we know nothing about what such land was called (other than *ke-ke-me-na*) and how much of it there was.

7. The *da-mo* of cadastre Eb/Ep (dealing with the locality known as *pa-ki-ja-ni-ja*) and that of cadastre Ea must be entities of the same nature but geo-graphically distinct. By chance, we happen to know about a third Pylian *da-mo*

(Un 718) associated with the locality known as *sa-re-pe-da*. In this case, the sources tell us not about its internal organization but about one of its collective obligations.

Agricultural offerings to Poseidon were expected from two groups of subjects who were clearly distinguished by both the text of the tablet and its physical arrangement. The first group include an individual named *e-ke-ra2-wo* (for 480 liters of wheat, 108 liters of wine, etc.),[28] and the *da-mo* (for 240 liters of wheat, 72 liters of wine, etc.). In the second, the *ra-wa-ke-ta* (72 liters of flour, 24 liters of wine, etc.) and the *ka-ma wo-ro-ki-jo-ne-jo* (72 liters of wheat, 12 liters of wine, etc.).

Thus far, this is the only text to mention the collective contributions required of a *dāmos* (*da-mo do-se: dāmos dōsei*). In this instance these are religious contributions. It is likely, however, that the *dāmoi* were also required to make fiscal contributions and that they were among the taxpayers who assured the palace in each district of a supply of farm products (series Ma, etc.).

8. The *dāmos* was not just a landed estate of which a portion was subject to being parceled out to tenants (§ 6), nor was it just a group of farmers liable for payments in kind to a temple or perhaps the palace (§ 7). It was also an administrative entity endowed with a legal personality. We learn this from the curious mention of a case[29] in cadastre Eb/Ep for *pa-ki-ja-ni-ja*, concerning a significant plot of land[30] held by the priestess *e-ri-ta*.

Ep 704.5: *e-ri-ta i-je-re-ja e-ke e-u-ke-to-qe e-to-ni-jo e-ke-e te-o da-mo-de-mi pa-si ko-to-na-o ke-ke-me-na-o o-na-to e-ke-e* . . .

Eb 297: *i-je-re-ja e-ke-qe e-u-ke-to-qe e-to-ni-jo e-ke-e te-o ko-to-no-o-ko-de ko-to-na-o ke-ke-me-na-o o-na-ta e-ke-e* . . .

The first clause of the sentence is clear: *hiereia ekhei eukhetoi kwe etōnion ekheen theōi*, "the priestess holds (this parcel) and professes that she holds it for the goddess[31] as *e-to-ni-jo*."[32] The second clause is opposed to the first by *de*. In version Ep, this clause has a verb *pa-si* = *phāsi*, the subject of which has to be *da-mo: dāmos de min phāsi ktoināōn kekesmenāōn onāton ekheen*, "but the *dāmos* asserts that it holds it in usufruct on the grounds that it comes out of the *ke-ke-me-na* parcels." In version Eb, the second clause has no verb in the indicative: *eukhetoi* must be a common factor for both clauses. The subject of *ekheen* is not expressed (Ep: *min*) but may easily be inferred from the first clause. In both these respects, the Eb version is more rapid and elliptical than the Ep version. It is nevertheless correct and intelligible: *ktoinookhoi de* (that is, *min eukhontoi*) *ktoināōn kekesmenāōn onāta*[33] *ekheen*.

The difference between the two versions reveals the equivalence *dāmos* = *ktoinookhoi*. In the pending case (not yet settled at the time the inventory was made), one of the parties (the plaintiff) is the *dāmos*, or local collectivity, represented by the college of twelve *ktoinookhoi* (§ 6).

9. Let me digress for a moment to consider the word *ko-to-na* together with its derivatives and compounds. In Knossos,[34] we have three examples (Uf 981,

1022, 1031) of the formula so-and-so *ekhei ktoinān phutēriān (e-ke ko-to-i-na pu-te-ri-ja)*. But we know the word chiefly from Pylos (roughly 175 examples): cadastre Eb/Ep of the *ke-ke-me-na* lands of *pa-ki-ja-ni-ja* (in which our *ko-to-no-o-ko* appear), cadastre Eo/En of the *ki-ti-me-na* lands of *pa-ki-ja-ni-ja*, and other cadastral documents (Ea, Ec, Eq 59, Sn 64 + An 218, Wa 784). Generally modified by one of the two epithets *ke-ke-me-na* or *ki-ti-me-na*, the word occurs either in the rubric noun (with the genitive of the holder's name), in the accusative as object of the verb *ekheen*, "to hold," or in the genitive modifying *onāton* ("allocation in usufruct of a *ktoinā*").

From the root $*k^sei$- Mycenaean derives: a present $*kteimi$,[35] with verbal participles and adjectives *ktimenos* and *aktitos*;[36] an agent noun *ktitās*, with compound *metaktitās*;[37] and finally, the derivative *ktoinā*.[38] For the time being it seems to me that all these terms basically have an abstract rather than a concrete meaning; they concern landed institutions, not the physical location of buildings or crops. Properly speaking, *ki-ti-me-na* must have meant "foundation land," that is, land (probably belonging to a temple) distributed (in accordance with some kind of charter) among the members (of whom there were a definite number, on the order of a dozen) of a college of *telestai*. In Pylos, cadastres Eo/En and Es (even though the latter does not explicitly contain either *ki-ti-me-na* or *te-re-ta*) pertain to institutions of this type (two different temples). By contrast, the lands of the *dāmos*, which (apart from the portion reserved for collective use) were subject to a non-organic and much more varied distribution, were called "distributable lands" (*ke-ke-me-na*). Within this general framework, it must be admitted that the primary sense of *ktoinā* (*"foundation") was doubly inflected in Mycenaean. In the first place, it shifted from the abstract (institution) to the concrete (the result of applying an institution) and designated the "plot" (attributed to the *telestās* by the foundation charter). Furthermore, its use was also extended to cultivable "plots" of other origins, most notably those which came from the division of the *dāmos*.

The word survived, albeit weakly, in the Greek of the first millennium (perhaps in Boeotia, since there seems to be no other possible origin for the radical root vowel -*u*- transmitted by Hesychius, and surely at Rhodes, in inscriptions). This survival lasted in Boeotia until at least the third century (because *oi* > *u* did not take place prior to 250 there), and in Rhodes until the Roman era.

The gloss κτύναι ἢ κτοῖναι χωρήσεις προγονικῶν ἱερείων, ἢ δῆμος μεμερισμένος should probably be read[39] as κτύν<η>, ἢ δῆμος μεμερισμένος. A thousand years after our Mycenaean documents were produced, it preserved the memory of a land-distribution institution combining two traditions, which can readily be associated with the *ki-ti-me-na* and *ke-ke-me-na* lands of our tablets.

In Rhodes,[40] κτοίνα did not denote the "parcel" of land but retained the sense of "collegial community" (governed by a foundation charter). The members of the community were named κτοινᾶται (D) or κτοινέται (E; cf. Myc.

ko-to-ne-ta). The Rhodian κτοῖναι may have been fairly numerous, and a Camirean decree (D) arranged for a census. We know the names of one or two of them (A: Ποτιδαίων; E: Ματίων). The κτοίνα held regular assemblies (B 8), celebrated sacrifices (B 4), and voted on honorary decrees and the attribution of crowns (A, B, E, F); certain lands of the κτοίνα could be given as gifts (C 10).

In Mycenaean, *ko-to-na* served as the base of the compound *ko-to-no-o-ko* and the derivatives *ko-to-ne-ta, ko-to-ne-u*, whose respective meanings are worth examining more closely.

To judge by the correspondences between the summary (Eb 236+ 317+847+901) and the final draft (Ep) of the *ke-ke-me-na* cadastre from *pa-ki-ja-ni-ja*, the term *ko-to-ne-ta* (Eb 901) = *ktoinetās*[41] refers not to any holder of *ko-to-na* but to one who holds a parcel in usufruct taken from the *dāmos* (*o-na-to pa-ro da-mo*). The term *ko-to-no-o-ko* (Ep 301.2–14) = *ktoinookhos*[42] has a still more restricted sense and applies to a limited, legally privileged category of *ko-to-ne-ta*.

On the other hand, it is more difficult to determine the sense of the derivative *ktoineus*.[43] We have (in the plural) only one example (PY Be 995, scribe not determined), an isolated (and mutilated—the number is missing at the end of the tablet) element in a personal inventory, and we do not know the administrative subdivision of Pylos to which it pertains: *ko-to-ne-we* MAN, with[44] variety 103 of the ideogram MAN, reserved (to judge from the Knossos examples) for personnel of humble or servile condition. Were these perhaps slaves assigned to work the *ktoinai*?

10. In case of dispute about the distribution of land belonging to the *dāmos* (and therefore perhaps responsible for that distribution) the college of *ko-to-no-o-ko* could be called upon. How the members of this group were chosen we do not know. Nor do we know what administrative duties they had or what duties were assigned at this level to one or more representatives of the central government.[45]

Beyond what we can guess about the semiautonomous organization of the rural commune, can we assume that officials at higher levels (district? province?) were assigned to deal with issues pertaining to the *dāmoi*, or even that, at the state level, there was an official whose duties made him a symbol of the *dāmos* as a class (that of proper names, § 4) alongside the *wanax* and the *lāwagetās*?

In fact, for reasons related to the structure of the word itself, it is the *da-mo-ko-ro* that is at issue here. This, too, was an institution common to both Knossos and Pylos, but the two occurrences of the word at Knossos tell us nothing, and the two examples from Pylos (Ta 711.1, On 300.7) are difficult to interpret.

While the occurrence of *da-mo-* in this compound is certain (but hard to interpret: *dāmoi* or *dāmos*), the second term, *-ko-ro*, is ambiguous, hence its meaning is uncertain. [. . .]

11. The title (Ta 711.1: *o-wi-de pu2-ke-qi-ri o-te wa-na-ka te-ke 85-ke-wa da-mo-ko-ro*) of inventory Ta of movable property leads to the following observations:

a) Apparently one has to distinguish between regular inventories, required for the palace's annual accounts, and occasional inventories. The latter category includes the two Pylian inventories, whose titles begin with the formula *hōs wide* so-and-so (with the name of the inspector assigned to do the inventory) and continue with an indication of the circumstances in which each inventory was made. In the case of Eq 213.1, this is *o-wi-de a-ko-so-ta to-ro-qe-jo-me-no a-ro-u-ra a2-ri-sa*.[46] In the case of Ta 711.1, it *is o-wi-de pu2-ke-qi-ri o-te wa-na-ka te-ke 85-ke-wa da-mo-ko-ro*.[47] In one case the occasion is made explicit by a participle *trokweomenos*. In the other, it is by a temporal proposition (*hote thēke*).

b) Starting with the idea that the movable property inventoried in series Ta was from a royal tomb, L. R. Palmer interpreted *wa-na-ka te-ke* as "rex sepeliuit." In order for a sovereign to preside over a funeral, it must have involved the burial of an important personage, probably a member of the royal family. Since there is no indication that 85-*ke-wa* of An 192 and Jo 438 was one, another 85-*ke-wa* may have been involved, a personage of high rank designated (exceptionally in Mycenaean) by an individual name plus patronymic. Hence we may assume that *Dāmoklos = Dāmokleweios*. Now, it so happens that On 300 gives a list of functionaries (first for the Near Province and then for the Far Province): first local officials (one *ko-re-te* per district), then a *du-ma*, and then a final personage; the list for the Far Province has for this last personage (with no indication of his duties) *te-po-se-u*, which is an anthroponym. Hence we may assume that he was a provincial governor (too well known to require mention of his position). Furthermore, since the list for the Near Province (which included the capital, Pylos) ends symmetrically with *da-mo-ko-ro*, we may look upon the son of Damocles who is the 85-*ke-wa* in question as the governor of the province of Pylos, a position that would have qualified him to preside over a royal funeral.

c) This construction depends on two independent assumptions: the funerary interpretation of *wa-na-ka te-ke* and the hypothesis that *da-mo-ko-ro* is a proper name. There is no reason why we cannot accept the first of these assumptions while rejecting the second, for if *da-mo-ko-ro* meant something like "provincial governor," Palmer's general theory would remain intact. In fact, I am inclined to reject both assumptions.

d) To be sure, series Ta inventories luxury items whose rich decoration is minutely described. Occasionally, however, it also mentions objects in poor condition, such as the tripod (641.1) whose supports were damaged by fire (*ti-ri-po . . . a-pu ke-ka-u-me-no ke-ra2: tripos . . . apokekaumenos skelea*). It is hard to accept that this rules out the possibility that these items were destined for the throne room without also ruling out the possibility that they come from a royal tomb. Furthermore, there is not a single example in Greek of *theinai* used without qualification in the sense of "bury."

e) In Greek, moreover, a hypocoristic (such as *Dāmoklos* would be) is never linked to another anthroponym as a patronymic designation. In Mycenaean, as well as in the Aeolian of the first millennium, this function was fulfilled by adjectives ending in *-ios*: *di-ko-na-ro a-da-ra-ti-jo* (D. *Adrastios*, PY An 656), *a-re-ku-tu-ru-wo e-te-wo-ke-re-wi-jo* (*Alektruwōn Etewokleweios*, PY An 654), *ne-qe-u e-te-wo-ke-re-wi-jo* (N. E., PY Sn 64), *ro-u-ko ku-sa-me-ni-jo* (L. *Kursamenios*, PY An 516), etc.

f) In my view, it is best to stick to the traditional interpretation according to which *wa-na-ka* is the subject, 85-*ke-wa* the object, and *da-mo-ko-ro* (a designation of office) the attribute of 85-*ke-wa*, which gives θῆκε the well-established senses of "*instituit*," "*creauit*." But this requires further explanation.

g) We are dealing with an inventory of the royal treasury (which may have contained objects in poor condition awaiting repair or replacement). The official previously assigned to the treasury was a certain 85-*ke-wa*. He is transferred to another post and named *da-mo-ko-ro*. He is replaced by one *pu2-ke-qi-ri*. Given the value of the items in question, an inventory was of course drawn up when one official replaced another in charge of the treasury; this was an occasional inventory (see "a," above), hence the formula *hōs wide . . . hote.*

12. We have no idea how civil, military, or religious powers were delegated at any level of Mycenaean society. The texts offer no solid evidence of, for example, a hereditary[48] attribution of functions or an elective one or one determined by drawing lots. The only document that mentions a designation (and then only in an incidental way) is our Ta 711, in which we see the *wanax* appoint a *dāmokoros*.

In the absence of any terms of comparison, it is difficult to judge the hierarchical rank of the *da-mo-kor-o*. If the sovereign himself decided which officials to appoint, how far down the hierarchy did he intervene (at the province level? the district level? and so on)? What proof is there, moreover, that *wa-na-ka te-ke* was not an administrative formula in general use, which applied not only to direct appointments by the sovereign but also to appointments made in his name by others at lower levels of the hierarchy?

13. We come now to the evidence of On 300, a mutilated and hard-to-interpret text. This mentions a distribution of the (unidentified) staple 154 to the principal functionaries of the Near Province (lines 1–7) and the Far Province (lines 8–12), in each case listing first the district prefects (*ko-re-te-re*), then a *du-ma* (lines 6 and 12), and finally a *da-mo-ko-ro* (line 7) and *te-po-se-u* (line 12) respectively.

There are gaps in the text. Furthermore, it is not entirely consistent with the "canonical" administrative structure, for if (by interpreting the gaps) we come to the conclusion that there were nine *ko-re-te-re* in the Near Province, there were certainly only six (rather than the expected seven) in the Far Province.

What is more, the drafting of the text is not homogeneous: for the Near Province, we find (line 2) in the midst of the *ko-re-te-re* (designated by title and district only) an anthroponym (*a-pi-a2-ro*), and we do not know whether this was or was not the name of a *ko-re-te* and, if it was, why this name was indicated in this particular way. Another disparity: the *du-ma* in line 6 was supposed to be designated not only by name *[du]-ni-jo* but also by title and location; the one on line 12 can have been designated, apart from his title, only by his name or his location (the latter being more likely). And the final disparity is that one list ends with an appellative (*da-mo-ko-ro*, line 7), while the other ends with an anthroponym (*te-po-se-u*, line 12). Taken together, these observations undermine one's confidence in the rigor of the text's presentation.

With these reservations in mind, however, we may assume that the information in On 300 is symmetrical for the two provinces and in each case arranged in ascending hierarchical order. If this is correct, the text would list, for each province, first the district officials (*ko-re-te-re*), then two provincial functionaries (whose respective jurisdictions we do not know), a *du-ma* and a *da-mo-ko-ro*. On grounds of symmetry, we might conclude that *te-po-se-u* (line 12) was a *da-mo-ko-ro*. With reference to Ta 711, we might then infer that the *da-mo-ko-ro* of the Near Province (line 7) was or was about to be *85-ke-wa*.[49] Thus to the extent that we can rely on On 300, we may assume that the *da-ma-ko-ro* was an important personage (but not the only important personage) at the provincial (as opposed to state) level of the hierarchy. Nothing in the sources or in our analysis of the word allows us to say anything more about what his duties may have been, however.

Correction (June 1965): Piecing together fragments of the Knossian tablets (results still unpublished) has revealed a coherent subseries in the C tablets (ideogram: HOG). A hog is awarded to (or a hog is supplied by) functionaries designated by title: *a-to-mo, du-ma,* and *da-mo-ko-ro* (the last example comes from X 7922 completed by another fragment). The similarity between the Knossian and Pylian institutions now appears better at the level of the *du-ma* and *da-mo-ko-ro*.

TRANSLATED BY ARTHUR GOLDHAMMER

NOTES

[1] KN B 822: [. . .] *si-ra-ko qi-ri-ja-to* [. . .] *do-e-ro* MAN 1 (with variety *103* of the ideogram MAN reserved, it appears, for persons of subaltern or servile condition): S. *priato doelon,* "S. bought a slave."

[2] In the catalog of slave women PY An 607, where (exceptionally) the ancestry of the individuals in question is indicated, all have either a slave father or a slave mother or both.

[3] Most recently in a brilliant essay by Yoshida 1964.

[4] Recall the 140 or so tablets or fragments in series Sc from Knossos, recording the assignment of armor, chariots, and horses to various "equestrians."

[5] On the uniqueness of the *ra-wa-ke-ta*, see below, § 4.

[6] In particular, the only two *temenē* that we know of are the *wa-na-ka-te-ro te-me-no* (an area evaluated at 3600 liters of seed) and the *ra-wa-ke-si-jo te-me-no* (1200 liters), and the two were linked in PY Er 312.

[7] Either by name, as in *ku-ro₂* (Ea 814), *ru-ko-ro* (Ea 132, 782, 823, 882, 1424), or by occupation, as in *a-mo-te-u* (cartwright, Ea 421, 809), *ma-ra-te-we* (plural in *-ēwes*, of uncertain meaning; Na 245), *su-qo-ta* ("hog breeder": Ea 822). One or the other for the mutilated word beginning with *e[* in Eq 59.

[8] Add Na 245, which locates the *ma-re-te-we ra-wa-ke-si-jo* at *e-wi-te-wi-jo*. Unfortunately the other instances of the toponym (Mn 456, Vn 130) do not allow us to situate this town or even to determine which of the two provinces it belonged to.

[9] Nevertheless, if the reconstruction is correct, one personage *[wa-na]-ka-te-ro* may appear in Eb 903; but cadastre Eb/Ep, like Eo/En, concerns the *pa-ki-ja-ni-ja* district, and there are a number of people with allocations who appear in both cadastres.

[10] See note 6, above.

[11] Derivative only attested (not *ra-wa-ke-ta*): As 1516, *ra-wa-ke-<si>-ja*; E 1529, *ra-wa-ke-si-ja*; F 288, *ra-w-a-<ke>-si-ja*: X 154, *ra-wa-ke-si* [. . . ; in two of the four examples (As, F), lapsus by scribe (character omitted).

[12] The *basilēwes* of the Mycenaean age were not yet (or no longer) local magistrates. We know nine at Pylos by name: *a-ke-ro* (Jo 438), *a-ki-to* (Fn 50, 867), *a-pi-ka-ra-do* (Ae 398), *a-pi-qo-ta* (Jn 431), *a-ta-no* (Fn 50), *e-ri-ko-wo* (Jn 845), *ke-ko* (Fn 50), *pa-qo-si-jo* (Jn 601). For Knossos, in addition to As 1516, see K 875, which lists six *basilēwiai*.

[13] Ea 71, 756, 781, 817, 821.

[14] Ea 305, 480, 757, 801, 802, 806, 809, 922, 1042; Eq 59.2 and 3.

[15] Mention of *pa-ro da-mo* (Ea 52, 136, 258, 259, 480, 773, 778, 808, 816, 824; Eq 59.4 and 7) or *da-mi-jo* (Ea 803; cf. § 1 g and note 17).

[16] Usufruct (*o-na-to*) was the right generally granted with allocations of *ke-ke-me-na* lands (except, apparently, those granted as *e-to-ni-jo*: Ep 704.5 = Eb 297, Ep 539.14 = Eb 473). Usufruct (*o-na-to*) was also the right granted with any parcel (*ki-ti-me-na* or *ke-ke-me-na*) transferred to a third party by the original beneficiary.

[17] The preparatory cadastre Ea once (803) uses a different formula (*e-ke da-mi-jo = ekhei dāmion*) in speaking of a certain *ka-do*, but I do not believe that its meaning was different from *e-ke pa-ro da-mo*.

[18] Prepositions marking origin were construed with the dative in Mycenaean (as well as in Arcado-Cypriot); *pa-ro da-mo* corresponds in meaning to Attic παρὰ δήμου.

[19] Only known exception: the priestess *e-ri-ta*, having received an *o-na-to pa-ro da-mo* evaluated at 48 liters of wheat (Ep 704.3 = Eb 409), transferred a fraction (18 liters) to a *te-o-jo do-e-ra* named *u-wa-mi-ja* by way of *ke-ra = geras* (Ep 704.2 = Eb 416). This is also the only known use of γέρας in Mycenaean.

[20] An *e-to-ni-o* (reading uncertain [. . .]), was in any case different (see note 16) from an allocation of usufruct; two are known: one (contested) by *e-ri-ta* (with the rank of *i-je-re-ja*), the other by *a-pi-me-de* (with the rank of *e-qe-ta*); they were considerable (468 and 652 liters respectively).

[21] A *ka-ma* (reading uncertain; probably neuter in *-as*, to judge by the derivation *ka-ma-e-u*) was an allocation of usufruct under special conditions (not very clear to us): obligation of *wo-ze-e*, etc. In Ep 301.2–14, ten *ka-ma-e-we* are enumerated (two with allocations on the order of 1,200 to 1,5000 liters). There are grounds for adding the *klāwiphoros ka-pa-ti-ja* (Ep. 704.7), the allocation of which (on the order of 1,250 liters, apparently) was a *ka-ma*, to judge by the obligations attached to it (*wo-ze-e*, etc.). A *ka-ma-e-u* (like a *te-re-ta* in cadastre En) could transfer to a third party a portion of his land (as in Ep 617.12 = Eo 173.2 = Ep 539.5, for the benefit of *po-so-re-ja*; Ep 617.14 = Eb

1347, for the benefit of *we-ra*[.], Ep 539.5, for the benefit of *me-re-u*); but (in proportion to the portion transferred?) the obligations of the *ka-ma-e-u* passed to the new *onātēr*.

[22] Eleven of the twelve Eb tablets pertaining to this category have survived. In all of them, scribe 41 has indicated *ko-to-no-o-ko*. But in Ep 301 scribe 1 omitted any such notation for the first five names on his list (lines 2–6). He changed his mind (and the blank line 7 may indicate this change) and completed the list (lines 8–14) with an indication of *ko-to-no-o-ko* beside each of the seven names. Then he tried to correct the beginning of the text by clumsily adding *ko-to-no-o-ko* to the first name in the small space left above line 2. Finally, he decided not to attempt this difficult correction for lines 3–6 (perhaps in the belief that the addition of *ko-to-no-o-ko* on line 2 would be extended to the other names as well).

[23] Allocations whose amounts are indicated: 174 liters (I), 84 liters (X), 72 liters (XII), 60 liters (II), 48 liters (III, IX), 12 liters (XI), 6 liters (VIII).

[24] Originally, fourteen *te-re-ta* (*telestai*) shared the *ki-ti-me-na* land, and the title of En 609 retains a trace of this state of affairs. But series En lists only thirteen *te-re-ta*. Textual differences (concerning the *o-na-te-re*) between Eo 224 and En 609.10–18 show that changes took place between the preparation of preliminary tablets Eo (scribe 41) and final version En (scribe 1). In the meantime, two lots of *pa-ra-ko* and *ta-ta-ro* were combined into one and transferred to *a-ma-ru-ta*.

[25] In the list that follows, the first number is the *ko-to-no-o-ko* allocation and the second the allocation from other sources: *a-da-ma-o*, 48 + 216 liters; *a-i-qe-u*, 72 + 144 liters; a_3–*ti-jo-qo*, 174 + 188 liters; *ka-tu-ro2*, 12 + 60 liters; *pa-ra-ko*, 84 + 120 liters; *wa-na-ta-jo*, 60 + 242 liters.

[26] In one case (Ep 617.10 = Eb 159), the drawing of lots is mentioned in connection with the assignment of a *ka-ma*, which passed from the hands of *si-ri-jo* to those of *pe-re-qo-ta*: *[pe-re-]qo-ta pa-de-we-u [e-]ke-qe ka-ma o-na-to si-ri-jo-<jo>-r-ake* (Ep: *si-ri-jo*[sic]; Eb: *si-[ri]-jo-jo*); *onāton Silioio* (uel *Sirioio*) *lakhe* is an explanatory parenthesis added to the standard formula *e-ke-(qe) ka-ma*.

[27] Ea 922 (for an amount of 12 liters): *a-pi-a₂-ro e-ke* (*Amphialos ekhei*) *ke-ke-me-na ka-to-na-no-no* [sic]; Ea 801 (for an amount of 132 liters): *ku-ru-me-no-jo me-ri-te-wo ke-ke-me-[na- ko]-to-no a-no-no*.

[28] His function is unknown, but his importance was considerable (to judge by Er 880, Un 219, Un 718, etc.). As for his name (stem in *-vn*, gen. *-wo-no*, dat. *-wo-ne*), I do not agree with Palmer that this comes from *Ekhelāwōn*. For one thing, there are no other examples of an amplification by *-ōn* of a second term such as *-lāwos*. For another, because ra_2 is equivalent to *ri-ja* (and one has *[e]-ke-ri-ja-wa* in Qa 1292). [. . .]

[29] This was noted long ago, and the two texts have been treated to much discussion and commentary. [For further insights on these essential texts, see Muellner 1976—EDS.]

[30] See n. 20; 468 liters according to Ep, 474 liters according to Eb; scribe 1 in Ep probably made a slip.

[31] Another possible interpretation (assuming that the goddess herself held the parcel): *eu-khetoi kwe etōnion ekheen theon*.

[32] See n. 20.

[33] This plural can perhaps be explained by the fact that the priestess has two allocations of *ke-ke-me-na* lands, one of them (Ep 704.3 = Eb 409) modest (48 liters), whose *o-na-to pa-ro da-mo* character is not challenged by the plaintiff while the other is the subject of the litigation in question. Text Eb can then be read: "the kt. state that the priestess has nothing but these allocations in usufruct."

[34] For Knossos there is nothing equivalent to the great Pylian cadastres. Nevertheless, we do have attestations of *ko-to-i-na* and *ki-ti-me-[na]* (X 7753), *ke-ke-me-na* (UF 835, 993; X 664, 7732, 7913), *te-re-ta* (Am 826; B 779, 7036; Uf 839, 990; X 1018), etc. Recall that (except in the final syllable), the Knossian scribes (unlike the Pylian ones) often wrote the second element of diphthongs in *i*: hence *ko-to-i-na* (KN) instead of *ko-to-na* (PY).

[35] It would later be replaced by *ktizō*; 3rd pl. *ktiensi* (*ki-ti-e-si*, PY Na 1179; *ki-ti-je-si*, PY Na 520).

[36] PY Er 880, Na 537, 925, 1088: *a-ki-ti-to*.

[37] PY An 610 and 624: *ki-ti-ta* and *me-ta-ki-ti-ta*.

[38] The Hesychian tradition is to put the accent on the root, and there is no major reason for discarding it. One does have ποι-νή, but also θοί-νη [. . .].

[39] When *oi* became *u* in Boeotian, *ai* had already shifted to *ē* more than a century earlier, hence my correction κτῦν<η>. The two other corrections were previously discussed by various commentators on Rhodian inscriptions.

[40] From west to east: A) *IG*, XII. 1. 1033 (Karpathos, temple of Poseidon at Porthmos; 2nd c.); B) ibid., 746 (Rhodes, Siana; 1st c.?); C) ibid., 736 (Rhodes, Rhonkion; 3rd c.); D) ibid., 694 (Rhodes, Kamiros; 3rd c.); E) ibid., 157 (Rhodes, city of Rhodos; 1st c.); F) *BCH*, 10, 1886, 261 (Rhodian Pereus, Phoenix; a relatively late and often faulty text, with slips such as πτοίνας for κτοίνας).

[41] Note that these derivatives of names, of which there are no examples in Homer, were already Mycenaean, in which one finds derivatives not only of thematic names but of other nominal types as well.

[42] Hiatus maintained either by sense of the composition or because of the initial etymological aspiration of -*(h)okhos*. Cf. Myc. *wa-tu-o-ko* (anthroponym, PY Ea 136) = *Wast-w(h)okhos*, etc.

[43] In Mycenaean as in later Greek, names in -*a/ā* gave rise to derivatives in -*eus*, in which the -*a/ā* was elided. The opinion of some scholars to the contrary notwithstanding, neither *ka-ma-e-u* nor *e-ka-ra-e-u* derive from themes in -*a/ā*.

[44] Only known example in Pylos; cf. series B from Knossos.

[45] Was it an *e-qe-ta* (*hekwetās*) who was assigned to supervise the *dāmos*? For *pa-ki-ja-ni-ja*, in the cadastre of the *ke-ke-me-na* land, *a-pi-me-de* (Ep 539.15 = Eb 473), who was probably the *e-qe-ta* mentioned in summary Eb 317, was the only important "civil" as opposed to religious official. He enjoyed a substantial *e-to-ni-jo* (552 liters). Scribe 1 ended the list in Ep with him; this list begins with the *ko-to-no-o-ko*.

[46] The rest of the tablet confirms that this is an inventory of cultivable land (*aroura*); *a-ko-so-ta* is a personage frequently mentioned elsewhere (An 39; Cn 40 and 719; Pn 30; Un 267; Va 482). [. . .]

[47] Ambiguous case (nominative or accusative?) for *wa-na-ka* (which can be read as *wanax* or *wanaka*, although the expected accusative would be **wa-na-ka-ta* = *wanakta*) and for the last two words. Syllabogram 85 remains controversial. *85-ke-wa* is a male anthroponym like *a₃-me-wa*, *wo-ne-wa*, *ke-re-wa*, *qe-re-wa*, *pu-re-wa*, *a-e-se-wa*, *i-pe-se-wa*, *da-te-wa*, *e-te-wa*, *a-ne-le-wa*, etc. Two other texts mention him (An 192, scribe 22: list of men; Jo 438, scribe not identified, inventory of gold). Series Ta is the work of scribe 2.

[48] It is chiefly alongside the names of the individual *hekwetai* that we find derivatives in -*ios* whose value [. . .] was probably patronymic: *a-re-ku-tu-ru-wo e-te-wo-ke-re-we-i-jo*, etc. This may have been a hereditary dignity, justifying the unusual onomastic formula: *Alektruwōn* would then be *hekwetās* as son of *Etewoklewēs*, etc.

[49] Can we explain the textual differences by assuming that On 300 was drafted when the post of *da-mo-ko-ro* for the Near Province was still vacant pending the appointment of *85-ke-wa*, whereas *te-po-se-u* was already on duty in the other province?

LOUIS ROBERT

Inscriptions from Lesbos

1960

In his lifetime, Louis Robert was acknowledged as the premier expert in Classical epigraphy, the study of inscriptions. In the following article he demonstrates the broad humanistic relevance of this subdiscipline of Classics. By tracing the precise geographical location of a place called "Mesa" in an inscription found on the island of Lesbos, Robert reconstructs a wealth of historical details with far-flung relevance, extending even to the social contexts of the poetry of Sappho and Alcaeus. See further Nagy 1993, 221–225.

We must look more closely [. . .] at the "Aeolian goddess" and the Lesbian triad of Alcaeus' poem. Before the lines naming the members of the triad, the fragment begins with these mutilated lines:

> . . .]ρά . α τόδε Λέσβιοι
> . . .] εὔδει[λ]ον τέμενος μέγα
> 3   ξῦνον κάτεσσαν, ἐν δὲ βώμοις
> ἀθανάτων μακάρων ἔθηκαν . . .

> to her the inhabitants of Lesbos
> dedicated this great and conspicuous
> precinct as a common sanctuary
> and built in it altars of the blessed immortals . . .

The Lesbians thus consecrated a common sanctuary that included the altars of the triad.[1] This interpretation is quite certain and does not depend on how one fills in the blanks in lines 1 and 2. Where on the island was this Lesbian sanctuary? Identifying the site is, I believe, important.

A false step was made early in the study of this question. The word εὔδειλος, equivalent to the Homeric and poetic εὐδείελος, "plainly visible,"

From "Recherches épigraphiques, V: Inscriptions de Lesbos," in *Opera Minora Selecta*, vol. 2 (Amsterdam: A. M. Hakkert, 1969–90), pp. 816–31; first published in *Revue des études grecques* 73 (1960): 285–315.

oriented scholars in a certain direction. Believing, rightly or wrongly, that the two epithets μέγα and ξῦνον sufficed for τέμενος, the editor detached εὔδειλον, which is perfectly acceptable. But he then arbitrarily took εὔδειλος to mean a situation on a height and restored: [ὄρος κὰτ'] εὔδειλον, "on a conspicious mountaintop." Scholars subsequently referred to the site as a "high place" and "peak sanctuary." This was the πρῶτον ψεῦδος, "first deception."

Later I will discuss the very indirect link that the commentators established with "Mount Pylaion." Alcaeus, however, makes a very different point, and the difference is important: the sanctuary, he says, was established by "the Lesbians" for their "common" existence, ξῦνον. Because this was a federal sanctuary, Alcaeus was able to seek asylum there after fleeing his homeland.

Now, it so happens that the federal sanctuary of the Lesbians is or ought to be well known, and its precise location has been determined. This identification is based on two inscriptions from the second century [CE], which are of the utmost interest for our purposes. A treaty establishing the συνθήκη, "alliance," among the cities of Mytilene, Methymna, Antissa, and Eresos, found in Delos, was concluded ἐμ Μέσσωι, "in Messon," and the name εἰς Μέσσον, "to Messon," appears repeatedly in the document as τῶι ἴρωι τῶι ἐμ Μέσ[σωι], "in the sanctuary in Messon."[2] Foreign judges from Miletus, Samos, and Aigai who came to settle disputes between citizens of Methymna and Eresos in application of the federal συνθήκη and of a ἐπισυνθήκη, "treaty and an addition to the treaty," among the cities of Lesbos came εἰς μέσσον, "to Messon." This is a place name and not an expression εἰς μέσσον, ἐμ μέσσωι, "to the middle, in the middle," as the editors of these documents believed. It was the site of a temple discovered by Boutan and excavated by Richard Koldewey.[3] The place has kept its name to this day—in the form Mesa. It is located toward the center of the island, close to the end of the great Gulf of Kalloni, which extends inland almost far enough to cut the island of Lesbos in two (the Euripe of the Pyrrhaians), some three miles north of the city of Pyrrha. Koldewey remarked on its isolated location: "The magnificent edifice was isolated in solitude." The identification of this place with that mentioned in the inscriptions of Delos and Miletus was made by Wilamowitz, and I made the same identification independently with the necessary evidence, at the same time grouping and interpreting the various inscriptions in order to reconstitute as fully as possible the history of the Lesbian confederation, previously thought to have originated in the imperial era. Since then, these results seem to have become the common property of scholars chiefly thanks to *IG* XII suppl., in which the inscriptions of Delos and Miletus were reproduced in accordance with our interpretations.[4] Meetings and deliberations of the confederation took place in this isolated sanctuary of Messon near the center of the island. This was where federal judges did their work.[5] Federal holidays were also celebrated here, of course. To the portrait I drew of the Lesbian confederation and its center at Messon I added a text from Hesychius μεσοτροφωνίαι ἡμέραι ἐν αἷς Λέσβιοι κοινὴν θυσίαν ἐπιτελοῦσιν, *"mesostrophōniai* days: days on which Lesbians performed a common sacrifice." I think that these were the days when the Lesbians stayed at the sanctuary of Messon to celebrate a solemn federal sacrifice at least once a year. The place was brought to life by the panegyrics of Lesbians from all the cities of the island on the shores of the Euripe in the valley of Messon.[6]

For scholars not disdainful of "epigraphic" publications and therefore aware of the existence and location of the federal sanctuary of the Lesbians at Messon, an inevitable question arises: What was the connection between this sanctuary and the federal sanctuary mentioned by Alcaeus as a place where he sought and found asylum?[7] It would not be reasonable to assume that there were two major federal sanctuaries. Now, this status is as well established for the sanctuary of Messon, which existed for no other reason than to serve as a federal sanctuary, as for the sanctuary in which Alcaeus stayed. Furthermore, what the surviving text of Alcaeus' poem says corresponds point-for-point with Messon. Λέσβιοι τέμενος μέγα ξῦνον κατέσσαν, "the Lesbians dedicated a great common sanctuary." [. . .] Moreover, one line in the new fragments of Alcaeus concerning his exile tells us: φεύγων ἐσχατίαισι. This does not mean that he went "to the end of the world," as it was initially understood. He was, as R. Goossens rightly observed, "at the edge of the territory."[8] The ἐσχατιαί in a Greek city was the region beyond the cultivated area of domains and farms occupying the plains and valleys; it was the region "at the end," land that produced little and that was used only intermittently and with difficulty, located near or in the mountains that bordered all Greek cities. This region touched and merged into the frontier region, the area of mountain and forest that separated the territory of two cities and was left to shepherds, woodcutters, and charcoal burners.[9] A Polish scholar [V. Steffen] conjectured that the ἐσχατιαί of Alcaeus' poem were located near Pyrrha. In fact, we already know from a scholium that Alcaeus stayed in Pyrrha while in exile.[10] Messon was some twenty miles from Mytilene as the crow flies, but it was necessary to cross the mountains to reach it. North and east of the valleys that opened onto the Gulf of Hiera stretched wooded mountainsides without a single village. This was the "Tschamilik" of the maps, the forest of pines.[11] We can travel there with the geologist L. de Launay, from Agiassos via the Megali Limni to Pyrrha and the Kalloni region, passing close to Mesa.[12] We then know what Theophrastus meant by τὸ Πυρραίων ὄρος τὸ πιτυῶδες, "the pine-covered mount of Pyrrha."[13] Such were the paths by which Alcaeus fled, such were the ἐσχατιαί, and it was here that he encountered the tyrant's soldiers.[14]

Of course Messon was not a "peak sanctuary" or "high place." The Lesbian sanctuary was practically on the shores of the Gulf of Kalloni, at one end of the gulf and a little more than half a mile from the coast. It stood thirty feet above sea level.[15] It nevertheless deserved the adjective εὔδειλος or εὐδείελος, applied either to the sanctuary itself or to the place in which it was located.[16] Readers may have the pleasure of judging for themselves by looking at the handsome drawing in which the architect R. Koldewey[17] reconstructed how the temple must have looked *in situ*.[18] The map of vegetation shows a plain that is an oasis of grain fields and olive groves on the edge of the "Tschamilik," while the forest resumes to the north.[19] The temple and plain stand out, εὔδειλος, plainly visible beyond the edge of the jumble of vegetation on the mountainside.[20] This is εὔδειλος, plainly visible, *conspicuus*, without being perched on a peak. In my view, the word could equally well be applied to a sanctuary in an open plain. It would apply quite nicely to the temple of Claros, which stands out when one comes to the coast from inland and catches sight of it in the bare coastal plain without a mountain or even so much as a hillock to raise it up. The same is true of the Heraion of Samos when one approaches it from the sea or mountain. After Mesa the plain widens out along the short of the gulf; it is the most beautiful plain on the island. When ships passed through the narrow straits of the Gulf of Kalloni and proceeded toward the far shore, the sanctuary of Messon and its region stood out as εὔδειλος.[21]

I therefore believe that the sanctuary of Alcaeus has been identified and that it has already been excavated. There is no need to search for a mountain to excavate. Based on numerous findings, Koldewey fixed the date of the temple as the first half of the fourth century.[22] He noted that the high water table prevented him from excavating in depth in order to uncover the remains of an earlier building on the site.[23] There was one.[24] But in the time of Alcaeus there was only one *temenos* with altars. Whatever the exact date of construction of the temple, it marked an important moment in the history of the Lesbian confederation. The construction of the "magnificent temple" in the solitude of the Gulf of Pyrrha (whose federal character resolves the mystery of why it was built near the small town of Pyrrha) proves that the confederation existed at the time and that it was vigorous, prosperous, and confident of the future.[25]

Unfounded hypotheses have been put forward about the deity worshipped in this beautiful temple. We now know what gods to place here. It was because "the Aeolian goddess" was worshipped here along with Zeus and Dionysus that the people of Mytilene, which was increasingly the dominant city in the confederation, and of Lesbos, identified that great goddess, mistress of harvests, with the princess whose husband Germanicus they had also deified. [Robert develops this argument in an earlier part of the article, not included here.]

The confederation was still in existence in this period, although its political importance had vanished. It is inadvertently mentioned in a passage from a few decades earlier, and there is no reason why it should have disappeared under Tiberius—on the contrary. It was [τὸ κοινὸν τὸ Λ]εσβίων that erected the monument to a great man, perhaps the famous Potamon. The honored personage, heading an illustrious lineage,[26] had filled many priestly

offices for both the city and Lesbos, τᾶς τε πόλιος καὶ τᾶς Λέσβω. The confederation would strike coins in the second century under Marcus Aurelius
and Commodus.[27] There would be a *Lesbarch* (λεσβάρχης, "president of the
council of Lesbos").[28] This has been known for a very long time. This persistence of federal life explains why a mythical figure such as that of the island's
eponym, Lesbos, endured for some time. A scholiast tells us that Lesbos was a
wife of Makar, the founder of Lesbos. On a coin that names the benefactor
Sextus the "new Makar," his wife Andromeda is called a "new Lesbos." They
were "new founders," κτίσται.[29] The inscription of the "Lesbarch" at
Amastris also corroborates the persistence of the confederation: L. Caecilius
Proculus, *pontarch* (ποντάρχων, "president of the provincial council of Pontus") and *Lesbarch*, is also called υἱὸν τῆς Λέσβου, πρωτεύοντα τῶν
ἐπαρχειῶν, "son of Lesbos, champion of the provinces." He therefore bears
the honorific title of "son of Lesbos"—corresponding to the title "son of the
city" accorded to benefactors adopted by the city, υἱὸς πόλεως, υἱὸς δήμου,
"son of the city, son of demos," like υἱὸς τῆς βουλῆς, τῆς ἐκκλησίας, τῆς
γερουσίας, τῶν νέων τῆς μητροπόλεως, "son of the council, of the assembly, of the senate, of the youth, of the metropolis." This title could be
awarded by the provincial assembly, hence υἱὸς Μακεδόνων, "son of the
Macedonians."[30] The *Lesbarch* had received the title "son of Lesbos" from
the Lesbian confederation over which he presided.[31]

In closing, I would like to indicate briefly why there has been so much discussion of "Mount Pylaion" and what has been concluded about the cult of
Hera.

Only one text mentions a Mount Pylaion on Lesbos. It is by Strabo, not in his
description of Lesbos but in a passage on the Pelasgoi, concerning the origins of
Kyme, XIII 621: Λέσβιοι δ᾽ ὑπὸ Πυλαίῳ τετάχθαι λέγουσι σφᾶς τῷ ὑπὸ
τοῦ ποιητοῦ λεγομένῳ τῶν Πελασγῶν ἄρχοντι ἀφ᾽ οὗ καὶ τὸ παρ᾽
αὐτοῖς ὄρος ἔτι Πύλαιον καλεῖσθαι, "the Lesbians say that they were
marshaled under Pylaios, who was, according to the poet, the ruler of the
Pelasgians, and that after him a mountain on Lesbos is still called Pylaion."
This text contains no topographical indications, and for a long time no identification was proposed. Everything came from a very ingenious article published by K. Tümpel.[32] A gloss of Hesychius gives: Πυλαίιδες αἱ ἐν κάλλει
κρινόμεναι τῶν γυναικῶν καὶ νικῶσαι. Πυλαίιδες: "women who participated in a beauty contest and won." Tümpel compared this with two accounts of beauty contests on Lesbos. They took place on the island[33] and, more
precisely, in a sanctuary of Hera.[34] If this sanctuary of Hera on Lesbos bore the
name "Pylaion," the "Pylaiïdes" of Hesychius would be Lesbians. The connection comes from Strabo's "Mount Pylaion." [. . .]

The parallel may be tenuous, but I find it appealing. However, nothing indicates that this sanctuary of Hera is "on Mount Pylaion." According to
Tümpel's theory, there is supposed to be a connection between Mount Pylaion

and the sanctuary of Hera; that is all. The sanctuary might well be located in a plain, like that of Hera at Samos, and Mount Pylaion might loom nearby. Yet this is the source of the phrase repeated by all the commentators on Alcaeus about the sanctuary of Hera located *on* Mount Pylaion, said to be a "peak sanctuary."

Hence if one adopts Tümpel's combinations concerning the "Pylaïdes," there is no difficulty about locating this sanctuary in the plain, as at Mesa-Messon.

Since the first editor, moreover, it has been accepted that the principal deity in the triad invoked by Alcaeus was Hera, disguised by the appellation "Aeolian goddess." This was partly for reasons of consistency: the epithet πάντων γενέθλαν, "the source of all," and the protection of the Aeolians. Above all, the fragment of Alcaeus mentioning the triad has been associated with another fragment found at the same time according to which the exiled poet was abiding in μακάρων ἐς τέμενος θεῶν, "the precinct of the blessed gods"— precisely the place of Lesbian beauty contests:

> οἴκημ<μ>ι κ[ά]κων ἔκτος ἔχων πόδας
> ὄππαι Λ[εσβί]αδες κριννόμεναι φύαν
> πώλεντ᾿ ἐλκεσίπεπλοι, περὶ δὲ βρέμει
> ἄχω θεσπεσία γυναίκων
> ἴρα[ς ὀ]λολύγας ἐνιαυσίας

> I abide in a safe haven,
> where the long-robed Lesbians come
> to be judged for their beauty,
> and all around resounds the divine echo
> of the sacred yearly cry of women[35]

Finally, a small fragment of Sappho seems to name, after Hera, Zeus and the amiable son of Thyone (Semele).[36] This is supposedly the same triad as in Alcaeus and the same sanctuary, hence Hera must be Alcaeus' "Aeolian goddess."

For my part, I see no *a priori* difficulty in grouping this collection of texts in this way. I would therefore concede that the Lesbian beauty contest took place in the sanctuary of Messon-Mesa. Such contests would surely have been no more out of place here, in this pleasant plain by the sea in the center of the island, than in some "peak sanctuary." Hence I would grant that the goddess of the sanctuary was sometimes worshipped under the name "Aeolian goddess" and sometimes identified with Hera.[37]

[. . .]

I myself was struck by one fact. Why did Alcaeus, who invoked Zeus Antiaos and Dionysus Omestes by their names and cult epithets, use a circumlocution for Hera? Above all, the inscriptions pertaining to the two Agrippinas show, I believe, that the cult included an "Aeolian goddess," known as such, and not Hera. Doubtless one has to acknowledge a double denomination for the great goddess of fertility, Karpophora, who reigned at Messon where the sea and the moist, fertile land came together in a region comparable to that of the goddess of Samos. In my view, it is difficult to completely separate fragments G 1 and G 2 of Alcaeus. It was from G 2.24, that I took φεύγων ἐσχατίαισι, "fleeing to the borders of the region," which fits the Pyrrha region so well and which comes four lines before μακάρων ἐς τέμενος θεῶν, "in the precinct of the blessed gods," and then the mention of the women of Lesbos. It is also difficult to ignore the connection that one suspects from the debris with the fragment of Sappho.

In any case, these questions are not essential for the study I have presented here. The beauty contest in the sanctuary of Hera would enrich our image of the sanctuary of Messon.[38] In any case, the important thing is that I have connected the Alcaeus fragment with the federal sanctuary of the Lesbians at Messon and described the poet and partisan's place of refuge topographically and visually.

TRANSLATED BY ARTHUR GOLDHAMMER

NOTES

[1] [Bibliography in support of the argument that the *temenos* "sacred space" is not a temple-building.]
    [. . .]

[2] *IG* XI 4, 1064, A I 5, and B I 32.
    [. . .]

[3] Robert Koldewey, *Die antiken Baureste der Insel Lesbos* (1890), pp. 47–61 and Plates 18–26. The excavation took place in 1885–1886. Koldewey considered these ruins as the most important in Lesbos. See Boutan [. . .] 311: "These are probably the most extensive and at any rate the best preserved ruins on the island."
    [. . .]

[4] *IG* XII suppl., 136 (treaty in Delos), 139 (inscription of the Delphinion) and 120 (treaty between Rhodes and the Lesbians, which I explained and applied to the history of the confederation).

[5] The texts of the two inscriptions imply the existence of a number of buildings for meetings, magistrates, irregular tribunals, and of course housing in this isolated location. See Koldewey's remarks on the few remains [. . .] and note their place on the map [. . .].

[6] [. . .] The dictionary of Liddell-Scott-Jones, s. v., notes: "name of a festival at Lesbos."

[7] I noticed this same point in reading the papyrus of Alcaeus and confirmed my idea a decade ago after rejecting the suggestion that Alcaeus' sanctuary was "on a mountain." It therefore pleased me greatly to find another scholar with the same interpretation: L. A. Stella, "Gli dei de Lesbo in Alceo fr. 129 P," *La Parola del Passato* 11 (1956): 322–23.
    [. . .]

[8] [. . .] An ἐσχατιαί is a frontier zone, a region remote from any center, a wasteland. And in the passage from Sophocles *Philoctetes* (144: νῦν μὲν ἴσως γὰρ τόπον ἐσχατιαῖς προσιδεῖν ἐθέλεις ὄντινα κεῖται) in which we find an identical use of the dative of place ἐσχατιαί, the τόπον so characterized is simply an "out-of-the-way place." The expression φεύγων ἐσχατίαισιν may mean that Alcaeus was exiled "to the edge of the territory," and this was indeed the impression given by the first verses of the poem. [List of other attestations of the sense of 'frontier zone'.]
[. . .]

[9] I tried to describe this region in *Hellenica* VII, chap. 16: "Epitaphe d'un berger." I shall give a more detailed account in my *Frontières grecques*, based on acts of arbitration, of all texts concerning the use of the Greek mountains and the cult sites found in them. On the ὄρη δημόσια, mountains in the public domain, see *Hellenica* XI-XII, pp. 196-197.
[. . .]

[10] During an earlier exile: π(ερὶ) τὸν Ἀλκαῖον . . . φθάσα[ν]τες πρὶν ἢ δίκη[ν] ὑπο[σ]χεῖν ἔφ[υ]γον [εἰ]ς Πύρρ[α]ν (ed. Lobel-Page, scholium at E 3). [. . .]

[11] See the beautiful map by H. Kiepert in R. Koldewey, loc. cit., Pl. 30, and ibid., Pl. 31, the map of vegetation in color. This should be complemented by the map in P. C. Candargy, *La végétation de l'île de Lesbos* (Paris, 1899), pp. 12–13.

[12] L. de Launay, *Chez les Grecs de Turquie* (Paris, 1897), p. 47.

[13] *Historia Plantarum* III, 9.

[14] I take this from the fragment of scholium D 2 (Lobel-Page): ὁ μεταξὺ Πύρρας κα[ὶ] Μυτιλήνης τ]ῶν δορυφ[ό]ρων τινας π[.

[15] Koldewey, loc. cit., 47. Over the years silt deposits have probably moved the land further into the gulf. Boutan, loc. cit., 313, noted that one traveled from Mesa to Kalloni "across a plain that did not exist in antiquity. All signs point to land of recent formation: the sea also receded nearly two leagues at this location." [. . .]

[16] It is generally accepted that the word can apply to "a shore." [. . .]

[17] On Koldewey's life and work, see W. Andrae, *Babylon, Die versunkene Weltstadt und ihr Ausgräber Robert Koldewey* (Berlin, 1952); on Koldewey's stay in Lesbos after the excavation of Assos, see pp. 33–37.

[18] Loc. cit., Pl. 18, 2. See also p. 47, the drawing of the uncovered ruin in its setting. For a very detailed map of the plain of Mesa, see Pl. 18. 1. The temple is "on the lowest of the hills," p. 47.

[19] Loc. cit., Pl. 31.

[20] See L. de Launay, loc. cit., 83, on plains bordering the gulfs of Kalloni and Hiera, which give "the sense of horizontality of which one feels the need from time to time when confronting uneven terrain."

[21] The word λόφον does not trouble me, for it could well be applied to a hillock thirty feet above sea level. [. . .] Koldewey's phrase about the temple looking like an island in times of flood. What is more, deposits of silt probably increased the distance between the temple and the sea, which was probably closer to if not actually on the coast in antiquity.
[. . .]

[22] Koldewey 57–58.

[23] Koldewey 47. This is one problem with excavating temples located on plains. Koldewey also noted that the torrent "from the heights of the Tschamilik" with its two tributaries was capable of transforming the whole valley into an impassable swamp in wintertime.

[24] Koldewey 59.

[25] It would be very interesting to know if examination of the architecture could help resolve the issue of the date. It would be historically important to be able to go back as far as Alexander.
[. . .]

[26] L. 1, τὸ ἀπύγονον Πεσίλεος.———L. 6, [πρ]ογόνων τῶν συνστασαμένων.
[. . .]

[27] [Bibliography.] Among the types: a female figure holding a model of a temple.

[28] In an inscription of Amastris, in Paphalagonia [references].
[. . .]

[29] Because the heroes Makar and Lesbos were husband and wife, it is certain that Sextus and Andromeda were as well.
[. . .]

[30] [Bibliography on] a high priest of the imperial and agonothetic cult of the koinon of Macedonia. υἱὸν Μακεδόνων καὶ τῆς πατρίδος, πρῶτον τῶν ἀπ' αἰῶνος τού[τῳ] τειμηθέντα τῷ ὀνόματι. The editor compares this with the title υἱὸς τῆς Ἑλλάδος in Sylloge 854. The title υἱὸς τῆς Λέσβου ([. . .]) also provides the most exact parallel for the situation of these presidents of the koinon.

[31] The inscription and coinage shows that Lesbos at this time took the heroine Lesbos for its eponym and not the hero Lesbos. [Bibliography.] The heroes Lesbos and Makareus, if not Makar, are associated with Aeolus.
[. . .]

[32] K. Tümpel, "Lesbiaka, 5, Pylaiides," Philologus (1891): 567–68.
[. . .]

[33] Oldest text: Theophrastus of Eresos in Athenaeus, XIII 610 a: κρίσεις γυναικῶν . . . περὶ . . . κάλλους . . . καθάπερ καὶ παρὰ Τενεδίοις καὶ Λεσβίοις.

[34] Scholia to Iliad 9.128: παρὰ Λεσβίοις ἀγὼν ἄγεται κάλλους γυναικῶν ἐν τῷ τῆς Ἥρας τεμένει λεγόμενος καλλιστεῖα. Anth. Pal. IX, 189 anonymous epigram: ἔλθετε πρὸς τέμενος γλαυκώπιδος (not ταυρώπιδος) ἀγλαὸν Ἥρης / Λεσβίδες. ἀβρὰ ποδῶν βήμαθ' ἑλισσόμεναι / ἔνθα καλὸν στήσασθε θεῇ χορόν· ὕμμι δ' ἁρπάξει / Σαπφὼ χρυσείην χερσὶν ἔχουσα λύρην. / Ὄλβιαι ὀρχηθμοῦ πολυγηθέος. ἦ γλυκὺν ὕμνον / εἰσαΐειν αὐτῆς δόξετε Καλλιόπης. In fact, there is no trace here of a beauty contest, and girls could form a chorus in the sanctuary of Hera or any other sanctuary. If the poet did not allude to it, it was because it was not on his mind. Nevertheless, this text is cited everywhere, most notably in all recent studies of Alcaeus, in support of the beauty contest in the sanctuary of Hera. [Bibliography.]
[. . .]

[35] Poetarum Lesbiorum fragmenta, ed. Lobel-Page, fr. 62. [. . .]

[36] Poetarum Lesbiorum fragmenta, ed. Lobel-Page, fr. 17.
[. . .]

[37] What has been said about the goddess dominating the triad, based on Alcaeus and Sappho, is quite correct. It is easy to understand why the sanctuary might have been named for the goddess alone. If the combination of the Pylaiides and Mount Pylaion is correct, there is no reason why the name Pylaion might not have been given to one of the heights above Mesa.

[38] Elsewhere, moreover, the author contests the notion that there was actually a "triad" (pp. 324–25) and treats Dionysus separately. These observations do not seem convincing to me.
[. . .]

[39] If Tümpel is correct, I would call Mount Pylaion a height above the sanctuary. [. . .]

LOUIS ROBERT

Eulaios: History and Onomastics

1962

*Robert's classic article illustrates the explanatory power of epigraphical and
prosopographical approaches in the Classics. Robert's methodological emphasis on underlying systems is summed up in this striking "rule of archaeology," as he calls it: "He who knows only one name knows no name. One
has to know a thousand in order to know one."*

Ａll science is science of the particular, as my friend Fernand Chapouthier
used to say. I shall therefore begin with a very specific fact, an inscription, a name.

The inscription in question is from Samothrace. It was recently included in
the published findings of the American archaeologists who excavated the sanctuary of the Kabeiroi. Most of the inscriptions from the sanctuary of the Great
Gods are lists: lists of *theōroi* or lists of initiates, *mystai*, or *epoptai*. They therefore seemed monotonous and uninteresting, even to their recent editor. Number 47 of the new publication names the initiates of the Macedonian city of
Beroia, Veria.

Ἐπὶ βασιλέως Θεοδώρου . . . μύσται εὐσεβεῖς Βεροιαῖοι
Τιβέριος Κλαύδιος Εὔλαιος
Οὐλπία Ἀλεξάνδρα ἡ γυνὴ αὐτοῦ,
Γά(ϊος) Ἰτύριος Πούδης = Gaius Iturius Pudens
δοῦλοι Κλαυδίου Εὐλαίου Στάχυς, Παράμονος. Θηβαΐς

during the rule of the king Theodoros . . . pious initiates from Beroia:
Tiberios Klaudios Eulaios,
Ulpia Alexandra, his wife,
Gaios Ityrios Pudes = Gaius Iturius Pudens,
slaves of Klaudios Eulaios: Stakhys, Paramonos, Thebais

From "Eulaios, histoire et onomastique," in *Opera Minora Selecta,* vol. 2 (Amsterdam:
A. M. Hakkert, 1969), pp. 977–88; first published as *Epistēmonikē Epetēris tēs philosophikēs
Skholēs tou Panepistēmiou Athēnōn* (1962–3), pp. 519–29.

Then the date: the year 261 of the Macedonian era, which corresponds to 113 of the Christian era. The editor warns that "these names call for little commentary." Here I shall study only the name of the first personage.

The first publication, by the director of the excavation some twenty years ago, gave: Τιβέριος Κλαύδιος Εὐάλιος. The recent editor proposes Εὔλαιος. "On line 1 as well as line 10 (the slaveowner) AL and LA are both possible epigraphically (that is, based on what seems to be written on the stone), and Εὔλαιος is in itself a more plausible name." That is the sum total of commentary on the name. Hence the name does not appear to be certain, and Εὔλαιος was preferred only because it was "more plausible" than Εὐάλιος considered "in itself."

This method is woefully superficial. All science is science of the general. The name Εὔλαιος must not be considered "in itself," that is, as an isolated example. We must look for comparisons, for other examples, in order to treat this case as part of a series, a larger collection. He who knows only one name knows no name. One has to know a thousand in order to know one: this fundamental rule of archaeology broadly understood is worth repeating.

With a dictionary of proper names, even a very old and outdated one, we can easily identify two personages named Eulaios in historical and literary texts. Based on this evidence, Otto Hoffmann judged the name to be authentically Macedonian in his 1906 book on the Macedonians. Plutarch, in his treatise *How to Tell a Flatterer from a Friend*, recounts that after the battle of Pydna, Εὖκτος καὶ Εὔλαιος, ἑταῖροι Περσέως ("Euktos and Eulaios, the guards and companions of Perseus") reproached the fleeing king and were stabbed by him. In the *Life of Paulus Aemilius* he points out that this crime occurred in Pella and that the two personages were "heads of treasury" (Εὖκτον καὶ Εὔλαιον, τοὺς ἐπὶ τοῦ νομίσματος). Here, then, we have an Εὔλαιος among the high officials of Macedonia during the reign of Perseus and as ἑταῖρος (guard and companion) of the king.

Polybius mentions another Eulaios at the court of Philometor, and Diodorus following Polybius and Saint Jerome following Porphyry identify the same person, who, along with Lenaios, was Philometor's tutor. Polybius, followed by Diodorus, paints a very dark portrait of these two as both greedy and militarily incompetent. After fomenting war against Antiochus IV, they were responsible for the king's shameful retreat, without a fight, to Samothrace. The name Eulaios is abbreviated on some bronzes of Ptolemy Philometor, and there is no other in this coinage.

This Eulaios was "perhaps Macedonian," according to Ion Russu, who published a list of Macedonian names in 1938. Yet most historians have portrayed Eulaios and Lenaios as adventurers of barbarian origin and former slaves. Nevertheless, despite the hostility of the ancient tradition concerning them (for Polybius detested courtiers and offered only caricatures of the ministers of Philopator, Antiochus III, and Philip V), it is worth noting that nowhere in the sources is Eulaios characterized as Oriental. Diodorus distinguishes "Eulaios the eunuch" from "Lenaios the Syrian," "the Coelesyrian former slave." In Polybius, Eulaios is a eunuch, a σπαδῶν, not a Syrian or "Kuzistani." To maintain, as Walter Otto does, that "Eulaios, too, was probably an Oriental" is to contradict the few existing texts. If Eulaios was a Macedonian name, Ptolemy's tutor was of Macedonian origin. Calling him a "Kuzistani," that is, an Oriental from Susiana, as Bevan does, is hardly justified by saying that the Susa river bore the name Eulaios. The name of Philometor's tutor does not resemble any "Oriental" or Semitic or Iranian name—whether in its original form or transcribed into Greek.

On the contrary, we find other, characteristic examples of the name Eulaios in Macedonian inscriptions. In 1939 and 1948, Nicolas Vulic published lists of ephebes from Derriopos, near Prilep (Prilepi), dating from 74 to 107 [CE]. One of these ephebes was an Εὔλαιος Ἀντιγόνου, "Eulaios son of Antigonos." In the published photograph, Jeanne Robert recognized that Εὔμιος Πετιλίου, "Eumios son of Petilios," was Εὔλαιος Πετικίου, "Eulaios son of Petikios." These lists are, moreover, of great interest for Macedonian onomastics, although no one has noted this. On them we find typically Macedonian names such as Ἀρριδαῖος, Κόρραγος, Ἀδαῖος, "Arridaios, Korragos, Adaios," along with names favored in Macedonia such as Λιμναῖος, Ὀρέστης, Αἰνείας, "Limnaois, Orestes, Aeneas," and significant family groups such as Κάσσανδρος Ἀντιγόνου, "Kassandros son of Antigonos." We see the collection of names to which the two Eulaioi of Derriopos belonged.

The name also occurs elsewhere in Macedonia, namely, in Beroia. Russu's list refers to a 1912 publication. In fact, the inscription was already known to Delacoulonche in 1858. It is an honorific inscription from the city of Beroia concerning a woman, Domitia Iulia, the wife of Titus Flavius Caesennianus Εὔλαιος. The statue was erected by Tiberius Claudius Εὔλαιος. Not only do we have here two additional Macedonian examples of the name Eulaios, but the inscription copied in Beroia features the same Tiberius Claudius Eulaios, who was *mystēs* at Samothrace. Clearly, in order to understand or even accurately read the inscriptions of Samothrace, one has to look at other inscriptions as well. If one is interested in Macedonian names, one has to look at Macedonian inscriptions and onomastics.

When one does this, the reading of the name Εὔλαιος in the inscription from Samothrace is confirmed, not by the damaged stone but by an inscription from Beroia naming the same person, and Εὐάλιος is no longer tenable. The Macedonian character of the name is no longer in doubt: I have not found any instance of this name in the inscriptions other than the five attestations from Beroia and Derriopos.

In view of all this, the editors of the *Life of Paulus Aemilius*, and most recently Ziegler, were clearly right to adopt the correction Εὔλαιος for the Εὔδαιος of the manuscripts. This correction was due to Coray, who relied on the Εὔλαιος in Plutarch's other work. Furthermore, W. Crönert was wrong to propose correcting this Εὔλαιος to Εὔδαιος by considering these names "in themselves" and without even relying on the manuscripts of the *Life of Paulus Aemilius*.

We are now in a position to assess theories about the origins of Ptolemy Philometor's tutor. This high personage bore a Macedonian name. If he had hailed from Kuzistan, Polybius surely would have criticized him for it, just as he incriminated Lenaios for being "Syrian." He could not be attacked for his origins or birth but only for his status and function: "Eulaios the eunuch and Lenaios the Syrian." This leaves only the type of argument briefly alluded to by Pierre Jouguet: "The name Eulaios is Macedonian, but it is unlikely that this eunuch was Macedonian by birth." I do not see why. Among the descendants of the Macedonians in Egypt, there were people of all sorts, and they were not immune to the blows of fate, so that Eulaios may have become a eunuch by accident or illness, or he may have been made a eunuch deliberately.

Furthermore, his Macedonian origins are quite consistent with his high functions at the court of the Lagidai. As W. Otto has observed, Eulaios was the young king's "nurse," *nutricius* in Latin, τιθηνός in Greek. He was, in Caesar's phrase, the *nutricius eunuchus*, just as Potheinos was later for Ptolemy XIV. This explains his precocious influence and promotion to the post of tutor. But it was excellent that he was Macedonian—the ruling class—in addition to being a eunuch. This background is an important detail for the study of the court of Alexandria in this period, despite the rhetorical backbiting of Polybius and his modern successors, such as Bevan.

In this way, anthroponymy, working with modest, "banal" inscriptions such as lists of *mystai*, ephebes, and honorific inscriptions, can contribute to political history by shedding light on the origins of Ptolemy Philometor's tutor. . . .

I still have to discuss the river of Susa, whose name suggested that Eulaios might be Kuzistani. This river was called "Ulai" in Hebrew and in Assyrian inscriptions. It appears in the form Εὔλαιος in Arrian and Pliny. "The river that the Greeks called Eulaios," wrote Pierre Jouguet. Indeed, I believe that if the Greeks chose to give this precise form to the indigenous name of the river, it was because they adapted it "in Macedonian style."

Certain Greek inscriptions found in Susa itself since 1903 have shown that the city had become "Seleucia on the Eulaios," Σελεύκεια πρὸς τῷ Εὐλαίῳ. It was founded as a Greek city. In these Hellenistic foundations, Macedonian colonists played a major role. Thus in the second century, in the Attalid foundations of Philadelphia of Lydia and Apollonis of Lydia, coins from these cities bore the Macedonian shield as an emblem. In the case of Apollonis, I have shown how lists of ephebes from the first century [BCE] featured Macedonian names. In the absence of a monetary type, anthroponymy alone is enough to prove a Macedonian settlement, for the names Ἀρειδαῖος, Πρεπέλαος,

Ἀμύντας, Δρεβέλαος, "Areidaios, Prepelaos, Amuntas, Drebelaos," were found there. [. . .]

In the foundation of cities in the late fourth and third century, the Macedonian component was obviously no less important, quite the contrary. Thus, on the banks of the Euphrates, in Doura (renamed Europos), Franz Cumont noted such Macedonian names as Ἀρύββας, Κρατέας, Ἀδεῖα, Δαδαῖα, Ἀδαῖος, "Arubbas, Krateas, Adeia, Dadaia, Adaios."

In Greek inscriptions from Susa I have found Macedonian names or names favored in Macedonia, such as Κράτερος (Krateros) and Νικόλαος (Nikolaos). The most typical, however, is the very rare name Δρακας (Drakas). [. . .]

Onomastics is thus sufficient, despite the absence of any historical text, to prove that there was a Macedonian settlement on the Eulaios in Seleucia. It seems clear to me that the indigenous name for the local river was adapted to a form familiar to Macedonian ears.

In passing I might mention another Macedonian trace in Iran. My friend Daniel Schlumberger has informed me about a previously unknown rock sculpture at Bisutun. It depicts Herakles in the midst of a banquet. An inscription indicates that this Herakles Kallinikos was dedicated, as I decipher it, in honor of a Seleucid functionary with the title "Chief of the High Satrapies" by a Greek named Hyakinthos, son of Pantaukhos. The latter name is found chiefly in Macedonia and Thessaly.

Thus the name Εὔλαιος in an inscription from Samothrace, a name that was not corroborated and seemed unworthy of further comment or research, has taken us first to Macedonia, then to the Macedonian court in Alexandria, and finally to the remote mountainous border region of Iran, to the Macedonians of Seleucia, and to the ancient city of Susa.

Allow me to claim a little more of your attention for a much briefer look at a second name and, finally, a conclusion.

A long time ago, in the *Revue des études Grecques* of 1934, I compared a historical text that discussed the cult of an Apollo *Kōmaios* in Naucratis with the name Κωμαῖος (Kōmaios). I concluded that Apollo's epithet could not be corrected, since it was corroborated by the name, and that the name was to be explained as "theophoric" since it was the epithet of the god. I found the anthroponym *Kōmaios* in several Ionian cities: Athens, Colophon, Ephesus, Keramos, Abdera, and Thasos. I also considered the month *Kōmaion*, attested in Colophon. The following group was thus established: Apollo *Kōmaios*, the month *Kōmaion*, and the name Κωμαῖος (Kōmaios), just as one has Dionysus Λήναιος (Lēnaōs), the month Ληναιών (Lēnaiōn), and the name Λήναιος (Lēnaios).

My analysis seemed to be corroborated by an inscription from Thasos published in 1958. In that city, the home of a series of Κωμαῖος (Kōmaios), this precious new text revealed the existence of a festival known as the *Megala Kō-maia*. The editor noted this confirmation but hesitated about the relation of the *Kōmaia* with Apollo. After remarking that "one might be tempted to think above all of Dionysus," he observed as I had done that "the little evidence that has been collected favored the hypothesis" of an Apollonian attribution. His conclusion, however, was that "it is not out of the question that Apollo presided over these Great Kōmaia of ancient Ionian tradition." This formulation was so cautious that it asserted next to nothing: "It is not out of the question." Nothing can be built on such uncertainties, for, alas, practically nothing in the world is out of the question.

In fact, I connected *Kōmaios* to Apollo because the text concerning Naucratis named an Apollo *Kōmaios* and the epithet *Kōmaios* had not yet been attached to any god other than Apollo. Shortly after the publication of my article, I promised to produce another text dealing, once again, with Apollo *Kōmaios*. Since that time, I placed the text in circulation but did not comment on it. Speaking of the great city of Seleucia on the Tigris, Ammianus Marcellinus reports that Lucius Verus's generals took from this city a *simulacrum Comaei Apollinis*. This divine statue was installed in the Temple of Apollo on the Palatine in Rome. It was supposedly from this Seleucid temple that the germ and plague that ravaged the Empire spread. If some identified this *Apollo Comaeus* with the one in Naucratis, others believed that the name designated "a god of the Babylono-Aramaic pantheon," such as Nebu. This is the Oriental mirage. There is no evidence that this *Apollo Comaeus* was not taken to Seleucia on the Tigris by its Greek worshippers when the city was settled by Greeks.

Thus two very explicit texts associated *Kōmaios* with Apollo and not with some other god. If anyone doubts that I was on the right track in associating the Ionian god *Kōmaios* (and therefore, now, the *Kōmaia* festivals of Thasos) with Apollo *Kōmaios*, those doubts can now be laid to rest by incontrovertible evidence that should put an end to all equivocation on the matter. This summer, the ephor of antiquities of Kavala, M. Lazaridis, discovered a dedication in the city of Philippi; he has been kind enough to send me a photograph together with the text. The inscription dates from the end of the fourth century or the early third century. It reads: Διόδοτος Ἐπιγένους Ἀπόλλωνι Κωμαίῳ καὶ Ἀρτέμιδι, "Diodotos son of Epigenes to Apollo Kōmaios and Artemis."

Is it possible to believe that the Apollo *Kōmaios* of Philippi is not the god of the *Kōmaia* of Thasos? It was also Apollo who gave his epithet to the Colophonian month and to all the Κωμαῖος citizens of the Ionian cities.

It is natural to assume that Apollo *Kōmaios* was taken from Thasos to Philippi. We find his cult in part of Macedonia.

Can we then guess the route that he probably followed to Seleucia on the Tigris? Are we not here seeing evidence of the Macedonians who settled in the new city founded by Seleucus I?

In fact, we have explicit evidence of what we should have assumed a priori about the Macedonian role in this foundation. In Book 5, Polybius mentioned the *adeiganes* of Seleucia on the Tigris. From Casaubon to the dictionary of Liddell, Scott, and Jones, scholars sought an Oriental origin for this word. Here is yet another instance of the Oriental mirage. In 1943, based on a new inscription from Laodicea in Syria naming the πελιγᾶνες, "council members," Pierre Roussel recognized that the term πελιγᾶνες was a Macedonian word designating a civic body, and that the word also appeared in Polybius's text about Seleucia on the Tigris. For the *peliganes* in Syria, he concluded that "this mention usefully calls our attention to the political role played by the Macedonian element in the colonization of the region, in which so many place names, rivers, and cities alluded to the mother country that it was possible to call it New Macedonia," to borrow an expression from Theodore Reinach.

The Apollo Kōmaios of Seleucia on the Tigris, who has been taken for an Oriental god seems to me to have been a Macedonian import, just as the (incorrect) *adeiganes*, taken to be an Oriental word, were a Macedonian institution, the *peliganes*. Here again on the Tigris, two words suffice to show the influence of the Macedonian element in these colonies of Alexander's generals and successors.

We thus come back to the Far East, to Mesopotamia, once again following the Macedonians, as with the names Eulaios and Drakas.

Unless new documents are unearthed, the history of Hellenistic colonization—which is no less interesting or important than the endlessly discussed history of archaic colonization—will progress through the study of anthroponyms. Detailed, informed study of Macedonian names shows how they spread through the Greek Orient, carried, in my view, by the descendants of Macedonians and not by mere fashion. These names enable us to identify centers of Macedonian colonization such as Apollonis in Lydia and Susa, and also, I believe, Dorylea in Phrygia and Stratonicea in the high valley of the Caicus. They also spread sporadically through the Greek cities of Asia Minor, because those cities granted πολιτεία to many officers of Hellenistic kings, often of Macedonian origin, who settled in them. I shall say no more; it would take another lecture to prove the point.

Have I succeeded in showing that history can and must avail itself of anthroponymic sources? By this I mean primarily inscriptions, and inscriptions seemingly of the most monotonous and banal sort, the small change of epigraphy. Frequently, progress in history comes not from a "great" new inscription that attracts everyone's attention, including that of those least prepared to understand (and I am not speaking of inscriptions such as the all too famous "decree of Themistocles," that scandalous stone, that touchstone of critical thinking, that sensitive balance for testing the *psychostasia* of historians), but from careful examination of where names originated and how they spread.

Of course, if anthroponyms are to be useful to historians, they have to be grouped, not considered individually, each name "in itself." Greek names have usually been treated from a linguistic point of view: Bechtel inserted names into contexts in order to understand their structure and explain them, but his work had its limits. Some scholars, like my great teacher Adolf Wilhelm, who, I hope, is still remembered and still revered, tried to eliminate some names as impossible while defending others from audacious corrections and completing mutilated ones: such activities helped to establish a sound, critical catalogue of anthroponyms. Beyond these necessary tasks, we have to restore names to their historical and geographical context and establish their chronology. It turns out that many names are more or less local, used only in one city or one region. Names teach us about cults, feelings, and fashions. They reveal movements of colonization and ethnic kinship and political and economic relations. We must establish not catalogues of names but the *history* of names and even *history by means of names*.

TRANSLATED BY ARTHUR GOLDHAMMER

NICOLE LORAUX

What Tiresias Saw

Dedicated to Renate Schlesier

1982

The essays collected in The Experiences of Tiresias *were written between 1977 and 1985; several of them originally appeared in psychoanalytic journals. They investigate the Greek "imaginary" as it provides evidence for a view of sexual difference that—in the face of a contemporary discourse of incompatible categories—could attribute to males aspects of the feminine, without undermining the virility that was self-evidently an inherent characteristic of the classical citizen-soldier and his model, the warrior-hero of myth and epic. Drawing on the texts of historians and philosophers as well as poets, Loraux's inquiry broadly shares with those of Vernant, Vidal-Naquet, and Detienne the widely ramifying project of interpreting the interaction between imaginative structures and the ideological premises and social practices of the classical period; more particularly, her investigation here participates, with those of H. Monsacré, M. Olender, Y. Thomas, and others, in the study of how gender is* embodied *in classical antiquity.*

"What Tiresias Saw" offers Loraux's characteristically synthetic and exhaustive inventory of sources, scholia, glosses, variants, analogues, and interpretations—here with the goal of establishing the precise nature of the vision that blinded Tiresias on Mount Helicon. The scholarly apparatus should not obscure, however, the degree to which this inquiry is unconventional. For Loraux's focus is not on the blind seer Tiresias, with his nearly inexhaustible ambiguities, nor on the character of his seeing. Rather, she explores the far more elusive object of that fatal sight on Helicon—and the pronoun is deliberately chosen: not whom, *but* what . . . Athena, bathing, is whom Tiresias sees—but *what* did he see when he clapped eyes on the nude Athena? A remarkable number of layers are stripped away by this analysis in order to render the body of the goddess apparent.*

From *The Experiences of Tiresias: The Feminine and the Greek Man*, trans. Paula Wissing (Princeton: Princeton University Press, 1995), pp. 211–26 ["Ce que vit Tirésias," in *Les expériences de Tirésias: le féminin et l'homme grec* (Paris: Gallimard, 1989), pp. 253–73; first published in *L'Eerit du Temps* 2 (1982): 99–116].

Who can fill in these two precipices with his eyes? One is afraid of
finding something virgin, untamed. The strong woman is best a
symbol; in reality she is frightening to behold.

—Balzac, *Beatrice*, Part 1

I magine the young Tiresias on Mount Helicon. It is midday. His childhood
is at an end, his existence as a blind seer already beginning. He saw, he lost
his sight.

But what Tiresias beheld on Helicon is not what he saw, in the most common version of the myth, on Mount Cyllene. Tiresias did not see the coupling
of two snakes. It follows that he was not transformed into a woman and did not
have to become a man once more, before being blinded for incautiously inter-
vening in a dispute between Hera and Zeus concerning the intensity of feminine pleasure.[1]

In the other version of the myth, the only one to be considered here, Tiresias
saw and was blinded. And the thing that, in a flash, destroyed his eyes forever is
the sight of Athena's body.

Whether a later invention by the Hellenistic poet or an ancient tale,[2] the
story is told by Callimachus. Accompanied by the nymph Khariklo, the divine
virgin has untied her *peplos* and is bathing in the water of a spring, the midday
silence all around her. The adolescent hunter and son of the nymph, Tiresias
approaches, led by an unquenchable thirst to the spring. And the unfortunate
one, without wishing it, saw what is forbidden to be seen. Full of rage, Athena
cries out, and night is already overtaking the child's eyes . . .

If the reader, in search of disquieting oddity, has come upon this tale, there is
no doubt that the blinded Tiresias is not in and of himself the main issue. Here
we are, as close as we can be, to the "terrifying childhood anxiety about losing
one's sight"[3] that Freud detected in "The Sand Man" and which he could have
sought in Callimachus's fifth *Hymn*. However, we intend to resist the temptation to fix on the castration complex, and it will not be Tiresias, the voyeur in
spite of himself or the blind seer, who will retain our interest here,[4] but the
blinding flash that shrouded the ephebe with night. In this way we may question the secret law by which seeing Athena's body means losing one's sight but
also, perhaps, acquiring the gift of divination. This inquiry leads to Athena
alone, the familiar and suddenly unknown goddess, the bearer of this "particular variety of the terrifying that goes back to what has long been known, long
familiar": Athena, by whom the strange is nothing else than a type of the well
known.[5]

Perhaps because they identify with heroes such as Herakles, Diomedes, or
Odysseus, whom the virgin goddess protects with all her solicitude, philologists are apt to highlight the qualities that make Athena the very figure of prox-

imity.[6] For Homer, it is true, as well as for the metopes of Olympia, Athena is *philē*—beloved, loving—and knows how to cultivate the bonds of familiarity that unite her with those under her protection.[7] But the poet is never mistaken. It is a "terrible divinity" (*deinē theos*) who climbs on Diomedes' chariot or who aids Herakles in his Labors.

Philē, deinē: there, in the tension between these two qualifiers, lies the familiar strangeness in the form of a goddess.

SEEING AN IMMORTAL, SEEING ATHENA

Speaking to the blinded Tiresias, Callimachus's Athena—kindly in all ways like the Athena of the philologists—explains that she has nothing to do with this punishment, which is certainly horrible but is a result of the ancient law of Kronos: one cannot behold the gods against their will (*Hymn* 5.101–2).

So, is this general law sufficient to account for Tiresias's story? The lesson is too clear, and the reader resists it, desiring to retain the full meaning of the catastrophe that replaced the light with night and perhaps not fully convinced of Athena's proclaimed innocence. For a moment let us admit that this is indeed a matter of not looking the gods in the face, of not beholding any of them against their will. It is necessary at least to observe that in the time of Callimachus the Homeric epiphanies in which a god only appeared to a mortal of his choice were over (in Book 16 of the *Odyssey*, in the case of Eumaios, Athena is visible only to Odysseus, and utterly incapable of contemplating the goddess against her will, Telemachus quite simply saw nothing). To save Tiresias's eyes, couldn't Athena have evaded his sight as she did with the unoffending Telemachus? That was the end, it is true, of the myth—and of its logic in which there is something irremediable about sight.

Therefore, Tiresias saw a god—more exactly, a goddess named Athena. The stubborn reader is not forbidden to wonder about what, in the mythic/ religious imagination of the Greeks, is implied for a mortal in the sight of a divine being,[8] particularly one endowed with the name of Athena. In fact, for a human to behold the faces of the gods, even when they are motivated by friendly intentions, is difficult, even dangerous.[9] In the *Iliad* Hera fears that Achilles will take fright at the sight of the Immortals in the midst of battle: "The sight of the gods in broad daylight [*enargeis*] can be borne only with difficulty," she explains (22.13).[10] *Enargēs:* a divine means of appearing; etymologically, this word speaks of the white brilliance of lightning, but Homer's commentators readily saw in it—too readily, perhaps—the corporeal presence of the god.[11] One can play at taking yet another step, to focus on the fear generated by the sudden emergence of the god, *enargēs,* and speculate about the terrors accompanying the face-to-face confrontation between man and the divine, those very emotions that the art of the archaic period expressed in the form of frontal representations.[12] But whether they care little for showing their divine bodies or avoid direct contact, the Immortals in Homer rarely appear *enargēs*, preferring to display themselves to humans in multiple forms where humans can recognize—generally, after the fact—that a god was there. As for identifying this apparition by naming the god, that is another matter. In Book 13 of the *Iliad*, Poseidon took on the traits of the seer Kalkhas to speak to the Greek warriors. Swift as a falcon, he is already long gone while Ajax is still speculating about the divinity momentarily concealed in human form. And if the hero, proud of having guessed the truth, concludes, "The gods easily let themselves be recognized," one must not be deceived. What Ajax "recognized" is the generality of the divine, deciphered in the "traces left by his footsteps." He no more recognized Poseidon than Aeneas, in Book 17, will identify the god that, in the character of a herald, held fast next to him to stimulate his courage as Apollo. By all evidence, since the time of Homer, the gods have been reluctant about displaying themselves in person.[13]

Now, with Athena, things are different. Since the initial episode of the *Iliad* (where Achilles instantaneously recognizes the goddess in the two terrible eyes that look at him),[14] up to the Athenian tragedies (where Athena is apt to practice epiphanies for the greater pleasure of her audience of citizens), by way of the *Odyssey* (where, when she pleases, she reveals herself *enargēs* to Odysseus), Athena apparently likes direct contact with mortals, and as accustomed as she is to the game of appearances, she is not above displaying herself in person, even if she intends to be visible only to her favorites. Perhaps this is the warrior-virgin's propensity for epiphany?[15] When, in the works of the poets, the gods cease to appear for a single hero and no longer hesitate to reveal themselves to one and all, the goddess will be all the more dangerous toward those whom she has not chosen.

This brings us back to Tiresias's adventure on Helicon. However, before returning to Callimachus, we will pause a moment to consider a most remarkable Euripidean epiphany, at the end of the *Ion*:

> Ah! to what god belongs this face flashing with light, emerging over the palace rooftop? Let us flee, mother, do not look at the divine except at the time when it is given to us to behold it. (*Ion* 1549–52)

Athena makes haste to stop Ion in his rush by adding that she comes as a friend. However, she does not reject the idea that there is a time for seeing the gods and a time for fleeing contact with them. Callimachus is of the same opinion, and if he insists on the highly involuntary nature of Tiresias's mistake, this attenuating circumstance is not enough to prevent the punishment. But what matters to me in each case is that, behind the generality of the warning (not to see the gods against their will), the crucial issue is to avoid the sight of Athena. Without a doubt, there is a considerable difference between seeing Athena and seeing any other god, and to understand this, it is necessary to investigate the specific relationship of the goddess with seeing and being seen. I will return to this point after more details have been resolved concerning the interpretation of Callimachus's text.

Suppose then that Tiresias has been blinded at high noon. Even before Athena takes refuge behind Kronos's harsh law, the reader of the *Hymn* has formed an opinion. The accident ("he saw the forbidden") was included in a warning addressed a few lines earlier to the citizens of Argos ("Whoever sees Pallas nude will behold the city for the last time"),[16] and the nymph Khariklo quickly learned this ominous lesson ("O my poor child! You saw Athena's breasts and flanks; you will not see the sun anymore"). Athena can indeed invoke the general nature of the law; the reader knows that Tiresias was blinded for having set eyes on Athena, and Athena in the nude.[17] For this imprudent male[18] has seen the naked body of the goddess, whose virginal modesty, Callimachus takes care to add, prevented her, in the far-off time of the judgment of Paris and the rivalry of the goddesses, from beholding her own image in a mirror.

At this point in the reading, a few seemingly simple questions need to be asked. The answers, however, are less obvious.

What does *seeing Athena nude* mean? In other words, what does one see when one views the naked body of Athena?

But also (a question we have already foreseen), generally speaking, what does it mean to *see* Athena?

Callimachus's text urges one to begin with the first question. I will heed the suggestion, taking care to remember to return to the second.

THE FORBIDDEN BODY OF THE PARTHENOS

A sharply delineated figure in the Greek imagination, the girl (*parthenos*) is threatened or frightening—which basically amounts to the same thing—and she must be hidden beneath the protective wrapping of clothing, of the veil. No goddess has more right than Athena to the title of *Parthenos,* and Tiresias, for having seen the goddess's breasts and flanks, discovered what no one, god or man, must ever know, so faithful is Athena to her vow of virginity. He saw a forbidden body (and perhaps *the* forbidden body).

There is, to be sure, another virgin goddess whose forbidden body was seen, and, for the imprudent mortal—Callimachus takes pleasure in emphasizing the fact—the result of the adventure was even worse. Athena took only Tiresias's sight; Artemis (the story is well known) pledged Actaeon to death. Actaeon and Tiresias. Or rather, Artemis and Athena. The text takes most of its meaning from the comparison between the two stories, which resemble one another, even though here the only purpose of the second—that of Artemis and Actaeon—is to shed light on the first. However, while Callimachus seems to be making Athena, this friend of manly heroes, into another Artemis by giving her nymphs for companions, the contrast between the two adventures is incontestably greater than the resemblance.[19] If, to punish the same fault, Athena takes away the wrongdoer's sight and Artemis his life, can the difference in their responses be explained only by the different functions assumed by each goddess—the latter as a huntress accustomed to killing and the former as having specific relationship to sight?[20] Another difference comes to mind, concerning the body of each virgin. Artemis loves bathing, and her nudity, which she willingly reveals to the gaze of her nymphs, is fundamental to her provocative chastity, which irresistibly attracts the hunter's desire. On the contrary, even the poets know little about Athena's body, and if Callimachus is to be believed, she is far from any thoughts of seduction when she gives her body an athlete's care. Aware of this discrepancy, Nonnos of Panopolis, the late imitator of Callimachus, will concentrate on the story of Actaeon, which is much more dramatic or explicitly erotic, and, making Artemis into "the goddess that one must not see" and the young hunter into her "insatiable beholder," he will follow the lover's gaze "moving over the chaste body of the virgin whom no one marries." For Artemis is endowed with a body (*demas*) completely exposed to view. In the case of Athena, however, this same Nonnos merely speaks of her "nude forms" (*eidos*, a way of referring to beauty in its immateriality). *Demas, eidos*: two virgin goddesses, two ways of having or not having a body. And, since it is Athena who interests me here, I need to note that she simply does not have a body, not even a body that she keeps to herself in the manner of Artemis. So how can one speak of Athena's naked body?

What did Tiresias see when he startled Athena at her bath? There is a strong temptation to suggest that what he saw had something to do with the discovery of bisexuality. Because first of all, in this version of the myth, Athena's body replaces a pair of snakes, a fairly clear symbol of the revelation of bisexuality, which Tiresias saw—and separated—on Mount Cyllene.[21] But Callimachus himself invites this interpretation, insisting on the virility of the virgin with the muscular arms who when she anoints her body shuns perfumes, unguents, and the mirror in favor of the oil used by athletes (*Hymn* 5.3–21).[22] What is there about the body of a virile virgin? Not surprisingly, a great silence surrounds this question. No Greek—least of all Callimachus—would dare imagine Athena's nudity, much less describe the body of the poliadic goddess in detail. To be sure, in Athens the Parthenos prefers the institutional use of the masculine name, *theos,* barely feminized by the article, to the feminine title of *thea* (goddess). She is *hē theos,* the female divinity. Of course Aristophanes will not miss any opportunity to poke fun at the city of Athens where "a *woman god* [*theos gunē*] stands fully armed, and Cleisthenes the invert . . . with a shuttle." But even the Athenian comic poet, however eager for gender-derived humor, would probably have rejected a joke made at her expense by a certain Theodorus. When one of Euclid's disciples observed that Athena "is not a god [*theos*] but a goddess [*thea*], because only males can be called gods," the audacious character was supposed to have objected, scandalizing Diogenes Laertius who was telling the story, "How did Stilpon find that out? Did he lift up her dress and look at the garden?"[23] One does not lift up Athena's robe, and Theodorus knows it full well, in the false ingenuousness of the philosopher who pretends not to know that *theos* denotes, beyond the difference of the sexes, the divine itself in its neuter state. But the anecdote is interesting, in what it reveals and in the Greeks' hesitation concerning the Parthenos and their refusal to go any further.

Perhaps the partisans of a bisexual Athena will return to the charge by evoking a late tradition in which what Tiresias really saw was the Palladion.[24] Now, it is known that this famous statue of Athena, with its eminently apotropaic virtues, held a lance in the right hand and in her left, a distaff and spindle (the right, the masculine side, the emblem of virility; the left, the sign of women). But Callimachus's text contains nothing to support this reading. There the myth of Tiresias is certainly the *aition* of the Argive custom of the bathing of Pallas—or, more exactly, of the Palladion—but if the poet, throughout the long description of the rite, confused the goddess and her idol, in the narrative of Tiresias's adventure all references to the Palladion have disappeared, and it is the goddess in person—*sōmatikos*, a scholiast would say—who blinds the careless one.

When it comes to Athena, it is better not to be too imaginative: one can muse about "the Virgin . . . as a phallic body,"[25] but above all one should temper one's reading of Callimachus by consulting other texts. Athena never looks at herself in a mirror? The reason is that she hated the mirror of the waters. One day, playing the flute, which she had just invented, she beheld her image on the water and saw her face disfigured like the Gorgon.[26] The goddess who enchants the philologists because—they innocently say—"she is a woman and it is as if she were a man"[27] is no stranger to worries about her beauty, she who could not bear to see herself ugly (*amorphos*) and threw far away the instrument that she would henceforth regard as an "outrage to her body" (*sōmati luma*)— for here, on the occasion of this episode, Athena has a body (*sōma*). Her austere admirers protest, of course:

> I cannot believe that the divine Athena, the all-wise was frightened by ugliness painful to the eyes and threw the flute from her hands. For how could the ardent love of appealing beauty have overcome her, she to whom Klotho assigned a virginity without marriage or child?[28]

But this connection suggests it. If the virile virgin hates mirrors, she hates them because she is a woman.

Athena is a woman. It must be repeated, no matter how great the temptation, from Callimachus to modern historians of religion, to erase this fundamental dimension of the figure of the Parthenos (the need for masculine desire to reassure itself about a woman whom one would not fear—in the end—

because she was not truly female at all!). That Athena is a woman—and a "large and beautiful woman"—was hardly a matter for doubt to Odysseus in the *Odyssey*. If the hero stresses his difficulty in recognizing the goddess immediately, able as she is to assume all shapes, it was enough, when the body (*demas*) became visible and Athena took on the likeness of a woman,[29] for Odysseus to instantly recognize her. Undoubtedly, reading this passage, it will be suggested that the goddess, always perceived in her appearances, has no body of her own; but the impression persists that Athena can only be identified by Odysseus as the goddess Athena in the form of a woman, and only in that form.

For want of solid evidence for a bisexual Athena, must one then be resigned to conclude with no further questioning that Tiresias indeed discovered that "this virile being is *only* a woman"? That he "caught by surprise this feminine nature that she hides beneath the external characteristics of a function—warfare—reserved for a sex that is not hers"?[30]

It is not evident that this sensible conclusion exhausts the meaning of the story. In search of what Tiresias saw, undoubtedly—I will return to this point—one must go beyond the too simple alternation between the secret virility of the virgin and the warlike appearance that conceals a woman's body. Above all, it is not obvious that a spectacle that the text is so careful not to spell out can be imagined.[31] Therefore, in order to move matters along, let me shift the question a bit. Since, in this attempt to "see Athena," we have gradually lost sight of the role of vision, I will consider for awhile what it is to see the goddess.

THE GODDESS, THE EYE, AND SEEING

The sight of the goddess: an ambiguous formula, but the ambiguity is inherent in Greek thought about vision where, in a complete reciprocity between seeing and being seen, catching sight of the god amounts to catching his eye—as if, in the final analysis, one saw nothing better than the other's eye; as if, with each glance, everything was played out between two gazes. It is for this reason that one recognizes Aphrodite by her delicate neck, her desirable breasts, but also—curiously—by her flashing eyes. It is for this reason that, for Euripides' Hippolytus, not seeing Artemis is the same as not seeing her eye.[32]

The Parthenos is far from breaking this rule. When, in the first book of the *Iliad*, she stays close to Achilles' side, visible only to him, it is by the terrible flash of the goddess's eyes that the hero immediately recognizes *glaukōpis Athēnē*, the virgin with the penetrating gray-eyed gaze.[33] Would it be that seeing Athena is exhausted in the sight of her piercing eye? Returning to a text by Callimachus, one could believe it for a moment: "No mirror either; her eye is still beautiful enough."[34] Perhaps there is enough terror in the eyes of Athena to make the goddess avoid her own sight. At least, if the game of sight is one of fascination, must one suppose that Athena has no intention of being caught in the trap of seeing, she who reigns as the all-powerful mistress over mortal vision? It is Athena who, in Book 5 of the *Iliad*, dissipates the fog from the eyes of Diomedes, and during the battle the hero will be able to distinguish gods from men (what distinction, then, does she wish to prevent Tiresias from making by blinding him?). Once again it is she, "the goddess with the Gorgon's eye, the unconquerable virgin of Zeus," who, in *Ajax*, beclouds the eyes of the hero she wishes to destroy. Finally, it is she, goddess-warrior, coming forth "shining with the flashing of her weapons, a bronze brilliance for the eyes," who from birth dazzles even the eyes of the Immortals.[35] How could she fail to punish the eyes of the mortal whose fault it was to see?

But if, as has already been suggested,[36] it is indeed under the authority of the Athena *Oxuderkēs* (with the penetrating gaze) of Argos that Callimachus places the story of Tiresias, we can bet that the son of Khariklo did not contemplate what was forbidden him for long. The disturbing light from the goddess's eye instantaneously blinded the careless voyeur.

Who has ever beheld Athena with impunity, without her deciding to cast the first glance? When, at the end of the *Ion*, her face, dazzling like the sun, appears before the terrified Ion, the goddess must explain that she is not an enemy, and even this explanation has an ominous sound, as if, in order not to immediately provoke desperate flight—as the aegis did in the *Iliad*—the slayer of the Gorgon, herself clothed in the Medusa's skin, must recall that she can also be kind. For we must resolve to leave the luminous benefactress of the philologists to speak of the Gorgon, or at least, of this black light that is Athena's Gorgonian aspect. Not only is the goddess the bearer of the aegis, thereby creating "in her opponent a crushing paralysis whose magical efficacy . . . overdetermined by the Gorgon's mask, with its deathly gaze that freezes all it touches into the immobility of stone"[37] (thus Iodama the priestess was petrified for beholding at night in the temple the goddess covered with the Gorgoneion); but as *Oxuderkēs* or *Glaukōpis* she has the serpent's piercing stare.[38] Better, the poets aptly name her *Gorgōpis* as if, in her gray eyes, metonymy of the Gorgon, were harbored all the evil power of the chthonian creature that she once had doomed to death. Piercing are the eyes of Athena *Oxuderkēs,* the eyes of the Palladion, the eyes of the cultic or apotropaic statues of the goddess;[39] but piercing too are the eyes of Pallas for the mortal who unexpectedly sees her. And yet, what did Athena fear from Tiresias's gaze? If by undressing her body the goddess abandoned the protection of the aegis, doesn't the Gorgon keep watch in Pallas's eyes?

Unanswerable questions, and perhaps, in this case, idle ones. For if the myth speaks of the goddess's naked body, that detail alone, when it comes to Athena, is sufficient to alert one to be careful not to neglect it. But this side trip concerning Athena's sight was perhaps not without benefit, in that it has definitely focused our attention on this unknown: the goddess's body. Since the reciprocity between seeing and being seen is itself enough to suggest that the spectacle of Athena is something dangerous, what more does one gain by undressing the goddess? What is it, then, about this body so suddenly glimpsed and then immediately concealed from view?

THE IMPOSSIBLE BODY OF THE PARTHENOS

And if seeing Athena's nudity were seeing an *adunaton*?

Assuredly, this is a bothersome proposition for the one who asks it as well as the reader, and one can attribute it to an immoderate taste for complications. It is included among those statements that one attempts to refute by resorting to the "evidence." Thus, readers hasten to demonstrate that Athena's body was simply that of a beautiful woman. Proof exists—the famous beauty contest of the goddesses judged by the shepherd Paris. A silver Etruscan plate depicts the three Immortal goddesses bathing before the fatal judgment of Paris: to the left and the right, Hera and Aphrodite, bare-breasted; in the center, in the simplest of garments, a beautiful woman, generously proportioned, with long flowing hair; at her feet are carefully arranged a helmet, a lance, a shield, boots, and a dress insistently proclaiming the bather's identity—yes, indeed, it is Athena.[40] But, let us say it outright, because nothing blinds the gaze, the "real" image, despite its realistic intent (and perhaps for that reason alone) does not succeed in convincing us of its reality, any more than does Claude Lorrain's depiction of the judgment of Paris, where Athena is the least clothed of the three goddesses, next to an undraped but modest Aphrodite and a Hera dressed from head to toe.[41] It is better to start over from another angle and note that traditionally the goddesses do not appear nude before Paris but endowed with their functional attributes—and those of Athena, among which are the helmet and breastplate, are part of her garments;[42] the Euripidean theme of the goddesses at their bath (which, in the *Cypria* was reduced to Aphrodite's toilette alone) certainly includes the obligatory reference to the "beauty" of the Immortals, but in the most general of terms and without the slightest detail;[43] and the only representation of Athena at her toilette in fifth-century Greek pottery shows the goddess washing her hands.[44] It certainly can be conceived that, in matters of this beauty competition (*morphē*), the desire to know at last what to believe about the forms of the Parthenos is acute indeed, but it is also a desire that in all likelihood will not be satisfied. There is nothing, in any event, that can prevent me from speaking of an *adunaton*.

Seeing the impossible, then: the body of a goddess who is never reduced to her body alone, because her being is in the multiple appearances that she assumes, in Homer, to deceive Odysseus or to be recognized, in the protective wrappings—breastplate, aegis, *peplos*—that in the minds of the Greeks are indissociably attached to her.

In Book 5 of the *Iliad*, according to the scholiasts, Homer would have shown Athena nude; but, more sensibly, with regard to a passage of Book 8 in which the same episode is repeated, a scholiast observed that "surprisingly, he does not undress the virgin." And it is perfectly true that the poet does not undress Athena. Of course, when she readies herself for battle, the virgin disrobes; but she slips into another garment without a pause, without a breath in the text. The reader can be the judge, in this passage from Homer:

> Athena, meanwhile, the daughter of Zeus the aegis-bearer, lets slide to her father's floor the supple and embroidered gown [peplos] that she has made and worked with her hands. Then, slipping on the tunic [khiton] of Zeus the assembler of clouds, she puts on her armor for battle, the source of tears. Around her shoulders she throws the awesome fringed aegis. . . .

The gown has already "slipped" to the floor without the text slowing down to describe the act by which the virgin undoes the fastenings—in the Hymn Callimachus will be more eloquent, and the scholiasts as well, who are intrigued by the fluid rapidity of this movement that ends before its beginning has even been mentioned. And, while in Book 14 Hera preparing to seduce Zeus is evoked in the desirability of her body, which she bathes and then anoints, here—time, it is true, is pressing since the warrior must reach the battlefield—there is no place for any description at all between the peplos that falls to the ground and the khiton that Athena dons. It will be added that peplos and khiton, the one a woman's garb meant for inside Zeus's palace and the other a manly tunic for war, are so to speak functional articles. The goddess is not concerned with adornment.[45]

Weapons, aegis, peplos: it is worth examining each of Athena's preferred coverings in turn.

The goddess's birth is a warrior's birth. Pallas springs forth from Zeus's august head bearing her bronze weaponry. Moreover, if a more explicit version of this story is to be believed, it is the swallowed Metis who, inside Zeus's body "conceived and wrought as a smith's true masterpiece" these arms from which Athena will not be separated: the bronze breastplate, but also the aegis where the goddess will later attach the Medusa's head.[46] A warrior's array, Athena's weapons are a kind of vestment. In fact, without the complete hoplite's armor with which the goddess was born, the lightly armed soldier is conventionally referred to as "naked" (gumnos). But arms clothe a man to such an extent[47] that a paradox claims that a courageous man stripped of his clothing is not really naked if he is armed with a spear and a shield, as the spear serves as his tunic and the shield as his cloak.[48] Athena's garb and weapons are consubstantial with her to such a degree that one sees less and less how the word gumnos could be employed to denote Athena's nakedness.

Things are no different with the aegis; for instance, a battle in the Homeric epic: weapons are driven deep into the warriors' bodies (Homer even attributes to javelins and arrows the desire to bite into men's flesh, indeed, to feed on it). While the gods cannot be killed, they are as vulnerable to wounds as mortals, and Ares, the god of murderous warfare, himself suffered on the day that Athena, fighting at the side of Diomedes, tore open his "beautiful skin" *(khroa kalon)*. In Book 21 he is engaged in single combat with the goddess on whom he intends to take revenge. He reaches only Athena's "awesome fringed aegis, over which even Zeus's thunder does not triumph," and again it is the goddess who will have the upper hand (398–408). Ares and Athena: between these two warriors is a world. Like human fighters, Ares has a body that can be bruised, soiled with dust and blood, and deeply gashed. Athena cannot be wounded because the aegis protects her, this magic weapon that wards off all blows. But also, Athena cannot be wounded, as if the aegis dispensed her from having a body. Magic invulnerability versus the vulnerability of bodies, aegis versus skin—inevitably the Warrior will triumph over the god of war. Aegis versus skin? While the Homeric aegis sometimes resembles a breastplate, the most traditional depictions of this divine weapon represent it as a skin: a goatskin but also, in a more ominous mode in other versions, the Gorgon's skin that Athena removed, or the skin of a Giant who, like the goddess, was named Pallas—or again Asteros. Therefore, Athena wears this talisman on her body, which cannot be grasped and to which the *Iliad* has not even once given the name of *khrōs* (the Homeric reference to the body by alluding to the envelope of skin surrounding it), and it would be apt to say that, brought back to its original status, the aegis is like the skin of the "artificial goddess."[49]

Last, the *peplos*: a woman's finery, one hopes that it is, all things considered, the most neutral of Athena's clothing, except that once again it is consubstantial with her. This is true not only because the bodies of virgins must be hidden (thus, the *korai* of the Museum of the Acropolis contrast the heavy folds of their *peplos* with the nudity of the *kouroi*). In many respects Athena, who is made up of what clothes her, transcends issues of concealment; in this she resembles the first Hesiodic woman, a bride in the form of a *parthenos,* whose beauty is all exterior, and whom in fact the goddess helped to adorn.[50] Not only can one never see the body of the Parthenos, who removes her *peplos* only to slip into another article of clothing. The important thing is that the connection between the goddess and her clothing seems even closer than usual. Book 5 of the *Iliad* explains that she worked this garment with her own hands and, knowing that Athena presides over the task of weaving, one would not be too surprised to discover that ordinarily a *peplos* served as an object to be circulated, rarely worn by the one who wove it, always given away. Thus, in Book 14, Hera will wear a dress that Athena wove for her; the same is true of all clothing, gifts in honor of marriage or engagement, that circulate between the sexes like the very symbol of exchange. Because she refuses this exchange, the Parthenos wears on her body the product of her work, taking back what her hand had made. The autarchic Athena, the goddess seems to live within a closed circuit, and there is no breach giving another access to her. Still—it must never be forgotten—this autarchic weaver needs multiple coverings with which she drapes her body, a body that is unknown to all and perhaps even to herself.[51] Her body is indissociable from what clothes it, to the extent that it lacks any contours except for those traced by the *peplos*.

We must return to our subject, even if we run the risk of discovering that what Tiresias saw remains shrouded in silence. Therefore, for the reader who is becoming impatient, wondering where all these paths away from Athena's body actually lead, and who demands, after all, some certainties (what can one see or say of the goddess's body, whether it be always dressed or not?), I will attempt to focus on the highlights of what can be seen and said about Athena's body. Once again, we will consult the Homeric poems, because they feature Zeus's daughter, to seek some indications on the part of the poet that he at least sees the Parthenos, even while her favorite Odysseus does not recognize her beneath the innumerable manifestations of her artistic performance.

When she appears other than as a tall and beautiful woman, the form well known by Odysseus, only the poet is able to discern Athena behind Nausica's friend, the young shepherd, or the wise Nestor. But the thing that enables Diomedes or Odysseus to identify the goddess is her voice: a sonorous presence, as unfleshly as an untamed *parthenos* would wish it; an opportunity for the reader to note the distance that so often extends between what the epic hero perceives and the vision of Athena that must be attributed to the poet (but at any rate, the reader is not allowed to perceive very much).[52]

Before going into what little can be said about Athena's physical presence, we will focus, as a counterexample, on the footsteps of the goddess who is most present in her own body—Aphrodite, of course. Assuredly, Helen recognizes her by her flashing eyes in Book 3 of the *Iliad,* but also by her wondrous throat, her desirable breasts—the very attributes that a man would probably identify with the goddess. But if Aphrodite's beauty is meant to be seen, it also happens, when in Book 5 the goddess of pleasure wanders out onto the battlefield, that she painfully experiences her body's vulnerability, in her skin—her flesh (*khrōs*)—where Diomedes' lance penetrated. Then the divine blood spurts forth, "her lovely skin blackens," Aphrodite moans, and in a corner of Olympus, Hera and Athena mock her, thinking that the goddess has cut her hand on a golden clasp while caressing a woman (*Iliad* 5.314–425). Aphrodite's body is vividly present, then, in all its corporeal dimensions. Therefore she is disrobed without too much difficulty. And if in the *Homeric Hymn* devoted to her, the goddess takes on the appearance of a virgin ignorant of the yoke in order to seduce Anchises, it is a good tactic for an immortal who does not wish to frighten the human male she desires—for indeed the text describes Aphrodite's disrobing at length.[53] One even catches a glimpse of the desirable body and fine skin of Hera, the shrewish wife of the father of the gods, when the goddess, bent on seducing Zeus, undertakes a formal toilette, "arranging all her finery about her skin" (*Iliad* 14.163–87). But in Athena's case, as we know, the body and its covering are never mentioned.

Based on the poet's depiction of the divine virgin, we will only be able to reconstitute an incomplete view of Athena. There are her eyes, of course, that gazed on Achilles at the beginning of the *Iliad*, her flashing eyes that Athena turns away after having triumphed over Ares (*Iliad* 21.415). There is her "beautiful hair"—but in the *Iliad* it belongs to the Trojan statue of the goddess, and on the Achaean side where she has her quarters, the goddess is not characterized by her tresses. But what is mentioned most of all about the goddess's body is what she covers with her aegis or her breastplate—what the warrior protects by donning his armor. In the much-quoted passage in which the goddess prepares for war, before draping the aegis over her shoulders and putting the helmet of invisibility on her head, she dons her armor (*thōresseto*). If *thōrax* first refers to the chest before it is used metonymically to refer to the breastplate, in the case of Athena we always have already moved to the second meaning of the word *thōrax,* in which the body is merely implied by the armor that encloses it.[54] Woe to Tiresias, who saw *stēthea,* Athena's breast, which this female warrior never forgets to clad in bronze.

And then, there are Athena's hands—the hands of a weaver who worked her own *peplos,* but above all the powerful hands of the warrior, which protect Diomedes from Ares' lance and are a sufficient weapon against the god of battles and his acolyte Aphrodite. But Athena employs the strength of her hands only on rare occasions—much more rare, in any event, than the translators of the *Iliad* would have it, in their overall wish to provide the goddess with more of a physical nature. Whether it is a god or a man whom she takes by the hand, it is always the other's hand, and not her own, that is mentioned. In fact, Athena has an incorporeal touch, which makes javelins and arrows glance off the heroes, without any movement on her part.[55] At most she resorts to her breath to protect Achilles from Hector's spite, but then we are informed that "she needed a very light breath" (*Iliad* 20.439).

A very light breath . . . and then two flashing eyes, often terrible, and powerful hands; and again, a *peplos,* a breastplate, the aegis. This would make up a *parthenos,* the Parthenos. Such at least is the Athena of the *Iliad.* In the *Odyssey,* we have suggested, she is nothing but a voice and semblances, unless she appears *enargēs* (but there the text is astonishingly discreet about what, in this flashing presence, one sees of the goddess).

Let us look no more. Athena's body cannot be encompassed with a description.

There is no hiding the fact that all this adds little definition to what Tiresias saw on Helicon. And, at the end of this survey, the question takes a different form: What, then, did the young Tiresias see, before he became forever old and blind as befits someone who was or will be able to decipher an enigma?

Was what he saw the Gorgon in Athena's eye? The phallic body of the virile virgin? Or the secret of a feminine body, the *heimliche Orte* of a well-hidden woman concealed behind the goddess's warlike wrappings like so many materializations of the forbidden? (In this case, the strangeness of the aegis concealed the familiar; and when it is beheld, the familiar is blinding.)

Unless, like Freud on the Acropolis,[56] Tiresias had seen "what cannot be seen," because there would be nothing to see of Athena's body or nothing that can be seen; because perhaps Athena's body, divested of those wrappings that surround the goddess, is nothing. A strange superficiality, the empty presence of the familiar goddess.

Put our minds at ease. To keep Tiresias from dwelling on his lost sight (vision?), as compensation the goddess gave him the superacute hearing of the soothsayer and, in the night of Hades, lucidity among the shades.[57] Since that time, no one has seen Athena's body, but clothed in the *peplos*, armed from head to toe, and equipped with the aegis, the Maiden, her body unapproachably distant but recognizable by her well-known silhouette, still watches over the doors of our modern senates where, as the friend of those men who debate and make war, the goddess of *mētis* appears, for our peace of mind, to incarnate Reason.[58]

Primordial mothers, dispossessed of their original power; Helen, married so many times but whose lovely body is perhaps nothing but a mirage, the immateriality of a ghost; Athena, whose wrappings make up her being. Three feminine figures, three ways of thinking about femininity in a negative register: as privation for the mothers, as illusion itself for Helen—sower of discord—as the mode of nonbeing for Athena.

Would this be the Greek image of femininity in which, if one discounts everything that men appropriate for themselves in their minds, only the negative remains for women? This would amount to restoring Greek women to history, which certainly does not mean abruptly giving them over to "reality" and History with a capital *H*—which facile positivisms liken to the real. But since here it was only a matter of discursive thought, we will focus on the historiographical genre, as a counterexample, to zero in on another(?) discourse on women.

Until now, the texts we have studied are essentially poetic and often marked with a mythic/religious seal. It has not escaped me that there is a great distance between these and the historic prose of a Thucydides, as well as a great risk of a shift in tone. But this is a risk we must accept. At the same time, we must remain open to the possibility that distance does not mean hiatus, and although this shift may restore greater ambivalence to the Greek representation of women, nonetheless the value it places on them is still negative.

TRANSLATED BY PAULA WISSING

NOTES

[1] On the canonical version of the story, see the material gathered by Brisson 1976.

[2] In lines 55–56 of *Hymn V (Bath of Pallas)*, Callimachus asserts that others have told the story before him; this statement is taken seriously by K. J. McKay, *The Poet at Play: Kallimachos, The Bath of Pallas* (Leiden [*Mnemosyne*, supp. 6], 1962).

[3] Freud 1964, 231.

[4] This does not mean that Tiresias as a figure was not utterly marked for this adventure.

[5] Freud 1964, 220, 222–26 (*Unheimlich/Heimlich*).

[6] Athena and Herakles: *Iliad* 8.362–69; and Diomedes: *Iliad* 5.116–17 and 809, 10.283–91; and Odysseus: *Iliad* 10.278–80; *Odyssey* 3.218–24, 378–80, 13.372. Athena, goddess of proximity: W. Otto, *Les dieux de la Grèce* (Paris, 1981), pp. 65, 71, 78.

[7] See E. R. Dodds, *The Greeks and the Irrational* (Berkeley, 1951), p. 35. To be sure, in Greek, "as in many languages, the word that would convey this particular nuance of the frightening is lacking," but in the word *philos* there is virtually much more disturbing unfamiliarity (see Slatkin 1988) than in *xenos*, the word for "foreigner" that Freud mentions (1964, 221). [. . .]

[8] On this question, see particularly {Buxton 1980, 30–32,} and Laurens and Gallet de Santerre 1986, 463–81.

[9] E.g., *Homeric Hymn to Demeter* 105ff.

[10] Or, to follow Pucci's translation (1985, 17 (1) and 1986, 8): "The gods are terrible in their fully blazing appearance."

[11] Thus, to comment on *Odyssey* 3.420 (where Athena has appeared *enargēs*), Eustathius says that "she has appeared corporeally" (*sōmatikōs*). On the difficulties involved with understanding the word *enargēs*, see Pucci 1986, 21–22.

[12] On the terror of the face-to-face confrontation and the Gorgon's mask that graphically embodies it, see Schlesier 1982, 23ff., Vernant 1985 and 1989, 119–20.

[13] From the *Iliad* to the *Odyssey*, the textual strategy of the epiphany is of course quite different, as Pucci noted (1986, 8), but this is not my point.

[14] Despite Pucci's arguments (1985, 176) in favor of maintaining the ambiguity (Achilles' eyes / Athena's eyes), I have made a choice: see n. 33 below.

[15] Otto 1981, 61.

[16] H. Kleinknecht, "*Loutra tês Pallados*," *Hermes* 74 (1939): 301–30 n. 316 [. . .], is interested in this echo from the sole perspective of the relationship between myth and ritual.

[17] According to Apollodorus, the version in which Tiresias "was blinded for having seen Athena totally naked" dates back to Pherecydes (3.6.7).

[18] Note that the prohibition against seeing Pallas in the nude is addressed to men (lines 51–54) and comes after a prohibition aimed specifically at women (lines 45–48). On the ritual dimension of the hymn and the question of bathing statues, see L. Deubner, *Attische Feste* (Berlin, 1956), and Ginouvès 1962, 283–84, 292–94.

[19] In Nonnos's *Dionysiaka* (4.337–45), the dying Actaeon expounds on the theme, suggested in Callimachus, of Athena's gentleness compared to Artemis's cruelty ("Happy Tiresias! For you have seen Athena's nude form without perishing").

[20] Such is the interpretation of K. J. McKay, *The Bath of Pallas*, p. 27.

[21] The pair of snakes and bisexuality: Brisson 1976, 55–56. Whatever Athena's affinities with the snake, one still cannot assert with Brisson (66) that "Athena can be likened to a serpent." It is better to base one's reasoning on the terms of the mythic sequences and observe 1) that, in this version, it is seeing—Athena equals seeing—snakes copulating; 2) that, in the best logic, for Tiresias seeing Athena is also equivalent to the two other sequences preceding his punishment (his experience of femininity, his role in the argu-

ment between Zeus and Hera): if one compares the two versions of the myth and reckons that Callimachus's version is a "condensed" version of the other, one has to take the method to its conclusion.

[22] According to Jouan (1966, 101), Callimachus would be alluding here to Sophocles' *Judgement*, where Athena was satisfied with oil while Aphrodite used a perfumed unguent.

[23] Athena is *hē theos* in the Athenian inscriptions; *theos gunē*: Aristophanes *Birds* 829–31; Theodorus's joke: Diogenes Laertius 2.116, where the garden is a startling metaphor in the context of the Parthenos's sexuality—mention is made of Aphrodite's "cleft meadows." *Theos* as a neuter designation for the divine per se: in Book 20 of the *Odyssey*, Athena, speaking to Odysseus or seated at his side, is the goddess with the blue-grey eyes (*thea glaukōpis*: 44, 393), but when she wishes to assert her divine essence, she states, "I am *theos*" (47).

[24] See Frontisi-Ducroux 1975, 104–106 and 110 (see the discussion about Palladion); description of the Palladion: Apollodorus 3.12.3.

[25] Quotation by G. Rosolato 1977, 135.

[26] To play the reed is to make the face of the Gorgon; see Schlesier 1982 and Vernant 1985, 56–58.

[27] Quotation in Otto 1981, 72.

[28] Account of the adventure and commentary in Athenaeus 14.616; see also Plutarch *Moralia* 456b (*amorphia*), Apollodorus 1.4.2 (*amorphon*), Clement of Alexandria *Paedagogos* 2.31.1 (*aprepes*), and Ovid's Latin variations (*Art of Love* 3.505; *Fasti* 6.699). Concerning the notion of *amorphia,* I am greatly indebted to the ongoing research of Maurice Olender.

[29] Even if it is not necessarily Athena's "true" face but one that she might adopt (Pucci 1986, 14–15). *Odyssey* 13.287–319 (and 16.157–64); in line 288 (*demas d'eikto gunaiki*), however, it would be forcing the text to translate it, as V. Bérard and P. Jaccottet have done, "She *resumed* the form of a woman," which amounts to prejudging Athena's "ordinary" form; at the most, the text permits one to understand, "She had taken on the form of a woman for a body."

[30] Brisson 1976, 34 (emphasis added). More subtly, Buxton, who accepts the basic premises of Brisson's argument, observes that to move from apparent masculinity to latent femininity "means a more radical transgression of the divine identity than would be the case with Aphrodite's 'transparent' femininity" {(1980, 31)}.

[31] In 1.88, *stēthea kai lagonas* (breast and flanks) has nothing descriptive about it; these terms simply situate parts of the human body, male or female.

[32] *Iliad* 3.396–97 (Helen and Aphrodite), *Homeric Hymn to Aphrodite* 181 (Anchises and Aphrodite), Euripides *Hippolytus* 86. On the reciprocity of sight, Frontisi-Ducroux 1975, 110.

[33] *Iliad* 1.197–205; in 1.201, with Otto and McKay and against Mazon (who sees Achilles' eyes there), I interpret *deinō osse* to refer to the eyes of the goddess; on *osse* as expressing the fiery gaze, see A. Prévot, "Verbes grecs relatifs à la vision et noms de l'oeil," *Revue de philologie* (1935): 271.

[34] *Hymn* 5.17, a passage that McKay rightly views as important. On the mirror (where one looks straight at oneself, in the form of a simple face), cf. J.-P. Vernant, "Résumé des cours et travaux," *Annuaire du Collège de France* (1979–80): 453–59, and Vernant 1989, 117–29.

[35] *Iliad* 5.127–28 (Diomedes); Sophocles *Ajax* 450 (*hē Dios gorgōpis adamatos thea*) and 51–52, 83–85 (Athena and Ajax); Orphic fragment 174 (O. Kern, ed.), with commentary by Detienne and Vernant 1974, 172.

[36] This hypothesis underlies the interpretation of *Hymn* 5 by K. J. McKay; on Athena *Oxuderkēs* in Argos (Pausanias 2.24.2) and *Ophthalmitis* in Sparta, see the remarks of L. R. Farnell, *The Cults of the Greek States*, vol. 1 (Oxford, 1896), p. 279.

[37] Quotation from Detienne and Vernant 1974, 173; story of Iodama: Pausanias 9.34.2.

[38] *Oxuderkēs:* it will be recalled that the root of *derkomai,* which expresses the intensity of the gaze, furnishes one of the words for snake, *drakōn; glaukōpis:* in Pindar's eighth *Olympian,* snakes are *glaukoi,* which the scholiast glosses as "terrifying."

[39] On the efficacy of the archaic statue's gaze: Frontisi-Ducroux 1975, 108–10; Plutarch *Moralia* 309i, quoting the historian Derkyllos, tells of the adventure of the Trojan Ilos, blinded for having saved the Palladion from a blazing temple and who recovered his vision after appeasing the goddess's anger; recall the prohibition made to the men of Argos against seeing Pallas (i.e., according to the scholia to Callimachus's *Hymn* 5, the Palladion that the Argive women bathe each year).

[40] See C. Calvi, "Il Piatto d'argento di Castelvint," *Aquileia Nostra* 50 (1979): 355–56, fig. 1. I thank Claude Bérard for having sent me, at François Lissarrague's request, a photocopy of this document "to show [me] what Tiresias saw."

[41] *Landscape with Judgment of Paris,* National Gallery of Art, Washington, D.C. (no. 2355).

[42] For Dumézil, Paris did not choose among three types of beauty but among the three functions.

[43] The three goddesses bathing: Euripides *Andromache* 284–86, *Helen* 676–78; they wash their gleaming bodies (*aiglaenta sōmata*) or simply their beauty (*morphan*); *morphē,* "form," as a word for "beauty": again, see *Trojan Women* 975 and *Iphigenia in Aulis* 183–84. On all of this, see Jouan 1966, 95–99.

[44] See C. Dugas, "Tradition littéraire et tradition graphique dans l'Antiquité grecque," *L'Antiquité classique* 6 (1937): 13 and fig. 6 (krater from the Bibliothèque Nationale, Paris). The opposition that provides the structure for the image, as in the case of Sophocles (n. 22), contrasts Athena, who is washing (content with water from a fountain), and her rivals, who adorn themselves.

[45] *Iliad* 5.733–38. Scholia to line 734 (*katekheuen*) first mention the detached clasps in terms analogous to those used by Callimachus (*Hymn* 5.70), then the disrobed goddess; see also the scholia to 8.385. On Athena in this passage from the *Iliad,* see Loraux 1981, 142–43.

[46] Athena born armed: Stesichorus fr. 62 Bergk, *Homeric Hymn to Athena* 4–5, Callimachus fr. 37 Pfeiffer. Mētis forging Athena's weapons: Chrysippus fr. 908 von Arnim. Cf. Detienne and Vernant 1974, 172.

[47] "The weapons, the garment of an individual, are connected to the individual and cannot be seen as abstract" (Gernet 1917, 222 n. 103).

[48] Plutarch *Moralia* 245a (*Virtues of Women*), with commentary by Ellinger 1978, 23.

[49] The aegis as the Gorgon's skin: Euripides *Ion* 987–97; as the skin of Pallas the Giant, or the Giant Asteros: Clement of Alexandria *Protreptika* 2.28.2, with commentary by F. Vian, *La Guerre des géants* (Paris, 1952), pp. 198 and 267 (where the Palladion of Ilion is covered with a man's skin); L. Koenen and R. Merkelbach, "Apollodorus (*Peri theōn*), Epicharm und die *Meropis,*" *Papyrologische Texte und Abhandlungen* 19 (1976): 3–26. *Khrōs* referring to the flesh penetrated by the weapon and pain: e.g., *Iliad* 11.398. The "artificial goddess": I have borrowed this expression from G. Dumézil (in *Le Festin d'immortalité*).

[50] Loraux 1981b, 84–86.

[51] To wit, the multiple occurrences of the verb *dunō* (to dig into, to slide into) concerning Athena: see for example *Iliad* 5.845; 8.378 and 387; 17.551.

[52] Pucci (1986, 9) stresses the difficulty of perceiving the gods' bodies, and especially, in the case of Achilles, of seeing Athena, this "white figure."

[53] *Homeric Hymn to Aphrodite* 161–67; however, the ellipsis of the very *instant* of disrobing invites further development of the point advanced by P. Friedrich (*The Meaning of Aphrodite* [Chicago and London, 1978], pp. 136–37) concerning nudity as a constitutive element of this goddess.

[54] *Iliad* 5.737; cf. 8.376 and Euripides *Ion* 993; *stēthos* is, for the warrior, what covers the breastplate (*thōrēx*): see *Iliad* 16.133 and 17.606; in *Ion* 995, Athena wears the Gorgon's skin on her chest (*epi sternois*); shoulders: see *Iliad* 5.738 and *Homeric Hymn to Athena* 14–15.

[55] Artisan's hand: *Iliad* 5.735; female warrior's hand: 5.836 and 853, 21.403 and 424; man's or god's hand, not hers: 4.541, 5.29–30 (except 21.286, where she acts with Poseidon); supplement on the body added by P. Mazon: translation of 1.197, 5.799, 21.397; Athena's incorporeal intervention: 11.437–38.

[56] According to Rosolato 1977, 138.

[57] Callimachus *Hymn* 5.119–30; Apollodorus 3.6.7.

[58] This article was originally published in *L'Écrit du temps* 2 (1982): 99–116, and has benefited from the comments of Luc Brisson, Claude Calame, and Claude Bérard concerning the "reality" of what Tiresias saw. I am grateful to each of them for the time they devoted to this discussion and have attempted to explain here why I persist in my view. Last, I owe much to my conversations with Piero Pucci on the question of epiphanies.

HÉLÈNE MONSACRÉ

The Erotic Images of War

1984

Elegant and terse, Hélène Monsacré's study achieves a tone gracefully matched to its subject, that of the Iliad's *subtle and delicate figurations of warfare as intimate interaction. (This translation omits part of the second section of this chapter, which details three principal sexual metaphors identified by Monsacré in the* Iliad, *comparisons that contrast: the "dance of Ares" with that of young men and women in peacetime; a woman's bridal veil with inviolate city walls; and the physical intimacy of marriage and of mortal combat.) Monsacré traces the vocabulary and imagery of love through a narrative of carnage, reaching a conclusion — "the eroticization of death" — rich with implications beyond the* Iliad *in terms of the inversion of values imposed by war.*

The erotic images of war in the *Iliad* could in themselves provide material for a study of considerable dimensions. The relationship of eroticism and war is a subject of vast magnitude. In this essay I shall simply try to underline a series of associations which figure in both the vocabulary of war and that of love. In examining the principal scenes where eroticism is linked with combat, I shall attempt to specify which categories in the epic are masculine and which are feminine. Three aspects are of particular interest: war as an amorous activity; the erotic metaphors of conflict; and, finally, the eroticization of death.

THE EROTIC REPRESENTATION OF CONFLICT

It is hardly necessary to insist on the parallel that exists between a duel of champions and "amorous conflict": in both cases, two bodies are joined. This analogy has been studied exhaustively by P. Guiraud in medieval and modern texts.

From "Les images érotiques de la guerre," in *Les larmes d'Achille* (Paris: Éditions Albin Michel, 1984), pp. 63–77.

The "military metaphor," he says, is so coherent and so pertinent that all the modes, means, and phases of combat and all the phrases that express them contain powerfully sexual images. The same holds true for the Homeric epic.

In fact, the warrior who hurls himself on his adversary is physically transformed at the moment of attack; he is completely absorbed by his desire to meet his opponent, to establish touch with him. He attacks him with his lance, which he has every intention of driving into his body. Of course, the warrior's goal is to accomplish the exploit that will assure his fame, but on a more immediate level it is also to satisfy his desire to possess the adversary. For during combat, the spirit that drives the warrior is similar to the power of lust. Nestor evokes "the desire for war" and Achilles stimulates the ardor of the Myrmidons by reminding them of their taste for fighting: "Here is the day of the hard task, the day of the fight you once craved." Hector, absent from the battlefield, is missed by his troops — "the Trojans bitterly regret his absence" — as though during wartime only the masculine realm were subject to the power of love.

In fact, in certain ways, the meeting on the battlefield has the appearance of a love tryst, as Emily Vermeule has shown in a recent study.[1]

In a clash of bodies, certain feminine physical characteristics are attributed to the warrior. His skin (khrōs) is beautiful (kalos), tender (terēn), like that of a young girl (parthenikēs terena . . . khroa), or the Muses of Mt. Helicon, or the flowers of the field (teren' anthea poiēs).[2] His skin is also fine and white like lilies (leirioeis),[3] luminous like the voices of the muses, or the sound of crickets. As for his throat, it is fragile, delicate (hapalos), like the cheeks of the captives of Achilles,[4] or the fine skin of a parthenos, a virgin.[5]

Kalos, hapalos, terēn, leirioeis: so many epithets, which, emphasizing the delicacy of his skin, turn the warrior into a potential love partner. Whiteness of the face and body is the typical characteristic of women who live indoors. When Hector draws attention to the pallor of Ajax's skin he is, in a way, treating him as a woman; diminishing his valor by granting him no more strength than that of an unarmed woman.

And, in fact, the Iliad presents other instances of an ironic comparison between death struggle and lovers' tryst. In order to arouse Zeus's erotic desire, Hera slides beneath her own robe the charmed girdle of Aphrodite: "in it reside tenderness, desire, the lovers' rendezvous." In the world of war — that is, of men — the "'rendezvous' of the champions" away from battle (promakhōn oaristun),[6] designated by the same term (oaristus) that impels the warriors to combat.

In combat, bodies meet and mingle. "There is no better way than meeting, body to body, entwining our arms, our passions,"[7] as in love. In both cases, the verb meignumi expresses the union. There is another similarity: in both instances, one partner is overcome by the violence of the other. In the act of love, the woman is overcome by the man: Thetis, in sharing the bed of Peleus, submitted to him (*damassen*).[8] The unfortunate warrior, subjugated by the strength of his adversary, is overcome as well.

The enemy, like the erotic partner, is possessed by his opponent, at his mercy. The functional analogy of the two themes is clear in the *Iliad*: erotic activity serves as a model for war, which borrows from its diction.[9]

In the discourse of war it is possible to discern yet other sets of associations in which a sexual connotation is evident: the juxtapositions of a dance of young people with the dance of Ares, a wife's veil with the battlements of a city, marriage between man and woman with the union of combat.

[. . .]

THE EROTIC METAPHORS

The Dance of Ares

To stimulate the ardor of his companions, Ajax reminds them that "Hector has invited his people not to a dance but to a battle." The reference to the dance (*khoros*) serves here to ward off any suggestion of softness: war is not a diversion and the only agility allowed is that of a clash of arms. To confuse the battlefield with a *Khoros* is to forget to be a man, to cavort in the sphere of the "sweet hymeneal acts" of Aphrodite. In fact, in the epic, in contrast to the world of war, *khoros* is associated with peace.

On the shield of Achilles, Hephaistos has depicted several dance scenes, one of which evokes a group of young people dancing. The emphasis is on the sweetness of the scene, the beauty of the young maidens, the harmony of movement—all indicate that the young men and women are under the protection of Aphrodite, the goddess who presides there.

Evoking the ballet that two warriors perform is a metaphorical way of saying that hand-to-hand combat is a dance to the death. Since the battlefield is the chosen place of masculine activity, the only possible—that is, virile—dance is the dance of Ares. As Hector says to Ajax before hurling himself upon him, "I know how to dance body-to-body the cruel dance of Ares." The force of this analogy emerges even more clearly if one is aware that it is mangy dogs who dance and cavort around the cadavers, since this kind of sport is their exclusive privilege.

Among the threats and curses which the Trojans and Greeks hurl at each other, the ironic allusions to the "dance of Ares" and the "feast of dogs" are prominent and serve to drive the warriors on to greater exploits. When Priam mourns the loss of Hector his first words are reproaches to his remaining sons. Those who died with Hector were brave men (*aristoi*), he says, those still living are "liars, dancers. They excel only in beating the ground in rhythm." Among those sons is Paris. Once again, the figure of Paris is linked to the effeminate.

Paris, after a duel interrupted by Aphrodite, seems to have returned from a ball rather than from the field of battle.

The Veils of a City

In a superb image, Homer offers a parallel between the veils of a chaste woman and the unscalable walls of a city. Achilles, urging Patroclus to return to camp as soon as the Trojans have been repulsed from the ships, dreams aloud of conquering Troy with his friend alone: "And then we alone, the two of us, would emerge from the ruin so as to be the only ones to lift the holy veil from the brow of Troy." By evoking the holy veil, Achilles compares Troy, the city that has remained inviolate, to a captive he has conquered whose veil he forcibly tears off. In a profound study of Homer's use of the word *krēdemnon* (veil), M. Nagler demonstrates how the chastity of women can symbolically be assimilated to the safety of a city. In both cases, the integrity of the "veil" (a piece of fabric or a rampart) is the guarantee, and the male warriors are protectors as well as assailants. Here, too, the warrior's masculine power is conveyed by a sexual image: in the poetic context of the *Iliad*, to capture a city whose ramparts are destroyed is the equivalent of violating a woman whose veil has been torn.

The same image is used in the *Odyssey* to recall the victory of the Greeks over the Trojans: "When we tore the brilliant veils of Troy," says Odysseus, remembering the sack of the city. The metaphor that turns a city into a woman is doubly significant if we remember that in the world of the *Iliad*, the pillage of goods and the rape of women go hand in hand: "I spent bloody days in warfare," says Achilles, "fighting other men in order to take their women." Indeed, this correspondence is at the very heart of the epic: we note that at the moment when Troy succumbs and Hector dies, the two queens of Troy discard their veils. Hecuba laments "throwing her splendid veil far from her," and Andromache lets the shining bonds slip from her forehead: the diadem, the headdress with its plaited ribbon, and finally the veil, which golden Aphrodite had given her on the day that Hector of the gleaming helmet had led her from the house of Eetion. These two unveilings prefigure, even as they bear witness to, the fall of Troy. Gesture here serves to illustrate metaphor.

The allusion to Andromache's wedding veil accentuates the dramatic and symbolic character of the episode. The effect is striking: a black cloud of sorrow envelops Andromache, replacing the shining veil, Aphrodite's gift, which has slipped to the ground. This veil had been the visible sign of her status as wife and virtuous woman. From now on, no longer protected by Hector, she will be at the mercy of the assailing Greeks. The fall of her *krēdemnon* corresponds, in the feminine sphere, to the dishonor suffered by Hector, as his body is dragged through the dust. The system of values operative in the metaphor of the city-woman finds expression in the actions of the real world.

The Wedding of the Combat

On the battlefield, the allusion to marriage is made explicit on several occasions. In every case, it is a question of differentiating what takes place in the combat of warriors from that which happens in peacetime between men and women. At the very moment when two of the Trojan warriors die, Homer evokes their recent or imminent marriage. It is a way of recalling the inexorable menace that hovers over the hand-to-hand combat of the warriors. Iphidamas, expiring under Agamemnon's blows, is a young man who has just married. The theme of marriage frames his appearance: he has left the marriage chamber for the plain of Troy "where he, pitiful, falls into a deep, leaden sleep, far from the woman whose hand he has won, in return for defending his city. He has not seen the reward he expected from his wife." The connection of the themes of marriage and war is already realized here, and the digressions are all the more significant.

The death of Othryoneus at the hand of Idomeneus is also marked by allusions to marriage. Othryoneus had wanted to take one of Priam's daughters as his bride. To replace the *hedna* (the presents that a suitor offers to the parents of a young woman), which he could not pay in exchange for her hand, he promised a heroic act that would expel the Greeks. Idomeneus triumphs over him by suggesting a wife without the customary gifts: "Follow me then: we will go to our ships to come to terms for the wedding: we shall not, I assure you, look for gifts." [. . .]

The metaphorical transformation of battlefield into a place for courtship paradoxically allows the poet to direct the attention of his audience to the only pertinent place, the combat zone. On the plain of Troy, a warrior can achieve glory or death, but he cannot obtain a bride. Homer plays with the mixture of the two realms—combat and marriage—so as . . . to insist that on the battlefield the only marriage possible is with Thanatos, a death with a feminine face.

WAR AT THE HEART OF THE EROS-THANATOS POLARITY

"We are not allowed to love one another, you and I," says Achilles to Hector at their moment of confrontation.[10] There are many points in this aggressive encounter at which the power of Eros intervenes. Without attempting a comprehensive analysis of the relationship between Eros and Thanatos in the *Iliad*—an analysis that is beyond the scope of this study—let us focus on Hector, whose death is the culminating moment of the poem. Hector is, in fact, at no time more beautiful, more desirable, than at the moment of his death.

Achilles attentively observes—perhaps even admires (*eisoroōn*)—the "beautiful skin" of Hector before burying his spear "in his delicate neck."[11] After he has killed him, he strips him of his armor, and it is at this moment that the beauty of Hector's naked body is most apparent: "The sons of the Achaeans came running from all sides. They admired his body, the enviable beauty of Hector."[12]

Hector, lying in the dust, is like an erotic partner, "sweeter to the touch" (*malakōteros amphaphasthai*) than ever.[13] His "dark hair," his "charming head" are the features on which the poem chooses to end the story of Hector on the battlefield.

From the plain of Troy to the bier erected inside the walls of the city, past the ship of Achilles, Hector's body is subjected to various assaults that do nothing to damage either his beauty or his integrity. Even though Achilles drags Hector's body in the dust every day, he cannot vilify or mutilate it. In fact, a series of divine interventions, playing on the twofold theme of dissimulation and manipulation (magic unguents) preserve the corpse. [. . .]

Aphrodite and Apollo join together in their efforts to preserve the suppleness and integrity of Hector's body by eliminating the risks of dismemberment and putrefaction. The theme of freshness as opposed to dryness appears repeatedly in the story of Hector's dead body. The intervention of Apollo as preserver recurs in two other passages. The god spreads his golden aegis[14] over the body so as to ward off corruption. In death, Hector retains his splendor, the freshness of his youth:

> There he is, all fresh, with the blood that covered him washed off, unsoiled, all his wounds closed, all those he received—and how many warriors drove their bronze spears into him.[15]

Oion eerséeis—quite fresh, or more precisely "as though bathed in dew." This vegetal reference is not meaningless. In fact, the theme of dew, and more generally, that of freshness and of vegetal growth, sounds throughout Hector's trajectory in the last three books of the *Iliad*, from the moment his mother calls to him from the Skaian gates until the moment she grieves over him on his bier. Hecuba chooses to refer to the life she has given as the shoot that she has caused to grow, displaying her *lathikēdēs* breast, "which causes the forgetting of sorrow,"[16] in order to dissuade Hector from confronting Achilles and thus to deflect from him certain death. And when she recovers his body, she again resorts to a vegetal image to describe the freshness of his body:

> And here you are today, lying in your house, fresh-faced, as though life had just left you, like those whom Apollo comes to strike with his gentle arrows.[17]

C. P. Segal[18] has emphasized the paradoxical use of the adjective *hersēeis* or *eersēeis*. A rare occurrence in the *Iliad*, it appears only in the passage of the hierogamy in Book 14 during which the earth brings forth a bed of "lotos bathed in dew" and in the description of Hector's dead body. Hector's corpse is surrounded by vegetal, and more generally, erotic symbolism, for the noun and the adjective "dew" and "dewy" are closely associated with life, with growth, and with beauty. When Hecuba sees "in the corpse of her son a beauty compa-rable to that of dew and flowers,"[19] she is summarizing the ideal of the war-rior's heroic death: to die, after a great exploit, at the height of one's youth and beauty.

At the end of the *Iliad*, we find Hector lying down, this time "on an open couch,"[20] beautiful in death as Paris was in love, he too on a couch, but alive.[21] It is perhaps here that we find the clearest instance of the opposition between Paris and Hector. The beauty of Paris, lyre-player and dancer, in his bedroom in the middle of the day, in a clearly erotic context, is a sign of his cowardice. The freshness of Hector's body, so sweet to the touch, though mauled by Achil-les, is a sign of heroism: because of his heroism he remained dear to the gods,[22] who allowed his beauty not only to outlive his death, but even to increase pre-cisely at the moment his life ends.

War thus stands at the very heart of the Eros-Thanatos polarity. Eros and Thanatos provoke the same physico-psychological transformations. Love's passion, like death, envelops those it afflicts;[23] it conquers them, loosening their limbs. [. . .]

Notes

[1] Vermeule 1979, 99–105.
[2] *Odyssey* 9.449.
[3] *Iliad* 13.830.
[4] *Odyssey* 17.123, 449.
[5] *Works and Days* 519.
[6] *Iliad* 13.291 and 17.288.
[7] *Iliad* 15.509–10.
[8] *Iliad* 17.432.
[9] Vermeule 1979, 101–2.
[10] *Iliad* 22.265.
[11] *Iliad* 22.327.
[12] *Iliad* 22.369–71.
[13] *Iliad* 22.373.
[14] *Iliad* 24.20–21.
[15] *Iliad* 24.419–21
[16] *Iliad* 22.83.
[17] *Iliad* 24.757–59.
[18] Segal 1971.
[19] Ibid., 70.
[20] *Iliad* 24.720.
[21] *Iliad* 3.382, 391–92, 447–48.
[22] *Iliad* 24.423–24.
[23] Eros: *Iliad* 3.442, 24.294; Thanatos: *Iliad* 5.68, 16.350.

MAURICE OLENDER

Misshapen Priapus

1986

The god Priapus's most innate characteristic is also his most visible, namely,
his huge erect penis. Short and disproportionate, Priapus negatively defines
the norm of godly beauty. This disproportionality, and thus ugliness, has,
like beauty, its own correspondences in virtues: Priapus is incontinent, im-
potent, and immoderate. His immoderation shows itself in the garrulous-
ness of the inscriptions carved upon his likenesses. In these inscriptions, the
god displays a constant need to assert that he is, in fact, a god. He also dwells
upon his appearance (which is marked entirely by his ithyphallism) and
compares his body with those of the other gods. This inferiority complex
derives from the fact that Priapus has no metamorphoses available to him,
and no disguises; he is both owner and tenant of his phallus.

Olender's study was part of a collection (including papers by Frontisi-
Ducroux, Loraux, Malamoud, M. Moscovici, and others) that, under the
title Corps des Dieux, *explored how the corporeality of divinity was imag-*
ined in antiquity: beyond the gods' functions and spheres of influence, what
were the specific properties (and limits) of their anthropomorphism? What
formal features do human beings, in taking their place on a spectrum "be-
tween beasts and gods" lend to, and borrow from, the species on either side?
Together with other analyses of human physicality (e.g., Sissa 1990), these
investigations of the immortal body complemented the highly influential
prior studies (Vernant 1982; Loraux 1975, 1978) of the representation of
the bodies of epic heroes who perished in a "beautiful death" and the sup-
port such images later provided to a developing civic ideology.

When Vasari praised the garlands painted by Giovanni da Udine in
the loggia of Psyche in the Farnesina, he detected the presence of
Priapus in the vegetal motifs. In his description of the profusion of
fruits and vegetables, the name of the god with the obscene member denoted
what the painting did not show. The god's phallic body did not appear in the

From "Priape, le mal taillé," in *Le temps de la réflexion* 7 (1986): 374–88.

loggia of Psyche. Thanks to the painter's "grace" and Vasari's pen, Priapus came to life in the description:

> Above the figure of a Mercury in flight, he [Giovanni] has portrayed Priapus as a gourd surrounded by convolvulus with eggplants as testicles. Next to this, he has painted a bunch of large figs, one of which, overripe and split open, has been penetrated by the tip of the gourd. It is impossible to imagine a more graceful capriccio.[1]

As a sexual metaphor, Priapus figured in any number of garlands in which fruits and vegetables were used to represent sexual union during the Renaissance. The ancients never camouflaged Priapus this way, never disguised his massive body as something else. Among the gods Priapus's body was unique. Although surrounded by satyrs, Pans, and other hybrids of man and beast, Priapus was radically anthropomorphic. From birth, moreover, he was distinguished by the enormous size of his phallus. From the first the child was equipped with an oddly oversized *membrum virile*. The ancients associated this oversized member, a mark of ugliness, with attitudes suggesting shame and immodesty. Their descriptions of Priapus's strange body hinted at certain requirements of life in society. They expressed the aesthetic and ethical norms of a community that liked to think of its gods as handsome and well proportioned: figures reflecting the splendor of the divine—polished, gleaming, lustrous statues.

In a parody, Lucian described an assembly of gods ordered hierarchically in terms of the substance (gold, silver, ivory, bronze, or stone) and artistic quality (*tekhnē*) of their statues by Phidias, Alcamenes, Myron, or Euphranor. Far below these came the host of crude gods fabricated without art (*atekhnōs*).[2]

Priapus was represented by a misshapen statuette of mediocre wood. To judge from the texts, his birth seems to have coincided with the carving of a crude effigy that was immediately dubbed "Priapus": "I used to be the trunk of a fig tree, a useless piece of wood [*inutile lignum*], when an artisan, unsure whether to turn me into a stool or a Priapus, decided to make the god" (Horace *Satires* 1.8).

How could a god have such an ugly, shameful body? How could a *theos*, a *divus*,[3] live in such a worthless shell? Reduced as it often was to its most basic essentials, the god was nothing more than a stake driven into the ground, a stake carved in the most rudimentary but essential fashion, for the effigy was always distinguished by its phallus. If Priapus was often confined within garden walls, he also lived trapped inside his crude body.

For Theocritus and Leonidas of Tarentum, both poets of the third century [BCE], as well as for many other Greek and Latin authors[4] the ridiculous little figure with its stiff member served to protect herb gardens or small orchards by frightening away birds, thieves, and anyone else bent on doing violence to the treasures that this modest rural warden was meant to protect. According to Diodorus, he was also supposed to ward off the evil eye by acting as a *baskanion*, or amulet, to repel the envious and chastise "anyone who might cast an evil spell over the fine objects that a man possesses."[5] Thus statues of Priapus with their repellent members were apotropaic objects, capable of warding off evil.

From birth, Priapus's deformed body played a crucial role in determining his fate. His congenital ugliness figured in representations of the god, whose behavior made society wince. Let us briefly revisit the scene of his birth.

That scene began in excess only to end in shame: Aphrodite, returning from Ethiopia, struck Zeus as being possessed of extraordinary beauty (*kallos ametrē-ton*). The two coupled, whereupon Hera, overcome by boundless jealousy, began to worry that the child born of their union might be more beautiful than all of Zeus's other offspring. She therefore touched Aphrodite's belly, and her magic caused the child to be born deformed (*kakomorphos*). [. . .]

The story goes on to say that Priapus was born "misshapen" (*amorphos*), "jumbled" (*asēmos panu*), "shamefully ugly" (*aiskhros*), and "fleshy to the extreme" (*perissosarkos*). His mother, the beautiful Aphrodite, sees with her own eyes (*heōrakuia*) that this child will bring her nothing but shame, reproach, and opprobrium (*psogos*). She then takes the child and tosses it onto a mountain, where a shepherd finds it and brings it up in the belief that the reason for its malady is to make the land and flocks more fertile. As to the nature of this malady (*pathos*), the scholiast indicates that it is an affliction of the sexual organ (*to tou aidoiou*).

Two other texts recount the birth of the child with the repulsive body that makes its mother ashamed. One of these contains an important variant.[6] In this text, after coupling with Dionysus, Aphrodite also couples (*emigē* in both cases) with handsome Adonis. When Dionysus returns, Aphrodite plaits him a garland and goes out to meet him but feels shame (*aideomai*) at the thought of going off with him because she is already married. She then retires to Lampsacus to give birth. Once again, jealous Hera intervenes. With her hand she places a curse on Aphrodite's womb, causing the birth of a deformed (*amorphos*) child named Priapus. This time, however, Aphrodite does not abandon the baby in the mountains but rejects him, turning her back on the child and refusing to recognize (*aparneomai*) him.

Finally, another text insists on the fact that Priapus, son of Dionysus and Aphrodite, is the image (*eidōlon*) of a child with a member (*aidoion*) too big for his age; the member is also referred to as the *phallos*.[7] Let us pause at this point to remark that in the iconography, when Priapus is depicted as a bald old man with an outsized penis, he is characterized by the same phallic disproportion that already defined him in his cradle. As his small body grows old, it adds the characteristics of old age to those of childhood without undergoing any true metamorphosis.

In rejecting the misshapen child to which she has just given birth, Aphrodite tries to avoid the shame occasioned by the sight of the newborn. Her disgust and shame are the result of an ugly, misshapen body dominated by its sexual aspect. The ancient texts link Priapus's misshapen ugliness to his obscene, shameless behavior. In the ancient world, ugliness, like beauty, drew on both the aesthetic and ethical registers by evoking perceptible correspondences.

Now we are ready to see how Priapus not only became a garden god but came to be confined to the garden. Ultimately, in fact, Priapus came to be identified with the wood of his rustic idol, which in a sense imprisoned him inside his image.

A brief scholium by Servius to Virgil's *Georgics* informs us that Priapus was expelled from Lampsacus, his native city, because of the size of his *membrum virile* (*pulsus est propter virilis membri magnitudinem*), whereupon he was accepted by the gods and made god of gardens.[8] If we wish to learn more, we must consult the humanist Noël Conti (1520–1582), who cites many ancient authors on the subject of Priapus. Among them is Posidonius of Apamea (first century [BCE]), from whom Conti took the following tale.[9]

Time had passed. Priapus, now adolescent, haunted the women of Lampsacus, his native city. He was now the man (*vir*) with the big instrument (*ingens instrumentum*), perfect for engendering new citizens. As such he was well liked by the ladies of Lampsacus. This favor earned him the hatred and jealousy of all the other males, and his envious rivals issued a decree banishing him from Lampsacus. Saddened, the women of the town petitioned the gods for help. After a time during which nothing happened, the men of the town discovered that their sexual organs were afflicted with a serious malady. At this point someone was dispatched to the oracle at Dodona to seek advice about how to remedy the disease. The oracle replied that the malady would end only when Priapus had been called back home. This was done at once. Temples were now built and sacrifices made in honor of Priapus, who had meanwhile been declared god of gardens.

Effigies of the god have remained in gardens ever since, like the Priapus of the following epigram, who confesses that he is there for no reason but simply because he has been stuck in the ground by custom. Let us heed what the statue is saying. Here as elsewhere in Greek and Latin *priapea*, the god is loquacious, whether scoffing at passersby or complaining about his threatened place as guardian:

> For no reason [*eis to kenon*] other than to conform to custom [*nomou kharin*],
> Eustochides has stuck me, Priapus, here to watch over his desiccated vine-
> stocks with this big embankment all around. If anyone comes, he will find
> nothing to steal but me, the guardian.[10]

His outsized phallus, which has marked him from birth, has thus gotten him rejected by his mother and then thrown out (*pulsus est*) of his native city.

When he returns in less outlandish form, Priapus seems menacing but is in reality a harmless garden decoration. From now on, this god, the legitimate[11] son of Aphrodite and either Zeus, Dionysus, or Adonis (depending on the version) would be hastily carved from any old piece of wood. Columella advises his readers "to honor this god carved in the trunk of any old tree,"[12] and Horace describes a Priapus carved from the worthless wood of the fig tree. The fact that the immodest god was often carved from the wood of the fig tree is significant, because the semantic field of this tree and its fruit illustrates various aspects of the god's obscenity.

When Theocritus indicates a path by a brook ("take the path by the oak trees"), Priapus suddenly appears. His "statue, just carved in the wood of a fig tree," is still covered with bark. In another text, as witness to his recent fabrication, Priapus points to a tree, a poplar, which stands to his left, as the source of the wood from which he is made.[13] Sometimes, in one of the countless puns with which the *priapea* are filled, the god points out that once his phallic scepter has been detached from the tree, it will no longer sprout leaves.[14] Sometimes the god addresses a passerby: "As you see, I am wood [*sum ligneus*]."[15]

The garrulous god feels compelled to comment endlessly on the shape of his body. Sometimes he compares himself to the other gods ("each of us has his own particular shape") in order to point out that the distinctive feature in his case is none other than the phallus. At other times he complains that he is nothing but a miserable piece of wood with a shape that makes him *seem* more fearsome than he is.

If a passerby looks too closely at his statue, Priapus describes it in surprising detail: "I am made of the wood of the fig tree, neither filed smooth nor cut to the red line but hacked out by an uneducated shepherd with his hook."[16] In other words, this is not a polished statue; its maker has not even taken the trouble to smooth the green wood with a file. Indeed, these details are consistent with the whole of his body, since the god is carved out of a block of wood like a club, and the mark of his identity is that he is a single piece. The words that describe the wood of the statue suggest that the god has a monolithic body as hard as it is insensitive.[17] The weapon (*hoplon*) that grows in the hollow of the groin is nothing other than a club (*rhopalon, clava*).[18]

Once carved, the statuette had to be erected.[19] Sometimes the farmer who carved it bestowed a name on the piece of wood. For example, the god tells the story of how one day, just after his raw wood (*lignum rude*) had been carved, the *vilicus* said: "You be Priapus."[20] Here, the naming of the god defines his identity. Just as Horace's artisan "decided" to make a Priapus rather than a stool, the farmer transformed an ordinary piece of wood into a distinctive god. Between his renunciation (*aparneomai*) by his mother at birth and the need to name his image in order to recognize it, Priapus occupied a special place among the gods that neither Diodorus nor Strabo doubted, even if the latter insisted on the fact that Priapus was a god of recent times, a late arrival with whom "Hesiod was unfamiliar."[21] The loquacious god of the *priapea* expressed this difference in his own way, complaining that he never met Penelope. But, he says, "in those days I had not yet been carved."[22] Priapus sometimes exaggerated his marginality by pointing out that he was honored and greeted as a *divus minor*, because, when compared with his elders (*maiorum*), he was the last of the gods.

Priapus is therefore a god with problems of representation. In his characteristic style of self-derision, the garrulous idol constantly repeats that its crude, shapeless wood is the divine body of Priapus. This strange need for a god to assert that he is a god is matched by his constant concern with his appearance, his need to look like what he professes to be, as if his identity were entirely a prisoner of his appearance and his need to frighten passers-by with his terrifying (*terribilis*) member.[23] [. . .]

In many respects, Priapus's image is that of a paralyzed god rather than a force in action. The child is cast out at birth. As an adolescent, he is sent into exile. And his effigy is a sort of scarecrow hastily thrown together and enclosed within a garden. This is a three-stage operation. In the first stage, a statue is crudely carved, generally from a single block of wood, by the relatively unskilled hands of a shepherd or peasant or, less often, an artisan. Then the statue is erected by sticking it in the ground. Finally, the phallic stake is named Priapus.

Priapus's arrival thus seems to coincide with the hewing of his idol. Apart from his birth and his adolescent banishment from Lampsacus, which results in his becoming god of gardens, he does not seem to have an identity distinct from the wooden figure of which people ask questions, a figure the poets portrayed as an astonishing ventriloquist: a body reduced to an endlessly loquacious phallic marker. Encased within a piece of wood, a carelessly carved log, incarnated in and by his effigy, Priapus bore no resemblance whatsoever to those unconstrained and mobile gods Hermes, who could be anywhere, and Dionysus, who lent himself to countless epiphanies and who sometimes, after arousing someone's desire, had the dramatic power of making himself impossible to grasp, even invisible. Compared with this father, with his multiple apparitions and changing masks, forever veiling what he revealed, Priapus was immobile and always on display, frozen in his visibility. So easy was he to grasp that his figure, more menaced than menacing, was in constant danger of being spirited away or even burned on the household hearth.

Although the gods' corporeal envelopes were the subject of endless games and innumerable metamorphoses, Priapus was incapable of the slightest movement or the least transformation. At once owner and tenant of his phallus, hamstrung by his tumescent member, he was nailed to his stake. Priapism, the malady to which the god lent his name, was looked upon by ancient physicians as a form of *paralysis*,[24] a fact that adds an additional element to the image of the rigid god if we assume that the nosographic vocabulary is not independent of either common social values or shared knowledge. Priapus's *membrum vir-ile*, like his statue, seems stuck, incapable of changing its state. Such changeless-ness is unnatural for this member, and Aristotle regards it as a "morbid alteration," because the organ is defined by nothing other than its mobility, that is, by the fact that it "increases and diminishes in volume."[25] [. . .]

When ugliness affects the representation of the body, disgust enters the pic-ture in two main ways: through the vileness of death, which causes the battered or defiled body to decompose, and through excessive, untrammeled sexuality in defiance of propriety, restraint, and decency. To abandon reserve is to make body, mind, and spirit ugly. In the first sense, *aiskhros*, which in later texts de-scribes Priapus's physical appearance and manners, already referred in the Ho-meric texts to both a physical mark and a form of behavior or social condition.[26]

The hideous and the ugly could manifest themselves not only in shame and infamy but also in the sort of derision and laughter that obscenity and lewdness could provoke. In ancient representations these terms were closely associated with excesses apt to disrupt the equilibrium required by beauty and decency. Words for ugliness and indecency, together with the reactions of laughter and disgust to which they gave rise, allow us to probe certain sensitive areas of social deviancy.[27]

The concrete manifestations of Priapus's ugliness correlate with the fact that he is a god whose visible body determines all his speech and action. The an-cients produced a series of representations of Priapus revealing both his ugli-ness and indecency, showing him to be an incontinent fellow as garrulous as he was impotent, a god utterly without mastery. He shamed everyone but never felt ashamed himself. Perhaps this was because, as Plutarch puts it, "he who is shameless [*anaidēs*] is not pained by what is shameful [*aiskhros*]."[28] [. . .]

Because he displays what ought to be hidden and shows off what should be kept under wraps, Priapus typifies the ugliness of impropriety. His all too vis-ible behavior is characterized as *turpis*. This term belongs to the Latin lexicon of moral and physical ugliness, often revealed by sight; it could also express indecency or obscenity that lacked charm and was repellent. Priapus's inde-cency is characterized by his absolute lack of self-control. He cannot restrain himself or hide his organ, and his language is just as incontinent. He endlessly rehearses the same threats and obscene litanies. The rhetoric of the *priapea* is as ridiculous as its threats are ineffective.

Theognis was aware of how few men were never tempted by anything vile (*aiskhros*), and he pointed out that decency (*aidōs*) was a matter of facial expres-sion as well as speech. And at the other extreme of ancient times, Plutarch criticized indecency (*anaideia*) in the voice and debauchery (*akolasia*) in the male organ, both being forms of ugliness to which Priapus was subject: lewd-ness and idle gossip. Plutarch further associates the two images by remarking that those who indulge to excess in sexual pleasure have sterile sperm, "just as the talk of gossips is fruitless and yields nothing." Priapus's display of his organ does not lead to fatherhood any more than his garrulous tongue hits any target effectively.

[. . .] Ultimately, Priapus's phallus was not just visible but all-consuming. It not only filled up his tiny garden but permeated all the prose that the ancients wrote about him for more than half a millennium in *priapea* that attest to the abdication of imagination in favor of repetition. The god's significance was reduced to his visible armature, to a figure whose only intrinsic quality was apparently to represent the visible. Prisoner of what he displayed, wholly identified with his unchanging form, Priapus seemed to come down to the exhibitionism that defined him, the ithyphallism that set him apart among the gods from birth. [. . .]

Although gods sometimes transgress the limits of their bodies and change from one type to another, Priapus is like a mortal in that he undergoes no metamorphosis. Nor does he appear and disappear or experience transfiguration. He is not only changeless but unambiguous—carved from a single block, like a club. Devoid of suppleness, metaphor is beyond his grasp. Strictly required to offer nothing of himself but what is visible, he shows everything and reveals nothing. Homogeneous to excess, in body and in word, Priapus is merely lewd, rigid, petrified.

Decency can play with indecency. Covering up can be followed by uncovering. Thus the garment that covers the body (or certain intimate parts of the body) serves as a garment of modesty, yet at the same time allows access to others governed by rules of propriety that may be broken but within limits. It is just such a garment that Priapus lacks, and this lack condemns him to a state of solipsism in which the only possible communication is sterile repetition. Or, just as unlikely to encourage decency, the iconography shows Priapus in a position of anasurma, his garment pulled back in such a way as to reveal his member. Priapus's statue is literally never unveiled. It is in a state of perpetual exhibition. Hence its physical envelope is all the more constraining. It is obscenity petrified.

We are a long way from the garlands painted by Giovanni da Udine in the loggia of Psyche in the Farnesina.

TRANSLATED BY ARTHUR GOLDHAMMER

NOTES

[1] Giorgio Vasari, *Le Vite dei più eccellenti pittori scultori ed architettori*, vol. 6 (Florence, 1906; repr. 1973), p. 558. [. . .]

[2] Lucian *Zeus the Tragedian* 7. [. . .]

[3] Priapus was both *daimōn* and *numen*.

[4] Primarily in the Greek *Anthology* and in a Latin anthology known as the *Corpus priapeorum*, whose poems are said to date from the late first century [CE] [. . .].

[5] Diodorus Siculus 4.6.4.

[6] Scholia to Apollonius of Rhodes *Argonautica* 1.932, ed. C. Wendel (1935). [. . .]

[7] Nonnos scholia 40 [. . .]. See also *Souda*, s.v. *Priapos*.

[8] See Servius at 4.111, ed. G. Thilo, vol. 3 (1887), p. 328.

[9] Natalis Comes (Noël Conti), *Mythologiae sive explicationum fabularum libri decem* (Paris, 1605). [. . .]

[10] Lucian *Anthology of Planudes* 238.

[11] According to the scholia to Euripides' *Alcestis* 989 (ed. E. Schwartz, vol. 2 [1891], p. 239), a god is legitimate (*gnēsios*) if both of his parents are divine.

[12] Columella *Agriculture* 10.31–34.

[13] *Corpus Priapeorum* 85.

[14] Ibid., 25.

[15] Ibid., 6, 43. [. . .]

[16] *Anthology of Planudes* 86. [. . .]

[17] *Anthology of Planudes* 242. . . .

[18] Ibid., 242. [. . .]

[19] The verb *histēmi*: *Anthology of Planudes* 236; verb *tithēmi*: ibid., 238. [. . .]

[20] *Corpus Priapeorum* 10: *tu Priapus esto*.

[21] Diodorus Siculus 4.6.4; Strabo 13.1.12.

[22] *Corpus Priapeorum* 68.

[23] Columella *Agriculture* 10.33; *Corpus Priapeorum* 20.

[24] Caelius Aurelianus 5.9.90. [. . .]

[25] Aristotle *On the Parts of Animals* 689a.

[26] See Vernant 1979, 1365–74.

[27] Olender 1985.

[28] Plutarch *On False Shame* 528D–E.

YAN THOMAS

The *Venter*: Maternal Body, Paternal Right

1987

Ostensibly a survey of the term venter *in Roman civil law, Thomas's study offers a multifaceted example of the mental and social construction of a legally precise entity—the unborn infant, with rights that will come into force upon parturition—from the indissoluble organic complex of the mother, her uterine environment, and the (potential) child who inhabits it. Phenomena like cesarean section (in antiquity, usually fatal to the mother) and judicial injunctions to "nourish the womb" point to the absolute conceptual distinction between the maternal body and the contents of the uterus, which derived legal and civic status exclusively from the male parent, as the state was eager to guarantee in the case of his absence or death. The resulting perspective on male and female status here coincides with scrutiny of the human body and the function of its parts and metonyms.*

Omitted from this translation are sections on Greco-Roman precedent, juridical oversight of childbirth, and legal attitudes to abortion.

In Roman law a child who has been conceived but not yet born is called a *venter*. The word designates the invisible subject who, although he is still one with his mother, is already entitled to his own rights. The word's usage is specific. First of all, it does not refer to any kind of organic entity. *Partus* is the word used for embryo: the embryo already formed, which is proleptically considered as about to be expelled from the womb, if not already released from the mother. But no legal value is added to the obstetrical meaning: the *partus* is that to which the woman must give birth (*pario*). *Venter*, on the contrary, refers to nothing outside of law. By means of this legal fiction whose name is borrowed from that of the womb, jurists deduce a legal individuality, a network of rights contingent on the realization of birth (the birth that is itself a legal fact since it

From "Le 'ventre': Corps maternel, droit paternel," in *Le genre humain* 14 (1987): 211–37.

actualizes a provisional or resolutive condition). Furthermore, this way of qualifying *venter* belongs exclusively to Roman civil law. Everywhere else, a woman's *venter* is her womb: it is only within a legal context that the container, through metonymy, comes to signify the contained.

THE WOMB, THE CHILD, THE POSTHUMOUS CHILD

When a legitimate heir is expected—an heir to whom the law guarantees succession rights because he belongs to the masculine line of descent—the patrimonial status quo comes to an end. Through his birth, the newborn cancels the testament of his father who should have anticipated either instituting him as his heir or disinherited him nominally. He should have included in his will the following clause: "let the *venter* be disinherited" (*venter exheres esto*). "If the *venter* has been ignored" (*ventre praeterito*), the current heir loses his rights.[1] "To substitute for the *venter*" is to designate a second-rank heir in case the posthumous heir dies.[2] Similarly, in successions where no will has been drawn up, the *venter* is preferred to any other potential heir of secondary degree, whether a relative, the state, or the treasury: the "*proximus a ventre*," the individual next in line in the order of succession after the child to be born, is now set aside. Equally suspended are the rights of those who are "in the same degree as the *venter*,"[3] namely the brothers and sisters of the upcoming child or children, who still do not know how many joint heirs they will have. How many, within a single birth, will come to share the succession? How many will take their share of the common debts?

Through the essentially uncertain *venter*, legal fiction has to cope with nature, a nature that is sometimes so creative that boundaries are sometimes needed to check its excesses. For, if a woman from Alexandria gave birth to five children, and made the trip to Rome to be seen by the emperor himself, was this enough ground to decide that the heir, pending further information, should content himself with one-sixth?[4] [. . .] A reasonable legal solution, or average, is therefore instituted. Jurists decide that the number of children which the womb can conceal should not exceed three, that the heir who is "in the same degree as the *venter*" is entitled to enjoy one-quarter of the patrimony before delivery:[5] only then would it become clear whether his share would increase in relation to the lower number of children being born, or whether it would decrease proportionately should more children be born by some miracle.[6]

Legal circumspection, therefore, creates order where organic confusion rules; for, in the words of a famous jurist who conveyed Aristotle's opinion that quintuplets were no exception to the laws of nature, "so many can women's wombs contain."[7] The designation of the child to be born as *in ventre* or *in utero* is no stylistic convention. It is a formula used by jurists to overcome the obstacles which the uterine envelope poses to the law, to the father's right over the child, when the father is still alive, and especially to the child's right to succeed his father if the latter is deceased. The woman, then, ends up in the unlikely situation of having to embody the masculine line of descent herself: she forms a unit with the *venter*, since the latter designates both her and what is not entirely hers. The *venter* is "allowed provisional possession" of the inheritance, a process called *mittere ventrem*. In order to defend the rights of the child, a guardian *ad ventrem* is assigned to him. It is particularly in these circumstances that the one *in ventre* (whose legal individuality is derived from his father) is called *venter*, and that the law overcomes the opacity of the maternal body in order to regard the heir as already present in legal terms, appropriating the signifier to turn it against itself and applying the word for womb to the father's posthumous son. Correspondingly, the technical term designating a mother as parturient, *parens*, in legal language acquires the opposite meaning of father or ascendant in the paternal line of descent. When Isidorus, in a learned etymology drawn from an excellent antiquarian source, equates parents with parturients—*parentes quasi parientes*—he refers exclusively to the father who has the double function of founder of a line of descent—*initium generis*—on the one hand, and parent (sire) on the other. In this way, because he is the only agent of procreation, the father is its cause and the mother its matter.[8] Maternal status is apparently abolished by a permutation of the masculine and the feminine but, by means of this exchange, the law establishes the father as a substitute for the mother.

A learned linguistic confusion that serves an institutional function. At first glance, the law opts for the indivisibility of mother and child: the child whom she bears has no name other than that which contains it, no name, we should add, other than the woman as a whole, since she herself is reduced to *venter*. When the *venter* is allowed provisional possession, the initiative for the entire procedure rests with the wife: she is the one who, temporarily and under the supervision of a guardian, receives the property. There is indivisibility, therefore, but also division. We should not question the cohesion of a representation where the alternative between enclosing body and enclosed body is perpetually doubtful and makes it impossible to know exactly whether one or the other, or both, are concerned. [. . .]

The womb, the woman, the posthumous child: out of this organic network, the law strives to isolate a virtual subject—a legal subject, as we have already seen, and therefore incorporeal. By using the qualification *venter*, the law transforms a physical entity into a legal entity able to exercise its rights. The organic body of the womb turns into the legal body of a child about to be born: these two registers come together and trade places constantly as the pregnant woman's maternity and the dead man's paternity collide like two opposing elements.

This is the law's exclusive prerogative. Elsewhere, *venter* has but a single meaning: reproductive organ, pregnant woman. For a woman, *venter, uterus, alvus, matrix* are one and the same thing: a space which can be either full or empty, but always acts as a container. And this is no obstacle to saying that the son who has left his mother's *venter* still holds a title to it: "It is your own *venter*, Britannicus, which she flaunts": this is how Messalina, who shows herself bare-breasted in brothels, is being criticized for her behavior.[9] Far from constituting an abstract concept, the *venter* metonymy impresses maternity onto the body itself. This is why "striking the *venter*" is the best way to kill a pregnant woman, and especially to dispatch a mother—Agrippina begs to be stabbed in the very spot that had given birth to Nero: "and bringing her womb forward: strike the *venter*, she said."[10] [. . .]

To Nurture the *Venter*

In order to understand how a subject defined by law can borrow its name from that of the womb, one should first examine the maternal body. The pregnant woman is dual. She is herself, but in her there is this other being who, although he is organically part of her, does not legally participate of her substance. A legal entity has taken over the entire space, since, from now on, the *venter* is this other within herself. Let us not forget, in order to evaluate properly this radical otherness, that in law the *venter* is always the posthumous heir of a deceased male, whether husband or father.

Case law devoted to posthumous heirs is abundant and unusually complicated. This does not, however, necessarily mean that it was frequently resorted to. It only suggests that a Roman always had to consider the possibility of dying and leaving a wife behind him pregnant with his child: the law itself would require him to anticipate this eventuality. Because of the close attention they pay to rare occurrences, the jurists allow us to observe the high points of their normative universe. By devoting so much mental energy to those rare cases where a child would be born after the natural or civil demise of his father, jurists perform a theoretical operation. They isolate a hybrid phenomenon in order to isolate an essence. The hybrid originates from a dead man who will not exercise his paternity and from a woman who, because of her husband's death, loses her legal status as a mother: while marriage creates the mother, its dissolution terminates her function. The essence is that of the genealogical link. The latter appears at its most visible when, of the two poles that it binds together, the first does not exist any more and the other does not exist yet and can only be thought of as a link. Between a father's death and his son's birth, their abstract unity is realized within the *venter*'s receptacle. There is no other legal fiction in Roman law which better confirms the saying (used about inheritance rights) that father and son are one and the same person: *pater et filius eadem persona.*[11]

We have already said that the woman is divided between herself and the *venter*: during the procedure when she is granted provisional possession *ventris nomine*, she acts in the name of an invisible entity. But there is an entire casuistry relating to nourishment whose function seems to be to differentiate between the two natures. A common notion at the time is that the embryo feeds on the blood that flows back into the womb. But how is one to reconcile this nourishing blood dispensed by a mother's body with the legal principle requiring that all nourishment come from the father? It will be enough to isolate, from what the woman eats, the share that is specifically reserved for the *venter* and will be deducted from the patrimony: these are the "nourishments paid out to the *venter*."[12] [. . .]

One of the tasks entrusted to a guardian *ad ventrem* is to rule on the question of sustenance. He will take into consideration neither the woman's personal fortune nor her dowry, for what she lives on is not what the child feeds on: the latter's nourishment is deducted from his father's patrimony, and comes to him only from the latter. [. . .] Thus legal casuistry constructs a double flow of maintenance: that of the woman, and that of the father's child. There could hardly be a more radical separation. Jurists distinguish between the nature of the mother and that of the child to be born. The latter is in the father's sphere of influence; the father himself falls within the competence of the state: "Everything should be done to make sure that the child [*partus*] is born. The *venter* must be nourished, if not for his father, who is dead, at least for the state which he augments through his birth."[13] For the father, for the state: this captures the essence of the economy of Roman marriage, and the role of women within it. Because she has no civic function, she does not procreate directly for the state. She gives children to her husband who in turn acts as father for the benefit of the state.

The *venter* has so much autonomy in relation to the mother's body that to deny the *venter* provisional possession means to kill the child. "To deny maintenance" (*alimonia denegare*) and "starve to death" (*fame necare*) are equivalent: the newborn is killed by abandonment. Exposure, which consists in setting down a child in order to let him starve to death, represents the exact opposite of the gesture the father makes when he acknowledges paternity of his child: he raises him from the ground (*tollere liberos*) and orders that he be breast-fed (*ali iubere*). Thus the son is first raised, then nourished (*sublatus altusque*). His first nourishment, then, comes to him from his being accepted and integrated through this primeval gesture within the father's domain. In this way, the child owes his coming into life to his father who either performs the ritual in person if he is present, or delegates it if absent. It becomes understandable now why jurists, in the chapter entitled "on the granting of provisional possession to the *venter*," decided that if an heir *in utero* dies as a result of the stream of nourishment from his patrimony being cut off, this is death by starvation. [. . .]

Not to let him die of starvation: a matter of life or death that remains entirely foreign to the mother herself. It is as though the law did not even recognize that she could nourish the *venter* by herself. The legal alternative is either to nourish the posthumous child from the paternal inheritance, or to kill him the way children are exposed. For not to grant provisional possession to the *venter* means to deprive him of his birth:

> the cause of children who remain to be born should prevail over those who are already born. Indeed, everything must be done in order to facilitate the birth of a *partus*. For a child already born, the only necessity is to make him integrate the family [i.e., being granted provisional possession consecrates him as a legitimate heir]. As for the child who is still to be born, he must be nourished: if not for his father, who is dead, at least for the state which he augments through his birth.[14]

Thus, the institution alone allows the child to be born. It substitutes itself for the father who, had he been alive, would have performed the act of acknowledgment and ordered that his son be fed. The legal fiction allows the dead father to acknowledge paternity *in utero*. The child is allowed to draw nourishment from his father's patrimony as though he had already been delivered and separated from his mother by means of the paternal gesture.

THE SPLIT BODY

The case law concerning the maintenance of the *venter* acts as an effective aid to conceiving of the principle of division between paternal and maternal. One seldom sees an institution so exclusively dependent on fundamental notions of sexual reproduction. [. . .]

Jurists were not only able to isolate from the maternal body a subject which is both legally and—through the fiction of nourishments—biologically foreign to it; they were also able to insure that this learned sleight-of-hand be applied efficiently. Legal constructs work hand in hand with law enforcement but, this time, it is the policing of the maternal body, of the body as such—in the same sense as *contrainte par corps*. This enforcing of the law falls under the responsibility of the urban praetor. The praetor's edict strictly regulates the supervision of pregnant widows and, even more strictly, their delivery. Control is exercised by the dead husband's relatives. The stakes are twofold: first, relatives are given the means to verify that the widow is truly pregnant and that she is not getting ready to display a child who is not hers. They should also make sure that the child is raised according to his father's will. What is being prescribed is not only the staging of the delivery but also the separation. [. . .]

Under the reign of Marcus Aurelius, a husband whom his wife had repudiated came to suspect that she was carrying his child. He obtained a rescript from the emperor authorizing him to have his ex-wife examined by three mid-wives, and to have a guard stand at her side until delivery. Ulpian makes the following observation about this intervention by law, similar to the one that the praetor's edict prescribed concerning the pregnant widow: "The *partus* is an integral part of the woman and of her entrails. But as soon as he is separated from her [*plane post editum*], the man can, in his own right [*iure suo*] claim his son and, based on the praetor's edict, ask that he be presented to him or even carry him away. Thus the *princeps* grants his help whenever necessary." The *portio mulieris* or *pars viscerum* motif is reminiscent of the Stoic notion that the embryo is but a *meros tēs gastros* (part of the belly). But common opinion about embryos is used here to define birth legally as a complete rupture. Once the mother's indivisible body, which is placed under surveillance and subjected to constraint precisely because of its indivisibility, lets the son out, the father can appropriate him immediately. Once again the *venter* construct has to yield to the reality of organic fusion. The jurist, in turn, agrees to this fusion when nature, because it is too opaque for the law, requires a *contrainte par corps* and demands that "a partition be established between what comes before and af-ter," i.e., to consider and qualify childbirth as a legal event. Biological nature yields to legal nature, embryo to son, maternal body to paternal right.

Birth, then, is considered as a dissociation and sometimes made more dra-matic by the mother's death. If a rule of pontifical law prohibited that a preg-nant woman be buried before her fruit was liberated, it was not only, as a jurist from the classical period explains, because one ought to preserve "hope for a living being." The commentary is only trying to make what is but a funerary taboo conform to the rationality of jurisprudence: in order to subsume the rule under this general purpose, the woman would have to have reached the end of her pregnancy at the time of her death, a clause that the law itself does not specify. More likely to shed light on its meaning is the antiquarian saying used to explain the etymology of Caesar's name: of all births, the ones requiring cutting open the womb were also held to be the most auspicious. If Caesar owed his auspicious name to a cesarean, one may assume that, since the birth of a child required that his mother be sacrificed, the barren death of a woman was to be compensated by a substitute of birth: hence the excision of the fruit. [. . .]

INCARNATING THE ABSENT FATHER

The deceased or absent father: these are the extreme cases when the alterna-tive between *venter* fiction and *venter* policing comes into action, between the entire might of the law in the place of reality on the one hand, and an omni-present reality impervious to law on the other; in brief, between the two mean-ings of *venter*.

But what if the husband is not only alive but present as the mother's husband? The machinery of the law is at hand to invest the child with life. The child is born. As soon as he is separated from the womb, he is enveloped by the paternal power. The father can appropriate him legally even though he were to ignore everything of his birth. He derives this power from the state—which delegates it to him—and can only lose it with or by the state, when civil law formally breaks either the civic or domestic bond. [. . .] Any modification made to the son's status requires the formalities of civic mediation, and the passage of time does not in any way alter the imperishable bond that keeps him *in potestate*.

The father, therefore, is legally invested with power over his sons. He becomes so as soon as the *venter* ceases to perform its function. As far as civil law is concerned, the mother appears only under this title. When she is no longer able to appear as *venter*, she does not even exist any more. There are no maternal rights, no power, no legitimate claim to inheritance, no transmission of the name. Legally a woman is defined as a subject unable to transmit. As one of Ulpian's aphorisms has it: "She is the beginning and the end of her own family." *Caput et finis*: a mere segment.

Since all transmission has to be masculine, it is the father's responsibility to bring about the child's birth. First, because of the legal fiction according to which the son is "born from the father": a formula that does not refer to procreation, for to be born is not to procreate and because "born from the father" belongs to the machinery of adoption laws. Second, on account of a ritual that both replicates the legal mechanism and reveals its meaning. The father raises the child off the ground and, as Ennius puts it, "brings him to his chest." By doing this, the father fulfills a function that, among the plethora of female divinities specializing in supervising childbirth, a masculine deity performs: Jupiter, the father-god.

When the child exits the womb he does not immediately receive the female attention of midwives, nurses, and mother. [. . .] The child was either raised and fed at the father's behest, or, as we saw, was rejected and denied the right to live. The texts are numerous and consistent enough to help us reconstruct the stages of a ritual that had been performed on Cicero, Augustus, and Nero, which legal writers of the third and fourth centuries [CE] still mention. When on the ground, the child is naked: the coldness of the floor was sometimes supposed to trigger his first cry. But what does the "raising" mean? [. . .]

Tollere liberos designates both the gesture of raising a child from the ground and its legal equivalent conveyed by this metaphor: for "to raise the child" can just as well mean "to acquire paternal power." It does not matter, then, whether this right is a consequence of the ritual, or whether the ritual is only a way to signify this right. The essential remains: the primeval gesture is a masculine one. It cannot be separated from that most Roman of all institutions: *patria potestas*. It is on this model that the annalists fashioned the story of the primeval twins' second birth: after they have been exposed, and then breast-fed by the she-wolf, Romulus and Remus are taken in by the shepherd Faustulus, who hands them over to his wife to be fed. Just as the legal father, the foster father performs a gesture that implies its opposite: to raise the child and have him breast-fed is only one out of two options, the other being to deposit the child and let him starve to death. In this case, the twins experienced both these fates consecutively.

Everyone knows that they owed their salvation to the she-wolf who offered her teats at the Lupercal. But this first, purely animal maternity, is in stark contrast with the humanized, Romanized maternity of the wife to whom her husband hands over the children he has held. [. . .]

Tollere liberos: paternal institution, civic institution. First, the child is born from the maternal body; then the father brings the child under his own *potestas* (right) and, from there, to the tutelage of the state. In Cicero's own words, from his *Response to the Haruspices* (27, 57): "Nature ties us first to our parents, to the immortal gods, and to the fatherland. For as soon as we are raised to the light of day, we receive heavenly breath and are in our proper place registered within the state." *Parentes*, gods, and *patria* all contribute to the birth of a citizen. The former "raise" their sons, the gods breathe life into them, the state grants them their status. Worth noting is how much *patria* determines *parentes*: the masculine value of *parens* is thus increased twofold. For this initiation into life and the state, which he receives as soon as he exits the maternal body, the child has no other "parent" than his father.

One can understand why Roman legal casuistry was so obsessed with the figure of the posthumous child. In the absence of paternity's usual embodiment (i.e., the father), paternity is thought of as happening through the now dual body of the mother, a body containing a foreign incorporeal.

When she was pregnant with Augustus, Atia saw in a dream her entrails unfold all the way to the stars and wrap around the universe; lying by her side Octavius, in his own dream, was contemplating the sun rising from his wife's womb. For his mother, the birth of an emperor implied the image of her own body expanding infinitely; in his father's dream, it was announced by the appearance of a celestial body "emerging from Atia's womb."

TRANSLATED BY FLORENT HEINTZ

NOTES

[1] Respectively: *Digest* 28.3.3.5 and 29.2.84.

[2] Ibid., 25.4.3.

[3] Ibid., 5.4.3.

[4] Ibid., 46.3.36; contra: Ulpian *Digest* 29.2.39.6.

[5] *Digest* 5.1.28.5.

[6] Ulpian *Digest* 5.4.4, apparently contradicted by *Digest* 29.2.30.6.

[7] Julian *Digest* 46.3.36. Aristotle's opinion comes from *Hist. animal.* 7.4.36.

[8] Isidorus *Etym.* 9.5.4.

[9] Juvenal *Sat.* 6.124.

[10] Tacitus *Annals* 11.38.

[11] *Justinian Code* 6.26.11.

[12] *Digest* 25.6.1.7; 37.9.9.

[13] Ibid., 37.9.1.19.

[14] Ibid., 37.9.1.15.

CLAUDE NICOLET

Structure and Communication

1976

The final pages (the Conclusion) of Le métier de citoyen *highlight the importance of the census, which Nicolet views as providing the* ratio— *"a word that can be translated both as 'system' and as 'structure'"*—*of the Roman Republic. Not only did the census sort out the precise identity of the citizen in terms of the fiscal, military, and civic obligations that the state required, but it also established a class hierarchy that contained conflict effectively by apportioning rights and duties according to well-precedented categories. To articulate the numerous interrelations that involved the Roman citizen, moreover, Nicolet distinguishes two developments unique in the ancient world: first, a complex system of communication, ranging widely both geographically and socially, and, second, the associated, broad-based prominence of the language necessary to such communication, initially as political oratory and later via literacy. Sharing in part the* Annales *perspective as well as Paul Veyne's interest in the mental and social formulations that permit government, Nicolet shows how key dispositions and interests of the Roman citizenry helped to create the successful rule of the Republican oligarchies.*

I n this book, I have chosen to analyze Roman political life in the largest sense of the phrase, at the level of what may be called its civic base. I have, therefore, deliberately omitted the much narrower upper sphere that was the focus of the most obvious events on the political stage. [. . .] The social level whose point of view I have tried to adopt has seldom been explored until now, mostly because it eludes us for the most part in its particularity: plain citizens, nobodies who are only valuable as members of a larger group, appear only very rarely in sources that are generally no more than bare chronicles.

The preceding pages, although too cursory to cover the subject exhaustively, do allow us to reach several tentative conclusions that, I believe, are likely to

From "Structure et Communication," in *Le métier de citoyen dans la Rome républicaine* (Paris: Gallimard, 1976), pp. 506–28.

modify the rather stiff image of the Roman state long promoted by the study of public law alone. I should like to insist on a few points.

First, it appears that Roman civic life under the Middle and Late Republic constitutes a true structure, a coherent whole moved by a highly powerful internal logic. As is to be expected, every element within this structure remains in a relatively fixed position in relation to other elements; any change occurring in one of these elements will sooner or later cause others to be modified. We have seen how most of civic life takes place within three areas: the military, the financial, and the area of political decision. To be a Roman citizen means to have, in each of these three domains, a set of rights and obligations, to enjoy a certain number of privileges, and to endure a certain amount of inconvenience. The three domains are strongly connected, because it is both unthinkable and abnormal that a citizen should be either entirely excluded from, or completely oblivious of, the decisions affecting his life and destiny. Like any ancient state, the Roman state establishes a simple and highly conscious connection between the safety and prominence of the community on the one hand, and that of each of its components on the other. [. . .] In the end, all the demands made by the city (military, fiscal, and civic duties) are nothing but demands made by and for oneself. They are not imposed on the citizen from the outside, by a reality that would transcend him; on the contrary, they originate in the simple logic of a tacit contract that binds free individuals together. These necessary constraints are but a form of freedom. Because they are not arbitrary, but logically justified, they constitute a structure.

But even though every individual is thus, in theory, bound to the city by equal ties, in practice the degree of participation, or rather of constraint, will not be the same for all. [. . .] This is why the organization of the entire state is based on a central principle, the true keystone of the system, whose purpose is to distribute to everyone their rights and duties, their obligations and privileges, as accurately and strictly as possible, and in the interest of all. This is what the Romans call the *ordo* or—using a word that can be translated both as "system" and as "structure"—the *ratio* of the census. The census in Rome appears therefore, with all the various categories that derive from it, as absolutely central and fundamental. Everything depends on it: military levies, the calculation and payment of taxes, the organization of political assemblies, the access to magistracies and, generally, to the ruling class. [. . .] This voluntary hierarchy that the city establishes between citizens by means of the censors follows one main principle: the quest for "proportional" or "geometric equality." To rich, noble, and powerful individuals falls the share not only of providing the bulk of the military and fiscal effort, but also the main role in the making and enforcing of public decisions. Because they are overwhelmed by their lot, the poor are "relieved" of these various burdens and responsibilities.

We are entitled to call such a system a structure, because the test of history will show how strikingly interconnected all its elements are. Such as I have just described it, the census system functioned correctly until around the end of Hannibal's Punic war. From the middle of the second century onward, however, it becomes progressively desegregated. The first sector to crumble is the fiscal one: from 167 onward, success met in overseas campaigns allowed citizens to become exempt from direct taxation. The close link that existed between military effort and fiscal effort now disappeared: this came as an immediate advantage for the rich, who were the only ones who had to pay. Hence a source of unbalance. The poor will not wait long before claiming their own share. As soon as 133, it becomes necessary to distribute part of the public lands directly to them and, in 123, to provide them with a "subsistence level" supply of grain subsidized by the state. Soon a second section of the whole structure collapses: the rich could no longer remain the only ones subject to the "blood tax." To start with, they were not numerous enough; then, their warlike and military vocation tends to weaken slightly around the middle of the second century. But above all, precisely around this period, military campaigns, more and more often victorious, increase in appeal. This explains why in 107 Marius experiences no difficulty in finding volunteers, keeping in mind that he abandons the idea of requiring census qualifications and recruits plebeians. [. . .] From now on, part of the Roman civic population, the very class that pushes upward directly under the political class (for which a military transition remains an obligation), will cease to experience the life of military camps. There will also come a time when proletarian armies, which after 90 were recruited in regions of Italy only too recently naturalized, will feel more and more alienated from the traditions of Roman civic life. They will replace these values with their solidarity, their personal allegiance to a single leader, and their aversion for civilians, whom they consider expendable. As the events following the death of Caesar make clear, the military will thus turn into a dangerous instrument of civil war, a party or a state within the state.

When two of the main components in the civic structure undergo profound modification, the third element will not remain untouched for long. The way citizens participate in political decisions is also bound to change its nature. But in this area the process is less straightforward than in the two previous cases: the model cannot work as perfectly in a domain as complex as that of politics. To be sure, in the long term (on the scale of a century), the expected outcome will eventually occur: the mass of citizens, once exempted from military and fiscal duties, will be inevitably stripped of its role in political assemblies. Even though the *comitia* of the Roman people survive well into the first century [CE], they are, at this point, no more than a formality. [. . .]

This evolution, however, was not a linear one. Around the end of the second and beginning of the first centuries [BCE], popular influence on the process of political decision, including the influence of Rome's most impoverished classes, increases significantly. Legal guarantees ensuring individual rights by protecting citizens from coercion by magistrates are gradually refined until 123 [BCE].

Between 139 and 107 [BCE], the introduction of the secret ballot reforms and improves the electoral process, making it more "democratic." Until the social war of 90–89, the growing role of the tribunician assembly, in which distinctions of rank and fortune are less pronounced than in the centuriate assembly, clearly allows for large numbers of humble citizens to be heard. Moreover, most of the time political conflicts still unfold within the confines of legality: the use of violence is not yet a common phenomenon.

It is only in 101 that a law is first passed under the coercion of partisans armed with clubs. One has to wait until 88 to see, for the very first time, a Roman army march against the city to settle, against the advice of the *comitia*, a conflict over military leadership. However, in addition to the extinction or transformation of the structures discussed above, the electoral body also undergoes its own changes, which deeply modify the requirements for exercising political sovereignty. The massive influx of Italians into the city following the Social War, even though it takes more than a generation to occur, increases the civic body from 400,000 to a million men; moreover, this occurs without any noticeable increase in the actual number of voters in Rome itself. [. . .] It is understandable, then, that the political "discourse" emanating from comitial life gives the impression of becoming increasingly inadequate.

This is why I have tried to signal, as a counterpart to this process, the birth or development of another kind of political discourse that, more and more, will replace the old one. Although they are absent from the *comitia*, or underrepresented there, the truly urban masses—composed for the most part of freedmen, legally confined to the four tribes, or of recent citizens, uprooted proletarians who, consequently, exercise no leverage neither in the centuriate nor tribunician assemblies—will find a way to express themselves in a relatively effective although nonofficial manner, in circumstances less fortuitous than they appear. The Roman state, like the states of Hellenistic Greece, periodically assembles its masses for major ceremonies of religious or civic origins (triumphs, spectacles) whose regular occurrence constitutes a kind of civic liturgy. [. . .] Gathered with less order and hierarchy than in their official assembly, the citizens take advantage of their leader's conspicuous presence to voice their opinion, with surprising freedom in speech and behavior alike, about a particular person or issue. Even though lacking completely in any legal significance, these manifestations were both too frequent and too often repeated not to perform some regulatory function within the mechanisms of decision-making. At least for the political class, they represented an often irreplaceable barometer of public opinion. Indeed, they allowed the most skillful, or most fortunate, among that class to manipulate this opinion, and sometimes even to influence the outcome more efficiently than through traditional channels.

In the end, however, this parallel political discourse, which could either give or restore the right to express themselves to those who had been deprived of it, also experiences a number of disturbing malfunctions. There is but a short step between crowd and claque, between claque and armed mobs increasingly modeled after a military pattern whose lethal effectiveness, after Sulla's episode, had left its mark on the minds of many people. From Lepidus to Catiline, from Clodius to Milo, political chieftains (albeit second-rate ones) will all dream of imposing their own rule as leaders of their legions: for want of real legions they will sometimes levy sham armies which, little by little, will turn the Forum or Campus Martius into arenas for civil wars.

After focusing on the structures, one could devote a second series of comments to the mechanisms. In a way a political system is very much like a living organism or a machine (according to Easton's model)[1] meant to provide responses to external stimuli. We will see later on which kinds of questions and answers they are. But I should like to make a few statements first on how the system itself functions. At the outset, one is struck by the high level and high density of relationships, and therefore of communication channels, which, in every direction, consolidate the Roman civic body. About their number first: the demographic range of civic life is considerable and, from an ancient perspective, truly extraordinary. Without bursting at the seams, the Roman state was able for centuries not only to make several hundred thousand citizens live and act together, but also to make either individuals or numerous communities come together on a regular basis, to insure peaceful coexistence (and Romanization) within the mosaic of Italic peoples, and finally to secure the loyalty of all these men by allowing them relative access to both the upper echelons and the political class. [. . .]

On the other hand, these many men who, from now on, live together within the same body politic, are linked to one another by almost constant interactions, both spatial and temporal. The calendar of civic life, as we saw, is particularly busy. Even though the census occurs only every five years (except for those such as senators and knights who were likely to be called for it several times), almost every year sees a levy that, until 167, is accompanied by collection of taxes. Elections take at least fifteen days out of the year. A vote on bills of law could necessitate many more days (in certain years, up to twelve laws had to be voted on). Furthermore, one ought to remember that each of these procedures required several preparatory meetings; and although nobody was required to attend these meetings, entire crowds would sometimes flock to them. Games and spectacles recurred regularly and, by the end of the Republic, took several dozen days. To these one should add triumphs, funerals, and, as we saw, certain departures and arrivals of magistrates. Finally, law courts were in operation for most of the year, and important trials, which had deep political implications, became more frequent in the last century of the Republic. The citizen's physical presence was therefore required, or at least strongly recommended, much more frequently than in any of our modern democracies. Now, almost every one of these occasions required the displacement of several thousands, sometimes even tens of thousands, of individuals and their reassembly in the city. These movements were not restricted to Rome itself or to its suburbs: from the whole of Romanized Italy anybody who wanted to could come. One is under the impression that, as much or more than the needs of economic activity, civic life would have generated continuous migrations within Italy, causing groups and individuals to move on a regular basis. Politics truly irrigated the social body.

Furthermore, these movements were not inorganic, because they involved more than individuals. A strong structure, based on the census but also grounded in partially territorial communities, namely the tribes, placed every individual within a specific group. There and only there did his vote and opinion carry some weight. In a way, the Roman state appears as a segmented society. But solidarities function on several different levels at once. There is a geographic dimension to them: territorial or urban community, *municipium* or colony, tribe, region. This is where various influences and solidarities operate, around local interests and particularities that, even in the first century [BCE], were still very much alive. Now, it was often at Rome, both within the frame and under the pretense of Roman politics, that these conflicts were solved, or where these solidarities manifested themselves. People came to Rome in groups, gathering around one or more notables; they ran into each other, met again after a long time. They left reassured, motivated, resentful, or triumphant. [. . .] Horizontal and geographic solidarities seldom go without vertical and social solidarities—the entire game of clienteles, of matrimonial alliances, of services rendered or required, of patronages and friendships. These private ties, which the segmented nature of civic organization would instigate but never completely overlap, pervade the whole of Roman social life, and it was only natural that they should play a role in political life proper. Around leaders destined to occupy the first ranks, one meets with a medley of influences: groups or parties, some based on kinship, others on neighbors' ties, others yet even more frequent, based on personal loyalties sealed either on the battlefield or in the Forum, not to mention financial and economic bonds, or simply political and ideological affinities. Almost every individual is thus hemmed into a highly diversified network of relationships that is all the more dense, ramified, and sophisticated insofar as it acts as a constant point both of encounter and overlap for the political and social spheres, for the voluntary and the determined. We are light-years away from the medieval peasant bound to his parish, isolated by the surrounding forest of his lord, and confined in his own ignorance. These extremely dense relationships presuppose (and this is what really matters to me) an extremely high level of communication, an intense mental and social life. For between these men drawn into the same civic life, messages must have been circulating constantly; when taken together these messages represent a refined example of political language. We were able to observe that in the Roman state, as opposed to what may happen in other political systems, reciprocity is always implied. There is a constant dialogue

between the state and the citizen, between the state and the constituent, between the one who commands and the one commanded. Even an act as constraining as the recruiting of an army first requires that the person to be
recruited voluntarily declare himself to the *census*; even after this step, the con-
sul can still agree to examine special cases and, if absolutely necessary, can authorize an appeal (by means of a formal complaint) to the tribunes of the *plebs*
in order to counteract arbitrary measures. [. . .] Roman political life, said
Mommsen, is a true contract: it is necessary to consult with the people, therefore, to enunciate a question, and to obtain an intelligible answer. This process
necessitates communication and exchange of messages. Of these messages, we
have traces at our disposal that should not be disregarded: Roman politics primarily means oratory because, before it is even possible to ask questions, it is
necessary to explain, to enlighten, and eventually to persuade. To decipher
what survived for us of this political oratory in order to discover, through a
speech often badly transmitted, which audience it is meant to reach, will certainly be one of the new and exciting challenges posed for Roman historians in
the years to come. Certain fortunate occurrences such as Cicero's two speeches
on the agrarian law, one before the Senate, the other before the people, should
allow for a thorough analysis of both the cultural level and collective mentality
of each intended audience.

In this respect, we are in for a surprise. What we know about this political
discourse, as well as the analysis of both the techniques and procedures of *comitia*, leads one to think that the Roman electorate had reached a remarkably
high level of culture. The overwhelming presence of oratory, that is to say of
oral techniques of expression, should not make us forget that writing plays a
significant role in almost every instance of civic life. Declaration to the censors
means inscription in a register; bills of law and names of candidates are posted.
When using a ballot the voter himself must inscribe at least a few letters on it.
[. . .] All these clues give the impression of a civilization centered on the
written text—one might almost say a clerical civilization. [. . .] Graffiti,
electoral or otherwise, as well as private invoices from Pompeii show that the
literacy rate must have been high in this small town, at least among men. I
should also emphasize that this assessment fits in with the general conclusions
of some cautious historians about the level of communication that the Graeco-
Roman urban civilization had reached at its apogee.[2] With respect to both its
demographic density and level of culture, this civilization represents a stage in
development that Europe never again attained until the Age of Enlightenment. But should this really come as a surprise? The ancient city, as a political
and cultural center more than as a commercial or industrial hub, extends a
particularly dense network of connections over the rural world. A sufficiently
large portion of the population enjoys (for various reasons) enough leisure to
"invest" in education and culture. The very high level of development and rationalization reached by political life provided additional incentives to take full

advantage of this option. I once tried to show that social success (because it is always, in part, a political success) implies in Rome, well before a true bureaucracy begins to develop, a high level of culture. To belong to the large circle of citizens means the first step to success: it can hardly be reached without a minimum degree of education. [. . .]

Modern political science has introduced the concept of system into the study of political institutions (in the larger sense of the term); by system, it means, based on the model of an organism or (less convincingly) of a machine, an ensemble of elements combined in order to produce a given result. In other words, a system is meant to provide certain responses to "stimuli" or questions produced by the "external milieu." In the preceding pages, I have tried to analyze the political system of Republican Rome from a global point of view. One is entitled therefore, in conclusion, to address its effects, results, and functioning. To be sure, this point of view that I have deliberately adopted might not be the best there is: for it is obvious that the essential part of political decisions (those decisions that deeply and lastingly involve the social organism) was not taken mainly by those popular authorities that I have attempted to define. I have often insisted on the gap that exists, within the Roman civic body, between the mass of *cives* (which I have studied here) and what I have very approximately called the political class: i.e., roughly, the upper echelons of the state, senators, knights, publicans, scribes, and various retinues. Within the Roman process of decision-making, the main emphasis must of course be placed on the Senate, a particularly important deliberative and decision-making authority. [. . .] It is only at this global level that we will find an answer to the main question: how did the Roman institutions function, what were they worth, and what did they mean? It is a contemporary who gives the first answer, a statesman and a philosopher attuned to the methods and conclusions of Greek political philosophy: Polybius. His opinion is doubly interesting: first, because he comes at a dramatic time in history, when it is becoming clear that the entire inhabited world, sooner or later, is going to fall under the sway of Rome; also because the way he approaches human societies, their institutions and their evolution as organisms, is in a way very close to certain modern models. In Book 6 of his *Histories*, Polybius devotes a lengthy excursus to these issues. According to him, in the final analysis, any extensive society, any institution must be evaluated by the degree of cohesion they provide to the nation which makes use of them. The greater the "will to live together," the more social pressure will be exercised on the various parts forming the whole, the more interdependent the various state and government authorities will be. Put in a nutshell, the more centripetal forces prevail over centrifugal ones, the more chances there will be for a state to succeed. According to Polybius, the case of Rome is both privileged and exemplary in this respect, for two main reasons. First, with regard to the constitution, in the narrow sense of government authorities, these are so well combined that it is almost impossible to conceive of major conflicts arising between them. People, Senate, and magistrates each have their own reasonable share of autonomy, of decision-making privileges and duties. Most of the time everything conspires to make them get along and collaborate rather than clash in open conflicts such as the ones which other states were experiencing at the time. Second, on the more general level of institutions, namely the set of *moeurs et coutumes*, Rome in its entirety is pervaded by a collective "discipline," voluntarily accepted, which strengthens social cohesion considerably. This discipline is not only repressive; it successfully combines both incentives and prevention, rewards and punishments. Hence the Romans' dedication and patriotism in general.

Polybius's picture is clear and powerful. Some of its details can of course be questioned; one can emphasize the narrowness of its chronological framework, since it seems clear that Polybius himself, around the end of his life, was able to notice the first signs of malfunction in this system. At least he presents a coherent and attractive theory. But Polybius is writing around 150 [BCE]. The Roman Republic will live on for 120 more years, and it is precisely within these last years that the system will so obviously run amok. We see in succession a bloody conflict fought around the agrarian law, violence invading the Forum ever more openly, the era of civil wars fought by armies of citizens and suspended by brief attempts at establishing monarchic rule (Cinna, Sulla, Caesar)—all this ending in the establishment of a new regime very different from its predecessor: the Empire. All this is very well known, perhaps too well: for, distracted by the tramp of boots and the clash of weapons, one tends to neglect the true nature of those conflicts in which the Roman civic body was involved. These events, which are given pride of place in our history books, all concern power, whether attempts at monarchy, failed or successful, or the recruiting of the political class, and all occur somehow outside of the *populus*'s immediate sphere of interest. The role it played in this area was always very limited: it was restricted to choosing among candidates belonging to the ruling class in accordance with legal and traditional rules particular to this class. The Roman people never governed by itself, essentially because of the constitution of the census, which by setting up legal qualifications for the holding of magistracies put the latter beyond the reach of most of the *cives*. The *populus*, in this case, is barely an actor and almost exclusively a spectator.

It remains to be explained how in this typically oligarchic context this people, apparently dispossessed of its own affairs, was still able to keep participating, as long as the Republic lasted, in electoral or judicial rituals that seemed to concern only the political class and how it was even able to intervene so often with passion and violence to make its strength felt directly. [. . .]

The masses could dimly feel that beyond these games seemingly reserved for a very small number of people, there were realities at stake that concerned them directly. No doubt, we must avoid speaking—as has been done for too long ever since the nineteenth century—of political "parties" in Rome, and particularly of a "popular party." On the other hand, there is a political behavior that can quite accurately be labeled *popularis* (*populariter agere*) and that is perfectly defined both by theoretical texts, those of Cicero in particular, and by the actions of those who deserved this epithet. To be "popular" is to court the people, and—as Zvi Yavetz has brilliantly demonstrated—it refers to daily behavior and attitude, to the kind of language being used (simplicity, cheerfulness, absence of contempt, feigned interest in the people's pleasures and cares) as much as to political agendas and actions per se. [. . .] Although it is of course impossible to speak of a popular political "program," certain measures recur so frequently from the end of the second century onward, both in political discourse and practice, that they must somehow reflect some of the real issues that justified the citizens' sustained attention to the struggles in the Forum or those on the Campus Martius. Most obvious among these measures are those that provide the citizens, or at least a majority of them, with immediate and palpable benefits: after Tiberius Gracchus, the agrarian laws, after Gaius, the grain-supply laws, and similarly all the measures (laws, *senatusconsulta*, praetorian edicts) meant to fight usury and indebtedness. In principle, a political figure bent on winning over public opinion only had to "dabble in these questions" in order to become popular: the conservatives knew this well and, like Livius Drusus in 123, his son in 91, or even Cato of Utica, did not hesitate to outbid their rivals so as to prevent them from becoming too "popular." [. . .]

But the people were not only receptive to material advantages. In a way, the popular "program" comprises a certain number of political or judicial measures that simply aim at improving the political system by eliminating some of its most obvious inequalities: the *tabellariae leges*, for instance, which guarantee a greater freedom to vote, or the propositions of the tribune Cornelius in 67 (on privileges, on the *senatusconsultum*, or on the praetor's edict). The major struggle, fought between 75 and 70 [BCE], over whether the rights of the *tribunus plebis* should be restored (as far as we can tell from Sallust) shows that in spite of some hesitations the masses finally realized where their real interest lay.

Nevertheless, during the last thirty years of Roman Republican history the struggle, once more, changes its direction. A new issue appears, which sometimes carries more weight than the simple appeal to immediate material gratification of the citizens, namely the defense of the peace, in the face of the growing danger and the dreaded specter of civil war. Nothing is more typical in this respect than the political action of Curio the Younger during his tribunate in 50 [BCE], on the eve of the lethal encounter between Caesar and the Senate. Whatever the true motivations of this ambitious man who took up the legacy of Clodius, his repeated suggestions in the fall of 50 to avoid war and to dismiss the two generals aroused widespread enthusiasm. [. . .]

It is obvious therefore that as oligarchic as one imagines the Roman political system to be, it implied a certain degree of communication (and not only one-way) between the masses and the political class. Formally, initiative belonged for the most part to members of the latter class, either magistrates or candidates. One may at the most guess that they were constantly required to maintain some degree of adherence to their plans, and we have seen the role that language, both written and spoken, played in this process. But the system could also, within certain limits, work the other way around: the masses could in turn both obtain legal sanction for some of their most crucial claims and make known their own basic needs and preferences, so that the political system was forced to take them into consideration. The system did this in its own way, namely through the interplay of men and clans; every cause had to find a champion who, because he needed more than others to exploit his *popularitas*, was more inclined than others to defend the said cause. All things considered, the Roman political system was diversified enough to make sure that this function was always fulfilled by one party or another when there was need for it. Perhaps what was really at stake, for members of the political class, was their own *gloria* and *dignitas*. It is typical, however, that these essential notions, which define both the mentality and psychology of an entire social group, are also, by their nature, collective notions based on exchange and reciprocity. The average oligarchic Roman—be he a Catiline, a Clodius, or a Caesar—while hungry for glory, honor, and dignity, can only find them in others and never without a cost. The people, in Rome, was certainly not everything, but it was still something.

Nevertheless, the real issues in which the citizen body had something directly at stake form a kind of underground history. This aspect of history is seldom emphasized, although certain texts, which are used less often than they should be, do allow us to shed light on it. The first issue, one that it would be wrong to forget, is simply that of Rome's collective survival, and of its citizens' individual welfare. Ancient states lived in a dangerous world without international safeguards, and Rome, more than any other state, lived on the periphery of the Greek world. Hannibal's war had been the last in a series of wars in which everybody knew that they were not only fighting for their fatherland, but also for their life and freedom. One should not underestimate the kind of pressure that this feeling of danger would have exercised on collective consciousness and on the willingness to accept discipline. Naturally, with regard to what could be called foreign policy, there were other things at stake: various economic interests, for instance, or personal ambitions, which, even though they divided the political class and found a response among the masses, still remained secondary. This was the price to pay for the complete solidarity required by the ancient laws of war. This fundamental issue progressively disappeared when it became clear that the war had been decisively won and Rome was no longer under direct threat; it reappeared, though, in 171 and 106 with German invasions, and even around 63–58 with what came to be felt as a Gallic threat. It still remains true that, around the middle of the second century, the issue changes in its direction: from then on war becomes a source of profit—hence the rise of ever fiercer conflicts over the distribution of these profits. And here the people, taken as a mass, were directly concerned: with the agrarian law, with the issue of booty, with the use of money from taxes collected in the provinces. Although threatened for a while, the system's cohesion emerged ever stronger from every crisis, and each citizen felt that he played a part in the outcome. For the most part, it is precisely because this equitable distribution of profits meets with success that the civic body expands so extraordinarily. The success of "Rome, Inc." meets with envy. The redistribution of profits is significant enough for eager masses from the outside to crowd at the city gates. Centripetal forces are such that one has to elbow one's way into this paradise, the Roman state. One million Italians will force their entry into it by means of a highly paradoxical war, a kind of reversed conquest: after conquering Italy, Rome will yield to Italy because it has taken over the world. Progress in "democracy," social and political "struggles" are all determined by how constantly the organism grows and by how many repeated successes it meets with on the outside.

The other collective issue was liberty. It is worth noting here that the word is seldom used alone; it is most often supplemented with phrases such as *aequa libertas* and *aequum ius*, equality in law and equality before the courts. Roman liberty pays no attention to social and political inequalities, so long as equality before the law remains a given. Aristocracies are easily endured, personal power readily tolerated and even accepted, if they agree to preserve legal autonomy. But the status of citizen remains the only essential and sufficient safeguard to guarantee this freedom. The bloody episodes of civil war may compromise it at times, but it is remarkable to note how the various restorations which follow these episodes (Sulla and the Empire) all involve legal progress. One of the least paradoxical aspects of imperial monarchy will be to insure, somehow or other (and despite the disappearance of political freedom), a tolerable legal system. The right to appeal to Caesar (direct heir to the appeal to the people) and especially legal codifications will guarantee it. Until around the middle of the second century [CE], Roman citizens—ever more numerous incidentally—will feel equal before the law (even though in a state of common political bondage which, in the end, will bother them little). To be sure, the German Middle Ages for many long centuries obscured this crucial right that the Romans left us, but they never succeeded in eliminating it completely. It reappeared, triumphant, in the modern world: we are all Roman citizens.

TRANSLATED BY FLORENT HEINTZ

NOTES

[1] D. Easton, *A Systems Analysis of Political Life* (New York, 1965).
[2] {Chaunu 1974, 108–10.}

JEAN IRIGOIN

The History of the Text of Pindar

1952

This excerpt focuses on one of Irigoin's most important scholarly discoveries. He demonstrates that the sequence of four "books" in the canonical editions of Pindar's victory odes or "epinicians" (Olympian, Pythian, Nemean, Isthmian) reflects a sea change in the history of textual transmission: the transition of scroll (= volumen) to codex. In the course of this transition, an original sequence of Olympian/Pythian/Isthmian/Nemean odes, reflecting the descending chronological order of the traditional dates assigned to the founding of these athletic festivals, was disrupted. Irigoin reconstructs the "scroll-mentality" of the Library of Alexandria, which had organized Pindar's victory odes in terms of historical occasions; the later "codex-mentality" lost sight of the original Alexandrian taxonomy. Irigoin's work illustrates clearly the continuities and discontinuities of textual transmission.

The date of Didymus's commentary marks a terminus in work on Pindar. To be sure, the next century would not forget the Theban poet: his compatriot Plutarch would write his biography and Quintilian would hail his genius, characterizing him as *lyricorum longe princeps*. But the scholarly work of the grammarians appears to have been interrupted. In the second century [CE] a new form of commented edition appeared.

An event that occurred during the reign of the Antonines had a decisive influence on the history of Greek poetic texts. People began choosing among poets and even among works of the poets in whom they were interested, and out of these selections came editions. Of the nine lyric poets of the Alexandrian canon, or ten if one includes Corinna, only two were selected: Sappho for monodic lyric and Pindar for choral lyric. Within Pindar's work, the four books of the *Epinicians* were included and thirteen other books excluded from the selection.

From "Du IIe au IXe siècle," in *Histoire du texte de Pindare* (Paris: C. Klincksieck, 1952), pp. 93–121.

Although it is possible, as we shall see, to give an approximate date for the selection of the *Epinicians*, there is no indication of the person responsible for that selection. The selection of specific dramas of Aristophanes was probably the work of Phaeinos. A certain Dionysius played a similar role for the text of Euripides.[1] [. . .] The date of the Pindaric selection coincides with the philological renaissance that took place in the time of the Antonines, most notably in connection with the work of the grammarians and lexicographers from Apollonius Dyscolus to Harpocration and Phyrnichos. Their work should probably be seen as connected with the founding of Hadrian's Library (131–32 [CE]) and the creation, also in Athens, of state-sponsored chairs for the teaching of rhetoric and philosophy (176 [CE]). Since the fire in the library of the Museum at Alexandria, the importance of that center of philology had declined. With the advent of the Second Sophistic, Athens became the capital of Hellenic scholarship. Only previous scholarly work could justify the creation of a research and documentation center like Hadrian's Library and a teaching center like the University of Athens, and the creation of such centers must have given new impetus to work already in progress.[2]

Wilamowitz was the first to recognize the importance of this period for the history of texts.[3] On the basis of indirect tradition, he credited it with shaping the selections of poetic texts. Since then, the discovery of literary papyri has confirmed the hypotheses of Wilamowitz, although not enough notice has been taken of the fact. After the middle of the third century [CE], the papyri, with very few exceptions, mention only authors and works from the selections. Alcaeus and Bacchylides were excluded altogether from the selection of lyric poets. The most recent of their papyri date from the beginning of the third century. For Sappho, we possess papyri from the sixth and even seventh centuries. Only one papyrus of Pindar is from after the second century; it contains fragments of the *Olympians*. The fact that for fifty or at most a hundred years certain texts excluded from a selection probably made in Athens persisted in Egypt is by no means surprising. On the contrary, it confirms the idea that the philological work on which that selection was based must have occurred in the second century, sometime between 150 and 180.[4]

Examination of the indirect tradition may perhaps yield more information than Wilamowitz had derived from it. Plutarch (46–125 [CE]) cites Pindar nearly one hundred times: only twenty-three of these citations are from the *Epinicians*. Their distribution is as follows: *Olympians*, 7; *Pythians*, 7; *Isthmians*, 7; *Nemeans*, 2.

Lucian (120–180 [CE]) was still familiar with the first of Pindar's Hymns, which, according to the *Icaromenippus* (ch. 27), the Muses sang during a banquet. F. W. Householder's findings[5] show that two of Lucian's quotations from Pindar are from the *Epinicians* and two from other books. Lucian belonged to the generation that witnessed the emergence of the selection.

In the early years of the third century, Philostratus the Elder apparently knew only the edition of the *Epinicians*. In the *Imagines*, twenty-three of the twenty-eight allusions to odes of Pindar refer to the *Epinicians*. Indeed, Philostratus seems already to have been using a commentary fairly close to our scholia.[6]

Later, only the *Epinicians* remained familiar. To give only one example, from the early sixth century: Choricius of Gaza cites the *Epinicians* 30 times: *Olympians*, 11; *Pythians*, 12 (including 5 quotations of the same passage); *Nemeans*, 6; *Isthmians*, 1;[7] and other books only 3 times.

Pedagogical considerations were at the root of the selection. The classical poets, long used for purposes of teaching, gradually saw their role limited to that of textbook authors. Most of them were little read except as examples in the classroom, from primary school all the way through rhetorical training, and other literary genres, particularly the novel, replaced them as entertainment literature. Hence a need was felt for a selection from the vast range of poets published by the early Alexandrian philologists.[8] In the case of Pindar, the *Epinicians* seemed more interesting than the various religious odes because they were more human centered and lent themselves to historical commentary. Ten centuries later, Eustathius of Thessalonica would make the same point in his *Preface* to the *Commentaries on Pindar* (ed. Drachmann, vol. 3, p. 303). It is also likely that the persistence of the great Hellenic games favored the epinician odes. Note, however, that, to judge by the papyri of Pindar, the *Epinicians* were not particularly admired until the time of the selection. The *Paeans* are represented by five papyri, the *Epinicians* (*Olympians* only) by two, the *Partheneia* and *Dithyrambs* by only one. The indirect tradition confirms the evidence of the papyri. To be persuaded of this, one has only to consult the list of citations of Pindar by Plutarch. This situation is not unusual. In the case of Aeschylus, for example, the papyri containing plays from the selection are rare. All the evidence shows that the selection was not based on the public's taste or made in response to its demands but, rather, achieved in accordance with a concerted plan.

Themistius offers an interesting comment on the lyric poets used in early fourth-century teaching. In discussing his father's school, he mentions, after Homer, Plato, and Aristotle, the following authors: Menander, Euripides, Sophocles, Sappho, Pindar.[9] The two lyric poets studied, Sappho and Pindar, were from the selection.

The texts of the poets of the selection had to be annotated and commented if they were to serve the purpose expected of them. The Pindaric scholia of the medieval manuscripts can be traced back to commentaries compiled at the time of the selection. The date generally accepted for this work is the fourth or fifth century [CE]. I shall offer the following arguments in favor of the earliest date proposed (without proof) by Wilamowitz: (1) the evolution and degradation of this commentary over the course of the period extending to the end of the fourth century; (2) the absence, in common portions of the various versions of this commentary, of the names of authors or grammarians later than the end of the second century; and finally, (3) the existence, at the beginning of the fourth century, of a commentary very similar to one of those versions.[10]

A technical innovation seems to have facilitated the compilation of a commented selection. In the first century, the papyrus codex began to replace the *volumen*. In the latter, the space between columns of text left little room for comments, as can be seen in the papyrus of Alcman's *Partheneion* (1st century [BCE]) or that of Pindar's *Dithyrambs*. The papyrus of the *Paeans* exhibits a new formula that appears not to have survived. In the codex, however, the margins permitted the copying of fairly extensive commentaries. It is plausible that the text and commentary of the *Epinicians* were written on a codex at the time of the selection. Indeed, various commentaries on poets from Homer to Apollonius of Rhodes bear subscriptions indicating the compiled sources. The formula of these subscriptions regularly included the verb *parakeitai* or *paragegraptai*.[11] As P. Boudreaux has shown, these subscriptions refer to a marginal commentary; that is the meaning of *parakeitai* and *paragegraptai*. The precise indication of sources proves that the compiler was the author of the subscription. [. . .]

To be sure, the scholia of Pindar are not followed by a subscription of this sort, which tells us something about both the sources of the commentary and its presentation. But the scholia of Aeschylus and Sophocles did not fare any better. In Aristophanes and Euripides, only a few plays preserved their subscriptions.[12] Placed at the end of the commentary, these indications easily disappeared. Since the selections of different poets appear to have been established at the same time, conclusions based on the subscription of some can legitimately be extended to the others. Hence it is highly likely that, toward the end of the second century, the selection from the *Epinicians*, along with its commentary, was transcribed onto a papyrus codex. Instead of the seventeen scrolls containing the entire work of Pindar accompanied by various *hupomnēmata* (commentaries), a single codex presented a commented edition of the selection.[13]

The revival of rhetoric and the sophistic, and with it the use of poetic texts at various levels of teaching, led to the compilation of a selection from the *Epinicians*. The use of the codex, which made it possible for the contents of several scrolls to be included in one handy book, gave this selection a new physical presentation, which placed the text in constant proximity to its commentary.

One must bear in mind that the codex, which appeared in the first century, may also have been used for works excluded from the selection. An example is one of the papyri of the *Paeans* (PSI 147). Conversely, in the third and fourth centuries, the text of the selection and its commentary may have been separately transcribed onto *volumina*. But the archetype of the selection appears to have been a codex.

The edition of the selection, whose date was indicated earlier, contained the four books of the *Epinicians* together with a commentary, but a change in order occurred in the transition from *volumen* to codex. Owing to an error, the four scrolls containing, respectively, the *Olympians, Pythians, Isthmians,* and *Nemeans* were transcribed onto codex with the last two scrolls reversed: the *Nemeans* were placed before the *Isthmians*.[14] The original order was preserved in several passages of the commentary, which must therefore have been written prior to this accident. For example, I cite the Vatican *Life of Pindar* (ed. Drachmann, vol. 1, p. 6).[15] In the first argument of the *Isthmians*, the scholiast, after stating that all ancient games were held in honor of a dead man, mentioned three games, omitting the Nemean Games that were to be discussed later and dwelling only on the two he had already discussed, the Olympian and Pythian, in order to compare them to the third, the Isthmian (ed. Drachmann, vol. 3, p. 192).[16] Note also the relative frequency of citations from the *Nemeans* and *Isthmians*. Before the era of the selection, the *Isthmians* were cited more frequently than the *Nemeans*. In Plutarch, for example, we find seven citations from the *Isthmians* and two from the *Nemeans*. After the selection the reverse obtains; Choricius of Gaza cites the *Nemeans* six times and the *Isthmians* once.[17]

It is impossible to reconstitute the edition of the *Epinicians* in its original form. The titles of certain poems can certainly be traced back to this edition. These include:

Olympian 2: "for Theron of Acragas, winner in the chariot race"

Olympian 9: "for Epharmostos of Opous, winner in wrestling"

Olympian 11: "for the same [as the recipient of *Olympian* 10]; payment of interest [*tokos*]."

The text remains that of the vulgate stemming from the edition of Aristophanes of Byzantium, and it does not appear to have undergone significant change until the moment when the sequence of texts stemming from the edition of the *Epinicians* had bifurcated into two distinct versions. In it we find mistakes from various dates.[18] The interpolation at *Olympian* 2.48a is prior to the Alexandrian edition. The replacement of *kruphon* by *kruphion* at *Olympian* 2.177 occurred before Aristarchus. Other errors are probably more recent. [. . .]

Errors occurred in the colometrization. The basic colometry to which I shall refer in what follows is based on an analysis of the metrical scholia. Before Boeckh, Pindar's editors adopted this colometry, which goes back to Aristophanes of Byzantium. It was faithfully reproduced in the eighteenth-century editions of Beck and Heyne. In *Olympian* 5, colon 11 of the first strophe[19] is lengthened by one syllable (*heortais* | instead of *heor|tais*), and colon 6 of the third strophe is shortened by three syllables (*erkhomai* | *Ludiois* instead of *erkhomai Ludiois* |).

Must all these errors be attributed to the archetype itself? That is unlikely. The two versions that we will study later on probably came not from the archetype of the edition of the *Epinicians* but from a copy of that archetype. Errors must have been introduced into the text during the period between the constitution of the archetype and the final copy.

The real difficulties begin with the commentary. The scholia of the medieval manuscripts consist of various elements: extensive excerpts from Didymus's commentary, a few quotations from more recent authors, bits of paraphrase, metrical analysis of the odes, and numerous elementary explanations. The original commentary contained in the archetype of the edition consisted of the same elements but in different proportions. The scholarly explanations, which for us are the most interesting elements, were gradually eliminated in favor of grammatical explanations, which were more useful for students than learned commentaries. The use of the commentary in instruction has diminished its value, for us at any rate. The decadence that affected the work of the great Alexandrian philologists and of the grammarians of the Late Empire had its effects on the commentary of Pindar.

Fortunately, we at least possess two states of this degradation. Derivatives of the archetypal edition of the *Epinicians* can be divided into two groups. One branch of the tree culminates in the archetype of the Ambrosian version, so-called because its unique surviving representative is a manuscript in Milan, the Ambrosianus C 222 inf. (A). The other branch culminates in the archetype of the Vatican version, the earliest example of which is Vaticanus gr. 1312 (B). As I shall show, the two branches bifurcated at a very early date, in the late third or fourth century.[20] During the period between the edition of the *Epinicians* and the bifurcation of the two branches, the scholia deteriorated. After the division, each family continued to suffer the effects of this deterioration independently, ultimately culminating in the archetypes of the two versions. The scholia found in the two versions must go back to the archetype of the edition of the *Epinicians* or at any rate to one of its descendants prior to the constitution of the two families. In addition to the rare scholia given by Drachmann as common to both versions in *Olympians* 2 through 12, the only part of the *Epinicians* for which we possess an example of the Ambrosian version, there is a far greater number of scholia with the same content but sometimes in different forms. With few exceptions, these latter scholia supply interesting information.

Dating the archetypes of the versions is a delicate matter. The only certain elements in the dating are the *terminus post quem*, the edition of the *Epinicians* in the second half of the second century [CE], and the *terminus ante quem*, the beginning of the seventh century, at the dawn of an iron age of centuries during which all literary work came to a halt. In view of the two states of the commentary represented by the two versions, it seems possible, as I shall show, to date the Ambrosian archetype to the fourth century [CE] and the Vatican archetype to the beginning of the fifth. In the current state of our knowledge, it is impossible to be more precise.

Examination of the fragments of Aristarchus's commentary preserved by way of Didymus in each of the two versions clearly reveals the effects of the deterioration. In the scholia to *Olympians* 2 through 12, Aristarchus is cited seventeen times by the Ambrosian version only, seven times by the Vatican version only, and three times by both. Three times the Ambrosian version gives Aristarchus's remark without naming him. The Vatican version does the same seven times. The result would be the same if we looked at Didymus rather than Aristarchus. Thus each version left out some of the commentary from the edition of the *Epinicians*. Since the losses and omissions are more frequent in the Vatican version, it is probably later than the Ambrosian version. This hypothesis is corroborated by the use of a known formula. In order to mark a passage worth noting for mythological, historical, or simply grammatical reasons, the late-era commentators used a single sign, —, which can be interpreted as a call for a scholium. In the commentary we therefore find expressions like *to sē-meion, to sēmeion hoti, to sēmeion* —, *to* —, etc. This formula is never used in the Ambrosian version, whereas there are a dozen examples in the corresponding portion of the Vatican version.[21]

[. . .] As a general rule, we can say that the scholia of the Vatican version are more numerous than those of the Ambrosian version but contain less valuable information and more elementary explanations.

The second-century grammarian responsible for the edition of the *Epinicians* did not limit himself to compiling Didymus's commentary and the works of a few philologists while adding his own personal explanations. He also composed, or used, a complete paraphrase of the poems, which was cut up into pieces and inserted among the other scholia. By bringing these pieces together and using a little ingenuity, Lehrs was able to reconstruct the paraphrases of the ninth *Olympian* and the fourth and ninth *Pythians*. The Vatican version preserved these paraphrases more carefully than did the Ambrosian version, but the paraphrase goes all the way back to the edition of the *Epinicians*, as the presence of similar portions in both versions proves. [. . .]

The metrical analyses of the odes, colon by colon, may be the work of Dracon of Stratonicea, a grammarian who lived before Apollonius Dyscolus.[22] They apply to the four books of the *Epinicians* and are prior to the formation of the two versions, both of which reproduce them. The metrical scholia are based on the teachings of Hephaestion, hence one cannot place more confidence in them than one has in this metrician. The metrical preface found in some medieval manuscripts is ancient, but only the first part certainly belongs to the edition of the *Epinicians*: this is a note on the composition of the triad and the choreographic value of its elements (ch. c [Drachmann, vol. 3, p. 307]); the rest of the preface consists of a "Treatise on Feet," with an appendix on the iambic and trochaic meters (chs. d and e [Drachmann, vol. 3, pp. 307–10]), which may have been written for an edition of the tragic poets or of Aristophanes.

The edition of the *Epinicians*, which I have just briefly reconstituted, evolved fairly rapidly (the commentary in particular was changed considerably to suit the needs of teaching), culminating in the two versions that have come down to us through the medieval manuscripts.

TRANSLATED BY ARTHUR GOLDHAMMER

NOTES

[1] Quoted in the subscription of the scholia to *Orestes*. [. . .] In Irigoin's book, footnotes are not consecutive except on individual pages. — ED.

[2] The city of Athens had created a chair in rhetoric as early as the time of Antoninus Pius (Philostratus *Vitae Sophistarum* 1.23). A library dedicated along with its books to Athena, to the emperor Trajan, and to the city of Athens by T. Flavius Pantainos and his children has recently been discovered. [. . .] We even know the rules of the library and its hours of operation. [. . .] It is likely that the contents were mainly philosophical. T. Flavius Pantainos held the title of priest of "the philosophical Muses." [. . .]

[3] U. von Wilamowitz-Moellendorff, *Einleitung in die Altertumswissenschaft* (Leipzig, 1921), p. 185.

[4] The example of Sophocles and Euripides is particularly clear-cut. [. . .] From Sophocles, eight papyri, which range in date from the third century [BCE] to the second or third century [CE], yield plays eliminated from the selection of seven tragedies; twelve other papyri, which contain plays from the selection, range in date from the second to the fifth century [CE]. Euripides, the most admired of the tragic poets, is represented by sixty-two papyri. Fifteen of them, ranging in date from the third century [BCE] to the second or third century [CE], contain plays eliminated from the selection of ten tragedies; forty-six others, which contain plays from the selection, range in date from the third century [BCE] to the eighth century [CE]. Of the plays excluded from the selection, only *Melanippus Captive* and *Skiron* are found in papyri later than the third century [CE]. The small number of exceptions confirms the rule (besides these two papyri, there is also the fragment of *Phaethon* from a fourth-century parchment codex preserved in the Bibliothèque Nationale in Paris). [. . .]

[5] F. W. Householder, *Literary Quotation and Allusion in Lucian* (New York, 1941), p. 34.

[6] A list of Philostratus's sources can be found in the edition of the *Imagines* by the Philological Seminars of Vienna (1893).

[7] For the switching of the *Nemeans* and *Isthmians*, see below.

[8] Authors and texts not included in the selection did not disappear entirely. Anthologies, which had already met with great success, assured them a measure of survival. Furthermore, the libraries of certain scholars and collectors preserved specimens of the doomed texts. According to Ammianus Marcellinus (25.4.3), the emperor Julian read the odes of Bacchylides with pleasure (*lyrici Bacchylidis quem legebat iucunde*). We owe to this practice the survival of the nine plays of Euripides excluded from the selection: they are found in manuscripts L (*Laurentianus* 32, 2) and P (*Palatinus gr.* 287 and *Laurentianus conv. soppr.* 172). This was an antiquarian curiosity; the commercial editions that were current at the time confined themselves to the selections.

[9] Themistius *Orations* 20 (ed. Dindorf) [. . .]. According to Sozomenus (*Historia ecclesiastica* 5.18), the poets studied in class by Apollinarius of Laodicea were Menander, Euripides, and Pindar.

[10] [. . .] What is said here about Pindar can be extended to the other poets of the selection, in particular the tragic poets and Aristophanes. It is possible, however, that the

texts of the lyric poets, being less easy to read, were the first to be accompanied by commentaries. One thinks of the papyri of the *Paeans* and *Dithyrambs*.

[11] [Example of *parakeitai:*] subscription of Book 7 of the *Iliad* in the *Venetus A* (*Marcianus gr.* 454); [example of *paragegraptai:*] subscription of Aristophanes' *Birds* in the *Ravennas 429* and the *Vossianus gr.* F. 52; also of Euripides' *Orestes* in the *Parisinus gr.* 2713, in the *Marcianus gr.* 471, and in the *Taurinensis* B IV 13. [Another example of *parakeitai:*] subscription of Book 4 of the *Argonautica* of Apollonius of Rhodes, in the *Laurentianus 32, 9.*

[12] Aristophanes: *Clouds, Birds, Peace*; Euripides: *Medea, Orestes.*

[13] In the case of the scholia of Aristophanes, G. Zuntz has attempted to demonstrate the physical independence of the selection and its commentary ("Die Aristophanes-Scholien der Papyri I," *Byzantion* 14 [1939]: 545–614). In his view [. . .], the commentary was not linked to the text before 700 [CE]. His argument, based on the emergence of exegetical chains, does not take account of certain facts about classical texts: (1) the existence of marginal commentaries on certain papyri; (2) the significance of the subscriptions cited above; (3) the abandonment of the classical poets, from the seventh to ninth centuries [CE] (which would place the linking of text and commentary in the tenth century). For very different reasons, K. Weitzmann ("Illustrations in Roll and Codex," in *Studies in Manuscript Illumination*, vol. 2 [Princeton, 1947], pp. 119–20), also rejects the conclusions of Zuntz. A proof of another sort is provided by the fourth discourse of Themistius, delivered to the Senate on January 1, 357 [CE], in Constantinople. The orator praised Constantius for establishing a library and scriptorium. Among the products of that scriptorium, he mentioned, after the masters of Attic prose from Thucydides to Demosthenes, the commentators of Homer and Hesiod, and then various philosophers. I would read this as Themistius alluding to commented editions of Homer and Hesiod, that is, of the poets in general. C. Wendel, citing this passage ("Die erste kaiserliche Bibliothek in Konstantinopel," *Zentralblatt für Bibliothekwesen* 49 [1942]: 193–209), gives a different interpretation; for him, it involves the transition from the papyrus *volumen* to the parchment codex.

[14] I have found the same explanation in H. T. Deas ("The Scholia Vetera to Pindar," *Harvard Studies in Classical Philology* 42 [1931]: 1–78, esp. 49); our agreement confirms the plausibility of this explanation.

[15] Certain copyists corrected the text, either by restoring what seemed to them the normal order or by deleting the expression for "*Nemean* victors"; see Drachmann's critical apparatus.

[16] This example is taken from Wilamowitz, *Einleitung*, p. 185 n. 121. Calliergi, the first editor of the scholia of Pindar, corrected what he took to be an omission by inserting a note on the *Nemean* games; see Drachmann's critical apparatus.

[17] [. . .] Pindar's *Life* in verse (Drachmann, vol. 1, pp. 8–9), in which the *Epinicians* are cited first among the poet's works [. . .], is later than the edition of the selection. The hexameters of which the poem is composed are of a type comparable to the hexameter of Nonnos [. . .]. The two *Lives* in prose found in the medieval manuscripts (the Ambrosian and the Vatican) contain ancient elements, but it is not easy to say when they were written. Nevertheless, the order of the books of the *Epinicians* given in the Vatican *Life* seems to indicate that at least part of it was written prior to the reversal of the *Isthmians* and *Nemeans*.

[18] For this archetype, as for all the reconstituted or preserved manuscripts that will be studied below, I give only a selection of errors and corrections. The length of the text of the *Epinicians* and the volume of the manuscript tradition do not permit a full accounting.

[19] The metrical scholia distinguish three strophes, not three triads, in the fifth *Olympian*.

[20] The citation of Exodus 3:8 in the scholia to *Olympian* 1.157 c (Drachmann, vol. 1, p. 51) is not necessarily of Christian origin. This part of the Septuagint was written in the third

century [BCE]. We do not have the Ambrosian version of the first *Olympian*, moreover, and the Vatican version probably dates from the beginning of the fifth century.

21 This remark was made previously by Deas, "The Scholia Vetera," [see above] pp. 72 ff., but we do not draw the same conclusions. [. . .]

22 *Suda* ed. Adler, vol. 2, pp. 138, 25–28, s.v. *Drakōn*.

LOUIS GERNET

Dionysus

1953

"Dionysus and the Dionysiac Religion: Inherited Elements and Original Features" originated as a review article: the present translation omits some specific discussion of the Jeanmaire volume (1951) under review. Its subject is Dionysus—certainly the god most central to French and American Hellenic scholarship of the past three decades. Gernet's essay touches on many of the reasons why: the mystical and, literally, spectacular aspects of Dionysiac religion; its focus on the psychological category of mania, *with emphasis on therapeutic* katharsis; *and the "preeminent place" held by women in Dionysiac cult, which illuminates a fundamental "opposition of the sexes" functioning powerfully in religious life. The essay also makes an important statement about method. The material in the present volume amply demonstrates Jeanmaire's own practice, quoted here: "To comprehend in history is always to interpret texts (and sometimes monuments) by way of experimental forms of knowledge," which include such analytic disciplines as sociology, ethnography, and clinical psychology, as well as traditional philology. Gernet's sanction of this synthetic method expands into a formulation of the classicist's essential inquiry: "How are human realities grasped in history? There is an undefined series of human experiences in which Hellenism has an important place."*

[. . .] The author's investigation of traditional sources associated with the god's name examines first the beliefs and popular customs that have been placed specifically under Dionysus's patronage, and second the heortology or system of Athenian religious festivals, the only one about which we have considerable information. It is for this reason that he begins his book with a chapter entitled "Approaches to Dionysus." The purpose of this chapter, in its

From *The Anthropology of Ancient Greece*, trans. John Hamilton and Blaise Nagy (Baltimore and London: The Johns Hopkins University Press, 1981), pp. 48–70 ["Dionysos et la religion dionysiaque," in *Anthropologie de la Grèce antique,* ed. J.-P. Vernant (Paris: François Maspero, 1968), pp. 63–91; first published in *Revue des études grecques* 66 (1953): 377–95].

general and specific points, is to suggest areas of human activity where the conception of the god, the images evoked by it, and the accompanying emotional states manifest themselves with some immediacy. [. . .]

With regard to Dionysus's prehistory, the author makes a penetrating observation: if Dionysus became the god of the vine, there must have been some "vacancy for him to fill," for in continental Greece, viticulture appears to have developed and expanded without a well-defined religious patron. But the author could have said more. Although the mythology of the vine is meager (p. 24), both in legend and in certain ritual patterns there exists a clear thread of evidence concerning the inventor of the vine and wine; this myth did not at first or always involve Dionysus. The tale of the vine's "invention" contains a recollection of royal or kingly magic power, and everything develops as if, between the ancient period and the "archaic" period (the period of the new god), there existed, as in the case of already constituted divine personalities, no stage involving the service of a religious group such as the Eumolpidai or even the Phytalidai.

The system of Athenian festivals—and it is possible to refer to a system, since the festivals can be described as Dionysiac feasts occurring in winter— gives preliminary support to some very important conclusions. First, Dionysus is found to be the patron of rituals much older than himself: the *phallophoria* of the Rural Dionysia, the more or less disorderly procession (*kōmos*), and the use of masks. Although a "new god," he is strongly represented in these practices. As Jeanmaire says, "The feeling of divine presence is essentially the conception one has of his interventions" (p. 38). But the religious activities associated with Dionysus prove that one is dealing with a complex personality. The season of his feasts is one of intense popular activity and gives rise to the joy and consolation of festive celebrations. But traditionally this same reason also provides a period of contact with the world beyond, a world not only that the dead inhabit but that is also the source of the blessings they offer, or according to a Hippocratic text, "whence comes nourishment." The Anthesteria, especially, reveal this rich complexity of emotions. Another factor related to this is directly relevant to the religion of Dionysus. Earlier, Jeanmaire had pointed out that there was a prehistoric tradition of orgiastic rites in Greece, such as those associated with the cult of Artemis. But for us as well as for the Greeks, *orgiasmos*, "the celebration of orgies," suggests Dionysus most of all; according to the testimony from the festivals, it is associated with Dionysus himself. The Lenaean festival, more or less "in decline" by the classical period, could have gotten its name only from the *lēnai*, another name for the bacchants. (Jeanmaire cannot avoid mentioning the etymology *lēnos* = wine-press, even though he thinks that the linguistic arguments against it are irrefutable.)

As far as one can ascertain, then, these appear to be the most general characteristics of a divinity at once single and multiple—surely unique in the Greek pantheon. [. . .]

On the subject of orgiastic rites, Euripides' *Bacchae* offers a poetic tableau with a specifically didactic purpose, and within the context of other testimonia, one can place it geographically. The adventure of Skylas (Herodotus 4.78–80) provides an example from a frontier region of Greece of delirium and possession in a male *thiasos*. A century later, Demosthenes attests that, among members of a *thiasos* dedicated to a foreign god, Sabazios (but one with analogies to the Greek god), there existed a form of behavior similar to that observed in the cult of Dionysus (18.259). And in the vast area of the eastern Mediterranean, cult practices existed that characterized the bacchants of Greece as "an ancient Aegean substratum"—Asia Minor and its cult of the Magna Mater, Syria and its goddess, Canaan and its *nebi'im*. Perhaps these forms of orgiastic rites have to be distinguished. Even so, it is possible to show that in this region of the ancient world there was a similar kind of unity involving a yearning for ecstasy and trance. And if such a unity leads us to a period of prehistory, the classical problems are to a certain extent modified. When Rohde wanted to make Thrace the center for the diffusion of orgiastic practices, it was precisely because he needed to explain what he regarded as a disturbing element in an "Apollinian" Hellenism. It should be pointed out that for Jeanmaire the "origin" of Dionysus might be sought in Asia (surely he too easily minimizes the evidence from Greco-Lydian inscriptions concerning the name *Bacchus* [p. 58]); but for a historical understanding of orgiastic practices themselves, it is to his advantage to define an area or field of extension in which the Greek phenomenon, insofar as what is traditional rather than borrowed, should be situated.

This phenomenon can now be examined by itself; it can be defined as an act of possession. The Greeks speak of *mania* (madness) and they consider it divine. The *Bacchae* brilliantly illustrates such an interpretation and allows us to see the seriousness and profundity with which the Greeks invested *mania*. [. . .]

The language of Dionysiac religion is rich in words that are instructive. The term "dithyramb," for example, leads to an examination of another set of facts. Maenadism is a female phenomenon, but the dithyramb is a masculine one. Perhaps, as Jeanmaire suggests, behind this "opposition" there lies another that is geographical. It can at least be seen within a cycle of myth and ritual belonging to the Aegean islands (especially Naxos), which are more or less independent of continental Greece. It is, of course, a question not of dualism but of complementarity, and in fact the materials in the chapter on the dithyramb complement those in the preceding chapter on maenadism. The word *dithurambos* is an ancient one from the Aegean basin. In the classical period, it refers to a literary and musical genre that we know has a prehistory. Behind its standardized form, which has been shaped and assimilated by a Greek esthetic norm, one can detect several elements: memories that the word itself evokes, echoes of the pathetic, and, above all, the depiction of a very primitive Dionysus. These elements evoke a religious practice that, despite its original features, appears to resemble those making up the complex of maenadism and those that have been compared with them. Direct testimony—about the cult of Dionysus—or indirect (cult vocabulary) permits us to make a reconstruction. Its central act was the sacrifice of an ox; the dance to which it gave place was frenzied and "inspired." The ritual culminated in the victim's dismemberment and the eating of its raw flesh. In this case, too, clarification of these phenomena can be found in ethnographic parallels: for example, the *zikir*, as observed in the last century among Cairo confraternities, reveals the same kind of communal ecstasy: the *frissa* of the Aissoua, still practiced on occasion in North Africa, reaches its climax in a *diasparagmos* and omophagy.

In examining this typical pattern, Jeanmaire has observed something that triggers the study of an important phase of the Dionysiac religion, for it deals with its literary possibilities. He says that in a milieu that is above all civic, the religious drama easily takes on the character of an exhibition; and precisely because of the audience, the cyclical choruses tend to become *spectacles*. However, before the question of Dionysus's connection with the theater is raised, it is appropriate to explore in some depth a specific conception of Dionysus involving the actions he performs for souls and the means he uses. As has been seen, Dionysus has certain selected affinities with the world beyond and the world of the dead. The chthonian Dionysus appears as leader of a "chimerical hunt," and this conception of him is inseparable from that of his coterie, the demonic band, which is the mythical expression of the human *thiasos*. Even in our most common depictions, those containing the fantastic and burlesque figures of the satyrs, there still persist some connections with an equine demon whose very shape could be a symbol of the underworld forces (a theory Jeanmaire has developed following Malten's lead). At its most profound, this symbolism underlines the idea, or rather feeling, that the intoxicating ecstasy of Dionysus gives one access to a world that is supernatural. This is confirmed by the testimonies about the popularity, effects, and even specific character of a type of dance which is essentially bacchic—a dance that, for purposes of "purification" and "initiation," contains elements of *mimēsis* (Plato *Laws* 815C). Is this what the Attic theater owes to the cult of Dionysus?

Of the four theatrical genres that we know were performed during the great March festivals in the precinct of Dionysus, it is the satyr drama to which Jeanmaire devotes the most time. He postulates a "preliterary form" in which the imitation takes the form of orchestrated leaps and gambols. This would be the chorus of the possessed, which is the manifestation of the divine *mania* and at the same time the means of its cure. Although the author believes that satyrs of the type we find depicted in art are essentially characters of myth, he does not dismiss the belief that the mask played a role in this primitive stage, a role that Georges Dumézil has illustrated in his discussion of the Centaurs. In any case, there may have been an "organic relationship" (p. 312) between the cult of Dionysus and the origin of the dithyramb. As for comedy, it could naturally have been placed under the patronage of Dionysus, whose traditional festivities were accompanied by a frivolous form of behavior that issues in comedy. Only tragedy remains for discussion, and here Jeanmaire is reserved. [. . .]

He recognizes that commemoration of legendary events at anniversaries of heroes must have had an important role to play in the prehistory of tragedy. And he is strongly opposed to the thesis that states that there is a "primary and fundamental relationship" between Dionysus and the literary genre which circumstances ended up placing under his patronage. Notably it is impossible to admit that the initial themes of the tragic poems "dealt with the suffering" of the god.

Up to this point, little has been said about the mythology of Dionysus. Actually, this mythology in part eludes us, and in some respects is irrelevant for our understanding of the god's personality. For his mythology reveals no features that are original. In the portrayal of most Greek divinities, the strictly mythical element (which is rather limited) consists of themes or remnants of themes of obscure origin that, except for an occasional reference to a few moments in a cultic act, have lost their original significance and survive only in a poetic tradition in which they are freely embellished. Dionysus's case is admittedly rather peculiar. The themes of his myths happen to be very ancient; they are adapted for the use of a god who arrives late on the scene (p. 78), and they are organized into narratives in which archaism itself is a sign of artifice. But because the work of the imagination has been redirected, the intentions that now dominate them give these tales an emotional force that is certainly more vital than the tales of Zeus or even of Apollo. Dionysus has been provided with a biography that puts him in close contact with the human world, and with a "history" that is no longer a timeless myth. In the version that has turned out to be almost canonical—it is not the only one, nor is it likely the most ancient—mythical motifs of the thunderbolt and the second pregnancy are echoes of states of society and religious thought which are "primitive," but which essentially emphasize the eminent dignity of a god, who is the preferred son of the supreme deity, although he is like so many heroes born of mortals, and has close ties with men. Semele and Ariadne are avatars of goddesses (they can return to their goddess form); but depicted in their sufferings, they represent the element of the feminine that plays so large a role in the cult. On the other hand, the myth develops in two directions. From its beginning, the tale of such a god, because of his unique magical power, remained open-ended: a certain gospel-like quality asserted itself in developments that formed the data for a divine biography. This was at first spontaneous, but later on, contemporary history exerted its influence. Alexander's expedition to India inspired a new chapter in Dionysus's biography, and it enlarged his sphere of activity to fit the geographical and fantasy-filled world of conquest—and all this, of course, favored every form of

syncretism. Dionysus, it must be observed, was already by his vocation a conquering god, a god of lightning journeys; and the theme of his peregrination in
the East, even the Far East, is already present in the *Bacchae*'s prologue. In the
version found in Apollodorus's *Bibliotheca*, one that can be described as pre-
Alexandrian (p. 308), it is an integral theme.

But the mythopoeic process has also operated on another level, and there is
another sort of Dionysus which must be considered: the mystical Dionysus. It is
curious that for both the mystical and ancient Dionysus the tales told are of the
same kind. The basic myth is one of dismemberment of the god. This has been
specifically interpreted as a myth belonging to a "religion of salvation," itself
derived from "agrarian rites" (Cumont and Frazer complement each other
here). Jeanmaire offers a very judicious critique (p. 373ff.) of a theory that
makes much of vague analogies and employs a form of schematization which
is hardly applicable to the concrete themes in the legend of Dionysus. At the
very least, it can be said that the myth is connected with the practice of *diasparagmos*, and that, based on the facts of the cult, there has been speculation of a
gnostic type that finds in the destiny of the suffering but resurrected deity a
model and promise for his followers. [. . .]

There is a psychological theme that has a very important place in Jeanmaire's book and that seems to have furnished the point of departure for his
whole study: What is the significance of this phenomenon of *mania*? For Plato
felt obligated to defer to its magic power, and though he recognized that it
operated on various levels, he found its most authentic form dominated by the
name Dionysus. Surely this is a question about a human reality, as strange as it
may be to us at first inspection. How are human realities grasped in history?
Jeanmaire is one of those who poses such questions, and he has already touched
on them in *Couroi*. The reflection that precedes his analysis is worth quoting:
"to comprehend in history is always to interpret texts (and sometimes monuments) by way of experimental forms of knowledge, with the understanding
that our direct experience of man and social realities . . . must be supplemented and illuminated by disciplines that are basically descriptive in their
methods of inquiry. Here one is dealing, in the case of a religious form of behavior which has to do with what the ancients understood by the term 'orgy,'
with some psychological realities that depend in part on clinical observation,
and with the connection of these with social realities, the analysis of which
comes from ethnography or sociology" (p. 105ff.). In other words, human
events have many dimensions. So, in his own study, Jeanmaire devotes one part
of the effort to the psychological element that research in mental pathology
allows him to identify, and another part to the religious manifestations of a
mania that has analogues in other societies. [. . .]

There are some negative points to make. It is indeed necessary to leave
room, among the ancestors of Dionysiac religion, to phallic cults such as the

one found in the Rural Dionysia: obviously a very ancient heritage—although the symbol was never found to have occurred in the Aegean basin—which combines female fecundity and agrarian fertility within a "primitive" system of religious thought and behavior. Still, this element remains peripheral to Dionysiac religion in its most typical manifestations: for in maenadism, as in other aspects of the cult, the sexual aspect does not appear. There is no *libido* to speak of in this matter: in Euripides' play Pentheus's innuendoes always fall flat.

Nor does intoxication, at least in the current sense of the word, appear to be an essential factor of Dionysiac religion. One always thinks of Dionysus as the god of wine, and consequently as the god of intoxication: drinking bouts, to be sure, are an important part of those feasts that Dionysus perpetuated; the *kōmos* parade may indeed stagger occasionally. What we do not see, however, is that *mania* itself owes its power and its magic to the ingestion of wine (or, for that matter, of any other substance, considering how scant the evidence is on that matter). The maenads are not inebriated women—on this particular subject Euripides has Pentheus make yet another infelicitous innuendo; the bacchants, just as the celebrants of the ancient dithyramb, are not intoxicated individuals. In other words, what we are dealing with here is sheer delirium, a case of "collective ecstasy" of the kind Félice writes about in one of his better-known works. It is a kind of delirium, though, which is brought on by means of suggestion techniques, both traditional and collective: fever of the dance and hypnotic music.

What is the importance of *mania* within Dionysiac religion as a whole? Here one encounters a curious contradiction. On the one hand, *mania* sometimes appears as the essential element; for one should keep in mind that, even when the bacchic delirium remains confined to a small group, it can still affect the rest of society not only with a more or less benevolent curiosity, but also with participatory sympathy. In the function performed by the *thyades*, the idea is implied, and sometimes even made explicit, of a kind of delegation. Jeanmaire has emphasized the importance and dynamic value of "spectacle," which, even more than theater, is a major means of action for Dionysiac religion. After all, *catharsis* is meant for people other than the actors or performers: its most basic effect being to cure *mania* through *mania*. Delirium, therefore, fulfills a religious function that could be described as generic. [. . .]

The distinctive feature of Dionysiac religion lies in the extreme variety of psychological experiences that it either allows, or imposes on, its members. Suffice it to say, to make one realize the richness and possibilities it offered the Greeks, that the cult of Dionysus "fills up the gap" in its own way, for while it tends toward the most individual form of religion, it is partial to the Bacchanal and its overblown sense of social belonging (*thiaseuetai psukhan* [Euripides *Bacchae* 75]).

Yet another aspect of Dionysiac religion, although seemingly specific and episodic, might not be the least revealing. Jeanmaire emphasizes the role played by laughter within the "cathartic system" (p. 321), thus reminding us how important this issue of laughter is, which has seldom been treated ever since Salomon Reinach's outdated and slightly superficial study; but this in turn raises a more general question, that of the role of *play* and *paidia* in Dionysiac religion. Dionysus became a symbol par excellence for dramatic activity because he is both a god at play and one who makes others play. Even in a festival as popular as the Anthesteria, one could go so far as to say that he "plays" or toys with a certain ambiguity between the "real" world and the world beyond.

Jeanmaire successfully conveys to his reader not only a sense of this shifting reality that so pervades the cult of Dionysus, but also an impression of its unity. Thus, a little more light is shed on the meaning of *mania*: because *mania* is so emphasized at times, it can never be entirely missing from other occasions. To be sure, one has the feeling that this religion contains something murky: which does not mean that it aims at some kind of dizzying pantheism, or lives on the pressing need for communion with a world of mystery—there is seldom so much at stake for the Greeks; and Jeanmaire notes repeatedly that joy is always the keynote, never pessimism. There is something murky in this cult, however, because the god himself is still a disturbing one (p. 118) and because madness is his domain. The cult's own revivals and progress always involve those of orgiasm: the classical period itself witnessed a sudden increase in maenadism (p. 163ff.); all of a sudden, an entire army can be carried away in a divinely inspired fit of *furor*. Witness the history of Alexander—or his legend, which, in the end, is the same thing. With Dionysus, as far as one may think oneself to be from it, one is constantly on the verge of madness.

Nevertheless, this madness is of a good kind: the lesson taught by the *Bacchae* is that divine *mania* should be praised. Even the bacchants' name is revealing; it never ceases to teach us about the true nature of Dionysiac religion. And indeed, what has always struck the imagination about this cult is how important a role the female element plays in it. [. . .]

What lies at the base of all this is the opposition of the sexes. It functions in all forms of religious life, where it occasionally translates itself into symbolic antagonism. It can also be found in mythical transformations of ritual dramas, where hostility is carried as far as possible: for example, in festive practices involving the exchange of insults, or in myths such as those about the crimes of the Lemnian women and the Danaids. This is a very general concept that Dionysism utilizes; but it gives it an importance that ought to have its own special significance. There is something antimasculine as well as revolutionary in the *Bacchae*. The opposition of the sexes is less explicit in Dionysism, but perhaps more profound. Nothing characterizes its legends more than the liberation of women, whether promised or imposed: they are delivered from domestic life, its joys, and its life of servitude. What they realize, by the grace of Dionysus, is an "escape"; and the word appears many times in Jeanmaire. Its recurrence serves to point out one of the most obvious goals of Dionysism itself. And it is possible to understand woman's preeminent place in the cult because she is best suited to embody it: women are less involved, less integrated in society, and are called up to represent a principle that is opposed to society itself, but that society needs. Such a need, one has to believe, was keenly felt by the Greeks on a religious level. [. . .]

In spite of the commonplace quality of his myth and ritual, Dionysus dominates souls with force. It is because this aspect of his personality is affirmed in his case more than in that of any other. There must be profound reasons for this, and Jeanmaire brings some of them to light.

Dionysus is a god with many sanctuaries but very few temples (p. 20): he did not easily enter a form of civic religion that magnified and depersonalized divinity. This observation leads to another point that occurs as a leitmotif: except by accident or contrivance, Dionysus is foreign to the world of the affairs of the state; not hostile, but peacefully foreign. He alone among all the gods is associated with no function of the state; nor does he even figure in any moment of the past life of the city. The other side of this is his direct link with the world of nature, especially its wild and uncivilized side. [. . .]

Another definite characteristic of Dionysus is his rapport with the world of the dead. This is not to say that no other god has connections with it, but that Dionysus's is different. [. . .] His dealings with the world of the dead are those of a "ubiquitous" god, and his presence alone creates a sense of hereafter. [. . .]

What remains is the historical question. After uncovering the elements that seem integrated in Dionysism and that characterize it from its beginning, and after determining the cult's place and raison d'être within a system that is more or less directly known, a question still remains unanswered: how does one explain the success of a religion that Herodotus found "incompatible with the Greek temperament" and whose recent introduction he could only explain as a borrowing? Jeanmaire does not pose this question and it is admittedly an obscure one. But it cannot be avoided. The cult of Dionysus must have had its origin in a genuine religious *movement* with a fully deliberate desire for renewal; otherwise, how can the extraordinary popularity of a new god and his message be explained? In the history of his cult, Dionysus is a god of *revivals*, and such a trait must have been his from the beginning. Jeanmaire's claim— that the tales of resistance to the god, their violence and eventual defeat, are mythical themes—is probably true; but there must have been a more or less rapid diffusion of the cult, which involved the concept of a militant religion of conquest. In any case, it is not a religious movement that comes essentially from the outside. And the indirect testimony we have about it suggests that it is indeed a spontaneous movement. [. . .]

Even though it does not deal with some of these questions, the book still has its own value. One of its obvious merits, stated earlier, is the author's sense of history and his genuine ability to interpret historical events. In light of this, I admit some puzzlement at the skepticism of the book's last lines, where Jean-maire speaks of *"histoire inactuelle."* There is no such thing. There is an undefined series of human experiences in which Hellenism has an important place.

TRANSLATED BY JOHN HAMILTON AND BLAISE NAGY

JEAN-PIERRE VERNANT

The Masked Dionysus
of Euripides' *Bacchae*

1986

This essay, first published in a 1986 collection on Greek tragedy co-authored by Vernant and Vidal-Naquet (which also includes a collaborative paper on masks by Vernant and Frontisi-Ducroux), is among many that attest to the spirit of collective enterprise and intellectual cross-fertilization that was an early hallmark of the équipe *at the Centre de Recherches Comparées sur les Sociétés Anciennes. A shared interest in the particular images and symbols through which the Greeks represented their divinities has generated a rich set of studies, including those by Frontisi-Ducroux, Georgoudi, Loraux, and Olender (in this volume), as well as others by Detienne, Lissarrague, Sissa, and further contributions by Vernant. In this essay, Vernant analyzes the ambiguous function of the theatrical mask worn by the god Dionysus as an actor on the tragic stage, and explores its relation to religious masks representing the deity (or worn by his votaries) in civic religious ceremonies. Vernant's inquiry into the Dionysian mask broadens into an interpretation of Euripides' play that draws on perspectives from the anthropology of religion as well as from philology. This selection omits some history of the concept of "Dionysism" in later religious thought, as well as portions of Vernant's close reading of the* Bacchae.

Amid all the sources of evidence on Dionysus in fifth-century Athens, Euripides' *Bacchae* occupies a place of particular importance.[1] The richness and complexity of the work and the density of the text make it an incomparable document when it comes to trying to understand the particular features of the religious experience of the devotees of this god who, more than any other, assumes within the Greek pantheon the functions of the god of the mask. [. . .]

From *Myth and Tragedy in Ancient Greece*, trans. Janet Lloyd (New York: Zone Books, 1988), pp. 381–412 ["Le Dionysos masqué du *Bacchae* d'Euripide," in *Mythe et tragédie en Grèce ancienne deux* (Paris: François Maspero, 1972), pp. 237–70].

In the *Bacchae*, Dionysus takes the principal role. The poet sets him on stage as the god who himself stages his own epiphany there, in the theater, revealing himself not only to the protagonists in the drama but also to the spectators seated on the tiered steps, by manifesting his divine presence through the unfolding of the tragic drama—drama that is, moreover, specifically placed under his religious patronage. It is as if, throughout the spectacle, even as he appears on stage beside the other characters in the play, Dionysus was also operating at another level, behind the scene, putting the plot together and directing it toward its denouement. [. . .]

The constant interaction between the Dionysus of the civic religion—the god of the official cult—and the Dionysus of the tragic representation—the god who is the master of theatrical illusion—is right from the start underlined by the duality, or double persona, of Dionysus in the theater itself. On the *theologeion* he is present as a god; on the stage he is seen as the Lydian stranger "who looks like a woman"; the two are dressed alike and wear the same mask; they are indistinguishable yet distinct from one another. The mask worn by the god and the human stranger—who is also the god—is the tragic mask of the actor, the function of which is to make the characters recognizable as what they are, to render them visually identifiable. But in the case of Dionysus, the mask disguises him as much as it proclaims his identity; it literally "masks" him; at the same time, through his misidentification and secret, this prepares the way for his authentic triumph and revelation. All the characters in the drama, including the chorus composed of his faithful female Lydian devotees, who have followed him to Thebes, see only the foreign missionary in the theatrical mask that the god wears. The spectators also see that foreigner but realize that he is a disguise for the god, a disguise through which the latter can eventually be made known for what he is: a masked god whose coming will bring the fulfillment of joy to some, but to others, those unable to recognize him, nothing but destruction. The ambiguity of the mask worn by the stranger and by the god expresses the interplay between the two, underlining both the affinities and the contrast between on the one hand the *tragic* mask that sets the seal upon the presence of a particular character, giving him a firm identity, and on the other the *religious* mask whose fascinating gaze establishes an imperious, obsessive, and overwhelming presence, the presence of a being that is not where it seems to be, a being that is also elsewhere, perhaps inside one, perhaps nowhere. It is the presence of one who is absent. It is a "smiling" mask (434, 1021), unlike the usual tragic masks, a mask that is consequently different from all the rest, a mask displaced, disconcerting, and that, seen there on the theater stage, is an echo that calls to mind the enigmatic face of some of the religious masks of the god used in the civic religion.[2] [. . .]

It is noteworthy that there is absolutely no documentation on the Dionysism of fifth-century Athens to vouch for [. . .] a Dionysism systematically used to reverse the meaning of sacredness and the basic orientation of the official civic religion: no evidence of any ascetic tendencies, no rejection of the positive values of earthly life, not the slightest urge towards renunciation, no preoccupation with the soul or attempt to separate it from the body, no eschatological perspective at all. No hint of any preoccupation with salvation or immortality is to be found in the relevant rituals and pictorial representations or in the *Bacchae*. Everything is played out in the here and now. The undeniable desire to be free, to escape into an elsewhere is expressed not as a hope for another, happier life after death, but within the present life, through the experience of an extra dimension, an expansion of the human condition, which thereby accedes to a blessed otherness.

This view is confirmed by the analyses produced by anthropologists.[3] Apart from the Christian ecstasy of ravishment in solitude, silence, and stillness, they distinguish two forms of trance and possession that are, in many respects, diametrically opposed. In the first, it is the individual human being who takes the initiative, asserting his control over the situation. Thanks to the peculiar powers that he has acquired by various means, he is able to leave his body, which he abandons in a state of catalepsy to journey in another world from which he then returns to earth, remembering everything he has seen in the beyond. Such was the status of the "magi" in Greece, strange figures with their own life discipline, spiritual exercises, ascetic techniques, and reincarnation. They are more or less legendary figures who have more in common with Apollo than with Dionysus.[4]

In the other form of trance, it is a matter not of an exceptional human being ascending to the gods, but of the gods coming down to earth of their own volition, in order to possess a mortal, to ride him, to make him dance. The one who is possessed does not leave this world; he becomes other through the power that inhabits him. On this level, a further distinction should be made. In the *Phaedrus* (265a), where Plato tackles the problem of *mania*, he makes a distinction between two kinds: on the one hand, the delirium may take the form of a human sickness from which the victim must recover; on the other, it may be a divine state with a fully positive value of its own. A similar dividing line distinguishes between practices of a corybantic type on the one hand and the cult of Dionysus on the other. In the first case, it is a matter of individuals who are sick. Their critical state of delirium or prostration is the sign of a fault, the manifestation of an impurity. They are the victims of a god whom they have offended and who punishes them by taking possession of them. So what needs to be done, in the course of ritual, is to identify the god from whose vengeance the sick person is suffering so that he can be cured through the appropriate purifications, which can liberate him from his state of possession. In a Dionysiac *thiasos* there is no god to be identified and ejected; there is no sickness: the particular pathology of the individuals involved is of no concern. The *thiasos* is an organized group of faithful devotees who, if they use trance, turn it into a form of social behavior, ritualized and controlled and for which a preliminary period of apprenticeship is probably required. Its purpose is not to cure an individual's sickness, much less to deliver him from the evil of living in a world from which he longs to escape forever; instead, it is to procure a changed state of being, through music and dancing, for a group of people, in ritual costume, in a setting of wild nature either real or simulated. The aim is for this group momentarily to undergo the experience of becoming "other," within the very framework of the city and with its agreement, if not authority: "other" not in an absolute sense, but in relation to the models, norms, and values peculiar to the particular culture of that city.[5]

Nor could it be otherwise for Dionysism. The deity that Dionysus constitutes in the Greek pantheon does not represent a domain of reality separate from the world, a domain set in opposition to the inconsistency and inconstancy of human life. His position there is ambiguous, as is his status, which is more that of a demigod, however much he wishes to be a full god with all the privileges and attributes of one. Even on Olympus, Dionysus embodies the "other." If he had a mystical function, he would wrench men from the world of becoming and the sensible in all its multiplicity and project them over the threshold beyond which one enters into the sphere of what is unchangeable, permanent, one, and forever the same. But that is not his role. He does not detach human beings from earthly life through techniques of asceticism and renouncement. Rather, he blurs the frontiers between the divine and the human, the human and the animal, the here and the beyond. He sets up communion between things hitherto isolated, separate. His eruption into nature, the social group, and each individual human being, through trance and regulated possession, is a subversion of order. This subversion, by means of a whole range of prodigies, fantasies, and illusions, involving a disconcerting disorientation from everyday reality, projects one either upward, into an idyllic confraternity among all beings, the blessed communion of a golden age suddenly retrieved, or, on the contrary, if one rejects and denies him, downward, into the chaotic confusion of a terrifying horror.

As I have already explained, in this analysis of the *Bacchae*, I shall concentrate solely upon such features as may illuminate the figure of the masked god and the nature of his devotees' religion.

The Dionysus of the *Bacchae* is a god intent upon imposing his imperious, demanding, overwhelming presence upon this earthly world: he is a god of *parousia*. In every land, every city that he decides to make his own, he makes his entrance, arrives, is there. The very first word of the play is ἥκω: "Here I am, I have come." Dionysus always bursts in suddenly, as if erupting from somewhere else, somewhere foreign, a barbarian world, far away. His sudden coming is all-conquering, extending and establishing the cult of the god from city to city, from place to place. The entire tragedy, as it unfolds showing us the

Dionysiac epiphany, illustrates this "coming." It shows it on stage, where Dionysus performs both as a protagonist in the midst of other actors and as the organizer of the whole spectacle, the secret manipulator of the plot that finally leads to the Thebans' recognizing him as a god. But this epiphany is also addressed to the spectators whom the fiction of the drama includes, as if they were participants in the revelation of the god. Through the pity and terror that they feel for the victims, it allows them fully to perceive what is at stake and all that is implied. At the same time, thanks to the type of comprehension conveyed by the perfectly ordered tragic action, it affords them the same pleasure, the same "purification" that Dionysus grants to the cities where he chooses to appear once he is recognized, accepted, and integrated there.

This epiphany is not like that of ordinary gods, nor is it a "vision" analogous to the *epopteia* of the mysteries. Dionysus insists that he be "seen." The last words of the Prologue, which balance the "I have come" of the opening, call upon the "city of Cadmus to behold [ὡς ὁρᾷ Κάδμου πόλις]" (61). Dionysus wants to be seen to be a god, to be manifest to mortals as a god, to make himself known, to reveal himself,[6] to be known, recognized, understood.[7] This "manifestness" that must, in certain conditions, be a feature of the god's presence, is expressed forcefully in the fourth stasimon by the chorus of Lydian women devotees, who first state their desire that justice should "be manifest [φανερός]" (993), then declare what is for them a matter of principle: "My happiness depends upon pursuing that which is great and manifest [φανερά]" (1007). Next, they proceed to invoke the Dionysus of epiphanies, calling upon the god to show himself too, to make himself manifest: "Appear! [φάνηθι]" (1018). But Dionysus reveals himself by concealing himself, makes himself manifest by hiding himself from the eyes of all those who believe only in what they can see, in what is "evident before their eyes,"[8] as Pentheus himself puts it at line 501, when Dionysus is there before him, under his very nose, but invisible to him beneath his disguise. It is an epiphany allright, but of a god who is masked. To make Thebes accept his presence, to "appear" there, Dionysus has changed his "appearance," transformed his face, his external aspect, his nature.[9] He has donned the mask of a human being; he presents himself in the guise of a young Lydian stranger. Distinct from the god, yet at the same time identical to him, the stranger assumes the functions of a mask in the sense that, even as he conceals his true identity (from those who are not prepared to recognize him), he is also the instrument of the god's revelation: he manifests his imperious presence before the eyes of those who, in his sight and—as it were—face to face with him, have learned to "see what must be seen" (924): what is most manifest under the disguise of what is most invisible.

But how can the god and his devotee be face to face, looking straight into each other's eyes? After all, trance is collective: it occurs in a group, in the setting of a *thiasos*. Nevertheless, when the band of maenads surrenders jointly to the orgiastic frenzy, each participant acts on her own account, oblivious of any general choreography, indifferent to what the others are doing (as in a *kōmos*). Once the devotees have entered the dance, each as one elect is face to face with the god, totally submissive within herself to the power that possesses her and moves her as it will.

So although the epiphany of Dionysus can only be made manifest through the collective orgiastic behavior of a group, for each individual concerned it takes the form of a direct confrontation, a "fascination" in which, through the interchange of gazes and the indissociable reciprocity of "seeing" and "being seen," all distance is abolished between the devotee and her god, and they become united. In trance, the human being plays the part of god while god plays the part of human being. Momentarily, the frontiers between them collapse, blurred by the intensity of the divine presence, which, to be seen in all its immediacy before one, must first impose its dominion over one's eyes, and having won possession of one's gaze from within, transforms one's very mode of vision.

When Pentheus interrogates the Lydian stranger about this god whose missionary the young man claims to be, his question draws a clear line of demarcation between two contrary forms of vision: that of the sleeping dreamer, which is illusory and unreal; and that of the wide-awake, lucid man, with eyes wide open, which is authentic and irrefutable. "How did you see him? In a dream," he asks, "or face to face?" "ὁρῶν ὁρῶντα," the stranger replies: "Seeing him seeing me" (470). "I saw him seeing me": it is an oblique reply that displaces the question and stresses that the god's epiphany has nothing to do with the dichotomy that shapes the convictions of Pentheus, namely his distinction between on the one hand dreams, fantasies, and illusions, and on the other true vision that provides irrefutable knowledge. The "vision" demanded by the masked god is something far beyond those two forms of knowledge, of which it makes a mockery. It is based on the meeting of two gazes in which (as in the interplay of reflecting mirrors), by the grace of Dionysus, a total reversibility is established between the devotee who sees and the god who is seen, where each one is, in relation to the other, at once the one who sees and the one who makes himself seen. [. . .]

No other text so insistently, almost obsessively, repeats such a plethora of words signifying seeing and visibility: *eidos*, even *idea* (at 471), *morphē*, *phaneros*, *phainō*, *emphanes*, *horaō*, *eidō* (and their compounds). Euripides finds it all the easier to employ this vocabulary to suggest the whole range of multiple meanings, ambiguities, and reversals suggested by human experience confronted by Dionysus, given that the very same terms can be applied to ordinary, normal vision, to supernatural "apparitions" engineered by the god, to his epiphanic revelation, and to all the illusory forms of "appearance," seeming, misleading resemblance, and hallucination.

What the vision of Dionysus does is explode from within and shatter the "positivist" vision that claims to be the only valid one, in which every being has a particular form, a definite place, and a particular essence in a fixed world that ensures each his own identity that will encompass him forever, the same and unchanging. To see Dionysus, it is necessary to enter a different world where it is the "other," not the "same" that reigns. [. . .]

The epiphany of Dionysus is that of a being who, even in proximity and intimate contact with one, remains elusive and ubiquitous, never where he seems to be, never fixed in a definitive form: a god on the *theologeion*, a smiling young man on the stage, a bull leading Pentheus to his death, a lion, a snake, a flame, or something else again. He is at once and as much on the stage, in the palace, on Cithaeron, everywhere and nowhere. When the women of the chorus exhort him to manifest himself in his full presence, they sing: "O Dionysus, reveal yourself a bull! Be manifest, a snake with darting heads that see, a lion breathing fire to be seen."[10] Bull, snake that sees, lion to be seen [. . .] and the chorus's next words are: "O Bacchus come! Come, with your [masked] smile!"[11] Cast your noose about this man [Pentheus]." The mask, with wide staring eyes that fix one like those of the Gorgon, expresses and epitomizes all the different forms that the terrible divine presence may assume. It is a mask whose strange stare exerts a fascination, but it is hollow, empty, indicating the absence of a god who is somewhere else but who tears one out of oneself, makes one lose one's bearings in one's everyday, familiar life, and who takes possession of one just as if this empty mask was now pressed to one's own face, covering it and transforming it.

As has already been pointed out,[12] the mask is a means of expressing absence in a presence. At the crucial moment in the drama when Pentheus, perched in his tree, is up there in the sky for all to see (1073, 1076), the epiphany of the god takes the form of, not an extraordinary appearance, but a sudden disappearance. The messenger tells us, as an eyewitness, "Barely had they seen [him] . . . huddled at the top, when the stranger vanished":[13] he was nowhere to be seen. And from the sky, in a supernatural hush that suddenly falls on the heavens and the earth alike, there comes a voice[14] that identifies the god and urges on the maenads to attack his enemy. Dionysus is never more present in the world, never does he affect it more than at this moment, when, in contrast to Pentheus, exposed to all eyes, he escapes into invisibility. When present-absent Dionysus is here on earth, he is also in the heavens among the gods; and when he is up there in heaven, he is also on this earth. He is the one who unites the normally separate heaven and earth and introduces the supernatural into the heart of nature. Here again, there is a striking contrast between Pentheus's fall and the ascension of the god (underlined by the ironic use of the same terms and expressions to refer to both). [. . .] Whether the god rises to heaven, falls to earth, or leaps and flames between the two, whether he is man, flame, or voice, visible or invisible, he is always the polar opposite to Pentheus, despite the symmetrical expressions that are used to describe them both. He brings down to earth the revelation of another dimension to existence and grants our world and our lives direct experience of the elsewhere, the beyond. [. . .]

Dionysus cannot be pinned down in any form, he plays with appearances, confuses what is illusion and what is real. But his otherness also stems from the fact that, through his epiphany, all the cut-and-dried categories and clear oppositions that impart coherence to our vision of the world lose their distinctiveness and merge, fuse, changing from one thing into another.

Let us consider a number of them: first, male and female. Dionysus is a male god with a female appearance (*thēlumorphos*, 353). His dress and his hair are those of a woman, and he transforms the virile Pentheus into a woman by making him wear the costume of his devotees. Pentheus then wants to be, and seems to be, altogether a woman and is most gratified when Dionysus tells him: "So much alike are you, I could take you for your mother or one of your aunts" (927). The spectators are the more likely to share his view given that the parts of Pentheus and Agave would both be played by the same actor.

Young and old: in the cult of Dionysus, the difference between the two states is wiped out (206–209, 694): "Did the god declare that just the young or just the old should dance? No, he desires his honor from all mankind. He wants no one excluded from his worship," Tiresias declares (206–209); and the messenger reports that on Mount Cithaeron, he has seen them "all as one, the old women and the young and the unmarried girls" (694).

The far and the near, the beyond and the here and now: Dionysus does not tear one from this world, but by his presence he transfigures it.

Greek and barbarian: the Lydian stranger, from Asia, is a native of Thebes.

The one in a frenzy, the one who is mad (*mainomenos*) is also *sophos*, *sophistēs, sōphrōn*.

The new god (*neos*: 219, 272), come to found a cult hitherto unknown, also represents "customs and traditions hallowed by age and handed down to us by our fathers" (201); "whatever long time has sanctioned, that is a law forever; the law tradition makes is the law of nature" (895ff.).

The wild and the civilized: Dionysus makes one flee from the town, deserting one's house, abandoning children, spouse, family, leaving one's daily occupations and work. He is worshipped at night, out on the mountainside, in the valleys and woods. His servants become wild, handling snakes and suckling the young of animals as if they were their own. They discover themselves to be in communion with all beasts, both the wild and the domesticated, and establish a new and joyous familiarity with nature as a whole. Yet Dionysus is also a "civilizing" god. The chorus of his faithful Lydian maenads applauds Tiresias when he draws a parallel between Demeter and Dionysus. For the god is to what is liquid and potable all that the goddess is to what is solid and edible. The one by inventing wheat and bread, the other by inventing (279) the vine and wine, together brought to men (279) the means to pass from a wild life to a

civilized one. All the same, there is a difference between wheat and wine.
Wheat is entirely on the side of civilization, but wine is ambiguous. When it is
neat, it conceals a force of extreme wildness, a burning fire; when diluted and
consumed in accordance with the rules, it brings to civilized life an extra, as it
were supernatural, dimension: joy in the feast, with evil forgotten. It is a drug
(*pharmakon*) that makes pain fade away; it is the ornament, the crown, the
living, happy brilliance of the banquet (380–83), the joy of the celebration.

Like wine, Dionysus is double: most terrible yet infinitely sweet.[15] His presence, which is a bewildering intrusion of otherness into the human world, may
take two forms, be manifested in two different ways. On the one hand, it may
bring blessed union with the god, in the heart of nature, with every constraint
lifted—an escape from the limitations of the everyday world and oneself. That
is the experience extolled in the *parodos*: purity, holiness, joy, sweet felicity. On
the other hand, it may precipitate one into chaos in the confusion of a blood-
thirsty, murderous madness in which the "same" and the "other" merge and
one mistakes one's nearest and dearest, one's own child, one's second self for a
wild beast that one tears apart with one's bare hands: ghastly impurity, inexpi-
able crime, misfortune without end, without relief (1360). [. . .]

Dionysus does not wish to be the patron of a sect, a restricted group, an
association closed in on itself and confined within its secrets. He demands to be
fully accepted in the ranks of the gods of the civic community. His ambition is
to see his cult officially recognized and unanimously practiced in all the different forms it may assume (536, 1378, 1668). The *polis*, as such, must be initiated.
In this respect, the *thiasos* of the bacchants differs from the closed groups that
flourished in Athens toward the end of the Peloponnesian War and that celebrated the mysteries of foreign gods: Cybele and Bendis, Cottyto, Attis, Adonis, and Sabazios. The religious status claimed by Dionysus is not that of a
marginal, eccentric deity with a cult reserved for the brotherhood of sectarians
who are conscious of being different and pleased to be so, marked out for themselves and in the eyes of all by their nonconformity to the common religion.
Dionysus demands from the city official recognition for a religion that in a
sense eludes the city and is beyond it. He is out to establish at the very heart and
center of public life practices that, either openly or covertly, present aspects of
eccentricity.

The tragedy of the *Bacchae* shows the dangers that are involved when a city
retrenches within its own boundaries. If the world of the same refuses to absorb
the element of otherness that every group and every human being unconsciously carry within themselves, just as Pentheus refuses to recognize that
mysterious, feminine, Dionysiac element that attracts and fascinates him despite the horror that he claims to feel for it, then all that is stable, regular, and
the same tips over and collapses and the other, of hideous aspect, absolute otherness and a return to chaos, come to appear as the sinister truth, the other,

authentic, and terrifying face of the same. The only solution is for women to use the controlled trance, an officially recognized *thiasos* promoted to the status of a public institution, while men turn to the joy of the *kōmos*, wine, disguise, and carnival and for the city as a whole, in and through the theater, to make it possible for the other to become one of the dimensions of both collective life and the daily life of each individual. The victorious eruption of Dionysus is a sign that otherness is being given its place, with full honors, at the center of the social system. [. . .]

The text of the *Bacchae* presents a break and a contrast between the possession—well-being of the faithful and the possession-punishment of those who are impious. At the same time, and in contrast, it establishes a continuity between the oribasic practices of the Dionysiac religion and other aspects of it that have nothing to do with *mania*. In the very first stasimon, the chorus, faced with the impious Pentheus, glorifies Piety. As it sings the praises of Dionysus, it shifts the emphasis and expresses itself in different terms. The god who leads the *thiasos* is also the joyful god whose laughter resounds to the notes of the flute, who soothes anxiety and dispenses sleep by bringing forth the grape and wine and all the brilliance (*ganos*) of festivity. Dionysus delights in feasting, peace, and opulence: "To rich and poor he gives the simple gift of wine, the gladness of the grape" (417–23). This is a popular kind of wisdom, familiar to humble folk who aspire to no more than a peaceful life governed by reason (*to phronein*). Open to the deity, conscious of the brevity of human existence, and thinking ordinary mortal thoughts, they do not pursue the inaccessible but instead devote their lives to happiness. Wise enough to shun beings who believe themselves superior, they derive their well-being from making the most of the blessings that the god makes available to them.

Scholars have pondered on this relaxing of the tension as one passes from the ardent religious fervor of the *parodos* to the somewhat pedestrian sentiments expressed in the first stasimon. As Jacqueline de Romilly writes: "From mystic ecstasy we move to a cautious kind of hedonism."[16] The modern reader cannot fail to be aware of the drop in intensity. Perhaps it was less striking to the Athenian spectators who were more familiar with the various aspects of the cult and the multiple facets presented by the figure of Dionysus in the fifth-century city. At all events, one cannot help noticing that, after delivering his account of the stupefying prodigies and incredible miracles that he has witnessed on Mount Cithaeron, the messenger—apparently quite naturally—rounds off with a conclusion to the effect that: This is a great god and he is great above all in that "he gave to mortal men the gift of lovely wine by which our suffering is stopped. And if there is no god of wine, there is no love, no Aphrodite either, nor other pleasure left for men" (773–74). Is this irony on the part of the poet? In the third stasimon, which picks up the *makarismos* of the *parodos* and proceeds to celebrate the extreme well-being, indeed beatitude that the god dispenses to his devotees,[17] the tone is much the same. One should place one's faith, not in human knowledge (*to sophon*), but in the mysterious power of the deity (*to daimonion*), and in religious matters conform with the established tradition (*to nomimon*, 894–95). So what kind of felicity is the devotee of Dionysus really seeking? The chorus declares: "He who garners day by day [κατ' ἦμαρ] the good of life,[18] he is happiest. Blessed is he."

Fulfillment found in ecstasy, "enthusiasm," and possession; but also a well-being derived from wine, the joy of festivity, the pleasures of love and the felicty to be found in everyday life. All this Dionysus can bring if only men learn to welcome him and cities to recognize him, just as he can deal out misfortune and destruction if he is rejected. But in no circumstances does he ever come to announce a better fate in the beyond. He does not urge men to flee the world nor does he claim to offer a soul access to immortality achieved through a life of asceticism. On the contrary, men must accept their mortal condition, recognize that they are nothing compared with the powers that are beyond them on every side and that are able to crush them utterly. Dionysus is no exception to the rule. His devotee must submit to him as to an irrational force that is beyond his comprehension and that can dispose of him at will. The god has no need to explain himself. He is alien to our norms and customs, alien to our preoccupations, beyond good and evil, supremely sweet and supremely terrible. His pleasure is to summon up the multiple aspects of otherness around us and within us.

The Dionysus of the *Bacchae* is a god as tragic as human existence, to Euripides' way of thinking. But by showing his epiphany on stage, the poet renders both the god and life, whatever their contradictions, as intelligible as they can be.

The only way of acceding to an understanding of the masked god is to enter into his game oneself. And only a tragic poet is capable of doing that, having reflected on his art, conscious of the special skills at his command, since he is past master at casting the spells of dramatic illusion. Transposed to the stage, the magic ploys of the god undergo a transmutation. They harmonize with the techniques of the dramatist and the enchantment of his poetry and thus, be they most terrible or most sweet, they contribute to the pleasure of the dramatic spectacle.

Charles Segal has correctly perceived that the deliberate "modernity" of this, Euripides' last play, devoted to Dionysus, suggests a homology between the Dionysiac experience and the tragic representation.[19]

The drama of the *Bacchae* bears witness, through the epiphany of Dionysus, to the tragic dimension of human life. But at the same time, by "purging" the terror and pity prompted by the staged imitation of the actions of the god, it brilliantly reveals to the eyes of all the spectators the *ganos*, the joyous, dazzling brilliance of art, festivity, and play: the *ganos* that it is Dionysus's privilege to dispense here on earth, the *ganos* that, like a beam of light from another world, transfigures the drab landscape of our daily life.

TRANSLATED BY JANET LLOYD

NOTES

[1] The play was written during Euripides' stay with King Archelaus, in Macedon where the poet, already over seventy, visited in 408 and where he later died in 406. It was produced for the first time in Athens in 405, directed by Euripides the Younger, who was either his son or his nephew, as part of a trilogy that also comprised *Iphigenia at Aulis* and *Alcmeon* and that won Euripides a posthumous first prize.

[2] On this point, cf. the fine study by Foley 1980.

[3] Cf., most recently, Gilbert Rouget, *La Musique et la trance: Esquisse d'une théorie générale des relations de la musique et de la possession* (Paris, 1980; preface by Michel Leiris).

[4] On the affinities among "magi" such as Abaris, Aristeas, Hermotimus, Epimenides, Pherecydes, Zalmoxis as well as Pythagoras and the Hyperborean Apollo, cf. E. Rohde, *Psyche: The Cult of Souls and Belief in Immortality among the Greeks*, trans. W. B. Hillis (New York, 1966), p. 88ff.; E. R. Dodds, *The Greeks and the Irrational* (Berkeley, 1959); Detienne 1963, 69ff.

[5] Cf. on this point, the important article by Henrichs 1982, 143–47 of which are devoted to maenad rituals.

[6] δείκνυμι: 47, 50; φαίνομαι: 42, 182, 528, 646, 1031.

[7] γιγνώσκω: 859, 1088; μανθάνω: 1113, 1296, 1345.

[8] φανερὸς ὄμμασιν.

[9] 4, 54; εἶδος: 53; φύσις: 54.

[10] φάνηθι . . . ἰδεῖν / . . . ὁρᾶσθαι, 1017–18.

[11] γελῶντι προσώπῳ, 1021.

[12] Frontisi and Vernant 1990.

[13] οὐκέτ' εἰσορᾶν παρῆν, 1077.

[14] ἐκ δ' αἰθέρος φωνή τις, 1078; αἰθήρ, 1084.

[15] δεινότατος, ἠπιώτατος, 861.

[16] J. De Romilly, "Le Thème du bonheur dans les *Bacchantes* d'Euripide," *Revue des études grecques* 76 (1963): 367.

[17] εὐδαίμων, 902, 904, 911; μακαρίζω, 911.

[18] βίοτος εὐδαίμων, 911; cf. 426: εὐαίωνα διαζῆν, "he hallows his life."

[19] In particular in ch. 8, "Metatragedy: Art, Illusion, Imitation," in Segal 1982b.

STELLA GEORGOUDI

The Twelve Gods of the Greeks: Variations on a Theme

1995

Stella Georgoudi's article begins as an iconographical study, scrutinizing the famous altar built by Pisistratus the Younger to ornament the Athenian agora. But which twelve gods are depicted? (This translation omits an early section that catalogues arguments for and against Otto Weinreich's 1937 assertion that the twelve gods formed a "canonical" series, Ionian in origin, of six Olympian pairs.) Weighing political, visual, and literary evidence, Georgoudi puts special emphasis on problems of interpreting the shifting implications of the Hymn to Hermes. *She concludes by stressing the flexibility of Greek concepts of divinity, which the assembly of twelve appears to demonstrate both in the variability of its membership at different times and places and in the impregnable constancy of its benevolent collective identity—which "candidates" Philip of Macedon, Alexander, and Herakles confirmed in their divergent responses.*

During the last quarter of the sixth century [BCE], one of the most ancient monuments of the Athenian agora, the Altar of the Twelve Gods, was erected. Built by Pisistratus the Younger, grandson and namesake of the famous Athenian tyrant, this building fits in well with the building program started by the Pisistratids. [. . .] Up to this point, there was no great temple, no temple comparable to the one on the Acropolis, known as the "ancient temple" of Athena *Polias*, the worthy home of the city's protecting divinity, and whose construction has recently been linked to Pisistratus.

Clearly, because of its religious, political, and juridical functions, the Athenian agora progressively became a major center under the Tyrants. We could even say, without fearing to be too mistaken, that the Twelve Gods' arrival on

From "Les Douze Dieux des Grecs: Variations sur un thème," in *Mythes grecs au figuré de l'antiquité au baroque*, ed. S. Georgoudi and J.-P. Vernant (Paris: Gallimard, 1996), pp. 43–80.

the agora signals one of the first important acts that aimed, among other things, at transforming this space into a religious center—a center that would be, if not the equivalent of the Acropolis, at least worthy of it. It is also meaningful that Pisistratus built the altar and its precinct, about one meter high, near the Panathenaic way, which went from the Dipylon Gate to the Acropolis, crossing the agora diagonally. Thus, the famous Panathenaic procession—which would be immortalized on the Parthenon frieze in the fifth century [BCE] in its own iconographical language—had to go past the Twelve Gods. It is as if the founder of the cult of the Twelve Gods had meant to establish a firm link between this divine complex and the festival of the Panathenaia, a festival reorganized by the Pisistratids. The Altar of the Twelve Gods became a place of refuge very early on; this is where the Plataeans, when threatened by the Thebans in 519 [BCE], come to seek shelter and put themselves under the protection of the Athenians (Herodotus 6.108). Very early on, the Altar also becomes the official starting point of roads leaving Athens, the milestone from which all distances are measured. It is thus a kind of center, a nodal point of the city, which Pindar will later describe as the "navel" of holy Athens, the "fragrant navel [omphalon thuoenta] [where] all steps converge [polubaton]."

Yet who exactly are these twelve divinities honored in the Athenian agora? No document gives their names. They are simply called "the Twelve [hoi dōdeka]," and we speak of the Altar of the Twelve Gods, the Altar of the Twelve, or even of "the Altar of the Gods [ton tōn theōn bōmon]." [. . .]

Where does the concept of the Twelve Gods arise? [. . .] Some find the original model for the Twelve Gods in Mesopotamia or among the Hittites, others in Lycia or in Egypt. Herodotus himself, relying on the priests of Heliopolis, claims that the Twelve Gods' names are originally Egyptian (2.4).

Although different cultures use the number twelve, or even worship a group of twelve divine entities (whether or not in association with the twelve months or zodiacal signs), this is not evidence enough to give an atavistic profile of the Greek Twelve Gods. Some scholars, after a fruitless quest for an "archetype," turned their gaze back to Greece, and discovered there the first signs of the group. Although the Athenian cult is the only one that can be dated with any certainty, Greek thought links the Twelve with ancient times, with the distant past when institutions were created and established. The Twelve Gods are "contemporaneous" with the foundation of the Olympic games; in the "primitive" time of Cecrops, they help give shape to Athenian identity. [. . .] They are found on the outposts of heroic expeditions (the Bosporus altar), and they are also associated with the dawn of a new human race, a civilization at its beginning. Deucalion himself, the son of Prometheus, establishes a cult of the Twelve Gods by consecrating (hidrusato) an altar to them. This happens, according to tradition, right after the flood sent by Zeus to punish the violent and rash men of the Bronze Age, at the same time when Deucalion and his wife Pyrrha, following Zeus' advice, give rise to a new human race.

Deucalion is also a great inventor: he is the first (*prōtos*) "to found cities and build temples for the Immortals." Thus, simultaneously with this new beginning, the cult of the Twelve Gods is established by the only man whom Zeus thought worthy of being spared, precisely because of his "wisdom and piety."[1] [. . .] The Twelve Gods seem to provide an example for men to follow in order to base their relationships on friendship and cooperation. It is tempting here to link this with a decree in Mytilene about the reintegration of exiles (fourth century [BCE]): to promote harmony and well-being among citizens, the Council and the People invoke the Twelve Gods, Zeus, Concord (*Homonoia*), and Justice (*Dikē*), in this order.[2]

Does this nonconfrontational, antiagonistic aspect explain, at least partly, the Twelve Gods' absence from the Homeric poems? In a world of war and violence, in a world in which even gods fight and vie with each other, what place is there for this divine group that aims at friendly association and synergy? This is a difficult question, and it may be impossible to answer it. Unless we discard it by having recourse to a "historical" evolution: Homer, Hesiod, and the Lyric poets are simply unaware of the Twelve Gods, who must be a late "product" of Greek religion.

Nevertheless, this number "twelve" seems at work in the well-known episode in the *Iliad* (Books 20 and 21) in which Zeus incites the gods to enter the fight, each on behalf of his or her own side: Hera, Athena, Poseidon, Hermes and Hephaistos choose the Achaeans; Ares, Phoibos (Apollo), Artemis, Leto, the divine river Xanthos and Aphrodite side with the Trojans. Divided in rival groups, the gods "rush toward one another with a terrible din." Although these gods who are fighting each other do form with Zeus a group of twelve, it is in this case a fragmented whole. These divine powers strongly individualized, break the unity and coherence that is normally characteristic of the Twelve Gods. [. . .]

Even if supporters of the "canon" of Twelve "Olympians," divided into exactly six gods and six goddesses, refuse to take this episode of the *Iliad* into account, everybody agrees that there is a reference to the Twelve Gods in the *Homeric Hymn to Hermes*. Let us summarize the passage briefly: right after his birth, Hermes, the cunning and clever son of Zeus and the nymph Maia, abandons his "sacred crib"; he leaves the maternal threshold in Arcadia and starts looking for his brother Apollo's cows, which he finds grazing near Olympus, "on the shady slopes of Pieria." Hermes craftily and successfully steals fifty cows, which he brings back to the Peloponnese, by the banks of the Alpheios river. There, Hermes performs a sacrifice and divides the parts: he takes two cows from the stolen herd, kills and skins them, cuts up their "flesh heavy with fat," and roasts the pieces, with the chine and the entrails full of black blood. Later on, happy with his "beautiful work," he divides the meat into "twelve parts" (*dōdeka moiras*), draws lots, and adds a "perfect privilege" (*teleon* geras) to every one of them: probably a "meat privilege" (according to Benveniste's felicitous formula), carved out of *nōta gerasmia* (honorific chine) that were roasting on the fire, and that constitutes the choice piece in Greek sacrifice. Once Hermes has performed this division, he does not taste any of these "hearty and rich meats" despite the enticing smell. He goes to offer (*katethēken*) them into the "high byre," where just before he had crowded the bellowing cows together.

[. . .]

Most see the sacrifice performed by Hermes as an evolution from the sacred (*hieros*) to the profane (*hosios*), a transition that only a character like Hermes could bring about. [. . .] But all these problems of interpretation obscure the question of the Twelve Gods that is hiding behind Hermes' action. If we want to give this question the importance it deserves, we can understand Hermes' actions in different ways. From one particular point of view, Hermes naturally appears to be one of the Twelve Gods to whom he intends to give the twelve parts. Hermes does not need to become one of Olympus's inhabitants, or to obtain the glory, the *kleos*, promised condescendingly by Apollo, to secure his place in this group. The god will not earn his position among the Twelve "at the end of the tale." [. . .] Endowed from birth with "wonderful gifts," [. . .] knowing the "history" of immortal gods from their beginnings on earth, Hermes in the *Hymn* is from the start described not only as an Immortal (*athanatos*), but even more significantly as a god (*theos, daimōn*). And as a god of transitions and of the in-between, he, more than any other, knows both how to be included in the group of the Twelve, as a divinity who receives, as well as how, outside of the group, to be a divinity who offers. It is easier to understand the association between Hermes and Apollo in this context, especially as it concerns the presence of Alpheios, the river that offers the spatial frame for the young god's sacrifice. All three are included—let us remember—among the Twelve Gods honored not too far away at Olympia, the site bathed by the "plentiful and pleasing waters" of Alpheios. The god performing the sacrifice on the banks of this river does not accomplish a "rite of desacralization" for the benefit of men. On a "large, flat rock," he "slices" through the rich flesh of cows and divides it into twelve portions; he leaves to luck the task of assigning each piece to its recipient, without showing any preference for any single member of the divine group. He does, however, ensure that the division is as egalitarian as possible: each portion is composed of the same pieces of meat, put on a spit, and roasted together (*homou*); each portion includes a choice piece, which gives it its significance as "perfect privilege." [. . .]

Hermes, however, does not taste this meat, despite the enticing smell. The reason for this restraint is not that these portions belong to men by way of some "desacralization," nor because gods are normally satisfied by the "aroma" rising from their altars, but precisely because he is one of the Twelve Gods, who function in unison as a group: Hermes cannot be a "loner" and start the meal alone. For lack of a collective feast, not unlike those "equal feasts" (*daitas eisas*) in which Homeric gods participate, Hermes chooses to abstain from the mouth-watering meat, and to show solidarity with his eleven divine companions.[3]

This brief glance at the traces left by the Twelve Gods probably gives only a partial image of their presence and actions in Greece. It is sufficient, however, to make us wonder, even if only briefly, about the meaning of the cult of the Twelve Gods. Most of the work done on the topic seems to have been hindered by two claims: 1) the Twelve have to be Twelve *Olympian* Gods, and 2) their cult necessarily has a pan-Hellenic dimension.

Yet, except for one passage in Aelian (*Variae Historiae* 5.12), the Twelve Gods are never described as Olympians in epigraphical or literary sources. Plato, for example, never calls them *Olympioi*; in the *Laws*, by way of contrast, the *Olympioi*, that is, "those who hold Olympus" (10.904e), are placed on the same level as the celestial gods (*ouranioi*) without being identified with them. Plato contrasts the Olympian and "celestial" gods with the "chthonian" ones. But if this is the case, the Twelve Gods of the *Laws*, who must surely be among the gods "who hold the city" (4.717a), cannot be identified as a group with the Olympian gods, as some have maintained:[4] one of them, as we saw, Pluto, is obviously a chthonian god, who, according to Plato, is also a "great benefactor" for the human race. In fact, Pluto welcomes in his company only men whose souls are freed by death from all pains and desires linked with the body (*Cratylus* 403e–404a).

As for the pan-Hellenic character often attributed to the Twelve Gods, the example of Athens shows that this is hardly self-evident. Some have tried to contrast the Pisistratids with Cleisthenes by invoking precisely the Altar of the Twelve Gods in the agora. It has been claimed that Cleisthenes established a clear distinction between the Ten Eponymous Heroes and the "Twelve Gods dear to the Pisistratids." The cult of the Ten Heroes, founded and fostered by Cleisthenes, thus would be a "specifically Athenian" cult, a "national" answer to the "pan-Hellenic" cult established by the Tyrants. Similarly, Cleisthenes divides all the Athenians into ten *phulai*, choosing a decimal system rather than the originally Ionian duodecimal system. In other words, the Ten Heroes are pure products of democratic Athens who stand in opposition to the pan-Hellenic group of Twelve Gods, which originally comes from Ionia and was favored by the Pisistratids.[5]

A more detailed examination of the cult of the Twelve Gods, however, could very well lead to our reconsidering this conclusion. First, as I have shown, the supposed "transplantation" of the cult from Ionia to Greece proper is groundless. Moreover, the number twelve and its factors three and four are clearly extant in pre-Pisistratidean Athens. We need only mention the different systems of dividing up the Athenians that Aristotle places even before Solon (archon in 594–93): the four *phulai*, the twelve *trittues* (one *trittus* = the third of a *phulē*), or the forty-eight (twelve times four) *naucraria* (territorial and administrative divisions). We could also mention the Dodecapolis of Cecrops: according to Philochorus, Athenian historian of the fourth century [BCE], this legendary king was the first to gather the *plēthos*, the multitude of people who, until then, had been living scattered all over Attica, into twelve cities. The civilizing king's Dodecapolis would then have been the first synoecism, preceding that of Theseus. Some, of course, want to see a fourth-century fabrication in this tradition, but most agree that Philochorus's list must reflect some real fact of archaic Athens.[6]

Secondly—and this is the essential point—the Pisistratids were especially interested in developing *pan-Athenaic* cults rather than pan-Hellenic ones. [. . .] Despite some disagreements about specific details of the Pisistratids' religious policies, most experts agree that the Pisistratids gave a tremendous boost to civic cults. They also established Dionysos as a major god in Athens, and gave a remarkable civic dimension to his cult. They also promoted the cult of the Eleusinian goddesses, Demeter and Kore, in Eleusis as well as in Athens. They championed not only Apollo *Patrōos*, the divine ancestor of the Athenians, but also Apollo *Pythios*, the Delphic god; in Athens, the two sides of Apollo are closely connected, maybe even fused. They started to build the Olympieion, an enormous temple of Olympian Zeus, left unfinished until Hadrian completed it in the second century [CE]. The most important Athenian cults are concentrated in the agora, on the Acropolis and its slopes, and southeast of the city by the banks of the river Ilissos, where Thucydides places ancient sanctuaries (2.15.4). [. . .]

We should examine the foundation of the cult of the Twelve Gods in the framework of the Pisistratids' religious policy aimed at promoting civic gods. The Twelve Gods are established in this center of fusion and union, the agora, where they offer help and protection to all citizens, regardless of any particular ties maintained with specific gods entailed by membership in a family, *genos*, phratry, or religious association. The Twelve seem to have formed a group that is neutral and homogeneous, as it were, and in which both the city and its different component parts could recognize themselves. The divine group that dominates the agora from the sixth century [BCE] seems to be closely associated with the very origins of the city and its juridical institutions. According to some versions, the Twelve Gods are referees in the quarrel between Athena and Poseidon over Attica. According to another tradition about "ancient times" (*ta palaia*), Demosthenes tells how the Twelve Gods sat on the Areopagus Court to judge Orestes, and also one of their own, Ares (Demosthenes *Against Aristocrates* 66; Apollodorus 3.14.1–2). The Twelve also exercise this power of judgment in a less dramatic, not to say comical, setting when they banish Eros from their number because he "troubled" them by provoking dissent (Athenaeus 13.563b). The group of the Twelve Gods can prosper only in harmony and agreement.

[. . .] An altar of the Twelve Gods found near the outer borders of the Greek world imposes a divine *pan-Hellenic* presence on the barbarian gods. [. . .] Some tend to underestimate the Twelve Gods because they do not have sanctuaries or imposing temples, but only altars. We should not forget, however, that the altar is the place where the most important religious act, the sacrifice, is accomplished. Moreover, we should take into account the importance that was given to such altars dedicated to the Twelve Gods. The altar of Pisistratus, for example, is part of religious life in Athens from its foundation in 522 [BCE] to the sack of Athens by the Herulians in 267 [CE]. Recent discoveries have shown that the altar had not been abandoned for any length of time, contrary to what was previously believed, even if we admit that it was damaged by the Persians. Athens piously preserved and renovated the altar at least twice: during the last third of the fifth century [BCE], the monument is enlarged and adorned, and during the fourth century, a new precinct is added to the altar. It is significant that the fourth-century renovation takes place at the exact same time when the well-known monument of the Ten Eponymous Heroes is built. Beside this temporal coincidence, we should consider another striking detail: the new precinct of the Twelve Gods and that of the Ten Heroes are remarkably similar architecturally, as if the Athenians had aimed at creating a certain similitude, at least in appearance, between these two religious poles in the agora.

   [. . .]

What the Greeks call *hoi dōdeka* (*theoi*) seems to be a rather flexible group, probably composed of the principal gods of a city or region (some of whom, the most well known of the Greek pantheon, are found almost everywhere), or sometime of divinities who are significant in a particular mythical/religious context, as for example Alpheios or Kronos at Olympia, and Zeus *Eubouleus* at Delos. Yet even when the Twelve Gods are named, it is not obvious that they were considered as twelve separate divine entities, or a simple collection of twelve distinct individuals. Fused into this group, the Twelve Gods, according to circumstances and local particulars, act as a *whole* that incorporates all the characteristics and powers (*dunameis*) issuing from its twelve members. Besides its own individualized divinities, a city thus can establish a cult of a divine plural entity, a condensed pantheon, a group that establishes its own modes of actions, and delimits its own spheres of intervention in communal life.

If this is so, it should be easier to understand some ambiguous aspects of this group of Twelve.

First, it explains why the Ancients usually speak of *dōdeka theoi*, without naming the individual gods. Secondly, it helps us to understand why we also find the Twelve Gods represented symbolically, as well as anthropomorphically: on a base in Epidauros (fourth century [BCE]) where the Twelve Gods are represented as twelve small points drawn in a circle, below the inscription *duōdeka theōn* (*Inscriptiones Graecae*, vol. 4, 2.287).

Thirdly, it explains why the Twelve Gods are often evoked alongside other individual divinities, or sometimes associated with these divinities' cults: in Athens, the Twelve Gods are thus also the guests of Zeus *Eleutherios*, while in Megara, the sanctuary of Artemis *Sōteira* (the Savior) gives shelter to their statues, made by Praxiteles. In Cos, in the first century [BCE], the same person could hold the priesthood both of the Twelve Gods and of other civic divinities (Zeus *Polieus*, Athena *Polias*, Delian Apollo, and so on). In Hierapytna, in Crete, the Twelve are associated with Athena "of the city" and with Apollo *Dekatophoros*, "who receives the tithe," while in Magnesia, the divine group is honored alongside Zeus, Artemis *Leukophruēnē*, and Pythian Apollo during the great festival of Zeus *Sosipolis*.[7]

Although this seems somewhat paradoxical, or even abnormal, it seems clear that some of these individual divinities are at the same time members of the Twelve. Yet in the religious context, as we saw, they were often endowed with a specific epithet: while simultaneously being part of the group, these gods also act individually when vested with the powers given by a particular epithet. Thus they can be found outside of the group, and there affirm their individuality, their specificity, and their different spheres of action. Or they can separate themselves from the group when they become the protagonists in a story that implies the presence, intervention, and judgment of the Twelve Gods as a group: I am thinking here of Hermes in the *Homeric Hymn to Hermes*; or of the rivals Athena and Poseidon, each claiming Attica; and also of Ares, being judged for murder by the Twelve. But these divinities are simultaneously separated from the pairs that are integral parts of the group, and inside this *whole* that is able to create its own dynamics, and to impose a global divine presence that is coherent and harmonious.

Epilogue: Philip II of Macedonia not only wanted to conquer Greek cities and rule over Greece, he also wanted to become a god, though not just any god. He wanted to be one of the Twelve Gods, and become their *sunthronos*, to be "enthroned" among them. Thus he organized without hesitation a sumptuous procession at Aigai in Macedonia, during which he had magnificent statues of the Twelve Gods carried across the city, alongside his own image "worthy of a god" (*theoprepes eidōlon*). In this way, he presents himself to the astonished crowd as the "thirteenth" (*triskaidekaton*) god (Diodorus 16.92.5, 95.1). Later on, Alexander the Great would be more successful than his father in the business of deification: he arranges divine filiation for himself, he requires his subjects to bow down before him (*proskunēsis*), and he demands divine honors for himself. It seems that he too was obsessed with the idea of becoming the "thirteenth god." Many have advanced this claim, including the orator Demades, who proposed a vote before the Athenian assembly (in 324 [BCE]) to the effect that Alexander be considered as *triskaidekatos*. Demosthenes and others vigorously opposed this proposal, and Demades was fined 100 talents for "excessive impiety" (Aelian *Variae historiae* 5.12).

Philip and Alexander did not have the wisdom and moderation of Heracles. This glorious son of Zeus, deified after his death and welcomed among the gods, refused his father's suggestion to become one of the Twelve Gods. "That's impossible," he answered his father, since one of the Twelve would have to be excluded from the group. Heracles cannot accept an honor (*timē*) that implies another god's *atimia*, dishonor and deprivation of his rights (Diodorus 4.39.4). Besides, the idea of becoming the "thirteenth" god never occurred to him. Of course, Heracles chose the way of virtue . . .

TRANSLATED BY CORINNE PACHE

NOTES

[1] Lucian *On the Syrian Goddess* 12; Hellanikos of Lesbos *FGrH*; cf. Detienne 1990, 310.

[2] A. Heisserer and R. Hodot, "The Mytilenean Decree on Concord," *Zeitschrift für Papyrologie und Epigraphik* 63 (1986): 109–28. According to Lucian (ibid.), a "great friendship coming from Zeus [*diothen*]" existed between all the animals brought by Deucalion on his "ark."

[3] Scheid-Tissinier 1994, 276–78.

[4] For example, G. Morrow, *Plato's Cretan City: A Historical Interpretation of the Laws* (Princeton, 1960), pp. 434–36.

[5] About this theory, see the classic work of Lévêque and Vidal-Naquet 1964, especially 72–74, 96–98, 141–43.

[6] Philochorus in *FGrH* F 94 (with Jacoby's commentary); cf. D. Lewis, "Cleisthenes and Attica," *Historia* 1–2 (1963): 22–40; and U. Kron, *Die zehn attischen Phylenheroen* (Berlin, 1976), pp. 84–86.

[7] References in C. Long, *The Twelve Gods of Greece and Rome* (Leiyden, 1987), pp. 83 (Megara), 93 (Cos), 94 (Hierapytna), and 53 (Magnesia).

CLAUDE MOSSÉ

Heroes and Gods

1984

This chapter suggests ambivalence in Homer's conception of the hero. Aristocratic heroism—with its emphasis on the body of the hero: powerful, beautiful (cf. Loraux 1977, Monsacré in this volume), and precious by virtue of its vulnerability to "noble death"—is distinguished from an ethic that Mossé calls both new and "political" (arising in the city-state), one that emphasizes endurance, survival, judgment, and an agrarian pragmatism. Although most discussion of the gods has been omitted from this translation, the nature of heroic authority is, in Mossé's view, essentially related to the source of Zeus's omnipotence on Olympus.

Few texts have spoken to the human imagination as influentially as the *Iliad* and the *Odyssey*. [. . .] It is true that the language of the *Odyssey* is more prosaic, but this is precisely what makes the adventures of Odysseus so valuable for historians keen to learn about the social, economic, and political realities of "Odysseus's world." Although the poems should not be taken as literal reflections of the true story of the capture of Troy or even of colonial expeditions contemporary with their writing, it would be foolish to ignore the evidence they offer about a society that was indeed quite real.

It has been said that, for the Greeks, the *Iliad* and the *Odyssey* embodied a value system, namely, the heroic ethic that subsisted even in the democratic Athens of the classical period. The principles of that system were obviously those of a warrior aristocracy for which the virtues that become apparent in combat are essential, for it was in combat that the warrior could acquire *kleos*, the glory that made him immortal. To seek engagement in battle was the essence of the hero. [. . .] The "noble death" for which the warrior hoped, the death that would bring him *kleos*, ideally came in the prime of life, before the warrior's body suffered the decrepitude of old age. This was the case with Achilles, Hector, and Patroclus, who would consequently remain forever

From "Des héros et des dieux," in *La Grèce archaïque d'Homère à Eschyle* (Paris: Editions du Seuil, 1984), pp. 34–47.

young and handsome in human memory. Because the warrior's glory was coupled with eternal youth, his mortal remains had to be cared for in a particular way. Conversely, the worst injury that one could do to an enemy was to mutilate his body, as Achilles did when he dragged Hector's body, hitched to his chariot, through the dust in the hope that it would be devoured by dogs and vultures. Nevertheless, since Hector was, along with Achilles, the very type of the warrior hero and thus under the protection of Apollo, his body regained its original beauty, so that when the elderly queen Hecuba, his mother, addressed her son's body after Priam had retrieved it, she could say: "But now I find you fresh as pale dew, seeming newly dead" (*Iliad* 24.758ff.).

Physical beauty, maintained by attentive care and through the application of oils and unguents, was a corollary of the warrior ethic. Of course, as J.-P. Vernant has noted,[1] in combat it was primarily by the splendor of his arms that the warrior stood out: "What was resplendent in the body of the hero was not so much the bright charm of youth (*khariestatē hēbē*) as the luster of his bronze armor, the sparkle of his weapons, his cuirass and helmet, and the flame that burned in his eyes, the emanation of his burning ardor." Achilles, Homer said, was "resplendent in his armor" (*Iliad* 19.397). At rest, however, it was essentially physical beauty that differentiated the hero from the common man, from a man like Thersites, whom the poet is at pains to describe as "the ugliest man who ever came to Ilion" (*Iliad* 2.216). When Helen, atop Troy's ramparts, describes the Achaean heroes to old Priam, their fine appearance is what counts. For example, when Priam points to Agamemnon, he asks: "Come, tell me who the big man is out there, who is that powerful figure?" (*Iliad* 3.167). And he has this to say about Odysseus: "The son of Atreus stands a head taller, but this man appears to have a deeper chest and broader shoulders" (*Iliad* 3.193), while Ajax "towers head and shoulders above the Argive troops" (*Iliad* 3.225ff.). Ten years later, Odysseus's good looks charm Nausicaa, the daughter of the Phaeacian king, for Athena has made him seem "taller, and massive too, with crisping hair in curls like petals of wild hyacinth, but all red-golden" (*Odyssey* 4.230ff.). Even Menelaus, Helen's unfortunate husband, is a handsome blond man cherished by Ares and as good-looking as his rival Paris, "the like of the gods."

Nevertheless, the ranks of the heroes include a number of old men for whom war can no longer be a principal activity. The most celebrated of these is old Nestor, king of sandy Pylos, whose judicious counsel sometimes wards off serious conflict. In fact, elder heroes who no longer participate in battle have a different role to play. Having escaped glorious death, they put their wisdom at the service of the community. Even among the warriors, however, there are a few who stand out for their lucidity rather than for their battlefield prowess. In Troy, for instance, there is Polydamas "the shrewd," Hector's comrade and of the same age as he but who "excelled in handling . . . words" as Hector "excelled at wielding arms" (*Iliad* 18.253). Among the Achaeans it was of course Odysseus who played this role, sometimes joined by Agamemnon.

Did this represent a breach in the heroic ethic due to the intrusion into the realm of the hero of what may already be called the political (about which I will say more later on)? Had war, the occasion of "noble death," ceased to be the sole arena in which the heroic ethic could be exercised? It is interesting to observe that both the *Iliad* and the *Odyssey* contain signs not of a challenge to the prevailing value system but of a certain ambiguity toward it. Take, for example, Achilles' reply to Odysseus when the latter comes with Diomedes to urge him to reenter the fray: "I had small thanks for fighting, fighting without truce against hard enemies here. The portion's equal whether a man hangs back or fights his best; the same respect, or lack of it, is given brave man and coward. One who is active dies like the do-nothing" (*Iliad* 9.318). To be sure, this response was dictated by Achilles' annoyance at being obliged to give up his share of booty, the woman Briseis, to Agamemnon. Later, however, he clarifies his position: "Now I think no riches can compare with being alive, not even those they say this well-built Ilion stored up in peace before the Achaeans came. Neither could all the Archer's shrine contains at rocky Pytho, in the crypt of stone. A man may come by cattle and sheep in raids; tripods he buys, and tawny-headed horses; but his life's breath cannot be hunted back or be recaptured once it passes his lips" (*Iliad* 9.400ff.). This is echoed by a passage in the *Odyssey* in which Odysseus, visiting Achilles in the underworld and congratulating him on his glorious death, is told: "Let me hear no smooth talk of death from you, Odysseus, light of councils. Better, I say, to break sod as a farm hand for some poor country man, on iron rations, than lord it over all the exhausted dead" (*Odyssey* 11.488ff.). [. . .]

These ambiguities have occasionally been blamed on the psychology of individual heroes, whose distinctive personalities the poet presumably wished to bring out. Yet although it is true that Homer liked to individualize his heroes, this desire does not explain all the ambiguities, nor can it hide the contradictions within the heroic system of values embraced by both the poet and his audience. Furthermore, the emergence of a new ethic, that of the peasant-soldier of the nascent city-state, can be seen in a passage in the *Odyssey*. Odysseus confronts one of the suitors, Eurymachus, for daring to pose as his rival: "Eurymachus, we two might try our hands against each other in early summer when the days are long, in meadow grass, with one good scythe for me and one as good for you: we'd cut our way down a deep hayfield, fasting to late evening, or we could try our hands behind a plow, driving the best of oxen—fat, well-fed, well-matched for age and pulling power, and say four strips apiece of loam the share could break: you'd see then if I cleft you a straight furrow. Competition in arms? If Zeus son of Kronion roused up a scuffle now, give me a shield, two spears, a dogskin cap with plates of bronze to fit my temples, and you'd see me go where the first rank of fighters lock in battle" (*Odyssey* 18.366ff.). [. . .]

Does Zeus's omnipotence hark back to the Mycenaean era, when omnipotent kings reigned over the cities of Greece? Or was it nothing more than the power that the head of the family, the master of the *oikos*, exercised in his "household?" In other words, was Zeus's power over the other gods political or social? This question leads us to examine what Homer has to tell us about each of these realms of human activity.

TRANSLATED BY ARTHUR GOLDHAMMER

NOTE

[1] Vernant 1989, 41–79.

LAURENCE KAHN

Against the Rules:
A Performative Sacrifice

1978

The chapter excerpted here examines the Homeric Hymn to Hermes—*a text that, as the present collection attests, has proved extraordinarily rich for contemporary French scholarship (cf. Georgoudi, Leduc in this volume). Kahn here identifies what she sees as a key pair of opposed terms*—hosios *and* hieros—*that describe the act of sacrifice central to the* Hymn's *action. She argues (contra such interpreters as Jeanmaire and Benveniste) that Hermes' sacrifice is anything but normal and that the key terms above are deployed in special senses, so that "to miss these anomalies of usage" is to miss the essence of the sacrifice's—and the myth's—peculiar efficacy. Kahn charts a highly schematic opposition between "normal," Promethean sacrificial ritual and Hermes' singular act, and she underscores the spatial character of Hermes' special status as a god who defines frontiers (cf. Hartog in this volume) by placing himself at their limits, enjoying the power of reciprocal passage.*

There is only one full version of the Hermes myth. Variations on this version are always either lacunose or elliptical. [. . .]

As a counterpart to the myth's uniqueness, which may bring analysis to a halt, one should mention the reference to sacrificial and ritual vocabulary, as well as to the Promethean myth where the distinction between humans and gods rests on sacrifice, work, and procreative marriage: it is precisely to this organizational dichotomy that the terms *hieros* and *hosios* allude.[1]

In fact, studies devoted to the terms *hosios* and *hieros*[2] within the vocabulary of Greek sacrifice often rely on the *Homeric Hymn to Hermes*. This suggests that the use of *hosios* and *hieros* in this hymn is normal, that is, in keeping with all the semantic models describing sacrifices, or more precisely, that it complies with the model inaugurated by the Promethean sacrifice.

From "Contre les règles: un sacrifice efficace," in *Hermès passe ou les ambiguïtés de la communication* (Paris: François Maspero, 1978), pp. 41–93.

It appears, however, that the sacrifice Hermes offers to the Twelve Gods does not obey the rules imposed by this ritual: Hermes sacrifices divine animals stolen from Apollo without any kind of tithe; he slaughters them so that their blood does not gush out; the carving, roasting, and sharing of the flesh run against all the rules prescribing careful discrimination between the various parts of the meat; finally, he does not eat. It is, however, precisely during consumption that the *hieros/hosios* dichotomy should play its role, by defining the opposition between what belongs to the gods and what pertains to humans, by creating differentials, that is, order where the chaos of the Golden Age used to rule, in other words, by generating discontinuity where continuity prevailed. [. . .]

Thus, at first glance we may observe that the two main axes of the general scheme—the opposition between meats that are either *mēria* or *hosiē*, burned or consumed—are missing. Let us not forget that, through this very scheme, sacrifice allows—by means of a symbolic motif of sharing—both men and gods to come together for a common meal while distinguishing very sharply between them.[3] [. . .]

Armed with his *tekhnē*, Hermes manufactures the cooking fire and, even more important, he turns Apollo's divine cattle into a domesticated herd, a symbol of domestic livestock farming in the human sphere. This means that he has effectively moved from sacred to profane a herd, which, although it was originally always the same number, will from now on reproduce and multiply itself. To acknowledge Hermes' share of *timē* means accepting the following: that he is responsible for recirculating a commodity reserved for sacred use only; that, through him, these animals will no longer be immobilized as belonging to the gods but will circulate and generate profit among men; and finally, that these *hiera khrēmata* have fully become *hosia khrēmata*. To grant him his request for *timē* is to let him watch over the herd, which in fact happens at the end of the *Hymn*. The use of *hosiē timē* here, therefore, depends on the ambiguity of the speaker's position in his speech: where is Hermes speaking from? Is he god or man? As a thief he snatches Apollo's herd, as a thief again he threatens to seize the treasures; as the god of profit and trade Hermes receives his brother's *philotēs* in exchange for the promise (guaranteed by a great oath) never to rob Apollo again. Between the master of thieves and the god of trade lies both the distance that separates a man from a god, and their common denominator: the *"circulation of commodities."* Temple treasures, originally *hiera* used for profane purposes, are said to be *hosia*: it is within this movement from *hieros* to *hosios* that Hermes finds his home in Olympus. And even if he happens to be welcomed by Zeus, his *timē* will remain imbued with its technical aspect of which *hosiē* acts as the sign. Similarly, far from being a normal usage of *hosios*, the phrase *hosiē timē* adopts exactly the same movement of semantic relocation and condensation as *hosiē kreōn* or *admētēs*. To overlook these anomalies in usage is tantamount to overlooking the performative aspect of the myth. [. . .]

What is at stake in the performative action of space and word, in what we previously called the destruction/restructuring of the cosmos, is both the status of Hermes and that of the border itself. What divides the divine world from the human world is not a *no-man's-land*, a zone of uncertainty where beings of ill-defined status may move about: it is a sharply defined line of demarcation. Hermes' action constitutes no upheaval, not even a transgression of this fundamental polarity: chaos and anarchy would have arisen only if an undefinable entity had existed somewhere. The representation of Olympus after Hermes integrates it acquires even more coherence and structure. For the performative puns made on the terms *admētēs* and *hosios*, far from weakening their strong semantic charge, strengthen their power to differentiate.

These crucial points of the myth, these meeting points for various levels of meaning where multiple networks of signifiers fit into each other, are neither obscure nor blurred points: they are simply particularly dense. And it is this very density which should attract our attention: in this case, within a myth which tells us about passage, these points are precisely the various places where this passage occurs.

TRANSLATED BY FLORENT HEINTZ

NOTES

[1] Sokolowski 1955. [. . .]

[2] [. . .]; Jeanmaire 1945; Benveniste 1969, 2: 192–202.

[3] On the origins of *thuō* and fumigation, cf. Benveniste 1969, 2: 223–31.

CLAUDINE LEDUC

A Theology of the Sign in Greece:
The Homeric Hymn to Hermes (I),
Commentary on Lines 1–181

1995

This excerpt omits some of the detailed explication of the three inventions (the lyre, the door-hinge, and the herdsman's fire) by which, in Leduc's view, Hermes makes himself manifest in the Hymn, *and the hierarchy Leduc establishes among them.*

Two interrelated questions appear throughout this commentary: Should we understand Greek gods as powers lacking ontological unity? Is it absurd to suppose that divinities whose presence is well established on the Aegean shores very early on could manifest themselves as important powers in the Greece of city-states, while concealing an essential being coming from primeval times? Do divine myths belong exclusively to the order of discourse? Is it not possible to imagine a narrative that can—whether the speaker is aware of it or not—intermingle the expressible and the inexpressible, the representative power of words addressed to all and the revealing power of things that can be seen by everyone, a discourse on the divine and a semiotic theology?

[. . .]

My first suggestion concerns the appropriateness of a "preconceived classification" of Greek myths. After having subjected it "to the test of analysis," it might be possible to classify the myth of Hermes in this or that category. Yet I believe it would be profitable, before even putting it to the test, to be able to avail oneself of an analytical category encompassing all myths that focus on a divinity's *erga*, "activities." Why? Because to speak of gods in the context of a system in which the divine is not transcendental comes to much the same thing as to speak of the gods' immanence, and of their manifestations in beings

From "Une théologie du signe en pays grec: L'hymne homérique à Hermès [I], Commentaire des vers 1–181," *Revue de l'histoire des religions* 212 (1995): 6–49.

and things, no matter what the degree of consciousness of the speaker. The decoding of a god's *erga* implies a function that is not necessarily present in the analysis of other myths. It aims at understanding how the divine presence is expressed and perceived in the Greek world. The researcher will indeed, as J. Rudhardt puts it, always be unable to "relive for himself the inner experience" of which the myth was "both the expression and the instrument." But he can try to "comprehend" it and to accept the risk inherent in one's own subjectivity.[1] [. . .]

My second suggestion comes directly from the first: when a Greek myth's subject is a divinity's *erga*, the signs used cannot be simply reduced to words and to their "representative power." Myth can use different systems of communication to speak of a god, with or without the "speaking subject's" knowledge. A few years ago, specialists were fond of contrasting the myth/discourse [*discours*] of C. Lévi-Strauss or J.-P. Vernant, or the myth/speech [*parole*] of R. Barthes or W. Otto.[2] Using these two terms, I am tempted to say that myth focusing on a god's *erga* is biographical "discourse" and theological "speech [*parole*]." In order to make the logical explanation of Hermes' deeds clear—the need for conquering his own place and *timē* among the twelve Olympians—myth uses words, these "affectively neutral symbols," as Lévi-Strauss puts it. To stay with his terminology, we can also say that myth uses "symbols that are concrete and pervaded with affective values" in order to unveil if not the divine itself, which always stays ineffable, at least the perception of the divine that can be experienced and handed down by men.[3] It is left to the reader to grasp the demonstration of the myth/discourse [*discours*] and to "see" the mystery of the myth/speech [*parole*].

The experience of the divine in Greece, as it is expressed in myths telling the *erga* of the gods, is visual. This third suggestion is found in a long remark of J.-P. Vernant in *L'Homme grec*:[4] in Greek culture, he says, the act of "seeing" occupies a privileged place, at the summit of the most valued human abilities. . . . In the first place, to see and to know is one and the same. . . . In the tales of the gods' deeds, myth/speech [*parole*] provides something to be seen, and thus expresses and transmits the presence of the divine in human experience. At the risk of overusing Eleusinian terminology, I would argue that myth often has recourse to *epopteia*, and that this *epopteia* takes the place of theology.

Hermes' "childhoods" provide different objects of sight: objects and gestures imbued with everyday familiarity. Close examination of these concrete signs must not dissociate matter, form, and movement. It might be useful in attempting to decode this display to rediscover some suggestions made by G. Bachelard. The poet-epistemologist said that the humblest objects and the most elementary gestures express "images with which life's imagination is engaged," and that every gesture calls for matter, and all matter that has been "developed" contains a gesture.[5] This reference also brings to mind A. Leroi-

Gourhan, who founds his classification of techniques on manufacturing, that is, on the constant interaction between matter and gesture.[6]

My understanding of the first part of the *Homeric Hymn to Hermes* is based on these three premises, and my interpretation agrees with that of Laurence Kahn without putting it into question. This sequence recounts the first day and first night of Hermes in six episodes: the birth in the cave, the invention of the lyre, the theft of Apollo's cows, the invention of organic fire, the sacrifice of the cows, and the return to the cave.

The theogony of Hermes is unique insofar as it is the only timed theogony in Greek mythology. The passage under consideration (1–154) starts with the god's schedule: he was born "the fourth day of the first half," and "born in the morning, at midday he was playing the lyre, and in the evening he stole the cattle of far-shooting Apollo" (17–19). The passage ends with Hermes' return to the maternal cave at the end of the night: "then, glorious Hermes went hurriedly to his cradle, wrapping his swaddling clothes about his shoulders as though he were a feeble baby, and lay, playing with the cloth around his knees, and held his dear tortoise" (150–54).

Among all these facts, only one piece of information is clear: the god's day of birth! In Greece, the fourth day of the lunar month is dedicated to Hermes, as the third is dedicated to Athena, and the seventh to Apollo. By contrast, the newly born god's schedule has yet to be deciphered. What codes is the poet using, consciously or not, when he takes pain to show that Hermes is a god who performs a cosmic revolution in between two dawns, during which his physical appearance undergoes deep modifications?

The narrative explicitly states that Hermes' itinerary repeats itself daily: the god is born in the morning, plays the lyre at midday, steals cows in the evening, sacrifices after dusk, and goes back to his cradle at the end of the night, just before the cycle starts all over again.

The narrative also specifies that this itinerary is two-dimensional. Hermes moves in a circle between two cosmic levels. In the morning, the god is tightly wrapped up in his *liknon*, the winnowing basket that is his cradle. During the day, he is very active and all his deeds take place in the world above. At the end of the night, the god comes back to the world below, wrapped up in his cradle. Hermes' first day is thus formally presented as starting with an *anodos*, a going up, and ending with a *kathodos*, a going down. Hermes also moves in a circle between the center and the periphery. The god leaves Arcadia, where he is born, to go to Pieria, and then, after having crossed Boeotia, he goes toward Pylos, and finally back to his point of departure. Arcadia thus is the center of the world: Hermes' birth transforms the cave of Cyllene into an *omphalos*, a navel from which the world constructs itself. Pieria and Pylos, whatever their precise geographical locations, designate its outermost bounds. Boeotia's inclusion might give us a clue as to where the poem was composed. But is it a coincidence that Onchestos is the only named Boeotian site? This "charming grove" is in fact dedicated to Poseidon, who, in the Greek imagination, rules over outermost boundaries and revels in delimiting circular bounds. To come from a sanctuary of Poseidon comes to the same thing as coming from the end of the world.

The hymn also indicates that the daily cosmic revolution performed by Hermes is accompanied by deep transformations in his physical appearance. At night, when the god is in the cave, he is small, frail, and bound: he is still a *paidion*, an infant wrapped up in his cradle. In the daytime, as soon as he crosses the threshold of the cave and goes up into the world above, Hermes keeps growing both in strength and liveliness. He is a *kouros* at the peak of *hēbē* (adolescence), who improvises on the lyre (55–56). After the theft of the cattle, the old man remembers seeing a *pais* (209), a boy, yet Apollo is looking for an *anēr* (200), a grown man. Painters usually depict Hermes stealing the cows as a grown man, often bearded. The cow sacrifice is presented as a manifestation of the god's great strength (117). Thus, in the course of his daily revolution, Hermes completes the circle between the different stages of life: from *paidion*, to *kouros* and *anēr*, and back to *paidion*. [. . .] Greek gods typically have already achieved their *akmē* by the time of their birth: when Leto gives birth to Apollo in Delos (*Homeric Hymn to Apollo* 120–12), "the white linen" the goddesses use to wrap the *paidion* is not enough "to hold him," and he sets out, a perennial ephebe, hair flowing over his shoulders, having obtained his bow, lyre, and oracles. Because Hermes' story is unique among theogonies, his circular path between the different stages of life must be highly significant.

The cosmic/biological cycle that the very circular Hermes completes in the period between two dawns accomplishes a fusion of polarities. The correlation between these three oppositions—world above vs. world below, day vs. night, *paidion* vs. *anēr*—is so marked that we must never lose sight of it in attempting to decipher the myth.

The first twenty-four hours of Hermes' life are thus told in six episodes aimed at making the god known. Yet in the course of these six episodes, the myth, unbeknownst to later plagiarisms, but perhaps with the partial and intermittent complicity of the poet and his audience, uses two modes of communication.

The narrative is a biographical discourse. It discloses Hermes' filiation; then, indirectly, or, as C. Lévi-Strauss puts it, by practicing "intellectual tinkering" of the "savage mind," it explains how the god conquers his place on Olympos and his *timē*.[7] The discourse uses a clear sign—the refusal to eat meat during the sacrifice—to show how Hermes obtains his status as an Olympian, which is to say, a recipient of the *thusia*, the sacrifice introduced by Prometheus. It also brings together two events—the invention of the lyre and the cattle theft—in order to explain how, on the very following day, Hermes can become the god of trade.

The narrative displays concrete signs borrowed from daily life. [. . .] It suggests that to show Hermes' inventions, in a system of thought in which the divine is not transcendental and where the act of seeing has a privileged place, is to reveal the god's manifestation in human experience, and to create a theology of the sign.

The narrative, implicitly yet convincingly, evokes parallels between what it says and what it presents as objects of sight. The one conclusion about the common meaning of these signs that can be drawn from the biographical discourse about Hermes' origins is that information is not concealed. Certainly, the meaning of the sign displayed is never explicitly denoted, yet it is not silenced because it is concealed, but because the vision of the divine is an inner experience that must be lived by everyone as an individual encounter.

[. . .]

The narrative also offers three concrete signs, to be seen or guessed, by which Hermes manifests himself: the lyre, the fire, and the door's hinge, whose manufacture is presented as a mystery to be solved. The discourse about Hermes' origins, which situates the god's birth in the realm of biology and sexual reproduction, allows us easily to pinpoint the existence of this particular trait of meaning at the intersection of the signs displayed. These are the three figures, whose matter is organic and whose shape is a result of the union of two parts that evoke the above and the below, the masculine and the feminine sex organs. The contact between the active male part and the passive female part can be assimilated to a copulation that combines the above and the below. This copulation results in something, in all three cases, and something that is sonorous: "the wonderful sound of the lyre," the rotation of the door's hinge, and the crackling fire. Hermes' fire, which sparks out of two combined wood sticks, is a "living" fire whose organic matter situates it in the sphere of the biological and sexual reproduction of living beings. It grows: it is a child. By giving birth to fire, Hermes in a way gives birth to a representation of his own birth.

Hermes puts his glowing fire *eni bothrōi* (112), in a "pit." The term *bothros* (pit), for a Hellenist, is a clear indicator of chthonian ritual. We should not forget, however, that a series of analogies connects this pit to the discourse about the god's birth and his first two inventions: the organic fire tucked inside his *bothros* is comparable to the *paidion* Hermes tucked inside his cradle in the cave, to the "wonderful sound" of the lyre still potentially in the soundbox of the lyre, and to the movement of the door that comes out of the *holmiskos* (hinge). We should also take into consideration A. Neuberg's observation, made long ago: a fire in a pit represents—and has done so since the beginning of time—the most commonplace and frequent figure of daily life;[8] the shepherd lights a fire to delimit the boundaries of the area belonging to his social group, and there is also the fire found in the hearth at the core of the house.

[. . .]

Hermes asks the help of his older brother, Hephaistos, in order to make his fire glow and blaze in the *bothros*. This is a perfect example of Hermes' practical intelligence—of his *mētis*—which allows him to find quickly a solution for technical problems. As the Pantheon's blacksmith, Hephaistos can use the formidable bellows from his Etna or Mosychlos workshops. Why not avail himself of these tools? Yet this intervention probably results from less basic imperatives. The organic fire that Hermes extracts from his *pureia* is a timid spark that blooms slowly, like a flower or a small child. [. . .] Hermes needs Hephaistos's help to start his sacrificial fire, because he needs the unquenchable and purificatory flame that soars—the flame of bloody sacrifice and of the funeral pyre in Homeric diction—and this flame does not belong to his own sphere of activity, but to Hephaistos's. If my interpretation is correct, there seem to be two fires in the Greek imagination, rather than a constellation: there is the organic fire of Hermes and the *phlox* of Hephaistos, and they each are constructed differently.

The narrative of Hermes' first day thus focuses on three signs. The nativity discourse, which explains how Hermes guarantees a cosmic continuity based on sexual reproduction, also suggests that Hermes' immanence can be "seen" in these three amorous and fertile figures. The information is so transparent that it is difficult to imagine that the composer of the hymn could have unconsciously transmitted it.

By contrast, the poet and previous or subsequent speakers must have been unaware of how the poem offers us a glimpse of the *to ex hou*, this "thing out of which" the representation that later takes the shape of Hermes and his biography was constructed in the imagination of the Aegean people. Although the code is hidden, an analysis of the network secretly connecting the three signs displayed clearly reveals, I believe, Hermes in his substance and *genesis*.

[. . .]

The narrative of Hermes' first twenty-four hours implies that the signs offered to be seen do not all have the same symbolic value. By analyzing how the narrative unconsciously connects the lyre, the fire, and the hinge, we can come nearer the *to ex hou* of a construction of the Greek imagination that the poets narrating Hermes' childhoods have unconsciously inherited. This would suggest that the fire and the hinge could be considered as symbolic signs, while the lyre belongs with "the intellectual tools" used by minds still at the stage of bricolage or "tinkering."

There are so many definitions of "symbolic sign" that it is essential to specify that I refer to the one used by G. Bachelard and G. Durand. According to Durand, the symbolic sign, like the *symbolon* of the Greeks, is composed of two halves. The concrete half makes a secret and inexpressible half appear; it is both source and "epiphany of a mystery." A mind that ignores this contradiction, the incompatibility and irreversibility, sees contradictory and opposed meanings agglutinate in everyday beings and things, the immaterial and the material, day and night, light and shadow, above and below, center and periphery, matrix and penis, sexual reproduction and *tekhnē, paidion* and *anēr*, sleep and wakefulness, life and death. When the "mystery" becomes independent of the symbolic sign that begot it, it becomes "symbol," since a symbol by definition cannot refer to anything perceptible.[9]

What name can we give to this agglutinative mode of thinking that finds the source for its ideas in its everyday environment? "Symbolic thought," as the specialists of imagination call it? "Circular thought," in the manner of M. Daraki?[10] "Mythical thought," as M. Detienne suggests?[11] I don't know. "Mythical thought" is maybe a little too ambiguous, and the formula seems to exclude the possibility of finding two kinds of thoughts in one single myth: thought that connects polarities, and thought that splits them.

The analogy linking the three signs displayed is not limited to the meaning that is situated at their intersection by the discourse about Hermes' origins: the sexual reproduction of living beings that is the basis for the cosmos's continuity.

Displaying the lyre, the hinge, and the fire amounts to the same thing as displaying signs that refer to the *oikos* and the community of *oikoi*. It is undoubtedly possible to find these three objects outside of the home, but their use is closely linked to the household.

[. . .]

Tools of daily life, the fire, the lyre, and the hinge are found next to one another in the *oikos*, and in the times when there was a hearth in Greek houses, they were even placed next to each other in the *megaron*. The poet from Homeric society, perhaps in common with the Mycenaean poet, plays his instrument near the circular fire, which is located in the center of the *megaron*, and, facing the door that turns on its hinges, indicates the two poles of the world. The *oikos* and the space in which the group's *oikoi* gather lie at the intersection between the three signs displayed in the childhoods of Hermes.

To display the fire, the lyre, and the hinge, is the same thing as to display signs that refer to the junction between sexual reproduction and manufacture, the junction between *genesis* and *tekhnē*. These tools, which denote sexual union and sexual reproduction, also share this particularity, that they are objects made out of organic material, and that they require much *mētis*, much skill, experience, and dexterity. As is suggested in the writings of Theophrastus, the male part and the female part that compose it must be very precisely fitted to each other in order to be able to give birth to fire, music, or the coming and going of the door's hinge. Hermes, whose birth is biological, manufactures procreating objects out of biological matter. When *genesis* and *tekhnē* take over each other's shifts, we can suppose that technical manufacture and sexual reproduction are not thought of as opposites, but as compatible polarities. Hermes is manifest not only in a sexuality that is the basis of the cosmos's continuity, as can be understood from the narrative about his origins, but also in the continuity and reversibility of sexual reproduction and technical production. Hermes' three inventions are miraculous because they articulate *genesis* and *tekhnē*, Life and Art.

The fire in the pit and the hinge possess, by contrast, an analogous feature that distinguishes them from the lyre: their signified gives birth to an anthropomorphic representation.

The cosmic/biological cycle that Hermes accomplishes between two dawns is an anthropomorphic representation of the daily cycle of the fire of the domestic *eskhara*, "fireplace," or the shepherd's *bothros*. We only need to recall the outline of the itinerary that Hermes completes between the world above and the world below, day and night, *anēr* and *paidion*, and to remember the links made obvious in the analysis. The *paidion*, who sleeps tightly wrapped up in his cradle, is an anthropomorphic representation of the glowing embers that sleep at night hidden under their cover of ashes. The birth of the baby, who issues out of his mother and of the maternal cave, and the young, bright-eyed prankster who comes out of his cradle whistling are anthropomorphic representations of the embers waking up in the morning that kindle the logs on the *eskhara*. The *kouros* who plays the lyre at midday and the strong *anēr* who knocks the cows senseless in the evening are anthropomorphic representations of the growing strength of fire in the daytime, a strength that reaches its acme during the preparation of the evening meal. The *paidion* who sneaks in the door of the cave to find himself once again tightly wrapped up in his cradle is the embers that are gathered on the *eskhara* under a covering of ashes right before sleep.

The circular trip that Hermes completes between the cave of Cyllene and the outermost bounds of the horizon, which are denoted by the sunset and the moonrise, is an anthropomorphic representation of the hinges turning on themselves that open the door and indicate the limits of this world to the observer placed in front of the *thairos*. It is through analysis of these anthropomorphic representations, besides, that we were able to unravel the enigma of the sign without a name.

Although their signified give birth to anthropomorphic representations, the fire in the pit and the hinge are not interchangeable. The god accomplishes in fact two circular journeys: between the world of the above and the world of the below, and between the center and the two extremities of the horizon. The two signs, by contrast, are complementary. If the social thought that imagined the story of Hermes' travels has drawn these two circular journeys from the same central point—the cave—it is because thought links the meanings that have as their sources the fire and the hinge.

A social thought that "sees" the junction of all polarities—day and night, the above and the below, the matrix and the penis, the *paidion* and the *anēr*, *genesis* and *tekhnē*—in the cycle of fire represented by the cosmic revolution accomplished by Hermes is a thought that ignores separation and division, and represents to itself the cosmos as a Whole. "The imagination of life," as

Bachelard puts it, has always been deeply "engaged" in the image of the fire in the pit, the most commonplace and frequent thing in domestic space; there, it "sees" an *omphalos* where the continuity of the cosmos is expressed, and makes its vision material with the building of a circular hearth in the center of the house and in the middle of the community. But a circular fire installed in a circular hearth in the center of a house and of the community is the center of a cosmos lacking direction. From the fire in the pit, it is possible to build a world; yet it is not possible to build it in time and space. The social thought that represents the turning of the hinge as a journey made by Hermes from the center of the world to the two extremities of the horizon is thought that "sees" in the hinge the cosmic sign that makes possible the orientation of the world founded by the fire in the pit. The fire in the pit and the hinge are the signs that make possible the founding of the *oikoi*, and their integration in an oriented cosmos.

The signified of the lyre, by contrast, does not result in any anthropomorphic representation. The lyre is thus an image that thought still at the "tinkering" intellectual state uses to explain, very concretely, what things in the world of the gods can be included in the cycle of gift and countergift. The lyre is an instrument of the discourse about obtaining *timē* and the institution of exchange, and thus belongs rather to the realm of Laurence Kahn's linguistic analysis.

Hermes steals Apollo's immortal cows, and makes them cross over into the sphere of reproduction and death. So be it! [. . .] As E. Benveniste showed long ago, livestock in the prehistoric period is a form of circulating wealth. Livestock represents, in particular, what a man will pay in order to obtain a woman who will allow him to reproduce himself. A woman worth a great deal requires a great deal of oxen! By stealing fifty females fit for reproduction, and by leaving the bull (192–94), Hermes' theft clearly comes within the field of matrimonial gift and countergift: a herd that is bound to grow in exchange for a woman ready to bear children. To switch from cow-thief status to that of honest partner, Hermes should offer (according to the rules observed among men) either his daughter, his sister, or his mother—namely, females who are in his possession (*ktēsis*). But Apollo is a god and, unlike mortals, is not subjected to reproduction. Yet Hermes is a god too, and the joining together of *genesis* and *tekhnē* is within his grasp. Hermes, therefore, gives to Apollo, in exchange for his own cows, an instrument that he has made after his likeness, and that he owns, an instrument that will not allow his elder brother to beget children, but only to create music.

Fire in the pit and the hinge, however, are not the tools of some "intellectual tinkering." They are symbolic signs. The narrative of Hermes' first day and first night, which tells the story of the gods' heroic deeds, and which reveals both the fire and the hinge, refers—unbeknownst to its author and to those who preceded and succeeded him—to the two halves of a single *symbolon*, the center of the world as inhabited by the residential group. Fire in the pit and fire in the hinge stand for the concrete half. Hermes represents the secret half, invisible, intangible, inaccessible to human experience and inexpressible. It is impossible to display a symbol, yet it is possible to show its concrete half. It is this concrete half that the speakers of Hermes' childhood tales display without their knowing, as they build a biographical discourse on the symbol itself.

Hermes would therefore be the anthropomorphic symbol for the center of the world. As for the domestic fire (located on the circular hearth that, as it faces the door, receives its orientation in the middle of the house), it would function as Hermes' symbolic sign. J.-P. Vernant sees divine anthropomorphism as one way for the Greeks to think out the immeasurable distance between gods and men.[12] If my own hypothesis stands, then anthropomorphism would also allow Greeks to think out the "disenchantment of the world" (M. Gauchet's beautiful phrase),[13] namely the immeasurable distance between gods and things. When Hermes, by taking on human shape, moves away from the circular hearth where organic fire burns, it is the immaterial, the invisible, the inexpressible element that separates itself from what can be touched, seen, and expressed. The god takes off towards some inaccessible Beyond, and the hearth, once separated from the divine with which it was consubstantial, acquires its own status of "thing" located within the world of men. But this "thing" is still loaded with sacred power, since the god still consents to manifest himself within it. At the risk of sounding presumptuous and simplistic, I would be inclined to argue that the anthropomorphic representation of the divine (of this sphere first thought of as consubstantial to both beings and things) was a way, for social groups around the Aegean, to divide the human world from the Other world and to build a religious system.

My own hypothesis, which makes Hermes the symbol of a cosmic center embodied in the fire burning on the domestic hearth—a hearth that is itself both circular and oriented—seems incompatible with Vernant's theories on the unity of Hellenic gods, and on the couple Hermes–Hestia.[14] I believe it is enough to relocate my hypothesis in its historical context for it to become entirely compatible!

If Hermes is indeed, as I have tried to show, the symbol that has freed itself from the center of the world as embodied in the circular fire of the hearth, then Hermes possesses a certain "ontological unity." His substance, or "deeper being," as M. Delcourt used to say, corresponds to a certain imaginative construct that itself is built around the properties of the organic fire located at the center of the house and the inhabited space. Supporting this hypothesis further is beyond the scope of this commentary. What we need to demonstrate instead is that the whole of the series of mythical sequences centered on Hermes coincides with the network of symbolic relationships that gives structure, in the Greek imagination, to the representation of "pure" fire, the fire of fire technicians, of *thusia*, and of funerary cremation. Preliminary verification, based on the chapter that P. Lévêque and L. Séchan devote to Hermes in *Les Grandes divinités de la Grèce*,[15] raises the possibility that the *epiklēseis* of the god, or his areas of operation, may indeed coincide with the properties assigned to domestic fire in a Greek context. The master of fertility who helps both plants and herds to grow, the messenger of Zeus and the chthonic god, the Thief and the Traveler, seem to refer to organic fire, the kind of fire that grows between the upper and lower spheres, which not only rarefies and obliterates all organic matter, but also circulates between different worlds.

Does attributing a "deeper being" to Hermes contradict Vernant's theory, according to which Greek gods exist only to the extent that they are part of the entire divine system? Hermes' ontological unity, if indeed he has one, is one that he inherited from a very distant past, and that perpetuates itself as a structure of the unconscious. The imaginary construct that ended up taking the shape and name of Hermes must have started very early on on the shores of the Aegean, and it was handed over from generation to generation unbeknownst to "speaking subjects." C. Lévi-Strauss would have said that it was "thinking itself within" human beings, and without their knowing.[16] It seems to me that this unconscious transmission of an imaginary pattern is in no way incompatible with the conscious activity of a synthesizing social thought, the type of thought that "thinks within the myth," and uses it to establish, very progressively, a genuine religious system. Hermes moves away from the concrete sign that created him and, as the cosmos is being divided and functions are distributed between gods and humans, he joins the divine system. As the process of a long "disenchantment of the world" unfolds, Hermes acquires all the characteristics of divine "power."

How can we reconcile this interpretation (according to which Hermes, as a symbol, was generated by a symbolic sign embodied in the fire of the circular hearth) with Vernant's theory that sees Hestia as the city's *meson*, and Hermes as a marker whose movements are defined in relation to the *meson*? I believe that this incompatibility is only superficial: the *meson* is not the center of the world. The sign through which social groups express their own idea of where they are within the cosmos is closely connected to their mode of organization: furthermore, every social group, even those who deny it, is—as Lévi-Strauss says[17]—immersed in historical evolution. It is in the order of things, therefore, that the destructuring–restructuring of Greek societies, as they progressively shift from household-based to political structure, be also reflected in the representation of how they perceive the implementation of these changes in space and time. The fire of the circular hearth is the cosmic center of a society whose structure is based on individual households; these are, in turn, integrated within the king's household. In the "actual" social groups of the *Iliad* and the *Odyssey*, the circular hearth is an *omphalos* that allows the *oikoi* of the residential community both to sink their roots and orient themselves. The king's *eskhara* finds its reflection in the hearths of his subjects. It firmly roots them within the territory that sustains the *oikoi*, and incorporates them in the residential net-work. By the time city-states appear in Greece, kingship, household structure, and circular hearth remain only as a kind of "rubble" left behind by long-gone centuries. The high and rectangular hearth of the Prytaneion—the *Hestia koinē*—from now on indicates the *meson* of civic space and time; by reflecting itself in domestic *hestiai*, it defines residential space. But the *meson* is not one of the centers of the world: the *Hestia koinē* is in no way connected to the Under-world. As Plato very poetically puts it, "it has its roots in the sky" (*Republic* 10.616c). Since the material half of the sign that defines the social group changes both its form and meaning, it is only logical that a different anthropo-morphic representation be assigned to the signified. Hestia Prytanis is sitting, motionless, in the middle of the city on a high and rectangular hearth-altar. Her myth is confined to intimations of her virginity and of the privileged, or rather exclusive, relationship that she enjoys with Zeus, the god of heaven's luminous heights. To be sure, the relationship between Hermes and the center of the world does survive, although unconsciously, in collective imagination. But human beings, from now on, "think" the organization of their world both "into" the *meson* and into the anthropomorphic representation they gave it, Hestia.

Through this reading of the *Homeric Hymn to Hermes*, I have clearly tried to "understand" Hermes as well as the mechanics of the social thought that in-vented him. Yet, as J. Rudhardt says:[18] "To try and understand Greek religion is to give up on being objective. And abandoning objectivity, as we observe and interpret the words and behavior of other men, makes us vulnerable to a grave danger: that of attributing our own subjectivity to others, of drawing on the way we ourselves perceive and conceive of the divine, and even of drawing on those very theories that should help us avoid such a pitfall." It is quite possible that, by attempting to root the myths of Hermes, Athena, and Hephaistos deep within the concrete, everyday, and beautiful aspect of things, I am only trans-ferring onto them my belief in their emotional and poetic power.

TRANSLATED BY CORINNE PACHE

NOTES

[1] Rudhardt 1977, 314.

[2] Jourdain-Annequin 1989.

[3] Lévi-Strauss 1971, 597.

[4] Vernant 1993, 19–21.

[5] G. Bachelard, *L'Air et les songes* (Paris, 1943), pp. 297–300.

[6] A. Leroi-Gourhan, *Evolution et technique*, vol. 1: *L'Homme et la matière*, 2d ed. (Paris, 1971), pp. 18–9.

[7] Lévi-Strauss 1962, 26–33.

[8] A. Neuburger, *The Technical Arts and Sciences of the Ancients*, 2d ed. (New York, 1969), pp. 247–55.

[9] Durand 1984, 7–19, 10.

[10] Daraki 1985, 163–66.

[11] Detienne 1979, 145–47.

[12] Vernant 1989, 7–39.

[13] Gauchet 1985.

[14] Vernant 1971, 124–84.

[15] 1966, 269–83.

[16] Lévi-Strauss 1964, 20.

[17] Lévi-Strauss 1983, 1217–31.

[18] Rudhardt 1991.

FRANÇOISE LÉTOUBLON

The Mirror and the Loop

1983

This study of narrative structure in Homer—especially the Odyssey—
*argues for a sophistication and self-conscious reflexivity earlier denied to
archaic literature by classical scholarship. Using the associated concepts of*
mise en abyme *(Gide) and specularity (which carries a strong ironic suggestion) to invoke mirror images, Létoublon reveals a wealth of self-
referential narrative and juxtaposes its parallelisms with those of the loop
structure* (Ringkomposition) *most familiar as a feature of style in Herodotus. Although this translation is limited to comments on Homeric epic,
the essay goes on to propose combinations of these two narrative strategies
in the odes of Pindar and in Plato's* Symposium. *(Also omitted are the
author's varied modern analogies, which include Van Eyck and Velázquez,
Garcia Marquez, Proust, and Fellini.)*

> My lord, you played once i' the university, you say?
>
> —Shakespeare, *Hamlet*, 3.2

Reflexivity in literature and, more generally, in art is often attributed to
the modern era, to the seventeenth or sometimes even the twentieth
century. I would like to show that Greek literature was already reflexive as far back as the archaic period. Its reflexive character manifested itself, I
believe, in the use of certain compositional procedures that cannot readily have
been unwitting or unconscious.

Some literary works present themselves explicitly as wagers on the impossible: an impossibility of subject or structure. In my view, contemporary criticism often neglects the problem of structure or construes it solely in terms of
mise en abyme.[1] I would like to relate the problem of the reflexive narrative to
other techniques of textual construction and show that those techniques were
employed from the beginning of Greek literature. Even if we cannot say that
Homer wagered on an impossible architecture, I do believe that the *Odyssey* in

From "Le miroir et la boucle," *Poétique* 53 (1983): 19–36.

any case contains a technique for the exploration of possible narratives,[2] in a sense analogous to Bach's experimentation with keys in the preludes and fugues of *The Well-tempered Clavier*. This obviously assumes that the Homeric epic (or epics) is (are) constructed: the *Iliad* and the *Odyssey*, whether they are the works of just one author or of several authors to whom we shall continue to refer, as is conventional, as "Homer," were constructed at least at the moment when they were written down, and the *Odyssey* was constructed with reference to its elder sister text.[3]

THE *ILIAD* AS RING OR LOOP

[. . .] Various signs indicate that the *Iliad*, in the state in which it has come down to us, has the structure of a loop or ring (*Ringkomposition*): Book 1 of the *Iliad* and Book 24 (which is named for the last letter of the Greek alphabet, *omega*) are symmetrical in several respects: in Book 1, a father, Chryses, a priest of Apollo belonging to the Trojan camp, asks a Greek leader, Agamemnon, the supreme commander of the enemy forces, for his child, a daughter; in Book 24, another father, Priam, king and supreme commander of the Trojans, goes under divine protection to the Achaean camp to ask for his dead child, a son, from the Greek leader whom the ordeal of combat, especially single combat with the best of the Trojans, has shown to be the best of all, Achilles. This symmetry, already noted by Karl Reinhardt and Dieter Lohmann,[4] is reinforced by the symmetry of the scenes of supplication and solicitation among Achilles, Zeus, and Thetis. In Book I, after Agamemnon takes the prisoner Briseis, Achilles' share of the spoils, in compensation for the loss of Chryseis, Achilles asks Thetis, his mother, to beg Zeus's favor on his behalf. In Book 24 it is Zeus who asks Thetis to intercede with Achilles in order to persuade him to consent to the return of Hector's body to Priam. What is more, these two symmetrical structures are combined to form a chiasmus, which completes the circularity of the construction:

Book 1

Visit of a father to the commander of the Greek army; request for a living daughter in exchange for ransom; the request is denied.

Achilles asks Thetis to intercede with Zeus on his behalf.

Book 24

Zeus asks Thetis to intercede with Achilles. Visit of Trojan leader to the best of the Achaeans; request for a dead son in exchange for ransom; the request is granted.

The epic composition thus firmly links the end of the narrative to its beginning by means of symmetry and variations (living daughter and dead son, substitution of Achilles, the best man in combat, for Agamemnon, who is only a political leader, substitution of Priam for Chryses). A more careful search turns up additional symmetries: for example, in Book 9, ambassadors from Agamemnon bring conciliatory proposals to Achilles, and in Book 18, Thetis visits Hephaistos to obtain a new panoply. These may serve to buttress the work's architecture. Cedric Whitman's hypothesis that the *Iliad* has a geometric strcture seems to me to have some merit: it takes my hypothesis of a ringlike structure to its ultimate conclusion.[5]

Some episodes within the *Iliad* also appear to conform to a circular structure: the description of Achilles' shield suggests concentric circles in which nature and culture alternate.[6] As an object, the "real" shield was certainly round, and the last circle mentioned in the description, formed by the ocean, must have constituted the actual rim of the shield made by Hephaistos the artisan. There is, however, no indication that the world represented on the shield was arranged by the artisan in concentric circles: the Homeric description gives us only the outer circle. The others may be an effect of the descriptive technique: the work of art imitates the reality of the world, the description of the work of art imitates its reality, but distortion is possible at each stage of representation. Hephaistos's representation of the cosmos on the limited space of the shield implies a selection within the diversity of the real, and the linearity of the descriptive text, depicting viewed scenes within the space enclosed, as was the Greek cosmos, by the Ocean, produced the concentric circular structure in the description of the shield without necessarily implying that the scenes represented by Hephaistos on the surface of the shield were arranged in concentric circles. The circular structure of the description can be interpreted as a secondary effect of, first, the circularity of the world that the shield reproduces with its outer circle and, second, the linear character of literature, transposing the linearity of speech.

MISE EN ABYME AND THE STRUCTURE OF THE ODYSSEY

STRICT DEFINITION: PENELOPE'S DREAM

If, like Lucien Dällenbach, following Gide, one insists on a strict definition of *mise en abyme* as a narrative inserted into another narrative that the inserted component reproduces in whole or in part on a reduced scale,[7] the story of Penelope's dream in Book 19 of the *Odyssey* seems to provide a perfect model (and probably the first example in western literature): Penelope tells the disguised Odysseus about a dream she has just had. While she is tending her geese, an eagle comes and kills them all and then, speaking with a human voice, reveals that he is Odysseus and that the geese were Penelope's suitors.

The symbolism of the dream prefigures the actual events that are about to follow, that is, the end of the *Odyssey*. In this sense, Penelope's narrative, like any
account of a premonitory dream, reproduces in schematic form (using symbolism deciphered within the narrative itself by the eagle speaking human language) a portion of the principal narrative, which in this case it anticipates.

If one accepts Penelope's dream as the model and archetype of the narrative
en abyme, it is worth calling attention to one of its essential characteristics: the
mise en abyme in the *Odyssey* implies a play on the identity of the speaker (*énon-
ciateur*) and the dramatized subject (*allocutaire*) and thus a close connection
with the notion of *irony*:[8] Penelope recounts her dream to Odysseus without
recognizing him, and she refuses to believe in the dream's premonitory reality;
Odysseus, the true subject-agent of the dream, hides his identity and pretends
to be simply a well-meaning listener, yet he contradicts Penelope by asserting
that Odysseus will actually return and thus make the dream come true. An
analogous ironic structure can be found in other examples in the *Odyssey*, and
of course in the play that Hamlet stages to unmask Claudius as his father's
murderer—an instance of Shakespearean *mise en abyme*. Why is irony so often
present when one work is inserted in another if not to indicate symbolically the
distance between the author of the inserted work and the author of the larger
work? Distance, that is, between Hamlet and Shakespeare, or, in the *Odyssey*,
between Odysseus and Homer: Odysseus conceals his identity while asserting
the reality of the narrative prefiguring the events of which he will be the hero
and which will unmask him, while at the same time affirming the reality of the
premonitory narrative and of his false identity to the woman who is keener
than anyone else for his return and who therefore ought to recognize him,
namely, Penelope. The text of the *Odyssey* plays constantly on such failures of
the characters to recognize one another, as well as on mistaken and clandestine
identifications. Long before Socrates practiced irony as a philosophical technique, the epic bard was using it in the *Iliad*, and with Odysseus's constant lies
about himself in the *Odyssey*, the use of irony became almost systematic.

Broad Definition: the Mirror and What Lies Beyond, or the Virtual Image

The pictorial examples cited by Gide (Dutch painting and Velázquez's *Las
Meninas*) suggest that it might be better not to stick with the narrow definition
of *mise en abyme*, which implies that the inserted work contains nothing that is
not explicitly present in the larger work: the mirror in the Arnolfini wedding
painting shows the backs of the couple that one sees from the front in the painting. Because the mirror is convex, it also shows a larger portion of the room
than one sees in the painting, and, between the couple is another person not
otherwise visible, a visitor whom it is tempting to identify with the painter
because of the Latin inscription *Hic fuit Jan Van Eyck* above; but if the visitor is

Van Eyck, he has not portrayed himself as a painter.[9] The mirror in the center of *Las Meninas* shows the faces of people not otherwise visible on the canvas. If they are indeed the king and queen, then the painting is the reverse of what one would expect: it shows the painter, Velázquez, the canvas he is in the process of painting, but from the back, the children, attendants, and pets present for the sitting, and finally, in the background, behind a partially open door, an innocuous visitor who may well be the spectator looking at the painting that Velázquez is making, that is, you and I.[10] As for the scene that the author is in the process of painting, it is visible, or at any rate hinted at, only in the vague, distorted image in the mirror, the false center of the painting, and in the converging gazes of the various figures. Thus in the two most obvious and—deservedly—most celebrated pictorial examples of *mise en abyme*, the ironic dimension that results in a wavering between represented reality and image, between representing subject and spectator, is essential, just as in the Homeric model. [. . .]

ESSAY IN TYPOLOGY BASED ON THE *ODYSSEY*

There are any number of inserted narratives in the *Odyssey*, and obviously not all are instances of *mise en abyme*, any more than every play within a film or novel within a novel is one. The idea ceases to be interesting if it is overextended. Thus, for example, when the bard of the Phaeacians sings of the amours of Ares and Aphrodite and of Hephaistos's ruse to take them by surprise, it is not in my view an instance of specular narrative or *mise en abyme*.

THE *ODYSSEY* AND THE REFERENCE TO THE *ILIAD*

Several of the *Odyssey*'s narratives deal, however, with central events in the *Iliad*: when Telemachus goes to see Nestor in Pylos in search of news about Odysseus (*Odyssey* 3.31–488), stories are told about the returns of various Achaean commanders to Greece: Nestor himself, Menelaos, and, above all, Agamemnon. These stories resume at Menelaos's residence in Lacedaemonia (4.81–619). At the palace of the Phaeacian king Alkinoos, the bard Demodokos tells how the Greeks used a wooden horse to deceive the Trojans and capture Troy (*Odyssey* 8.499–520). These narratives (*récits*) do not strictly reflect the story (*histoire*[11]) of either the *Odyssey* or the *Iliad*, but, by alluding to the gap between the two epics (the *Iliad* ends with Hector's funeral, while the *Odyssey* begins in Ithaca ten years later, ten years whose story is told in brief snatches, rather like "flashbacks"), they are a device for allowing the *Odyssey* to establish itself as a continuation of the *Iliad* and for asserting that the two works constitute a single literary whole, what we would call a *text*. In the narrative set in Alkinoos's palace, as in Penelope's dream and the pictorial examples mentioned earlier, the relations between the characters are complex and ironic: it was Odysseus who had the idea of using the Trojan horse, and Demodokos, by recounting the episode, is therefore glorifying him without knowing that the stranger in whose honor the king has asked him to perform (and who himself suggested this episode!) is none other than Odysseus, who has once again concealed his true identity.

In Book 1.325ff., Phemios, the bard of Ithaca, tells the story of the Greek leaders' returns from Troy—an obligatory theme for any bard with his wits about him—and in so doing recounts the death of Odysseus, which has a dramatic effect, provoking an angry reaction from Penelope, while Telemachus defends poetry and absolves poets of blame for the disasters they recount. The theme is taken up again at the end of the *Odyssey*, when, after the slaughter of the suitors and of the soothsayer Leodes who had agreed to read the auspices for them, Odysseus spares Phemios at Telemachus's request (22.242–372) thus closing the loop by harking back to the opening theme, mimicking the circular structure of the *Iliad*. The allusion to Phemios's narrative not only states a theme that will come up again at the end of the epic but in a sense inverts the subject of the *Odyssey*, which is the return of Odysseus: here the mirror image is false and misleading. It reflects the reality that the suitors would prefer, not that of the story of the *Odyssey* (besides which it also serves a dramatic function: Odysseus's survival is presented at the beginning of the *Odyssey* as a problem for the reader or listener as well as for the characters in Ithaca). The theme of Odysseus's death is recalled in the stories told to Menelaos: tears are shed for him (4.113–14, 183–85).

THE STORIES TOLD TO ALKINOOS AND ODYSSEUS'S SELF-DRAMATIZATION

At the request of the Phaeacian king, who from the tears provoked by Demodokos's recitations has guessed his identity, Odysseus himself begins to tell of his adventures after leaving Troy (9.36ff.). Although some episodes in the *Odyssey* (for example the Calypso episode) are narrated "objectively" (5.1–261) by an omniscient narrator who hides behind the events he relates and speaks of all the characters in the third person,[12] other episodes are recounted through flashbacks, as in the "stories told to Alkinoos," which are presented through subjective, retrospective narration. The stay with Calypso is retold from this new point of view, but before Odysseus's true identity is revealed (7.242–62): when the narrator of the story about Calypso is asked about "his name and his people" by queen Arete (7.238), he does not answer and portrays himself as an anonymous shipwreck victim in search of asylum. After his identity is revealed (9.16–19) following Demodokos's performance and the recounting of the Trojan horse episode, Odysseus resumes his story well before the stay with Calypso, probably going all the way back to his departure from Troy, which links the time frame of his narrative to that of the Greek victory over Troy and thus to Demodokos's narrative. The narrative of the visit to Circe (12.1–144) has an "actantial" structure parallel to that of the visit to Calypso (Odysseus and his companions confront a female seductress, goddess, and sorceress). Since the visit to Circe is told to Alkinoos and the Phaeacians only by Odysseus, whereas the visit to Calypso is first recounted by the narrator and later recounted to the Phaeacians by an unknown shipwreck victim, we may assume that the variation in point of view is an artistic touch to avoid a tiresome repetition. Furthermore, when Odysseus comes to the point in the story of his return of his visit to Calypso, which he has already recounted in Book 7 upon his arrival in Phaeacia, he simply refers back to his original narrative, 12.447–52 (translation by Samuel Butler):

> Hence I was carried along for nine days till on the tenth night the gods stranded me on the Ogygian island, where dwells the great and powerful goddess Calypso. She took me in and was kind to me, but I need say no more about this, for I told you and your noble wife all about it yesterday, and it is hateful for me to say the same thing over and over again.

This multiple narration of the visit to Calypso, recounted first by the narrator, then by an Odysseus who is not really himself, and finally alluded to without narrative by the unmasked Odysseus, can be interpreted as a retrospective *mise en abyme* with variation in narrative point of view, to use Todorov's terminology, or voice, to use Genette's.[13] Furthermore, the narration of the visit to Circe can be interpreted as a retrospective *mise en abyme* that refers to actual elements of the story not present in the narrative: thanks to the temporal artifice that has the *Odyssey* begin when Telemachus, in Ithaca, turns twenty while Odysseus, simultaneously,[14] is at last allowed by the gods to leave Calypso, the stories told to Alkinoos are like a "condensing mirror" that concentrates the ten years that have elapsed between the fall of Troy and the present moment. It is as if the author deliberately avoided using the mirror to show us the same things that he reveals as narrator.

CIRCE'S PREDICTIONS: SPECULARITY TO THE SECOND DEGREE

When Odysseus recounts his visit to Circe, he tells the Phaeacians how the sorceress predicted the obstacles that he would encounter and told him how to avoid them: the Sirens, the Planctae rocks, and the island of the Cattle of the Sun (12.39–136). Then, in the same order, he recounts how those events came to pass in accordance with the prediction: the Circe narrative can be interpreted as a prospective *mise en abyme*, which refers to events that we witness later, not directly, by way of an objective narrative as in the case of Penelope's premonitory dream, but only indirectly, through Odysseus's narrative, which contains Circe's prediction as a mirror within a mirror.

TYPOLOGICAL CRITERIA OF THE SPECULAR NARRATIVE SUGGESTED BY THE *ODYSSEY*

The typology elaborated by Dällenbach and inspired by Jakobsonian linguistics (*mise en abyme* of the *énoncé*, the *énonciation*, or the code) strikes me as ill-suited to literary objects and not very fruitful in practice.[15] If one accepts the examples from the *Odyssey* proposed above, then it seems to me that the following typological criteria make sense:

—temporal criterion: prospective/retrospective
—modal criterion: specular narrative referring to narrative/to story (events not present in the objective narrative)
—reality criterion: specular narrative referring to real story/fictive (imaginary or fraudulent) story.

Penelope's dream would then be a prospective specular narrative referring to real story and narrative. The stories told to Nestor, Menelaos, and Alkinoos refer to the Achaean kings' returns and the fall of Troy, thus to the blank in the narrative between the end of the *Iliad* and the beginning of the *Odyssey*, hence these would be retrospective specular narratives referring to the real story. The epic of Odysseus's death told by Phemios would be a retrospective specular narrative referring to a fictive story. And Odysseus's narrative of his visit to Calypso reflects the actual narrative, whereas his account of his visit to Circe refers only to the reality of the story. Through an additional artifice, this image, whose actual model eludes us like the person in the mirror between the Arnolfini couple or the royal couple in the mirror behind the painter Velázquez, contains another mirror image, prospective at the moment of its production as text because it involves a prediction, but retrospective at the moment of its duplication in Odysseus's narrative: this image refers to an actual narrative, but in the second degree. [. . .]

[. . .] Greek literature was reflexive from the beginning. Homer's apparent use of various types of reflexivity (loop structure and several forms of specular narrative involving different criteria of time, mode, reality, and voice) demonstrates a deep understanding of the nature of the literary object and possible symbolic forms of reflexivity. [. . .]

TRANSLATED BY ARTHUR GOLDHAMMER

NOTES

[1] See especially {Ricardou 1967, 171–90,} and Dällenbach 1977.
[2] I am thinking of the title of C. Bremond's "Logique des possibles narratifs" (1966), which Bremond applies to characters or "actants" and I apply to the construction of literary works.

³ This, in my view, is the consensus of current Homeric research: see Svenbro 1976 and Nagy 1979.

⁴ See Reinhardt 1961 and Lohmann 1970, 204–5, and, without reference to the foregoing, Redfield 1975, 219.

⁵ {Whitman 1958, 249–84.}

⁶ First circle: cosmological background, earth, sky and sea, sun, moon, stars; second: human element, social, city in peace and city in war; third: humanized nature (agriculture, plowing, harvest, vineyards, husbandry); fourth: social recreation, dancing and acrobatics (the comparison of dancing with Theseus's towers in the Labyrinth reminds us of architecture, a cultural element, while the mention of a woman's value in oxen is a reminder of pastoral life and nature); fifth circle: Ocean (which forms the rim of the shield, just as it establishes the edge of the world in Greek cosmology). This analysis (suggested by Redfield 1975, 187–88) may be valid for the (literary) description of the shield but not necessarily for the design of Hephaistos, like the arrangement in concentric circles. It may be Homer who sees an alternation between "brute" nature and humanized nature, civilized humanity and humanity returned to a savage or denatured state, in the shield made by Hephaistos, or it may just be ourselves, following Redfield inspired by the analyses of Lévi-Strauss.

⁷ Dällenbach 1977.

⁸ The word εἰρωνεία does not appear in Greek before the fifth century, apparently, and its development appears to have been strongly influenced by the technique of Socratic interrogation (although the parallel with εἴρομαι, "to interrogate," may be a misleading etymology). See Chantraine, *Dictionnaire étymologique de la langue grecque, s. v.* In any case, the use of irony in Homer seems always to have been linked to the identity of the narrator.

⁹ See {Panofsky 1934} and Dällenbach 1977, 19–22.

¹⁰ The analysis of Foucault 1966, 19–31, is by now a classic. By beginning *Les Mots et les choses* with a description of *Las Meninas*, Foucault was suggesting that reflection began with the age of Velázquez. The discovery of symbolic forms of reflexive literature in the archaic period in Greece may at least in part refute the historical argument of the "archeology of knowledge."

¹¹ I am adhering to Gérard Genette's distinction between *histoire* and *récit* (see esp. {1972,} 71–73).

¹² After the invocation of the Muse that opens the *Odyssey* as well as the *Iliad*, the "I" of the Homeric narrator gives way to the third person: in the first four books we follow Telemachus from Ithaca to the Peloponnesus to Nestor's home in Pylos and to Menelaos's in Lacedaemonia, and then we follow Odysseus from Calypso's island to Phaeacia to Ithaca, all through objective narrative presented as representing reality (see the notion of "narrative mode" in Genette 1972, 183–224, and that of "voice," ibid., 225–66), or at "focus zero," ibid., 206–11). The focus of the narrative on Odysseus's point of view occurs only in the stories told to Alkinoos.

¹³ Todorov 1967 [. . .].

¹⁴ The analysis of the simultaneous action in the *Odyssey* concerning Telemachus on the one hand and Odysseus on the other begins with Aristotle *Poetics* 13.30, who speaks of a διπλῆν σύντασιν, "double structure," and continues with T. Zieliński, *Die Behandlung gleichzeitiger Ereignisse im antiken Epos* (Leipzig, 1899–1901), and Delebecque 1958, 1982.

¹⁵ See the critique of Dällenbach's typology in Bal 1978.

PIERRE JUDET DE LA COMBE

Remarks on Aeschylus's Homer

1995

*The hermeneutics of Jean Bollack's approach to Classical studies (see the
Introduction) have been vigorously continued and reshaped by a new generation of Classicists who apply a combination of rigorous philological and
philosophical methods to a wide variety of Classical topics. Two leading
exponents of this new school are Pierre Judet de La Combe and Philippe
Rousseau (author of the next selection). In this selection Judet de La
Combe explores the poetics of Aeschylus within the larger context of his
ongoing work in producing a definitive edition of the Aeschylean text, with
extensive and in-depth commentary.*

While preparing a philological commentary on Aeschylus's *Agamemnon*,[1] I became ever-more impressed with the pervasive presence of
Homeric words, formulas, themes, and even scenes in the diction
of this drama. Homer appeared to be much more referred to, or more "used" or
"rewritten," than previously supposed. The tragic text seemed to be the result
of an endless dialogue with epic, and its originality could not be determined by
mere internal analysis, as if this text could be seen as a closed semantic universe.
Instead, the way the *Agamemnon* constitutes itself had to be conceived as a permanent shift from text to text, as a perpetual interaction between different
genres and works of art.

The very large scale on which this intertextuality displays itself within this
drama prevents us from maintaining a distinction between literal and allusive
meaning.[2] In many contexts, we cannot consider allusion to be merely an additional phenomenon that one could choose not to read in the text: many times,
the literal meaning of a new compound adjective or of a difficult syntagma can
only be deciphered if we identify what Homeric word, or what precise verse in
the *Iliad* or in the *Odyssey*, is alluded to. In these cases, "Homer" does not represent a traditional poetic language or a traditional code, the technical knowledge of which could simply help us understand an obscure phrase: the

obscurity of the Aeschylean words is rather the sign of a specific relationship to a specific text.

For example, most modern editors consider as spurious the form *sphagēn* in the expression *ekphusiōn oxeian haimatos sphagēn* at line 1383 of the *Agamemnon*, which could be translated as "breathe out a sharp slaughter of blood" as Agamemnon is slain by Clytemnestra. Before deciding to eliminate the enigma that we read in these words, we may recall the difficult passage in the Homeric *Iliad* where wolves—that is, the Myrmidons—are said to be "vomiting a killing of blood" (*ereugomenoi phonon haimatos*, 16.162). This way, we may account for the odd use of *sphagē* (slaughter), which ordinarily appears in contexts of sacrificial killing. One text is an index to the other. The difficulty in the *Agamemnon* refers precisely to the difficulty in a verse from the *Iliad*. In a specific way, it interprets it and at the same time is interpreted by it. In the expression *phonos haimatos*, as the wording of Aeschylus shows by way of the "translation" *haimatos sphagē*, the word *phonos* retains its usual meaning of "gory killing."

I do not mean to say that Aeschylus's concern was above all philology and that he wanted to give us his own interpretation of a disputed Homeric passage. I would rather argue that this kind of reference to the *Iliad* implies the existence of a third element. The act of quoting and at the same time of transforming an Iliadic phrase (with *sphagē* for *phonos*) implicitly refers to a certain idea of what poetic language is, an idea that is asserted, vindicated through this indirect way of composing. In an authoritative manner, tragedy shapes its own language, as it builds up new possibilities of meaning through this interaction between syntagmata. The Aeschylean phrase vindicates the legitimacy of a syntagma where the word *sphagē* (slaughter) can be the complement of a verb that means "to breathe out." Agamemnon's murder is defined in a synthetic way, both as a savage death (*exphusiōn* normally applies to horses, and it recalls the idea of *ereugomenoi* as applied to the Iliadic wolves) and as a sacrificial death. We remain puzzled by this very strange use of *sphagē* only if we think that the poet needs to employ an already established code.

Even more striking examples of this kind of new semantic synthesis can evidently be found in the new verbal coinages that Aeschylus offers, and especially in his famous adjectival compounds. Several times, a new compound quotes and condenses, or reduces, a whole Homeric sentence. Innovation, then, means to stick close to tradition. This is the case with the well-known enigma *isotribēs* at verse 1443, where Clytemnestra insults Cassandra after her death and makes her look like a whore. We are certainly justified to read an obscenity in this word.[3] Even if the metaphor of *histos*, "mast," for "phallus" is not found in archaic poetry, the obscene meaning of the word imposes itself through the semantic construction of the passage (with Agamemnon described as a "charmer of Chryseis" at 1439, and the death of Cassandra as a sexual relish of luxury for Clytemnestra, *eunēs paropsōnēma tēs emēs khlidēs* at 1447, with *eunēs* as a definitional adjective). As Martin West points out, the word *isotribēs* is a

quotation from *Iliad* 1.31.[4] Here Agamemnon describes the future condition of
his captive, Chryseis, in Argos: he refuses to give her back to her father, because
she is supposed to live with him in Argos "going up and down at the loom
and attending my bed as my companion" (*histon epoikhomenēn kai emon lekhos
antioōsan*). Ironically, Clytemnestra implies that Cassandra played her part of
captive in an unusual way: the *histos* (loom) that she had to work with was set
on a boat, as a mast, and her social function was therefore totally undignified
(normally a woman, be she a wife or a captive, does not board ships). The new
coinage, *isotribēs*, presupposes an epic sentence and an epic situation that it
quotes and at the same time denies.

In such phrases, the so-called literal meaning has no real autonomy and cannot be opposed to a supposedly additional "allusive" one. Allusion grants its
meaning to the text. And if we adopt Giorgio Pasquali's expression *arte allusiva*
as Pietro Pucci does for the Homeric text itself,[5] we should understand *allusiva*
as a "definitional" epithet: it does not mean that this art shows an eminent skill
in literacy or in literary puns and double entendre, as learned poetry would,
but, rather, that tragedy constitutes its own language and differentiates itself
from other poetic genres in an indirect way. The literal meaning is therefore in
no way a fixed term that the interpreter could freely relate to other literary
meanings, that is, to other texts, in a free and open interplay that he could
control. By itself the tragic text is already an interpretation. Its openness presupposes a precise and definite relationship with tradition. To that extent, this
text forms itself in a double way. First, it analyzes the different meanings a
traditional phrasing could convey (this would represent a philological moment
within the poetic act of composing); second, these analytically unfolded meanings are resumed and modified in a new linguistic synthesis, which presupposes a new idea about the possibilities one can ascribe to language—and
actualize through language.

Thus the task of the interpreter is not only to understand what is being read,
to restore its meaning, but also, in order to do so, to account for this kind of
activity within poetic tradition. The interpreter must deal not only with meanings but also with the fact that a text achieves its own meaning in accordance
with the ideas it presupposes about the potentialities of language. To underline
this opposition, we could make use of the contrast posited by Julia Kristeva
(who had a different theoretical purpose) between *signification* and *significance*.
Significance would be the way a text becomes a linguistic event.

So, if we consider the emphasis that the Aeschylean text places on references
to Homer, we have to understand a kind of classicism at work here. Just like
any classicism, it does not imply any dependence on tradition. Rather, it re-
enacts tradition by working out two kinds of break.

First, it presupposes that a new poetic genre such as tragedy can break with
contemporary modes of speaking and of writing: at any given point, it has archaic language at its disposal. Homer, as a figure for archaism, appears to be a

renewed and useful starting point for displaying a critique about modern ways of thinking, such as cosmology, ethical or political theory, and even science.

Second, moving in an opposite direction, it presupposes that the past, to which the poet recurs in order to make the present controversial, has to fill a new function, and thus be modified. By way of this breaking both with the present and with tradition, tragedy highlights its own temporality, and its own currency: it seeks to prevail and to constitute itself as an autonomous, authoritative, and historical event.

I propose to read some passages of the *Agamemnon* where one can observe this double movement whereby a new meaning begins to impose itself. In doing so, I shall try to answer two questions:

—If we accept the idea that the history of poetry is a process of differentiation,[6] how does tragedy seek to differentiate itself from other forms of poetic discourse and from non-poetic discourse?

—What is the motive for this differentiation? In other words, what proper claim does tragedy raise against or in contrast to the already existing forms of discourse?

One of the most striking Homeric quotations in the *Agamemnon* is at verse 1480: here Aeschylus, as far as we know, is the first author to re-use the Homeric "gloss" for divine blood, *ikhōr*. The reference to *Iliad* 5.339–42 is obvious. In Homer the immortal blood, *haima*, of the gods is paradoxically defined as a blood that is not blood. The liquid that drips from Aphrodite's wound is black ("her lovely skin blood-darkened": *melaineto de khroa kalon*, 5.354), and the wound brings utter pain to the goddess (same verse), as it would also for humans. Nevertheless, gods are said to be "nonblooded" (*anhaimones*). They bleed *ikhōr*, and not *haima*, because "they eat no food, nor do they drink of the sparkling wine." The fact that Homeric poetry insists on defining this contradictory humor shows that it is dealing with a problematic term. Aeschylus remakes this passage almost word by word and, at the same time, applies the definition it contains to a new reality. This blood becomes metaphorical, and its immortality specifies the everlasting process of revenge within the lineage of the Atreidai. As Clytemnestra says to the elders, after the murder of Agamemnon: "Now you have mended the opinion that you uttered, by invoking the thrice-gorged daemon of this lineage. For from him comes a craving for blood to lap up, which is nourished in its lower belly. Before the old agony ceases, new blood flows" (based on Eduard Fraenkel's translation, except for the revised last sentence).

There are two problems. The first is with syntax: many editors take *ikhōr* as an appositive to "desire" (*erōs*). But they do so at the expense of a slight semantic inconsistency: the desire for blood would be blood itself, or any other humor. It is better to take *prin katalēxai to palaion akhos, neos ikhōr* as a nominal phrase. This option is strongly suggested by the strong antithesis *palaion/neos*. The words for "before the old agony ceases, new blood (flows)" are then supposed to explain the previous statement: they reveal by way of *ikhōr*, the immortal blood, the cause of this permanent desire for human blood in the belly of the lineage. Most modern interpreters translate *ikhōr* as "pus" or "sanies," a meaning they believe they find in the medical writings of the fifth century. In a recent paper, however, Jouanna and Demont have demonstrated that in Hippocrates "pus" and *ikhōr* are never assimilated.[7] The word *ikhōr*, as distinct from either "blood" or "sanies," always specifies a well-defined reality, *serum*. If we suppose—as they do and as I will not do—that Aeschylus was here using a medical term, then Clytemnestra seems to be saying that a wound remains open in the lineage's belly, which is then affected with an ulcer.

Moreover, Jouanna and Demont believe that such a technical meaning, *serum*—and not *blood*—should be read into the Homeric passage. It is not my intention to discuss here this new interpretation, which, I believe, is based on an erroneous interpretation of the relative clause *hoios per te rheei makaressi theoisin*, which they take as being restrictive: the goddess is dripping *ikhōr*—not any kind of *ikhōr* but the kind that runs in the veins of the blessed divinities. The immortal humor would then be a *species* of this fluid secretion, *serum*. But *hoios per te* normally conveys not a restriction but a clear identification: "precisely the one that." This interpretation, which asserts the existence of a generic *ikhōr*, would suppose that men also could have *ikhōr*. I prefer to stay with the usual interpretation, "blood" (I refer to the work of Georges Pinault, and the relationship he establishes between *ikhōr* and the verb *ikhainō*). In fact, the problem we have to face here is not so much to decide what was the original meaning of this word in Homer but rather to define the way Aeschylus, as an interpreter of Homer, reads it. Because of the sharp contrast he draws within his sentence between *ikhōr* and *haima* (in *haimatoloikhos*, a word which is, by the way, a condensed form of a Homeric sentence)[8] and because of the clear link he creates between a god (*daimona*) and this *ikhōr*, we are allowed to conclude that in *ikhōr* Aeschylus understood "divine blood." The craving for human blood, with the repeated violence from generation to generation, is explained by the vital strength, the ever-new energy of divine blood. The daemon performs two roles. First, he perverts human sexuality as he makes the human womb bring forth a desire for death and human blood (this desire is clearly generated by the daemon: *ek tou* recalls mythical genealogy). Second, he maintains this human desire with the strength of his own divine energy.

From this very short comment, we can draw two conclusions about the nature of Aeschylean classicism. As Aeschylus reasserts the validity of the Homeric meaning for the rare word *ikhōr*, he sets himself in opposition to the modern and technical usage: the physicians used it for *serum* and Philolaos will later understand it as bile. The word was surely not clear. As a gloss it begged for interpretation (this was already true for Homeric poetry). Against the medical solution for the enigma that it concealed—a solution that ruled out any kind of theological reference (through the idea of divine blood), the Aeschylean metaphor tries to prove that an original use of the word, as it has to be read in the *Iliad*, still makes sense. This return or recourse to tradition does not mean any dependence on a more traditional mentality, nor does it imply that Aeschylus was less "modern," less "enlightened," than the contemporary physicians. Rather, it points out that the way one refers to tradition differs deeply according to the genre of discourse that is chosen (in this case, poetry as opposed to medical theory). Differentiation, as we know, is of and by itself one of the modes of modernity.

And yet, conversely, the Homeric meaning has to undergo a deep transformation. It is uttered and reformulated by a tragic character (and not by a narrator, as in the *Iliad*), whose concern is not to explain divine purity, as with Homer, but to express his resentment against the steadiness of divine violence. Olympian essentiality (with the specificity of divine blood) manifests itself in a stubbornly compulsive desire for human murder. This new appraisal of divine power implicitly denies the legitimacy of any theoretical theology that would consider the gods in and of themselves, as is the case in the *Iliad*. As such, it properly belongs to tragedy, as a new genre.

Homerism thus assumes two functions. What has to be said by the chorus or by a character requires a Homeric phrasing because, on a semantic level, epic helps to identify what is at stake in a specific tragic situation. The heroic reference provides the categories whereby an action, an event, can be understood and symbolized. Much more so than previously recognized, the universe of tragedy, as far as its semantic components are concerned, is at one with the traditional, or epic, poetic world. The Homeric code supplies the symbolic material through which poetic identities can be constructed and communicated: as a model, it makes intelligible various kinds of reality by way of divine or human actions, of motives, of dramatic figures such as kings, warriors, messengers, and so on. Through this in many respects purposefully anachronistic use of epic, the idea of a consistent world can be brought to representation.

But this is only half of the allegorical process whereby tragedy repeats and reshapes epic ("allegorical" because it repeats *allōs*, "in another way," epic texts).[9] If epic serves as a still relevant scheme for fiction, it is almost all the time used in a negative way: almost any time a precise reference to Homer can be read, it brings with it a negative element. If the traditional heroic norm is necessary in order to warrant some reality for the tragic *muthos*, this norm at the same time cannot be maintained. The repetition of Homer thus becomes a means for figuring tragic disaster. More profoundly, it shows at work an aesthetic principle that would be proper to tragedy and according to which the contents that tragedy displays can only be represented in a contradictory way, through the epic code, and through the catastrophe brought about by its negation. In our passage, Clytemnestra talks about a divine nature, with its own

physiology, precisely because this immortal nature reveals itself through a series of disasters for mortal beings.

Sometimes, the repetition of Homer is wider, and more continuous. I propose to analyze briefly the striking repetition from the very beginning of the
Iliad, which we find in an ephymnium, the refrain in which the chorus, after
Agamemnon's death, accuses Helen of being the cause of the whole disaster
(1455–61): "Ah, you mad Helen, you who alone did destroy those many, all
those many lives, under the wall of Troy! Now you have crowned yourself
with the last and perfect garland unforgettable, because of a blood not to be
washed away; this garland, a Strife which was then in the house, strong-built, a
husband's bane" (based on Fraenkel's translation, except for the last sentence).

We immediately observe that the main themes of the Iliadic proem are
quoted and, moreover, that in both texts they appear in the same sequence. As
in the proem of the *Iliad*, the climax of this ephymnium is the epic theme par
excellence, *eris*. But, at the same time, this text entails a new interpretation of
the story the *Iliad* claimed to tell. Helen, who destroys the lives of the heroes,
plays the part of Achilles' anger, and, what is more unexpected, the part of Zeus
too: she brings to fulfillment (note *telean*, "the ultimate, the perfect," as applied
to the crowning) the outcome of the whole narrative (compare *Iliad* 1.5: *Dios
d'eteleieto boulē*, "and the will of Zeus was becoming fulfilled").

Before we try to determine the kind of relationship this text establishes with
epic, we need to deal with some syntactic difficulties.

First, we have to decide how the two accusatives *telean* and *polumnaston* are
to be construed. Many take them as epithets for an elliptical *psukhan*, which is
picked up from the previous sentence and which would then refer to Agamemnon's life, qualified as "perfect" and "unforgettable." But the chorus is not concerned here with the heroic deeds of the king but by the negative power that
must be ascribed to Helen. I would thus prefer, following Wilamowitz, Fraenkel, and Lloyd-Jones, to relate *telean* and *polumnaston* to the implied feminine
internal complement of *epēnthisō*: "now you have crowned yourself with the
last and perfect garland unforgettable."

Second, *di' haima anipton*, which has puzzled many editors (who delete *dia*),
must be causal: "because of" (it cannot be "in blood unpurgeable" or "with
blood . . ."). We have then to draw a clear distinction between the deed itself
(Agamemnon's murder) and the glory it produces (the garland Helen deserves
because of it). This temporal distinction within the *kleos* goes back to the
Iliad.[10]

The third and worst difficulty is *hētis* at verse 1460. The relative pronoun is
usually corrected (for example, *ē tis ēn* [Schütz], "in truth there was an Eris then
in the house"—Fraenkel). But it can be considered genuine if we take Eris as
its antecedent and if Eris is read as an apposition to the internal object of "you
have crowned" (*epēnthisō*). Helen's last and most perfect glory is the strife that
was settled in the house (with Clytemnestra).

I have chosen this passage not only because it is very close to the poetic program of the Iliadic proem but because it develops, I think, a critique of the potential of epic narrative itself, as opposed to tragic experience. Our task, then, should be to examine with more precision the nature of this critique.

In this refrain, the chorus interweaves two different poetic genres, lyric praise and, as we have already seen, epic. Addressed to a second person, Helen, it ironically celebrates a heroic victory, which is figured in the shape of a pan-Hellenic athletic achievement (*epēnthisō*). It is composed as a negative *ainos*, as a direct praise, which "applies to the here and now."[11] Formally, too, it keeps one of the main features of an *ainos*: a relatively high number of rare or newly coined words (*paranous, polumnaston, eridmatos*). But if the form of the *kleos* is lyric, its content belongs properly to epic: Helen's name recapitulates the entire narrative program of the *Iliad*. This shift from one genre to the other subverts the rules of epic symbolization. Granted, an everlasting memory (*polumnaston*) will be attached to Helen, as it is expected for Achilles and Hektor. The compound *polumnastos*, which Aeschylus could find in everyday language as a proper name,[12] means "much-remembered," as in Empedocles' poem about nature.[13] It is to be taken as an index, signaling epic *kleos*. But it also negates *kleos* in two ways.

First, instead of providing oblivion and relief from suffering, as Helen does in the *Odyssey* and as poetic Mnemosyne does,[14] this kind of memory will always remember disaster. Second, this word picks up Penelope's epithet in the *Odyssey, polumnastos*, where it has another meaning, "much-courted" (from *mnaomai* and not from *mimnēskō*).[15] Helen will gain epic glory precisely because she did not behave as a Penelope.

The new word *eridmatos* too expresses this two-sided relationship toward epic. With *eri-*, which we find only two times in the plays of Aeschylus, it is an emphatic Homerism (even if, as it is well known, verbal adjectives in *-tos* are in Homer prefixed with *ari-* and not with *eri-: arignōtos, arideiketos*). As for the meaning of *-dmatos*, I think that the old interpretation, which reads here the verb *demein*, "build," and not *daman*, is right: this is suggested by the presence of *en domois* and confirmed by the chiastic structure *en domois Eris | eri-dmatos*. The Strife appears to be "strongly, terribly settled" within the domestic settlement of the Atreidai. The heroic, epic strife that causes the death of many warriors on the open battlefield of Troy (*hupo Troiāi*) turns into a private, domestic quarrel. The etymology that the repetition *Eris—eridmatos* provides changes the content of the epic principle that is *eris*. No distinction can be made any more between the wife who has gone beyond the sea, so as to set in motion the heroic poem, and the wife who remained at home to kill the main actor of this story. Helen gives her name to both.

What, then, can be said, tentatively, about the purpose of such a precise "allegory" in Homer? In a certain sense, the way tragedy reformulates here some major epic themes implies a kind of critique directed against the narrative

mode of epic: at long last, the story of the Trojan war, with its episodes and its
many changes of fortune, culminates in a single horrible event. This last catastrophe provides its real meaning to the whole. Therefore, there is no room left
for any self-distancing narrator who would relate in detail the deeds of heroes.
All the epic matter is summed up in one single name, Helen, which cannot be
uttered without nonpraise and blame.

If we generalize—and many other examples would show that we are dealing here with a general tendency in tragedy—we could say that tragedy sub-
mits epic, as a form of discourse, to a very severe analysis: it denies the
legitimacy of a narrative that does not really take into account the fact that any
discourse is related to a particular, actual situation, and to a particular speaker,
that it makes sense because it is uttered here and now. In the present case, the
sense of the Trojan story can only be expressed and communicated through
blame, through a personal engagement of the speaker. The relevance of an
utterance depends not on what it says but on how it relates to the speaker's
situation. In other words, tragedy reactivates the relationship between utterance and occasion. In a stylized form, it recalls that occasion determines the
discourse. This is, for example, the main message of the famous "Hymn to
Zeus" at the beginning of the *Agamemnon*: theological discourse has to rest
upon human experience: *mathos* needs a definite *pathos* in order to make sense.

But it is not enough to discover the determining effects of this kind of critical reflection applied to discourse within the tragic diction itself if the aim of
the analysis is to identify the principle of the new symbolic form tragedy claims
to be. The analysis would remain too formal, too abstract, if it does not define
in a positive way the new claims that tragedy makes on already given poetic or
unpoetic forms. The reflection that is at work in these texts should also assume
an aesthetic function, if it is a real component of the poetic whole. I mean that it
must in a positive way give a chance to the expression and communication of a
new kind of experience.

So we have to take a further step, the last one. In order to reach a conclusion,
I stress two facts.

It is clear that when characters use the epic code, they do not make an epic
narrator of themselves. They express, rather, their own individual and temporal relationships with the world of epic. After the catastrophe, the chorus discovers in Clytemnestra a second Helen and in Helen the principle of the whole
Iliad. The Homeric code is distorted because it turns into a personal mode of
expression. Nevertheless, it keeps its original strength, and remains constraining, as it still provides the adequate symbols. Granted, Helen may be presented
as the real and negative cause of the epic grandeur, which is then destroyed. But
she is no more Helen than a name for a portentous mythical being, which out-
does any kind of individualization. Even if it is "deconstructed," as a mode of
discourse, epic still imposes the reality it builds, through the synthetic and symbolic figure Helen now is. The long and problematic narrative condenses in a

name and in an event. Thus, an individual pathetic situation—the disaster as it is lived and understood by the chorus—gets the density of the entire objectively and necessarily epic process it synthesizes.

To conclude this point: The critical analysis that tragedy develops (as it recalls that any discourse, even traditional, is relevant from a particular point of view, from a particular experience) assumes an aesthetic function as it clears the way for an objective, substantial self-representation of the individual, whose *pathos* appears to be the climax of a universal, constraining process. Epic in tragedy serves no longer to figure, to symbolize, a world, but to figure the individual relation to it: it gives to this relation the consistency of an identity.

But as we are dealing with dialogue, and so with controversy, the use of epic also serves another purpose. If it gives a public and intelligible form to the endless linguistic activity by which in an always open process a character tries to relate to his or her own situation, this form, as it has to go through contradiction, remains provisional and controversial, as we have seen in the two last passages we read: where the chorus accuses a daemonic Helen, Clytemnestra recognizes the divine blood of a daemon.

So epic, used as a massive and constraining—but at the same time always problematic—symbolic material, allows a new poetic form such as tragedy to represent individualities in a complex way, conceived in a new political context as discursive individualities, which at the same time must be recognizable through a traditional symbolic identity, however renewed and reshaped, and must remain beyond any kind of identification (otherwise speech, as an activity, would not make sense any more). In so doing, tragedy differentiates itself from all the prevailing contemporary kinds of generalizing discourses (myth, wisdom poetry, philosophy, political theorizing, and so on) which try to set theoretical or practical norms for individuals without really facing the question of individuality.

TRANSLATED BY THE AUTHOR

NOTES

[1] See Bollack and Judet de La Combe 1981–82, to be followed by a new edition of the episodic parts of the play, edited by Judet de La Combe.

[2] Allusion and intertextuality cannot be confused. Allusion implies a reflective and localized activity of the author, while intertextuality, according to the original definition of the word given by Julia Kristeva, points out the general condition of any textuality as being the result of a necessarily open and unlimited relationship with other texts. The two words refer to two opposite theories of poetic activity. I would in fact prefer the word allegory, understood as a definite and historical relationship to other texts, the rewriting of which serves as a condition for a new writing and can then be coextensive with a whole text. [. . .]

[3] As many editors did in the last century.

[4] [. . .] West refuses any obscene connotation, however, in line with a rigid conception of tragic style, where irony seems to play no part: Cassandra would be imagined here—and mocked—as a "complete shipboard wife." [. . .]

[5] Pucci 1987, 236 with reference to {Pasquali 1971, 11–20}.

[6] Nagy 1990.

[7] Jouanna and Demont 1981.

[8] *Iliad* 21.1–2.

[9] Allegory and intertextuality must here be understood as being opposite (see the note above). While in a strict sense intertextuality refers to a general condition that imposes itself on any text, as it incorporates and transforms a multiplicity of other texts in an ever open process that is determined by the anonymous and never achieved dynamics of language which produces meaning, allegory points out a gap, and a historical and individualizing activity in reference to a given and precise situation: see Bollack 1997, 93–103.

[10] Cf. at the end of *Iliad* Book 7 the analysis Hector gives of the temporality that underlies the spreading of *kleos*.

[11] Nagy 1989, 12.

[12] It was the name of Battos's father (Herodotus 4.150). [. . .]

[13] B 3 Diels-Kranz; 14 Bollack.

[14] In the Hesiodic *Theogony* (54–55).

[15] *Odyssey* 4.770, 14.64, 23.149.

PHILIPPE ROUSSEAU

Rewriting Homer: Remarks on the Narrative of the Chariot Race in Sophocles' *Electra*[1]

2000

As the new generation of the "hermeneutic school" (see the Introduction), both Pierre Judet de La Combe (in the previous selection) and Philippe Rousseau display a keen awareness of American, British, and German trends in Classical scholarship. Having developed a philological model that transcends these trends, they have successfully applied it to a wide variety of textual and exegetical problems in Classical literature. In this selection, Rousseau explores the Classicizing poetry of Sophocles in terms of earlier poetic models, especially the Homeric tradition.

This paper does not venture a new explanation of one of the most admired, but also one of the most puzzling and debated passages in Sophocles' tragedies. The enigmas of the Pedagogue's speech are too closely connected with some of the central questions raised by the *Electra* as a whole to be resolved by merely considering the way it relates to the Homeric narrative of the chariot race in the *Iliad*. I shall content myself with taking a closer look at an already well-known feature of the speech, that is, its obvious Homeric coloring.

[At this point, Rousseau surveys the previous scholarship on the subject, with special reference to the editions of R. L. Jebb (*The Electra of Sophocles*, revised and edited, with additional notes, by R. H. Mather [Boston, 1894]) and J. H. Kells (*Sophocles. Electra* [Cambridge, 1973]).]

Jebb looked for a clue in the many features that call to mind the Homeric poems and cautiously suggested that the poet's aim had been to produce for the stage the epic version of Orestes' return to his homeland. [. . .] The basic assumption of Jebb's interpretation led him to give priority to the *Odyssey*, and to treat the verbal echoes of the *Iliad* as a stylistic device meant to give a Homeric coloring to Sophocles' drama.

Leaving temporarily aside the more general implications of Jebb's theory, I suggest that the relationship between the Sophoclean and the Homeric narratives is even closer than he thought it to be, and that the Athenian poet has done more than, to quote Kells's opinion, borrow freely from the *Iliad* for his composition. The differences as well as the similarities make sense in a process that can be described as an explicit attempt to rewrite—and rectify—the Homeric narrative of the chariot race.[2]

First, I shall argue that in its overall composition as well as in the particulars of its diction, the fallacious account of Orestes' death is meant to be perceived by the audience as an echo of the Iliadic chariot race. Second, I shall choose one of several identifiable differences between the Sophoclean and the Homeric narratives in order to give an idea of Sophocles' understanding and use of his model. Finally, I shall pose some questions about the relevance of these observations to the interpretation of the Pedagogue's speech in the *Electra*.

Let us start with a specific observation: Orestes' Pedagogue enters the action when Clytemnestra has just finished her prayer, and he brings to the queen the apparent fulfillment of her half-concealed and monstrous wishes. His appearance immediately reminds the audience of the stratagem devised at the beginning of the play. The first reaction of both Electra and Clytemnestra when they hear of Orestes' purported death signals ironically to the listeners that the queen's undoing is approaching at the very moment she believes herself to be safe. When the false stranger, answering the pressing demand of his interlocutor to give a true account of the way Orestes has met his death (678ff.), tells her that he has been sent to her for that very purpose (680), the hearer expects the Pedagogue to conform in his report to the instructions that Orestes had given him in the prologue (44–50).

These instructions have it that the Pedagogue will not only announce Orestes' death but also forge a false narrative about the stroke of fortune that led to the death of the young man. Without considering the mention of the oath and the meaning of the expression indicating that stroke of fortune (*ex anankaias tukhēs*), I draw attention to a small but interesting indication of the way the Pedagogue will be expected to construct his narrative. The phrase *ek trokhēlatōn diphrōn kulistheis* has attracted some attention from the commentators, especially the word *trokhēlatōn*. Kells goes so far as to suggest that this ornamental epithet hints at the idea of ornamenting the story of Orestes' death, but nobody seems to have been aware that this expression is probably coined as an explicit *allusion* to, or a *quotation* from, the *Iliad*. We may consider the expression at 23.394 (= 6.42): *autos d' ek diphroio para trokhon exekulisthē*. This expression describes the fall of Eumelos from his chariot after Athena has broken the yoke of his horses. The "allusion" gives a clear signal that the future narrative will be closely related to the celebrated Homeric chariot race.

If we consider the organization of the two narratives, we are in a better position to appreciate the full extent of Sophocles' explicit debt to Homer.

Let us first look at the composition of the Pedagogue's speech:

First event: the foot race (*dromos*), 684–87.
Other events: victories, praise of the hero, 688–95.
[*Gnōmē*, 696–97]
Chariot race, 698–756.
    Opening of the event, 698–700.
    Catalogue of the charioteers, 701–710.
    Drawing of lots and placement of the chariots at their starting points,
       709–710.
    Start of the race (all together), 711–19.
    Orestes' driving, 720–22.
    First accident, 723 + 724–30.
    The Athenian's behavior, 731–33.
    Orestes' behavior, 734–35.
    Keen and evenly matched contest between Orestes and the Athenian,
       736–40.
Second accident: Orestes' fall, 741–42 + 743–48.
From the spectators' standpoint: Orestes' death, 748–56.
Orestes' funeral (pyre and tomb), 757–60.
Conclusion, 761–63 (cf. 680).

Let us now compare the plan of the preceding speech with the narrative of
the Funeral Games in the *Iliad*:

Patroklos's funeral (pyre and tomb), up to line 257a.
Opening of the games, 257b–61.
Chariot race, 262–652.
    Opening of the event, 262–86.
    Catalogue of the charioteers, 287–351.
    Drawing of lots and placement of the chariots at their starting points,
       352–61.
    Start of the race (all together), 362–72.
    "First contest" (Eumelos vs. Diomedes), 373–400.
        Keen and evenly matched contest between Eumelos and Diomedes,
           375–81.
        Divine interventions, 382–93.
        Eumelos's fall, 394.
        Eumelos is bruised, 395–97.
        Diomedes' dash to victory, 398–400.
    "Second contest" (Antilochos vs. Menelaos), 401–47.
    From the spectators' standpoint (Eumelos's fall?), 448–98.
    The arrival, 499–533.

Disputes and settlements, Nestor's narrative about some earlier funeral
    games, 615–52.
Boxing, 653–99.
Wrestling, 700–39.
Foot race, 740–97.
Fencing, 798–825.
Weight-throwing, 826–49.
Shooting, 850–83.
Spear-throwing, 884–97.

It is immediately obvious that the plan followed by Sophocles is not so much
different from the Homeric one but is its exact opposite. The *Iliad* begins with
the funeral, and continues with the chariot race, describing a first series of
minor events, then the foot race, and then finally a second series of minor
events. Sophocles, on the other hand, puts his narrative in the reverse order,
starting with the foot race, giving a brief summary of the other events, and then
describing at length, as in Homer, the chariot race, finishing with the funeral.
His account is more concise, and the disposition is the converse of his model's.
Still, the Homeric pattern is fully recognizable.

The events are singled out by the Pedagogue: the foot race and the chariot
race. The corresponding episodes in Homer are explicitly linked by some
structural similarities highlighted by a few verbal iterations. The foot race
seems to mimic the first race in a more humorous way: they both begin with
some mention of Patroklos (280f., 748f.); they both follow the same basic pattern (after the opening of the event and the presentation of the runners: starting
points and indication of the turning post [757 = 358]; keen contest between
Ajax and Odysseus during the first half of the race; decision during the second
half [768 = 373] provoked by Athena's intervention; part played by Antilokhos,
etc.).

The Homeric and the Sophoclean narratives of the chariot races share the
following elements:

—a catalogue of the charioteers (five in the *Iliad*, ten in the *Electra*)

—the mention of a drawing of lots and the placement of the chariots at their
starting points

—a description of the charioteers driving in a pack at the beginning of the
race

—dramatic events happening when the charioteers have lasted past the
middle of the race, after the turning of the post in the *Iliad*, and after six of the
twelve courses have been completed in the *Electra*

—a decision resulting from two successive events presented in two "episodes" clearly distinguished from one another, even if the distinction is sharper
in the *Iliad*

—a scene, toward the end of the narrative, in which the narrator brings into focus the behavior and reactions of the spectators of the events, implicitly requiring from the audience that they place themselves into the vantage point of those spectators in order to watch the conclusion of the race.

Such a parallelism in the general compositions of the two races is highlighted by a string of verbal echoes of a type quite similar to the one already noted for lines 49f. of the *Electra*. Most of these allusions have been pointed out by Jebb, so that we may deal with them in quick order.

[The author cites *Electra* 709–19, *Iliad* 23.358 (= 23.757) and 23.362–72.]

But there are also many more allusions of the same kind scattered throughout the Pedagogue's narration of the race, for example at *Electra* 723 (*kai prin men orthoi pantes estasan diphroi*), and we need to take into account the more hazy—but no less effective—Sophoclean *arte allusiva* involved in the nebula of sound echoes and etymological and semantic affinities associated with the borrowing of Iliadic motifs. For example, the Athenian "holds back" (*ankōkheuei*) his horses in order to allow the flood of wreckages to pass by in a way quite similar to Menelaos' avoidance of a collision with Antilokhos, and there may very well be other reminiscences of this sort.

I have already made note of the fact that in both narratives the major events happen when the charioteers have gone round half the course. The intended relationship between the two accounts is made explicit in the wording of *Electra* 726 (evoking *Iliad* 23.373).

Jebb has underscored the close connection between Orestes' safe driving during the first part of the race and the fatal mistake leading to his death on the one hand and, on the other, Nestor's instructions to Antilokhos.

[The author cites *Iliad* 23.334–43, *Electra* 720–22 and 743–46.]

The correspondences are so clear and the resonances are so explicit that we cannot be in any doubt that they were intended to be perceived as such by the audience. The Athenians would have thought that at lines 720ff. Orestes drove as Nestor had told "him" to do, and at lines 743ff. he had done precisely what Nestor had explicitly warned "him" against.

Finally, let us observe one more echo of the description of Eumelos's accident as it really happens (*Iliad* 23.392f.) and as it is imagined by Idomeneus (23.467f.) in the description of Orestes' fall (*Electra* 748f.): the breaking of the chariot allows the horses to split and bolt apart on the track.

To sum up briefly so far: the narrative in Sophocles' tragedy bears such a close and explicit relation to the Homeric episode that it could be said to have been built from within the latter, with the specific purpose of drawing the attention of the audience to its intertextual implications.

Having highlighted the most obvious similarities between the composition and the diction of the two narratives, we must now turn to their differences.

I have already drawn attention to the fact that the whole description of the Pythian Games follows a pattern of succession which is the exact opposite of the Funeral Games: starting from the *dromos* it moves through a brief summary of the other events and a magnified description of the chariot race toward the death and the funeral of Orestes.

Another feature of the Sophoclean account of the race that makes it look very different from its Homeric model concerns the manner in which the narrator, that is, the Pedagogue, focuses on his hero. Here the *Iliad* is obviously quite different. Hinting at an observation to which I shall return later, I wish to mention immediately that the Homeric narrator has also placed his real hero, Achilles, at the focal point of the narrative, not as the main *actor* in the events themselves but as the privileged *spectator* to whom these events are offered as a mirrored image of his own fate.

The Homeric passage that Sophocles has used to mould his own narrative is itself composed in a very particular way and could hardly be defined as the *standard*—or the "typical"—epic account of a chariot race. To put it as briefly as possible: the narrator lets his audience expect the story to be told in a way that is quite different from the one he actually chooses for the narration. In the description of the preparation for the event itself, from Achilles' call for the charioteers to come forward until the actual start of the race, he contrasts what we are expected to take as two paradigms of a victorious race, and at the same time two traditional ways of telling the story of a heroic chariot race.

According to the first of these paradigms, put in Achilles' mouth, success depends on the natural strength of the horses, that is, fundamentally on their genealogy or pedigree. Nestor on the other hand criticizes Achilles' view of a "normal" race (23.319; cf. 285f.), and the old king goes a long way to describe the *terma* or "post" chosen by Achilles and also to instruct his son on how to drive around it.

At the turning post, the order based on the innate quality of the teams can be upset and the expected loser can become the winner if he knows how to play his game. The expected function of the turning post in the narrative is again emphasized by the narrator before the start of the race (23.358–61) and by Idomeneus near the end (462–68). But there is no mention of the *terma* or "turning post"—nor any suggestion that it might have played a part in the final result—in the narration of the decisive events leading to Diomedes' victory over Eumelos and to Antilokhos's victory over Menelaos. There is not a hint that Eumelos breaks his chariot while he wheels around the post, nor that Antilokhos overtakes Menelaos there.[3]

On the contrary, the Homeric narrator takes great care to tell us that these events happen after the bend at the extremity of the course, when the charioteers are on the last leg of the race (23.373f).

Let us now consider how each of the two main events in the race is told. In the first scene, the horses—and the gods—are the agents; both drivers are passive. From the very first line of the second scene the initiative lies entirely with the drivers. The first episode is built in accordance with the Achillean standard, but it somehow disproves its validity insofar as it ends up with the defeat of the owner of the best team. The second one has a great deal to do with Nestor's view about driving the chariot, but Antilokhos's victory is flawed and the "winner" would be the loser in the end but for his opponent's royal generosity. In consequence neither Achilles' nor Nestor's paradigms of excellence are proved to be valid. Success has been achieved through divine arbitrariness on the one hand and human treachery on the other. If the epic sense of a worthy life requires some close correlation between valor and deeds, that "transparency" turns out to be somewhat clouded in the mirror of heroic life provided by the narrative of the chariot race at the Funeral Games.[4]

The sophistication of Homeric poetry is evident precisely in the emphasis on the function of the turning post in a chariot race *en général*—possibly reminding the audience of many epic songs narrating such an event—but it lets the narrator report the dramatic episodes of the race without even mentioning the post or its influence on the behavior of both horses and drivers. In other words, an explicit blank in the narrative signals to the attention of the audience the "effacement" of the *sēma* from the narration of the race. The *sēma* of the turning post is the symbol of the plenitude of a hero's sense of achievement.

Let us then look at the manner in which the Sophoclean narrator tells of the heroic death of Orestes at the Pythian Games. The Pedagogue's story is cast in the Homeric mold, but it profoundly modifies his model. The question I intend to address now is how he makes the change, and why. And, more specifically, I will examine whether these transformations reveal something about the way Sophocles understood the Homeric narrative as I have briefly described it. The first difference is so obvious that it may seem trivial to mention: whatever the underlying implications of the Homeric episode, the content of the story is not sinister in itself; the narrator slowly moves away from the dark images of death and burial toward the happier tableaux of a smiling Achilles (23.555), of the brightening of Menelaos's disposition (597–600), of Nestor's joy in the gift of a cup (624 and 647), and, later on, of the laughter of the Achaeans, Achilles included, at the comic sight of the lesser Ajax's athletic accident (784).

The Pedagogue's narrative, fictitious as it may be, is the story of Orestes' death and leads climactically from the picture of the splendor of the Pythian Games, from the dazzling appearance of the young hero, from the celebration of his fortune, to the description of his fall, the horror of the crowd at the spectacle of his fate, his defaced body, and the grief on the occasion of his funeral.

The presentation of the first accident (724–27) emphasizes the action of the horses. So also with the Homeric narrator, when he tells of the competition between Eumelos and Diomedes: the horses are the subject of the verbs *pherousin* (725) and *sumpaiousi* (727). But the difference is immediately apparent: in the Sophoclean race the gods have no part in the events leading to the collision and the wreck of eight of the ten teams. The accident is caused by the rash movement of the Athenian's colts, and the fault is explicitly traced back to a flaw in their nature, their being "hard-mouthed" (*astomoi*). Conversely, from verse 731 onward, the description of the race follows Nestor's paradigm. The stress is on the actions of the two drivers: separately or together they are subject of all the verbs from *paraspāi* (732) to *helissetai* (746). And just as the first accident reveals affinities to the paradigm of Achilles through the fact that it was due to a natural deficiency on the part of the horses, the second is caused by a mistake of the heroic driver.[5]

In this episode too, the differences between the two accounts are obvious. Orestes falls and dies because he has engaged in a maneuver that leads him to commit the kind of error that Antilokhos had been warned by Nestor to avoid at all cost. In the Homeric narration, the failure of Nestor's paradigm can be blamed on the fact that Antilokhos somehow went beyond his father's advice and "cheated." He is stripped of his "victory" and nearly loses his prize because his behavior has violated the heroic code of conduct, on social and moral grounds, not because of a technical mistake. At the time of his trick he could certainly not be said to have been unaware of what he was doing and that he was somehow wrong to act as he did. Orestes' failure is of a very different nature. The perfect charioteer, driving his horses in accordance with Nestor's paradigm, nevertheless commits an unaccountable "error" in driving, which causes his death.

Let us now consider the settings of the accidents in Sophocles' drama. They are both said to have occurred at one or the other extremity of the race course, when the chariots are wheeling around the turning post. This is precisely the place where Nestor thought it possible for a driver to win the race or to break his chariot. The Homeric narration, as we have seen, takes great care to avoid any mention of the post when it informs the audience of Eumelos's fall or Antilokhos's "trick." The Pedagogue does the contrary. He makes clear for the two women that the Athenian's colts bolted and whipped around at the end of the sixth and the beginning of the seventh lap, that is, at the bend close to the starting point, and that Orestes' horse was turning around the post when his driver inadvertently struck the pillar and broke the axle of his chariot. Considering the close and manifest dependence of his speech upon the *Iliad* and the implications of the Homeric narrative structure, we can hardly suppose that the explicit mention of the post in his relation of the events is coincidental.

But how should we then interpret this "rectification" of the epic tale? The shifting of Eumelos's fall and Antilokhos's maneuver from the place where one would have expected them to happen to an unspecified location in the first case and, in the second, an accidental crack in the ground somewhere along the track, was intended in the Homeric narrative as a poetic device to question the intelligibility of the heroic achievements. Its significance could then be construed to be a challenge to the principle of epic poetry itself, insofar as the purpose of *epos* is to "sing of men's fame" (*klea andrōn*, as at 9.189). The events must somehow bear witness to his valor. What if his success can only be ascribed to some arbitrary intervention of a god or to some deceit or treachery on the part of men? Sophocles brings back the accidents to the place where, according to Nestor's instructions to his son, a driver wins or loses the race on his own merits, the place also where the heroic charioteer who dares to hug the turning post risks the breaking of his wheel if he does not take care to avoid striking the post.

One explanation for Sophocles' decision could be that, being as unaware as the later scholiasts of Homeric narrative intentions, he assumed that in his model the decisive events were really meant to happen at the turning post as one expected it to be the case, and that he simply wanted to correct some sort of technical fault in the epic narrative by making his own narrative clearer and more in line with the poetic and ethical expectations of both his audience and that of epic.

I suggest rather that Sophocles knew well what was intended by the Homeric narrative, and that he worked out his rectification in accordance with the purpose of his own plot. The Pedagogue's account of Orestes' death is a fallacy directed at Clytemnestra and incidentally at Electra. The son of an epic hero whose death was itself a challenge to the epic concept of heroic destiny, Orestes is made to meet his fate through an *anagkaia tukhē* of a nature as paradoxical or ambiguous as his father's had been. The narrative presents its "internal" audience, the characters on the stage, with the picture of a hero's short-lived career and death. Orestes' achievements must bear witness to his nature (cf. verse 686). Therefore the Pedagogue's story is cast in the frame of the traditional epic narration of a chariot race as it is sketched by Nestor and shown at the background of the Homeric episode. The valor of the *driver* appears in the way he hugs the turning post but makes sure that he does not hit it (720–22) as well as in the careful planning of his race (734f.; cf. *Iliad* 23.322–25). There cannot be any uncertainty about the legibility or the transparency of his heroic deeds. At the same time the rounding of the post conceals a danger for the unwary, and an accident may occur there if the charioteer is bold enough to keep hard to the stone but does not take care to avoid the shock. The pattern allows the Pedagogue who cannot pretend to have seen the gods, to tell his audience of Orestes' fall and death in such a way that he may speak in a general manner of some divine intervention, as hinted at in verses 696f., without mentioning it in the narration of the particular circumstances of the accident. The hero's unawareness of his mistake remains unaccounted for.

For the "external" (that is, for the theatrical) audience who can identify the epic model of the Pedagogue's speech, the rectification of the Iliadic narration offers an example of the nature of a tragic destiny as Sophocles understood it. Orestes' accident is devised as a kind of symbol of the tragic error. He falls because of a "mistake" that can hardly be ascribed to a lack of skill on his part: on the contrary, his downfall seems to be brought about by his acting in conformity with the standards of excellence that should have given him full success.[6] This could be said of Orestes' fate as it was presented in at least a part of the tradition and especially in Aeschylus's *Choephoroi*.

I could further elaborate on other aspects of the Sophoclean use of Homer's narration of the chariot race in the *Iliad*, but that would take me far beyond the scope of this essay.[7] From my study it seems already possible to discern something of Sophocles' manner and purpose in devising the fallacious report of Orestes' death. The difference between the two intended audiences of the speech is an important element for this interpretation.

The Pedagogue addresses two women whose feelings are poles apart when he begins his report. They do not know of the treachery devised by Orestes nor of the *Iliad*, but they belong to the heroic world and can be assumed to have the same experience of heroic poetry as any of the heroes. The Pedagogue somehow sings to them a song of praise and sorrow, and the epic format of his speech is a sign of the beguiling effect on the listeners' hearts. It cunningly pretends to have been intended to bring pleasure to Clytemnestra. Still, its poetic power works to the opposite effect and drives her to question her own feelings in line with the provocative conclusion of the (false) witness, until the latter forces her to confess, if only in a devious way, that Orestes' demise causes her to be relieved of her daily anguish and to be actually happy. The epic forgery[8] serves as a trial of her true self. It confronts her with what ought to be for her the most grief-laden picture in order to reveal the most secret part of her soul, and to condemn her for her expected joy at the news (consider Electra's observation at 804–807). Therefore it is constructed in accordance with what the *Iliad* indirectly points out as the "typical" pattern for the narration of a heroic chariot race in order to bring in to full light the heroic nature of Orestes and the horror of his death. In other words, the Pedagogue is shown to hold *his* audience spellbound and to deceive them through the fact that he recites his tale in the traditional noncritical, ante-Iliadic mode of heroic poetry.

The external audience, on the other hand, the people in the theater, are made conscious at once of the intended deceit and of the textual interplay between the *Iliad* and the tragedy. How did they link the two facts together if they did? Simply insofar as they were reminded of the deceitful power of epic narrative, in line with many passages in the epic tradition itself? I doubt it. As we have seen, Sophocles does not only refer to the *Iliad*, he actually rewrites, *in a specific manner,* the Homeric episode. The fundamental point is that, in this process of rewriting, he does not merely innovate by creating a new and unexpected form out of his own material. He works on a pattern that the *Iliad* itself designates not only as a possible way of telling the story but also the expected or traditional way of doing it. By doing so, if one assumes as I do that Sophocles did not misread his epic model, he deliberately "introduced" his character's story-telling into the "literary" past or the "prehistory" of the narration of the chariot race at the Funeral Games, as a form from which the *Iliad* had already distanced itself, and one is bound to believe that he expected his audience to be aware of his purpose. The many allusions to or quotations from the Homeric text in the diction as well as in the composition of the Pedagogue's speech are not only meant to give an epic coloring to the narrative but to hint at the central differences between the two accounts and to work, in conjunction with the fictitious and deceitful aspect of the latter, as an invitation to listen to the story from the critical standpoint of the *Iliad* itself.

If this is the case, how ought we to understand the fact, noticed above, that Orestes' death exemplifies the "tragic" concept of human destiny?

Notes

[1] This article has not been published before. Some notes have been omitted for brevity.

[2] [The author debates Létoublon 1990.]

[3] [. . .] Rousseau 1992.

[4] [. . .] Ibid.

[5] The exact nature of Orestes' "mistake" is not clear. Was he wrong in giving some slack to the left-hand horse? Should he have noticed that in so doing he would hit the turning post? Nestor's instruction to Antilokhos seems to imply that the driver ought to give some slack to the right-hand horse and, correspondingly, to keep a tight rein on the left-hand horse in order to avoid touching the post. But it might be argued that Orestes' fault as described here is only in the fact that, while giving some slack to the left-hand horse at the right moment, he has not guarded against the danger of hitting the stone. Whatever the option, there is no doubt that the word that conveys the essence of the tragic "mistake" is the verb *lanthanei*.

[6] Consider *Iliad* 16.844–54. The meaning of the episode would be more explicit if, following Jean Bollack's interpretation (vs. that of Jebb), we read line 743 not as the description of Orestes' mistake in driving but merely the indication, nonetheless significant, of the circumstances of his tragic unawareness. We must assume that Sophocles read in Nestor's instructions to his son that, in order to keep as close as possible to the pillar, the driver had to give some slack at some stage to the left-hand horse but was warned to be very careful not to touch the stone in doing so.

[7] For example, there is the triple occurrence at verse 742 of the word *orthos*. Compare Nestor's recommendation to Antilokhos, 23.335f.

[8] [Note refers to poetic references to *pseudea*, "falsehoods," in Hesiod *Theogony* 27, as discussed in Blaise et al. 1996.]

PART III

Divergences of Approach or Subject

CHARLES DE LAMBERTERIE

Milman Parry and Antoine Meillet

1997

Milman Parry's publications on oral traditions underlying Homeric poetry were republished in a single volume by his son, Adam (MHV = Parry 1971). Like the father, Adam Parry was a distinguished Classics scholar, but he did not share the ethnographic interests of his father. The son's introduction (MHV ix–lxii) does not fully reflect this vital aspect of the father's work. The direct continuator of Milman Parry's research on Homer and oral traditions was Albert B. Lord, whose The Singer of Tales *(Cambridge, Mass., 1960; new ed. 2000, by Stephen Mitchell and Gregory Nagy, with new introduction) remains the definitive work on what is commonly called the "Parry–Lord theory." A vital aspect of this "theory" is linguistics, as represented primarily by the French scholar Antoine Meillet. This extract documents Parry's intellectual debt to Meillet, which is noticeably underrated in Adam Parry's introduction to his father's work (see also the new introduction by Mitchell and Nagy to the 2000 edition of Lord's book).*

In 1924, a young American named Milman Parry, twenty-two years of age and a recent graduate of the University of California at Berkeley, where he had taken his B.A. and M.A. degrees, arrived in Paris with his wife and infant son with the intention of pursuing a doctorate in letters.[1] As to why he chose to go to France to do his doctoral work, opinions vary. Most likely there was no teacher in his native country in whom he had full confidence. The allure of Paris may have played a part: the "school of Paris" had achieved considerable renown, and in the years after World War I the city was the international metropolis of arts and letters. But for a student who wished to do research on Homer, there must have been a more specific reason. According to his son Adam Parry, Milman Parry came to Paris with the intention of

From "Milman Parry et Antoine Meillet," in *Hommage à Milman Parry: Le style formulaire de l'épopée et la théorie de l'oralité poétique*, ed. F. Létoublon (Amsterdam: Gieben, 1997), pp. 9–22.

studying under Victor Bérard but soon realized that Bérard was not the man
he was looking for:

> He had gone to Paris to study with Victor Bérard. Bérard's notion of Homer
> turned out to be far from Parry's own, and he did not wish to direct his work.
> The theses were in fact written under the supervision of Aimé Puech,
> who was of great help to him in the composition of his work and who, after
> Parry's death, published a brief but affectionate testimonial to him. He
> was supported and encouraged by M. Croiset (1846–1935), the author (with
> A. Croiset) of the famous *Histoire de la littérature grecque*.[2]

Puech [1936] published the obituary to which Adam Parry alludes in the *Revue
des études grecques*. It is indeed "brief but affectionate," but it also contains a
rather different version of Parry's story. Puech does not mention Bérard, who
to many orthodox academics was an amateur in philology, more a politician
than a scholar. Instead, he assigns the leading role to the brothers Croiset, who
at the time were the preeminent Greek scholars in France:

> Parry came to France after reading the *Histoire de la littérature grecque* by
> Alfred and Maurice Croiset, and, determined to become a Homer scholar,
> went to see Maurice immediately upon arriving. Croiset, a professor at the
> Collège de France confronted with a doctoral candidate, felt it necessary to
> put the young man in touch with a professor at the Sorbonne, so he sent
> Parry to me. I was immediately drawn to his youthful ardor, by the elegance
> of his mind as well as by his personality, and also by the clear conception he
> had already formed of his project. While he worked on his thesis, I had the
> pleasure of receiving him almost every Sunday and of conversing with him
> about the progress of his work. He was already very sure of his ideas, and I
> discussed them with him not to modify them but to encourage him to strive
> for greater depth and subtlety.[3]

Parry defended his doctoral theses at the Sorbonne on May 31, 1928. The chair-
man of the jury was Antoine Meillet (1866–1936), professor at the Collège de
France since 1906. The other members were Joseph Vendryes (1875–1960),
professor at the Sorbonne since 1907; Maurice Croiset (1846–1935), the Nestor
of Greek studies in France and professor at the Collège de France since 1893 as
well as administrator of that institution from 1911 to 1929, when he retired;
Aimé Puech (1860–1940), Parry's thesis advisor and professor at the Sorbonne
since 1893; and Louis Méridier (1879–1933), professor at the Sorbonne since
1918 and director of the *Revue des études grecques* since 1922.

Under the regulations then in effect, Parry was required to present two theses in order to obtain his doctorate in letters. His principal thesis was entitled
L'Epithète traditionnelle dans Homère. Essai sur un problème de style homérique,
while his complementary thesis dealt with *Les Formules et la métrique
d'Homère*.[4] Interestingly enough, the importance of these works seems to have
escaped nonlinguist Hellenists, none of whom deemed it necessary to review

Parry's work for the *Revue des études grecques*. And while Puech, as we just saw, was favorably disposed to Parry's work, his brief mention of it in his obituary note was rather vague and suggested a certain embarrassment. He indicated that the work was important, to be sure, but since he really failed to grasp how and why it was important, he limited himself to praise of Parry's intellectual abilities:

> As the subject of his research he chose *formulas* in Homer's poetry. He stud-
> ied these in relation to the composition and transmission of the poems. He
> combined great knowledge with great finesse and forged his own method.
> Year after year he published articles that complemented and revised the re-
> sults of his thesis.[5]

Puech, on the other hand, published brief but substantial notes on certain of Parry's post-thesis articles, but he merely alluded to the content of the thesis itself. His most explicit analysis appeared in a review of "Homer and Homeric Style" [Parry 1930 = *MHV* 325–64]:

> In a very interesting study on *L'Epithète traditionnelle* in Homer (Paris,
> 1928), Milman Parry for the first time subjected the characteristic *formulas*
> of Homer's style to systematic examination. With great ingenuity and clarity
> he showed how the bards developed systems of proper names plus epithets to
> fill a portion of the verse, thereby greatly facilitating their task. In this pio-
> neering work and still more in subsequent studies, Parry drew on his obser-
> vations to propose general conclusions about the nature of ancient epic
> poetry, which he viewed exclusively as improvisation made possible solely by
> the inexhaustible wealth of formulas on which each individual bard could
> draw, a wealth of formulas that had been amassed slowly over a long period
> of time.[6]

Although Puech accepted the analysis of the system of formulas, he felt that Parry's general observations were "not without a certain excess," because they gave the impression "that in the uniformly traditional fabric of the epic style, there was no room for the expression of individual talent or genius." And he concluded that Parry, sensitive to criticism on this point, "has perhaps not yet conceded enough but is aware that certain concessions must be made."

This benevolent but puzzled reaction is symptomatic of a certain literary tradition in the academic world, where the concern with steering a middle course made people afraid of the wrenching revisions of the conventional notions of authorship and literary work that Parry's analyses threatened to make necessary. Indeed, what was so astonishingly modern about Parry's project was that he proposed to study how a text "functioned" in abstraction from all the rest. Such an approach obviously could only shock the defenders of "individual genius," who feared the thought of Art being degraded to a merely mechanical exercise.

By contrast, Antoine Meillet and his student Pierre Chantraine praised Parry in no uncertain terms. In his review of Parry's theses, Meillet reacted as a linguist, that is, a scientist unwilling to settle for impressionistic epithets, and was quick to grasp what was new in Parry's work. Here is the first paragraph of his review:

> These two doctoral theses, defended in Paris by an American Hellenist, are worthy of consideration by linguists because of their precise appreciation of the character of Homeric language. The oral style of Homer was fundamentally different from the style of modern written literature. The modern author who addresses a reader reading a text is not considered to be an artist unless he expresses himself in a personal manner. Horace provided the theory of this method when he spoke of the *iuncturae novae* by means of which the meaning of shopworn words could be rejuvenated. By contrast, the Homeric bard sang before an audience. His subject matter was traditional, and his language was no less so. The listener would have been disconcerted by new means of expression. He was glad to find familiar formulas constantly repeated. The bard, who was continually improvising, could express himself in verse—and Homeric verse, ill-adapted to the structure of Greek, presented constant difficulties—only if he had a large number of examples in mind. To take a well-known example, he had to know, for instance, that in epic poetry one said *patrida gaian, patridi gaiēi*, but *patridos aiēs*. [. . .] That is why I said that Homeric language was entirely formulaic. This assertion scandalized certain philologists, but it accurately captured something quite real, something obvious to anyone with a sense of the Homeric style and to anyone who recognizes that the style of a personal artist like Pindar is of a different species from the impersonal style of anonymous bards constrained by the exigencies of oral recitations chanted to the accompaniment of instruments that marked the rhythm. We have no way of knowing whether the Greek bards used written memory aids or at what date the Homeric poems were set down in writing. The essential facts are that these poems were intended to be recited and that they were based on ancient oral semi-improvisations, similar to the improvisations of those who recite Serbian epic songs, hence that formulas were both necessary for the storytellers who made up their texts as they went along and expected by listeners who found that these formulas eased the effort of following along.[7]

If I quote this text at such length, it is because historians have, I think, thus far failed to appreciate its import, which was considerable in several respects:

1. What Meillet admired above all in Parry's work was its "precise appreciation of the character of Homeric language." In plain language, what this meant was that Parry the student had followed the lead of Meillet the teacher, who therefore awarded him a good grade. It is revealing in this respect that Meillet used this occasion to defend his own ideas against attack from various quarters. Indeed, in the first chapter of *L'Epithète homérique*, Parry paid sustained homage to Meillet's views on Homeric language and formulaic diction and noted,

as did Meillet in his review, that those views had met with a rather chilly reception. By asserting that "Homeric language is entirely formulaic," the linguist Meillet inevitably shocked the delicate sensibilities of humanists who felt that such a position slighted the genius of the Artist.[8]

In a scholar with a personality as strong as Meillet's, such an attitude is hardly surprising. Nevertheless, his review should not be seen as self-glorification coupled with condescension toward his student. Such pettiness was apparently not in Meillet's character, and he never dreamt of denying Parry's originality. It was simply that in a review intended to be read by linguists, he concentrated on the aspects of Parry's work that would be of interest to his audience while hinting that the work contained many other things as well. In fact, Parry's central preoccupation was with the *aesthetic* aspects of Homeric style. Through a series of contrastive studies on the use of epithets in Homer and in the work of poets such as Apollonius and Virgil, he attempted to show "how the ideal of the traditional style differed from that of the individual style."[9] Meillet was also sensitive to this aspect of the question, as the allusions to Horace and Pindar in his review indicate. In fact, one of Parry's achievements was to eliminate the artificial distinction between the linguistic approach and the literary approach to the Homeric poems and to show that a rigorous linguistic analysis necessarily leads to new conceptions of literary form. The linguists were quick to recognize this essential fact, which seems to have escaped most of the Hellenists who read Parry. Besides Meillet, there was also his pupil Pierre Chantraine, the beginning of whose review I quote:

> It has long been acknowledged that the epic style was wholly determined by the constraint of the dactylic hexameter. This has been shown in the articles by (M.) K. Witte and (M.) [A.] Meillet and by M. K. Meister in his book *Die homerische Kunstsprache*. But the meter not only governed the linguistic structure of the poems but also shaped its literary form. It led to the elaboration of a traditional style. M. Parry's great merit is to have given a definitive proof of this fact by means of a methodical inquiry based on a solid foundation of statistics.[10]

Despite some reservations, most notably about the stiffness of some of Parry's demonstrations, Chantraine concluded that Parry's work "will free us from some acquired habits" and "transform Homeric philology."[11] Three years after publishing this review, Chantraine himself wrote an article on the Homeric formula that was intended as a complement to Parry's analyses, since it attempted, "by means of an inverse and complementary process," to "consider formulas no more detached from their context but within a given passage," which made it possible to reveal "the flexibility and variety of the system." Through a series of examples he showed that the work of the bards involved adapting traditional formulas to particular contexts.[12] This study was important because it was the personal response of a great Homer scholar to a question that Parry had raised at the beginning of *Epithète* concerning the relative share of the tradition and the poet in epic diction.[13] Furthermore, it paved the way for the now well-known works about the suppleness of the formulaic system.

2. We are accustomed to associating the name Milman Parry with the theory of "oral composition." In fact, orality is never discussed in Parry's early works, and it is conspicuously absent from his two doctoral theses. This often misunderstood point deserves emphasis. It was in fact Meillet who, in the review just quoted, was the first to perceive the implications of Parry's analyses before Parry himself was aware of them. On this point we have the incontrovertible testimony of Parry himself in his study of the Yugoslavian bard Ćor Huso, at the beginning of which he sketches out a brief intellectual autobiography and explains how he came to be interested in this oral poetry:

> My first studies were on the style of the Homeric poems and led me to understand that so highly formulaic a style could be only traditional. I failed, however, at the time to understand as fully as I should have that a style such as that of Homer must not only be traditional but also must be oral. It was largely due to the remarks of my teacher (M.) Antoine Meillet that I came to see, dimly at first, that a true understanding of the Homeric poems could only come with a full understanding of the nature of oral poetry. It happened that a week or so before I defended my theses for the doctorate at the Sorbonne, Professor Mathias Murko of the University of Prague delivered in Paris the series of conferences which later appeared as his book *La Poésie populaire épique en Yougoslavie au début du XXe siècle*. I had seen the poster for these lectures but at the time I saw in them no great meaning for myself. However, Professor Murko, doubtless due to some remark of (M.) Meillet, was present at my *soutenance* and at that time M. Meillet as a member of my jury pointed out with his usual ease and clarity this failing in my two books. It was the writings of Professor Murko more than those of any other which in the following years led me to the study of oral poetry in itself and to the heroic poems of the South Slavs.[14]

My point is obviously not to attribute everything that one finds in Parry to Meillet. Murko's influence was decisive in directing Parry's attention to the Slavic epic. There was also the work of Marcel Jousse, who was one of the first scholars to take an interest in "oral style" and whose work Parry discovered during his stay in Paris.[15] But Meillet's role—and it was crucial—was to have established a connection between two areas that a priori had little in common. Let me repeat the final sentences of the paragraph of Meillet's quoted above: "The essential facts are that these poems were intended to be recited and that they were based on ancient oral semi-improvisations, similar to the improvisations of those who recite Serbian epic songs, hence that formulas were not only necessary to storytellers, who made up their texts as they went along, but also expected by listeners, who found that such formulas made the stories easier to follow." To be sure, Parry was not the first to discuss orality in connection with

Homer: J. Latacz has shown all that Parry's theories—developed, I reiterate, only after his doctorate—owed to nineteenth-century German Homeric philology, of which Parry's work was the logical culmination.[16] Meillet's stroke of genius was to have steered Parry's thinking in this direction before Parry thought of it himself (so far as one can judge from the content of his theses as well as from his own statements) and to have established a bridge between the Homeric poems and the Serbian epics, that is, between the oral poetry of the past and that of the present. Meillet's flash of insight was nothing less than a research program assigned to Parry, an anticipation of the future work of the young doctor of letters. Meillet's questions would in fact preoccupy Parry to the end of his life.[17]

As Parry himself acknowledged, Meillet's role was therefore decisive in orienting Parry's scholarly work once his thesis work was out of the way. It is no longer possible to argue today, as A. Parry did in the introduction to his father's *Collected Papers*, that Parry found in Meillet nothing more than a teacher well disposed to ideas that he, Parry, had conceived on his own. To quote A. Parry:

> The professor at Paris whose ideas were most in harmony with Parry's own was Antoine Meillet (1866–1936), who was primarily a linguist and as such more disposed to see the language of Homer as the product of a tradition than most straight Homerists. Meillet gave Parry confidence in following out his intuition that the structure of Homeric verse is altogether formulary; but he cannot be said to have vitally affected the direction of his thought.[18]

In challenging this way of writing history, I have no intention of contesting Parry's originality or turning him into a mere epigone of Meillet. It is important, however, to stress that it was Meillet who set Parry on the course that he so brilliantly followed. The work of J. Latacz and J. M. Foley on the history of the "oral theory" has shown that Parry's work rests on two "columns" (as Latacz calls them): the first is the German philological tradition, exemplified most notably by G. Hermann, J. E. Ellendt, H. Düntzer, and K. Witte, with whose substantial work on Homeric formulas Parry was intimately familiar, while the second is the study of oral epic and improvisational technique exemplified by M. Murko and E. Drerup (and Drerup was well aware of what such research could potentially contribute to our understanding of the Homeric poems).[19] But there would have been no spark in Parry's mind, no uniting of subject areas that might easily have remained alien to each other, without the breadth of vision, encyclopedic culture, intellectual curiosity, and synthetic gifts—in a word, without the genius—of Antoine Meillet.[20] In this connection, let me mention a well-known precedent: when Ferdinand de Saussure discussed his research on anagrams with his former student Meillet, Meillet immediately had the idea of comparing it with methods used by Johann Sebastian Bach, an insight with far-reaching consequences:

I understand, of course, that one might have so-to-speak *a priori* doubts. But he subscribes to our conception of a rationalist art. I do not know if you have seen a thesis from here on the *Esthétique de Bach* by André Pirro. Here we see how preoccupations as seemingly puerile as the preoccupation with anagrams obsessed Sebastian Bach yet did not prevent him from writing highly expressive music, indeed helped him to shape an expressive form.[21]

Thus, in a paradox more apparent than real, Parry's aesthetic concerns were most enthusiastically embraced by a linguist.

Meillet expressed his views on Homeric language in a large number of works, articles, and reviews. The simplest way to gain an overall picture of those views is to read Chapter 6 of his *Aperçu d'une histoire de la langue grecque* [fourth edition, 1935], which is entitled "Homeric Language." The first edition of this work was published in 1913, but the chapter in question was substantially revised and expanded for the third edition, published in 1930, just after Meillet discovered and developed an admiration for Parry's research.[22] Meillet clearly hoped to bring together all his work on the subject. He found a worthy continuator in the person of P. Chantraine, who produced a remarkable overview that included the essentials of Meillet's teaching.[23] Rather than follow Meillet's writings step by step, I shall attempt to focus on what Parry himself found inspiring, to judge by the way in which he conceived his research on Homer.

1. A necessary prelude to any linguistic study is a careful philological examination of the Homeric text and its history. Meillet devoted a major article to this question: "Sur une édition linguistique d'Homère."[24] This was a magisterial lesson in methodology that remains valid today and certainly one of the best things ever written about Homer. Despite the title, the article was not a review. Indeed, it was essentially programmatic in character. Meillet set out to show what method an editor of Homer would have to adopt in order to take account of the results of linguistics. Starting with a series of examples (geminates, digamma, infinitive, etc.), he showed that the most important thing of all was to free oneself from "all the illusions of the traditional text," which was the result of "a whole series of adaptations and rearrangements" and in many instances of "little more value than an ancient commentary." Even if we cannot always claim to restore a more satisfactory original text, "there is reason to doubt the traditional text."[25] This way of approaching the vulgate strikes me as quite sound, and I fear that certain recent studies in which one finds an unhealthy and superstitious respect for the *textus traditus* may well signal a true regression in this area.

It is important to avoid a possible misunderstanding. When Meillet used the terms "original text" and "traditional text," he in no way meant to restore a primitive core of the epic by chipping away at interpolated episodes, as some scholars did during the era of the "Homeric question." His purpose was essen-

tially linguistic. Nevertheless, such an undertaking implied the need for a doctrine concerning the literary composition of poems. Here is a brief passage
from Meillet that may have inspired one of Parry's central ideas in *Epithète*,
namely, the radical difference between the work of an author and the product
of a tradition:

> It should not be forgotten that between the initial composition of the text and
> the date when it was definitively established, there was a time when it was
> fluid. Not all literature should be judged according to the canons of classical
> literatures: there are times when it seems natural to adapt texts to the needs
> and customs of the moment, as in the case of French medieval literature.
> At no time since the edition has Virgil's text been fluid. By contrast, the
> Homeric poems, composed of formulas that were the common property of
> all bards, must have been subject for some period of time to extensive revi-
> sion whose extent and location are impossible to gauge.[26]

2. From the nineteenth- and early twentieth-century German philological
tradition, Meillet took and developed the idea that Homeric language was not
the language of a specific place or time but an anachronistic and artificial idiom
largely conditioned by exigencies of meter.[27] Among the great names in this
tradition, mentioned earlier in remarking that Parry was thoroughly familiar
with their work, a special place has to be set aside for Kurt Witte (1885–1950),
the author of the celebrated formula that the language of the Homeric poems is
"ein Gebilde des epischen Verses."[28] In the first five volumes of the journal
Glotta (1909–1914), Witte published a series of articles on Homeric language
that quickly became classics, even as Meillet was taking up the same questions
from a very similar point of view. For proof of this assertion, it is enough to
look at the article entitled "Du Caractère artificiel de la langue homérique,"
which shows how much Homeric language owed to a literary tradition that the
bards transmitted from generation to generation.[29] A few years later, Meillet
established that the use of a hypocoristic such as *Patroklos* has to do with the
ametrical character of the expected form *Patrokleēs* in the nominative (cretic
rhythm).[30] Such an analysis is damning for any well-meaning literary commentary that might speculate about the semantic value of such a hypocoristic.
In his review of Parry's theses, Meillet cites without further details the case of
the alternation between *patrida gaian* and *patridos aiēs* as a "well-known example" of the effect of verse on language, but in fact he is referring to Witte's
remarks on the "inflection of Homeric formulas."[31] It is certainly no accident
that Parry's celebrated article on "The Homeric Language as the Language of
an Oral Poetry" begins, in A. Puech's quite accurate characterization, with "a
review of ancient theories on Homeric language, a category to which all theories prior to K. Witte and Meillet are relegated."[32]

The inevitable conclusion that emerges from these analyses is that one cannot speak rigorously of Homeric *language* if by that term one means a system

precisely situated in space and time, of what is called in French tradition an *état de langue* (state of language). This point did not escape Meillet:

> Homeric language is ill suited to a synchronic type of study because it is not homogeneous. In it we find traditional formulas or orders representing a prehistoric state of affairs along with very free types no doubt close to the current usage of the authors. What makes Homeric language so valuable for studying the history of Greek in fact rules out the study of a definite *état de langue* such as can be carried out with profit in the case of Attic, for example.[33]

Not so very long ago, hasty readers of Saussure invoked his name in support of the claim that in matters of syntax and diction particularly, only synchronic studies deserved to be called scientific; happily this is no longer the case. Vast treasures of imagination have been squandered on vain attempts to find a common denominator capable of accounting for all the senses of a particular word in Homer while refusing on principle to look at what came before and after. This shows that these lines of Meillet have lost none of their pertinence.

3. In regard to Homeric formulas Meillet held a clear-cut doctrine that "scandalized certain philologists," as he himself proclaimed with a certain visible pleasure on the grounds that the truth of his doctrine was "obvious to anyone with a sense of the Homeric style."[34] Here is the text that touched off the powderkeg:

> The Homeric epic is entirely composed of formulas that the poets passed on to one another. Take any fragment, and you will soon see that it is composed of verses or fragments of verses that occur verbatim in one or more other passages. And even the lines that do not turn up piecemeal in other passages have the character of formulas, and it is probably only by accident that they were not preserved elsewhere. It is true, for example, that verse 1.554 of the *Iliad* does not occur anywhere else in the *Iliad* or the *Odyssey*, but this is because no other opportunity arose to make use of it.[35]

The same doctrine can be found only slightly attenuated in *Aperçu*:

> This poetry is so formulaic that even when one comes upon an expression that does not occur anywhere else, it seems as though it is by accident.[36]

The use here of the indicative "is" in the final clause shows that the author had no intention whatsoever of moderating his view.

At the beginning of *Epithète*, Parry lent his teacher support by tracing the history of the question:[37]

> Although Homeric critics have been forced to acknowledge that there is a certain formulaic element in the *Iliad* and the *Odyssey*, they remain divided about a question of the utmost interest: what proportion of Homeric diction must be ascribed to tradition and what proportion to the poet? . . . One can judge the situation by noting the opposition that (M.) Meillet aroused

when he voiced the opinion that the Homeric style is completely formulaic. Meillet wrote: [the quotation of Meillet 1923a, 61 follows: see n. 35 above]. Commenting on these lines, A. Platt wrote (*Classical Review* 38 [1924]: 22) that "on page 61 what is said about the epic is such that the reader can scarcely believe his eyes."

There is admittedly something paradoxical and even provocative about Meillet's doctrine. When we speak of formulaic expressions and lines in Homer's epics, what first comes to mind is the repetition characteristic of these poems. In our minds, *formula* is associated with *recurrence*. Hence it is strange to find a line not repeated anywhere else described as formulaic. In my view, however, the idea is valid, so long as it is properly understood. Consider the example cited by Meillet, verse 1.554 of the *Iliad*. It is indeed unique, but its constituent parts are not randomly distributed in the line. [. . .]

It is therefore perfectly correct to say that in *Iliad* 1.554 the poet is truly composing and that, far from mechanically repeating traditional formulas, he demonstrates genuine originality. But he creates by stitching the elements of the line together according to traditional patterns. In other words, what is formulaic is not the finished formula but the mechanisms that the bards used to compose expressions and even entire lines. What we see here is not so much the "ready-made" Homeric text with its many repetitions but the rules that precede the composition of that text. It is beyond the scope of this paper to expand on this point. Let me simply refer the interested reader to Bryan Hainsworth's important recent study, which goes into all these questions in detail.[38] Furthermore, Michael N. Nagler has shown that by cataloguing the procedures that gave rise to Homeric expressions and phrases, one can construct a veritable "poetic grammar."[39] To be sure, this sort of reasoning attaches a new meaning to the word "formula," rather different from the traditional meaning, and the danger is that in so doing the term may become too flexible and consequently less incisive. It must be granted, however, that defining "formula" purely in terms of quantitative repetition also has its limitations. If one adopts such a narrow view, it becomes difficult to draw a line between what is formulaic and what is not. What is more, the Homeric poems are only the surviving portion of an epic tradition known to have been far more extensive. Meillet's provocatively paradoxical "formulaic even though unique" thus turns in the end to be quite fruitful.

It is no distortion of Meillet's thought to interpret it as I have just done. The excerpt from *Origines* that I quoted earlier continues as follows: "The Homeric epic was a form of poetry composed by professionals using learned formulas, and it would have been difficult to compose it in any other way with the traditional lines that were used."[40]

To be sure, this statement contains a contradiction: what it meant for a bard to be truly a master of his craft was that he had acquired a skill that allowed him not simply to repeat his elders, as a simple apprentice would, but to compose. But his creative contribution was supplied within a traditional framework. Here as in so many other areas, what is interesting is not so much the result (in this case the text of the Homeric poems as we know them) as the procedures that made that result possible. The philologist's goal should therefore be to grasp the poet at work. To conclude, let me quote a statement of Michael Nagler's that I like because it cuts through so many false issues: "All is traditional on the generative level, all original on the level of performance."[41]

TRANSLATED BY ARTHUR GOLDHAMMER

NOTES

[1] See Adam Parry, Introduction to *MHV* ix.

[2] Ibid., xxiii.

[3] Puech 1936, 87–88. Maurice Croiset received as fine a eulogy from the Académie des Inscriptions et Belles Lettres as he could have wished for: he was called ([1935]) "the acknowledged master of Greek studies in our country." The writer added: "He supervised and controlled everything." [. . .]

[4] Parry [1928a, b; full bibliography in *MHV*].

[5] Puech 1936, 88.

[6] Puech 1932, 326. [. . .]

[7] Meillet 1929, 100–101.

[8] Parry 1928a, 9–10 [= *MHV* 8–9], quoting from Meillet 1923a, 61.

[9] Parry 1928a, 28 [= *MHV* 23], with many similar instances throughout the work (e.g., 180–81 = *MHV* 144–45, etc.). The title of the thesis was also revealing in this regard: the author proposed to study the "epithet *in* Homer" as well as "*in* the *Argonautica*" and "*in* the *Aeneid*" (29ff., my italics) rather than *by* Homer, as he is sometimes incorrectly believed to have written.

[10] Chantraine 1929, 294. The importance of this review was recognized by A. Parry (Introduction to *MHV* xxiii n. 3).

[11] Chantraine 1929, 299.

[12] Chantraine 1932, citations p. 122.

[13] Parry 1928a, 9 [= *MHV* 8], passage cited below, note 37.

[14] *MHV* 439 (posthumous publication, by way of A. Parry).

[15] See A. Parry in *MHV* xxii; M. Parry cites Jousse three times: at the beginning of the (two-part) major article in which he speaks for the first time of "traditional oral style" and "oral poetry" in connection with Homer (1930, 78 = *MHV* 270 n. 1), and in two later studies [*MHV* 377 and 445].

[16] Latacz 1979, 25–44.

[17] That is, in his son's reserved and painful words (*MHV* xli), until the "accidental gunshot" that ended his life in Los Angeles in December 1935 at the age of thirty-three, a few months after his return from a research trip to Yugoslavia.

[18] Introduction to *MHV* xxiii (a passage that immediately follows the one cited in n. 2).

[19] See Latacz 1979, 1–23 ("Einführung"), esp. 9–12; also Foley 1988, chs. 1 and 2.

[20] Meillet's name is barely mentioned in the work of J. Latacz cited in notes 16 and 19. On the other hand, Foley (1988, 6, 9, 20, 27) speaks of Meillet several times as Parry's "men-

tor" and emphasizes his role in fostering Parry's interest in orality, but he does not cite
Meillet's review of Parry's theses.

[21] Excerpt from a letter from Meillet to Saussure (February 1908), quoted by Jean
Starobinski (1971, p. 159), with this very pertinent remark: "It may not be irrelevant
to point out that in Bach's technique, the letter-notes corresponding to the bass motifs
often spell out a signature or homage." This aspect of Bach's technique has since been
the subject of a number of now classic studies [. . .].

[22] The last edition published during Meillet's lifetime was the fourth (1935), which was
virtually identical to the third; Parry's thesis is cited in the bibliography on p. xvi.

[23] Chantraine 1949 (text of a lecture delivered in 1940). [. . .]

[24] Meillet 1918a.

[25] Ibid., 286, 301.

[26] Meillet 1923b, 59; cf. Parry 1928a, 19–44 (= *MHV* 17–36) and passim (see above, note 9).
Note the parallel that Meillet draws between the Homeric poems and the French literature of the Middle Ages. Nagy 1997 shows how enlightening this parallel is and how
Homerists can profit from a study like that of Zumthor 1972 which considers the notion
of "flux" (*mouvance*), reminiscent in some ways of Meillet's "liquidité." See Zumthor
1972, 65–75, esp. 68: "For the archaic period, prior to 1100, the very notion of author
seems to elude us at times."

[27] Meillet even came to the conclusion that the dactylic hexameter was of foreign origin,
for otherwise it would not have been so ill adapted to the natural rhythm of the Greek
language (for example, 1923a, 6off.: "bold but no doubt necessary hypothesis," ibid., viii).
This thesis has recently been challenged, apparently with good reason, but this is not the
place to take up the issue. (See now Nagy, "Is There an Etymology for the Dactylic Hexameter?" in *Mir Curad: Studies in Honor of Calvert Watkins*, ed. J. Jasanoff, H. C.
Melchert, and L. Oliver [Innsbruck, 1988], pp. 495–508.—EDS.)

[28] K. Witte, "Homerische Sprach- und Versgeschichte: Die Entstehung der ionischen
Langzeile," *Glotta* 4 (1913): 209–242. [. . .]

[29] Meillet 1908–1909.

[30] Meillet 1918b, 28–29.

[31] Meillet 1929, 100 (cf. above, note 7); Witte, pp. 112–13 (in "Zur Flexion homerischer
Formulen," *Glotta* 3 [1912]: 110–17).

[32] Puech 1934, 261 on Parry 1932, 1ff. (= *MHV* 325 ff.). See also, in the same sense, the passage from P. Chantraine cited above, note 10.

[33] Meillet 1923c, 61.

[34] See above, note 7.

[35] Meillet 1923a, 61.

[36] Meillet 1935, 176.

[37] Parry 1928a, 9–10 (= *MHV* 8–9).

[38] {Hainsworth 1993, 1–31 ("Introduction. I: Formulas").}

[39] Nagler 1967, 269–311, developed in Nagler 1974. [. . .]

[40] Meillet 1923a, 61.

[41] {Nagler 1974, 26.}

EMILE BENVENISTE

The Medical Tradition
of the Indo-Europeans

1945

Emile Benveniste applies Georges Dumézil's methods of reconstructing so-
cial realia primarily on the basis of linguistic evidence. (On the relevance of
Dumézil's methodology, see Introduction, note 2.) This piece is generally
recognized as a methodological tour de force in comparative linguistics as
applied to traditions mediated by the classics.

Did the notion of "medically treating a disease" exist in the common Indo-European language? If proof of such an assertion requires showing that the same term was used in all the Indo-European dia-lects, doubt would seem to be in order: we find almost as many expressions as there are languages. Yet the Indo-European expression does exist: it is estab-lished by the correspondence of Latin *medeor, medicus*, "to heal, healer," and so on, with Avestan *vi-mad-*, "to treat a sick person." However, the forms of the root **med-* elsewhere reveal rather different meanings: Oscan *meddiss*, "judge"; Greek μέδομαι, "to care for"; μέδων, "lord, chief"; μήδομαι, "to decide"; Old Irish *midiur*, "to decide, judge, consider"; Gothic *mitan*, "to measure"; Ar-menian *mit* (<**mēdi-*), "thought." We must look for the fundamental meaning that might possibly be the origin of senses as diverse as "judging," "governing," and "healing."

A first indication is provided by one of the nominal forms of **med-* in Latin, which best accounts for all the observed facts: *modus*, "measure." Here we have the notion of "measure" but conceived differently than in *metior, mensura*, "to measure, measurement." This is a measure that is *imposed* on things and as-sumes understanding, reflection, and authority; it is not a measure of mensura-tion (as in *mensis*, "month") but a measure of *moderation* (cf. *modus: moderor*, "measure, moderate"), applied to that which violates or ignores a rule. This is

From "La doctrine médicale des Indo-Européens," *Revue de l'histoire des religions* 130 (1945): 5–12.

why *modus* has a moral sense that can be seen clearly in its derivative *modestus*, "moderate, modest," as well as a sense of "reflection," proved by the frequentative *meditor*, "to reflect, consider," and a value of authority, apparently in the verb *moderari*, "moderate, apply restrictions, govern."

In Greek, the senses of "having concern" (μέδομαι), being "chief" (μέδων), and "to settle on a plan" (μήδομαι) all lead back to the idea of "authoritatively taking *measures* appropriate to the situation." This sense also explains why Oscan *med-diss*, literally "he who pronounces the **medo-*," designates the judge, and Oscan *med-* corresponds to Latin *ius* in *iudex*, "judge." It is more attenuated in Gothic *mitan*, "to measure," but it survives, still perceptible, in *us-milan*, "to conduct oneself, to live," *us-mel*, "conduct," which assume a sense such as "to adopt a rule of life." In more recent times all that remains is the notion of "decision, judgment" in Old Irish *midiur*, "I judge, I reflect," and that of "thought, reflection" in Armenian *mit*.

We can now see that the sense "to care for, to heal" in Latin *medeor* and Avestan *vi-mad-* simply restricts the broader sense of **med-*, which can be defined as "to take measures of order with authority and reflection; to apply a deliberate plan to a confused situation." Here we have the point of departure as well as the obvious explanation of the sense "medical." Now, the fact that this technical sense can be found at the two extremities of the zone, in two conservative languages that retained so many vestiges of the common language, is proof that in the Indo-European period the forms of **med-* served to express the notion of "medicine" and that in very early prehistoric times the Indo-European peoples had elaborated a certain technique for the treatment of diseases.

Furthermore, the values that enter into this definition help us to gauge the intellectual level of this technique. It is clear that Indo-European "medicine" assumed reflection, competence, and authority. The "treatment" of diseases called on the same capabilities and required "measures" of the same order as the command of men or the exercise of magistracy. It was quite different from the medicine of primitives. At the level of culture suggested by this lexical analysis, the physician in no way resembles a witch doctor; he is a man of thought.

It is therefore legitimate to ask whether the practice of medicine, which the vocabulary tells us was fairly advanced in the Indo-European era, rested solely on an empirical basis. Was there also a medical *doctrine* common to the Indo-European peoples? Although the question has yet to be explicitly posed, it is justified by certain historical parallels. Were not the Assyrians and the Chinese familiar, if not with medical "philosophy," then at least with a general notion of diseases, their causes and cures?

In fact, we find a clear statement of such a theory in the Avesta. It is modestly presented as a purely practical classification of curative procedures. These are of three kinds: the "medicine of the knife" (*karəto.baēšaza*), the "medicine of plants" (*urvarō.baēšaza*), and the "medicine of charms" (*mąθrō. baēšaza*).[1] The fact that three types of disease are here distinguished by specifying the treatment appropriate to each leads us to believe that those who treated patients with the knife, with plants, and with charms were already coordinating their practice in terms of a rudimentary theory.

This inference is confirmed, and the interest of the Iranian example is increased, by the existence of a similar tradition in ancient Greece, which Pindar recorded. This correspondence has been noted previously[2] but without detailed analysis, and over the years it has been forgotten. It is worth taking another look at this important text in *Pythian* 3 (47–55). When Hieron of Syracuse was afflicted with a grave disease, the poet evoked Asclepius, whom his father Apollo plucked as an infant from the pyre where his mother Coronis was to die and entrusted to the Centaur Chiron "so that he might teach him to heal the painful maladies of men" (διδάξαι πολυπήμονας ἀνθρώποισι ἰᾶσθαι νόσους). Here are the procedures that Chiron taught Asclepius:

τοὺς μὲν ὦν, ὅσσοι μόλον αὐτοφύτων
ἑλκέων ξυνάονες, ἢ πολίῳ χαλ-
      κῷ μέλη τετρωμένοι
ἢ χερμάδι τηλεβόλῳ
ἢ θερινῷ πυρὶ περθόμενοι δέμας ἢ χει-
      μῶνι, λύσαις ἄλλον ἀλλοίων ἀχέων
ἔξαγεν, τοὺς μὲν μαλακαῖς ἐπαοιδαῖς ἀμφέπων,
τοὺς δὲ προσανέα πί-
      νοντας, ἢ γυίοις περάπτων πάντοθεν
φάρμακα, τοὺς δὲ τομαῖς ἔστασεν ὀρθούς.

All who came to him with ulcers born within their flesh, wounded somewhere by shining bronze or hurled stone, or with bodies ravaged by the heat of summer or the cold of winter, he delivered each of them from his pain, sometimes by healing them with gentle charms, sometimes by giving them healing potions or by applying various remedies to their limbs, and sometimes he set them on their feet by means of incisions.

Here Pindar reveals an ancient tradition that has all the earmarks of a *school myth* intended to legitimate teaching supposed to be of divine origin. Note, first of all, the internal consistency of this classification. There are three types of disease: the "spontaneous ulcer" that the body engenders by itself; "exhaustion" of the organism from the effects of heat or cold; and "wounds" caused by weapons. There are also three types of treatment, each corresponding to a particular type of disease. "Charms" are applied to "wounds." In the *Odyssey*, for example, the son of Autolykos uses a charm to staunch the flow of blood from Odysseus's wound: ἐπαοιδῇ δ᾽ αἷμα κελαινὸν ἔσχεθον (19.457). "Plants" applied to the limbs or imbibed in potions heal the exhaustion of the body. And "incisions" are used for ulcerous sores. Remedies and ailments exhibit a pattern that indicates thoughtful elaboration. Now, it so happens that the medical practice of the Avesta was based on the same classification: the "charm" (ἐπαοιδή) corresponds to the *maθra-*, "plants" (φάρμακα) to *urvara-*, and "incision" (τομή) to the "knife" (*karəta-*). Since the treatment procedures are identical, we may conclude that bodily afflictions were classified according to the same categories.

The significance of this concordance is not diminished by the objection that these three procedures are common to all medicine and that people of all ages have resorted to incantations, simples, and knives. In the first place, the problem is not to gauge the originality of Indo-European medicine but to establish that there was one and that it was defined by identical traditions in Greece and Iran. The more important point is that these three procedures, which, taken separately, are indeed found everywhere, are here grouped and coordinated as parts of a *doctrine* that was a distinctive possession of the Indo-European peoples. So far as we know, no other ancient medicine reveals such a hierarchical relationship of three treatments *linked* together in an organic whole encompassing the science of simples, the dexterity of the practitioner, and the curative power of incantations. The originality lies in the classification of methods of treatment, which assumes a unified concept of bodily afflictions.

Together, these two items of evidence would suffice to justify the reconstruction of a common doctrine. We propose to add a third to the list. We find it in the *Rig Veda* (10.39.3), admittedly in a form whose relation to the doctrine in question is not immediately apparent. But the ideas are indeed the same. In a hymn of the Tenth Mandala, the Aśvins are invoked as healing gods in the following terms: . . . "You are the ones, O Nāsatyas, who are called healers of what is blind, of what is meager, and of what suffers from a fracture."[3]

The Nāsatyas are presented as healers of three types of disease whose names, coordinated by *cit-*, in some way cover the whole range of curable ills. These three adjectives were not chosen at random among those denoting infirmity of some kind. Each one corresponds to one of the three treatment procedures mentioned above.

The blind man . . . is afflicted with a malady reputed to be divine, which of course was often taken to be a sign of supernatural sight or poetic inspiration (Tiresias, Homer). Only a god could heal it, or a "charm."

The meager man . . . suffered from a consumption that ate away at his body. The appropriate treatment for his weakness was medication with plants, which nourished and healed.

The "broken" man . . . , that is, the man with a fracture, required the care of a surgeon.

Unintentionally, merely by reproducing what must have been a traditional theme, the Vedic poet has in fact offered us a mirror image of the doctrine contained in Pindar and the Avesta: whereas the latter two sources spoke of remedies while the poet speaks of maladies, both maladies and remedies correspond to the same system of classification. The *Rig Veda* therefore refers, albeit in a brief and remote allusion, to the same Indo-European conceptions, whose antiquity it therefore corroborates.

The doctrine may therefore be considered to have been established by three independent and concordant attestations. It sets forth a series of practices constituting a summa of medical knowledge, a summa that by virtue of its origins is a mythic "totality" embodied by a healing god: Apollo in the legend of Asclepius, Aryaman in Mazdean medicine, and the Aśvins (Nāsatyas) in Vedic medicine.[4] Each of these peoples adapted a doctrine inherited from a common past to its own mythology, a doctrine whose very expression shows that it could not have been reinvented in each case.

Indeed, it is not merely on a priori and empirical grounds that this doctrine should be imputed to the Indo-Europeans. It seems possible to identify deeper relationships that link it to a broader classification. This way of coordinating the afflictions to human life and the remedies that combat them in triplets appears to depend on the same principles that organize the three states of society and, more generally, the tripleness of the universe.[5] Note that each of the three medicines has as its instrument the symbolic attribute of one of the three social classes: the charm (Greek ἐπαοιδή, Avestan *mąθra*) for the priest-magicians; the knife (Avestan *karǝta-*, cf. Greek τομή) for the warriors; plants (Avestan *urvara*, Greek φάρμακα) for farmers. It is hard to believe that these similarities are accidental. Only the figurative values of these three elements are to be considered; their function is of course to heal, not to represent. But the relation between malady and remedy suggests that both are complementary aspects of an *ambivalent* representation of social attributes. Incantations cast spells—or heal them; iron wounds—and removes the cause of the wound; plants poison—or nourish. In each case healing virtue is only half of the power of the attribute, whose very ambiguity is essential to this complex symbolism. With the same arrow Rudra and Apollo can bring either pestilence or salvation. Hence the malady and its corresponding remedy must be considered together in each of the three aspects in which they traditionally figured. Doing so will help us to see better the symbolic relation between the three divisions of the medical doctrine in question and the three divisions in terms of which society organized itself and conceived of its structure.

TRANSLATED BY ARTHUR GOLDHAMMER

NOTES

[1] Vendidad 7.44; cf. also Yaši 3.6 [. . .]

[2] J. Darmesteter, *Ormazd et Ahriman, leurs origines et leur histoire* (Paris, 1877). H. Güntert, *Der arische Weltkönig und Heiland* (Halle, 1923). H. Hirt, *Die Indogermanen: ihre Verbreitung, ihre Urheimat und ihre Kultur* (Strassburg, 1905–1907), v. 2, pp. 5–15.

[3] See also *Rig Veda* 1.112.8, where similar praise is addressed to the Nāsatyas but in less precise terms: "the rejected(?), the blind, the paralytic."

[4] For an etymological interpretation of the name Nāsatyas as healers, see Güntert, p. 259.

[5] See my article on this: "Symbolisme social dans les cultes gréco-italiques," *Revue de l'histoire des religions* 129 (1945): 5–16 [translated in this volume as "Social Symbolism in Greco-Italic Cults," pp. 439–47].

CHARLES MALAMOUD

The Work of Emile Benveniste:
A Linguistic Analysis of
Indo-European Institutions

1971

*Emile Benveniste continued the intellectual legacy of Antoine Meillet (for
his influence, see the extract from Lamberterie in this volume) in applying
comparative linguistics to the realia of the Greco-Roman world. In this
review of Benveniste's* Le vocabulaire des institutions indo-européennes
*(Paris, 1969), Malamoud offers a general guide to Benveniste's methodol-
ogy and rhetoric of argumentation.*

L inguistics, together with its semiological and semiotic generalizations,
became a model for the human sciences in the 1950s. It also supplied the
natural sciences, such as genetics, with explanatory models, or at any
rate metaphors. In the movement that made the science of language and of
languages the central reference for so many disciplines, the linguist Emile Benveniste played a decisive role in France.

Since the publication of his *Problèmes de linguistique générale* in 1966, readers
not normally drawn to the specialist journals in which Benveniste usually pub-
lishes have been able to become familiar with his work. The book is an anthology of texts published between 1939 and 1964 representing only a portion, but
no doubt the most significant portion, of Benveniste's work in general linguistics. These articles can, I think, be divided into two groups illustrative of the
double process by which linguistics has been able to achieve the preeminent
status so often granted to it today (to the point where an ideology of linguistics
has begun to emerge).

The major fact is that the theoretical position of linguistics as the science of
language has been consolidated over the past several decades. Emile Benveniste

From "L' oeuvre d' Emile Benveniste: Une analyse linguistique des institutions indo-
européennes," *Annales Economies Sociétés Civilisations* 3–4 (1971): 653–62.

contributed to that consolidation by discovering and solving certain key problems, which form the subject matter of one of the two groups of texts just mentioned. Among these are "Sur la Nature du signe linguistique" (1939); "Structure des relations de personne dans le verbe" (1946); "Le Système sublogique des prépositions en Latin" (1949); "La Phrase nominale" (1950); and "Être et avoir dans leurs fonctions linguistiques" (1956). This group also includes texts dealing with the history and present situation of linguistics. It takes up the first part of the volume. Benveniste's doctrine is clear: a stranger to the controversies that marked the succession of schools (and fashions) in the evolution of linguistics after World War I, he chose to base his thinking on the ingenious but elliptical, enigmatic, and sketchy work of Ferdinand de Saussure. Benveniste recognized the full consequences of Saussure's axioms that language is a system of signs and that linguistic expression is "the highest form of a faculty inherent in the human condition, the ability to symbolize." This theoretical orientation enabled Benveniste to resist the behaviorist wave that swept over linguistics, especially in the United States, from 1930 to 1950, and to calmly accommodate the most genuinely innovative work to appear since that time, as if transcending it in advance. The remainder of the anthology forms a second group of texts, which focus more directly on how linguistics relates to other disciplines. Significantly, these papers were first published in journals of philosophy, psychoanalysis, and sociology. They include, primarily, "Don et échange dans le vocabulaire indo-européen" (1951); "Communication animale et langage humain" (1952); "Remarques sur la fonction du langage dans la découverte freudienne" (1956); "Catégories de pensée et catégories de langue" (1958); "La Philosophie analytique et le langage" (1963). This list of titles alone is enough to suggest the types of subjects examined, which range from the specific role and function of language in human activities to the contribution that linguistic analysis of the essential features of words can make to the understanding of culture and social structure.

As important as Benveniste's work on general linguistics has been, however, it is only one aspect of his scientific work. Since 1925, when his remarkably precocious career began, Benveniste has written a substantial number of articles and books dealing with the comparative grammar of the Indo-European languages. In *Les Origines de la formation des noms en indo-européen* (1935) and *Les Noms d'agent et noms d'action en indo-européen* (1948), he set forth a powerful theory of the Indo-European root and revealed the semantic value and function of certain nominal suffixes: both his concrete results and new methods had a profound impact on the study of this linguistic group. Moreover, although he has written one or more articles on each of the Indo-European languages, the Iranian languages (primarily Avestan, Old Persian, Middle Iranian, and Ossetic) are in some sense his specialty. Every year he devotes one of his weekly lectures at the Ecole des Hautes Etudes to the languages of this group.

Le Vocabulaire des institutions indo-européennes, the book that is the subject of this article, belongs to both the "general linguistic" vein of Benveniste's work and the "comparative grammar" vein. To be sure, the lexical material studied in the work is purely Indo-European. And insofar as formal analysis is involved, the methods used are the classical techniques of comparative grammar. Still, both the overall plan of the work and some of its particular arguments illustrate a series of theses set forth in *Problèmes* (p. 25): "Individual and society naturally determine one another in and through language. . . . Society is possible only through language; and through language also the individual. . . . Expression (*langage*) always occurs within a *language (langue)*, within a specific, defined linguistic structure. Language and society are inconceivable without one another. . . . Through language, man assimilates culture and perpetuates or transforms it. Like each language, moreover, each culture employs a specific symbolic apparatus with which each society identifies." [. . .]

What exactly is the book about? Is it about Indo-European society as it must have existed before it fragmented into the many peoples who spoke the various Indo-European languages that have come down to us in written texts? To a certain extent, yes. But can one assign to the initial prehistoric phase everything that can be found in each of the societies that grew out of it, and nothing more? That would amount to very little, and one could not even be certain of the inventory obtained in this way, for there were Indo-European populations that left only fleeting traces, and we cannot be sure that their evidence, if we could only lay our hands on it, would confirm or refute the results obtained elsewhere. And the evidence that we do possess is not all of equal value. In regard to what we believe to be the original state of things, some cultures were more faithful than others, or more faithful in some respects than in others. There is general agreement that the social structures and what Georges Dumézil has called the ideology of the Indo-Europeans were better preserved in Rome and in India than in Greece. But to say this is to imply that we already know what the original state was. In fact, we have filtered the available empirical data in such a way as to construct a model, and then we have used that model to reinterpret and reorganize the same data, thereby, when all is said and done, refining and systematizing our filtering procedure. The result is not, properly speaking, a vicious circle but a complex dialectic, the effect of which is always to make what is most consistent seem most plausible. It would be nice some day to hear the theory explicitly formulated. It cannot be said that Benveniste avoids the issue. After defining (vol. 1, p. 8) the back-and-forth procedure of comparative grammar, he poses the question in the clearest possible terms in regard to the vocabulary of religion (vol. 2, pp. 179ff.): "Here we encounter the same difficulties of method that we saw with respect to other institutions. The problem is to deduce the Indo-European reality from the lexicon. If we limit ourselves to that portion of the vocabulary which can be defined completely and directly in terms of regular correspondences, the object of study will slowly dissolve before our eyes. . . . Because of the nature of its method, comparative grammar tends to eliminate distinctive developments in its search for the common source. This approach leaves only a very small number of Indo-European words." Benveniste's subsequent remarks offer no clear way out of this dilemma, however:

> We can nevertheless learn from the Indo-European religious vocabulary without restricting our search to correspondences verified across the whole range of languages. We shall attempt to analyze the essential terms of the religious vocabulary, even when the religious value of the terms considered appears in only one language, provided that they can be interpreted etymologically. We will find, in fact, that the religious value of a term is often perceptible in only one language. It then becomes important to find out to what extent it is a survival and to what extent it constitutes a new development.

These rather mysterious statements become clearer when we look at the paper to which they serve as an introduction. By what criterion can we decide that a particular form or meaning is a survival or an innovation? Fidelity to the etymological value of the word is the key. [. . .] This acrobatic approach, which calls for prodigies of analysis and inference, nevertheless clearly illustrates both Benveniste's goal and his method.

The goal: Benveniste does not propose to give a detailed, concrete image of the common Indo-European society comparable to the image one might seek to give of a historical society. In this respect, he diverges from a tradition (found mainly among German scholars) of relating linguistic, primarily lexical data to archaeological data and other historical information in order to reconstruct the *realia* of the common period. Scholars working within this tradition asked such questions as where the territory of the Indo-European nation was located (in Central Asia, the Baltic region, or southern Russia), when and how its diaspora came to pass, and what resources, indeed, more generally, what productive forces were available to primitive Indo-Europeans. They also wondered about their social organization and religious representations, but these they examined in terms of historic and ethnographic probabilities rather than on the basis of internal evidence, which could only be linguistic. Benveniste's ambition was different: "The historical and sociological aspects of these processes I leave to others" (vol. 1, p. 10). His aim was to apply the back-and-forth interpretive procedure of comparative grammar to systems of ideas. In this way he hoped to construct a matrix, an explanatory model capable of engendering the observed facts about Indo-European societies as revealed by analysis of their vocabulary. The goal was thus to discover not common Indo-European institutions but the institutions of the historical Indo-European peoples in so far as those institutions perpetuated and revealed structures of the common period or could be interpreted as transformations of those structures.

There was also a further complication: the common Indo-European language, having been at one time a concrete, living tongue, had changed over the course of its history (which ended in what we regard as prehistoric times). By the same token, the people who spoke this language also experienced change in the centuries that preceded their diaspora. What is more, that diaspora did not occur all at once but over an extended period, with fairly long intervals between separations. And just as the descendants of those who left first preserved in their language traces of an archaic form of the common language (I am thinking primarily of Hittite), analysis of the institutional vocabulary in some ways suggests that primitive Indo-European society itself went through a series of states of civilization. This is the case, in particular, in regard to kinship relations, to which Benveniste devotes a detailed study (in the part of the work that seems to me least problematic and most classical, both in the form of the argument and the theses set forth, which does not mean that it is not also quite brilliant). The author shows (vol. 1, p. 275) that Indo-European society "was certainly, as has always been claimed, patriarchal. But in this as in many other respects, various signs point toward a series of superimposed systems." [. . .]

Material *realia* are linked directly to a given site and state of civilization. The languages spoken by populations that have moved away from that site and changed their way of life preserve few traces of it in their lexicon, and these are largely inert. By contrast, the institutional vocabulary is a much more robust legacy. Note that here the word "institution" is to be understood in a very broad sense: "not only the classic institutions of law, government, and religion but also the less obvious institutions that can be discerned in techniques, ways of life, social relations, and speech and thought processes. The subject is essentially unlimited" (vol. 1, p. 9). Surely the term was not chosen for its plasticity alone. Or, rather, the choice was in itself a thesis. Interpersonal relations (hence also feelings) are already social relations. To give, take, or exchange (goods or services), to have trust, to make friends: in order for such actions and psychological dispositions to occur and be named, society must already exist. They, too, are the objects of penetrating analyses in this book, analyses that show how these notions are shaped by the whole social structure and how they change (partially, as we shall see) when a historical variation of the social structure takes place. (What is more, study of these changes makes it possible to analyze facts that at first seemed simple.)

We have seen how the author carved up this "essentially unlimited subject." The plan of beginning with the economy and moving on first to the kinship system (where the biological and the social converge), next to social differentiations as such, then to the political sphere, and finally to law and religion, superstructures par excellence, might seem to be compatible with the by now traditional approach of historical materialism. This impression needs to be corrected at once: the sequence of chapters implies no causal or hierarchical relations among the examined phenomena. Furthermore—and the point bears emphasizing because the distinction is at times elusive in the text itself—the facts analyzed here are ideas and the words that name them. Since this places us squarely in the realm of representations, it is impossible to isolate the economic or to assign it the role of ultimately determining instance: "If one believes that economic notions stem from needs of a material order that must be satisfied, and that the terms that render those notions can only have a material sense, one is gravely mistaken. Anything that has to do with economic notions is connected to much broader representations that bring into play the whole range of human relations and relations with deities." It should come as no surprise, then, that the chapters grouped together under the head "economy" contain studies of hospitality, personal loyalty, credit and belief, gratuity and gratitude along with others dealing with husbandry, the idea of wealth, prices, and wages.

Here as elsewhere in this book, Benveniste's research stands the traditional view of the matter on its head. The Indo-European word *peku, represented by Sanskrit paśu, Latin pecus, and German Vieh, is usually understood to mean "livestock." This has been held to be the initial sense, whereas the sense of "money" is derived from it in certain languages. But Benveniste shows that the fundamental sense, the one that explains all the others, is "movable personal property" and, in particular, that the sense "livestock" is merely a secondary specification "associated with social structure . . . and forms of production" (vol. 1, pp. 47ff. and 59). Another surprise is in store for us in the vocabulary of purchase and sale: it seems that these activities originally pertain to persons, not material objects. More than that, evidence from the Germanic tongues (especially Gothic) suggests that "to buy" was originally "to redeem": in other words, to pay the price for a man was to deliver him. To buy an object, to buy (or redeem) a man: there is indeed a metaphorical relation between the two notions. But in going from common Indo-European (and the earliest attested forms of the historical Indo-European tongues) to our own culture, the sense of the metaphor was reversed.

Not all of Benveniste's analyses lead to seemingly paradoxical conclusions. But all do show that society is "always already" there before personal sentiments come into play and that, in the ancient Indo-European languages (or at any rate in the epic texts that best preserve the initial ideology), "what we take to be a psychological, affective, and moral terminology actually points to the relations between the individual and other members of his group" (vol. 1, p. 340).

This principle of interpretation enables Benveniste to answer questions that have long tormented philologists. Take, for example, the Greek adjective *philos* (vol. 1, pp. 337ff.). This word, which can mean "beloved," is also (in Homer) the equivalent of a possessive adjective, "my own" (or "your own," "his own"). The problem is to determine the relation between these two values: which accounts for the other? So long as the question is posed exclusively with these two terms, each of the two possible solutions seems reasonable but neither is truly convincing. Everything becomes clear, however, if, as an attentive reading of the texts suggests, we interpret *philos* as "a person to whom we are bound by a mutual commitment of hospitality." This relationship is of an institutional order: it involves the status of the host in Homeric society. It stipulates that between two men united by *philotēs* there is an affinity sanctioned by an oath, which creates bonds of affection made manifest by the ritual gesture of welcome and recognition, the *philēma*, or kiss. If, in light of this result, we examine the passages in which *philos* is traditionally interpreted as a possessive adjective (his hands, his knees, his heart), we can restrict the sense and understand that the nouns qualified by *philos* designate "welcoming" parts of the body (hands, knees) worthy of belonging to a *philos* person on whose hospitality, friendship, and loyalty one may count.

When we look at things from this angle, we find that in ancient Indo-European cultures, the individual characterized by a certain quality was defined as a member of a group of people sharing the same characteristic—not a logical group but a social group. I am: I belong to my group. The very notion of "self," "the expression a person uses to define him- or herself as an individual and to refer to him- or herself" (vol. 1, p. 332), which is rendered by the Indo-European form **swe* and its derivatives, "is not limited to the person but originally posits a small group of intimates. . . . This subjectivity is stated in terms of membership." We are led to this conclusion by study of the whole range of derivatives: for example, **swesor*, the word for "sister," one of the rare kinship terms that lend themselves to analysis, can be analyzed as *swe-sor*, whose strict sense is "a female member of the social group **swe*," where **swe* is "the social segment . . . within the 'large family' to which the masculine members belong" (vol. 1, p. 215). "Social institutions are the source of the concepts that seem most personal. In the great lexical unity . . . that arises from the term **swe* institutional values are coupled with values referring to the individual, thus laying the groundwork for a higher degree of abstraction, the grammatical person" (vol. 1, p. 332).

The group defines the meaning of "inside" and is distinguished from everything outside itself. Benveniste returns more than once to the distinction between same and other, inside and outside, which in fact seems to be the major function of the vocabulary of institutions. When it came to the noun for "door," most Indo-European languages, even those most notable for lexical innovation, retained forms that were a direct continuation of the common prototype (vol. 1, pp. 311ff.). A "door" was not merely a part of the physical structure of a house. It was of course a passageway, the key part of the walls erected around the family group, the point at which outside confronted and threatened inside. Beyond the door, "at the gate," begins the stranger and the strange, as indicated by the Latin derivation from *fores*, "door," to the adverbs *foris* and *foras*, "outside," and the adjective *forestis*, "exterior, foreign." (One regrets that Benveniste did

not consider another Latin word that completes but at the same time compli-
cates this picture: the word *forum*, which separates the notions of exterior and
foreign. The forum is at once a place external to all the groups of a city yet
shared by them as a common interior. One dreams of the sparkling exegesis
that Benveniste might have written of the paradoxical French expression *for
intérieur*, which refers to one's innermost self.)

The richness and consistency of the vocabulary pertaining to "door" stand as
a symbol, indeed almost a symptom, of a fact that cannot fail to strike the
reader: many of the institutions studied by Benveniste (including religious rites
and representations) have the function of consecrating territorial boundaries,
zones of competence, and levels defining the status of individuals. What matters, apparently, is to delimit the concentric circles of "social membership" (vol.
1, pp. 293ff.) and to establish a hierarchy among the individual's multifarious
allegiances. But the fact that we have remarked on does not concern individuals alone and is not simply a matter of preserving differential group identities.
Acts, too, are grouped in classes (a preliminary distinction divides the sacred
from the profane: see vol. 2, pp. 179ff.). Institutions whose function is to cir-
cumscribe interiors are also responsible for drawing a line between the normal
and the abnormal. Invariably, the legislative efforts of human sovereigns as
well as the creative efforts of deities involve sorting, dividing, imposing structure on shapeless material and thereby determining and establishing limits. A
significant example is provided by the pair of Greek adjectives *thesphatos/
athesphatos* (vol. 2, pp. 140ff.). Literally, *thesphatos* means "pronounced by a
god." More precisely, the adjective is applied to things to which "a limit has
been assigned by divine pronouncement" (vol. 2, p. 141). It was through a later
and somewhat insecure development that the value "pronounced by a god"
turned into the rather savorless "miraculous, prodigious." (As for *athesphatos*,
its proper sense is "to which no limit has been set," and from that initial sense it,
too, took on the meaning "miraculous," thus rejoining its opposite.)

I have tried to show the ground covered by Benveniste's research in the book
under review. His conclusions, sometimes disconcerting, often bracingly paradoxical, and always stimulating, only partially account for the value of the
work. The work also illustrates the application of a method about which a few
words need to be said because, oddly enough, it is above all the method that is
rich in doctrinal implications.

What is original about this book is its ability to achieve results of interest to
historians and anthropologists on the basis of purely linguistic data. Linguistic
and not philological: the point here is not to reconstruct a social structure (as
one might do from a series or set of events) on the basis of contemporary accounts and interpretations recorded in texts. Benveniste dwells on texts only
insofar as they provide the context necessary for full understanding of the

words they contain. But the words are what counts: words which, when considered in terms not only of their intrinsic structure but also of the combinations into which they enter and the substitutions they allow, define notions. (Among linguistic facts, only words can directly or indirectly tell us about institutions and therefore inform us about the civilization or the community under study. Other aspects of language—phonetics, morphology, syntax—are not relevant. Meillet once wrote that "what needs to be determined is what social structure corresponds to a given linguistic structure and how, in general, changes in social structure are reflected in changes in linguistic structure." Benveniste, who quoted this passage on page 14 of *Problèmes*, clearly states how and why this program proved to be unachievable.)

Words, then. In the semantics of a word, Benveniste distinguishes between signification and designation. He attached great theoretical importance to this distinction, a rudimentary form of which can be seen in certain of the essays collected in *Problèmes* (pp. 117 and 127ff. especially). It is repeated with emphasis in the present book, yet neither term is ever defined. We learn something about what is at stake from the discussion on page 127ff. of *Problèmes*, where we find a distinction between sense and designation which suggests that in this context "sense" and "signification" are largely synonymous. "Sense" is the property that a linguistic element possesses "as signifier to constitute a distinctive, oppositive unit delimited by other units and identifiable by native speakers. . . . This 'sense' is implicit, inherent in the linguistic system. [. . .] But language also refers to the world of objects . . . every statement, and every term of every statement, thus has a reference, knowledge of which is implicit in the native use of the language. [. . .] This distinction is sufficient to indicate the difference between 'sense' and 'designation.'" The important fact is that sense (like signification) is intralinguistic, whereas designation defines a relation between a word (to focus on this particular class of linguistic units) and an extralinguistic object.

In the present book, whose goal Benveniste describes as "studying the formation and organization of the vocabulary of institutions" (vol. 1, p. 9) and not the institutions themselves, what is essential is to isolate the *signification* of words from their *designation*. To study the designation of a word is to study its referent, that is, the reality to which it refers. By contrast, to grasp the signification of a word one must examine its place in the vocabulary as a whole. For example, when we look at the Greek word *hēgemōn* (leader, commander) in terms of designation, we ask about the status and powers of the man who bore this title (under specified historical conditions). When we examine the word's signification, however, we try to clarify the way in which it relates to the various meanings of the verb *hēgeomai*, "to lead, to believe" (see vol. 1, pp. 10 and 151ff.). In this case, the relation between the noun and the verb is clearly perceptible to the native speaker of Greek, even if he is not capable of making it explicit or explaining it. We may therefore conclude that he is, to some extent at least, conscious of the signification of each of these terms. But the other examples that Benveniste gives of this distinction are different: the Greek word *drus* designates the oak in Attic. An examination of the Homeric uses of the word and comparison with the word *doru* show that the initial meaning is "wood" and that "oak" is merely a secondary specification. In the Germanic languages, the same Indo-European root yields, on the one hand, the names of trees (cf. English *tree*) and, on the other hand, terms that can be translated as "faith granted, trust" (cf. German *Treue*, etc.). Benveniste shows (vol. 1, pp. 103ff.) that all these terms derive from the Indo-European root **dreu-*, signifying "firm, solid." And this is the *signification* of the derivatives, whereas in the historical languages we perceive only the designations, which are sometimes divergent. Is the signification therefore accessible in this case to the English speaker who notices the resemblance between *true* and *tree*? By contrast, the Greek speaker will achieve only a first level of understanding of the signification if he notices the "tree" and the "wood" in the "oak." But only the etymologist can determine the ultimate signification! Benveniste, moreover, does not hesitate to state this explicitly: "Through comparison, and by means of a diachronic analysis, we thus bring out a signification where initially we had only a designation. The temporal dimension thus becomes an explanatory dimension."

We see, then, that not only is signification intralinguistic, but it also involves degrees of depth that coincide with the age of the levels considered. Speakers are quite generally unaware of the signification of the words they use, although the range of variation is, it seems to me, quite wide. Etymology thus regains the primacy that it seemed to lose when structure became the fundamental notion of linguistics, in large part thanks to Benveniste himself, who continues to invoke it, and also after Saussure sharply contrasted synchrony and diachrony. What is more, we are again confronted with the old-fashioned and forgotten problem of "linguistic sentiment," which is raised by the question of how signification relates to the unconscious, or, rather, to degrees of consciousness.

Clearly, the method adopted in this book, a method described in all too brief remarks, calls for substantial theoretical elaboration, which Benveniste or his exegetes need to provide. This theoretical work is all the more necessary in that it is not of concern solely to linguists.

Indeed, institutions exist only through the (systems of) words that name them. If the signification of a word, beyond its designation, is in the last instance revealed by etymology, then there is reason to believe that the fundamental sense of a living institution in a specific period of history is that assigned by its denomination, understood in its etymological sense. This is not a deduction from the text: the author himself, after describing his project ("to recover the primary notion of institution as a latent structure, buried in linguistic prehistory") states that "in this way one can shed new light on the foundations of many institutions of the modern world in the economy, society, law, and religion."

In other words, the weight of the past, the presence of the past, is above all the weight of words. Scholars must now attempt to verify Benveniste's assertions by examining the etymology of modern institutions. It will be interesting to see if they can link the present and the past by tracing things back to where Benveniste leaves off. Georges Dumézil gave an indication of how this might be done when he analyzed the tripartition Party-Army-Masses as a revival of the functional tripartition characteristic of Indo-European ideology.

What Benveniste called institutions coincides in part with what Dumézil dubbed ideology. In any case, the use of these terms raises a series of issues that must be confronted head on: it used to be generally accepted that the notion of Indo-European was purely linguistic. In other words, the only relation among the Indo-European-speaking peoples of the globe was this commonality of language, the fact that the language of each was a transformation of the same initial language. If we now take it for granted that language conveys notions which in themselves gave shape to institutions that have remained robust (through a sort of historical unconscious) over the centuries and in spite of changing conditions, then we must grant that the notion of Indo-European is also "cultural," or, in other words, that the peoples who today speak one of the Indo-European tongues share certain common cultural traits. Questions then arise: How and to what extent do institutional notions resist historical change? And what effects did the bilingualism that so many societies have experienced in the course of their history have on the (quasi) unconscious but active system of significations, and therefore on culture and institutions?

TRANSLATED BY ARTHUR GOLDHAMMER

EMILE BENVENISTE

Social Symbolism in Greco-Italic Cults

1945

Comparative linguistics is closely linked to other humanistic disciplines in twentieth-century French academic traditions. As a premier linguist of his generation, Benveniste here tries his hand at applying linguistic methods of reconstruction to the sub-field of Classical Religionsgeschichte.

The division of society into three classes—priests, warriors, and farmers—was a principle of which the ancient Indo-Iranians were fully aware and which in their eyes possessed the authority and necessity of a natural fact. This classification governed the Indo-Iranian world so profoundly that its actual domain extended well beyond its explicit statement in hymns and rituals. It has been shown[1] that various representations outside the sphere of the social per se were compatible with this principle, to the point where any attempt to define a conceptual totality tended unconsciously to borrow the tripartite framework that organized society. In a series of brilliant studies, Georges Dumézil traced the origin of this classification back to the Indo-European community by detecting its presence in the myths and legends of ancient Western Europe and in particular in Roman religion (this is the subject of his book *Jupiter, Mars, Quirinus*).[2] The purpose of this paper is to add some new observations to this body of research, observations that confer a symbolic significance on certain formulas and practices of the Italic and Hellenic cults and thereby connect those cults to social representations. The data used are generally well known. This is my excuse for the somewhat schematic nature of the text, whose purpose is not to recount the facts yet again in detail but rather to interpret them.

I. UMBRIAN TRIADS

In the Umbrian religion, as we know it from the ritual of Iguvium,[3] the number three is pregnant with meaning: it governs the order of ceremonies, offer-

From "Symbolisme social dans les cultes gréco-italiques," *Revue de l'histoire des religions* 129 (1945): 5–16.

ings, and invocations, and we have a triple circumambulation of the site, a triple lustrative sacrifice, deities grouped in triads, triple formulas, and so on. This fact is well known and has many parallels.[4] But the undeniable "mystic" virtue of the number three is not the only issue. In several of these groupings, each term in fact refers to a social class, and the entire enumeration reconstitutes the totality of the society.

A clear example of this is: *nerf arsmo ueiro pequo castruo frif pihatu*, [Lat.] *principes et sacerdotes, homines et pecudes, capita[5] et fruges piato* ["he (you?) shall ritually purify rulers and priests, humans and cattle, roots and fruit"].[6] The sentence contains three groups of two nouns juxtaposed in *dvandvas*: *nerf arsmo* designates the representatives of religious kingship; *ueiro pequo* (Av. *pasu vira*), the *uiri* considered as husbandmen in a situation in which divine favor was being asked for the productive forces of the society;[7] *castruo frif*, the fertility of the soil.

In this context we will include a divine triad that poses a broader problem. I am speaking of the three "Grabovian" gods, who, according to their common epithet, share the characteristic of being "gods of the oak,"[8] whatever such a denomination might mean: Jupiter, Mars, Vofionus: *iuue grabouei . . . marle grabouei . . . uofione grabouie*, [Lat.] *Jovi Grabovio, Marti Grabovio, Vofiono Grabovio*. As has long been noted, this Umbrian triad parallels the Roman triad Jupiter, Mars, Quirinus.[9] But if the first two names are identical, the discordance between Quirinus and Vofionus, coupled with the difficulty of specifying the role of the Umbrian god, poses a serious obstacle to comparison of the two groups. Accordingly, Giacomo Devoto limits himself to the following remark: "In trinitate grabovia Vofionus locum tenet quem Quirinus apud Romanos: natura tamen eius bellica probari non potest."[10]

The allegedly "bellicose" nature of Quirinus is no longer tenable. Analysis of his name assigns him a quite different function. *Quirinus* is the god of the *Quirites*, citizens gathered together in a *curia*. These three words have a common base: **couiria*, "meeting of the *viri*," of which a masculine form **co-uirio-* is attested by Volscan *covehriu*, "conventu."[11] In contrast to Jupiter and Mars, who represent, respectively, magical kingship and military might, Quirinus embodies a class of citizens, a "third estate," whose work is essentially rural. For a more detailed analysis of its role in the Roman triad, which reflects the threefold nature of Indo-Iranian society, see the previously mentioned work by Georges Dumézil.[12]

What do we do, then, with Vofionus, who occupies a symmetrical place in the Umbrian triad? All we know about him is what we think we can deduce from his name. *Vofion-* is explained etymologically as the god of offerings, of wishes, *qui oblationem votivam facit*, through a comparison with Umbr. *vufru*, "votivus," and Lat. *uoueo, uotum*. But what can a god of offerings, or a god laden with offerings, represent? Where do we find such a god, honored with such high rank?[13] This interpretation, which does not appear to be supported

by any known parallel, does not touch on the god's essential function and over-
looks the relation with the other two gods. A fortiori, therefore, we cannot
understand Vofionus's position in relation to Quirinus. Albrecht von Blumenthal correctly noted that the explanation of Vofionus in terms of *deus votorum*
failed to take account of the close relationship between the Grabovian triad and
the Roman triad.[14]

We shall therefore attempt to give an interpretation of this divine name that
takes fuller account of the god's importance and function. The Umbrian form
vofion- can be based phonetically on the prototype **leudhyon-*. Each feature of
this reconstruction can be proven: for the treatment *u-<l-*, cf. *vuku, uocu-* =
Lat. *lucus*, and *uaper, uapers-* = Lat. *lapis*; for *o, u,* representing ancient **-eu-,
-ou- (confused since common Italic), cf. *tuta, tota* = Gothic *þiuda*, etc.; for *f* <
*dh, cf. *rofu, rofa* = Lat. *rufus*, Gothic *rauda*, [and] *rufru*, "rubros," <**reudh-*, Gr.
ἐρυθρός. Hence there is no reason why *uofion-* cannot be traced back to
*leudhyon- (or **loudhyon-*). More than that, an ancient **leudhyon-* (**loudhyon-*)
could not yield anything in Umbrian other than *uofion-*, a derivative of the
same type as Lat. *curio*. According to his name, Vofionus must therefore be
either a god of "growth," comparable to the Latin *Liber* (**leudheros*),[15] or, what
comes to the same thing, a god of the nation, the popular community (Old
Slavic *ljudije*, "*gens*," OE *leod*, German *Leute*, etc.). In this role, he would indeed be the equivalent of Quirinus, god of the "people" and a fructifying deity.

If this analysis is correct, we have restored in Umbrian mythology the same
triple grouping that attests the survival of the Indo-European structure among
the Romans in the form of the trinity Jupiter-Mars-Quirinus. Hence this is an
Italic heritage, but one that was adapted early on to differentiated societies.
With the changes in social terminology that occurred in the Italic regions and
indeed among most Indo-European peoples, the gods of society took on new
names without changing their functions. Thus Quirinus and Vofionus, who
occupy the same place in the trinitarian hierarchy, symbolize the same activity
and the same class despite the difference in their names.

II. AGRARIAN LUSTRATION IN ROME

We know about agrarian lustration rites in the old Roman religion from a passage in Cato (*De agricultura* 141), which, though frequently cited, is still worth
looking at once again. The passage prescribes leading the three animals of the
suovetaurilia around the field and offering to Mars a prayer whose terms are
prescribed. The essential part of this prayer runs as follows:

> Mars pater, te precor quaesoque uti sies volens propitius mihi domo familaeque
> nostrae, quoius rei ergo agrum terram fundumque meum suovetaurilia
> circumagi iussi, uti tu morbos visos invisosque, viduertatem vastitudinemque,
> calamitates intemperiasque prohibessis defendas auerruncesque; utique tu

fruges, frumenta, vineta virgultaque grandire beneque evenire siris, pastores pecuaque salva servassis duisque bonam salutem valetudinemque mihi domo familiaeque nostrae.

Father Mars, I pray and beseech you to be kindly and favorable to me, my home, and my household. For this purpose I have ordered that a *suovetaurilia* be led around my land, ground, and farm so that you will prevent, ward off, and remove seen and unseen illness, barrenness, destruction, disaster, and unseasonable weather, so that you will allow my crops, grain, and vineyards to flourish and turn out well, and so that you will keep my shepherds and flocks healthy and give good health and strength to me, my home, and my household.

This passage abounds in double and triple expressions, which are ordinarily held to be redundancies typical of archaic formularies and their obsession with detail. In fact, the repetitions are quite varied in character. Some of the repetitions in the first part of the prayer are meant to define unambiguously a feeling, act, or object (*volens propitius, precor quaesoque, agrum terram fundumque*). Others are enumerative (*mihi domo familiaeque, fruges frumenta vineta virgultaque*, etc.). But—and this is what I wish to demonstrate—still others establish hierarchies. In them we recognize distinct notions coordinated in a structure that is not merely formal.

The enumeration of woes includes three terms with two members each: *morbos visos invisosque – viduertatem vastitudinemque – calamitates intemperiasque*. It is no accident that there are also three verbs: *prohibessis defendas averruncesque*. There is every reason to believe that nouns and verbs correspond analytically and that, with respect to the sense of the passage, they constitute units that balance one another. The woes are divided into three distinct species, each of which is symbolic:

morbos visos invisosque, visible or hidden maladies, are matters for the science of the priest-magician. The god is asked to "prohibit" (*prohibessis*) them, and the verb used is one frequently employed in deprecations: *di prohibeant! Jupiter prohibessit!* etc.;

viduertatem vastitudinemque, depopulation and devastation, are ravages caused by war (the old term *viduertas* is properly speaking the act of taking the life of a spouse). Hence the second verb is *defendere*, "to repulse by force of arms"; cf. *defendere hostes*, "to repulse the enemy," in Ennius;

calamitates intemperiasque are clearly scourges that damage the harvest and must be "swept away" or "turned aside" (*averrunces*). In the guise of a redundant formulation, then, what we find in this enumeration is an arrangement ordered in accordance with the social categories. Each class is defined by the particular woe that threatens its representatives. The totality of evil is socialized and decomposed into symbolic species. This representation also takes us back to the Indo-European past. We have already detected it in India and Iran, where it expressed itself in the form of prayers and wishes.[16] In *Taitt. Samh.*, I, 1, 13, 3, we read: *pāhí prásityai pāhí dúristyai pāhí duradmanyaí,* "keep [me] from subjection! keep [me] from wicked offering! keep [me] from bad food!"[17] Darius echoes this when he implores Ahuramazda's protection for his country (inscr. of Perspeolis, *d* § 3): *imām dahyāum ahuramazdā pātuv hačā haināyā hačā dušiyārā hačā draugā,* "may Ahuramazda keep this country from the armed enemy, bad harvest, the spirit of falseness." If there is a difference, it has to do only with the fact that the Sanskrit and Persian formulas have a general value, whereas the Roman prayer is intended in particular to ensure the prosperity of the field and the expression of wishes is adapted to that purpose. With this caveat, one can establish a comparison among the three phraseological series: *morbi visi invisique* corresponds to Skr. "bad offering," to Old Per. "spirit of perversion"; *viduertas vastitudoque* to Skr. "subjection (to the foreigner)," to Old Per. "armed enemy"; *calamitates intemperiaeque* to Skr. "bad food," to Old Per. "bad harvest."

In the second part of the Roman prayer, the same structure reappears, but this time the whole range of desired benefits is analytically enumerated for each item. The hierarchy is identical but reversed: *utique tu fruges, frumenta, vineta virgultaque grandire beneque evenire siris* . . . herald the health of the crop; . . . *pastores pecuaque salva servassis,* that is, in second place as in the Umbrian prayer and with the same expression (see below), the class of "men," in this case husbandmen; . . . *duisque bonam salutem valetudinemque mihi domo familiaeque nostrae,* the last class, that of priests, is represented by the person making the offering, who is in fact the person making the sacrifice, and the favor that he is asking is expressed in a *bona salus* formula, both terms of which are equally pregnant with religious value: *salus* is the Latin expression for the notion of "integrity" that is so important in all religious phenomenology, and the epithet *bona* adds its special force (cf. *boni di, bona fides, bonas preces precari, bene dicere,* etc.). Compare this phrase with the one that begins the prayer: *Mars pater, te precor quaesoque uti sies volens propitius mihi domo familiaeque nostrae,* and it appears that the *bona salus valetudoque* that it is asking, in both sequences, for *mihi domo familiaeque nostrae* will be the proof of the god's favorable dispositions (*volens propitius*). The sacrifice that he is offering will confer upon him the "integrity" that is a sign of divine favor because it is itself a divine virtue.

It can hardly be doubted that Cato's text, with its consecrated form, perpetuated quite archaic concepts that established a symbolic parallel between the society and the ceremonial act. But this prayer was only the first act of a "sacrifice" that also included a solemn ritual, the offering of the *suovetaurilia*.

III. THE *SUOVETAURILIA*

The sacrifice offered to Mars consisted of three animals: a pig, a sheep, and a bull. It was consistently designated by the term *suovetaurilia*, which hypostasized in a single word three words in the ablative, fixed and juxtaposed in the form they had in the ritual: *suovetaurilia* is in a sense the nominal transposition of the locution *su ove tauro* (*facere*). Modern historians have always viewed this grouping as a simple fact, and no one to my knowledge has asked whether this choice of animals was somehow necessary. There must be some reason for such a selection, however. Other animals (such as dogs, horses, or birds) might have been sacrificed, or perhaps only one of these three. Why choose precisely these three, why sacrifice all of them, and why offer them up to Mars?

The answer to the first two of these questions can already be found in the analysis I have proposed of the prayer that preceded the sacrifice. By virtue of a necessary liaison, the ritual was governed by the same representations that ordered the invocation. We need only prove that each of the animals did indeed have the symbolic significance that this liaison suggests. Now, it so happens that in light of very ancient data preserved in the religious literature, we can verify the correspondence between each animal and the god to which it was consecrated.[18]

The pig (*sus*) was the sacrifice that belonged to the Earth. Macrobius (*Saturnalia* 1.12, 20) says of Tellus: *sus praegnans ei mactatur, quae hostia propria est terrae.*[19] The ovine, sheep or lamb (*ovis*), was immolated to Jupiter from time immemorial. It will suffice to recall two important pieces of evidence. First, the *ovis Idulis* of which Festus says: *Idulis ovis dicebatur, quod omnibus idibus Jovi mactabatur.* And second, the offering of the *ovis* to Jupiter to consecrate the most solemn form of marriage, the *confarreatio*, over which the *pontifex maximus* and the *flamen Dialis* presided.[20]

Finally, the bull (*taurus*) belonged to Mars, to whom it was solemnly sacrificed at the Capitol and the Forum Augusti. Roman scholars claimed that, apart from Neptune and Apollo, only Mars was entitled to the sacrifice of a bull and that Jupiter in particular was not so entitled.[21]

We are thus assured that the whole social structure was involved in the *suovetaurilia*, with each class taking part in the sacrifice through the animal symbolizing its specific god, while the entire ceremony—prayer and offering—bestowed its benefits on the society as a whole, whether by purifying the people gathered on the Field of Mars or the victorious legions before the triumph or simply the family field.

It is not fortuitous that this sacrifice of three animals also existed in Greece at a very early date. The τριττύς or τρίττοια include three male animals: bull, ram, boar.[22] In the *Odyssey*, they are immolated together to Poseidon:

ῥέξας ἱερὰ καλὰ Ποσειδάωνι ἄνακτι
ἀρνειὸν ταῦρόν τε συῶν τ' ἐπιβήτορα κάπρον (11.130–1)

But the sacrifice could also be offered to other gods: it is mentioned in connection with Apollo, Asclepius, the Dioscuri, etc. It was usually to consecrate a solemn oath, as we learn from the scholiast of a Homeric text (T 197): πρὸς δὲ τὰ ὅρκια τρισὶν ἐχρῶντο Ἀττικοί, κάπρῳ κριῷ ταύρῳ. This assertion is corroborated by Demosthenes,[23] who described the oath-taking in a judgment for homicide: στὰς ἐπὶ τῶν τομίων κάπρου καὶ ταύρου. It is also corroborated by a prescription of Cos: τὰ δὲ ὁρκωμόσια ἔστω ταῦρος κάπρος κριός. τέλεια πάντα.[24] Although the correlation noted above between the sacrifice of certain animals and the cult of a specific god does not obtain in Greece,[25] there can be no doubt that the τρίττοια was a survival of the same past to which the *suovetaurilia* belonged and must be interpretable in the same way. When Mars was invoked and honored with the *suovetaurilia*, it was to repel the various kinds of evil that might pose a threat to the society and the fruits of the earth on which it depended.[26] It was the god's warrior functions that were addressed. In the *Odyssey*, moreover, Poseidon receives a triple sacrifice because of his function: the navigator who wishes to escape the perils of the sea owes the god on whom his fate will depend a sacrifice that symbolically sums up the entire human condition. In other circumstances, however, that sacrifice goes to a different god such as Apollo or the Dioscuri, and so on. In each case it is a question of placing the entire society under the protection of the god who is most effective under the circumstances.

IV. THE LIBATION TO THE DEAD

I believe that the same representations can also be detected in yet another practice: the libation that the Greeks offered to the dead, the χοή. Traditionally, this consisted of three liquid offerings: wine, honey, milk.[27] Each of these substances has an intrinsic meaning. *Wine*, whether it was called οἶνος or μέθυ, was the beverage of the strong, of warriors. *Honey* was famous for its purifying and inspirational virtues; the nourishment of seers, it was reputed to confer prophetic gifts and to place the celebrant in a spiritual relationship with his god. *Milk* was the ordinary offering of farmers and shepherds. Hence it is not presumptuous to link exalting wine, purifying honey, and nourishing milk respectively to warriors, priests, and cultivators. Here, again, the offering epitomizes the whole range of figurations in terms of which the society represents itself. If the homage in this case is offered to the dead, the reason is probably to be sought in the relationship between the dead and the living: it was essential that the framework of society be extended to the dead who once lived in that society, and in order to do this one allowed them to partake of the nourishment essential to the living. In return, the society of the living was rejuvenated and solemnized through consecration by the dead. In the Greek religion, which was so profoundly transformed that it offers little for comparatists to grasp, a trait like this one enables us to recognize the same tripartite organization that we know from Ionian and Attic traditions about the beginnings of Hellenic society.

TRANSLATED BY ARTHUR GOLDHAMMER

Notes

1 Benveniste 1938.

2 Dumézil, *Jupiter, Mars, Quirinus: Essai sur la conception indo-européenne de la société et sur les origines de Rome* (Paris, 1941).

3 Quotes are from G. Devoto, *Tabulae Iguvinae* (Rome, 1937).

4 See G. Devoto, "Contatti etrusco-iguvini," *Studi Etruschi* 6 (1930): 243 and *Tab. Ig.* 192.

5 Or perhaps *fundos*, ["farms"] as it was customarily translated.

6 VI a 30 (Devoto, "Contatti etrusco-iguvini," 188; cf. 197).

7 In a passage of the *Avesta* (*Yašt* 19.32), *pasu vīra* is also in an intermediary position, between the *dvandva āpa urvaire*, "water and plants," and the unfortunately murky expression *uye x^varaye*, "the two foods (?)." At issue are the boons of the golden age that the reign of Yama represents in the Mazdean traditions. If *uye x^varaye* referred allusively to felicity of a spiritual order, the Avestan sequence would parallel the Umbrian triad, with the same middle term (*pasu vīra-veiro pequo*).

8 P. Kretschmer, *Festschrift Adalbert Bezzenberger* (Göttingen, 1921), pp. 89ff.

9 Devoto, "Contatti etrusco-iguvini," 183.

10 ["Vofonio- occupies the same place in Grabovian triad and Quirinus in the Roman one; yet his bellicose nature cannot be proven"], ibid., 237.

11 Kretschmer, " Lat. *quirites* und *quiritare*," *Glotta* 10 (1919): 147–57.

12 Dumézil, *Jupiter, Mars*, pp. 74ff.

13 We cannot adduce the Roman *Agonius*, who Festus says was *deum praesidentem rebus agendis* in the old ritual; cf. agonia, "*hostia*." In the first place, this is only a distant memory, and if this god existed, it was to watch over a particular aspect of the sacrificial ritual, the killing of the victim, and guide the arm of the priest responsible for the immolation.

14 A. von Blumenthal, *Die Iguvinischen Tafeln: Text, Übersetzung, Untersuchungen* (Stuttgart, 1931), p. 61.

15 On *Liber*, see Benveniste 1936.

16 Benveniste 1936, 540–49.

17 I would not have known this mantra, which is buried in the vast literature of ritualism and which no exegete had noticed, had I not stumbled upon it by chance in the *Altindische Grammatik* of Jakob Wackernagel and Albert Debrunner (Göttingen, 1957), vol. 3, p. 15 d 39, where it is cited along with other grammatical examples in a discussion of the forms of the genitive.

18 All the necessary details about offerings can be found in the very well-informed article by M. Krause, "Hostia," in *Paulys Real-Encyclopädie der classischen Altertumswissenschaft*, ed. Georg Wissowa (Stuttgart, 1931) supp. v. 5, pp. 236–82. There is no need to reproduce the large number of literary and epigraphic references that Krause systematically assembled. See esp. pp. 264ff. on the *suovetaurilia* (and on the equivalent form, *solitaurilia*, whose meaning is less clear).

19 Krause, "Hostia," p. 253.

20 Ibid., pp. 255ff. Note, moreover, that the sacrifice of a sheep figured in numerous magical acts and fertility rites. See N. Thomas, "Animals," in *Encyclopaedia of Religion and Ethics*, ed. James Hastings (Edinburgh and New York, 1908–1915), vol. 1, p. 527.

21 On these offerings, the essential texts are gathered in an old article by P. Stengel, *Neue Jahrbücher für Philologie und Pedagogik* 133 (1886): 329–31. See also the article Τρίττοια by L. Ziehen in *Paulys Real-Encyclopädie*, vol. 13, p. 328.

22 *Contra Aristocratem* 68.642.

23 R. Herzog, *Abhandlungen der Preussischen Akademie der Wissenschaften* 6 (1928), p. 14, cited in Ziehen, *Paulys Real-Encyclopädie*, p. 328.

[24] See P. Stengel, *Die griechischen Kultusaltertümer* (München, 1920), p. 122. In general, the pig was sacrificed to Demeter and the bull to Poseidon, bull-god. But the sheep was the most common offering and had no specific attribution.

[25] On Mars Gradivus and Averruncus, see R. Stark, "Mars Gradivus and Averruncus," *Archiv für Religionswissenschaft* 25 (1939): 139ff.

[26] With variants depending on the time and place (e.g., water substituted for wine, mixture of milk and honey, etc.). [. . .]

[27] See Dumézil, *Jupiter, Mars*, pp. 252ff. Though beyond the scope of this article, I should like to mention two late medieval survivals of these conceptions. Toward the end of the ninth century, Alfred the Great added this observation to his translation of Boethius: "A populated territory: that is the work with which a king concerns himself. He needs men of prayer, men of war, and men of labor." In the fourteenth century, moreover, one could read this in an English sermon (G. R. Owst, *Literature and Pulpit in Mediaeval England* [Cambridge, 1933], p. 553, quoted along with the previous quotation by H. St. L. B. Moss, *The Birth of the Middle Ages* [Oxford, 1935], p. 271): "God made clerics, knights, and tillers of the soil, but the Demon made burghers and usurers." With the growth of cities, guilds, and commerce, the ancient order in which the preacher saw the natural order came to an end.

PATRICE LORAUX

Thought Takes Form

1993

In this essay, at the same time playful and dead serious, Patrice Loraux views the syllogism not only as a mechanism of demonstration but also as a historical eventuality produced by the mind of Aristotle. In other words, Aristotle gets credit (and gives himself credit) for inventing the syllogism, but once it has been invented, the syllogism becomes no longer an invention but something discovered that has always been.

In the Prior Analytics, *Aristotle defines his theory of the syllogism. In the* Posterior Analytics, *he moves on to consider the actual process of demonstration, which for him is a form of syllogism. Thus he emphasizes the deductive aspects of proof. Besides deductive proof or* apodeixis, *Aristotle also recognizes the importance of inductive proof or* epagōgē *(Posterior Analytics II ch. 19). Approaching the universal is an inductive process, full of trial and error, whereas the process of syllogism becomes an ostensibly perfect machine once Aristotle has defined it. In Aristotle's words, his invention of the syllogism was a* ponos *or "ordeal." Historically, this process may have been inductive, even though the product is viewed as the discovery of deduction.*

BARBARA CELARENT

All men are mortal: thus . . . ; therefore . . . This is thought at its most boring. "Impossible not to be overcome by boredom when hearing such a syllogism; it must be due to its useless form . . ."[1]

[. . .]

It is a subject that has notoriously fallen into disuse. The fate of the syllogism is perhaps even harsher than oblivion itself—the question of being having only fallen into oblivion—since the syllogism, which everyone knows by heart, evokes only indifference. But it may be the fate of all the great subjects of phi-

From "La pensée prend forme," in *Le tempo de la pensée* (Paris: Editions du Seuil, 1993), pp. 292–327.

losophy to end up very close to indifference. At the *utmost* limit of interest, without any effective way of being reused, the syllogism cannot arouse anyone's passion except that of logical technicians, and it is barely remembered as a matter of interest in the world at large.

Let us beware, because we are already on the wrong track. We are not concerned here with the figures (*skhēmata*) of the syllogism, which are indeed deadly boring, but with its definition, which is perhaps less fresh in our minds.[2] It looks like a Greek ontological sentence, and includes some of its highest determinations: the assumption (*ta keimena*), the something (*tode ti*), the other (*to heteron*), the result (*to sumbainein*), and finally, the necessary (*to anankaion*). How could such a dense *logos* be transformed and give rise to such mechanical figures? Here already are the beginnings of a bit of history.

Yet, and most importantly, this is a *logos* that excludes us: it takes place without us, it is a discursive process that produces newness by the very virtue of its assumption.[3] The "we" must not be part of it; if it were, it would disturb the movement of the *logos*. [. . .] This is the most difficult thing to accept: the syllogism takes place without us, and because it doesn't involve us, we lose interest: indifference. This is a well-known story: all men are mortal, etc. . . , but we do not have the courage to bring it to its conclusion. Thought falls out of our hands. We disturb the syllogism, and the syllogism, in turn, bores us.

Of course, the syllogism is also a very distant memory from school.[4] It made us aware of its form, and it is through it that thought first takes form in us:

device composed of sentences semantically fixed and deprived of all playfulness;

necessary chain of a necessity without content or with a rationally laughable content;

very supervised transformations of conclusive configurations.

Yet nothing really that invites analytical attention. It is indeed difficult to arouse interest. [. . .]

Therefore, and this is a promise, you will hear the other history of the syllogism. [. . .]

It is, in fact, traditional to see the syllogism as an object without history, as many other Aristotelian objects, at the same time fallen into disuse, and accepted as such forever. This, at any rate, is the history that has been constantly maintained: that they appeared without accidents, that is to say that they were reached without hesitation, without regrets, without breaks, without returns. [. . .] We know that the syllogism has not made one step backward from the time of Aristotle on, but neither did it take any step forward.[5] It emerged all at once, in its entirety, forever: a true Greek form.

All this is standard. No accidents, no snags. Yet there is nothing either that could attract analytical attention. [. . .]

It is indeed tempting to link the two motifs: it is because it lacks history that the syllogism is without interest, because nothing ever happens to it, because it produces no effect, and especially so since there is only one word in Greek, *pathos*, "what happens to someone, something experienced, misfortune, feeling of the soul, accident in the philosophical sense."[6] As a result, there could only be a history of the syllogism if, in one way or another, it could be made pathetic.

[. . .]

There was a time—roughly the Classical Age—when some were attempting to topple the syllogism from its high pretense of being a rational tool able to grasp the main objects of ontology. Yet it eventually fell under the blows of a system of disqualifying predicates, as well as from indifference: empty, powerless, ridiculous, etc. All the same, this is something akin to a history, an object that leaves real movement far behind, and accentuates the feeling of pure form through its very motionlessness.

In short, we needed time to come to the same conclusion as Aristotle, who himself says that the *sullogizesthai* is without history, or more exactly, without prehistory. Usually, Aristotle likes to rebuild, if not simply to build, slowly clearing a path through history for rational objects, by establishing a chronology of remarkable moments in their evolution, as he does, for example, for the idea of cause.[7] But in this case, there is nothing before, and Aristotle speaks of his *ponos* (of his labor) as if the syllogism itself, for lack of being able to do it historically, had to clear its path *through* Aristotle himself.

[. . .]

Oh, if only we could add some *pathos*, some event, some affect! Neither the pompous *pathos* of Aristotle when he reports on the act of birth of the syllogism, nor Kant's soberly acknowledged indifference, but something entirely different.

The syllogism, as you know, contains another history. This is the logician's promise in order to stave off boredom; it is left to another to understand that there are more than one way of understanding "to contain."

It contains all the great Greek discursive passions, but I won't say any more for now.

[. . .]

The *Posterior Analytics* is a text full of passion that needs to be neutralized at all cost: an entire system of unpredictable discursive passions that gravitate around the syllogism, this logical object that, for a time, wanted itself as powerful as science. Passions, *pathē*: events as well then, and perhaps a little history too. From this point on, the history of the non-prehistory of the syllogism, which Aristotle decreed in order better to give rise to the pure form in all its novelty, can begin.

Provided that we read the *Posterior Analytics* with feeling, which we do not often do. With feeling, that is to say pathetically. In short, this is a way of going against Aristotle's injunction that there is nothing to be said about the syllogism before it appears.

The Syllogism on the Moon

The *Posterior Analytics* themselves already suggest another history of the real syllogism, almost a little pathetic. And if it took place anywhere else, if we brought it on the moon at the time of an eclipse, the last sublunary event, the first eternal event? To be sure, we would lose nothing, inasmuch as the universe—and this is its definition—is the same always and everywhere.[8] This is no fiction, but Aristotle's own text. At the time of an eclipse, on the moon, the history of the syllogism would be at its shortest. It would take place simultaneously with the event itself. Instantaneous history. From the act of perceiving would immediately come knowledge of the universal.

[. . .]

The syllogism, then, at the light of the eclipse, will happen without history. Not only one instant of reflection to understand what is happening. Science as a lightning strike, absolutely simultaneous with the event. Aristotle's secret dream, his fantasy science, is to give rise to an *agkhinoia* (readiness of mind) that would allow us to come upon the middle term in an *askeptos* time—a moment of time so short that it cannot be observed.[9] On the moon, the syllogism does not walk; it goes faster than the act of walking, the only tempo that Greek man can observe. And, at the same time, the syllogism swiftly shuts inside itself the possibility to seize its human progress. We are robbed of the necessary time to grasp the time of the syllogism. While it is impossible to imagine its history, this mixture of event and effect might very well be its basis.

The occurrence will have concealed its history.

Coming Back to Earth

Let us bring the syllogism back among us, bipedal walkers of knowledge. As soon as it returns, it will already find it very difficult to happen, to become effective, and to reach the end of true principles. For this is science: to make principles come out of themselves, until we get at something new. [. . .] We shall have the syllogism at our disposal in *slow motion*, as if its movements were broken up into pieces. Not the artificial syllogism of the *Prior Analytics*, but the syllogism in a real situation as it faces up to a complete series of events. We are going to follow the passion of the syllogism, if it wants to become an event of this world, there where it will acquire history.

[. . .]

The *Posterior Analytics* narrates all the episodes—hardly better linked than those of the *Iliad*, which for Aristotle is the worst example of a unity badly held together[10]—where, at every step, what is necessary for the syllogism is the ability to disentangle itself from the whole network of wily impulses threatening to throw it off track, or, even worse, to paralyze it. In short, a text full of suspense, where what follows threatens not to happen with every step taken. This is extremely serious, and we see what is at stake: how to pursue the assumption to the end, through numberless obstructions, whose meaning we do not even grasp. We too often speak of the *Posterior Analytics* as a theory of demonstration: it is rather a step-by-step struggle—a true battle in the military sense—with what never ceases to delay the occurrence of the demonstration. And this, in fact, constitutes a history, the risk of reaching a dead-end inherent in every step. Yet Athena, doubtless, keeps watch over the syllogism, just as she does over Odysseus.

TECHNICAL-LOOKING BLUNDERS

Let us give a catalogue of all the situations in which the syllogism is at risk of a fatal wrong step, and let us make it sufficiently large and Homeric in style so as to impress the reader. It is a long story.

Not to be tricked by the argument of the *Meno*.
Not to be worried by the idea that principles, because they have not been proven, might communicate some uncertainty to their conclusions and resist the sly requirement of integral proof, including principles.
Not to yield to the temptation of an ultra-general proof that would straddle genres, a coarsely misguided step.
Not to superimpose proof and question.
Not to believe oneself compelled to prove assumptions along the lines of "why does a wall not breathe."
Not to give way to the infantile vertigo of infinite sequential interlocking of predicates ("Athenian" entailing "man" entailing "living," etc.).
To hold on firmly against the desire always to find more intermediate terms, and indeed there is even a word to name this particular delirium or fantasy of compactness, *puknosis*.
Not to slip toward the side of substantified accidents; the Ideas, this vain droning, are not far.
Not to mix up the fact and the why.
Not to contaminate the definition and the proof with each other.
Not to hope to offer proof of the essence.
Not to combine proof, division, induction.
To handle with the greatest care the syntagms of reduplication of the type: principle of principle.

This list is being offered for rhetorical purposes, only to dramatize, or better to make obvious the fragility of the demonstrative occurrence in face of all the opportunities to lose itself that are given to it. [. . .] Nothing tragic has happened so far, the syllogism has only been delayed. Aristotle naturally argues, in order to contain the risk, to avoid false paths. Nothing surprising, except the fact that the argument itself always ends up leaning on a system of predicates that a logician would probably consider too weak. To put a stop to this collapse of the discursive, Aristotle invokes the sense—natural in a normally educated man—of the absurd, the ridiculous, the useless, the undoable. [. . .]

[. . .]

The risk of stumbling, therefore, exists at every step, and, in order to counteract this, Aristotle uses, just as so many boundary stones, the most prosaic predicates of common sense in the matter of successful effectivity. Beware! Absurd, ridiculous, etc.

Process Without Consequences

But, seriously, what harm exactly would a misguided step cause? Where would we find ourselves? What would be the consequences? And, pitiless, as always, Aristotle dryly proffers the list of all the quasi-processes—if there is only an appearance of a beginning of any—that ruin ipso facto the idea of conclusion. There again, everything is done in order to impress, including the technical terminology. One more step, and there is:

The *petitio principii*.
The blocked division.
The proliferation of intermediaries.
The infinite walk (*eis apeiron*), opened up by the Third Man.
The situations of the type: movement of movement.
The fantasy of a science of everything.
The overload of discursive channels where knowledge moves in both directions.
The lulls of verbiage, oxymoron, simple changes of terminology.
The *ekthesis*, this manner of putting away that engenders the Platonic Idea when it is badly practiced.
The obvious question.

Enough! If all these things are threatening simultaneously, the syllogism will never occur.

The proof itself is indeed hardly without history; parasitical appeals happen at every step of the process, as if to interrupt its constant and natural course; and if we questioned a little before assuming? And if we spent a little more time on the principles, so as to radicalize them? And if we tested the ground before putting our foot down?[11] And if to reach the goal were more difficult than we suspected? Etc. Are these suggestions interesting? They are more like swerves that will stop shortly, or rather immediately, or that reach a state of panic, but not before it has stopped the movement of the proof.

[. . .]

At first sight, there is nothing concerted in these maneuvers, but rather some operational awkwardness that should be easy to rectify every time. And if a completely different history of logical life were hidden under this? We say that we acquire discursive *habitus* in school—a mistaken way of putting it since it is rather a matter of learning how to resist the assaults of a few sly invitations of style: ask yourself, then, why man is a man.[12] Because we may come to believe that it is beautiful to *dare* to question identity. It looks like the temptation of a mischievous spirit. Where does the voice that silently utters these "profound" questions, these radical suggestions, these models of scrupulous caution, and these fatal encouragements come from?

THE GUARDIANS OF COMMON SENSE

Aristotle warns us against procedures that spontaneously distract the syllogism and prevent it from starting.

It is absurd (*atopon*) to attack common sense, to pursue questions when one is in the process of stating.

It is impossible (*adunaton*) to practice the dichotomy, this enticing generation of empirical differences, by auto-specification of the universal.

It is ridiculous (*geloion*) to question the evidence, and to ask for example if there are any *phainomena*.

It is useless (*akhrēston*) to waste one's operational time with repetitions.

It is empty (*kenon*) to be satisfied with simple semantic variations—a trick Plato delights in—that do not bring the syllogism one step forward.

Here is a complete network of predicates with mixed values—let us say: logico-anthropological—in which human experience of the impossible diffracts itself in various modes. It is a question, in short, of giving rise to affects in which, for man, the logico-ontological impossibility converts itself into a feeling of impracticability. We must understand its meaning, as Aristotle constantly enjoins us.

[. . .]

Discursive temperance is under guard of a *paideia* (education) that dissociates itself in advance from the citizen who theorizes about all kinds of effective heroism, and suggests that the syllogism can only appear in the civic context. It is civility itself to know how to bring something to its conclusion reasonably. This is why Aristotle calls *apaideutoi*[13] these rude men, these savages, all those who, like that Antisthenes, rattle the limits of common sense under the guise of pernicious radicalism, to please themselves or to make an impression. Common sense: the delicacy never to pervert, by which we can assure the affinity between phenomenality's modes and the pertinent discursive forms. In front of the spectacle of living beings, we do not ask the question: are there animals? It is only if this question is withheld that we can state the assumption: all animals are mortal. [. . .]

It is a matter of countering a concerted attack against the ordinary rule of common sense that, as such, must lose neither the sense of the questionable nor the sense of experience (we can never deduce all the varieties of bees from the Bee—the bee in itself—but we must be patient enough to encounter them), nor the sense of the difference between *pathos* and *pragma*, a state of affairs and a state of myself, nor the sense that in between two points there is a sur-mountable space (*diastēma*), nor the sense of the chronology of actions (we cannot go up and down simultaneously), nor the sense of the verbal solution (to be banned), not the sense—and this one is critical—that we must know when to stop.

Discuss all of this, and you will become deep philosophers, but the syllogism will wait a long time before it appears in this world.

Something Moved

Here, of course, a surprise is awaiting us.

The *same* predicates (ridiculous, etc.) that used in the past to prevent us from reusing any syllogism that would have aimed at some effectivity now can be found there again as they were, but this time in the syllogism's service, allowing it to occur in its entirety when it seeks to seize an effective content, by protect-ing it from disruptive discursive influences. Something then has imperceptibly moved into the nonhistory of the syllogism, and it is the entire defense system that is now differently framed; the same formal determinations that prohibited us from using it as a tool, there help in giving birth to it by protecting it from the most extravagant maneuvers. This very light shivering is the only thread that we could use to write a prehistory of the syllogism, or "how it will occur despite everything."

The Syllogism Is Not Positive

One remark: we have to respect the order of the tale if we do not want to nullify the dramatization of the *Posterior Analytics*. [. . .] The understand-ing of the false step comes before the understanding of the step, and demands it. We could have thought that the syllogism was a positive object par excel-lence, a process that can reach its term without the mediation of unreal mo-ments. Is the syllogism the first fully positive state of Greek discursiveness? Not really, if we discover that it was tempted to hide itself at every step.

[. . .]

This is quite a story, then, and we begin to worry: where does the syllogism take its form? Did it descend among us in order to put itself in this awkward position, or has Aristotle, ever since the sublunary, projected up there the ideal *skhēma*, instantly free from all resistance? Let us bet that Kant—even though Kant knew better than anyone else what empty progress means—believed that Aristotle invented the syllogism on the moon, which led him to think that it was acquired all at once, without regret and without effort. Aristotle—who himself is not unaware of what it costs man to walk straight, that is, logically— reminds us how he himself created the syllogism out of his labors: the syllogism can take place down here only against a concerted system of resistances. They all share a family resemblance. They all set the bar of logical action a little higher. Always a little bit "more": a few more questions, a little more radical- ism, slowness, intensity.

Be that as it may. Yet the time they spend trying to comply is just as much delay for the syllogism: meanwhile, it still has not occurred.

HATRED OF THE CONCLUSION

Yet the syllogism wants itself to be a simple thing, a natural thing even, and to guide true principles to their end without problems or delays, and by means of its own resources. In short, without having recourse to us, it is the productive autonomy of science by the most direct path. Everything takes a turn for the worse when we intervene in the rhythm of logical process. We are people with problems, all of us, Greeks, tall and short, physicists, Eleatics, etc., and even these loners without a culture, such as an Antisthenes, etc. We have more than one trick in our bag. For example, we drop a great, sublime sentence into the silence, a sentence very dense and very deep in meaning that says everything in two words—*hen panta* (a Whole)[14]—and then we withdraw, leaving it to its fate: it is up to you, the *epigonoi*, to ensure both its meaning and its conse- quence. Or rather, in the din of arguments, we let a little question slip, a little question that draws everything to a standstill. Great *pathos* and small mischief: two American Indian–like nicknames for a philosopher. Imagine your delight: we are done with any *natural* consequence, this much too prosaic thing. Unless we, Platonists, would rather see you thrown into a panic by a never-ending and boundless consequence. But you have understood: deep down, we all share the same hatred of the conclusion, and we do everything to prevent it from happening.

[. . .]

The word *pathos* is indeed the pivot: let the event perish (the natural occur- rence and its temporal order) if this produces affect, by which I mean the in- tense sensation of thinking. *Anairein* is a key word in Aristotle, to engage in maneuvers that destroy the naturalness of the "there is." The still undeclared, and perhaps unperceived, objective of all those agitators is to make thought experience hyperbolic affects—even if they should produce the loss of all "there is"—which can be felt only beyond discursive common sense. Go beyond, and the apparatus of knowledge will be thrown into turmoil; go beyond, and the syllogism will never be.

To do in order to do in vain: a gesture against nature par excellence, and in agreement with the Aristotelian doctrine. Here we may suspect some acts motivated secretly not by the eventually enlightening desire to give birth, but rather by a fantasy of abortion, of things never brought to their conclusion, but always misplaced, premature, sterile. For what benefit, despite everything?

ARISTOTLE PATIENTLY

Everyone was working on his own behalf. There were the enigmatic ones, the worriers, the cautious, the overexcited, the stutterers, the ambiguous, the mystics, in short, all the great actors of the philosophical drama, and everything was flying in all directions.

Aristotle conducts his inquiry (*historia*) diligently. By linking, gathering all these microprocedures (and nothing is more familiar to Aristotle than the drawing up of lists—lists of anything, always homogeneous lists—here the list of endless procedures), it is possible to sense that with them, we have just entered a region of turbulence, a singular and insensitive turbulence where operative rectitude is thrown into a panic. Everything starts to be interrupted, to run into circles, to be endless. [. . .] We just came under the influence of the *apeiron*.

[. . .]

This ongoing mutation of the very structure of a logical operation, this sign of instability of the procedure, as if we continued a proof with a fable, or even songs, forewarns Aristotle about one requirement: a procedure, in order to stay such, must be homogeneous and stable for the length of time it exists.

It has been said that Aristotle emphatically speaks about his own labor on behalf of what we mistakenly call the invention of the syllogism; he even says that he spent a great deal of time, since there was nothing before it. It is true that he did force himself to catalogue the processes that do not work, and to elucidate their mechanisms (why does dichotomy not work? It is a different case from the overloaded discursive channel when the same discipline tries simultaneously to produce results and to reflect on its principles). Yet he sees instantly that one and the same law is at work through all these *amēkhaniai*. Then appears the cool strength of the syllogism, precisely when we persist in thinking along with Kant that it came too early, all at once, apparently painlessly and forever, an exemplary case of nonhistory. Classically, we credit this promptitude to him because he did not concern himself with its content.[15] Of course, we understand the outline of the reasoning: as long as Aristotle concerns himself only with the *form*—which is considered prior—it was easy, but problems start when we try to grasp the object. Yet, before we can let go of the form, we must, and this is what Kant underestimated, be done with the affects of *apeiron*, these great disrupters of form.

UNDER THE INFLUENCE OF THE *APEIRON*

The *apeiron* is the only real opponent that has, until now, thwarted all attempts to produce this act: stating the true to its conclusion. It is not a Not-something with uncertain boundaries, but a tight system branching out into discursive micro-skids, polymorph and sly, for which all of them, Physicists, Megarians, etc., are semiconscious agents, semiwarned, those who worry too much or too little about the follow-up or the possibility of taking one step, or who mistake words for acts, without fear of stuttering. This great cloud of *missed* acts— here, we place the most strictly Aristotelian element and a souvenir of Freud on the same semantic channel—constitutes the archive of the *apeiron*, and, at the same time, of the syllogism. They share common archives.

It is important to note that the *apeiron* does not simply appear around the corner like the great Other, unexpected and astonishing. No, it is something much more deliberate, much more precise. Aristotle grasped that there were some specific, definite, quasi-procedures that produce indeterminate effects. These maneuvers are very effective, if not active, provided that each one pretends to be the only one and to operate without the other's knowledge. As long as we consider it as it wants itself to be considered, the indeterminate-undifferentiated, whose major effect is a feeling of dizziness, the *apeiron* operates with impunity, masked by an absence of proper features and a plurality of volunteer spokesmen. Its work: subtle and perverse. That by doing, nothing occurs. To end heroically somewhere in the non-occurrence. To do in order to undo effectuation. All this is done under the illusory cover of a feeling of discursive superpower through tetanization of the channels of knowledge. You will be similar to perverse gods. You will feel—sublime and terrible feeling— the edges of your apparatus of knowledge vacillate with a horrible precision. Yet we would never have believed that this was what Antisthenes wanted, despite his trickster tendencies.

But all calms down as soon as Aristotle lists the ways taken by the indeterminate. By bringing forth precision—that is *the* precision—about the clandestine life of the *apeiron*, he details its maneuvers. Despite the repeated claim that there is no difference in the *apeiron*,[16] Aristotle still succeeds in producing a detailed spectrum of endless actions, those stillborn procedures. In a way, the indeterminate that comes out of the absence of assumption is very different from the indeterminate that comes out of the discursive circle, different from the powerlessness to pursue empirical differences, different from the infinite in action, different from the power that eternally remains power, different from the syntagm "science of all things," different from the void of a word that has too many meanings, different from the flight without end, etc. The *apeiron* might be worse than a *pollakhōs legomenon*, a term that qualifies itself as *pleonakhōs*.

Facing this flood of indeterminacy, Aristotle will soon suddenly say: stop! Or in Greek: *anagkē stēnai*.

ANANKĒ STĒNAI

Even though Aristotle regularly attacked its principle, he may in fact have invented only one thing: the before is really "before" the after, and the after comes immediately "after"; there is indeed a prior and posterior. Yet this *husteron proteron* structure is not stable, and when it is left to itself—like all Greek things, in fact—it is disrupted by its own effect, and time is affected by its constitution and is thrown out of joint, but maybe this is precisely what time is: the self-disruption of the *proteron husteron* by reciprocal affects of ecstasies. We must then keep watch on time itself, and for this purpose, Aristotle will invent all sorts of distinction, as well as, for example, the syllogism.

There is indeed a genuine "before" the syllogism, which confirms, without any paradox, Aristotle's claim that we can say nothing about the syllogism before him. Before, it is the generalized rule of the *apeiron*, not a universe in which nothing happens, but rather an intense turmoil full of flashes, flashes of sparkling discourses, but also flashes of weapons and local *agons*.

To happen at all, the syllogism will have to contain—as we said before—another history, which we now know: the history of what is never able to end and to procure knowledge, the history without stable archives of the *apeiron*. The syllogism will not occur as properly known rational knowledge unless it will contain all that, in terms of *logos*, strives in countless ways not to end, until it is realized into nonhistory. Of course, it is not so much a question of content, as we would understand the content of a formal object; rather, the syllogism contains, in a hoplite sense, the hostile upsurge of an enemy outnumbering it. The syllogism is then just as a resistance line that holds on and does not yield: it resists the resistance of realization.

Anankē stēnai. We know the canonical translation: "we must stop . . ." in the movement toward the infinite; but *histēmi* is also the hoplite verb that means that the fighter holds on and does not yield. Here, the continuous chain of the primary actions state-pursue-attain must hold without flinching, without sinking. It needs to be able to know how to stop the infinite revival of the question, be capable of a completely effective movement, know how to state a *therefore*. This is, in short, the very health of logical effectuation.

THE SYLLOGISM IS LATE

The syllogism is not much farther away. The slowness of our tale contrasts starkly with the factual brutality of the *Analytics*: "there is syllogism when . . ." We only succeeded in parodying Aristotle's *ponos*, or rather we tried to restore its *pathos*. Tradition (Kant) admires how precociously the syllogism was produced: early enough, indeed, but we need to see that this precocity includes a certain lateness. The syllogism occurs later, despite everything, than if we were on the moon, the night of an eclipse. [. . .]

The imperceptible lateness of the syllogism is the work of time itself, the lapse of psychic time that always tried to come between the moments of the necessary chain. All the problems of philosophy arise out of these temporal lapses. [. . .]

Therefore, if we want a syllogism, no pause. Beware of the *apeiron*: if the divine dies as an object of love—this is classical doctrine—the indeterminate turns away our overtures, and thus it is that it seduces, like a perverse First Mover.

THE INSTANT OF THE SYLLOGISM

Things now will go very quickly. In one instant, the syllogism will "take," that is it will stylize the outline of the Greek discursive movement: the stated assumption, which interrupts questioning and stops meanings; the pursuing, which brings among them the unique bound of the concluding, which stays deaf to the continuous indefinite revival of the meaning. In one instant, thought takes form. And this is what a form is: the simultaneous and ideally imaginable conjunction of all these moments. All the Greek ontological turmoil is fixed in one instant, or rather formalized.

Aristotle spoke of his *ponos*. Be that as it may. He needed much time[17] to unmask one after the other the soul of these maneuvers that wanted, each in its own way, performance rather than result. Yet it is only in one instant—this unnoticeable (*askeptos*)[18] lapse of time—that it is possible to perceive that all these attempts are alike: they allow the *apeiron* to cause, as its paradoxical task, the non-occurrence. [. . .]

It was true, then, that the syllogism did not take place the instant before. The syllogism, or rather the full positivity of the assumption. The "there is" without sentences, as common sense understands it. There are animals. No argument please. Don't ask me about the Great Animal. [. . .]

Aristotle understands: if the assumption is not followed up *immediately* with the consequence to pursue it and avoid infinite elusion, it flows backwards— maybe even regresses—ipso facto on itself by questioning itself, and we will then need to question the unquestionable evidence that principles are always ready to fail. If there is only one instant of hesitation about what has been attained, it is the conclusion itself that is delayed until hell freezes over. In one split second, Aristotle stops the *pathos* of philosophical acts.

And this was the syllogism, impassive event.

We would not perhaps have suspected that the syllogism took place so near the *apeiron*, very close to it, and, like all Greek objects, the real syllogism—that is a science bound to operative control—will have been heroic. Aristotle took some calculated risks: to work near unlimited operations is not without danger. Nothing brushes against the *apeiron* without risking the non-occurrence, if only in the prestigious mode of a fantasy of superpower. [. . .] The syllogism almost did not take place, and this is the starting point from which to reunderstand it, and this is where it becomes fascinating.

Aristotle has conquered, and is understandably proud:[19] before me, nothing happened as far as syllogisms are concerned. In contact with the strongest discursive self-affects, there where the power of knowledge flows back onto itself to experience its own superpower hindered by the forms of surprise, paradox, or dizziness. Against those, Aristotle proffered the syllogism, but the moment has been pathetic. It was simply a question of depathizing the *logos*, in one instant and on all fronts—to anaesthetize it. The tragedy is over. The *logos* enters the era of effective occurrence as a banal event. All men are mortal; thus . . . ; therefore . . .

[. . .]

Aristotle would seem to be a slow thinker, who does not shirk the delays of resistance, and of a case by case type of philosophy. Yet as far as the syllogism is concerned, he overtakes the others. They were endlessly debating, enjoying the strength of powerlessness and the delay itself; he made one instantaneous bound of necessity go through all these centers of useless exploitation of the *logos*. All the past wrong-headed processes were in fact imbued with a crazy idea: to force one to experience the dizziness of the *apeiron* by a systematic disturbance of the march (this Greek existential of spatio-temporality in which man grasps what it means to occur by schematizing it with his own body).[20] This translates into singular performances, as much in the sense of exploit as in the counter-effectuation that unmakes by making the very possibilities of effectuating, by destroying the movement, nature, knowledge.[21] In short, performances in non-occurrence, the least Aristotelian object possible, where enjoyment is at rest. How to stop all this?

Until now, there had never been any operation in the strict sense—a procedure that has been truly stabilized in its process—it was always a turmoil of maneuvers that concluded a pact with the *anairein*, the Greek verb that expresses the ruin of everything that is at the same moment in question. Everything that was listed earlier as logical mistakes, technically impeachable, was masking an ontological game that was also a children's game: to state / not to state, *tithenai/anairein, darstellen/fortstellen*.

Yet, we are less than one step away from the syllogism.

All at once, in one instant, forever, and on the entire Greek theater of operations in which thought ties its power to the limits of its practice, Aristotle stops everything. This was the dizzying instant of form, the day on which thought took form as a flash. Form that calls itself *skhēma*, disposition/dispositive. Thought has made its own arrangements.

The assumption (*ta keimena*), what we do not discuss, going to the end of itself, that is to say to something else (*heteron*), which it produces by virtue of its disposition (*skhēma*), without any other intervention or delay, especially not a delay of reflection: here is the syllogism in person.

[. . .]

A fundamental Greek law: Nothing persists if it is not watched. Aristotle then will avoid delays between primary actions of the discursive, simply to let them take place, against their own tendency to ruin themselves by rumination. More time between the state-pursue-attain, quick without telescoping all the instances into each other. This simultaneity is the *skhēma* itself, a term that signifies the being held together (*ekhesthai*) of the entire stated assumption. Or, if we prefer, it is time transformed into logical space, that is to say into a disposition not to grant time the possibility of corrupting itself by being affected by its own structure, the *after* already affecting the *before* of an irretrievable lateness. At any rate, when aporetic ontology reappears in Aristotle, this disruption will be everything.

A *skhēma*: the *skhēmata* of the syllogism. Dispositions of sentences, places assigned to desemantized meanings, only quantified (all, some, none), regulated transformations, everything in a moment too quick to give time to think. These are what we call the figures of syllogism.

It is true indeed that there is no positive prehistory of the syllogism, no time when, because of its not being there yet, it could already be foreshadowed by a clearing that would prepare the *skhēma*. Before itself, it does not take place at all, insofar as it can be contained in its entirety in the instant of the connection between the sentence that formulates the absolute ontological compactness and a disused logical space. The *skhēma*, first conversion of the time of logical act into operative spatiality. And, later on, we can have all the syllogistic conversations we want.

This is the eternal instant of the syllogism, an event (*pathos*) in the history of discursive effectuation that signals the end of the era of the *aesthetics* of acts of *logos*. Daring feats in discursive exercise are ended for now, and the great masterpiece of dialectics, as Hegel calls the *Parmenides*, is behind. Ended as well are the experiences in which thought sought to enjoy itself for its own glory by affecting its embarrassments.

This was the work of an instant, for the quasi-formal, born by operating—on the entire Greek field of operations—the simultaneous and faultless rejection of all the *logos*'s tendencies to abandon itself to perverse affects and its infinitely free games with its own potential for surprise. The passion for clever thinking-games without conclusion falls into disuse. The "miracle" of form among the Greeks may be a result of this successful and permanent rejection, without regrets, and without progress either, as traditional history puts it. This has yet to be seen.

The structure of thought—the form—then is acquired forevermore. From now on, the syllogism occurs, in one instant, forever, as a natural phenomenon of logos in this world of accidents. The history of *logos* that did not take place—that had no place—is over. There is no more *atopon*. Here, Aristotle requires admiration and indulgence. We enter, or so we think, the history without history of the syllogism.

THE MOMENT AFTER

Then, in one instant, the syllogism has conquered; the enemy is vanquished. Now free, it suddenly becomes insane; an available tool, it starts dreaming of seizing the highest rational objects, and it will become an object of ridicule. Revenge of the *apeiron*. Here is history back to its starting point. Eternally, from now on, the syllogism will be boring.

TRANSLATED BY CORINNE PACHE

NOTES

[1] Hegel, *Science de la logique*, trans. S. Jankelevitch, vol. 2, p. 35.

[2] *Prior Analytics* 1. 24b.

[3] *Topics* 1. 100a.

[4] Lettter of Hegel cited by J. Derrida, "L'Âge de Hegel," in Derrida 1990, 181.

[5] Preface of the second ed. of the *Critique of Pure Reason*.

[6] Chantraine, *DELG*, s.v. πάσχω.

[7] Kant, *Critique of Pure Reason*.

[8] *Posterior Analytics* 1. 87b.

[9] *Posterior Analytics* 1. 89b.

[10] *Posterior Analytics* 2. 93b.

[11] Wittgenstein, *Investigations philosophiques*, para. 375. [. . .]

[12] *Metaphysics* 6. 1041a.

[13] *Metaphysics* 3. 10005b.

[14] Heraclitus 50.

[15] See *Critique of Pure Reason*, preface to the second ed.

[16] See the critique in *On the Parts of Animals* 1. 3.

[17] *Sophistic Arguments* 34.

[18] *Posterior Analytics* 1. 34.

[19] *Sophistic Arguments* 34.

[20] See "Le Tyran boiteux," in Vernant and Vidal-Naquet 1986, 45–49.

[21] *Metaphysics* 8. 1047a.

JACQUES DERRIDA

Khōra

1987

In this reading of Plato's Timaeus, *paying special attention to the passage on the* khōra, *Derrida pursues Vernant's discussion of the opposition between* muthos *and* logos. *In his exploration of the rhetorical and philosophical problematic encoded in Plato's myth about beginnings, Derrida also offers a model of poststructuralist response to, and critique of, the structuralist method informing Vernant's work.*

> Myth thus involves a form of logic that can be called, in contrast to the logic of non-contradiction of the philosophers, a logic of the ambiguous and equivocal, a logic of polarity. How can one formulate, let alone formalize, the operations of reversal that transform one term into its opposite while maintaining various distanced points of view on both? It fell to the mythologist to transform this weakness into a result by turning to linguists, logicians, and mathematicians for the missing tool: a structural model of a logic that was not the logic of binarism, of yes or no, a logic different from the logic of the *logos*.
>
> —Jean-Pierre Vernant, "Raisons du mythe,"
> in *Mythe et société en Grèce ancienne* (1974), p. 250

As is well known, what Plato designates by the name *khōra* in the *Timaeus* seems to defy this "logic of non-contradiction of the philosophers," this logic "of binarism, of yes or no." Hence it might come under the head of this "logic different from the logic of the *logos*." The *khōra*, which is neither "perceptible" nor "intelligible," belongs to a "third genus" (*triton genos*, 48e, 52a). About it one cannot even say that it is *neither* this *nor* that or that it is *at once both* this *and* that. Timaeus's stated embarrassment manifests itself in another way: sometimes the *khōra* appears to be neither this nor that,

---

From "Khōra," in *Poikilia: Études offerts à J.-P. Vernant* (Paris: Editions de l'École des Hautes Études en Sciences Sociales, 1987), pp. 265–96.

sometimes both this and that, but this alternative between the logic of exclusion and the logic of participation may, as we shall have occasion to discuss at length, be no more than a temporary appearance and a consequence of rhetorical constraints. The *khōra* is apparently alien to the order of the "paradigm," the intelligible, immutable model. Yet although it is "invisible" and without perceptible form, it "participates" in the intelligible in a very embarrassing, indeed an aporetic (*aporōtata*, 51b), way. At least, Timaeus adds, we will not lie, we will not utter falsehood (*ou pseusometha*) in stating this. The prudence of this negative formulation gives us pause. Is not lying, not uttering falsehood, necessarily to speak the truth?

In this preliminary discussion, we would also do well to remember that the discourse on the *khōra*, as *presented*, derives not from the natural or legitimate *logos* but from a hybrid, bastard, even corrupt form of reasoning (*logismoi nothoi*). It is characterized "as in a dream" (52b), which can just as readily deprive it of lucidity as confer upon it a power of divination.

But does such discourse therefore come under the heading of myth? Can one gain access to the thought of the *khōra* while trusting to the alternative *logos/muthos*? What if that thought also called for a third type of discourse? And what if, perhaps as in the case of the *khōra*, that call for a third type was merely a digression to indicate a type beyond type? Beyond the categories and above all beyond the categorical oppositions that allow us to treat or speak of it in the first place?

Here, then, as a token of gratitude and admiration, is a homage in the form of a question to Jean-Pierre Vernant. It is addressed to the man who has taught us so much and helped us to think not only about the opposition *muthos/logos* but also about the constant inversion of poles, to the author of *Raisons du mythe* and *Ambiguïté et renversement*: How are we to conceive of that which, transcending the regularity of the *logos*, its law, and its natural or legitimate genealogy, nevertheless does not strictly speaking come under the head of *muthos*? Beyond the clear-cut and late-to-emerge opposition between *logos* and *muthos*, how are we to conceive of the necessity of that which, in *giving rise* to this opposition as to so many others, sometimes seems not to be subject to the law of the very thing that it *situates*? What about this *place*? Is there something to *think about*, as I have just so glibly stated, and to think about in terms of *necessity*?

The oscillation that I have just been discussing is not just one oscillation among others, an oscillation between two poles. It is rather an oscillation between two types of oscillation: double exclusion (*neither/nor*) and participation (*simultaneously and . . . , both this and that*). But can we legitimately transport the logic, paralogic, or metalogic of this super-oscillation from one realm to another? It originally pertained to types of being (perceptible/intelligible, visible/invisible, form/formless, icon or mimeme/paradigm), but we have shifted it to types of discourse (*logos*) or of relation to what is or is not in general.

The grounds for such a displacement are probably not self-evident. It depends on a sort of metonymy: types of being for types of discourse. It is always difficult, however, and particularly in Plato, to separate the two problematics: the quality of the discourse depends primarily on the quality of the being about which it speaks. Discourse, as the relation to what is in general, is qualified or disqualified by that to which it relates. Furthermore, the metonymy is justified in terms of *type*, from one type to another, from the question of types to the question of types of discourse. Now, the discourse on the *khōra* is also a discourse on type (*genos*) and on differences of type. Later we will take up the question of type in the sense of a genus or people (*genos, ethnos*), a theme that comes up at the beginning of the *Timaeus*. In the narrow context that concerns us at the moment, that of the passage concerning the *khōra*, we again encounter two types of type. The *khōra* is a *triton genos* in relation to the two types of being (immutable and intelligible/corruptible, changeable, perceptible), but it also seems determinate in relation to sexual type: Timaeus speaks about it as "mother" and "nurse." He does so in a mode to which it would be unwise to attach a name too hastily. Almost all the interpreters of the *Timaeus* rely unquestioningly at this point on the resources of rhetoric. They calmly speak of metaphors, images, and comparisons.[1] They ask no questions about the rhetorical tradition that provides them with a range of highly useful concepts, all of which are based, however, on the distinction between the perceptible and the intelligible that is precisely what can no longer be accommodated within the conception of the *khōra* and that Plato unambiguously suggests is that which is most difficult for that conception to accommodate. This problem of rhetoric is clearly not a secondary issue here. [. . .]

The discourse on *khōra* thus plays a role in philosophy analogous to the role that *khōra* "itself" plays in that about which philosophy speaks, namely, the cosmos formed or informed in accordance with the paradigm. The necessarily inadequate figures for describing *khōra* will henceforth be taken, however, from this cosmos: receptacle, imprint bearer, mother, or nurse. We shall see why these figures are not really even true figures. What they bring us close to philosophy cannot speak about directly in the mode of vigilance or truth (true or plausible). Dream is intermediary between the two, neither one nor the other. Philosophy cannot speak philosophically about that which resembles its "mother," "nurse," "receptacle," or "imprint bearer." As such, it can speak only of the father and the son, as if its father engendered it all by itself.

Once again we have at least a formal homology or analogy: in order to conceive of *khōra*, we must revert to a beginning earlier than the beginning, the birth of the cosmos, just as the Athenians must be told about their origins, which their own memory has not preserved. The formal aspects of the analogy are clear: a concern for architectural, textual (histological), and even organic composition is presented as such a little later on. It *recalls* the organic motif of the *Phaedrus*: a well-composed *logos* should resemble a living being. Timaeus:

Seeing, then, that we have now prepared for our use the various classes of causes which are the material [*hulē* is a word that Plato never uses to characterize *khōra*, a point I want to mention in passing in anticipation of the problem raised by Aristotle's interpretation of *khōra* as matter] out of which the remainder of our discourse [*logos*] must be woven [*sunuphanthēnai*], just as wood is the material of the carpenter, let us revert in a few words to the point at which we began [*palin ep'arkhēn*], and then endeavor to add on a suitable ending [*teleutēn*] to the beginning [*kephalēn*] of our tale [*tōi muthōi*]. (69a)

[Introduction to a work in progress. Fragment.]

TRANSLATED BY ARTHUR GOLDHAMMER

NOTE

[1] On this point, which is key for our approach to the problem, we shall have a great deal more to say at various points, especially when we outline a history and typology of interpretations of *khōra*, or, rather, when we attempt to describe the law of their paradoxes and aporias. For the time being, note simply that in the two French works, published seventy years apart, that propose an overview of the question and end with a general interpretation of all past interpretations, the metalinguistic or metainterpretive use of the ideas of metaphor, comparison, and image is never questioned. No question is raised about the interpretive rhetoric, in particular about what it necessarily borrows from a certain Platonic tradition (metaphor as detour via the perceptible in order to gain access to an intelligible meaning), which makes these works unsuitable for providing a metalanguage for the interpretation of Plato, especially a text as unusual as the passages of the *Timaeus* about *khōra*. Rivaud speaks, for example, of a "host of comparisons and metaphors whose variety is surprising" (p. 296), and of "metaphors" and "images" related to the "idea" of the "in what" (p. 298), even if, against Zeller, he refused to "see only metaphors in Plato's formulations" (p. 308). See "La théorie de la χώρα et la cosmogonie du Timée," in *Le Problème du devenir et la notion de matière*, ch. 5 (Paris, 1905).

Luc Brisson speaks in turn of the "metaphor of the dream that Plato uses to illustrate his description" (1974, 197; see also 206, 207). He even systematizes the operational use of the concept of metaphor and proposes classifying all metaphors in the course of determining what he calls "the ontological nature of the spatial environment" (we will return later to this title and the project it describes): such a determination "poses a considerable problem, because Plato speaks of the spatial environment only in terms of a totally metaphoric language that eschews all technicity. That is why we will first analyze two series of images: one having to do with sexual relations, the other with artisanal activity" (208; see also 211, 212, 214, 217, 222).

My point, of course, is not to criticize the use of words such as metaphor, comparison, and image. These are often inevitable, for reasons that I shall try to explain here. I use them myself on occasion. But there are limits to the relevance of this rhetorical code, which must be scrutinized in itself and treated as a theme rather than a merely operational concept. These limits have to do with the fact that the concepts of this rhetoric appear to be based on "Platonic" oppositions (intelligible/perceptible, being as *eidos*/image, etc.) from which *khōra* escapes. The apparent multiplicity of metaphor (or of mytheme generally) signifies not that the literal meaning can be made intelligible only through such devices but that the opposition between the literal and figurative has lost its value.

Bibliography and Abbreviations

Alaux, J. 1995. *Le liège et le filet: filiation et lien familial dans la tragédie athénienne du Ve siècle av. J.-C.* Paris.

Anthropologie de la Grèce antique. See Gernet 1968.

Bal, M. 1978. "Mise en abyme et iconicité." *Littérature* 29:116–28.

Baudy, G. 1986. *Adonisgärten, Studien zur antiken Samensymbolik.* Frankfurt.

Before Sexuality. See Halperin, Winkler, and Zeitlin 1990.

Benveniste, E. 1936. "Liber et Liberi." *Revue des études latines* 15:51–58.

———— 1938. "Traditions indo-iraniennes."

———— 1945a. "La doctrine médicale des Indo-Européens." *Revue de l'histoire des religions* 130:5–12.

———— 1945b. "Symbolisme social dans les cultes gréco-italiques." *Revue de l'histoire des religions* 129:5–16.

———— 1949. "Noms d'animaux en indo-européen." *Bulletin de la société de linguistique de Paris* 45:91–100.

———— 1966. *Problèmes de linguistique générale.* Paris.

———— 1969. *Le vocabulaire des institutions indo-européennes.* Vol. 1, *Economie, parenté, société.* Vol. 2, *Pouvoir, droit, religion.* Paris. (*Indo-European Language and Society.* Trans. E. Palmer. London, 1973.)

Bergren, A. 1989. "The Homeric Hymn to Aphrodite: Tradition and Rhetoric, Praise and Blame." *Classical Antiquity* 8:1–41.

Bergren, A., and Zeitlin, F., eds. 1982. *Text and Contexts: American Classical Studies in Honor of J.-P. Vernant.* Special issue of *Arethusa* (15 [1982]).

Berthiaume, G. *Les Rôles du mageiros. Etude sur la boucherie, la cuisine et le sacrifice dans la Grèce ancienne.* Mnemosyne Supplements 70. Leiden.

Blaise, F., Judet de La Combe, P., and Rousseau, P., eds. 1996. *Le métier du mythe. Lectures d'Hésiode.* Paris.

Boedeker, D. 1984. *The Descent from Heaven: Images of Dew in Greek Poetry and Religion.* Chico, CA.

Bollack, J. 1975. "Ulysse chez les philologues." *Actes de recherche en sciences sociales* 6:9–36.

———— 1976. "Notes sur l'épisode de Planctes." *Actes de recherche en sciences sociales* 9:173–76.

———— 1977a. "Réflexions sur la pratique philologique." *Social Science Information* 16:375–85.

———— 1997b. *La Grèce de personne*. Paris.

Bollack, J., Bollack, M., and Wismann, H. 1971. *La Lettre d'Epicure à Hérodote*. Paris.

Bollack, J., and Judet de La Combe, P., eds. 1981–1982. *L'Agamemnon d'Eschyle: Le texte et ses interprétations*, vols. I–III. Lille.

Bollack, J., and Wismann, H. 1972. *Héraclite; ou, La séparation*. Paris.

Bonnefoy, Y., ed. 1981. *Dictionnaire des mythologies et des religions des sociétés et du monde antique*. Paris.

Bonnet, C. 1987. "Echos d'un rituel de type adonien dans l'oracle contre Moab d'Israël (*Isaïe* 15)." *Studia et exempla linguistica* 4:101–9.

———— 1988. *Melqart: Cultes et mythes de l'Héraclès tyrien en Méditerranée*. Louvain and Namur.

Borgeaud, Ph. 1979. *Recherches sur le dieu Pan*. Rome. (*The Cult of Pan in Ancient Greece*. Trans. K. Atlass and J. Redfield. Chicago, 1988.)

Bourdieu, P. 1972. *Esquisse d'une théorie de la pratique: Précédé de trois études d'ethnologie kabyle*. Geneva.

Bouvier, D. 1987. "Mourir près des fontaines de Troie: Remarques sur le problème de la toilette funéraire d'Hector dans l'*Iliade*." *Euphrosyne* 15:9–29.

Bremond, C. 1966. "Logique de possibles narratifs." *Communications* 8:60–76.

Brisson, L. 1974. *Le même et l'autre dans la structure ontologique du* Timée de Platon. Paris.

———— 1976. *Le mythe de Tirésias: Essai d'analyse structurale*. Leiden.

Brulé, P. 1987. *La fille d'Athènes: la religion des filles à l'époque classique: mythes, cultes et société*. Paris.

Burkert, W. 1972. *Homo necans. Interpretationen altgriechischer Opferriten und Mythen*. Berlin. (*Homo necans: The Anthropology of Ancient Greek Sacrificial Ritual and Myth*. Trans. P. Bing. Berkeley and Los Angeles, 1983.)

Calame, C. 1977. *Les Choeurs de jeunes filles en Grèce archaïque*, vols. I–II. Rome. (*Choruses of Young Women in Ancient Greece: Their Morphology, Religious Role, and Social Function*. Trans. D. Collins and J. Orion. Lanham, MD, 1997.)

———— 1986. *Le Récit en Grèce ancienne: Enonciations et représentations de poètes*. Preface by J.-C. Coquet. Paris. (*The Craft of Poetic Speech in Ancient Greece*. Trans. J. Orion. Ithaca, 1995.)

Canto, M. 1989. Trans. and commentary. *Platon: Ion*. Paris.

Carlier, J. 1979. "Voyage en Amazonie Grecque." *Acta Antiqua Academiae Scientiarum Hungaricae* 27:381–405.

Casevitz, M. 1985. *Le vocabulaire de la colonisation en grec ancien: étude lexicologique: les familles des* ktizo *et de* oikeo-oikizo. Paris.

Cassin, B. 1995. *L'Effet sophistique*. Paris.

Cazeaux, J. 1980. "Anaxarète et Iphis (Ovide, *Métamorphoses* 14.698 sqq.) ou la pierre, le lin, le discours." In *Salamine de Chypre. Histoire et archéologie. Etat des recherches. Colloques internationaux du C.N.R.S.* 578. Paris.

Chantraine, P. 1929. Review of Parry 1928a, b. *Revue de Philologie* 55:294–300.

———— 1932. "Remarques sur l'emploi des formules dans le premier chant de l'*Iliade*." *Revue des études grecques* 45:121–54.

———— 1949. "La langue poétique et traditionnelle d'Homère." *Conférences de l'Institut de linguistique de l'Université de Paris*, vol. 8, 33–44. Paris.

———— 1956. *Etudes sur le vocabulaire grec*. Paris.

———— 1968, 1970, 1975, 1977, 1980. *Dictionnaire étymologique de la langue grecque*, I, II, III, IV-1, IV-2. Paris.

Chaunu, P. 1974. *Histoire, science sociale*. Paris.

La Cité des images: religion et société en Grèce antique. 1984. Institut d'archéologie et d'histoire ancienne, Lausanne and Centre de recherches comparées sur les sociétés anciennes. Paris.

Corbin, P. 1990. *Le village des cannibales*. Paris.

Cordero, N. 1990. "La Déesse de Parménide, maîtresse de philosophie." In *La naissance de la raison en Grèce,* ed. J.-F. Mattei. Paris.

Courbin, P. 1957. "Une tombe géométrique d'Argos." *Bulletin de correspondance hellénique* 81:322–84.

Cuisine. See Detienne and Vernant 1989.

Dällenbach 1977. *Le récit spéculaire: Contribution à l'étude de la mise en abyme*. Paris.

Daraki, M. 1985. *Dionysos*. Paris.

Darbo-Peschanski, C. 1987. *Le discours du particulier: Essai sur l'enquête hérodotéenne*. Paris.

———— 1995. "Humanité, guerre, ordre du monde. L'éthique des historiens grecs?" *Revue de synthèse* 116:527–52.

Delcourt, M. 1955. *L'Oracle de Delphes*. Paris.

DELG. See Chantraine.

Delebecque, E. 1958. *Télémaque et la structure de l' "Odyssée."* Paris.

———— 1982. *La Construction de l'Odyssée*. Paris.

Derrida, J. 1972a. *La Dissémination*. Paris. (*Dissemination*. Trans. B. Johnson. Chicago, 1981.)

———— 1972b. "La pharmacie de Platon." In *La Dissémination*. Paris.

———— 1990. *Du droit à la philosophie*. Paris.

Detienne, M. 1958. "La phalange: Problèmes et controverses." In *Problèmes de la guerre en Grèce ancienne,* ed. J.-P. Vernant. Paris.

———— 1960. "La notion mythique d'Aletheia." *Revue des études grecques* 73:27–35.

———— 1962. *Homère, Hésiode et Pythagore: Poésie et philosophie dans le pythagorisme ancien*. Brussels.

———— 1963a. *La notion de daimôn dans le pythagorisme ancien: de la pensée religieuse à la pensée philosophique*. Liège.

———— 1963b. *Crise agraire et attitude religieuse chez Hésiode*. Brussels.

———— 1972. *Les jardins d'Adonis: La mythologie des aromates en Grèce*. Paris. (*The Gardens of Adonis: Spices in Greek Mythology*. Trans. J. Lloyd. Hassocks, Sussex, 1985; reissued Princeton, 1994.)

———— 1973. "Le mythe: Orphée au miel." In *Faire de l'histoire*, ed. J. Le Goff and P. Nora. Paris.

———— 1977. *Dionysos mis à mort*. Paris. (*Dionysos Slain*. Trans. M. Muellner and L. Muellner. Baltimore, 1979.)

———— 1981. *L'invention de la mythologie*. Paris. (*The Creation of Mythology*. Trans. M. Cook. Chicago, 1986.)

————, ed. 1988a. *Les Savoirs de l'écriture en Grèce ancienne*. Paris.

———— 1988b. "L'écriture et ses nouvaux objects intellectuels en Grèce." In Detienne 1988a: 7–26.

————, ed. 1990. *Traces de fondation*. Louvain.

———— 1993. *Les Maîtres de vérité en Grèce archaïque*, 3d ed. Paris. (*The Masters of Truth in Archaic Greece*. Trans. J. Lloyd. New York, 1996.)

————, ed. 1994a. *Transcrire les mythologies: tradition, écriture, historicité*. Paris.

———— 1994b. "Ouverture" and "Manières grecques de commencer." In Detienne 1994a:7–21, 159–66.

Detienne, M., and Svenbro, J. 1989. "The Feast of the Wolves, or the Impossible City." In Detienne and Vernant 1989.

Detienne, M., and Vernant, J.-P., eds. 1968. See Gernet 1968.

———— 1974. *Les ruses de l'intelligence: La mètis des Grecs*. Paris. (*Cunning Intelligence in Greek Culture and Society*. Trans. J. Lloyd. Hassocks/Atlantic Highlands, NJ, 1978; Chicago, 1991.)

————, eds. 1979. *La cuisine du sacrifice en pays grec*. Paris. (*The Cuisine of Sacrifice among the Greeks*. Trans. P. Wissing. Chicago, 1989.)

Ducrot, O., and Todorov, Tz. 1972. *Dictionnaire encyclopédique des sciences du langage*. Paris. (*Encyclopedic Dictionary of the Sciences of Language*. Trans. C. Porter. Baltimore, 1979.)

Dumézil, G. 1978. *Romans de Scythie et d'alentour*. Paris.

DuPont-Sommer, A., and Robert, L. 1964. *La Déesse de Hierapolis Castabala, Cilicie*. Paris.

Durand, J.-L. 1986. *Sacrifice et labour en Grèce ancienne: Essai d'anthropologie religieuse*. Rome.

———— 1989. "Greek Animals: Toward a Topology of Edible Bodies." In Detienne and Vernant 1989.

Durkheim, E. 1910. *Formes élémentaires de la pensée religieuse*. Paris.

Ellinger, P. 1978. "Le Gypse et la boue. I. Sur les mythes de la guerre d'anéantissement." *Quaderni Urbinati di Cultura Classica* 29:7–35.

Faure, P. 1987. *Parfums et aromates de l'Antiquité*. Paris.

Festugière, A. J. 1972. *Etudes de religion grecque et hellénistique*. Paris.

FGrH. See Jacoby.

Figueira, T. J., and Nagy, G., eds. 1985. *Theognis of Megara: Poetry and the Polis*. Baltimore.

Foley, H. 1980. "The Masque of Dionysus." *Transactions of the American Philological Association* 110:107–33.

Foley, J. M. 1988. *The Theory of Oral Composition*. Bloomington.

Ford, A. L. 1992. *Homer: The Poetry of the Past*. Princeton.

Foucault, M. 1966. *Les mots et les choses: une archéologie des sciences humaines*. Paris. (*The Order of Things: An Archaeology of the Human Sciences*. London, 1970.)

———— 1972. *Archéologie du savoir*. Paris. (*The Archaeology of Knowledge: And the Discourse on Language*. Trans. A. M. Sheridan Smith. New York, 1972.)

Freud 1964. [1919]. "The Uncanny." In *The Standard Edition of the Complete Psychological Works of Sigmund Freud,* vol. 17, trans. and ed. J. Strachey. London.

Frontisi-Ducroux, F. 1975. *Dédale: Mythologie de l'artisan en Grèce ancienne*. Paris.

———— 1981. "Artémis bucolique." *Revue de l'histoire des religions* 198:29–56.

———— 1995. *Du Masque au visage: aspects de l'identité en Grèce ancienne*. Paris.

Frontisi-Ducroux, F., and Lissarrague, F. 1990. "From Ambiguity to Ambivalence: A Dionysiac Excursion through the 'Anakreontic' Vases." In *Before Sexuality*.

Frontisi-Ducroux, F., and Vernant, J.-P. 1990. "Features of the Mask in Ancient Greece." In *Myth and Tragedy in Ancient Greece*, ed. J.-P. Vernant and P. Vidal-Naquet. New York.

Garlan, Y. 1972. *La Guerre dans l'Antiquité*. Paris.

Gauchet, M. 1985. *Le désenchantement du monde: Une histoire politique de la religion*. Paris. (*The Disenchantment of the World: A Political History of Religion*. Trans. O. Burge. Princeton, 1997.)

Gauthier, P. 1976. *Un commentaire historique des* Poroi *de Xenophon*. Paris.

Genette, G. 1966a. *Figures: Essais*. 3 vols. in 2. Paris. (*Figures of Literary Discourse*. Trans. A. Sheridan. New York, 1982.)

———— 1966b. "Frontières du récit." *Communications* 8:152–63.

Georgoudi, S. 1990. *Des Chevaux et des boeufs dans le monde grec: réalités et représentations animalières à partir des livres XVI et XVII des Géoponiques*, with preface by M. Detienne. Paris.

Georgoudi, S., and Vernant, J.-P. 1955. *Mythes grecs au figuré de l'antiquité au baroque*. Paris.

Gernet, L. 1917. *Recherches sur le développement de la pensée juridique et morale en Grèce*. Paris.

———— 1945. "Les origines de la philosophie grecque." *Bulletin de l'enseignement public du Maroc* 183:1–12 (*Anthropologie de la Grèce antique*, 415–31).

———— 1948. "La Notion mythique de la valeur en Grèce." *Journal de Psychologie* 41:415–62 (*Anthropologie de la Grèce antique*, 93–139).

———— 1954. "Mariages de tyrans." In *Eventail de l'histoire vivante, hommage à Lucien Febvre*. Paris.

————, ed. and trans. 1954. *Antiphon: Discours: suivis des fragments d'Antiphon le sophiste*. Paris.

———— 1964. *Droit et société dans la Grèce ancienne*. Revision of 1955 ed. Paris.

———— 1968. *Anthropologie de la Grèce antique*, ed. M. Detienne and J.-P. Vernant. Paris.

Ginouvès, R. 1962. *Balaneutikè: recherches sur le bain dans l'antiquité grecque.* Paris.

Girard, R. 1972. *La Violence et le sacré.* Paris. (*Violence and the Sacred.* Trans. P. Gregory. Baltimore, 1977.)

———— 1978. *Des choses cachées depuis la fondation du monde.* Paris. (*Things Hidden since the Foundation of the World.* Trans. S. Bann [Books II & III] and M. Metteer [Book I]. Stanford, 1987.)

Goldhill, S. 1986. *Reading Greek Tragedy.* Cambridge.

Graf, F. 1991. "Textes orphiques et rituel bacchique: à propos des lamelles de Pélinna." In *Orphisme et Orphée*, ed. P. Borgeaud. Geneva.

Griffin, J. 1980. *Homer on Life and Death.* Oxford.

Halperin, D. M., Winkler, J., and Zeitlin, F., eds. 1990. *Before Sexuality: The Construction of Erotic Experience in the Ancient Greek World.* Princeton.

Hartog, F. 1980. *Le Miroir d'Hérodote: essai sur la représentation de l'autre.* Paris. (*The Mirror of Herodotus: The Representation of the Other in the Writing of History.* Trans. J. Lloyd. Berkeley and Los Angeles, 1988.)

Hartog, F., Schmitt, P., and Schnapp, A., eds. 1998. *Pierre Vidal-Naquet, un historien dans la cité.* Paris.

Henrichs, A. 1981. "Human Sacrifice in Greek Religion." In *Le sacrifice dans l'Antiquité*, Entretiens de la Fondation Hardt 27:195–242.

———— 1982. "Changing Dionysiac Identities." In *Jewish and Christian Self-Definition*, ed. B. E. Meyer and E. P. Sanders, vol. III. London.

Hiltebeitel, A. 1976; repr. 1990. *The Ritual of Battle: Krishna in the Mahâbhârata.* Ithaca; Albany.

HMP. See Létoublon 1997.

Humphreys, S. C. 1978. *Anthropology and the Greeks.* London.

Irigoin, J. 1952. *Histoire du texte de Pindare.* Paris.

Jacob, C. 1987. "Problèmes de lecture du mythe grec." In *Le Conte* (Colloque d'Albi), 389–408. Toulouse.

Jacoby, F., ed. 1954–1964. *Die Fragmente der griechischen Historiker.* Leiden.

Jacopin, P.-Y. 1988. "Anthropological Dialectics: Yukuna Ritual as Defensive Strategy." *Schweizerische Amerikanisten-Gesellschaft, Bulletin* 52:35–46.

Jamison, S. W. 1991. *The Ravenous Hyenas and the Wounded Sun: Myth and Ritual in Ancient India.* Ithaca.

Jeanmaire, H. 1939. *Couroi et Courètes.* Lille and Paris. Repr. ed. New York, 1978.

———— 1951. *Dionysos. Histoire du culte de Bacchus: l'orgiasme dans l'antiquité et les temps modernes, origine du théâtre en Grèce, orphisme et mystique dionysiaque, évolution du dionysisme après Alexandre.* Paris.

Jouan, F. 1966. *Euripide et les légendes des Chants cypriens.* Paris.

Jouanna, J., and Demont, P. 1981. "Le sens d'*ikhōr*" *Revue des études anciennes* 83:197–209.

Jourdain-Annequin, C. 1989. *Héraclès aux portes du soir: Mythe et histoire*. Centre de recherches d'histoire ancienne 89. Paris.

Judet de La Combe, P. 1991. "Espace public et individualité dans la tragédie: Sur l'*Agamemnon* d'Eschyle." *Hermes* 10:39–56.

———— 1994. "Zur Darstellung des Individuums in der griechischen Tragödie durch ein pragmatisches Verfahren." In *Individuum. Probleme der Individualität in Kunst, Philosophie und Wissenschaft*, ed. G. Boehm and E. Rudolph. Stuttgart.

Kahn, L. 1978. *Hermès passe, ou les ambiguïtés de la communication*. Paris.

———— 1993. *La petite maison de l'âme*. Paris.

Kirk, G. S. 1970. *Myth: Its Meaning and Functions in Ancient and Other Cultures*. Berkeley and Los Angeles.

———— 1974. *The Nature of Greek Myths*. Harmondsworth.

———— 1978. "The Spicy Side of Structuralism." Review of Detienne 1977. *Times Literary Supplement* 18 August 1978.

Laks, A., and Neschke, A., eds. 1991. *La Naissance du paradigme herméneutique (Schleiermacher, Humboldt, Boeckh, Droysen)*. Lille.

Lamberterie, C. de. 1997. "Milman Parry et Antoine Meillet." *HMP* 9–22.

Latacz, J. L. 1979. *Homer: Tradition und Neuerung*. Darmstadt.

Laurens, A. F., and Gallet, H. 1986. "Des hommes aux dieux en Grèce: Droit de regard?" In *Hommages à François Daumas*. Montpelier.

Leach, E. R. 1982. Critical introduction to M. I. Steblin-Kamenskij, *Myth*. Ann Arbor.

Leduc, C. 1995. "Une Théologie du Signe en pays grec: L'hymne homerique à Hermès [I], Commentaire des vers 1–181," *Revue de l'histoire des religions* 212:6–49.

Lejeune, M. 1955. *Traité de phonétique grecque*. 2nd ed. Paris. Superseded 1972 by *Phonétique historique du mycénien et du grec ancien*. Paris.

———— 1965. "Le DĀMOS dans la société mycénienne." *Revue des études grecques* 78:1–22.

Le Roy Ladurie, E. 1979. *Le Carnaval de Romans. De la Chandeleur au mercredi des Cendres, 1579–1580*. Paris. (*Carnival in Romans*. Trans. M. Feeney. New York, 1979.)

Lestringant, F. 1982. "Catholiques et cannibales. Le Thème du cannibalisme dans le discours protestant au temps des guerres de religion." In *Pratiques et discours alimentaires à la Renaissance*, ed. J.-C. Margolin and R. Sauzet. Paris.

Létoublon, F. 1983. "Le miroir et le boucle." *Poétique* 53:19–36.

———— 1990. "SURIMPRESSION: Sophocle entre Homère et Héliodore." *L'Information littéraire* 42:3–6.

————, ed. 1997. *Hommage à Milman Parry: Le style formulaire de l'épopée homérique et la théorie de l'oralité poétique*. Amsterdam.

Lévêque, P. 1988. "Pandora ou la terrifiante fémininité." *Kernos* 1:49–62.

Lévêque, P., and Séchan, L. 1966. *Les grandes divinités de la Grèce*. Paris.

Lévêque, P., and Vidal-Naquet, P. 1964. *Clisthène l'Athénien: essai sur la représentation de l'espace et du temps dans la pensée politique grecque de la fin du VIe siècle à la mort de Platon*. Paris.

Lévi-Strauss, C. 1958. *Anthropologie structurale*. Paris. (*Structural Anthropology*. Trans. C. Jacobson and B. G. Schoepf. New York, 1963.)

———— 1962. *La pensée sauvage*. Paris. (*The savage mind*. Chicago, 1966.)

———— 1964. *Le cru et le cuit*. Paris. (*The Raw and the Cooked*. Trans. J. and D. Weightman. New York, 1969.)

———— 1971. *L'homme nu*. Paris. (*The naked man*. Trans. J. and D. Weightman. London, 1981.)

———— 1972. Review of Detienne 1972. *L'Homme* 12:97–102.

———— 1979. *Claude Lévi-Strauss: textes de et sur Claude Lévi-Strauss*. Ed. R. Bellour and C. Clément. Paris.

———— 1983. "Histoire et ethnologie." *Annales Economies Sociétés Civilisations* 38:1217–31.

Lissarrague, F. 1990a. "The Sexual Life of Satyrs." In *Before Sexuality*.

———— 1990b. "Why Satyrs are Good to Represent." In *Nothing to do with Dionysos?*

———— 1990c. *L'autre guerrier: archers, peltastes, cavaliers dans l'imagerie attique*. Paris.

Lohmann, D. 1970. *Die Komposition der Reden in der Ilias*. Berlin.

Loraux, N. 1977. "La belle mort spartiate." *Ktēma* 2:105–20.

———— 1981a. *L'Invention d'Athènes*. Paris. (*The Invention of Athens: The Funeral Oration in the Classical City*. Trans. A. Sheridan. Cambridge, MA, 1986.)

———— 1981b. *Les Enfants d'Athéna: Idées athéniennes sur la citoyenneté et la division des sexes*. Paris. (*The Children of Athena: Athenian Ideas about Citizenship and the Division between the Sexes*. Trans. C. Levine. Princeton, 1993.)

———— 1981c. "La cité comme cuisine et comme partage." *Annales Economies Sociétés Civilisations* 36:614–22.

———— 1982. "Mourir devant Troie, tomber pour Athènes." *Informations sur les sciences sociales* 17:801–17.

———— 1984. "Solon au milieu de la lice." In *Aux origines de l'hellénisme. Mélanges Henri Van Effenterre*. Paris.

———— 1985. *Façons tragiques de tuer une femme*. Paris. (*Tragic Ways of Killing a Woman*. Trans. A. Forster. Cambridge, MA, 1987.)

———— 1986a. "Thucydide et la sédition dans les mots." *Quaderni di storia* 23:95–134.

———— 1986b. "Le corps vulnérable d'Arès." *Le Temps de la réflexion* (*Corps des dieux*) 7:335–54.

———— 1987. "Le lien de la division." *Le Cahier du collège international de philosophie* 4:101–24.

———— 1989. *Les expériences de Tirésias. Le féminin et l'homme grec*. Paris. (*The Experiences of Tiresias: The Feminine and the Greek Man*. Trans. P. Wissing. Princeton, 1995.)

———— 1990a. "Herakles: The Super-Male and the Feminine." In *Before Sexuality*.

———— 1990b. "Kreousa the Autochthon: A Study of Euripides' *Ion*." In *Nothing to do with Dionysos?*

———— 1993a. *L'Invention d'Athènes: Histoire de l'oraison funèbre dans la "cité classique."* 2nd ed. Paris.

———— 1993b. "Corcyre, 427, Paris, 1871. La 'guerre civile grecque' entre deux temps." *Les Temps modernes* 569:81–119.

———— 1995a. "Le procès athénien et la justice comme division." *Archives de philosophie du droit* 39:25–37.

———— 1995b. "La guerre civile grecque et la représentation anthropologique du monde à l'envers." *Revue de l'histoire des religions* 212:299–326.

Loraux, P. 1993. *Le Tempo de la pensée.* Paris.

Lord, A. B. 1960. *The Singer of Tales.* 2nd ed., with new introduction by S. Mitchell and G. Nagy. Cambridge, MA, 2000.

Lowenstam, S. 1981. *The Death of Patroklos: A Study in Typology.* Beiträge zur klassischen Philologie 133. Königstein.

Malamoud, C. 1971. "L'oeuvre d'Emile Benveniste: une analyse linguistique des institutions indo-européenes." *Annales, Economies, Sociétés, Civilisations* 3–4:653–54.

———— 1989. *Cuire le monde: rite et pensée dans l'Inde ancienne.* Paris.

Marouzeau, J. ed. 1927 and following. *L'Année Philologique: Bibliographie critique et analytique de l'antiquité gréco-latine.* Paris. The *Année* is now being electronically republished as *The Database of Classical Bibliography*, under the general editorship of Dee L. Clayman.

Marouzeau, J. 1927–28. *Dix années de bibliographie classique, 1914–1924.* Paris: Société d'édition "Les Belles Lettres."

Martin, R. P. 1983. *Healing, Sacrifice and Battle: Amēchania and Related Concepts in Early Greek Poetry.* Innsbrucker Beiträge zur Sprachwissenschaft 41. Innsbruck.

———— 1989, revised paperback version 1992. *The Language of Heroes: Speech and Performance in the Iliad.* Ithaca.

Mauss, M. 1968–1969. *Oeuvres.* Vols. I–II, ed. V. Karady. Vol. 1, *Les fonctions sociales du sacré.* Vol. 2, *Représentations collectives et diversité des civilisations.* Vol. 3, *Cohésion sociale et divisions de la sociologie.* Paris.

Mawet, F. 1979. *Recherches sur les oppositions fonctionnelles dans le vocabulaire homérique de la douleur.* Brussels.

Meiggs, R., and Lewis, D., eds. 1969. *A Selection of Greek Historical Inscriptions to the End of the Fifth Century B.C.* Oxford.

Meillet, A. 1908–1909. "Du caractère artificiel de la langue homérique." *Mémoires de la Société de Linguistique de Paris* 15.165–69.

———— 1918a. "Sur une édition linguistique d'Homère." *Revue des Etudes Grecques* 31.277–314.

———— 1918b. "Le témoignage de la langue homérique et les exigences du vers." *Bulletin de la Société de Linguistique de Paris* 21:28–30.

———— 1923a. *Les Origines indo-européennes des mètres grecques.* Paris.

———— 1923b. Review of K. Meister, *Die homerische Kunstsprache* (Leipzig, 1921). *Bulletin de la Société de Linguistique de Paris* 24:56–60.

———— 1923c. Review of H. Ammann, *Untersuchungen zur homerischen Wortfolge und Satzstruktur* (Freiburg, 1921). *Bulletin de la Société de Linguistique de Paris* 24:60–61.

———— 1925. *La Méthode comparative en linguistique historique*. Paris.

———— 1929. Review of Parry 1928a, b. *Bulletin de la Société de Linguistique de Paris* 29:100–102.

———— 1935. *Aperçu d'une histoire de la langue grecque*. 4th ed. Paris.

Meyerson, I. 1987. *Ecrits, 1920–1983: pour une psychologie historique*. Paris.

MHV. See Parry 1971.

Miralles, C. 1982. "El singular nacimiento de Erichthonio." *Emerita* 50:262–78.

ML. See Meiggs and Lewis 1969.

Momigliano, A. 1982. Review of Detienne 1981. *Rivista storica italiana* 94:784–87.

———— 1987. *Ottavo contributo alla storia degli studi classici e del mondo antico*. Rome.

Monsacré, H. 1984. *Les larmes d'Achille: Le Héros, la femme et la souffrance dans la poésie d'Homère*. Paris.

Mossé, C. 1983. *La femme dans la Grèce antique*. Paris.

———— 1984. *La Grèce archaïque d'Homère à Eschyle*. Paris.

Muellner, L. 1976. *The Meaning of Homeric EYXOMAI through its Formulas*. Innsbrucker Beiträge zur Sprachwissenschaft 13. Innsbruck.

———— 1996. *The Anger of Achilles: Mēnis in Early Greek Epic*. Ithaca.

Nagler, M. 1967. "Towards a Generative View of the Oral Formula." *Transactions of the American Philological Association* 98:269–311.

———— 1974. *Spontaneity and Tradition: A Study in the Oral Art of Homer*. Berkeley and Los Angeles.

Nagy, G. 1979. 2nd ed. 1999. *The Best of the Achaeans: Concepts of the Hero in Archaic Greek Poetry*. Baltimore.

———— 1982. Review of Detienne 1981. *Annales Economies Sociétés Civilisations* 37:778–80.

———— 1984. "Théognis et Mégare: Le poète dans l'âge de fer." *Revue de l'Histoire des Religions* 201:239–79.

———— 1985. "Theognis and Megara: A Poet's Vision of his City." In Figueira and Nagy 1985.

———— 1989. "Early Greek Views of Poets and Poetry." In *The Cambridge History of Literary Criticism* I, ed. G. Kennedy. Cambridge.

———— 1990. *Pindar's Homer: The Lyric Possession of an Epic Past*. Baltimore.

———— 1993. "Alcaeus in Sacred Space." In *Tradizione e innovazione: scritti in onore di Bruno Gentili* I, ed. R. Pretagostini. Rome.

———— 1994. *Le meilleur des Achéens: La fabrique du héros dans la poésie grecque archaïque*. Trans. J. Carlier and N. Loraux. Paris.

———— 1996. *Homeric Questions*. Austin.

——— 1997. "L'Epopée homérique et la fixation du texte." *HMP* 57–58.

Nicolet, C. 1976. *Le métier de citoyen dans la Rome républicaine*. Paris.

Nothing to do with Dionysos? See Winkler and Zeitlin 1990.

Olender, M. 1985. "Aspects de Baubo. Textes et contextes antiques." *Revue de l'histoire des religions* 102:3–55.

——— 1986. "Priape, le mal taillé." *Le temps de la réflexion* 7:363–89.

——— 1990. "Aspects of Baubo: Ancient Texts and Contexts." In *Before Sexuality*.

Palmer, L. R. 1980. *The Greek Language*. Atlantic Highlands, NJ.

Parker, R. 1983. *Miasma. Pollution and Purification in Early Greek Religion*. Oxford.

Parry, A., ed. 1971. *The Making of Homeric Verse: The Collected Papers of Milman Parry*. Oxford.

Parry, M. 1928a. *L'Epithète traditionnelle dans Homère: Essai sur un problème de style homérique*. Paris. = *MHV* 1–190.

——— 1928b. *Les formules et la métrique d'Homère*. Paris. = *MHV* 191–239.

——— 1930. "Studies in the Epic Technique of Oral Verse-Making I: Homer and Homeric Style." *Harvard Studies in Classical Philology* 41:73–147. = *MHV* 266–324.

——— 1932. "Studies in the Epic Technique of Oral Verse-Making II: The Homeric Language as the Language of an Oral Poetry." *Harvard Studies in Classical Philology* 43:1–50. = *MHV* 325–364.

Pasquali, G. 1951. *Stravaganze quarte e supreme*. Venice.

Pigeaud, J. 1981. *La Maladie de l'âme: Etude sur la relation de l'âme et du corps dans la tradition médico-philosophique antique*. Paris.

Préaux, C. 1959. "Du linéaire B créto-mycénien aux ostraca grecs d'Egypte." *Chroniques d'Egypte* 34:79–85.

Pucci, P. 1985. "Epiphanie testuali nell'*Iliade*." *Studi Italiani di Filologia Classica* 3:170–83.

——— 1986. "Les figures de la *mētis* dans l'Odyssée." *Metis* 1:7–28.

——— 1987. *Odysseus Polytropos: Intertextual Readings in the Odyssey and the Iliad*. Ithaca.

Puech, A. 1932. Review of Parry 1930 [= *MHV* 266–324]. *Revue des études grecques* 45:326.

——— 1934. Review of Parry 1932 [= *MHV* 325–64]. *Revue des études grecques* 47:261.

——— 1936. "Milman Parry." *Revue des études grecques* 49.87–88.

Puttkammer, F. 1912. *Quomodo Graeci victimarum carnes distribuerint*. Königsberg.

Ramnoux, C. 1959a. *La Nuit et les enfants de la Nuit dans la tradition grecque*. Paris.

——— 1959b. *Vocabulaire et structures de pensée archaique chez Héraclite*. Paris.

——— 1962. *Mythologie, ou la famille olympienne*. Paris.

Redfield, J. M. 1975. *Nature and Culture in the Iliad: The tragedy of Hector*. Chicago. 2nd ed. Durham, 1994.

Reinhardt, K. 1961. *Die Ilias und ihr Dichter*. Gottingen.

Robert, L. 1960. "Recherches épigraphiques, V: Inscriptions de Lesbos." *Revue des études grecques* 73:285–315.

——— 1962–63. "Eulaios, histoire et onomastique." *Epistēmonikē Epetēris tēs philosophikēs Skholēs tou Panepistēmiou Athēnōn*, pp. 519–29.

Rosolato, G. 1977. "What was Freud contemplating on the Acropolis?" *Nouvelle revue de psychanalyse* 15:125–39.

Rousseau, P. 1992. "Fragments d'un commentaire antique de la course des chars." *Philologus* 136:158–80.

——— 1995. *Dios d' eteleieto boulê. Destin des héros et dessin de Zeus dans l'intrigue de l'Iliade.* Thèse d'Etat, Université Charles de Gaulle - Lille III.

Rudhardt, J. 1986. *Le rôle d'Eros et d'Aphrodite dans les cosmogonies grecques.* Paris.

——— 1992. *Notions fondamentales de la pensée religieuse et actes constitutifs du culte dans la Grèce classique.* 2nd ed. Paris.

Saïd, S. 1982. "Féminin, femme et femelle dans les grands traités biologiques d'Aristote." In *La femme dans les sociétés antiques*, ed. E. Lévy. Strasbourg.

Samuel, P. 1975. *Amazones, guerrières et gaillardes.* Brussels.

Saussure, F. de. 1916. *Cours de linguistique générale.* Ed. Ch. Bally, A. Sechehaye, with the collaboration of A. Riedlinger. Paris. Critical re-edition 1972, ed. T. de Mauro. Paris.

Saxonhouse, A. 1985. *Women in the History of Political Thought: Ancient Greece to Machiavelli.* New York.

Scheid-Tissinier, E. 1994. *Les Usages du don chez Homère: vocabulaire et pratiques.* Nancy.

Schlesier, R. 1982. "Das Flötenspiel des Gorgo." *Notizbuch* 5–6:11–57.

——— 1988. "Lévi-Strauss' Mythology and the Myth." *Telos* 77:143–57.

Schmitt Pantel, P. 1992. *La Cité au banquet: histoire des repas publics dans les cités grecques.* Rome.

Schnapp, A. 1997. *Le chasseur et la cité. Chasse et érotique dans la Grèce ancienne.* Paris.

Schnapp-Gourbeillon, A. 1981. *Lions, héros, masques.* Paris.

Segal, C. 1971. *The Theme of the Mutilation of the Corpse in the* Iliad. Mnemosyne Supplements 17. Leiden.

——— 1982a. "Afterword: Jean-Pierre Vernant and the Study of Ancient Greece." In Bergren and Zeitlin 1982.

——— 1982b. *Dionysiac Poetics and Euripides'* Bacchae. 2nd ed. 1997. Princeton.

——— 1998a. "Frontières, étrangers et éphèbes dans la tragédie grecque: Réflexions sur l'oeuvre de Pierre Vidal-Naquet." In Hartog et al. 1998.

——— 1998b. *Aglaia: The Poetry of Alcman, Sappho, Pindar, Bacchylides, and Corinna.* Lanham, MD.

Sergent, B. 1984. *L'homosexualité dans la mythologie grecque*, with a preface by Georges Dumézil. Paris. (*Homosexuality in Greek Myth.* Trans. A. Goldhammer. Boston, 1986.)

Sissa, G. 1990. "Maidenhood without Maidenhead: The Female Body in Ancient Greece." In *Before Sexuality.*

———— 1997. "Philology, Anthropology, Comparison: The French Experience." *Classical Philology* 92:167–71.

Sissa, G., and Detienne, M. 1989. *La vie quotidienne des dieux grecs*. Paris. (*The Daily Life of the Greek Gods*. Trans. J. Lloyd. Stanford, 1999.)

Slatkin, L. 1988. "Les amis mortels." *L'Ecrit du temps* 19:119-32.

———— 1991. *The Power of Thetis: Allusion and Interpretation in the Iliad*. Berkeley and Los Angeles.

Sokolowski, F. 1955. *Lois sacrées de l'Asie Mineure*. Paris.

Soyez, B. 1977a. *Byblos et la fête des Adonies*. Leiden.

———— 1977b. "De l'apparition d'une crue à la saison des Adonies." In *Mélanges J. M. Vermaseren* 3:1188–93. Leiden.

———— 1981. "Musique des Adonies. Rapport archéologique à la connaissance du rituel adonidien." In *Adonis: Relazioni del colloquio in Roma*, ed. S. Ribichini.

Starobinski, J. 1971. *Les mots sous les mots. Les anagrammes de Ferdinand de Saussure*. Paris.

Svenbro, J. 1976. *La parole et le marbre: aux origines de la poétique grecque*. Lund.

———— 1982. "A Mégara Hyblaea: le corps géomètre." *Annales Economies Sociétés Civilisations* 37:953–64. See also Loraux 1981c.

———— 1984. "La découpe du poème. Notes sur les origines sacrificielles de la poétique grecque." *Poétique* 58.215–32.

———— 1988. *Phrasikleia: Anthropologie de la lecture en Grèce ancienne*. Paris. (*Phrasikleia: An Anthropology of Reading in Ancient Greece*. Trans. J. Lloyd. Ithaca, 1993.)

———— 1990. "The Interior Voice: On the Invention of Silent Reading." In *Nothing to do with Dionysos?*

Sznycer, M. 1981. "Phéniciens et Puniques, leurs religions." In Bonnefoy 1981.

Thomas, Y. 1987. "Le 'ventre.' Corps maternel, droit paternel." *Le genre humain* 14:211–37.

Thomas, Y., et al. 1984. *Du châtiment dans la cité: Supplices corporels et peines de mort dans le monde antique*. Paris.

Todorov, Tz. 1967. *Littérature et signification*. Paris.

———— 1967. *Qu'est-ce que le structuralisme? Poétique*. Paris.

———— 1971. "Le Récit primitif: l'*Odyssée*." In *Poétique de la prose*. Paris.

Trilling, J. 1983. *Aegean Crossroads: Greek Island Embroideries in the Textile Museum*. Washington, DC.

Vermeule, E. 1979. *Aspects of Death in Early Greek Art and Poetry*. Berkeley and Los Angeles.

Vernant, J.-P. 1962. *Les Origines de la pensée grecque*. Paris. (*The Origins of Greek Thought*. Ithaca, 1982.)

————, ed. 1968. *Problèmes de la guerre en Grèce ancienne*. The Hague.

———— 1974. *Mythe et société en Grèce ancienne*. Paris.

———— 1979. "*Pánta Kalá*. D'Homère à Simonide." *Annali della Scuola Normale superiore di Pisa* 9:1365–74.

————— 1982. "La belle mort et le cadavre outragé." In *La mort, les morts dans les sociétés anciennes*, ed. G. Gnoli and J.-P. Vernant. Cambridge and Paris.

————— 1985. *Mythe et pensée chez les Grecs. Etudes de psychologie historique*. 2nd edition, revised and augmented. Paris. The English-language version, *Myth and Thought among the Greeks* (London, 1983), is based on the 1st edition (Paris, 1965), and needs to be updated.

————— 1989. *L'Individu, la mort, l'amour. Soi-même et l'autre en Grèce ancienne*. Paris.

————— 1990a. *Figures, idoles, masques*. Paris.

————— 1990b. "One . . . Two . . . Three: Erōs." In *Before Sexuality*.

————— 1991. *Mortals and Immortals: Collected Essays*. Ed. F. Zeitlin. Princeton.

————— 1993. *L'Uomo greco*. Rome.

Vernant, J.-P. and Vidal-Naquet, P. 1972. *Mythe et tragédie en Grèce ancienne*. Paris.

————— 1986. *Mythe et tragédie en Grèce ancienne deux*. Paris.

Vernant, J.-P. et al., eds. 1974. *Divination et rationalité*. Paris.

Veyne, P. 1976. *Le pain et le cirque: sociologie historique d'un pluralisme politique*. Paris.

————— 1983. *Les Grecs, ont-ils cru à leurs mythes?: essai sur l'imagination constituante*. Paris. (*Did the Greeks Believe in their Myths?* Trans. P. Wissing. Chicago, 1988.)

Vidal-Naquet, P. 1981. *Le Chasseur noir: formes de pensée et formes de société dans le monde grec*. Paris. (*The Black Hunter: Forms of Thought and Forms of Society in the Greek World*. Trans. A. Szegedy-Maszák. Baltimore, 1986.)

————— 1986. "The Black Hunter Revisited." *Proceedings of the Cambridge Philological Society* 212:126–44.

Will, E. 1960. *Eléments orientaux dans la religion grecque ancienne*. Paris.

————— 1975. "Le rituel des Adonies." *Syria* 52:93–105.

Winkler, J. J., and Zeitlin, F., eds. 1990. *Nothing to do with Dionysos? Athenian Drama in its Social Context*. Princeton.

Yoshida, A. 1964. "Survivances de la tripartition fonctionelle en Grèce. *Revue de l'histoire des religions* 166:21–38.

Zeitlin, F. 1985. "Playing the Other: Theater, Theatricality, and the Feminine in Greek Drama." *Representations* 11:63–94.

————— 1996. *Playing the Other: Gender and Society in Classical Greek Literature*. Chicago.

Zumthor, P. 1972. *Essai de poétique médiévale*. Paris.